Fallen Glory

FALLEN GLORY

The Lives and Deaths of
History's Greatest Buildings

James Crawford

Picador • New York

Printed in the United States of America. For information, address Picador, 175 Fifth Avenue, New York, N.Y. 10010.

picadorusa.com • picadorbookroom.tumblr.com
twitter.com/picadorusa • facebook.com/picadorusa

For book club information, please visit facebook.com/picadorbookclub or e-mail marketing@picadorusa.com.

Library of Congress Cataloging-in-Publication Data

Names: Crawford, James (Writer on aerial photography), author.
Title: Fallen glory : the lives and deaths of history's greatest buildings / James Crawford.
Description: First U.S. edition. | New York : Picador, 2017.
Identifiers: LCCN 2016039186 (print) | LCCN 2016040493 (e-book) | ISBN 9781250118295 (hardcover) | ISBN 9781250118301 (e-book)
Subjects: LCSH: Lost architecture. | Ruined buildings. | Cities and towns—History. | BISAC: ARCHITECTURE / Buildings / General. | ARCHITECTURE / History / General. | HISTORY / World. | HISTORY / General.
Classification: LCC NA209 .C73 2017 (print) | LCC NA209 (e-book) | DDC720—dc23
LC record available at https://lccn.loc.gov/2016039186

Originally published in Great Britain by Old Street Publishing Ltd

First U.S. Edition: March 2017

10 9 8 7 6 5 4 3 2 1

CONTENTS

Introduction

Several years ago I visited the ruins of the palace complex of Knossos on the island of Crete. It was an early morning in September, but the sun was already very hot, and the surrounding olive groves throbbed with the scratching of the cicadas. I had just smashed my big toe against an ancient – and well hidden – flagstone, and was bleeding profusely into the ground: my inadvertent offering to a site that archaeologists believe was once used for human sacrifice. I liked to imagine I might be standing somewhere within the labyrinth built to hold the infamous mythological resident of Knossos – the Minotaur. Had I been one of the Athenian youths sent to feed the monster, I would have been in big trouble: limping through the maze in my cheap, plastic flip-flops, leaving a trail of blood in my wake. At the northern fringe of the ruins, I could see a broken chunk of portico propped up by three columns, each painted a deep orange. On the wall behind the columns, a bright fresco showed a bull bending its head to charge. This is one of the iconic show-pieces of the site, a fragment framed in a million tourist photographs, including my own. And it is a fake.

In 1900, the English archaeologist Sir Arthur Evans bought the entire site of Knossos and its surrounding land. He embarked on a massive programme of excavations, and then began what he called his 'reconstitutions'. There is nothing ancient about the portico. It is, in fact, one of the very first reinforced concrete structures built on Crete, and its construction was overseen by Evans himself.

Evans has come in for a great deal of criticism over the years. Some say he was carried away by his passion for classical mythology and lost track of his duties as historian and scientist. The less kind verdict presents him as an odious product of Victorian Britain: egocentric and supercilious, he is accused of creating a skewed account of the origins of Cretan civilisation that was more about his own repressed sexuality than the actual archaeology. I suspect Evans would never make my personal dinner party dream team – how do you cater for someone who, throughout his time on Crete, continued to import his food by the crate-load from England, and refused to drink the local wine? – but I can't help but feel some affinity with what he was trying to do at Knossos. After uncovering the remains of a building situated at the centre of one of the ancient world's most significant cultures, Evans wanted to go further still. I think of him standing among the excavation works, looking out at the surrounding amphitheatre of green, terraced hills, letting his mind wander back to the mid-second millennium BC. He wanted to know the story of this great palace. How was it born and how did it die? Who were its kings, princes and queens? What did they believe in? What was the basis of their faith? What formed the inspiration for their wondrous art? Evans' response to these questions was perhaps extreme and ill-judged, but I can't fault his enthusiasm. I feel the same whenever I'm confronted by a ruin, or by a story that begins 'where you are standing now there was once…' The scattered stones are not enough for me. I want to rebuild these fallen glories in my mind's eye and let them live again.

I have experienced this sensation in a number of places around the world. I remember climbing the steps of the Paris Metro at the Place de la Bastille, to be greeted by a blast of car horns and a buzz of scooters. I took a seat at a pavement café and looked out over a roundabout and past a bronze 'freedom' column to the glass and stone bulk of the Opéra National. But there was no trace of the Gothic fortress-prison that once provoked a revolution. The only remaining fragment of dissident spirit I could spot was some anti-Sarkozy graffiti, high on an apartment wall.*

In London, I have crossed the Millennium Bridge from the Tate

* My visit was before the *Je suis Charlie* marches in January 2015, since when the Place de la Bastille has once again been covered in 'dissident' messages.

Modern many times. Faced with Wren's masterpiece, I can't help but picture a different city skyline. If the Pudding Lane bakers had been less cavalier about fire safety, would Old St Paul's, one of the largest, most venerable – and most ramshackle – medieval Cathedrals in Europe, still crown Ludgate Hill in place of today's iconic, baroque dome?

Once, on a summer road trip through Andalucia as we drove west out of Cordoba, a Spanish friend pointed through our windscreen across a grass plain towards a complex of stone buildings in the foothills of the Sierra Morena. These were, he told me, the remains of one of the greatest palaces in Spanish and world history, the Madinat al-Zahara. It was early evening and, with the sun dipping, we took a detour to the ruins. The battery in my digital camera was dead, but I can still see in vivid detail the low light turning the stones red and the dramatic panorama across the plain. I imagined the last caliph enjoying this same view a thousand years earlier – perhaps just days before a civil war erased this dream palace forever.

There is no question that we invest our greatest structures and constructions with personalities. We care about buildings – sometimes, perhaps, more than we care about our fellow human beings. We shout with joy when we raise them up; we weep with sorrow when we destroy them. And, of course, we do continue to destroy them – buildings young and old, all over the world.

Even the longest human life barely exceeds a century. How much more epic are the lives of buildings, which can endure for thousands of years? Unlike the people who made them, these structures experience not just one major historical event, but a great accumulation of them, in some cases stretching all the way from the prehistoric era to the present day. In its lifetime, the same building can meet Julius Caesar, Napoleon and Adolf Hitler. What human could claim the same? If we let them, buildings have the potential to be the ultimate raconteurs. These are some of their stories.

PART ONE

GODS, HEROES AND MONSTERS

Are the gods architecture's greatest patrons, or its greatest enemies? Much has been built in their names. Just as much – very likely a great deal more – has been destroyed. Perhaps this is not surprising. What are gods if not the original architects? And there is, after all, nothing one architect dislikes more than the work of another…

Humanity's first great building myth is a case in point. The Tower of Babel was, it seems, sent to development hell by a god piqued at the audacity of his human creations. Yet even when plans have been handed down directly from heaven, the course of architecture has rarely run smooth. Time and again blueprints produced by divine hands have been misinterpreted by mortal masons. The gods have first commissioned and then abandoned some of their greatest works, from a palace in the hills of a Mediterranean island to a city on a desert plain on the banks of the Nile. These buildings have been inhabited and destroyed by a unique cast of heroes and villains – some imagined, others frighteningly real.

There is one place, however, that the gods have never yet left alone. A hilltop inside a city in an arid Middle Eastern landscape, where a great temple was built, demolished, rebuilt and then burnt to the ground, has become the setting for history's longest running property dispute. A dispute so intractable, some say, that it will only be resolved by the end of the world.

1. MAKE A NAME FOR YOURSELF!

The Tower of Babel – Iraq
(Born 5000 BC – Died 323 BC)

2. MODERNISM'S LABYRINTH

The Palace of King Minos – Crete
(Born 1900 BC – Died 1200 BC)

3. THE FIRST WAR MEMORIAL

The Citadel of Mycenae – Greece
(Born 1700 BC – Died 1150 BC)

4. THE SUN CITY ALSO RISES

Akhetaten – Egypt (Born 1348 BC – Died 1331 BC)

5. JERUSALEM SYNDROME

The Temple of Jerusalem – Jerusalem
(Born 950 BC – Died BC 70)

Chapter One

Make A Name for Yourself!

The Tower of Babel, Iraq (Born 5,000 BC – Died 323 BC)

'And the whole earth was of one language, and of one speech.

And it came to pass, as they journeyed from the east, that they found a plain in the land of Shinar; and they dwelt there.

And they said one to another, Go to, let us make brick, and burn them thoroughly. And they had brick for stone, and slime had they for mortar.

And they said, Go to, let us build us a city, and a tower, whose top may reach unto heaven; and let us make us a name, lest we be scattered abroad upon the face of the whole earth.'

Genesis 11: 1-5[1]

In southern Iraq, halfway between Baghdad and the Persian Gulf, and twenty kilometres to the west of the city of Nasiriyah, a massive, blocky structure rises above the sand flats. It is approached by a dusty tarmac road lined by rusting lamp-posts, slanting electricity poles and roll after roll of barbed wire. A few hundred metres to the south is Tallil Air Base, a vast military complex covering an area of over thirty square kilometres and surrounded by twenty-two kilometres of security perimeter.[2] Once the home of Iraq's Soviet-built, MiG fighter squadrons, Tallil was seized by U.S. forces in March 2003, and held until December 2011. The huge building is visible from almost every corner of the base. Over the years, American soldiers were taken on guided tours – a rare chance to leave behind the Pizza Huts, Burger Kings and Taco Bells[3] that had sprung up around their living quarters, and to experience the culture and history of the country they were occupying.[4]

The structure on the edge of the airbase is made from baked mud-bricks held together by bitumen – the semi-solid form of petroleum that occurs naturally throughout Iraq, a residue from the country's vast oil deposits. At first sight it most resembles a giant sandcastle.[5] Three staircases, each of a hundred steps, converge at a single point below the top of the building – the façade for an even larger block of bricks behind, rising inwards to a wide, flat roof. In the original design this was merely the first and largest layer of a building that continued skywards in a series of stepped terraces decreasing in size towards the summit. Today, only this base remains. In the shadow of the walls a ramshackle hut once sold souvenirs to the U.S. soldiers. From the top, you can see for miles across a flat and near-empty desert plain: the dry wastes between the Rivers Tigris and Euphrates. This place was once known as Mesopotamia, from the Greek meaning 'land between the rivers'.

What did those American troops think about when they were up there? Their guides may have told them that they were standing on the remains of one of the world's first skyscrapers, a temple at the heart of what was one of the largest cities on earth; indeed, that they were standing on the building that may have inspired the legend of the Tower of Babel. And the reason those soldiers were there – to put it in the crudest terms – was because, in America, in what is currently one of the greatest cities on earth, two colossal towers had been destroyed by an act of deliberate and catastrophic violence. From their high vantage point the soldiers would have been able to see, had they known what they were looking for, the place where it all began. Twelve miles to the south, in the heart of the Iraqi desert, is a jumble of sand mounds concealing the world's urban Eden: the first ever city.

That prototype city, and the cities that followed, brought people together as never before. They made them live in complex, cooperative societies, which needed new ideas to keep the people in order: government, law, organised religion, writing, art, and architecture. Cities gave birth to civilisation. But as they accumulated wealth and increased in size, they had to be defended and fought for. Rulers soon learned that they could increase their power by taking other cities by force, then subordinating them to the will of the greatest one: the 'capital'. From the start, cities – and the architecture they created – went hand in hand with war.

Just after 11am on the morning of 8 April 2003, the last remaining antiquities staff evacuated the National Museum of Iraq in Baghdad.[6] For almost three weeks the city had endured an incessant aerial bombardment from the coalition forces of *Operation Iraqi Freedom* – the now infamous 'shock and awe' treatment. Cruise missiles sought out strategic targets, in particular the palaces and administrative offices of Saddam Hussein and his Special Republican Guard. Above the city, smoke and dust cast up from the air-strike ruins mingled with thick black clouds from a ring of trench pits of burning oil around the central districts – an attempt to disorientate missile guidance systems.[7]

By the early days of April, soldiers and militia from the ruling Ba'ath Party and the 'Fedayeen of Saddam' were preparing for the imminent ground invasion, sandbagging buildings, bridges and traffic intersections to create thousands of defensive positions. The National Museum complex covers over eleven acres in the Karkh district at the heart of Baghdad. Its main entrance lies on the road running from the central train station across the al-Ahrar Bridge to the market and financial centre on the east bank of the Tigris: a key strategic location in any battle for control of the city.[8]

The Geneva Convention prohibits the use of cultural sites for military purposes, but its protocols were ignored and the entire museum was turned into a stronghold. Firing positions were dug into the gardens and courtyard in front of the main entrance, a second-floor storeroom was co-opted as a sniper's nest, and the roofs of the library and the Children's Museum were adapted to conceal troops armed with rocket propelled grenades (RPGs). One building was even converted into a command post, stocked with a series of military situation maps to allow for live, strategic tracking of the fighting across the city.[9]

Inside the museum, preparations were equally advanced. Here, however, staff worked to protect one of the finest and most extensive collections of antiquities in the world. For months they had been moving precious artefacts to secure storerooms. By the start of the conflict only the largest objects – heavy sculptures and massive wall friezes – remained in the public galleries. Sandbags surrounded these exhibits, and the ancient statues were trussed up in slabs of foam padding.[10]

Dr Donny George Youkhanna, the museum's Director-General of Research, and Dr Jabber Khalil Ibrahim, president of the Iraqi State Board of Antiquities and Heritage, had planned to stay in the basement for the duration of the battle, and had stockpiled food and water to last for two weeks. At the final moment, however, the two men's nerve failed. When Dr Jabber saw RPG-carrying Iraqi soldiers take up positions in the front garden, he decided that the situation was too dangerous, and evacuated the remaining staff. George and Jabber were last to leave. They passed through the museum, ensuring that all storage rooms and main doors were locked, exited through the back door of the compound, and crossed to the east side of the Tigris to another building belonging to the Board of Antiquities. Their intention was to return a few hours later, when, they hoped, the fighting would be over. But the advancing U.S. troops closed all bridges in the city, and for five days, no one was allowed to cross.[11] The National Museum was on its own – exposed, unprotected and about to become a battlefield.

On 9 April, a tank company from the U.S. Third Infantry Division advanced to an intersection 500 metres to the west of the museum. Their orders were to keep the intersection open as a support route for troops fighting in the northern districts of the city. Within seconds they were taking fire from the museum buildings. The unit's commander estimated that there were between 100 and 150 Special Republican Guard and civilians armed with RPGs and AK-47s in and around the compound. For the next two days the fighting was so intense that the U.S. soldiers did not leave the insides of their tanks.[12]

On the evening of 10 April, as the battle continued out on the streets, a group made their way unnoticed into the rear of the museum. Breaking though a bricked-up window, they navigated the empty hallways to find a passage leading down to the underground storerooms. After opening a secure metal door, they were confronted by an entryway sealed shut by cinder blocks. They demolished a section of the wall, and, using lit plastic packaging and foam padding as makeshift torches, passed through two pitch-dark storerooms to reach a back wall lined with metal safes and locked cabinets. Inside the cabinets were tens of thousands of ancient Greek, Roman, Arabic and Islamic gold and silver coins, and a substantial portion of the world's most precious collection of 'cylinder seals'.[13] These tiny objects – not much more than an inch tall and often no bigger than a human thumb – were first made in Mesopotamia 5,500 years ago, out of materials ranging from clay and limestone to semi-precious stones like agate, carnelian and lapis lazuli. Each one is unique, bearing intricate carved symbols that would once have been pressed and rolled into damp clay as a personal signature or 'seal'. The most exquisite items sell for hundreds of thousands of pounds on the international antiquities market. The right handful could be worth millions.

The thieves had acquired a set of keys to the safes and cabinets – a fact later held up as evidence that they had received help from a member, or members, of museum staff – yet at the crucial moment they dropped them. As the unventilated basement filled with fumes from the burning packaging, they mounted a furious and ultimately fruitless search. The keys were later found hidden under one of the hundreds of empty plastic boxes that lay scattered across the floor.[14] A catastrophic loss was averted only by this simple mistake. The thieves did not, however, leave empty-handed. The plastic boxes had contained precious jewellery and cylinder seals: 5,542 pieces of jewellery and 5,144 seals were taken – a third of the museum's entire collection of cylinder seals.[15] If the contents of the safes and cabinets had also been removed, it might have ranked as the greatest museum theft in modern history. Nevertheless, the robbers were able to make their escape with a staggering number of rare antiquities, none of them too large to carry away in an average-sized rucksack.

A jasper cylinder seal, showing monstrous lions and lion-headed eagles, from the Uruk period of Mesopotamia (4100 BC - 3000 BC)

Early in the morning of 11 April, another group of thieves entered the museum. Their interest was in the show-piece items from the public galleries. Over the course of a few hours, some of the world's greatest cultural treasures – objects dating back to the very birth of civilisation – were stolen. The exquisite 5,000-year old Mask of Warka, the earliest known naturalistic sculpture of a human face, was removed from a restoration room, along with the Golden Harp of Ur, a beautifully decorated wooden instrument dating from 2,600 BC, topped by the solid gold head of a bull. The world's oldest carved stone vessel, the 5,500-year-old Sacred Vase of Warka, was toppled out of its glass display case and hacked away from its base. And the Bassetki Statute, an incomplete figure cast in pure copper some 4,000 years ago, was dragged from the upper storey of a public gallery, shattering every step of the mezzanine's marble staircase on its way down to the ground floor.[16]

The Mask of Warka (c.3000 BC), also known as the 'Sumerian Mona Lisa'

Rumours of unrest at the museum quickly circulated among the international press in Baghdad. The first camera crews to arrive at the complex captured a perfect scene of cultural devastation – a mob of looters running through the shattered hallways of the public galleries. This third wave was made up of residents from the local neighbourhood, opportunists taking advantage of the fall of the city to steal what remained. By this point it was largely stationery and office supplies from the museum's administrative buildings.

The media had one of their first great scoops of the war. 'Museum treasures now war booty' reported the *Associated Press*.[17] *Reuters* led with 'Plunder of past in new Iraq'[18]; the BBC with 'Iraqi art "stolen to order"'.[19] The *New York Times* reported that it had taken 'only 48 hours for the museum to be destroyed'[20], and according to the *Independent* 'not a single pot or display case remained intact'.[21] Expert academics were on hand to provide context. With an impressive eye for specificity, Eleanor Robson, Oxford professor and council member of the British School of Archaeology in Iraq, explained: 'You'd have to go back centuries to the Mongol invasion of Baghdad in 1258 to find looting on this scale'.[22]

She continued by comparing what had happened to 'blowing up Stonehenge or ransacking the Bodleian Library'.[23] Piotr Michalowski, Professor of Ancient Near Eastern Languages and Civilisations at the University of Michigan, went even further, calling the pillaging of the Baghdad Museum 'a tragedy that has no parallel in world history; it is as if the Uffizi, the Louvre, or all the museums of Washington D.C. had been wiped out in one fell swoop'.[24]

Not everyone in the coalition hierarchy saw this as such a catastrophe. At a news briefing on 11 April, U.S. Defence Secretary Donald Rumsfeld appeared to blame television news programmes for exaggerating the scale of the thefts: 'The images you are seeing on television you are seeing over and over and over. And it's the same picture of some person walking out of some building with a vase. And you see it twenty times. And you think, my goodness, were there that many vases? Is it possible that there were that many vases in the whole country?'[25]

The answer to Rumsfeld's question is yes, it is possible that there are that many vases. Or there were. As Abdul Zahra al-Talagani, the media director for Iraq's Ministry of State for Tourism and Archaeology, put it, 'Iraq floats over two seas; one is oil, and the other is antiquities'.[26] The National Museum is like one great archaeological oil well, but the many thousands of precious objects held within its collections are a fraction of what is still waiting, undiscovered, out in the deserts. There are sites where excavators have scarcely been able to move without stepping on 4,000-year-old potsherds, or where archaeologists have found so many ancient artefacts that they have reburied them at the end of a dig season.

The thefts at the museum did not occur in isolation. They were feeding an international black market trade in Iraqi antiquities – a trade which dates back hundreds of years, but which had been growing again at a steady rate since the 1991 Gulf War.[27] Saddam's regime imposed the death penalty for stealing an antiquity – substantially curtailing, for a time, the looting of archaeological sites. But the dealers remained patient, and their opportunity came with the 2003 conflict. As law and order broke down, Iraq's archaeology was opened up to organised crime.[28]

Ancient sites came under the control of the looters and antiquities dealers. Armed gangs – frequently linked to paramilitary groups – provided 'security' for their workforces. Many of the labourers were farmers who had left their families and jobs behind to live on the sites and search for antiquities. Work began before sunrise and halted during the searing heat of the day. Second shifts started in the late afternoon or evening, often running throughout the night, with the excavations lit by lamps powered by car batteries. This was not the painstaking archaeology of the brush and the trowel – the diggers took to their tasks with heavy shovels and hammers, often destroying as much as they recovered.[29] Finding a cylinder seal or a carved tablet could net a looter $50.[30] The potential rewards for the dealers were, of course, much greater. On 5 December 2007, an 8cm-high limestone carving of a lioness was put up for auction at Sotheby's in New York. Described by the auctioneers as 'one of the last known master-works from the dawn of civilisation', the 5,000-year-old 'Guennol Lioness' sold for $57 million to a private collector, making it, at that time, the most expensive sculpture in history.[31] It did not take long for this news to reach Iraq.[32]

Although the exact provenance of the Guennol Lioness remains unknown – some suggest it is Iranian in origin – it was reported as having been found near Baghdad. In the weeks after the sale, newspaper articles quoted dealers in New York recommending antiquities as *the* new growth area of investment.[33] In 2008, *Fortune* magazine ran an article titled 'Really Old Money', explaining that 'the new darlings of the art market are ancient artefacts. It's a wild, high-stakes game with a shady past. Playing it could make you rich – or get you arrested'.[34] The appetite for antiquities has rarely been greater, and it continues to be fed today. Poor, ordinary Iraqis work day and night to unearth fragment after fragment of their ancient ancestry. More and more are doing so on behalf of the militant religious army, Islamic State. The propaganda films of millennia-old objects and buildings being smashed to pieces with drills and bulldozers to illustrate the fate of all 'heretical' cultures are only half the story. As it advances through Iraq, Islamic State is simultaneously gathering up artefacts and selling them to the highest black market bidders.[35] A new term has emerged to describe this trade – 'blood antiquities'.[36] Such is the sad fate of the world's first civilisation.

Few places have a cultural history as deep and rich as Iraq. It occupies the same land as ancient Mesopotamia, and its natural borders have remained unchanged over the millennia: the mountains of Anatolia to the north, the snow-capped Zagros range to the east, the Persian Gulf to the south and the vast Arabian desert to the west.[37] Yet for almost all of the last 2,500 years, this territory has been in foreign hands.

Most recently, of course, it was held by the American-led coalition, whose nearly eight years of occupation ended with *Operation New Dawn* and the withdrawal of the last U.S. forces in December 2011. Before that, the occupation of Iraq can be traced back in time from the British, who controlled the country from 1920 to the revolution of 1958, through the Ottoman Empire, the Mongols, the Muslim caliphs, the Romans and the Greeks, until finally you reach 539 BC, and the fall of the famous city of Babylon to the Persian armies of Cyrus the Great.

It was at the city of Babylon that the fortunes of Iraq turned. In the sixth century BC, Babylon was a cosmopolitan metropolis, the urban centre of the world, and a place of unprecedented architectural wonder. The ancient kings, Nabopolassar and Nebuchadnezzar II, drew on their empire's vast reserves of material wealth – and the skilled and unskilled manpower from many conquered and resettled populations – to create a colossal monument to civilisation. The evidence of an advanced society is to be found not only in the grand palaces and broad boulevards of the city, but also far out in the surrounding countryside. A system of canals and irrigation channels – some built so long ago that their existence was attributed to the gods[38] – made the land's sun-baked soil rich and fertile. Babylon was a seat of art, learning, politics and culture, as well as of political and military power.

Writing around a century after its fall to the Persians, the Greek historian Herodotus only reinforced Babylon's unrivalled reputation for splendour. He described a vast city standing on a broad plain, constructed in an exact square with each side '120 stades' in length. It was not only 'sheer size which renders Babylon unique,' he wrote, 'but its design as well: the city is unlike any other of which we know. First there comes a moat, deep and broad, filled with water, and enclosing the entire city; then there rises a wall, 50 royal cubits thick and 200 cubits high... The wall also features a hundred gates, fashioned out of solid bronze: door-posts, lintels and all'.[39] His account is wonderfully vivid, but the dimensions recorded by Herodotus seem improbably large. The 'two-hundred-cubit wall', for instance, would have risen up nearly 100 metres – a third of the height of the Shard in London. And the '480 stades'[40] circuit of the city is roughly equivalent to a distance of 80 kilometers.[41] By way of comparison, the M25, which almost perfectly encircles Greater London and its population of 8.3 million, runs for 188 kilometres.

What is certain is that Babylon captured the Greek imagination. Four centuries after Herodotus, Diodorus Siculus, author of the *Bibliotheca Historica*, produced a tantalising description of one of the city's most enigmatic architectural features: the famous 'hanging gardens'. To this day – and alone among the Seven Wonders of the Ancient World – the existence of Babylon's gardens remains unconfirmed by archaeological discovery.

Diodorus' account may explain why: 'When the ascending terraces had been built, there had been constructed beneath them galleries which carried the entire weight of the planted garden and rose little by little one above the other.' As the city itself crumbled and disappeared beneath the sands, how could anything have been left of this series of landscaped platforms rising into the sky? Diodorus went on to describe the advanced engineering techniques employed to ensure that the elevated gardens were watertight: first a layer of reeds and bitumen was covered by baked bricks bonded by cement, and then a thick seal of lead was applied. 'On all this again earth had been piled to a depth sufficient for the roots of the largest trees; and the ground, when levelled off, was thickly planted with trees of every kind that, by their great size or any other charm, could give pleasure to the beholder.'[42]

Most magnificent of all, however, was the building created as the centrepiece of Babylon. The city's walls may have cast a long, solid shadow, and its elevated gardens may have amazed by their architectural ingenuity, but both were dwarfed by this one structure – a man-made 'mountain', visible to travellers for miles across the plains. Here's Herodotus again:

> 'A tower of solid brick has been constructed, a square stade in size, and on top of this there stands another tower, and on top of that a third in turn, and so it continues, right the way up to the eighth. Sculpted into the exterior of these eight towers, winding its way to the very summit, is a staircase; and midway up this staircase is a resting place complete with benches, where those who are making the ascent can sit down and catch their breath. In the very topmost tower there is a huge temple'[43].

Herodotus was describing the Temple of Etemenanki; its name means 'the House which is the Foundation Platform of Heaven and the Underworld'.[44] This structure was a 'ziggurat': a temple tower common to Mesopotamia for over a thousand years, designed to rise upwards in a series of large, inward-sloping blocks. With each new level the blocks – ascended by a network of external stairways –

decreased in area as the building increased in height, making an exaggerated, 'step pyramid'. Such towers were always placed in the centre of cities, acting as ever-visible portals between heaven and earth. At the 'skyscraping' summit, kings could approach the gods. And at the same time, gods could make their descent to earth.

In Babylon, the ambition of Nabopolassar and his son Nebuchadnezzar was clear – *their* ziggurat, in *their* city, would be the greatest ever constructed. It was the Mesopotamian way to seek immortality through astonishing feats of architecture, a tradition passed down from the civilisation's mythical beginnings. The *Epic of Gilgamesh*, the world's oldest known work of literature, was written on clay tablets in Mesopotamia over 4,500 years ago. This story told of Gilgamesh, king of the city of Uruk, and his quest to the ends of the earth to challenge the gods and discover the secret of everlasting life.[45]

After a series of increasingly perilous adventures, and with his hopes at last extinguished, the inevitability of man's fate is made clear to Gilgamesh: 'You will never find that life for which you are looking. When the gods created man, they allotted to him death, but life they retained in their own keeping'.[46] As he returns to Uruk, exhausted and disconsolate, Gilgamesh looks up at his city's great walls. In that instant he sees in his building works the spark of immortality. A man's time on earth may be set, he realises, but in architecture his name can live forever.

Generation after generation of Mesopotamian kings followed the example set by Gilgamesh. As an extra measure they had the bricks used in their buildings stamped with their own names. When Nabopolassar and Nebuchadnezzar came to build Etemenanki, this meant a lot of autographed bricks – the estimates range from 17 to 45 million.[47] Nabopolassar also included a baked-clay cylinder in the foundation of the building, with an inscription which gave a full account of his endeavours:

> 'I fashioned mattocks, spades and brick-moulds from ivory, ebony and wood, and set them in the hands of a

> vast workforce levied from my land. I had them shape mud bricks without number and mould baked bricks like countless raindrops... I commissioned the wisest experts and the surveyor established the dimensions... The master builders drew taut the measuring cords, they determined the limits... I rolled up my garment, my kingly robe, and carried on my head bricks and earth. I had soil baskets made of gold and silver and made Nebuchadnezzar, my first-born son, beloved of my heart, carry alongside my workmen earth mixed with wine, oil and resin-chips. I constructed the building... raised its top as high as a mountain... I made it an object fitting for wonder.'[48]

Nabopolassar may have presided over the laying of the foundations, but he never saw his temple raised 'as high as a mountain'. Instead it was Nebuchadnezzar who completed the construction of Etemenanki many years after his father's death, building it up to its full height and cladding the entire structure in blue-glazed brick.[49] The two royal architects were indeed destined for immortality – but not in a way they could ever have imagined. The story of Babylon and its tower would be passed on and on, travelling though history from generation to generation, right up to the present day. Yet those who told it were not full of admiration for the scale and ambition of the city.

During his 43-year reign, Nebuchadnezzar sacked and plundered Jerusalem, destroying the sacred Temple of Solomon and taking the Jews into captivity. The kings of Mesopotamia may have been enthusiastic patrons of art and architecture, but they were also firm believers in the demonstration of power through military force and conquest. The Hebrew population was transported to the capital of the Babylonian Empire. And their revenge was to pass the story of the city down through the generations where it found a place in perhaps the most famous book of all – the Bible.

The biblical accounts of Babylon – *Bab-el*, as it was known in Hebrew – depict a city and a civilisation gone wrong. All around them the prophets saw the signs of corruption, decadence and excess. The Book of Daniel tells the story of the years of captivity, and recounts gleefully the fear and tension of a city on the brink. Most sensational is the scene at Belshazzar's feast, when a divine hand appears and produces the famous 'writing on the wall' – a prophecy of the imminent destruction of Babylon. Belshazzar, a successor of Nebuchadnezzar, demands that Daniel translate the glowing script. To the horror of the king, 'whose knees smote one against another', Daniel reads out that 'God hath numbered thy kingdom, and finished it; thou art weighed in the balances and art found wanting. Thy kingdom is divided, and given to the Medes and the Persians'.[50]

The Book of Daniel was written several hundred years after the Persian invasion of 539 BC, so the author already knew the ending, but it was told so artfully that it became embedded in language and culture. The retelling of the story in the Bible made Babylon synonymous with societal breakdown, civilisation on the edge. It held up the city's extravagant architecture as the epitome of human foolishness and arrogance. And the greatest example of this overweening pride and ambition was Nebuchadnezzar's colossal ziggurat. The temple of Babylon was seen as the prototype for the Tower of Babel – the work of architecture that challenged the authority of God.

Certainly that was what scholars and travellers believed for thousands of years after Babylon's fall. The Persian armies may not have laid waste to the city, but their invasion marked the end of Babylon's position as the world's pre-eminent metropolis. In the fourth century BC, Alexander the Great overthrew the Persian King Darius III and seemed set to once again return the city to its former glory, making it the capital of his vast Empire. Work began on restoring the great works of architecture – in particular the Temple of Etemenanki, which had been damaged and had fallen into disrepair. The Greek historian Strabo wrote that ten thousand men spent two months levelling the structure and clearing the ruined remains in preparation for rebuilding.[51] Yet Alexander died in 323 BC, before work could begin. One of his last acts had been to destroy all that was left of the Tower of Babel. Babylon limped on for several hundred more years – until around the seventh century AD – before it was finally abandoned and left to disappear beneath rising silt and storms of dust and sand. By this time, the biblical Hebrew texts had been translated into Greek and Latin.[52] The real Babylon was gone, and in its place grew a city of myth – a city where, it was said, they once built a tower so high that its top reached the heavens.

Hanging in room ten of Vienna's grand Kunsthistoriches Museum is an oil-on-panel painting titled the *Tower of Babel.* This is the work of the great Flemish Renaissance artist Pieter Bruegel the Elder, and it is the second of at least three paintings of the building he produced between 1553 and 1568. The first – a miniature on ivory completed in 1553 while Bruegel was working in Rome – is now lost. The third, 'small' *Tower,* finished sometime between 1563 and 1568, hangs today in the Museum Boymans Van Beunnigen in Rotterdam. The Vienna *Tower* is by far the largest work of the three, its panel measuring just over a metre by a metre and a half, and it was completed in 1563.[53] Likely a commission for the Holy Roman Emperor Rudolph II, the painting is renowned for its inventive and startling composition. The enormous, half-built tower dominates the centre of the picture, its top skirted by thin wisps of cloud. The newly completed, circular walls of the left side of the tower are a pristine, pale gold. On the right, the construction opens up to reveal a darker, reddish interior with a dense, honeycomb structure, like a beehive.

There are workmen on every level of the tower: operating heavy lifting machinery to raise huge blocks of masonry; perched on ladders and scaffolds; sculpting stone and chopping wood. Makeshift thatched-roof houses cling to the exterior as sleeping quarters for the vast workforce. Men and women cluster around braziers high up on the superstructure, and grand new archways are strung with laundry washing lines. The tower is surrounded by a port city – but even this city's tallest buildings are dwarfed by the very first level of the tower. In the foreground, on a hillside overlooking the scene, a haughty king is presented to a group of cowering, exhausted stonemasons.

Bruegel was playing a game with his painting, teasing the viewer to pick at its many threads to uncover his true meaning. The architecture of the colossal central tower is clearly influenced by the artist's time in Rome: its seven arcaded tiers are a direct reference to the Colosseum, and the power, ambition – and collapse – of antiquity's greatest empire.[54] A closer look reveals that the tower's construction is an exercise in futility. Even though it has already risen so high, not one section is complete from top to bottom. As new walls are built, others appear already to be crumbling away. The chambers inside the building have no obvious use or purpose. The tower is out of control, grotesque in its scale – it is architecture as a disease, a cancer.

The surrounding port is strongly reminiscent of Antwerp, Bruegel's home when he produced the painting. By the mid-sixteenth century, the Flemish town had grown into a prosperous and cosmopolitan trading hub. Its highly developed banking system made it Europe's financial centre, its streets were filled with the chatter of many different languages, and its reputation for tolerance had brought a great inflow of religious refugees. But Antwerp was also under the control of King Philip II of Spain, and by extension, the Church of Rome. Having succeeded his father Charles V in 1556, Philip embarked on a policy of heavy taxation designed to suppress Protestantism and all other non-Catholic religions. Four years after Bruegel finished his painting, ten thousand Spanish troops travelled north on a mission to 'cleanse' the Low Countries. The proud king who stands in the foreground of Bruegel's painting can be read as a symbol of all ambitious leaders whose arrogance blinds them to the inevitable failure of their endeavours. But it is also Philip II – the foreign ruler who stubbornly refuses to acknowledge both the political and religious rights of the people of Antwerp, and his inability to hold back the tide of the Reformation.[55]

The Tower of Babel was a popular subject among the Flemish and Dutch artists of the sixteenth and early seventeenth centuries. Painters such as Hendrick van Cleve, Tobias Verhaecht, Joos de Momper and Lucas van Valckenborch also produced fantastical and nightmarish visions of the tower. And just like Bruegel's paintings, their artworks were coded political statements. For the Protestants of the Low Countries, Rome and its all-powerful Church were the 'new Babylon' – as corrupt and as oppressive as the city they read about in their Bibles.

For more than a thousand years, the only sources of knowledge about Babylon and its tower were the Bible and classical writers like Herodotus. The earliest medieval European account comes from the Spanish rabbi Benjamin of Tudela in the twelfth century. He told of visiting the ruins of the 'Tower of Babel', and described a structure with a base two miles long, and which was 400 feet tall. A spiral path built into the tower led to the summit, 'from which there is a prospect of twenty miles, the country being one wide plain, and quite level'. The rabbi added that he could see the results of God's 'Heavenly fire which struck the tower' and 'split it to its very foundations'.[56] Writing in 1300, the Italian historian Giovanni Villani said that the tower measured 80 miles round, was 12,000 feet high, and 3,000 feet thick[57].

That same century, the traveller Sir John Mandeville claimed that the tower was an astonishing 64 furlongs in height, although he was unable to confirm this by sight, the locals having warned him that the remains were set in a land that was 'all desert and full of dragons and great serpents'.[58] Those who came later to Mesopotamia could barely find any traces at all. In 1575, just over a decade after Bruegel completed his painting, the German botanist and physician Leonhart Rauwolff wrote in *A Collection of Curious Travels and Voyages* that, when he journeyed to the region and was directed to the site of the tower, all that greeted him was a mound 'half a league in diameter, and so mightily ruined and low, and so full of vermin that have bored holes through it, that one may not come near it within half a mile'.[59]

Low, 'mightily ruined' mounds may have been a disappointment to medieval and renaissance travellers, but visitors to Mesopotamia in the nineteenth century viewed them with great significance. In December 1811, Claudius James Rich, a young agent in the British East India Company and amateur antiquarian, journeyed to a site around fifty miles to the south of Baghdad, near the city of Hilla. He wrote of how he 'found the whole face of the country covered with vestiges of building, in some places consisting of brick walls surprisingly fresh, on others merely a vast succession of mounds of rubbish, of such indeterminate figures, variety and extent'.[60]

Rich spent ten days in the region, setting down his observations in a short 'memoir', and putting his cavalrymen to work as surveyors with tape and line to measure the extent of the site. The result was the first modern archaeological record of the ancient city of Babylon. The physical remains were all but gone, but Rich was still captivated. 'Instead of being disappointed at the difficulty of ascertaining any part of the original plan of Babylon,' he wrote, 'from its present remains we ought rather to be astonished at the grandeur of that city which has left such traces, when we consider that it was nearly a heap of ruins two thousand years ago.'[61]

Other explorers soon followed the path taken by Rich to Babylon, including the Victorian archaeologist Austen Henry Layard – who would go on to uncover the famed city of Nineveh – and his Iraqi assistant Hormuzd Rassam, who later unearthed the first clay tablets containing the *Epic of Gilgamesh*. They carried out cursory excavations of the city, but were deterred by the sheer volume of debris[62]: the accumulated rubble of so many crumbling, mud-baked bricks. Other sites promised more immediate discoveries. Layard's subsequent finds at Nineveh included giant statues of winged bulls with human heads, and intricate wall carvings depicting long-forgotten wars, all of which were heaved into crates and floated down the Euphrates to their final destination – the British Museum.

For a time Babylon was considered too diminished to yield the sort of discoveries that would lead to fame and fortune. It was not until March 1899 – almost a century on from Rich's survey – that it became the site of a major archaeological dig. The driving force behind the work was Robert Johann Koldewey, an architect and art historian who had been searching throughout the Middle East for a suitably large site to excavate on behalf of the Royal Museum of Berlin and the newly-formed German Oriental Society.

Babylon was the perfect fit for Koldewey. It was almost certainly the largest archaeological dig yet undertaken[63] – he was tackling an entire city, after all – and it forced him to develop new standards and techniques for archaeological survey. Even then, the success of an excavation can still rely to some degree on luck, and Koldewey enjoyed the most auspicious of starts: one of the very first trenches of the dig unearthed the walls of the 'Processional Way', Babylon's most sacred street.[64] Lined with blue, lapis lazuli-glazed bricks and decorated with life-size figures of striding lions in white and gold, this broad avenue once passed through the 'Ishtar Gate' – dedicated to the goddess Ishtar and the entry point to the inner city – to lead on to Nebuchadnezzar's Temple of Etemenanki. Remarkably, as they dug deeper, the excavators found large sections of this avenue still intact, with thousands upon thousands of the colourful glazed bricks floating preserved in each successive layer of sand.[65]

The excavation of Babylon became an obsession for Koldewey. From the moment when the first spade bit the earth in 1899, he spent almost all of the next decade-and-a-half overseeing the huge dig site. A whole railway system was built and a locomotive brought from Germany to help with the removal of the immense quantities of debris. Hundreds of men were engaged year-round in tasks ranging from earth-moving to measured drawing. Excavations continued even after the outbreak of the First World War, and did not finally end until March 1917.[66]

Koldewey died in 1924, the year after he published his excavation report on Babylon, but the results of his methodical and systematic approach to archaeology are still on spectacular display today in Berlin's Pergamon Museum. The thousands of decorative tiles discovered during the dig were numbered individually and transported to Germany. In 1930, after years of cleaning and restoration work, the Pergamon unveiled a complete reconstruction of the 18-metre-high Ishtar Gate, along with large sections of the Processional Way.

As they put this massive, three-dimensional jigsaw back together, they discovered a long inscription by Nebuchadnezzar, explaining how he had replaced the previous city gates to make way for this new structure:

> 'I pulled down these gates and laid their foundations at the water table with asphalt and bricks and had them made of bricks with blue stone on which wonderful bulls and dragons were depicted... I hung doors of cedar adorned with bronze at all the gate openings. I placed wild bulls and ferocious dragons in the gateways and thus adorned them with luxurious splendor so that people might gaze on them in wonder'.[67]

Once again, Nebuchadnezzar was searching for immortality through architecture, and once again he found it in circumstances that he would never have expected. People still gaze on his gate in wonder, but thousands of years later and thousands of miles away from the spot where it was first built – on another continent, in the heart of another capital city, set inside a great work of 20th-century architecture.

Koldewey's excavation of the Ishtar Gate was a triumphant success, but his search for the Tower of Babel was more problematic. In 1876, George Smith – an assistant at the British Museum who first deciphered the cuneiform script of the *Epic of Gilgamesh* – had translated a clay tablet referring to a great temple tower in Babylon called Etemenanki.[68] This cuneiform text set out the composition of the city's entire temple district as a series of mathematical problems, giving values for the length and breadth of buildings, and then asking the reader to use these to work out the areas.

The result was an unusually precise set of dimensions for Etemenanki. Smith's translation revealed a building with a base of 91 square metres, which rose upwards in a series of seven stepped storeys, with each new base decreasing in size from 78 square metres at the second storey, down to 24 square metres at the summit. The height of the building was recorded on the tablet as measuring the same length as the base: 91 metres. Here, it seemed, was the truth behind the Tower of Babel, revealed in, of all things, an ancient maths test for aspiring Babylonian surveyors and architects.[69]

Koldewey and his team were eager to find the remains of this temple.

Yet when they arrived at its probable location, they were confronted by the sunken, mud-brick core of a levelled building, submerged in a pit of groundwater. The German archaeologists realised they were not the first to dig among the remains. In the 1880s, local people had burrowed into the structure's dilapidated base to remove its baked-brick mantle for building materials. In the process, the site had sunk below the water table. It was not until January 1913, fourteen years into the dig, that the water subsided enough for them to access the foundations.

Koldewey's colleague Friedrich Wetzel was put in charge of the exploration. He worked on the site for just under six months, producing a preliminary survey that had still not been followed up by the time the expedition was called off in 1917.[70] Few physical artefacts were recovered, but Wetzel's work did reveal one significant measurement. Just as the cuneiform tablet had described, the length of the temple base was 91 metres. It may have been reduced to a square pool of oily water, but after nearly two thousand years in obscurity, Nebuchadnezzar's temple was finally reintroduced to history.

In 1978, Saddam Hussein began rebuilding the city of Babylon.[71] Archaeological accuracy was of little importance to him – only the symbolism mattered. He simply built on top of the ancient remains, adding layer after layer of cement and mortar to the baked mud and bitumen-sealed bricks that had endured for millennia.

His aim was to demonstrate to the people of Iraq that he was a successor to the Mesopotamian kings of old. In particular he modelled himself on Nebuchadnezzar, whom he saw as a great warrior-leader – the conqueror of Jerusalem, no less – and whom he described, with crude historical simplicity, as 'an Arab from Iraq'[72]. Massive, state-sponsored images, murals, sculptures, and even laser light-shows[73] mimicked the artwork of antiquity, depicting Saddam in heroic profile – his nose supposedly lengthened to make it more like Nebuchadnezzar's – or carrying a traditional worker's basket on his shoulders. In the modern versions Saddam's basket was not filled with clay as with his 'ancestors', but cement.[74] Just like Nebuchadnezzar before him, many of his new bricks were stamped with an inscription, a message for posterity stating that: 'In the reign of the victorious Saddam Hussein ... the guardian of the great Iraq and the renovator of its renaissance and the builder of its great civilisation, the rebuilding of the great city of Babylon was done.'[75]

On a man-made hill overlooking the ancient city, Saddam built a brand new palace: a huge, ugly imitation of a ziggurat, surrounded by miniature palm trees and rose gardens. Its high walls and ceilings were decorated with murals of Babylon and the Tower of Babel, and the fixtures throughout were plated with gold. In December 2009, almost three years to the day after Saddam was executed, government officials reopened his palace to the public, charging an entry fee of 1,000 dinar – around 75 pence – for them to walk among its bare, echoing halls. There was even the opportunity, for £150 a night, to stay in the marble room where Saddam is said to have slept.[76] For a time, it was suggested that the palace would be turned into a hotel and conference centre, even a casino, but so far it has remained empty, save for the occasional curious visitors.

Saddam's construction works at Babylon provoked condemnation among the international archaeological community. Yet in a sense he was only following Mesopotamian tradition. It was common for their buildings to be levelled and reconstructed on exactly the same spot, with each subsequent version larger and more advanced than the one before. The remains of previous buildings were honoured by being preserved in some form in the foundations, but the structures that rose visibly towards the sky were, almost without exception, brand new. Saddam himself described his work as the 'third reconstruction of Babylon'[77] – following on from Nabopolassar and Nebuchadnezzar, and from Hammurabi, the author of the first ever written codes of law, who had raised the first incarnation of the city to greatness around 1700 BC.

Intriguingly, in the 1960s the German archaeologist Hansjörg Schmid discovered the remains of three successive buildings in the foundations of Etemenanki. The oldest formed part of a tower base of mud brick about

65 metres square, which appeared to have suffered considerable damage. Superimposed on this was a newer mantle of mud brick attached to the previous structure by timber beams, with a 73 metre square base. These were the traces of the temple towers that came before Etemenanki; the last layer, part of Nebuchadnezzar's 91 metre square base, was made up of the baked bricks so extensively pilfered for building materials by locals in the nineteenth century.[78]

Saddam never got the chance to add his own bricks to the pile. The Tower of Babel did not rise from its ruins. Instead, Iraq once again braced itself for foreign invasion. On 21 April 2003, coalition military units moved in to occupy the city of Babylon. In the months that followed, it was transformed into a major military base – known as 'Camp Alpha' – and became a temporary home for at least 2,000 troops. A large helicopter landing zone was built in the heart of the ancient inner city, and acres of the site were levelled to be covered with imported gravel. In December 2004, Dr John Curtis, Keeper of Middle East Collections at the British Museum, was granted access to visit the site for three days. His subsequent report was a damning assessment of the condition of Babylon.[79] Dr Curtis found broken bricks inscribed with the name of Nebuchadnezzar lying in spoil heaps throughout the site. Thousands of tonnes of earth – much of it containing valuable archaeological material – had been used to fill sandbags. Military vehicles had crushed the original brick surface of the Processional Way, and tank fuel was found seeping down into the subterranean layers of the ancient city. Long trenches had been dug around the Temple of Etemenanki as 'anti-tank precautions', with the displaced earth containing fragments of pottery and brick marked with cuneiform inscriptions.[80] Dr Curtis stated that it was not possible for him to determine when, and by which forces, the damage had been caused, but the conclusion was obvious – war had returned to Babylon, and placed what remained of its ancient architecture under immediate threat. The political symbolism of occupying the city had not been lost on the commanders of the coalition. Thousands of years after it first rose to prominence, Babylon still mattered.

At almost the same time as the war broke out in Iraq, researchers working with a private antiquities collection in Norway were beginning to examine and decipher an inscription found on a broken fragment of polished, jet-black stone. This slab – known as a 'stele' – measures 47 centimetres high and 25 centimetres across, and is shaped roughly like a gravestone, with a smooth, flat face and a rounded top. The upper portion of the stele is taken up with three carved images: a standing figure holding a staff and wearing the royal clothing of ancient Mesopotamia; a detailed profile of a huge, stepped temple-tower; and a ground plan of the tower.[81] Below the carvings, on a more damaged portion of the slab, is a partially erased cuneiform inscription.

The Tower of Babel stele © Schoyen collection

As the translation of this inscription progressed, the significance of the discovery began to emerge. The text reveals the standing figure to be Nebuchadnezzar, 'King of Babylon', and it names the temple-tower as Etemenanki. It then goes on to detail how he came to build his great temple: 'In order to complete Etemenanki to the top, I mobilised all countries everywhere, each and every ruler who had been raised to prominence over all the people of the world... The base

I filled in to make a high terrace. I built their structures with bitumen and baked brick throughout. I completed them, making them gleam bright as the sun.'[82]

The stele has been dated to the sixth century BC, and is believed to have been placed within the foundation structure of Etemenanki. Its journey from the base of the tower to a private collection in Oslo remains unclear. At some point in the last two-and-a-half thousand years, after the fall of Babylon and the steady disintegration of Etemenanki, it must have been discovered and removed – and then sold into the antiquities market. The researchers have conjectured that the occupying Persians might have claimed it as war booty, and that the partial erasure of the inscription could suggest that the conquerors intended to add new text to the stele.[83] It may then have re-emerged two thousand years later during the Mesopotamian 'antiquities rush' of the nineteenth and early twentieth centuries, just another artefact in an archaeological dig somewhere distant from Babylon.

Whatever its exact provenance, the stele is an extraordinary discovery. This is the only contemporary image of Etemenanki that has ever been found – a blueprint in stone for the great ziggurat that came to be known as the Tower of Babel. Although George Smith had revealed the probable dimensions of the Tower with his cuneiform translation in the late nineteenth century, its appearance had remained a confusion of classical accounts, biblical narrative, and artistic fantasy. This stele appears to show Babel as it really was – not the impossibly high structure that provoked God's wrath, but an architectural masterpiece of the classical world, and one of the most important monuments in the history of urban living.

There is a postscript to this story of the Tower of Babel. In the books of the prophets Daniel and Jeremiah a clear connection was made between Babylon, Nebuchadnezzar's temple, and the structure that caused God such displeasure: a connection that has persisted up to the present day. Yet the very first mention of the tower comes in Genesis. And according to the latest scholarship, it is likely that the Genesis stories pre-date the construction of Etemenanki by hundreds, if not thousands, of years.

The earliest books of the Bible are a compilation of oral traditions – narratives passed from generation to generation before they were written down in any form. Their sources were wide-ranging and disparate, and often borrowed from even earlier cultures.[84] The famous biblical story of Noah and his Ark, for instance, is drawn from the *Epic of Gilgamesh*: the clay tablets discovered in Mesopotamia in the nineteenth century tell the story of a great flood sent by the gods to wipe out all of humanity save for one man, Utnapishtim, and his family, who built a boat and took into it 'the seed of all living creatures'.[85]

We now know that the *Gilgamesh* account of 'the Flood' dates from at least 2000 BC, and it is generally accepted as having inspired the Bible story.[86] We cannot say for certain that the Tower of Babel does not have a similarly distant origin[87]: not least because, according to Genesis, it was the descendants of Noah who 'journeyed from the east' to the 'land of Shinar' – meaning Mesopotamia – to build a tower 'whose top may reach unto heaven'.

So if Etemenanki was not the inspiration for the story of the Tower of Babel, then what was? To answer that question, we need to return to the solitary building on the fringes of Tallil Air Base. This huge, ruined structure – and sometime tourist attraction for coalition troops – has a history stretching back much further than Nebuchadnezzar's Babylon. It was once the greatest ziggurat in Mesopotamia, built at the end of the third millennium BC in the city of Ur. Today it sits in an arid wasteland, but in ancient times it would have commanded a very different outlook. The course of the Euphrates has shifted significantly over the last few thousand years, so that it now runs ten miles further to the east. Ur was once on a branch of the river, leading into a lagoon that fed the Persian Gulf.[88] Access to the sea made the city a major trading centre, and by 2100 BC it was the capital of an empire stretching across all of southern Mesopotamia, and was possibly the largest city in the world. The first two kings of Ur – Ur-Nammu and his son Shulgi – reigned for sixty-five years between them[89]. What better way to demonstrate the wealth and glory of their kingdom than by raising a ziggurat bigger than any before?

They started with a huge brick base, 61m long, 45m wide, and 15m tall.[90] This was the first of three levels rising skywards. At the very top, at a height of around 30m, was the scared shrine to Nannar, God of the Moon.[91] The completed structure must have been a truly awe-inspiring sight. Shulgi was so proud of his efforts that his people – or perhaps more likely, Shulgi himself – proclaimed him a god. The ziggurat would have towered over the newly-built city of Ur, and been visible for many miles across a country of grain fields and long grasses irrigated by the waters of the Euphrates. It is hard to imagine a much greater transformation than from this abundant environment to the desolate landscape of today. Yet the glory of this original temple tower and its city was rather short-lived. Around 2000 BC, Ur was sacked by an uprising of two disaffected western provinces of its own Empire – Elam and Shimashki. The fall of the city was captured in vivid detail in a 500-line poem written in the immediate aftermath, known as 'The Lamentation over the Destruction of Sumer and Ur':

> That on the two banks of the Tigris and Euphrates, bad weeds grow,
> That no one set out for the road, that no one seek out the highway,
> That the city and its settled surroundings be razed to ruins
>
> [……]
>
> The country's blood pools like bronze or lead,
> Its dead melt of themselves like fat in the sun,
> Its men laid low by the axe, no helmet protects them,
> Like a gazelle taken in a trap they lie, mouth in the dust

[......]

The dogs of Ur no longer sniff at the base of the city wall.[92]

Ur was rebuilt, but it never regained the political influence it once held as the capital of an Empire. The fame of its temples, however, and its status as a site of scared pilgrimage did persist. Successive rulers of Mesopotamia thought it prudent to honour the gods by repairing and maintaining the architecture of Ur's religious precincts.[93] Indeed, one-and-a-half thousand years after it was first built, Nebuchadnezzar himself commissioned extensive reconstruction work on the ziggurat. And two-and-a-half millennia on from that, Saddam Hussein ordered the erection of a massive brick façade around what remained of the original base. Here was a structure older than the Bible, rising higher above the land of Mesopotamia than any other before, built by a king claiming to be a god – and part of a city destroyed after it had displayed an excess of ambition, wealth and pride. Could the ziggurat of Ur have been the inspiration for the Tower of Babel? The parallels seem compelling, particularly when you consider that a city called Ur is mentioned in the Bible as the birthplace of Abraham, son of Noah and father of the Jewish people.[94]

Twelve miles to the south of the ruins of Ur, even further into the wasted desert, seven heaped sand mounds break the flatness of the plain. If you are reading this book in a city, look up for a second and take in everything around you: the dense rows of high buildings, the hum and buzz of relentless traffic, the packed press of a tube carriage, the low, never-ending sprawl of the suburbs. All this began somewhere. Unlikely as it may seem, it was here in Iraq, in a place called Eridu – the 'first city' of Sumerian myth – in a landscape that today seems as far removed from humanity and progress as anywhere you could imagine. A great ziggurat once rose up in Eridu, built by Amar-Sin, son of Shulgi, as a counterpart to the temple of Ur.[95] It was, however, never completed, its construction halted by the fall of the empire. This looming, half-built 'skyscraper' across the plains from the city of Ur is an even stronger candidate for the original Tower of Babel. The eerie, abandoned building site must have made a powerful impression on the people of Mesopotamia who came after the destruction of Ur – perhaps so powerful that they passed on its fate as a tale of architectural ambition undone by man's hubris.

The Tower of Babel disappears into the clouds in Gustave Doré's 1865 engraving 'The Confusion of Tongues'

Eridu was excavated between 1946 and 1949 by Fuad Safar of the Iraqi Directorate General of Antiquities, with the British archaeologist Seton Lloyd acting as adviser.[96] According to an ancient Mesopotamian creation myth found – in its earliest form – on a 3,600-year-old clay tablet, it was at Eridu that mankind began.[97] Unlike Eden in the Bible, however, Eridu was no garden of paradise. From the very start it was a city, built by the god Marduk, the creator of everything. It was first home to the gods, who found it to be 'the dwelling of their hearts' delight'. Marduk then made man to serve the gods and to live with them in the city.[98] The excavation had set its sights high. Eridu was more than just the potential place of origin for Mesopotamian culture. Here, it was suggested, could be the very beginnings of civilisation itself.[99]

Work began on the largest of the sand mounds, and soon uncovered the remains of an extensive terraced structure. Bricks inscribed with the names of the kings of Ur were raised out of the rubble, appearing to confirm that this was the ziggurat half-built by Amar-Sin at the end of the twenty-first century BC. The archaeologists probed deeper. Beneath one corner of Amar-Sin's ziggurat, they discovered the walls of another large structure, which they were able to date back much further – to 3800 BC. This find was itself of huge significance, but they did not stop there. The excavators wanted to keep going below these remains, to see if anything else could be detected. No fewer than seventeen further layers of building works progressed down into the earth, before, at the lowest level, the traces of what Safar and Lloyd called a 'primitive chapel' were uncovered, around 3 metres square, resting 'on a dune of clean sand'.[100] Opposite the door of this structure was a pedestal, and in one wall was a tiny alcove, perhaps intended for a sacred statue or sculpture. The proposed date for these remains was around 5000 BC. Here, it seemed, was the first temple, in the first ever city.

Every one of the eighteen buildings was made of sun-dried brick – a material always in the process of crumbling back into the earth. The response of the architects of Eridu, however, was not simply to patch up and repair. Instead they kept adding and adapting, each time making a structure larger and more advanced than the one before. Such was their enthusiasm that they did this at least once every century over the course of more than a millennium.[101] Buildings were pulled down and their foundations levelled to create elevated platforms, and new structures were erected on top, always rising higher above the earth. As the temple grew, so too did the city, spreading across the landscape to bring more people inside its streets and walls. Just like Ur, ancient Eridu was fed by the Euphrates, and it once sat on a lagoon of fresh water emerging naturally from the earth. This was known as the 'apsu': a divine, life-giving water source, whose presence at Eridu made the city the most sacred in Mesopotamia.[102]

The layers of building works at Eridu provide an elegant and unique demonstration of the history of urbanism. Unlike others of their time, the people of Eridu were never satisfied with what they had created. They strove relentlessly for improvement. The fabric of the past was enshrined within their new works, but they did not let tradition stand in their way. They believed that things could always be better, and that man had the power within himself to innovate and create. The excavation at Eridu uncovered the fragments of what may have been the world's first city. But it also revealed something more important. Here, on one small square of earth, is the archaeology of an *idea*. The history of Eridu is the history of progress and ambition.

The Tower of Babel is a central figure in this same history. Whether the story can be traced to a single, real building or not is beside the point, because its true foundations can be found at Eridu. This mound of ancient sand and brick in the Iraqi desert *is* the tower – or rather, it is what the tower represents. Its height is not measured in metres, but in the tide-marks of successive buildings – seam after seam of architectural evolution that rise up through the centuries. Perhaps the story of Babel was meant as a warning that progress should never proceed unchecked. Or it may have been inspired by jealousy and a dread fear of change. Either way, some fragment of the tower has always been present, every time man has looked to build something new. It is both the angel and the devil on the architect's shoulder. It whispers, 'Beware, don't let ambition be your downfall'. And in the same breath it says, 'Build up to the heavens and don't look back. Go to it. And make a name for yourself.'

CHAPTER TWO

MODERNISM'S LABYRINTH

The Palace of King Minos, Knossos, Crete
(Born 1900 BC – Died 1400 BC)

In February 1893, Arthur Evans – archaeologist, collector, journalist, traveller, and Keeper of the Ashmolean Museum in Oxford – picked his way through the stalls of the Shoe Lane bazaar in Athens. With him was John Myres, a young scholar working at the British School of Archaeology.[1] As the two men moved through the narrow streets below the Acropolis, antiquity dealers brought forward tray after tray of artefacts for them to sift through. This was also the leather-work district of the city, and the air around was thick with the pungent smell of the tanneries.

Evans lingered at one stall, where a collection of three- and four-sided stones had caught his attention.[2] Removing his glasses, he held the stones just a few inches from his eyes and stared at the tiny symbols engraved in their surfaces. He had seen similar markings before, on a handful of curious artefacts held by his museum in Oxford.[3] Evans was something of an expert in numismatics – the study of currency and ancient coins – and his extreme myopia had the advantage of allowing him to study small objects in near-microscopic detail.[4] The more he looked, the more he became convinced that the symbols represented some obscure form of writing – a script that no one had ever seen before. He asked the dealer if he knew where the stones had been found.

'*Kriti*,' was the answer.[5] The stones were from Crete.

In March 1894, Evans made his first visit to Crete. His journey by steamship from Athens took him far out into the Aegean. There is no more appropriate way to arrive in Crete than by sea. For millennia, it has been the keystone of a bridge of islands running eastwards to join Europe to Turkey and the Middle East. To the south, there is nothing for hundreds of miles until the coasts of Libya and Egypt.

Evans' steamship approached the island from the north-west.[6] His first sight of Crete was the pale silhouette of the *Lefka Ori* – the 'White Mountains' – a range of imposing limestone peaks, still snow-capped in late spring and early summer, that surge up from the coastline to a height of over 2,200 metres. Further east, he could pick out the impressive bulk of Mount Ida – the summit of the island at 2,456 metres, and said to be the birthplace of Zeus. Just beyond the mid point of the northern coast, Evans' steamer turned in towards the sheltered harbour of the Cretan capital, Heraklion. Immediately behind the port was another mountain, Juktas. Evans had been told that, if you stood in the right place at the right time of day, you could discern in Juktas's rocky outline the profile of a recumbent Zeus – his broad forehead and pointed nose; the great expanse of his beard.[7]

Evans was captivated by Crete. He found the port of Heraklion a striking blend of east and west. A massive wall surrounded the city, built by the Venetians. The spires of old Christian churches rose up over the rooftops. But so did a series of mosque minarets – a sign that the Ottoman Turks were the current lords of Crete. There were fragments of structures and stonework going back much further, to the Byzantines, Arabs, Romans, and classical Greeks. Evans could see in Heraklion's architecture the constant push and pull of history, the relentless clash of races and cultures.[8]

His first destination was the city's bazaar, where he bought twenty-two stones carrying similar markings to those he had found in Athens. The following day he visited Ioannis Mitsotakis, the Russian vice-consul to Crete.[9] Mitsotakis had been collecting artefacts on the island for a number of years, and had recently found a gold signet ring in the hills above Heraklion, near a place called Knossos. The ring was engraved with more of the curious symbols, as well as depicting what appeared to be an ancient scene of worship involving a god, an obelisk and a tree. Evans negotiated a price with Mitsotakis, and later in life described the ring as one of his 'most precious spoils'.[10] Rather than pass it on to the Ashmolean, he kept hold of it himself for the next forty-four years.[11]

The name Knossos was familiar to Evans, as it was to any classical scholar. In the *Odyssey,* Homer had singled it out in his description of the island: 'In the middle of the wine-dark sea, there is a land called Crete, a rich and lovely land washed by the sea on every side; and in it are many peoples and ninety cities... Among the cities is Knossos, a great city; and there Minos was nine years king, the boon companion of mighty Zeus.'[12] Writing in the fifth century BC, the Greek historian Thucydides claimed that Minos was the 'earliest of those known'[13] to establish a navy and that he used it to control the Aegean and colonise and rule over the islands of the Cyclades. In the *Iliad*, Homer identified the grandson of Minos, Idomeneus, as the lord of Crete, who sailed with eighty ships to support Agamemnon of Mycenae in the siege of Troy.[14]

There was also a darker side to Knossos. According to Greek legend it was the site of a vast underground labyrinth, built by Daedalus, a brilliant inventor, master-craftsman and architect. At its heart was an abomination – a creature born of an unnatural union between Minos' wife Pasiphae and a bull: the Minotaur. Every year Athenian youths were sent in tribute to Crete, and cast into the labyrinth to feed the Minotaur, until Theseus – with the help of Minos' daughter, Ariadne, and a ball of twine – killed the monster and escaped.

The myth was told by Ovid, Plutarch, Virgil, Apollodorus and many others. Although it reached the height of its popularity in the seventh and sixth centuries BC, when the final battle between Theseus and the beast was a common subject of vase-paintings, the story has persisted right up to the present day. Its symbolism remains potent: man first tries to conceal his shame where it cannot be found, before he comes to realise that the only way to overcome his troubled past is to confront it head on.[15] The Minotaur is the dark side of the psyche, the beast within us all.

The legend certainly made a lasting impression on the Romans. A regular discovery in the fields and olive groves of Crete were coins dating back to the Roman occupation of the island. On one side they had the word 'Knosion' or the abbreviation, 'Knos'[16]; on the other was a labyrinth symbol or an image of a man with the head of a bull.[17] Many early explorers travelled to Crete in search of Minos and his labyrinth.

The Italian monk Cristoforo Buondelmonti carried out the first modern survey of the island in 1415. Roaming across the landscape for eleven weeks, he recorded an ancient underground quarry on the slopes of Mount Ida, and concluded that this was the dark lair of the monster. Over the centuries, others followed Buondelmonti to explore the mountain caves, with one of the most vivid accounts of the experience coming in 1779 from the French explorer Claude-Étienne Savary: 'We walked with precaution in the doublings of this vast labyrinth, amid the eternal darkness that reigns throughout it, and which our torches could hardly dispel.'[18] Just like Theseus, Savary and his companions unravelled a ball of twine as they went. It was little wonder that 'the imagination raise[d] up phantoms; it figure[d] to itself precipices under the feet of the curious, monsters placed as sentinels'.[19]

Others had marked out a different location for the labyrinth of Daedalus. Just two decades after the visit of Buondelmonti, the Cordoban traveller Pero Tarfur identified a site three miles outside of 'Candia' – the old name for Heraklion – as the labyrinth, where 'many other antiquities' could be found.[20] In 1834, Robert Pashley, an antiquarian and Fellow of Trinity College, Cambridge, travelled to Crete and agreed with Tarfur that a hillock of ruins 'in the immediate neighbourhood of the site of Knossos' called to mind 'the well-known ancient legend respecting the Cretan labyrinth, the locality of which is uniformly assigned to this city'. For the sober-minded Pashley, however, there was 'no sufficient reason for believing that the Cretan labyrinth ever had a more real existence than its fabled occupant.'[21]

In the nineteenth century, the locals called the site of Knossos by the Greco-Turkish word *kephala* – meaning 'big head'[22] – and in April 1879, a local merchant pleasingly named Minos Kalokairinos decided to dig down into the soil to see what he could find. Almost immediately he hit what appeared to be the traces of a massive rectangular building. Walls began to emerge from the earth, and on one side of the mound he found what seemed be a storeroom, containing giant, five-foot-tall ceramic jars known as *pithoi*.

A thousand metres to the south of *kephala,* through a wooded area that he christened the 'Forest of Jupiter', Kalokairinos discovered a large underground quarry. What else could it be, he speculated, other than the labyrinth?[23] After three weeks, these tentative excavations were called to a halt by the Cretan parliament, who feared that the ruling Ottomans would claim any significant finds as the property of the empire, and remove them to the Imperial Museum in Istanbul.

Kalokairinos may have been barred from further digging, but this did not deter him from publicising his discoveries. He sent samples of the *pithoi* to London, Paris and Rome[24] – indeed, the metre-tall terracotta jar he gave to the British Museum is still on show today in room twelve of the Arthur Fleischmann gallery. Interested parties began to descend on Knossos, and Kalokairinos was more than happy to show them around the site. W. J. Stillman, a former American consul to Crete, returned to the island on behalf of the Archaeological Institute of America to report on what had been unearthed. At Knossos he described 'huge blocks of hewn stone, gypsum and sandstone,' and remarked that 'the structure is the earliest example of the style commonly known as Hellenic that I have ever seen.' His tantalising conclusion was that he was 'at a loss to attribute this work to any other period or any other use than that which would belong to the Daedalian Labyrinth.'[25]

Stillman's rather breathless account piqued the interest of the German archaeologist, Dr Heinrich Schliemann, who had achieved worldwide fame for his excavations of 'Priam's' Troy and

'Agamemnon's' citadel of Mycenae. Schliemann's goal was to use archaeology to uncover the truth behind Homer's epic poems. The prospect of excavating another Greek legend was too good to miss. Even before visiting Knossos, he entered into negotiations to buy the site. Schliemann was exceptionally wealthy, but he was also a shrewd businessman, and he baulked at the prices quoted for the land. He suspected that the owners were attempting to cheat him by, among other things, listing more olive trees than the property contained.[26] Nevertheless, his efforts to acquire Knossos continued for several years, right up until his death in 1890. A report in the *Athenaeum* recalled a wistful Schliemann visiting the site and staring at 'a huge building peeping, but what it was... he could not tell, and thus he was obliged to go away without having dug his spade into the ground.'[27]

On 19 March 1894, Evans hired a local guide and rode out of Heraklion towards Knossos. They left the city through the great gate of the old Venetian fortress, and began to climb up a series of clay slopes still wet from the heavy rains of early spring. As they picked their way higher into the foothills above the city, they travelled past the vineyard estate of a Turkish monastery, and then through the fallen, fragmentary remains of *Colonia Julia Nobilis*, a Roman town built in the early years of the first century AD.[28] Here and there were the stones of villas, temples, aqueducts and bathhouses – even the sweeping curve of a theatre. Evans paid these ruins little notice. As his guide led him over the summit of another hill, he caught his first glimpse of Knossos. Half-hidden by pine trees was a wide, rounded knoll, lying in a hollow above a river valley, and surrounded on three sides by gentle hills strung with vineyards and olive groves.

Evans rode down to the tree line, tethered his horse, and walked out into the centre of the knoll. He later recorded in his diary that it was 'brilliant with purple white and pink-ish anemones and blue iris'.[29] Climbing down into the trenches dug by Kalokairinos fifteen years before, he saw great sandstone blocks overgrown with soil and weeds. As he cleared away the earth, touching the ruins for the first time, he was able to make out a distinctive sequence of rock-cut symbols and engravings. To his intense excitement, these looked exactly like the tiny, indecipherable markings on the stones from the Athens bazaar. Evans had not come to Crete looking for King Minos or the Labyrinth; instead he was following 'a clue to the existence of a system of picture-writing in the Greek lands'.[30] Remarkably, without any need for excavation and within just a few minutes of arriving at Knossos, he appeared to have succeeded in tracing this clue back to its original source.

Evans had planned to spend a fortnight on Crete. This turned into forty days. In that time he travelled across the remotest and wildest reaches of the island, looking for more signs of ancient remains, visiting isolated towns and villages, and asking everywhere for examples of the engraved stones.[31] In this last endeavour he met with particular success. Thanks to what Evans called a 'happy accident of Cretan superstition,'[32] he was able to collect a large number of the stones on his travels. It turned out that it was a custom for the women of Crete to seek out these particular artefacts and wear them around their necks, believing that they helped with milk production during breast-feeding. Evans described how he 'made a house-to-house visitation in the villages, and by one means or another prevailed on many of the women to display their talismans... Ladies of a certain age were not altogether averse to parting with their 'milk stones' for a consideration, but with the younger women it was a more delicate business'. Often he found that his requests were refused by first-time mothers. 'I would not sell it for ten pounds!' he was told. 'Don't you see my baby?''[33]

On 25 April, Evans sent word to the *Athenaeum* that, from the engravings on the walls at Knossos, and through collection and close examination of the 'milk stones', he had produced a catalogue of eighty different symbols belonging to two separate, and previously unknown, scripts – which he called Linear A and Linear B. His note emphasised the importance of this discovery: 'The evidence supplied by these Cretan finds shows that long before the time when the Phoenician alphabet was first introduced into Greece, the Aegean islanders, like their Asiatic neighbours, had developed an independent system of writing.'[34]

Evans believed he had found an entirely new civilisation on Crete – and not just any civilisation. 'I do not think that it is too much to say that the 'baneful signs' of Homer are here before us,' he wrote.[35] 'The golden age of Crete lies far beyond the limits of the historical period.'[36] His implication was clear. Here was a new origin point for the classical world, and by extension all of western civilisation. To Evans, deep down we were all Cretans.

In 1895, Evans returned to the island with his young colleague John Myres. The two men continued to search for traces of a lost culture, exploring in particular the Lasithi Plain, a flat expanse of farmland set high in the Cretan mountains. Here they discovered a string of ancient fortifications, and abundant evidence that 'these remote uplands harboured more than one walled city'[37]. Among the weathered ridges were crumbling watchtowers, a great 'military' road, even a shattered acropolis, which seemed 'to have been deserted before the dawn of history.'[38]

In assessing this extensive defensive network, Evans referred to the fortifications of the mountainous region of eastern France recently annexed by Germany during the Franco-Prussian War: 'We might be on the Vosges instead of the Cretan mountains,'[39] he wrote. It would take another four years of persistent negotiation, fighting off claims by rival archaeology schools and securing the support of no less than Prince George of Greece, before it was all his. Not that he had ever been in any doubt. One day he and Myres hiked up to a hill overlooking the site. As the two men sat and ate their lunch on the grass, Evans turned to his friend and announced, 'This is where I shall live when I come to dig Knossos.'[40]

Arthur Evans was born in 1851, and grew up in the small industrial town of Nash Mills near Hemel Hempstead in Hertfordshire. His father, John Evans, was an archetypal Victorian patriarch – on the one hand a captain of industry running a flourishing paper-mill business; on the other, a prolific amateur scientist pursuing often ground-breaking research in the fields of archaeology, geology, palaeontology and anthropology.[41]

Over the years John amassed a vast collection of coins, fossils, flint implements and prehistoric bronzes, transforming his family home into a museum. Evans spent his childhood in a kind of time capsule, in a place where ancient history was all around him – even, as his half-sister Joan recalled, in the air he breathed.

> 'The house in those days had a scent that was all its own: a scent compounded by the spiciness of leather bindings, the sour smell of flints, the slight acridness of rusted bronze, the faint aromatic incense of carpets and hangings from the East ... The perfume of jasmine might blow in at the window, and rose petals might drift through the open door; but the essential scent was the dry smell of Time itself.'[42]

While still a schoolboy, Evans accompanied John on archaeological digs, and he soon inherited his father's enthusiasm for collecting and his ceaseless appetite for work and travel. Educated at Harrow and then Brasenose College, Oxford, where he read history, Evans would interrupt his studies with 'Long Vacations'[43] – deliberately arduous journeys on foot or on horseback into hard terrain and 'primitive' countries throughout Europe. Roughing it appealed to the romantic in Evans.

It was a journey to the Balkans in 1871, made when he was just twenty years old, that really ignited Evans' adventurous, liberal spirit. As he traversed the Slavic landscape, moving from Slovenia to Croatia and on past Zagreb, he fell in love with the region's history and architecture – Muslim, Venetian, Byzantine, Roman – but even more so with the people. At that time, Bosnia-Herzegovina was still part of the Ottoman Empire. Yet everywhere he travelled, he encountered the signs of revolution. Local uprisings were met with bloody reprisals. There were stories of torture, murder and looting; villages destroyed and refugees marching across the country.[44] Evans admired the spirit and tenacity of the Bosnians, and cast them as heroic figures struggling against oppression and brutality.

In 1875 he returned to the Balkans with his brother Lewis, and compiled the notes from this journey into a book: *Through Bosnia and the Herzegovina on Foot, During the Insurrection, August and September 1875*. The brothers journeyed with only their knapsacks, sleeping kit and a revolver each. Evans' account is a fascinating travelogue, but it is shot through with romanticism. His ardent hopes for a peaceful and independent future Balkan state lead him to view the political struggles through an idealised and questionable version of the region's ancient past. In particular he waxed lyrical about the ancient 'Republic of Ragusa' – modern day Dubrovnik – as the 'Athens' of the Balkans, evoking a peaceful, maritime society that had lived thousands of years before, and which supposedly proved that the Slavic people were 'capable of the highest culture and civilisation'.[45]

This marriage of myth and modernity reached a peak in Evans' narrative of crossing the mountains of the Dinaric Alps. On arriving at a beautiful glade, alive with flowers, butterflies and insects, he imagined he had entered the domain of the fairies and nymphs of Europe's 'old world', who were the true agents of revolution: 'they are singing the fates of men; they are weaving destinies; they are watching with motherly tenderness over the heroes of the race, who... are dreaming on of better days... till the guardian nymph shall rouse each warrior from his sleep to sunder for ever the chains of the oppressors.'[46] In his enthusiasm, Evans had invented a mythology like that of the Greek Gods on Olympus: on a 'fairy mountain' at the pinnacle of the Balkan landscape, the fortunes of men and nations were being decided.

Over the next few years Evans became a prominent spokesman for this Slavic revolution. In 1877 he was appointed as the Balkan correspondent to the *Manchester Guardian*. From his base in Ragusa, he captured in a series of impassioned dispatches both the wider political climate and the experiences of individual people caught up in the troubles. When not interviewing insurgent leaders or detailing the squalor and hardship of refugee camps, he roamed the countryside, excavating obscure burial mounds and the remains of Roman buildings, collecting Greek coins, visiting medieval castles, and transcribing old Bosnian inscriptions.[47]

At the end of his first year as a reporter, while he was covering the outbreak of war between Turkey and Montenegro, Evans heard that the historian Edward Freeman, an old Oxford friend and mentor, was in Ragusa with his two daughters. Eager not to miss their visit, he rode overnight on horseback from the Montenegrin highlands back to the Dalmatian coast. Freeman's eldest daughter, Margaret, had met Evans years before in Oxford, but the robust and passionate figure who appeared in Ragusa was an altogether more exotic and appealing proposition.[48] In February 1878, with Evans briefly back in England, the two announced their engagement. The manner of their celebration was typical of Evans: the pair travelled to London to view Schliemann's new exhibition of antiquities excavated from the fabled city of Troy.[49]

For the next four years, Evans continued as Balkan correspondent, living in Ragusa with his new wife in the *Casa San Lazzaro*, a grand Venetian house he had acquired overlooking the sea. By 1882, the region still appeared no closer to freedom – it had passed first from the Turks to the Russians, and then on to the control of the Austrian Empire. Evans' journalism became still more politicised, and then strayed into activism: gatherings of people known to be sympathetic to the Slavic cause became a regular occurrence at the *Casa San Lazzaro*.[50]

The Austrian authorities soon tired of Evans, and on 7 March, he was arrested and held in the city's local jail.[51] He was released after seven weeks, but was expelled immediately from the country and barred from ever returning to Ragusa or Austria. To the relief of his family Evans decided to return to England – yet his half-sister observed wryly that a, 'heartfelt prayer went up from Nash Mills that Arthur would not take to Celtic archaeology and try to right the wrongs of Ireland.'[52]

The family's prayer would be answered. Instead Evans turned his attention to righting the wrongs within his own *alma mater* of Oxford. In 1884, at the age of thirty-three, he was appointed to the keepership of the Ashmolean Museum. At that time the museum was regarded by the university authorities as more of an irritant than an asset – a relic that had suffered from years of neglect and disorder. Evans, however, saw only opportunity. Here was the chance to establish the Ashmolean as a centre for archaeological studies, and he spent much of next decade pouring his energies into its revival, a task that took him from the macro-politics of the Balkans to the micro-politics of institutional academia. The ultimate transformation of the museum was as much a testament to his patience as it was to his tenacity.

The keepership was also a perfect fit with Evans' *wanderlust*. The conditions of residence not only made travel possible – they also presumed it, on the basis that it would lead to new acquisitions. The only firm requirement was for Evans to give occasional public lectures on the progress of his studies.[53] At the same time as rebuilding the museum, he was also constructing a new home, which he called 'Youlbury', on a sixty-acre estate in Boar's Hill near Oxford. This great Victorian mansion was completed in 1894, tragically too late to receive the Evans family. Margaret Evans died of tuberculosis in March 1893, and never had the chance to enjoy the house, garden, lake and woodland her husband had created for her.[54] Youlbury would always remain a base for Evans, a place where he could return after his travels. But it was never really home. Instead, another home – his spiritual home, perhaps – was still waiting for him, out across the 'wine-dark' sea.

In the spring of 1929, the young archaeologist and Cambridge Blue John Pendlebury arrived in Heraklion with his new wife, Hilda. Evans' chauffeur was waiting at the harbour to greet them.[55] The couple were driven out of the city and up into the hills along a rough, twisting valley-road that led towards Knossos. Near the end of the track, the car reached a small, lime-washed cottage sitting behind a stone wall. This was where Pendlebury was to stay during his visit. The building was known affectionately as the *Taverna*, and sat just a few metres through the trees from Knossos.

From the *Taverna*, a path climbed up a steep slope through cypress, olive groves and clusters of oleander and bougainvillea. Fragments of ancient statuary had been arranged among the trees and within sight of the path – the remains of a shrine, a broken column, or a fractured plinth. A headless statue of the Emperor Hadrian which Evans had found in the ruins of a nearby Roman villa rested in the shade, toga slung over one arm.[56] Near the top of the path a building emerged from the summit of the hill. It was wide, blocky and rectangular, with a low, flat roof that stood out against a backdrop of pine trees. Its windows boasted dark shutters, and at its rear it dropped down into the earth, with bedrooms sitting below ground level, designed to provide a cool refuge from the heat of the Cretan summer. At the front of the house, a terrace was surrounded by a garden filled with dwarf iris, palms, honeysuckle, roses and jasmine.[57] This was the house that Evans built in 1906 as his Cretan home, on the exact spot where he had once told John Myres that he would live. Known as the Villa Ariadne – after the daughter of King Minos – it was here that Evans, the new lord of Knossos, held court.

Arthur Evans (left) at Knossos in 1900 with two other members of the original dig team – Theodore Fyfe and Duncan Mackenzie.

Pendlebury did not know it, but he was being groomed to take over as curator of the site. At 78 years old, Evans had lost none of his energy or enthusiasm – but his time on Crete was coming to an end. Knossos had been a near all-consuming passion, and had entirely dominated the second half of his life. His report on the dig, *The Palace of Minos,* already stretched across two weighty volumes, and number three was on the way. The fourth and final instalment was still five years from publication. Evans had grown more concerned with his book than with the excavation of Knossos. By this time what mattered most to him was his interpretation of the site that he was billing as the most important archaeological discovery of the twentieth century: the origin point of European civilisation.

The dig had begun almost three decades earlier, on 23 March 1900. Evans had only managed to secure full ownership of Knossos at the turn of the century, his negotiations having been held up by the short, yet brutal Greco-Turkish war of 1897. Crete won its independence, but at a considerable cost – a series of Muslim-Christian massacres had devastated much of the island.[58] As in the Balkans, he was witnessing a modern society torn apart by the collapse of the Ottoman Empire. And as in the Balkans, he would try to use the past as a balm to heal the wounds of the present. When Evans and his party left Heraklion on the first day of the excavation, they met a large group of Cretans looking for work on the dig site. He instructed his foreman to choose men and women in an even mix of Christians and Muslims, so that, as he put it, the work at Knossos might be a symbol 'of the future cooperation of the two creeds under the new regime in the island'.[59] For Evans, resurrecting their ancient past would begin the process of reconciliation for the divided people of Crete. At just past eleven o'clock that day, a British military tent was pitched on top of Knossos, a Union Flag raised above it, and the ground was broken for the first time.

Just a few inches into the grass and soil, the tops of walls started to emerge. As they dug a little deeper, the excavators began to uncover fragments of frescoes. Working even further down into the earth, they found that the walls were up to two metres high. Still streaked with red paint, they formed a room lined with benches made of gypsum – a soft, grey-white mineral rock – facing a large, square basin. Perhaps the most extraordinary discovery was a small, elaborately-sculpted gypsum chair, with a high back fashioned into a leaf shape.[60] Evans stood over the chair as it was hoisted from the soil. This, he announced immediately to his excavation party, was 'the oldest throne in Europe'[61] – and the sunken tank was a royal bath.

The pace of the discoveries was breathtaking. Great deposits of clay tablets – some whole, some in pieces – were brought out of the earth. 'The cry is still they come,' Evans wrote home to his father.[62] Hundreds grew into thousands, all of them marked with the same form of picture writing he had first seen in the Athens bazaar. 'It is extremely satisfactory,' he continued, 'as it is what I came to Crete seven years ago to find.'[63] It was a telling letter: what had once been revolutionary to Evans was now merely satisfactory, a single component of something much bigger. He could now glimpse that Knossos was more than just a library of lost scripts.

As the dig continued, it became clear that the heaped hillock of earth concealed a massive and complex structure – unequivocally a palace to Evans' mind – covering an area of more than six acres.[64] In fact this was not just the remains of one 'palace', but of several, a sequence of architectural adaptations and reconstructions indicating that people had lived continuously on this one spot for many hundreds, perhaps even thousands of years, going back to the fourth millennium BC. Evans also coined a name for his civilisation. If the site of Knossos was indeed the Palace of Minos, then the people who had once lived within its walls should follow their famous king – and so he christened them 'Minoans'.[65]

Within weeks of the start of the dig, the excavators unearthed their first picture of a Minoan. As they cleared away the dirt from the surface wall of a long corridor section, a figure, painted on the stonework, became visible. 'A great day!' wrote Evans in his diary. 'The figure was life size with flesh colours of a deep reddish hue... The profile of the face was of a noble type... In front of the ear is a kind of ornament and a necklace and bracelet are visible... It is far and away the most remarkable human figure of the Mycenaean age that has yet come to light.'[66]

Throughout the remains of the palace, more fragments of ancient artwork emerged. There were frescoes of flowering olive trees, figures 'gathering saffron', groups of 'court ladies' sat in lively conversation. To Evans' intense excitement, there was also a 'great relief, in painted stucco, of a charging bull'[67] – thought to have once covered the north portico of the palace. The bull motif recurred throughout the site, in other frescoes and reliefs, and particularly in engravings on clay tablets.[68] Most unusual of all was a fragmentary painting that appeared to show a figure engaged in an elegant somersault over the horns of a charging bull, with another figure waiting behind the animal to catch them. Here, surely, was a record of some ancient and incredibly dangerous sport or ritual – it has been questioned whether such an act of 'bull-leaping' is even possible. To Evans it was an eerie echo of those mythical Athenian youths sent each year in tribute to face the Minotaur. He was rapturous. 'What a part these creatures play here!' he wrote.[69]

Spectacular archaeological discoveries and classical legends were coming together at Knossos in an intoxicating mixture. Evans struggled to maintain his scientific equilibrium. His romantic side began to dominate. 'There can be little remaining doubt,' wrote Evans to *The Times,* 'that this huge building, with its maze of corridors and torturous passages, its medley of small chambers, its long succession of magazines with their blind endings, was in fact the labyrinth of later tradition which supplied a local habitation for the Minotaur of grisly fame.'[70] It was October 1900 when Evans composed this letter – just a few months into the dig, and yet already he was blurring the boundaries between fact and the imagination. Increasingly, Knossos was turning into an excavation of Evans' own psyche.

In 1929, Evans walked Pendlebury on a tour though Knossos. Every section of the excavated palace was named with a picturesque flourish. There was the Room of the Throne, the Hall of the Colonnades, the Room of the Lotus Lamp, the Court of the Distaffs, the Megaron of the Double Axes, the Hall of the Jewelled Fresco, the House of the Fetish Shrine and the Room of the Lady's Seat.[71] Evans had not stopped at embellishing the ruins of Knossos with evocative titles; he had embarked on rebuilding them. Pendlebury had never seen a dig site like it in his life. No one had. Everywhere, fragments of the palace had risen again from the earth: walls, floors, stairways, columns, colonnades, porticos and roofs. And all of them sharp-edged and gleaming against the hard blue Cretan sky.

It was their newness that gave them away. Each structure was made out of reinforced concrete – the building material of the modern world employed to recreate an ancient palace of the Bronze Age. 'Very confusing' had been Pendlebury's immediate reaction to this hybrid Knossos in a letter home to his father after an earlier visit in 1928, and 'spoilt in places by Evans' restorations'.[72] No wonder he was confused. The Palace of King Minos was one of the very first concrete buildings to be constructed on Crete. The Villa Ariadne – Evans' house on the hill – was the other.[73]

It had not been Evans' original intention to rebuild Knossos in this way; the project of reconstruction was, in some respects, an accident of circumstance. There was evidence throughout the site that the final incarnation of the palace had been consumed by fire[74] – even down to the black scorch-marks that still marked the walls of the 'throne room'. It appeared that timber frames had once supported the upper storeys of the building. These had disintegrated almost completely over the centuries, but their place had been taken by massed heaps of clay and rubble. As digging cleared this debris, however, it also removed everything that was preventing the upper levels from crashing down into the lower.

Evans first used wooden beams and posts as scaffolding to ensure that the excavated structures remained in the exact places where they had been found. It was soon obvious that these props were inadequate for the Cretan climate: they rotted away over the course of a single season. Next they tried brickwork and custom-cut slabs of masonry – a time-consuming and very expensive process.[75] In 1905, a series of harsh winter storms threatened all of these makeshift structures with collapse. The prospect so horrified Evans that he enlisted the services of Christian Doll, an architect who had studied at Cambridge.

Doll had two immediate tasks: one was to find a lasting solution to the problem of protecting the site, and the other was to build a permanent residence for Evans at Knossos – the Villa Ariadne. For the latter, Doll introduced to Crete a fashionable new building material: reinforced concrete.[76] As Evans watched the superstructure of his villa rise up on the summit of the hill overlooking Knossos, he realised he had his answer.

Concrete allowed the protective shelters to evolve into what Evans liked to call 'reconstitutions'. After the First World War, the pace of this work increased considerably, with Doll replaced by Piet de Jong, a Dutch architect and artist. In a journal article for the Society of Antiquaries in 1926, Evans admitted that 'to the casual visitor who first approaches the site... the attempt may well at times seem overbold, and the lover of picturesque ruins may receive a shock'.[77] Two years later, however, as he presented his most recent concrete additions to the Royal Institute of British Architects, he was rather less circumspect. 'It is not too much to say,' Evans began his address, 'that in the last few years the site of Knossos has renewed its life'.[78]

The result was stark and – to many observers – quite unsettling. Concrete is a utilitarian building material: severe, bold and unashamedly functionalist. It would become a favourite of Le Corbusier, the Swiss-French architect and self-styled doyen of modernism who came to prominence in the 1920s with a new world view that imagined cities and homes as 'machines for living'. It is a great irony that Evans appeared to have 'unearthed' this vision for the future as the very beginnings of western European architecture. If you believed the 'reconstitutions' of Knossos, then Le Corbusier wasn't breaking new ground, merely going back to first principles. The English historian R. G. Collingwood was particularly scathing in his assessment: 'The first impression on the mind of a visitor is that Knossian architecture consists of garages and public lavatories'. For Collingwood there was 'no taste, no elegance, no sense of proportion', just a building fit for 'comfort and convenience – a trade, not a fine art.'[79] It was a review that would have made Le Corbusier proud.

Evelyn Waugh came to Knossos in February 1929, while on a Mediterranean cruise. His verdict was a customary mixture of caustic description and acerbic wit: 'I think that if our English Lord Evans ever finished even a part of his vast undertaking, it will be a place of oppressive wickedness,' he wrote, continuing:

> 'I do not think that it can be only imagination and the recollection of a bloodthirsty past which makes something fearful and malignant of the cramped galleries and stunted alleys... these rooms that are mere blind passages at the end of sunless staircases; this squat little throne set on a landing where the paths of the palace intersect... is not the seat of a lawgiver nor the divan for the recreation of a soldier; here an ageing despot might crouch and have borne to him, along the walls of a whispering gallery, barely audible intimations of his own murder.'[80]

The buildings constructed on the ruins of Knossos – some even reached several storeys high – may have been cast in bare concrete, but they were not without decoration. As Evans explained in the fourth and final volume of *The Palace of Minos*, it was the 'duty of the excavator to preserve, wherever practicable, the history of the building by replacing *in situ* – even when it entailed some reconstruction of the walls – replicas of the fresco designs as completed from the existing fragments.'[81] To create the replicas, Evans employed two Swiss artists, a father and son team, both called Émile Gilliéron. Their work on the frescoes created a sensation: here were vivid scenes of an ancient, lost world, depicted in an artistic style that was fluid, free and joyous. In one, an athletic young prince, wearing a crown of flowers, stands in a field of lilies. In another, a group of glamorous palace women sit talking, their hands held up in excitement over some choice piece of gossip. There is immediacy to these paintings – and a sense of familiarity and universality.[82]

Today these scenes remain some of the most recognisable representations of early European culture, featuring, as the Cambridge

Classics professor Mary Beard puts it, on everything from postcards and posters to T-shirts and fridge magnets.[83] And they seem custom-made for mass-reproduction – that twentieth century 'gift' to all artworks. Their enduring popularity is perhaps due to the fact that we can see ourselves in these figures, still recognise our own lives in a culture so distant in time. This familiarity was so pronounced that some questioned the exact degree of 'restoration' involved. As Waugh once again commented, 'It is impossible to disregard the suspicion that the painters have tempered their zeal for accurate reconstruction with a somewhat inappropriate predilection for covers of *Vogue*.'[84]

He was right to be suspicious. Often only the smallest fragments of the original frescoes were actually found – a few square inches here and there, and sometimes with no evidence that they even belonged to the same painting. The rest of the jigsaw was left to the imaginations of Evans' modern artists. In the most extreme example, the fresco given the name the 'ladies in blue' was first created by the elder Gilliéron from a handful of paint chippings, which showed upturned hands, and faint glimpses of clothing. The heads and the outfits were all his own work. Yet this version was itself seriously damaged by earthquake in 1926, and so the fresco we know today is a reconstruction of a reconstruction, carried out by Gilliéron's son.[85] The queer result of all this architectural and artistic licence was that the ancient ruins of the Palace of Minos were gradually beginning to fuse with a distinctly modernist mansion[86] – its walls covered in fresh Art Deco-style murals. Evans was quite unable to recognise, let alone acknowledge, that in his 'reconstitutions' time was very much out of joint. Indeed he openly expressed wonder at the glaring anachronisms. 'These scenes of feminine confidences, of tittle-tattle and society scandals,' he wrote of the 'court ladies' frescoes, 'take us far away from the productions of Classical Art in any age. Such lively genre and rococo atmosphere bring us nearer indeed to quite modern times'.[87] He had lost himself too deeply in a labyrinth of his own making.

From the start there had been something of the gentleman's club about Evans and his entourage at Knossos: the ageing widower and his team of bachelor excavators, architects and artists. They enjoyed midday lunches in the long, cool dining room of the Villa Ariadne, and convivial dinners on the terrace beneath hoods of fragrant jasmine. Evans imported ox tongues, caviar, foie gras, plum puddings and jam from the Army and Navy store in London. For drinks there was whisky, gin, French wine – Evans refused to drink the local Cretan grape – and champagne.[88] Over the years, however, this club began to shift towards something more akin to a cult. Men like the Gilliérons and de Jong were as much disciples as colleagues, inspired in their work by Evans' increasingly vivid reconstructions of Minoan society as a pacifist utopia.

In his introduction to *The Palace of Minos,* Evans made clear that, over the course of his excavations, he had come to understand that the dark tales of sacrifice at Knossos – embodied by the Minotaur myth – were a false history: 'The ogre's den turns out to be a peaceful abode of priest kings, in some respects more modern in its equipments than anything produced by Classical Greece.'[89] And to Evans the labyrinth – that dread work of architecture bringing death to anyone unfortunate enough to enter it – was really a dance floor, a place of joy and celebration. He recalled a passage in the *Iliad* describing Achilles' great bronze shield, its surface covered with delicate engravings of vineyards, ploughed fields, wedding parties and harvest banquets; wonderful vignettes of peace and tranquillity, and a stark counterpoint to the death and destruction on the fields of Troy.[90] One of the scenes on the shield was 'a dancing circle, broad as the circle Daedalus laid out on Knossos' spacious fields, for Ariadne the girl with the lustrous hair.' Here beautiful young men and women linked hands, and danced in 'rows crisscrossing rows – rapturous dancing'.[91] Evans obsessively searched for Ariadne's dance floor, locating it at several different parts of the ruins of Knossos – wherever there were broad, paved areas that would allow space for any kind of performance. Every year on a common island feast day, he made his workmen re-enact the scene, encouraging Christians and Muslims to join hands and move together in a meandering dance that mimicked 'the mazy turns of the labyrinth'.[92] To Evans, the ease with which his men took to this ritual was evidence that it had somehow survived across the millennia to remain part of island life; a shared pagan heritage transcending modern religious division.[93]

At the spiritual centre of Evans' pacifist Minoan society was a 'mother goddess', whom he described repeatedly in *The Palace of Minos* in long passages straying from science into sermon: 'She presides over births and fosters the young both of land and sea,' he wrote, continuing: 'Like Artemis, she combines the attributes of nurture and of the chase'. He envisaged the goddess as 'central to the cult of the Palace and of Minoan Crete as a whole... standing on her sacred peak with her pillar temple behind her.'[94] Female figures appeared repeatedly in artworks, sculptures and clay tablets discovered on site. Perhaps even greater numbers appeared on the antiquities market as forgeries – objects that may well have been the work of the Gilliérons.[95] After all, the line between 'restoration' and 'fake' had already been so blurred that the Swiss artists may have struggled to appreciate the difference.

Evans' excavation of Knossos became a political and philosophical act. As war once again descended on Europe, he had a deep personal need to believe there was hope for civilisation, that the continent's common ancestry could ultimately point to a peaceful future.[96] His 'Minoans' were half archaeological reality, and half antiquarian wish-fulfilment. In 1899, Joseph Conrad published *Heart of Darkness*, a short novel set on the Congo River. Its bleak perspective on colonialism and imperialism suggested that civilisation is always built upon – and frequently sustained by – unmentionable cruelties. Evans was the antidote to Conrad's character Mr Kurtz, the mysterious, troubled figure waiting at the end of the Congo.

At Knossos Evans saw the opportunity to establish the first Europeans as un-warlike, artistic and benevolent – western civilisation sprung from a utopia set on a bountiful island at the centre of the Mediterranean Sea. His repulsion at the violence of the modern world – from the Balkan and Cretan conflicts to the First World War – sent him searching for evidence of better days in Europe's deep past.[97] Even before the dig had begun, he was interpreting Minoan archaeology based on this theory, and suppressing evidence to the contrary. This included the extensive series of military fortifications he discovered in 1895 whilst travelling across Crete with John Myres. At Evans' Knossos, there was no place for 'the horror'.[98]

During the first six months of 2013, sharp-eyed travellers on London's Underground – or those with the energy to lift their eyes up from the morass of the daily commute – would have noticed a series of unusual signs that had appeared at various places throughout the network. Each of the 270 signs – one for every station – displayed a unique monochrome version of the labyrinth, with a red 'X' sitting at the exit (or entrance). Produced in vitreous enamel, the material used for signs throughout the Underground, they are the work of the contemporary artist Mark Wallinger, commissioned as part of the celebrations for the Tube's 150th anniversary.[99]

The Victoria Station labyrinth © Mark Wallinger

In Wallinger's vision, the X is the cue to enter the labyrinth, and embark on a single, meandering path into its centre and back out again: a route that echoes the Underground traveller's journey. 'Mostly we go about our business, journeying to work on the Tube and return home along a prescribed route,' he explains. 'The seeming chaos of the rush hour is really just the mass of individuals following the thread of their lives home.'[100] Wallinger's inspiration came directly from the symbols recurring on the coins and engravings from Knossos: the pattern of the Cretan labyrinth, which bears a strong resemblance to the two hemispheres of the human brain. For Wallinger, the traveller's journey is both physical and mental: a descent into the transport arteries of London, and also a space into which their imagination can wander.[101] The labyrinth of Knossos – the labyrinth of Evans – still endures. In one of the modern world's great cities, it has become a familiar symbol marking the start and end of the working day for millions of people.

Perhaps this contemporary development should come as no surprise. The Palace of Minos was one of the sensations of the early twentieth century, and became a touchstone for the foremost artists, architects, writers and philosophers of the age. Evans may not have realised it, but he was excavating Minoan and modernist culture at the same time. In 1913, the Greek-born, Italian artist Giorgio de Chirico completed a series of five paintings that situated a statue of Ariadne within a spare, near-empty landscape where modernist-looking reconstructions of classical architecture – rows of columns and archways – cast long, mournful shadows. The parallels with Evans' concrete additions to Knossos are obvious: even more so given that de Chirico was once a student of none other than Émile Gilliéron. Whether the paintings shaped Evans' construction work or vice versa, it is hard to say.[102] Regardless, this blurring of the artistic boundaries between the past and the modernist present had a profound influence on the surrealist movement of the 1920s.

Pablo Picasso was an admirer of de Chirico, and was also fascinated by another key aspect of the symbolism of Knossos – the Minotaur. His interest in the bullfight was spurred to another level by Evans' excavation of the labyrinth.[103] The bull and the Minotaur emerged as common motifs in his work, most famously in his *Guernica* mural, a massive, kaleidoscopic, Cubist response to the destruction in 1937 of an entire Spanish town by German bombers.

In the late 1930s, with Europe once again threatening to tear itself apart, Knossos became for many a cherished vision of life before the fall.[104] When the American writer Henry Miller visited Crete during a tour of Greece in 1939, he was unmoved by criticisms of the way the Palace had been reconstructed: 'However Knossos may have looked in the past, however it may look in the future, this one which Evans has created is the only one I shall ever know. I am grateful to him for what he did.' More important to Miller was what it represented to a continent on the brink of war: 'Knossos in all its manifestations suggests the splendour and sanity and opulence of a powerful and peaceful people... I felt as I have seldom felt before the ruins of the past, that here throughout the long centuries, there reigned an era of peace... In short, the prevailing note is one of joy.'[105]

In the aftermath of the Second World War, Evans' view of Crete as a pacifist paradise filtered down to subsequent generations, in whose imaginations it grew still more vivid and extreme. In the nuclear age, the island was embraced as the potential site of a new Eden in the event of a global holocaust. For the flower-power peaceniks of the Sixties and Seventies, it was where civilisation could begin again, a chance to return the western world to its creative, feminist origins.[106] Indeed, if you venture off the beaten track in Crete today, you can still find many traces of this once vibrant, now somewhat grubby, counter-culture. There is no need for Ariadne's ball of twine – just follow the scent of hashish and patchouli to the heart of a tie-dyed labyrinth.

Evans brought the Minoans onto the world stage just at the point when they could be consumed by a new monster: the mass media. In *The Palace of Minos* he went into exhaustive detail about Minoan culture and society, painting one of the most evocative pictures of an ancient civilisation that archaeology has ever known. Yet there was still a mystery over what happened to the Minoans. The ruins of Knossos had been left undisturbed for thousands of years before Evans embarked on his dig. Nevertheless, the stark reminders of the final moments of the Palace were still everywhere to be seen. The building had been ravaged by fire. There were blackened walls and floors, fragments of charred timber. From the positioning of the scorch marks, it was even possible to work out that on the day of the blaze – some time in the fourteenth century BC – the wind had been blowing strongly from the south.[107]

Evans attributed the end of the Minoans to a natural catastrophe – specifically, to an earthquake. Subsequent archaeological research has confirmed that there was a cataclysmic event, but that the Palace was repaired and rebuilt in its aftermath. Sometime in the seventeenth or sixteenth centuries BC, the island of Thera – the modern day tourist destination of Santorini – was torn apart by a massive volcanic explosion. Huge quantities of rock, fire and sulphuric acid were propelled twenty miles up into the atmosphere. Only a hundred miles away, Crete would have been rocked by a sequence of massive earthquakes, and smashed by the colossal force of a gigantic tidal wave.[108] For a time the impact on Minoan – and Mediterranean – civilisation would surely have been devastating. But it was not fatal. The Palace of Minos recovered and grew again.

John Pendlebury, Evans' successor at Knossos, had a different theory. He believed that an act of man rather than of god had brought about the end of Europe's first civilisation. In the war-torn early years of the twentieth century this must have seemed a depressingly familiar scenario – which perhaps helps to explain why Evans opted to discount it as a possibility. Pendlebury, however, was a different breed of archaeologist to Evans: he was a rationalist and a man of action. In his book *The Archaeology of Crete*, he felt perfectly able to recreate the last moments of Knossos as it fell to an invading force from the mainland:

> 'Now there is a name which is always associated, if not with the sack of Knossos, at least with the liberation of its subjects – Theseus. Names have a habit of being remembered when the deeds with which they are associated are forgotten or garbled... On a spring day, when a strong south wind was blowing which carried

> the flames of the burning beams almost horizontally northwards, Knossos fell. The final scene takes place in the most dramatic room ever excavated – the Throne Room. It was found in a state of complete confusion. A great oil jar lay overturned in one corner, ritual vessels were in the act of being used when the disaster came. It looks as if the King had been hurried here to undergo too late some last ceremony in the hopes of saving the people. Theseus and the Minotaur! Dare we believe that he wore the mask of a bull?'[109]

Even Pendlebury was getting carried away with the dramatic possibilities. Unlike Evans, though, he was able to rein himself in, ending this thrilling account with the reminder that 'such imaginings' are 'not suitable to archaeology'.[110] In a tragic irony, Pendlebury would experience first-hand what it was like to defend Crete from an aggressive army from the mainland. At the outbreak of the Second World War, he joined Military Intelligence, becoming a leading figure of the island's resistance. On 20 May 1941 German paratroopers targeted Crete for the first airborne invasion in history. Pendlebury was wounded in the fighting and found refuge in the cottage of a local woman. When he was tracked down by German soldiers and refused to respond to interrogation, they lined him up against a wall and shot him dead.[111]

'Here I am still alive,' said Evans when he heard the news, 'and that young man with all his promise is gone.'[112] Evans despaired of the modern world and its incessant cruelties. Knossos was his retreat from the belligerence of the twentieth century, and his optimistic history of the Minoans clearly struck a chord. Like Henry Miller, many were 'grateful to him for what he did.'

In more recent years, however, a shadow has been cast over Evans' Cretan paradise. In her 1973 memoir *The Villa Ariadne,* Dilys Powell, the British journalist, film critic and wife of the archaeologist Humfry Payne, described the 'pall of history pressing bloodstained and heavy on summer days' at Knossos.[113] Powell spent several dig seasons on

Crete after her husband was appointed director of the British School of Archaeology at Athens in 1929. 'For me it had always been afternoon in the Palace, late afternoon,' she wrote, 'the pines solid and gold-fringed in the dying sun, and as I clambered about the reconstructed passages something sacrificial in the air; one half-expected a roll of drums. In those days it had been comforting to escape from the deserted labyrinth back to the company at the Villa.'[114] Powell felt dread where Henry Miller had sensed joy. In the late 1970s, in a cave on Mount Juktas, the three-thousand-year-old remains of a young man were found tied and bound to a stone altar with a bronze dagger lodged in the chest.[115] In the mid-1980s, at a site close to Knossos, the ancient bones of two young children aged roughly eight and eleven were discovered bearing marks that are consistent with butchery.[116] Could it be true that the peace-loving Minoans practised human sacrifice and cannibalism? Somehow, despite all Evans' best efforts, the spectre of the savage Minotaur once again raises its great, horned head.

Chapter Three

The First War Memorial

The Citadel of Mycenae – The Plain of Argos, Greece (Born 1700 BC – Died 1150 BC)

In the small village of Mykines, several hours' drive south-west of Athens on the Peloponnese peninsula, there is a small, nondescript guest-house run by a man called Agamemnon. Even for those with superficial knowledge of the classics, this name should be familiar. Agamemnon was the legendary king in what the poet Hesiod called the 'Age of Heroes'[1] – a warrior-leader who united the disparate tribes of Bronze Age Greece, and led them across the 'great gulf of sea'[2] to modern-day Turkey, where they laid siege to the city of Troy.

Agamemnon's guest-house – that of the present-day Agamemnon, that is – was opened in 1869 by the current owner's great-great-grandfather, and it is called *La Belle Helene:* the beautiful Helen. The name refers, of course, to Helen of Troy, or more accurately 'Argive Helen', the Spartan queen from the plain of Argos, who first married Menelaus, Agamemnon's brother, before eloping to Anatolia with her new lover, the Trojan prince, Paris. Soon afterwards Agamemnon set off in pursuit with a thousand ships.

La Belle Helene was the second residence in Greece to be granted a hotel licence, and for a long time it was the only guest-house in the region. Over the years it has developed a peculiar mythology of its own. Fragments from the visitors' guest book, now browned with age and held in glass frames on the lobby walls, provide a deliciously bizarre roll call of heroes and villains from the modern world. There are the signatures of the philosophers Jean Paul Sartre and Karl Jung, the Beat poets Jack Kerouac and Allen Ginsberg and the photographer Cecil Beaton. The composers Claude Debussy and Benjamin Britten came, as did Virginia Woolf and Roger Fry. William Faulkner was a guest, Agatha Christie stayed many times, and Henry Miller passed through on his delirious tour of Greece just before the outbreak of the Second World War.

Three names in particular are likely to stop guests in their tracks: Heinrich Himmler, Herman Goering and Joseph Goebbels.[3] Why did the head of the Gestapo, the commander-in-chief of the Luftwaffe, and the Reich Minister for Propaganda travel to a tiny pension in a near-deserted corner of the north-eastern Peloponnese?

The answer is war.

Among the towering limestone mountains that rise from the floor of the Argive plain, sits a shrine to man's insatiable lust for conflict and conquest. On a rounded hilltop, reached by a steep walk uphill from *La Belle Helene,* are the ruins of a colossal citadel. Its now shattered walls were so big that they were said to have been built by the Cyclops, an ancient race of giants. The poet Homer identified this place as Agamemnon's palace-fortress, the greatest ever constructed in Bronze Age Greece. It was 'Mycenae, rich in gold'.[4]

For western European civilisation, this place is war's ground zero – the spiritual home of every 'hawk' who ever took up arms and marched across continents in the footsteps of Agamemnon, the one-time 'lord of men.'

On the evening of 18 June 1922, Alan Wace, Director of the British School of Archaeology in Athens, led an excavation team up the steep, rocky slopes of Hagios Elias, the higher of the two mountains behind the ruins of Mycenae. They set up camp for the night, and in the morning began searching for the ancient remains said to have been left behind on the summit, soon finding traces of broken-down walls.

Wace was a rationalist, deeply suspicious of the romantic streak that had consumed archaeology in the late nineteenth and early twentieth centuries. Yet even he could not help but inject a touch of the sublime into his excavation report. He begins soberly enough: 'The peak of Hagios Elias is so high, so precipitous and so isolated, that it makes an ideal watch or signal station'. From his high vantage point, he could see the beams of a modern lighthouse sweeping over the waters of the Gulf of Corinth. 'How many years ago' he wondered, had watchmen 'suddenly seen the red glare leap out' on some distant peak, and 'then themselves lit the beacon to rouse the burghers of Mycenae below?' Could they be camping on the very spot that marked 'the last in the chain of fire signals which... announced the fall of Troy'?[5]

Wace's vision of a watchtower was inspired by a famous play written nearly 2,500 years earlier. In 458 BC, the Greek dramatist Aeschylus produced *Agamemnon*, his take on the tragic events said to have occurred at Mycenae following the end of the Trojan War. The play begins at night, with a watchman at a lonely lookout point. He has been at his post for ten years, and knows 'the stars by heart... our great blazing kings of the sky'; yet he fights to stay awake, in the hope that he will at last see 'the signal fire breaking out of Troy.'[6] If the spine of peaks to the east lights up one after the other with burning beacons, it will mean victory for the Greek armies – and the end of the city of Troy. As the watchman cries 'for the hard times come to the house, no longer run like the great place of old', a brightness appears in the east, 'some godsend burning through the dark.'[7] It is the precious news that he has been waiting for. His great king, Agamemnon, is coming home.

Also waiting is Clytemnestra, Agamemnon's wife and the half-sister of Helen. She, however, has a darker purpose. In order to obtain fair winds for the journey to Troy, Agamemnon was forced to sacrifice their daughter Iphigeneia to the gods. For a decade the queen of Mycenae has nursed her wrath; now, finally, she has her chance for revenge. She lays a sacred purple cloth beneath the feet of her returning husband: a deliberate attempt to trick him into an act of hubris to anger the gods. Later that night, after a great feast, Agamemnon rests in his royal bath to wash off ten years of war and travel. Clytemnestra and her lover Aegisthus slip into his chamber, stab him to death, and throw his bones to the dogs and the vultures.

This play, the first part of a trilogy known as the *Oresteia* – after Agamemnon's son, Orestes – is a meditation on justice, crime and punishment, and an attempt by Aeschylus to dramatise the lives of legendary figures of old to make sense of the personal and political ethics of his own era.[8] Yet it is shot through with a sense of dread and foreboding, not just for the fate that awaits Agamemnon, but also for the mysterious cataclysm that engulfed all of Bronze Age Greece. Some seven centuries before the play was written – and just after the time when the Trojan War was said to have taken place – Mycenae was destroyed in a great fire. A whole civilisation went with it, as palaces across the Mediterranean and the Peloponnese were sacked and ruined. Whether through some self-destructive, anarchic civil war or an outside invasion – the cause remains uncertain – the glittering, golden light of the Mycenaeans was extinguished. What followed were four centuries of darkness. Agamemnon's death cries marked the beginning of the end, and, as Aeschylus' watchman foretold, 'the rest is silence.'[9]

Was Agamemnon a real person? This question is almost impossible to answer. What we do know, however, is where he came from. Around the eighth century BC, Greece began to re-emerge from the ruins of the Bronze Age. Cities and palaces were gone, and writing appeared to have vanished completely. Instead there was a land of tiny scattered settlements – basic, humble and insular.

Gradually, however, the silence was broken, and in the most compelling fashion. Storytellers travelling between communities shared accounts of a collective past, populated by a large and fantastic cast of heroes and gods. The Trojan War was one of the most popular tales, and the great conflict and its aftermath were turned into two epic poems – the *Iliad* and the *Odyssey* – by a man, or a number of men, using the name of Homer. Recited again and again by the light of village hearths, these poems supplied a glamorous origin story for classical Greece, offering a fractured people a tantalising glimpse of former glories. Characters were at the heart of Homer's work: powerful men and women burdened by real flaws, passions, tensions and contradictions. They loved, hated, fought and betrayed each other, and through them Homer explored deep questions about morality and what it meant to be human. So skilful was the storytelling that, to the rapt audiences, these people were powerfully, vibrantly alive.

Many communities still lived in the shadows of the old Bronze Age ruins, at once attracted to and intimidated by the sheer scale of the ancient walls. As Homer's poems evolved into a universally accepted gospel, these sites took on a sacred, religious significance. At Mycenae, countless offerings were placed in or around the remains of the citadel: helmets, shields, weapons, vases, figurines and wine cups. As writing slowly returned to the Greek civilisation, these objects began to be inscribed with Agamemnon's name, or just with dedications to 'the hero'.[10] Around a kilometre to the south of the citadel, a shrine – complete with an altar to carry out the animal sacrifices that recur over and over again in Homer's tales – was built to his memory and filled with more offerings. Another shrine was built to the north, this time to Agamemnon's spiritual father: Ares, the god of war.[11]

Mycenae became a centre where the universal spirit of the warrior hero was celebrated.[12] Homer had portrayed Agamemnon as a deeply ambivalent character, yet this seemed of little consequence when it came to his fame and veneration. He may have been stubborn, selfish, belligerent and arrogant, but he was also charismatic and powerful. One of the central dramas of the *Iliad* concerns the devastating consequences of a petty dispute between Agamemnon and Achilles over the captured slave-girl Briseis. Rather than harm his popular reputation, however, this squabble merely emphasised Agamemnon's role as a man of greatness. His implacable will had marshalled an entire people to undertake their greatest military campaign, and his actions, however self-interested, had a direct bearing on the lives and deaths of many thousands of Greeks and Trojans. Agamemnon was a giant in every sense: mind, body and spirit. His super-sized personality demanded respect and admiration across the ages.

For many visitors to the ruins of Mycenae – and people have been coming now for over two and a half millennia – the sheer scale of what remains is seen as proof enough of Agamemnon's existence. Among the Bronze Age palace-fortresses discovered on the Greek mainland, Mycenae is unrivalled.[13] First built some time around the seventeenth century BC – on top of earlier settlements which themselves date back perhaps another thousand years[14] – it grew over the centuries to become the power base for all of Greece, its aloof and aggressive mountain providing the perfect symbol for an ambitious, war-like civilisation.

In the thirteenth century BC, at the peak of its grandeur, Mycenae would have made a powerful impression on any visitor. Reached by crossing the flat scrub-land of the Argive plain, the citadel emerged with shocking suddenness, half-concealed at the opening to the Arachneion mountain range. Its massive, pale-gold stone walls – made out of giant slabs each weighing at least 3 or 4 tonnes – were in places over 7 metres thick and 12 metres in height.[15] At the very summit of the hilltop was the grand *megaron*: the great hall and royal throne room. A paved road with grooves for chariot wheels, shadowed on either side by upward-sloping, ramp-like walls, led to the imposing entrance to Mycenae, the famous Lion Gate.[16] Above a pair of massive 20-tonne stone uprights[17] and a giant lintel, a triangular sculpture showed two lions standing facing each other, their front paws resting against a Greek column. Today, the heads of the lions are gone, but the rest of the gate remains – the earliest piece of monumental sculpture still standing anywhere in Europe.

Only a member of the warrior-elite would have been granted an audience with the king and queen in the royal apartments. There, in the opulent decoration and rich furnishings, the might and the artistic brilliance of the Mycenaeans came together. This was a culture that believed in confrontational displays of wealth, recognising that power could be exercised as effectively in the domestic setting as on the battlefield. The palace would have been a riot of colour, with polished walls and floors decorated in striking patterns of blue, red, yellow, gold and pink.[18]

In the great hall, beyond a huge, circular, central hearth fire surrounded by wooden columns clad in bronze, stood intricately decorated thrones sculpted from rock crystal and inlaid with precious stones. Frescoes depicted glorious battle scenes of warriors on a broad plain, watched from above by women waiting on the ramparts of a high citadel. (Waiting, perhaps, for the return of husbands and sons gone to fight in Troy?[19]) Homer's description of 'Mycenae rich in gold' was accurate. This was a gilded fortress, dripping with the spoils of conquest: solid gold drinking cups, jewellery, daggers, swords and armour.

The Mycenaeans were always outward-looking. That is in the very nature of any ambitious, martial society – why rest when there are still many more worlds out there to conquer? There is ample evidence of their influence throughout North Africa, from Phoenicia to Syria and Palestine – even hundreds of miles down the course of the Nile at Amarna, in broken pots found in the remains of the 'sun city' of the heretic Pharaoh, Akhenaten. Traces of the Mycenaeans have also been found in Spain, Sicily, Cyprus, Croatia, Georgia and Bavaria, as far west as Cornwall and as far north as Scandinavia. Indeed, it has been suggested that for a time the Norse warriors adopted the razor blade in imitation of the clean-shaven look of their Greek counterparts.[20]

Their capital, Mycenae, may have been hidden deep in the mountains of the Peloponnese peninsula, but this was still a sea-faring, world-travelling people. The first month of the Greek year in the late Bronze Age was *Plowistos* – the month of sailing.[21] The older Minoan civilisation on Crete may have been one of the Mycenaeans' first great overseas conquests. A century or two later, Troy may have been their last.

Over time the burnt-out ruins of Bronze Age Mycenae were resettled, although it was far from the splendid fortress it had once been.

Rather, its people were squatting among the bones of the past, cowed by the legendary reputations of the warriors who centuries before had occupied its corridors and halls. In the fifth century BC, Greece erupted into two devastating wars. The first saw the city states unite – as they had during the invasion of Troy – to repel, against overwhelming odds, the massed forces of the Persian Empire. The second was the bitter and brutal Peloponnesian War, which pitted Athens against Sparta, city-state against city-state, in a self-destructive conflict that ultimately ushered in the end of classical Greece.

Mycenae was an early casualty of this civil war. Besieged, starved out and then sacked by Argos in 470 BC[22], its people were sold into slavery, and large sections of its citadel walls were dismantled. While playwrights like Aeschylus and historians like Herodotus continued to look back to the legends of Agamemnon and Troy in an attempt to understand the chaos engulfing their own era, the physical remains of the 'golden age' were dwindling fast. Mycenae was fortified briefly again in the third century BC – by the Argives, the same people who had sacked it a century and a half earlier – and, as conflict followed conflict, the shrines to Agamemnon and the war god Ares were resurrected.[23] The arrival of the Romans, however, saw the final abandonment of the site. The golden citadel was reduced to a peaceful rest stop for lonely shepherds and their flocks.

It seemed that the cult of the hero was coming to an end. In the *History of the Peloponnesian War,* written by the Greek historian Thucydides in the fifth century BC[24], Bronze Age Mycenae had already been reduced to a bare and basic fortress, and Agamemnon is portrayed as the biggest and baddest of a thuggish bunch of warlords.[25] Perhaps centuries of war had stripped the romance from the mythical warriors of old. They were not supermen, just men. And where was the glory in repeating, over and over again, the naïve mistakes of mere mortals?

Yet heroes are nothing if not resilient. Coming back to life is one of the things they do best. Agamemnon lay dormant for some 1,500 years – not so much forgotten as dismissed as a figment and a fairy tale – until, at the end of the nineteenth century, he re-emerged in a burst of sudden, violent glory.

On 25 November 1876, a telegraph reached *The Times* from the Peloponnese peninsula, informing the newspaper of the tantalising discovery of human remains in a series of 'grave-shafts' found just beyond the Lion Gate, inside the walls of Mycenae. The message came from Heinrich Schliemann – a one-time grocer's apprentice turned millionaire amateur archaeologist – and it told of 'golden masks' covering the skulls of three male bodies. In one of the masks 'remained a large part of the skull it covered'.[26] Schliemann then sent an updated telegraph to a Greek newspaper. After viewing the man beneath the mask, he had come to the conclusion that, 'this corpse very much resembles the image which my imagination formed long ago of wide-ruling Agamemnon.'[27] The media soon paraphrased this announcement as the wonderfully romantic – though sadly apocryphal – line: 'Today, I gazed upon the face of Agamemnon.'

Misquoted or not, Schliemann would have approved of the sentiment. He had a talent for self-mythologising.[28] Who better than a modern hero to find the supermen of the past? Indeed, if you believed his autobiography – written when he was nearing sixty years of age – it was a simple matter of destiny. As a seven-year-old living in the town of Mecklenburg in northern Germany, Schliemann recalled receiving as a present from his pastor father a book called *Universal History* by Dr Georg Ludwig Jerrer. As he read through this huge volume, he kept returning to one engraving: a picture of the city of Troy and its great walls consumed by flames.

His father told him that Troy had been destroyed so completely by the invading Greeks that its remains had disappeared without trace. Confused, he told his father he was mistaken: 'Jerrer must have seen Troy, otherwise he could not have represented it here.'[29] His father replied that it was just a 'fanciful picture', but Schliemann was not satisfied. He asked if it was true that Troy had massive walls, and his father agreed that it was. 'If such walls once existed,' he said, 'they cannot possibly have been completely destroyed: vast ruins of them must still remain, but they are hidden away beneath the dust of ages.'[30] His father was not convinced, but he told his son that one day, when he was older, he should go and dig them up, so that he could see for himself. 'The pickaxe and spade for the excavation of Troy and the royal tombs of Mycenae,' wrote Schliemann, 'were both forged and sharpened in the little German village in which I passed eight years of my earliest childhood.'[31] It was the origin story that every good hero needs.

Yet Schliemann, perhaps without realising it, was already a 'superman' of his own age: a swaggering industrialist, ruthless in business, driven by success, insecure, vain, obsessed with fame but at the same time paranoid that the intellectual establishment would never accept him. He had risen from humble beginnings to accumulate a fortune. He left his 'hapless and humble' job in a grocer's shop to work as a cabin boy and then, after a shipwreck washed him up on the coast of Holland, found employment as a book-keeper for an import and export firm in Amsterdam. By his mid-twenties, he had established his own business. From trading indigo in St Petersburg, he moved on to gold in California, cotton and tea in the American South during the Civil War, and saltpetre and brimstone – the raw materials for gunpowder – across Europe at the outbreak of the Crimean War.[32] By his early thirties, he had taught himself fifteen languages, from Russian, French, English, Polish, Swedish and Norwegian, to Hebrew, Latin and modern and ancient Greek.[33] This last allowed him to read Homer in its original text, and in the summer of 1868, at the age of forty-five, he travelled to Turkey to look for the ruins of Troy.

The career of Schliemann the archaeologist is shot through with a seam of enormous good fortune. His very first expedition took him to the Menderes River in the Dardanelles, in the north-west of Turkey. He picked and prodded around a mound of sand and rubble known as Hisarlik, but soon left, bemused by what he had seen. It was only a meeting with Frank Calvert, an English expatriate and consular agent who had lived in the region his whole life that reignited his interest.[34] Calvert put forward the theory that Hisarlik contained 'the ruins and debris of temples and palaces which succeeded each other over long centuries'[35] – and that it was the strongest candidate for the site of the ancient city of Troy. Schliemann was suddenly convinced by this reasoning, despite the fact that, judging by letters written to the Englishman in the autumn of that same year, he could not remember very clearly what Hisarlik looked like, or whether he had even visited it at all.[36] This did not stop him producing a vivid – and deeply revisionist – account of his time in Turkey.

'As soon as one sets foot on the Trojan plain,' he wrote, 'the view of the beautiful hill of Hisarlik grips one with astonishment. That hill seems destined by nature to carry a great city'.[37] From his lodgings in a nearby town he described a splendid panorama of the whole Trojan plain:

> 'With the *Iliad* in hand, I sat on the roof of a house and looked around me... I imagined seeing below me the fleet, camp and assemblies of the Greeks; Troy and its Pergamus fortress on the plateau of Hisarlik; troops marching to and fro and battling each other in the lowland between city and camp. For two hours the main events of the *Iliad* passed before my eyes until darkness and violent hunger forced me to leave the roof... I had become fully convinced that it was here that ancient Troy had stood.'[38]

The first serious investigations began at Hisarlik in 1871. Schliemann dipped into his millions to employ some 150 workmen on site each day.[39] Hundreds of tons of rock and rubble were removed, but his amateurish approach to archaeology meant that the dig was part excavation, part desecration.[40] In fairness, however, this was one of the most complex sites ever to have been worked on in the modern era. Just as Calvert had predicted, it was a confusion of layers and strata of many different buildings and 'cities' though time. Although Schliemann struggled to understand the technicalities of what was emerging from the earth, he was in no doubt about where he was. In August 1872, he announced to the world that he had found the walls of Troy; they had risen from beneath the sands of Hisarlik still bearing the marks of the great fire set by Agamemnon and his troops in the final sacking of the city.

'I have solved a great historical problem,' wrote Schliemann. 'The civilized world will acknowledge my right to re-christen this sacred locality; and in the name of the divine Homer I baptise it with that name of immortal renown, which fills the heart of everyone with joy and enthusiasm: I give it the name of "TROY"'.[41] We know now that Schliemann was digging down too far and too fast, wiping out many layers of remains in his race to the bedrock of Hisarlik. Ironically, he oversaw the destruction – not the discovery – of much of Homer's Troy.

Blundering and naïve as he was, Schliemann's determination, work ethic – and of course his money – delivered results. A year after unearthing the 'walls of Troy', he made the discovery that would ensure his worldwide fame. According to the account in his book *Troy and Its Remains*, one morning he spotted flecks of copper and gold in the rubble of a wall he was excavating. At first he did not draw anyone else's attention to it, instead dismissing his workmen for an early breakfast. He then took out a large knife and set about digging into the earth himself.

First he uncovered a copper shield, which put him instantly in mind of the shield carried into battle by the great Greek warrior Ajax. Next came a collection of gold and copper salvers and cauldrons. As he worked on, he realised that each of these vessels was filled to the brim with a quite remarkable range of ancient artefacts. There were cups, goblets and dishes of gold, silver and bronze; copper lance-heads; thousands of gold rings and bracelets; gold headbands and earrings; and, most impressive of all, a golden diadem, or headdress, made up of 8,000 tiny fragments of gold threaded on to a delicate golden string.[42] Schliemann christened this hoard the 'Treasure of Priam' and named this final, spectacular piece the 'Jewels of Helen'. As he pulled each gleaming artefact from the ground, he described how he then loaded it into the shawl of his young Greek wife Sophia, who stood by his side, watching eagerly. This last detail was another Schliemann fiction. Sophia was not even in Turkey when he made his discovery. She was in Athens.[43]

The 'Treasure of Priam' turned out to be as controversial as it was sensational. (Indeed, it remains so today, with some academics suggesting that some or all of the artefacts from the hoard were faked deliberately by Schliemann. The finds are currently in the vaults of the Russian State Museum, where they were deposited after being taken as war booty from Germany at the end of the Second World War.)[44] In breach of his agreement with the Ottoman authorities, Schliemann smuggled the 'Treasure' out of the country, a fact that only became apparent when a photograph of Sophia wearing the 'Jewels of Helen' appeared in newspapers around the world. As a result he was banned from excavating on Turkish soil, and forbidden from returning to Troy. The resultant fame and glory proved adequate compensations – and besides, Troy was just one site from the *Iliad* and the *Odyssey*. There was a whole world of Homeric legend out there, still waiting to be found. If Schliemann could no longer explore the city at the heart of the war, he would travel instead to the place where it first began, and to where a conquering hero had once returned, only to fall victim to a brutal, vengeful murder. He was on his way to Mycenae.

Schliemann had always been a believer in the literal truth of Homer. As far as he was concerned, Mycenae was the crime-scene of one of the most shocking events in early antiquity: the murder of Agamemnon, the 'lord of men' himself. He came to the citadel as much as a detective as an archaeologist, determined to solve the mystery of one of history's most notorious cold-cases. Schliemann's main source material was a book written in the second century AD by Pausanias, a Greco-Roman from the west coast of Turkey. His *Description of Greece* was a work of early archaeological survey – a comprehensive guide to all of the monuments and remains that could be found littered across the country. And in his account of Mycenae, he had left a tantalising reference to the death – and burial site – of Agamemnon.

Schliemann (top right, with cane) at the Lion's Gate, 1884/5

Pausanias provided a list of all of those who had been murdered alongside their king, which included the captured Trojan princess and fabled prophetess Cassandra, the royal charioteer Eurymedon, and Teledamus and Pelops, the infant twins of Agamemnon and Cassandra. Mycenae, he concludes, contained:

> '…the graves of all those who on their return from Troy with Agamemnon were murdered by Aegisthus after a banquet which he gave them… Clytemnestra and Aegisthus were buried at a little distance from the wall; for they were deemed unworthy to be buried within the walls, where Agamemnon himself and those who had been murdered with him were laid.'[45]

The scholarly consensus was that Pausanias's 'wall' was the very faint fragment marking the perimeter of Mycenae – not the huge, Cyclopean blocks that still formed the ruins of the main citadel itself. Within this wider, outer circuit were a number of large and impressive 'beehive'-shaped stone tombs. Although empty of bodies and artefacts, perhaps as a result of some ancient grave-robbing, these were assumed to be the most likely candidates for the last resting place of any great king and his retinue.

Against all received wisdom, however, Schliemann interpreted Pausanias as meaning 'within' the wall of the fortress itself, and directed his workmen to begin digging a trench just inside the Lion Gate.[46] Almost immediately they struck a series of upright stone markers arranged in a circle nearly 100 feet in diameter. Incredibly, a number of these stones were marked with clearly visible carvings of warriors and chariots.[47] With mounting excitement, Schliemann began excavating beneath these 'grave-markers', discovering five deep shafts dug straight down into the bedrock. Within these narrow, underground tombs, were the remains of some eighteen bodies: men, women, and two infants. They were covered completely in gold.[48]

Thin, golden sheets lay over the bodies like shrouds. There were headdresses of golden plate strung on fine copper wire; one 'gigantic' golden crown covered with thirty individual golden leaves; hundreds of thick, round gold plates shaped with elaborate and beautiful decorations of concentric circles, spirals, stars, flowers and butterflies. There were gold ornaments in the shapes of lions, stags, bulls and griffins; swords and daggers in gold and bronze decorated with exquisitely detailed inlays of gold, silver and lapis lazuli, including two sheaths showing strikingly vivid scenes of hunting and battle. The women wore delicate gold frontlets, and were dripping with gold bracelets, earrings and hairpins. In one grave, Schliemann described bodies 'literally smothered in jewels.'[49] The two infants were wrapped in paper-thin blankets of gold. It was in the first of the five graves – although the last to be fully excavated – that there came the greatest discovery. Here were three men – their bones so large that they assumed, for Schliemann, quite heroic proportions – each wearing golden breastplates. Two had their faces covered in golden masks of such distinctive and acute detail it seemed that they could only have been fashioned as portraits.[50]

One mask depicted what Schliemann described as 'altogether Hellenic' features: 'well-proportioned lips', a 'long thin nose running in a direct line with the forehead', and 'moustaches whose extremities are turned upwards to a point, in the form of crescents.'[51] It was the look of a matinee idol. The other showed a fat, round face with beady, porcine features: a typical henchman. When the masks were removed, the face beneath the 'Hellenic' mask turned to dust on contact with the air, but the other 'had been wonderfully preserved... both eyes perfectly visible, also the mouth, which... was wide open and showed thirty-two beautiful teeth.'[52] Schliemann was ready to identify the still intact remains as Agamemnon, but the media was quick to christen the handsome, moustachioed mask as the 'face of Agamemnon'.[53] In the popular consciousness, the less attractive portrait was conveniently brushed aside, and the intact remains were joined with the heroic visage. This may not have been a deliberate sleight-of-hand on the part of Schliemann, but there is no doubt it suited his sense of aesthetic order. Agamemnon became a composite of two of Mycenae's finest finds – an archaeological 'cut and shut'. [54]

One of the less heroic death masks found by Schliemann at Mycenae © National Archaeological Museum of Athens

In Schliemann's words, 'the news that the tolerably well preserved body of a man of the mythic heroic age had been found... spread like wildfire through the Argolid, and people came by thousands from Argos, Nauplia, and the villages to see the wonder.'[55] The parallels between the dig site and the legends were remarkable. Schliemann was convinced that he had discovered the tombs of Agamemnon, Cassandra, Eurymedon and their compatriots – the royal entourage that 'had been murdered simultaneously'.[56] Eurymedon had been a charioteer, and carvings of chariots covered one of the grave markers. The tombs were filled with the most beautiful and ornate weaponry, a sure sign that these were the warriors who had returned from history's greatest battle. Cassandra and Agamemnon's newborn twins were said to have been murdered alongside their mother – and he had unearthed the bodies of a woman and two infants, wrapped in gold.

For the media the story was irresistible. On 18 December 1876, *The Times* talked of the 'splendid revelation' that, 'the great KING of MEN who found a bard in HOMER' now had 'his royal state once more shown to the world by Dr SCHLIEMANN.' It continued that 'the hero himself, AGAMEMNON remains and is found to be just such a giant as a hundred chiefs would choose for their leader – a head and shoulders taller than all. The bones must have been iron to survive to this day.'[57]

Schliemann's excavation report on Mycenae, published in 1878, even had a preface from the British Prime Minister, William Gladstone, a former classics scholar. Gladstone did not stint in his praise: 'There was, in ancient poetry, a Destiny stronger than the will of the Gods... To me, on this occasion, Dr Schliemann is the... organ of that Destiny.' Having examined the evidence, he concluded that the only 'rational presumption' was that 'this eminent explorer has exposed to the light of day, after 3,000 years, the memorials of Agamemnon and his companions in the Return from Troy'.[58]

A legend had been exhumed from the pinnacle of Mycenae, in a real site that combined awe-inspiring opulence with gruesome, fascinating murder. Schliemann appeared to have found not just the possessions, but also the actual bones of Agamemnon. A fairy tale was revived in glorious, shocking detail. The implications were immense. Just as they had been in classical Greece, Homer's epic tales were suddenly being employed as historical reference points and potent political metaphors. *The Times* concluded that the return of Agamemnon had come at just the right time. 'What is it that all of Europe is looking for?' it asked. 'It is the KING of MEN, the great head of the Hellenic race, the man whom a thousand galleys and a hundred thousand men submitted to on a simple recognition of his personal qualities and obeyed for ten long years'.[59] Fresh out of the ground, the Lord of Mycenae was instantly being rallied to the cause against an unstable Ottoman Empire[60] – the latest occupiers of the Trojan plain. Here was a perfect role model for the renewal of age-old hostilities: 'the man to head the entire Greek race and the races mixed with it in their impending struggle with the remnants of the Asiatic power.'[61] After all, why reanimate a hero if you are not going to call on him to fight?

In the Britain of the Victorian and Edwardian eras, Homer's works were popular 'classics'. Every public schoolboy was familiar with the *Iliad* and the *Odyssey*, and the poetry – with its emphasis on honour, discipline, athleticism and courage in the face of death – spoke across the ages about what it meant to be a gentleman and a scholar at the height of Empire. The elite of British imperialism, who saw themselves as the vanguard of a new Athens, looked on the supermen of the ancient world not as demi-gods, but as kindred spirits.

In February 1915, the Mediterranean Expeditionary Force sailed off to fight the Turks and the Germans on the Gallipoli peninsula, just across the Dardanelles from Troy. It was a brutal, bloody campaign recalling Agamemnon's massive, seaborne assault on Priam's ancient city. For some, the parallels were immediate and even joyous. As he considered the prospect of passing through the Greek islands on his way to the Turkish front, the young poet Rupert Brooke wrote of how he would recite Homer and feel the 'winds of history' following him 'all the way.'[62] In a letter home, he wondered, with schoolboyish excitement, if the campaign would take him to the legendary battlefield: 'Perhaps the fort on the Asiatic corner will want quelling and we'll land and come at it from behind and they'll make a sortie and meet us on the plains of Troy? It seems to me strategically so possible... I've never been quite so happy in my life, I think'.[63]

Brooke died of sepsis before he even made it to combat. But in lines written in a notebook on his last voyage, he still imagined how this 'Great War' – perhaps the 'greatest' since Homer's time – would be the first to awaken the heroes of old: 'They say Achilles in the darkness stirred.../ And Priam and his fifty sons/ Wake all amazed, and hear the guns/ And shake for Troy again.'[64] Patrick Shaw-Stewart, an Old Etonian and classics scholar at Oxford's Balliol College, sailed with Brooke and was there to preside over his fellow poet's burial in an olive grove on the Greek island of Skyros – rather ironically the very island where Achilles was hidden by his mother in the vain hope that he would not be conscripted by Agamemnon to go to his death at Troy.

As he re-read the *Iliad* on his way to Gallipoli, Shaw-Stewart experienced a mingled sense of nostalgia and ominous familiarity. In the midst of a 'Hell of ships and cities' brought on by a 'Fatal second Helen' – a global war – Shaw-Stewart made clear that in this new Troy, he hoped to have the greatest of the old heroes on his side: 'I will go back this morning/ From Imbros over the sea/ Stand in the trench, Achilles/ Flame-capped and fight for me'.[65]

In 1916 Maurice Baring, the Eton- and Cambridge-educated poet, and a scion of the famous banking dynasty, composed a verse in memoriam of a friend who had been killed in action with the Royal Flying Corps. As he looked upwards to the biplanes duelling in the skies, he saw 'Such fighting as blind Homer never sung/ Nor Hector nor Achilles never knew/ High in the empty blue.'[66] For Baring, when men took to the skies like gods, it was the sign that history had finally found a conflict to outstrip the great battles of the Trojan plain.

The romantic streak evinced by these young poets and writers did not survive the conflict. Neither, of course, did a great many of the poets themselves. What beauty or glory could be found in the horrific realities of trench-warfare, with its seemingly endless round of shelling, shrapnel, barbed wire and senseless death? There was no chance to seek immortality here. 'Who will remember,' asked Siegfried Sassoon, one of the most famous war poets of them all, 'the unheroic Dead who fed the guns?'[67] The First World War marked the beginning of the end of Britain's Empire. In the aftermath, Homer-inspired delusions of heroism were put aside as one of many 'childish things' from a more innocent age.

While the boyish arrogance of Troy was being reborn on the nineteenth-century playing fields of Eton, Rugby and Harrow, Agamemnon's memory was being put to still more insidious uses on the European continent. In 1887 a classics professor turned philosopher called Friedrich Nietzsche made a bizarre yet explicit link between his own German ancestry and Homer's Greek heroes. Behind this was the theory of the 'Aryan race': a fair-haired, light-skinned people from the central Asian steppes, said to have invaded and settled in India in ancient history, before migrating through the Middle East and into Europe.[68]

In his book *On the Genealogy of Morality,* Nietzsche took up this idea and stretched it beyond credulity to construct a breed of aristocratic warriors who recurred throughout history:

> 'At the centre of all these noble races we cannot fail to see the blond beast of prey, the magnificent blond beast avidly prowling round for spoil and victory... The deep and icy mistrust which the German arouses as soon as he comes to power, which we see again even today – is still the aftermath of that inextinguishable horror with which Europe viewed the raging of the blond Germanic beast for centuries.'[69]

It was a crude, yet horribly compelling mythology, creating a purity of creed and purpose for Nietzsche and the German people where none really existed.

In 1918, Nietzsche's theories were echoed in a bestselling work of historical scholarship written by a retired German schoolteacher called Oswald Spengler. His *Decline of the West* provided a grand, sweeping, almost operatic treatment of world history – and, as the title suggests, it did not reach an optimistic conclusion about the state or fate of Western Europe.[70] This in no way lessened its popular appeal. Within a few years of publication, it had sold over 100,000 copies and been translated into a host of different languages.

Spengler's novel approach was to analyse the patterns of successive civilisations as they rose, declined and fell, and turning this into a compelling universal story. In particular, he focused on the idea of competing cultures as the forces for historical change. 'I see' he wrote, 'the drama of a number of mighty Cultures, each springing with primitive strength from the soil of a mother-region to which it remains firmly bound throughout its whole life cycle; each stamping its material, its mankind, in its own image; each having its own idea, its own passions, its own life, will and feeling, its own death.'[71] Early in his history, Spengler looks to Mycenae, which he describes, as it began its ascendancy, as 'darkly groping, big with hopes, drowsy with the intoxication of deeds and sufferings, ripening quietly towards its future.'[72]

At the same time, he told of a decadent society across the Aegean Sea, 'snugly ensconced in the treasures of an ancient culture, elegant, light, with all its great problems far behind it'.[73] These were the Minoans of Crete, whose capital was the great palace complex of Knossos. For Spengler, it was at moments like these, when 'the men of two cultures have looked into one another's eyes', that their true natures are revealed. 'I see it before me,' he wrote, 'the humility of the inhabitants of... Mycenae before the unattainable esprit of life in Knossos, the contempt of the well-bred of Knossos for the petty chiefs and their followers, and withal a secret feeling of superiority in the healthy barbarians, like that of a German soldier in the presence of the elderly Roman dignitary.'[74] Spengler saw clear parallels between Mycenaean and German *culture*: a tendency towards hard work and 'bearish morning vigour'[75]; a belief in the simple virtues of strength and vitality; a distrust of the effete and the overly refined. From there, it was no great leap to suggest that not just values were shared, but also ancestry, and DNA.

In Spengler's postwar Germany humiliated by defeat and crippled financially by reparations payments, there certainly was something 'darkly groping, big with hopes, drowsy with the intoxication of deeds and sufferings'. In February 1920 the National Socialist German Workers' Party was founded by a group of extreme right-wing, anti-communist agitators. In the summer of that same year a peculiar symbol made its debut as the official party emblem – an equilateral cross with four arms each bent at ninety degrees. Its origins could be traced back thousands of years to the Indus Valley, and its name was derived from a Sanskrit word, the literal interpretation of which was 'to be good.' It was the swastika.[76]

The swastika's adoption by the National Socialist German Workers' Party – the Nazis – came through a garbled interpretation of the works of Nietzsche, Spengler and even Schliemann. Nietzsche had linked the great figures of Homeric epic, both Greek and Trojan, with his modern concept of man in a world without God. Warriors like Agamemnon, Achilles and Hector were the first *Übermenschen* – the first 'supermen'. He believed that the ambition of humanity – and Germany – should be to look back to the 'Age of Heroes' to rediscover this former greatness. Spengler created a historical narrative grouping together the Mycenaeans, the Trojans and the Germans as the children of a shared culture. And Schliemann, at times unwittingly, provided the physical archaeological evidence.[77]

The swastika had appeared on artefact after artefact unearthed at Troy. Not long after these discoveries, Émile-Louis Burnouf, a close colleague of Schliemann's and the Director of the French School of Archaeology in Athens, began asserting that the swastika was the enduring mark of the Aryan race.[78] Schliemann, who in fact had barely noticed the symbol up to this point, then claimed that while excavating the ruins of Troy, he had immediately 'recognised the mark as the exceedingly significant religious symbol of our remote ancestors'.[79] The Oxford Professor of Assyriology, A. H. Sayce wrote in the Preface to Schliemann's final report on Troy that 'we now know who the Trojans originally were... Aryans'[80], while another contributor, Karl Blind, referred to them as a 'Teutonic tribe'.[81]

With the Trojan heroes Priam, Hector and Paris now identified as 'brethren in blood and speech' by Sayce and others, the next task was to make the connection to Agamemnon and the Greeks. While Schliemann claimed that 'a number of swastikas' were found engraved in the pottery at Mycenae, he did not offer any illustrations in his excavation reports. And in his analysis of the seven hundred golden discs found in the citadel's grave shafts, he described symbols bearing only the vaguest resemblances as 'derived' from the swastika.[82] This did not stop Burnouf from concluding that the Mycenaeans were clearly one of the 'prehistoric dynasties of the Aryan races.'[83]

In the 1920s, Schliemann's swastika artefacts from Troy and Mycenae were put on display in Berlin. At the same time the German pre-historian, Otto Grabowski, published *The Secret of Swastikas and the Cradle of the Indo-Germanic Race,* a book of skewed scholarship ending with the chilling promise that the dark winter of the German people would soon end in a 'morning which approaches under the light of the swastika'.[84] Hitler, writing in *Mein Kampf* in 1925, described the symbol as 'the mission of the struggle for the victory of the Aryan man'.[85]

It was in this febrile atmosphere of archaeological and nationalistic myth-making that Himmler, Goebbels and Goering made their way to Mycenae. They stayed at *La Belle Helene* because that was where Schliemann, their glorious countryman – and good *Übermensch* – had boarded throughout his excavations. And as they climbed up to the ruins of the citadel, they were hoping not only to see the tomb of a legendary warrior from antiquity, but also to recognise themselves reflected back across the millennia. Agamemnon had become the model for the Nazi super-soldier.

How do we make sense of Mycenae today? A place that has belonged to so many over the years, but which now belongs to no one – perhaps least of all the Mycenaeans and the Greeks. The poem *Mycenae* by the Greek Nobel Laureate George Seferis, ends with the lament: 'Not even the silence is yours / here where the millstones have stopped turning'.[86] The fortress has become a void and a vacuum. Its king and its warriors have fought for so long and for so many different causes that they now seem less like heroes and more like mercenaries: weary soldiers dragged dead-eyed from conflict to conflict. That is, of course, if they ever existed at all.

Today we know for certain that the face that Schliemann 'gazed upon' beneath the golden mask could not have been Agamemnon's. The grave shafts and their remains have been dated to around 1600 BC, 400 years before the era of the Trojan War.[87] The similarity between Pausanias' account of the burial site and Schliemann's excavations was just a remarkable coincidence. Homer's epic tales, brought so tantalisingly close to archaeological reality in the late nineteenth and early twentieth centuries, have now ebbed back towards the realms of myth.

In the latter half of the twentieth century, archaeology moved further and further away from the romantic passions of men like Heinrich Schliemann. A more sober scientific approach aimed to separate myth from hard fact, preferring the stories told by physical objects rather than blind, unauthenticated poets.[88] A breakthrough in the analysis of the Mycenaean script – known as Linear B – revealed extensive records not of great deeds and conquests, but of grain production and taxation.[89] The Mycenaeans were reassessed as a civilisation of traders and farmers rather than warriors, ruled over by diligent but dull bureaucrats. The citadel of Mycenae was steadily pacified, and its great walls were recast not as practical defences built in times of war, but as purely ornamental symbols of power and status.[90] Instead of being laid to rest, the heroes of Mycenae were disarmed and sent back out to work in the fields of the plain.

In the twenty-first century, the picture is shifting once more. There is a place for warriors again in the mountains of the Peloponnese. For years now the students of West Point, the elite US military academy, have been studying the *Iliad* as part of their literature courses. Robert Fagles, the late, award-winning translator of Homer, even visited the institution to read out the first lines of the Greek epic to some 1,000 students. The influence of the 'Age of Heroes' can still be found in today's theatres of conflict. In 2007, a NATO offensive in Afghanistan – aimed at forcing the Taliban out of Helmand province – was named *Operation Achilles.*[91]

When the American novelist Henry Miller visited Mycenae in the autumn of 1939, he found it 'closed in, huddled up, writhing with muscular contortions like a wrestler.' As he stood among the remains, 'trying to understand what happened here over a period of centuries', he described feeling like a 'cockroach crawling about amidst dismantled splendours'.[92] And he wondered if our own, modern world would one day suffer the same fate. At Mycenae, there was nothing left 'save these ruins... scattered relics in museums, a sword, an axle, a helmet, a death mask of beaten gold.' For Miller, the citadel was a perfect vision of fallen glory, where 'spades and shovels will uncover nothing of any import' and 'everything that is unmasked crumbles at the touch'.[93] Ruins could never live up to their reputations, and certainly not the ruins of mighty Mycenae.

Yet, as he stood on the summit of the citadel, Miller imagined a time when he would have been able to see on the plain below 'gods who roamed everywhere, men like us in form and substance but free, electrically free.' According to Miller, when these gods

> '...departed this earth they took with them the one secret which we shall never wrest from them until we too have made ourselves free again. We are to know one day what it is to have life eternal – *when we have ceased to murder.* Here on this spot, now dedicated to the memory of Agamemnon, some foul and hidden crime blasted the hopes of man.'[94]

Mycenae is Europe's original war memorial. To try to divest it of its military significance is futile. But a shrine to war need not always inspire its visitors to seek out new glories on the battlefield. It can also prompt reflection on the catastrophic effects of conflict. The Cenotaph, the Tomb of the Unknown Soldier, the white marble graves of Normandy, the thousands of poignant monuments in village squares across the continent, inscribed with the names of local boys who marched off to fight – perhaps all can trace their origins back to this ring of giant, broken walls clustered around an Argive hilltop.

Some may still judge Mycenae as a symbol of the never-ending cycle of war. Others, however, may follow Miller, and look instead among the wreckage for the gaps that exist between wars – seeing in the ruins the glimmer, and the hope, of peace.

CHAPTER FOUR

THE SUN CITY ALSO RISES

Akhetaten, Amarna – Egypt
(Born 1348 BC – Died 1331 BC)

A husband and wife sit opposite each other, playing with their three young daughters. One daughter sits on her mother's knee. A second rests in the crook of her mother's arm, reaching up to touch an earring. The father holds the third daughter in a tender embrace, lifting her towards his face to kiss her. Above them all is a full, radiant sun. It is a typical, happy domestic scene – it could be any family, anywhere, anytime. But it is not any family.

This picture, carved in relief into a pale-white slab of limestone, is almost three-and-a-half-thousand years old. It was discovered buried in the pebble-strewn sands of a flat desert plain on the banks of the River Nile. Today it sits, spotlit, on a plinth in Berlin's Neues Museum. The husband in the carving is the Pharaoh Amenhotep IV, although by the time this picture was commissioned he had changed his name to Akhenaten. The wife is Nefertiti: along with Cleopatra, the most famous – and famously beautiful – woman in Egyptian history. There is no other scene like this in the art of antiquity, in Egypt or anywhere else. Royalty were never shown behaving in such a relaxed, informal and intimate manner. This was something new, something unusual. In the Eighteenth Dynasty of ancient Egypt, after a millennia and a half of ingrained cultural conservatism, one man – Akhenaten – decided to break the mould.

The limestone slab showing Akhenaten, Nefertiti and three of their daughters beneath the rays of the sun (c.1340 BC)

Until around 150 years ago, however, nothing at all was known of this royal family. They did not appear on the lists of Pharaohs discovered by archaeologists digging at the sacred sites of Saqqara and Karnak.[1] Their omission, it turned out, was quite deliberate. Elsewhere, on tombs and palace walls, hammers and chisels had been used to deface their statues and remove their names from inscriptions.

And it was not just these official records that were erased. In the desert where the limestone carving was found, Akhenaten and Nefertiti built a new city from scratch. Perhaps 40,000 of their subjects came with them.[2] A decade and a half later, they were all gone. The city was dismantled, stone by stone. And no one ever returned.

At dawn in Egypt's Nile Valley, the sun rises over the waters of the Gulf of Suez. Its light climbs above the arid spine of the Red Sea Hills, and then races westwards across hundreds of kilometres of empty desert. On the east bank of the Nile, near the ruins of the ancient city of Hermopolis and some 300 kilometres to the south of Cairo, a wall of sheer limestone cliffs rears up from the valley floor to trace the course of the river.[3] This escarpment hugs the waterline as it continues southwards, before curving abruptly away from the Nile for a distance of 12 kilometres – retreating to 5 kilometres from the river at its furthest point – then bending back to meet the bank.[4]

The result is a half-moon of flat, yellow-orange sand enclosed by 100-metre-high rock walls on one side and the Nile on the other. The only break in the cliff face comes in a series of 'wadis': steep-sided valleys that have cut down through the limestone plateau to the desert floor. The deepest of these wadis is found at the centre of the encircling cliffs, and it is through this gap that the morning light first hits the plain. Viewed from the right spot, the disc of the rising sun framed by the 'V' of rock becomes a gigantic representation of the Egyptian hieroglyph *akhet* – the horizon.[5]

Now imagine this same place on a morning 3,300 years ago. The dawn sun that crests the cliff edge does not look down on an empty flatland. As the shadow cast by the bluff shortens, it reveals a sprawling city. The light bounces off great clusters of mud-brick houses – some whitewashed, others baked dark brown by the heat – which sit alongside large villas. Many buildings are several storeys high. There is no apparent order to this city. It runs close to the riverbank and parallel to the water for several kilometres, and it is cut through by the curve of a wide, central road. But beyond this basic layout, it appears to have grown in a haphazard fashion. To modern eyes, what it resembles most is a shanty-town or a *favela*, its square and rectangular blocks of houses crashing against each other at oblique angles and irregular heights. The comparison is unsatisfactory, however: this is no slum city. The sprawling residences of the very richest and most powerful officials and dignitaries press up against the tiny cubes occupied by the lowliest servants. All the buildings appear to have grown up through this same organic, unregulated process.[6]

The only exception is at the heart of the city, where two giant, rectangular structures lie at right angles to one another. The larger building is a massive palace that runs for over half a kilometre between the main road and the Nile. In the morning sun it glitters with vibrant colour. A huge central courtyard – its floor and pavements made of painted and varnished gypsum – is filled with red-granite and quartzite statues of the royal family, and tall gilded columns shaped in a variety of plant forms.

Every wall here is bright with exquisite painted scenes of nature and palace life: a kingfisher dives in the rushes; papyrus, cornflowers and poppies on a riverside; lily ponds alive with fish, ducks, butterflies, dragonflies and grasshoppers[7]; women play musical instruments and brush each other's hair; vine leaves and grapes grow from a yellow earth.[8] The level of detail is stupendous, so that it is easy to overlook that this palace is not finished. Parts of walls are still missing the inlaid tiles of intricately carved hieroglyphs. Stone plinths are empty, waiting for the new statues that are still being sculpted to stand on top of them. The courtyard at the centre of the palace is clearly intended to hold a crowd, a place for the people to come to see their king.[9] This morning, however, it is empty.

Instead, the people have gathered in the other colossal edifice that dominates the city. It runs almost directly west to east across the desert plain and its tall outer wall is a whitewashed, mud-brick perimeter 800 metres long by 300 metres wide. The main entrance is in the centre of the west wall: a stone gateway 22 metres high, flanked by flagpoles topped with long, colourful cloth streamers fluttering in the morning breeze. Once through the first gate, there is a large courtyard with water-filled foot basins for washing. Beyond this is a processional way: a series of courtyards of decreasing size, punctuated by tall columns sculpted in the shape of papyrus buds, and studded with row after row of hundreds of small, rectangular limestone tables.

Outside these inner courtyards, on otherwise empty ground leading to the outer walls, are more of the tables – 365 on each side, to represent every day of the year. In the sixth and final court, on a raised, gypsum platform, is a large golden table. This is not the end of the structure, however. A final section can be found at the perimeter's eastern edge, 300 metres further on, through an avenue of carved sphinxes.

This smaller enclosure culminates with a raised platform and an altar table, but also features a colossal statue of the seated king.[10] One other key detail: every room, corridor, column and courtyard in this vast structure is open to the sky. There are no roofs.

On this morning all the limestone tables, as well as the raised altars, are piled high with 'offerings'. Some are loaded with joints of meat, poultry, fruit, vegetables, and loaves of bread. Large bouquets of flowers and bowls of smoking incense rest on others. There are bronze and clay jars filled with water, wine and beer. At the head of the processional way, on the raised platform, Akhenaten and Nefertiti stand side by side. The golden table in front of them overflows with food, flowers and precious jewellery. The royal princesses wait behind their parents, shaking metal rattles known as *sistras.* As the first rays of the sun appear above the rim of the cliffs, and the light floods over the roofless buildings, groups of men and women begin to sing and clap their hands, to wave olive branches and beat drums. [11] Courtiers kneel on the ground, or bow down. The new god of the new Egypt has arrived: the one god that Akhenaten has decreed should replace all the others. *The Aten.* The sun.

Relief fragment of Akhenaten putting his hands up in worship to his god, the Aten (c.1340 BC). © Altes Museum, Berlin

From the moment that he rises in the east, until he finally dips behind the thick fringes of date palms on the banks of the Nile to the west, the Aten shines down on the city. There is no shade and no respite on this semi-circle of desert. It is just as Akhenaten wanted. 'Every eye beholds Him without hindrance while He fills the land with His rays and makes everyone to live,' he proclaims.[12] It was the Aten who directed the Pharaoh to this empty stretch of land, which he 'had created for Himself that he might be happy therein.' And it was in his honour that Akhenaten decreed a brand new capital city for Egypt.'Heaven was joyful, the earth was glad, every heart was filled with delight,' declares the author of an inscription found at Amarna.[13]

At least for a while.

In 1798, Napoleon Bonaparte launched an ambitious, and ill-fated, invasion of Egypt: a campaign aimed at cutting off British trade routes to India. As 50,000 troops crossed the Mediterranean, a group of 150 prominent scientists and scholars, known as the *corps de savants*, travelled with them. Their tasks, which were initially confined to map-making and survey work to support military operations, soon extended to exploring and recording the enigmatic, often monumental remains left behind by the Pharaohs. Napoleon saw much to admire in the ruins of the Nile valley, not least the evidence of millennia-old egos apparently close to his own in size. Whether or not the *savants* were part of the French emperor's commitment to Enlightenment principles, or a propaganda stunt to add a gloss of intellectual legitimacy to an act of wanton imperialism, their work remains the foundation of modern Egyptology.[14]

Over three years of war, disease and extreme hardship, the *savants* mapped, sketched and documented a staggering number of archaeological remains: the pyramids, tombs, colossi, obelisks and sphinxes that have come to define this ancient civilisation in the popular imagination. The results were published between 1809 and 1829 in a vast, 22-volume work called the *Description de l'Égypte*.

Buried deep within this magnum opus is a sketch made around 1799 by an group of *savants* who had journeyed down the Nile by boat. At a site known as Tell el Amarna – or more simply Amarna – a plain of extensive, scattered ruins was clearly visible from the river, set against a backdrop of tall, limestone cliffs. The surveyors briefly made landing, produced a quick drawing of the whole site and an elevation of the largest building remains, and then moved on. Their plan showed a significant settlement, laid out in a rectilinear grid, and dominated by a handful of massive structures.[15] As we have seen, this grid was a complete inaccuracy – imposing rational order on an original layout where none had existed – and the end result, when set against the many more visible wonders of the region, seemed unremarkable. Nevertheless, this sketch represents the moment that the modern world rediscovered Akhenaten and his city.

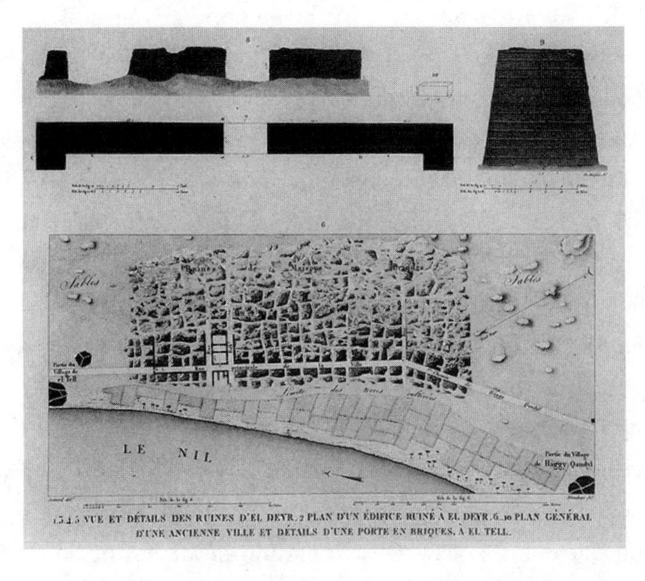

The first known map of Amarna, made by Napoleon's *savants in* 1798/9, and published in the *Description de l'Égypte*

The next explorer of note to visit the site was the English archaeologist, John Gardner Wilkinson. He also sketched a plan of the central district of the city – which can still be seen today in Oxford's Bodleian Library – but his main interest was in a series of open, rock-cut tombs found in the cliffs at the northern edge of the site. News of the tombs spread, and a steady trickle of antiquarians began to make their way to Amarna. The Scotsman, Robert Hay, later Laird of Linplum, took a team of copyists there in the early 1830s. The French draughtsman, Nestor L'Hôte followed in the 1840s, as did the esteemed Prussian Egyptologist, Richard Lepsius.[16]

Amarna was not an easy place to reach or explore. The locals of the impoverished villages strung along the Nile to the immediate north and south were unfriendly and often outright aggressive towards foreign visitors.[17] Apart from a fertile ribbon of cultivated land set right against the riverbank, the plain leading to the cliffs was a rocky wasteland, exposed throughout the day to the relentless sun and heat. Yet increasing numbers of antiquarians braved this harsh and hostile environment to visit Amarna, impelled by the desire to see for themselves what Wilkinson had first discovered in the tombs. This was not, at least in the popular sense of the word, treasure. It was art.

The carvings decorating the chamber walls were unlike anything seen before in the archaeology of Egypt. Artworks uncovered in other tombs and temples followed a rigid and formal style – stiff, conventional, and entrenched by century after century of repetition. Yet what they found at Amarna were reliefs of a royal family engaged in ordinary scenes from their day-to-day lives: relaxing with their children, commuting to a temple in the family chariot, sharing wine over the palace dinner table.[18] The works were characterised by fluidity and movement, a commitment to realism that had more in common with classical Greece than ancient Egypt. At the top of almost every scene was a common motif: the image of a full, radiant sun shooting out dozens of rays, each ending in a hand or an *ankh*, the hieroglyph for 'life'. So common was this symbol on the tomb walls, that it became customary for early visitors to Amarna to refer to the people who once lived there as 'Disc-worshippers'.[19]

Further study of the engravings revealed even more peculiarities. In some reliefs, the bodies of the royal family were distorted or deformed: heads and necks were unnaturally elongated, and all the physiques, including that of the Pharaoh himself, were distinctively feminine, with narrow waists, voluptuous bellies and hips, and swollen thighs. Once again, this exaggerated style was unprecedented. The standard artistic 'rules' of ancient Egypt allowed only for idealised, flawless depictions of royalty. Yet here were portraits that seemed to verge on caricature.[20]

A contemporary statue of Akhenaten found at Karnak (c1340 BC)

What the archaeologists could not find, however, were names for the distinctive figures depicted in the artworks. The tombs had clearly been entered by others over the centuries, and had suffered from the random vandalism of looters and squatters. Yet it gradually became clear that there was a pattern to the damage caused. It was almost impossible to find an image of the king and queen where the figures had not been defaced, and where the inscriptions bearing their names had not been scored out by chiselling.[21] This work appeared to be systematic and intentional, a sign that great lengths had been taken to remove any record of the existence of the royal couple. Here was a tantalising mystery. What had they done? What transgression – or crime – had deserved such treatment?

As the nineteenth century progressed, the answer began to emerge. A group of names was found to recur in the artworks and inscriptions. Those who had come to erase all traces of this family had overlooked certain references etched into the more inaccessible corners of the tombs. The archaeologists learned that there was a king called Akhenaten, who, at some stage in his early career, had been known as Amenhotep. There was a queen called Nefertiti, a name that translates as 'the beautiful one has come'. There was a god called 'Aten' – the divine embodiment of the sun's disc. And there was a name for the ruins that littered the Amarna plain: Akhetaten, 'the Horizon of the Aten'. The city of the sun.

The bare bones of a story could now be put together. There had been a Pharaoh, the son of Amenhotep III, who decided to reject the prevailing religion of Egypt. In the fifth year of his reign, around 1347 BC, referring to a great 'evil'[22], he abandoned the capital of Thebes – home to generations of kings – and sailed the entire royal court northwards along the Nile to the empty desert of Amarna. It was here, as an inscription by Akhenaten revealed, 'that the Aten desires that there be made for him a monument with an eternal and everlasting name.' He added: 'I shall make Akhetaten for the Aten, my father, in this place.'[23]

One of the most important discoveries came in a tomb cut into in a low plateau in the cliffs at the southern boundary of Amarna. One of nineteen tombs dedicated to officials of the royal court, this was built for Ay, 'Overseer of the Horses of His Majesty'– and perhaps also the father of Nefertiti.[24] On the wall of the entrance hall was a long inscription, which took the form of a universal prayer to the Aten. Known today as the 'Great Hymn', it is believed to be the work of Akhenaten himself. It is no exaggeration to describe it as a masterpiece of early literature. This was, in essence, the manifesto of the Pharaoh's new faith. In the hymn, the Aten is described as the single creator and lover of mankind and nature, not just in Egypt but across the whole world:

> 'O Sole God, like unto whom there is no other! Thou didst fashion the earth according to thy desire when thou

> was alone – all men, all cattle great and small, all that are upon the earth that run upon their feet or rise up on high, flying with their wings. And the lands of Syria and Kush and Egypt – thou appointest every man to his place and satisfiest his needs. Everyone receives his sustenance and his days are numbered. Their tongues are diverse in speech and their qualities likewise, and their colour is differentiated for thou hast distinguished the nations.'[25]

The hymn includes a wonderful description of the Nile valley as viewed from above – as if from the viewpoint of the sun, looking down – before ending with a message placing Akhenaten right at the heart of his new religion: 'Thou art in my heart, but there is none other who knows thee save thy son Akhenaten.' Here the Pharaoh makes it clear that he is his god's emissary on earth, and in so doing casts himself as semi-divine.

Two thousand Egyptian gods were reduced to one.[26] Akhenaten clearly saw himself as a visionary, taking the mythology out of religion, simplifying and cleansing the very idea of the divine. This would have been a radical step at almost any point throughout ancient history. Yet it is truly extraordinary that it emerged of all places in Egypt, where, as the early-twentieth-century archaeologist Stanley Casson put it, 'from start to finish... foreign ideas were quietly but firmly suffocated, while internal unorthodoxy was violently strangled.'[27] Unquestionably Akhenaten's new religion would have caused huge division in Egyptian society, in particular among the royal court and the priesthood. The sudden uprooting of the faithful and the loyal from Thebes to Amarna suggests a dramatic split. Akhenaten's break from tradition may well have sown the seeds of civil war. In legal texts written more than a century later, the Pharaoh is called 'the criminal of Akhetaten'[28] and his reign is referred to as 'the rebellion'.[29] Then as now, one man's vision is another man's heresy.

In the late nineteenth and early twentieth centuries, the rediscovery of Akhenaten, his city and his god, fired the imaginations of many archaeologists and scholars. One of the best articulations of the appeal of the 'rebel' Pharaoh came in 1909 from the American Egyptologist James Henry Breasted. 'There died with him such a spirit as the world had never seen before,' he wrote. To Breasted, Akhenaten was 'a brave soul, undauntedly facing the momentum of immemorial tradition, and thereby stepping out from the long line of conventional and colourless Pharaohs, that he might disseminate ideas far beyond and above the capacity of his age to understand.' His rather wonderful conclusion was that Akhenaten, 'in an age so remote and under conditions so adverse, became not only the world's first idealist and the world's first individual, but also the earliest monotheist, and the first prophet of internationalism.'[30] As eulogies go, it is hard to top.

There are, however, consequences to 'stepping out from the long line' of history. Akhenaten's personality and motives have become fair game for increasingly elaborate – and sometimes outlandish – speculation. We are desperate to find out what made this original *individual* tick. And, as is often the case, the conclusions say as much about our own modern prejudices as they do about Akhenaten himself.

The pioneering English Egyptologist, Flinders Petrie, who worked for a full dig season at Amarna in 1891, had set the tone for Breasted and his contemporaries. He held up a phrase found everywhere on the wall and tomb inscriptions – *Ankh eh maet*, meaning 'Living in truth' – as the *credo* of Akhenaten's reign. For Petrie, the worship of the sun as a source of life-giving energy, as opposed to a distant, half-human and half-animal being, demonstrated an unprecedented appreciation of basic scientific principles. 'It was a philosophic view and determination,' he wrote, 'which anticipated the course of thought by some thousands of years.' The truth in Akhenaten's religion was the truth of science; and the truth of his domestic life – captured in such intimate detail in the Amarna style of art – was the truth of a moral idealist. As Petrie continued:

> 'His affection is the truth, and as the truth he proclaims it. Here is a revolution in ideas! No king of Egypt, nor of any other part of the world, has ever carried out his honesty of expression so openly... Akhenaten stands out as perhaps the most original thinker that ever lived in Egypt, and one of the great idealists of the world.'[31]

Perhaps Petrie saw a kindred spirit in this near 3,500-year-old philosopher, moralist and naturalist. A patron of the arts and committed pacifist with a keen sense of entitlement, Akhenaten might have made a good Victorian.

The bold claims for this 'man out of time' reached far beyond the archaeological community. Sigmund Freud was fascinated by Akhenaten. In his 1939 book *Moses and Monotheism,* he speculated that the Pharaoh was, in effect, the inventor of God, and that Moses had been a former Atenist priest, who fled Egypt after Akhenaten's death, taking the concept of a single deity with him.[32]

In more recent times, there has been a swing in scholarly opinion. Far from a utopian and an idealist, Akhenaten has been cast instead as a megalomaniac: a deranged cult-leader, whose obscure mission to build a new city for his god forced extreme hardship on a servile population, who had no option but to follow their leader.[33] As the modern Egyptologist, Donald B. Redford puts it, 'For all that can be said in his favour, Akhenaten in spirit remains to the end totalitarian. The right of an individual freely to choose was wholly foreign to him. He was the champion of a universal, celestial power who demanded universal submission, claimed universal truth, and from whom no further revelation can be expected. I cannot conceive a more tiresome regime under which to be fated to live.'[34]

Others have focussed on the strange art of the period in an attempt to gain greater insight into the life of Akhenaten. To the archaeologist and journalist, Arthur Weigall, writing in the early twentieth century, the distorted, feminised portraits of the Pharaoh captured the sensuality and sensitivity of a man who was a poet and artist first, and a ruler second. 'His head seemed too large for his body,' wrote

Weigall. 'His eyelids were heavy; his eyes were eloquent of dreams. His features were delicately moulded, and his mouth, in spite of a somewhat protruding lower jaw, is reminiscent of the best of the art of Rossetti.'[35]

Rather than seeing these portraits as 'expressionistic', some modern experts have wondered whether they were anatomically accurate, and to speculate that Akhenaten may have suffered from some kind of genetic abnormality, the product of centuries of royal inbreeding. Theories have ranged from a disorder of the endocrine system and a malfunctioning pituitary gland – a condition known as Fröhlich's Syndrome[36] – to a hereditary disorder of the connective tissues, elephantiasis or hydrocephalus.[37] There has even been the suggestion that he was a eunuch. Yet another delightfully anachronistic theory has it that he was a transvestite or transsexual: a skirt-wearing high priest of 'camp', and the world's first gay icon.[38]

Of course, there is another way to explore the motives of Akhenaten – through his architecture. The city of Amarna was the physical realisation of a vision. Akhenaten ascended to the throne during one of the most prosperous periods of ancient Egyptian history. He could draw on incredible resources and manpower. And the site of Amarna was the original clean slate. Here was the opportunity to create the city of his dreams, the city that had been described to him by his supernatural father, the Aten. Barry Kemp, Emeritus Professor of Egyptology at Cambridge, has spent three decades excavating Akhenaten's city. According to Kemp, 'Amarna is where he put his vision into practice. The place itself ought to tell us something about transformation, about converting dreams into reality.'[39]

It began with boats – the massed flotilla of Akhenaten's court landing on the thin arc of marsh and date palms on the east bank of the Nile.[40] It is hard to imagine what the people must have thought as they stood looking out over the wide expanse of empty sand, walled in by high cliffs. This was their new home. We do not know if they went by choice. Were they willing disciples, converts to a new and exciting religion, or weary officials, pandering to a particularly extreme pharaonic whim? There are no written records to tell us. Perhaps the first night was spent gathered round the fires of a massive, tented village. But by the next day, the lines of building plots would have been laid out, and the brick-making would have started in earnest.[41] It is likely that the city's first buildings emerged at extraordinary speed.

As Flinders Petrie discovered during his season of excavations at Amarna in 1891, a simple mud-brick hut can rise from nothing in a matter of hours: 'The boys make a huge mud pie, a line of bricks is laid on the ground, a line of mud is poured over them, another line of bricks is slapped down in the mud so as to drive up the joints; and thus a wall of headers, with an occasional course of stretchers to bind it, is soon run up. The roof is made of boards covered with durra stalks to protect them from the sun; and the hut is ready for use, with a piece of canvas hung over the doorway.'[42] Whole neighbourhoods must have appeared within days. The archaeological remains suggest a construction free-for-all, a race to occupy, build and expand largely unregulated by the state. If Akhenaten was a totalitarian, then he showed an unconventional lack of interest in the fine details of civic planning.

There was, however, a blueprint of sorts for the city. Cut directly into the rock of the limestone cliffs both to the east and west of Amarna, were sixteen giant boundary markers. When newly carved, these would have shone a startlingly bright white against the escarpment wall. The markers comprised life-size statues and reliefs of the royal family worshipping beneath the disc and rays of the Aten, arranged around long and detailed inscriptions that set out Akhenaten's vision for his new city. The inscription on the very first one begins with a date: 5 years, 4 months and 13 days into the reign of Akhenaten. It describes how 'on this day', the Pharaoh 'mounted a great chariot of electrum, like the Aten when He rises on the horizon and fills the land with his love, and took a goodly road to Akhetaten, the Aten's place of creation.'[43] An elaborate ceremony was then performed to honour the Aten, before Akhenaten summoned his courtiers and laid out his plans.

The rest of the inscription appears to be a transcript of this foundation speech. The Pharaoh describes how the city of the Aten will be made in this place and nowhere else, and will never be allowed to expand beyond its boundaries to the north, south, east and west. He then lists the buildings that he will create for his god: a 'House of the Aten', a 'Mansion of the Aten', a 'House of Rejoicing', a 'Sun-Temple', and for himself: 'Apartments of the Pharaoh' and the 'Apartments of the Queen'.[44] He goes on to reveal that a Royal Tomb will be created in the eastern hills of Amarna, a place where he, Nefertiti and their first-born daughter Meritaten will eventually be buried, along with the priests of the Aten, state officials and courtiers. This statement was of huge significance. For a thousand years, the tombs of the Pharaohs had been cut into the hills above Thebes – it is probable that one had been prepared for Akhenaten already. Yet the new ruler was making clear that the future of Egypt lay in his still-to-be-built city, and that a new 'Valley of the Kings' would be created in the steep-sided desert wadi to the east, which every morning framed the rising sun.

This first carving became a template for the others that followed. The Pharaoh would ride out on his chariot to the cliff walls to set the location of each new boundary marker, and then workmen would begin the arduous job of cutting into the rock, and repeating the original inscription – subtle variations appearing over time as Akhenaten tinkered with the specifics of his vision.[45] It was a suitably grandiose beginning for the city, and on reading the inscriptions it is easy to imagine a gleaming metropolis rising clean and new out of the desert sands. For a time this may well have been the case. But it was short-lived. The prime building material of Akhetaten was mud-brick and desert rock – quick to erect, but subject to rapid wear and tear. Structures would have remained pristine only for a matter of months, weeks, sometimes just days. Mud bricks and mud plaster are unavoidably soft, prone to scratches, cracks and ultimately disintegration. The occasional downpours of desert rain would have discoloured whitewashed exteriors, leaving muddy rivulets in walls, and loosening ceiling plaster. Dust would have been a permanent problem, from the desert sands blown through even the smallest gaps in window shutters, as well as from the decay of the buildings themselves.[46]

Even the wall paintings of Akhenaten's Great Palace make reference to the issue: showing servants sprinkling floors with water, and then sweeping at the surfaces with brushes made of river reeds.[47] The new city would not have looked new for very long. The extremes of desert weather – intense daytime heat, and sharp night-time frosts – would have taken an immediate toll, making every building appear tired. As quickly as it was put up, the city of the sun began to fall down.

Even after Akhetaten had been constructed, its maintenance alone must have required a substantial workforce. And it is here, perhaps, that the Pharaoh's true vision for his city emerges. There is no obvious external workers' encampment visible in the remains.[48] Instead the population of the city itself appears to have carried out all the construction and ongoing repair work. Aside from the giant temples, palaces and villas of the officials, it seems that Akhetaten was one vast integrated workers' encampment, where the many builders, stonemasons, plasterers, painters, sculptors and painters all lived on site.[49]

Evidence has emerged of a huge number of small 'factories', mass-producing everything from glass, pottery and textiles, to jewellery and sculpture. Indeed, it was in the remains of one of these studios that excavators discovered the most famous artefact from Amarna: a life-sized, painted limestone bust of Queen Nefertiti. In 1912, a dig team of the German Oriental Society led by Ludwig Borchardt unearthed an ivory horse-blinker from a rubbish pit, bearing inscriptions that identified the horse – and the building where it was found – as belonging to Thutmose, 'Chief of the Sculptors'. Breaking into a sealed storage area, they came upon a large collection of plaster casts and half-finished statues of body parts, heads and busts made from gypsum plaster, limestone and quartzite. The most spectacular piece was pulled from the sands upside down, from the exact spot where it had fallen thousands of years before from a collapsed timber shelf, thought to have been the victim of termites. Once the millennia of dirt had been cleaned away, the excavators realised that it was not just any face that they had found. It was the city's queen

– seemingly a master study created by the chief sculptor for others to follow.[50]

For a long time a bit-part in the Amarna story, Nefertiti suddenly became the star attraction. The haunting beauty of the face in the bust – symmetrical features, long, swan-like neck and high, prominent cheekbones – made the object a worldwide sensation when it was first displayed in Berlin in 1924. Borchardt saw peace and serenity in the sculpture he had discovered, recognising in Nefertiti 'the epitome of tranquillity and harmony'.[51] Half a century later, the feminist writer and critic Camille Paglia was not so sure: 'This is the least consoling of great artworks. Its popularity is based on misunderstanding and suppression of its unique features. The proper response to the Nefertiti bust is fear.'[52]

However we interpret individual works produced by Thutmose – and some are clearly masterpieces of ancient art – taken as a whole the objects found in his studio demonstrate the all-pervading influence of Akhenaten, his royal family, and his new god in the everyday life and functions of the city. Yet at the same time, the residential and manufacturing districts of the city were allowed to grow in an extremely haphazard and unchecked fashion, according to no predetermined plan.

It is hard to dismiss the suspicion that the real reason for this was that the Pharaoh was completely indifferent to the domestic arrangements of his workforce; that their only role was as a resource to help him realise his higher cause – the celebration of the Aten through great new works of art and architecture. As long as his major construction projects continued at pace, and his 'factories' kept up their relentless output, then he had no cause for concern or intervention.

This suspicion is hardened by some of the most recent archaeological discoveries. In 2006, excavators unearthed a cemetery in a desert valley beyond the southern rock tombs in the limestone cliffs.[53] As they worked through the site, they realised that perhaps as many as 3,000 people were buried there.[54] As the human remains were painstakingly removed, pieced together and analysed, a picture started to emerge of the state of health of the people who lived in Amarna, and it is far removed from Akhenaten's vision of the city as a bountiful idyll of sunlight and nature.

The bones bear witness to widespread childhood malnutrition, spinal injuries, stunted growth, and early death.[55] The citizens of Akhetaten were shorter than other Egyptians of the time, and few lived beyond the age of 35. Two-thirds of the recovered skeletons belonged to people who had died before they had reached 20.[56] For some this indicates a darkness at the heart of Akhenaten's city of light. They point to the fact that, on almost every carving of a ritual scene found in the Amarna tombs, there is a prominent military and police presence.[57] Perhaps this was standard practice in Egyptian capitals. But there is a more sinister possibility – that the construction of Akhetaten and the worship of the Pharaoh's new cult were conducted at spear point. That the city was less of a religious enclave, and more of a spiritual concentration camp.

In the twelfth year of his reign Akhenaten held a great ceremony in his new city, receiving dignitaries from foreign states from across Africa, Asia and the Aegean. The event is commemorated in extensive detail in relief carvings in the Royal Tomb. The artworks show the Pharaoh sitting hand-in-hand with Nefertiti on a golden throne raised on a special platform built in the desert to the east of Akhetaten. The couple's six daughters stand on either side, with the two youngest cradling pet gazelles. Representatives from Syria, Palestine, Libya, Nubia and Kush come before the royal family, offering a dazzling array of gifts.[58]

According to an elaborate carving on the wall of the Royal Tomb, there were animals ranging from horses and long-horned cattle to lions, antelopes and cheetahs. The gifts included gold and silver, ostrich feathers and eggs, and furniture fashioned from ebony logs. Slave women and handcuffed political prisoners were also put on display, escorted by armed guards. For entertainment, there were wrestling and boxing matches, stick fencing bouts and acrobats.[59]

And of course, above them all, the ever-present disc of the sun shone down. This was the high point of the Amarna period, a joyous celebration held at the centre of the sacred desert land of the Aten, in the city that Akhenaten had built in his honour. The Pharaoh and his beautiful wife ruled over a vast empire, seemingly worshipped and adored by their subjects, and at the same time led a blissful domestic life. Yet this was the last glimpse of peace and happiness in the reign of Akhenaten.

From this moment on, the picture of what happened at Amarna grows more and more obscure. Another carving in the Royal Tomb shows that, later that same year, there was a family tragedy: Meketaten, the Pharaoh's second daughter, died during childbirth. Courtiers and officials are pictured mourning beside the deathbed, while Akhenaten and Nefertiti weep, cry out, and pour dust over their heads in an open display of grief.[60] Around the same time, Akhenaten's mother Queen Tiye also died. In the years that follow, the visual record of the royal court becomes faint and fragmentary. Two years later, in the fourteenth year of Akhenaten's reign, Nefertiti disappears; whether she is dead or not remains unclear. Meanwhile, political unrest had begun to afflict the extremities of the Egyptian empire.

A collection of 350 diplomatic letters inscribed on clay tablets – discovered in 1887 by a peasant woman digging at Amarna in the ruins of a structure known as the 'House of Correspondence of the Pharaoh' – give a vivid account of a great empire fraying at the seams. The threat of mounting Hittite aggression in the north is portrayed in a series of increasingly desperate missives. Another set of tablets shows Akhenaten ignoring pleas for help from his allies in the Mesopotamian kingdom of Mitanni, before relenting and dispatching troops, but too late. A letter reports that the Mitannian king Tushratta has been overthrown and murdered by his own son; shortly afterwards this territory too fell to the Hittites. To the east, dispatches warn that Egyptian control of Syria and Palestine is on the verge of collapse.[61]

In the midst of this, in the seventeenth year of his reign and just after the grape harvest, Akhenaten died.[62] We know nothing of the cause or the circumstances. Presumably his body was buried in the Royal Tomb cut out of the rock of the desert wadi – but if it was, it was later removed. It has never been recovered.

The identity of Akhenaten's successor is a matter for intense, and unresolved, scholarly debate. Ankhkheperure was the name of the new Pharaoh, who was also known as Smenkhkare and Nefernefruaten, which is identical to a longer variation of Nefertiti's name. Had the 'beautiful one' outlived her husband and seized power in Egypt for herself? Some suggest that Ankhkheperure was the husband of the eldest royal daughter, Meritaten. Others believe that it was Meritaten herself who had taken the throne. Both Meritaten and Nefertiti's claims are supported by a letter found in the ruins of the Hittite capital of Hattusa in Anatolia. This appears to be a desperate plea from an Egyptian queen to the Hittite king, saying her husband has died and asking to marry one of his sons to avoid the indignity of having to wed a 'servant'.[63]

Whatever the truth, Ankhkheperure's confused and confusing reign only lasted for two or three years. The next to take the throne is perhaps the most famous Egyptian Pharaoh of them all – the boy king, Tutankhamun. Either a son, or perhaps half-brother, of Akhenaten, Tutankhamun became Pharaoh at the age of ten, guided by the long-standing general Horemheb, and Nefertiti's father Ay.[64] One of his first actions was to announce the end of the Aten cult, in a pointed decree that placed all the blame for Egypt's disarray squarely with Akhenaten and his god.

> 'The temples and the cities of the gods and goddesses... were fallen into decay and their shrines were fallen into ruin, having become mere mounds overgrown with grass... The gods were ignoring this land. If an army was sent to Syria to extend the boundaries of Egypt it met with no success at all. If one beseeched any goddess in the same way, she did not respond at all. Their hearts were faint in their bodies, and they destroyed what was made.'[65]

Amarna was abandoned after a lifespan of just sixteen or seventeen years.[66] The entire population departed as one, leaving many of their belongings behind. This may have been either a military eviction or a delighted exodus from the desert plain. The mud-brick houses were left to their own steady disintegration. The stone buildings, on the other hand – the great Aten temples and the Pharaoh's vast palace – were levelled to their foundations. It was an organised and comprehensive demolition, with many of the well-cut stone blocks taken away and incorporated in other construction sites up and down the course of the Nile. The names and portraits of Akhenaten and Nefertiti were struck out, and the many statues of the royal family were smashed. The political, spiritual and artistic rebellion of Amarna was brought to a swift and decisive end. What remained of the city crumbled into the sands, its ruins left untouched until the arrival of Napoleon and his *savants* three thousand years later.

Tutankhamun may have overturned one of the most unusual and intriguing episodes in Egyptian history, but his fame derives not from what he did in life, but from how he was received by death. The discovery by Howard Carter in 1922 of the young Pharaoh's fantastically opulent tomb was one of the archaeological sensations of the twentieth century. His reign had only lasted around a decade, and ended in suspicious circumstances, with his skull bearing the marks of a possibly fatal head wound.[67] His close advisor, the veteran general Horemheb took power, ruling for 27 years and continuing to erase from the official records all traces of the Amarna Pharaohs who had preceded him – up to and including Tutankhamun himself.

The Aten was blamed for failing Egypt in its time of need. But the sun god had neither deserted the country nor its king. He was there the whole time – rising and falling each day, always visible, always watching. Perhaps he just did not care. Perhaps Akhenaten did not care either.

At start of the chapter I offered a vision of a city at worship. But there is an alternative. Rather than the great temple filled with the citizens of Akhetaten waiting for the dawn, there is just the Pharaoh and his family. The colossal open-air structure dwarfs their tiny figures – they stand on their own at the head of this vast stone edifice, which is nearly 1,000 metres long and built to face the rising sun. Across the city, the ordinary people remain hard at work, mass-producing artworks for the palaces and temples, and supplying the vast amounts of food and produce that are offered daily to the sun god on the thousands of limestone tables. These gifts to the Aten are left to his rays: the fruit shrivels, withers and bursts in the heat, meat goes bad. Later, servants suffering from malnutrition come to clear away the waste. They are forbidden from eating the food, which is sacred and intended solely for the Aten.

And so it goes on, the next day, and the day after that, and the day after that. It is a nightmarish vision, but after all, anything is possible in the life of the first 'individual'. As Egypt crumbled around him, did the Pharaoh simply carry on with his family life in his vast sun palaces and temples, indifferent and indolent, concerned only by the theological principles of his new faith? Perhaps, as some scholars have suggested, Akhenaten was nothing more than 'a tyrant who just happened to have good taste in art.'[68] If this is the case, he may well have been history's first, but he was certainly not its last.

Yet we cannot escape the fact that Akhenaten created something *different*, at a time when different was dangerous. This, in itself, makes him worthy of special attention. The modern interest in his religion and the city he built for it is hardly a surprise. We are eager to recognise him as a man ahead of his time. Perhaps the sun cult awakens in us some ancient, hard-wired spiritual need? To adapt Voltaire's famous line, if Akhenaten's god did not exist, would we today, in any case, want to invent him? Does Amarna, as some have speculated, mark the very start of the environmental movement?

Amarna was a beginning. As such, it is also a place of pilgrimage. The question is, will any pilgrims come? If so, who will they be? At the conclusion of his landmark study of Amarna, Barry Kemp imagines a handful of white-robed foreign tourists arriving at the ruins of the great Aten temple, and gathering together to worship. 'Akhenaten's chosen and unlikely self-image as the beautifully sculpted freak has already gained in modern times compelling iconic status,' he writes. 'Amarna's heyday may yet lie in the future.'[69] There is a long history of counter-cultures that grow, almost from nothing, to dominate the world. Think of Jehovah, Jesus and Allah. Before all of them there was Akhenaten, and his one god, the Aten.

The old gods fade and die; at least this is how history tells us it has always been. But as Akhenaten told his subjects 3,500 years ago, we cannot forget the sun, or deny that it sustains all life on our planet. Will the Aten become a figurehead for the evangelists of clean and renewable energy – someone to pray to in the event of a future worldwide ecological catastrophe? The sun god can play the waiting game. One of these mornings, people may once again look to the horizon, squint against the dawn glare, and remember.

Chapter Five

Jerusalem Syndrome

The Temple of Jerusalem
(Born 950 BC – Died AD 70)

On a morning some 4,000 years ago, in a land at the far south-eastern corner of the Mediterranean Sea, an elderly father set out on a journey with his only son. Along with two servants and a pack donkey, they travelled for two days into a barren range of hills, picking their way over slopes of loose rock and through a maze of dry riverbeds and gorges. On the third morning, the father saw in the distance the place he had come to find. He told his servants to wait with the donkey, and he and his son continued on alone. From a hilltop, the servants watched the man – who some said was over one hundred years old – lead his son down into the valley and then back up a slope to a bare summit.

Lit by the morning sun, the two figures bent down to their work, making a small altar from stones and wood. To the servants' astonishment, the father then bound the son's hands and feet, and the son lay down on the makeshift altar. From his cloak the father produced a knife, brandished it above his head, and began to bring it down. At the last instant, the killer blow was halted. The old man raised his eyes skywards before turning back to his son on the altar, cutting his bonds and setting him free.

When the pair returned to the servants, the father, whose name was Abraham, explained what had happened. God, he said, had set him the ultimate test of his faith. He had been asked to sacrifice his only son, Isaac. As he was about to strike, a voice had called out to him saying, 'Do not lay your hand on the boy.' By offering Isaac, Abraham had shown his true devotion, and God promised that his descendants would be 'as numerous as the stars of heaven and as the sand that is on the seashore'. They would be God's chosen people. At that moment, on an empty hilltop known as Mount Moriah, a new religion was born.[1]

Nearby, on another hillside, was a tiny walled village built around a natural, underground spring. It was called Urushalimmu – after Shalim, the god of the evening star.[2] Urushalimmu was a remote outpost in a blasted landscape, far from any trade routes, hard to reach, and exposed year-round to extremes of hot and cold. Yet, as a consequence, it was easy to fortify and defend, and was a secure haven in times of trouble. Urushalimmu may not have expected or wanted visitors. But for the next four millennia, visitors kept coming. Like Abraham, people were compelled to travel to this place, to view it from a hillside, and to see their destiny below. Urushalimmu – now better known now as Jerusalem – would become the centre of the world.

On 7 June 1967, Israeli Defence Force Colonel Mordechai 'Motta' Gur sent out a radio message to his battalion commanders from a position on the Mount of Olives, above the City of Jerusalem. 'We occupy the heights overlooking the Old City. In a little while we will enter it. The ancient city of Jerusalem which for centuries we have dreamt of and striven for – we will be the first to enter it. The Jewish nation is awaiting our victory. Israel awaits this historic hour. Be proud. Good luck.'[3]

It was the third day of the 'Six Day War', the conflict between Israel and the combined Arab forces of Egypt, Syria and Jordan for supremacy – territorial and spiritual – at the very heart of the Middle East. Gur and his paratroopers had been advancing since before the dawn, and by the time the sun had risen, the Israelis had managed to encircle the entire city. From his vantage point Gur watched artillery strikes shake the ancient stone walls of Jerusalem, and as he moved downhill through the Garden of Gethsemane – according to the Gospels, the scene nearly 2,000 years before of Judas' betrayal and Jesus' arrest by the Romans – Sherman tanks opened fire at point blank range on a bus blocking the Lion's Gate, a stone bastion leading into the Old City. With the way clear, Gur jumped aboard a half-track, sped past the tanks and the still burning bus, and led his unit into the narrow cobbled streets ahead. They made their way up the Via Dolorosa – the same route Jesus had walked, carrying his cross, on the way to his crucifixion.[4]

The advance was being broadcast live on 'Voice of Israel Radio'. Listeners could hear gunfire, shouted commands, soldiers' running footsteps and bullets ricocheting off stonework. Then a voice rang out clear over the army wireless: it was Gur, speaking the lines that, for Israelis, are perhaps the most famous of the 1967 war. 'The Temple Mount is in our hands! I repeat, the Temple Mount is in our hands!'[5]

The Temple Mount – known in Arabic as the *al-Haram al-Sharif*, or Noble Sanctuary – is a vast, rectangular, stone platform built on a narrow spur of rock rising out of the Kidron Valley west of the Mount of Olives. Four massive retaining walls, each several hundred metres in height and length, enclose a plaza almost 37 acres in area, which forms the entire eastern section of the Old City of Jerusalem.[6] The Temple Mount is dominated by one structure: the huge, golden-roofed Dome of the Rock, a masterpiece of Islamic architecture dating from the seventh century AD. As its name suggests, this building has at its heart a bare slab of the landscape's original rock. To Muslims, this is the spot where the prophet Mohammed ascended to paradise. To Jews, it is the summit of Mount Moriah, the very place where Abraham offered his son Isaac as a sacrifice to God.

Gur was met beneath the shadow of the Dome by Anwar al Khatib, the Jordanian governor of Jerusalem. He told Gur that the last of the Jordanian army had withdrawn, and that there would be no more resistance. Israeli soldiers were flooding into the Old City, and they were all rushing towards one place: a section of ancient wall on the western, outer edge of the Temple Mount. As Gur and his men made their way down a set of steps to a narrow lane, the shout came over the radio, 'The Western Wall! I can see the Wall.' Exhausted and overcome with emotion, paratroopers collapsed weeping against the stones, while others began to unite in prayer and song.[7] This section of wall was all that remained of a temple first built nearly 3,000 years before – a temple designed to be the sole vessel for God on the earth, and which had been raised, ruined, rebuilt, demolished, rebuilt again, and then finally destroyed. In the absence of any other physical remains, this narrow stretch of pavement and this fragment of wall had become the Jewish people's most sacred and holy site. For nineteen years, the Israelis had been denied access to the wall. Now they had fought their way back to what they believed was rightfully theirs.

Except nothing is simple in the history of Jerusalem. Every claim of ownership is met by an equally vociferous counter-claim. No city in the world has been more fought for and fought over. It belongs to everyone and it belongs to no one. And at the heart of this eternal struggle is the Temple Mount. It is, as the Israeli historian Gershom Gorenberg puts it, 'the most contested piece of real estate on earth'.[8]

The day after the 1967 war ended, Amos Oz, the Israeli writer, novelist and journalist, arrived in Jerusalem in his paratrooper's uniform, still carrying his sub-machine gun. 'I tried my hardest to feel... like a man who has driven out his enemies and returned to his ancestral inheritance.' But even in the euphoria of victory, he could see that, just as much as Jerusalem was his home, it was also home to Muslims and Christians. 'I walked the streets of East Jerusalem like a man who has broken into a forbidden place. City of my birth. City of my dreams. City of aspirations of my ancestors and my people. And here I was stalking its streets clutching a sub-machine-gun, like a figure in one of my childhood nightmares: an alien man in an alien city'.[9]

Chief of Staff Lt. Gen. Yitzhak Rabin – a future Prime Minister of Israel – entering the old city during the Six Day War of 1967, with Moshe Dayan and Uzi Narkiss. © Ilan Bruner

Some time around 1000 BC, David, the first king of the Israelites, marched an army to a ridge overlooking an imposing fortress known as Zion. This stone bastion, set at the heart of the city of Jebus, was thought to be impregnable. So confident were the Jebusites of their ability to withstand any assault that they taunted David by lining the battlements with the blind and the lame.[10]

David, however, was a man who relished a challenge. Said to be 'ruddy' with 'beautiful eyes', and 'handsome' – just as Michelangelo imagined him in statue some 2,500 years later[11] – David was also 'skilful in playing, a man of valour, a warrior.'[12] As a boy, he had defeated the Philistine champion Goliath with one flick of his trusty slingshot. His charisma and his ego demanded that Zion would fall. How David succeeded in bringing this about is obscure: the biblical account at this point becomes particularly vague. The most common explanation – borne out, to some extent, by archaeological evidence – holds that Joab, one of David's most trusted lieutenants, scaled a near vertical 'water shaft' that led from the base of the city's outer wall into the centre of the fortress.[13] Under cover of darkness, Joab despatched the surprised sentries and opened the city gates from the inside. In the end, the city was taken without much of a fight.

Jebus was renamed the City of David, only later reverting to its 'pagan' name of Jerusalem.[14] David had already united the northern tribes of Israel and the southern tribes of Judah, and because this mountainous stronghold had previously belonged to neither faction, it made perfect political sense to establish it as the capital of the newly minted kingdom of Israel.[15] As well as an administrative capital, David intended it to be the centre of religious life for his people. To put the seal of divine approval on the city, he sent for the Ark of the Covenant, a sacred casket made of acacia wood and gold which held the tablets of the Ten Commandments: God's law, spoken to Moses on Mount Sinai, and inscribed in stone.[16] David, flamboyant as ever, led the procession of the Ark into his city. Wearing only a priestly loincloth, he danced and leapt before the casket – a display of such ostentatious worship that it moved David's wife Michal, looking down on the scene from the window of their house, either to laugh at him[17] or to 'despise him in her heart'[18], depending which account you read.

Until that time, and apart from a period of capture at the hands of the Philistines, the Ark had been kept in a large, elaborate and moveable tent known as the 'Tabernacle' – which itself sat within a temporary courtyard of fabric walls some 150 feet long by 75 feet wide.[19] The inner surface of the Tabernacle was made of fabric, and the outer of animal skins bleached white by years of desert sun. At its entrance there was a richly coloured curtain and a screen of linen, and beyond them an ornamental veil embroidered with flowers and intricate patterns. Behind the veil was both the centre of the temple and of the whole Jewish faith: the Holy of Holies, the resting place of the Ark, and the earthly dwelling place of an invisible, intangible God. For centuries – ever since Moses had led the Israelites out of Egypt – the Tabernacle had moved across the desert, a nomadic temple for a nomadic people.[20] Now

David wanted to set down roots, and create something permanent. 'I am dwelling in a house of cedar,' he exclaimed in the Book of Samuel, 'but the Ark of God stays in a tent'.[21]

To the north of David's city was a small hill that rose steeply out of the Kidron Valley. Olive groves wound around its slopes, and on the flat summit was a threshing field circling a bare slab of rock: this was Mount Moriah, where Abraham was said to have bound his son for sacrifice. A Jebusite by the name of Araunah owned and worked this land. He offered to give it to the king for free, but David was insistent that he would buy it for a price – fifty shekels of silver.[22] This was where he would build the first ever temple for the God of Israel.

Or he would have, had the God of Israel not intervened. David was allowed to choose the site, draw up the plans, hire the labour, and gather the building blocks of the temple – many thousands of expertly hewn stones, great quantities of iron and brass, and giant trunks of cypress and cedar-wood from Lebanon[23] – but he was deemed unworthy of the job of constructing this most holy of sanctuaries. God told him: 'You shall not build a house for my name, for you are a warrior and have shed blood.' Instead, the honour would fall to David's son, Solomon.[24]

Remembered now as the 'wisest' of men, the young Solomon had not been shy of shedding some blood for his own political gain, including ordering the murder of his elder half-brother, and purging dissenters at the political heart of his father's court.[25] From this point on in the biblical account, however, he becomes something of a cipher – the great and majestic ruler of the golden age of the kingdom of Israel.

Solomon's Temple took the basic layout of the tented Tabernacle, and translated it into a magnificent structure of white Jerusalem stone and cedar-wood, overlaid with 'pure gold'. According to the Old Testament's Book of Kings, it was 30 metres long, 10 metres wide, and 15 metres high[26], and, as the Jewish-Roman historian Josephus wrote in the first century AD, the perfection of its walls was such that 'to the beholder there appeared no sign of the use of mallets or other work tools, but all the material seemed to have fitted itself together naturally without the use of these things.'[27] Set within a stone-walled enclosure, as the Tabernacle had been surrounded by a great screen of fabric, the main Temple was entered through a gateway of two bronze pillars known as Yachin and Boaz. These towering columns, decorated with sculptures of pomegranates and lilies, had been cast by Hiram, a master-builder from the land of Tyre. Once inside, the Temple was divided into three cedar-panelled chambers: the *ulam* or porch; the *hechal* or main sanctuary; and finally, the *dvir*, the Holy of Holies.[28] This small, cubed room, guarded by two winged cherubim fashioned from olive-wood and gold, was designed explicitly as the resting place for the Ark of the Covenant.[29]

Once the Temple was complete, around 950 BC, the people of Jerusalem assembled to watch the priests carry the Ark from the Tabernacle to its glittering new home – a home which, as Josephus later imagined, must have, 'dazzled the eyes of those that entered by the radiance of the gold which met them on every side.'[30] As Solomon performed the consecration ceremony for the Temple, he declared to God, 'I have built you an exalted house, a place for you to dwell in forever.'[31] God in turn replied, 'my eyes and my heart will be there for all time... I will establish your royal throne over Israel forever, as I promised your father David.'[32] The construction of the Temple enacted a binding contract between God and the Jewish people. Solomon had built a permanent place for the divine presence on earth. And in return, God granted the people of Israel a sacred right of ownership over the land – an unbreakable lease, granted for eternity.

Solomon's building was unique. One of the key points of the architectural brief for the building, as outlined in God's commandments from Exodus, was that the Israelites should 'not make for yourself an idol, whether in the form of anything that is in heaven above, or that is on the earth beneath... you shall not bow down to them or worship them'.[33] This was a house for a God with no shape or form, yet whose presence was everywhere. Apart from the Ark of the Covenant, which contained only stone tablets, the space at the centre of the Temple was empty. Centuries later, Greeks and Romans who came to enter the Holy of Holies were astonished to find that there really was nothing to see.[34]

The Temple was not just the most sacred site of religious worship in Judaism – it was intended to be the *only* site. According to the Book of Kings, Solomon's later successors King Hezekiah and King Josiah abolished all worship outside of Jerusalem, and dictated that Solomon's Temple was to be the one shrine for all of Israel. For the vast majority of people, this meant that the basic rituals of their religion – the communal sacrifice of animal offerings on an altar – could be performed only after making pilgrimage to the capital city, deep in the Judean hills.[35] The entire focus of national spirituality and worship was turned inward: towards Jerusalem, towards the Temple, towards an empty cube containing the essence of God on earth. The result was a city – and a building – that became an irresistible magnet for the pious and the faithful.

In AD 33, a man called Joshua ben Joseph – later known, via Latin, Greek and Aramaic translations, as Jesus[36] – travelled to Jerusalem. A Jewish preacher and a holy man, he was part of a massive pilgrimage to the capital city for 'Passover': a commemoration of the time, as recounted in the Book of Exodus, when God's tenth plague of Egypt, which brought death to all first-born children, 'passed over' the Israelites. The scale of this festival was immense. Jews came 'from every nation'.[37] Josephus, a Temple priest in the first century AD, estimated the number of people descending on Jerusalem at two-and-a-half million. As part of the ritual celebration, every family had to sacrifice a lamb. A report sent back to the Roman Emperor Nero by a Syrian priest recorded 255,600 slaughtered in the city during one Passover.[38] The clamour and colour of so many pilgrims in one place was overwhelming. There was not enough space in Jerusalem to accommodate everyone, so tens of thousands lodged in nearby villages, or set up camps encircling the city. Roman guards were a constant, visible presence – this land was now a province of the empire. Such a gathering could easily spill over into civil unrest. The military kept a close watch on the crowds, and the festival simmered with tension.

Jesus approached Jerusalem from the heights of the Mount of Olives, and as the city was laid out before him, his 'Apostles' – provincials from Galilee who had never before visited the capital – were awestruck by what they saw. 'Look, Teacher, what large stones and what large buildings!'[39] Jesus, however, had visited Jerusalem many times. As they neared the city he wept for its future destruction at the hands of enemies who would 'set up ramparts around you and surround you, and hem you in on every side... they will not leave within you one stone upon another.'[40]

Jesus knew that Jerusalem had been destroyed before – his vision for the city's end had precedent going back some six centuries. In the generations that followed the glorious age of David and Solomon, a cancer had eaten away at the kingdom of Israel. Fifty years of civil war – as Judah and Israel split apart once more – were followed by a series of ill-fated and sometimes disastrous reigns where, as the Books of Jeremiah and Lamentations recount, the Jewish kings 'did evil in the sight of the Lord.'[41] Despite the attempts of some pious rulers to arrest the decline, there was a steady moral collapse, and religion became corrupted. Worst of all were King Ahab and his wife Jezebel, who converted Solomon's sacred Temple to a shrine for Baal[42] – lord of the Earth and god of fertility – and took part in rituals that involved the performance of sexual acts, self-harming and human sacrifice.[43] The prophet Isaiah was the first to warn the Jews that they risked God's wrath, predicting the fall of Jerusalem: 'your cities are burned with fire; in your very presence aliens devour your land; it is desolate'.[44]

Isaiah was also the first to consider life after the destruction of the city and its Temple – imagining a new Jerusalem 'in the days to come', where 'the mountain of the Lord's house shall be established as the highest of the mountains and shall be raised above the hills, all nations shall stream to it... for out of Zion shall go forth instruction, and the word of the Lord from Jerusalem'.[45] Isaiah's poetic vision almost seemed to welcome the coming disaster, because it would allow the kingdom of Israel to rise again, new and improved. This was an exceptionally potent idea, and it has persisted throughout the history of Jerusalem, right up to the present day – the apocalypse as both a fear and a yearning. The end brings a new beginning, and moves the faithful ever closer to the Kingdom of Heaven.[46]

Jesus was familiar with the teachings of Isaiah, and he knew that the prophet's predictions had indeed come true. In 586 BC, after an eighteen-month siege[47], the armies of the Babylonian King Nebuchadnezzar overcame Jerusalem. By this time, the people of the city were starving and racked by disease; according to the Book of Lamentations, some may even have resorted to cannibalism: 'The hands of compassionate women have boiled their own children; they became their food.'[48] Recently a team of archaeologists analysed a cesspool dating from the siege: they found that the normal city diet of lentils, peas, wheat and barley had been replaced by 'backyard' plants and herbs fertilized by human excrement – the ancient latrine was full of tapeworm and whipworm eggs.[49]

Jerusalem had been a constant irritant to Nebuchadnezzar – he had laid siege to the city several times over a sixteen-year period[50] – and he was determined that this would be his last visit to the Judean hills. The destruction was near absolute. Fire raged through the city, and in the aftermath battering rams were used to flatten any walls that were still standing. Solomon's Temple, the single shrine for the whole Jewish faith, was not spared. Its gold and silver was pillaged, its priests were killed in front of Nebuchadnezzar, and then it was burnt to the ground.[51] All the survivors were marched across the deserts and the plains to Mesopotamia and the city of Babylon to be slaves in exile. It should have been the end of the world: a city annihilated, a people scattered across the earth, and the one and only house of their god demolished.

Yet something remarkable happened. Adversity spawned a new piety among the Israelites. In exile, they experienced a painful period of introspection, and lamented their failure to live up to the spiritual idealism embodied in the construction of Solomon's Temple. As they 'wept' beside the rivers of Babylon[52], they still remembered their lost city and longed to return. It was their own failure to follow God's laws that had led them to their fate, and they would not make the same mistakes again. God was still waiting for them on the summit of Mount

Moriah. One day they would rebuild His Temple. This was both an architectural and a spiritual promise. 'Rebuilding the temple' – an idea first emerging during the Babylonian exile in the hallucinatory and feverish visions of the prophet Ezekiel – was a metaphor for keeping the faith.[53]

Almost fifty years later, the Persian King Cyrus overthrew Nebuchadnezzar's Babylonian Empire, and the Jews were set free. Some 40,000 exiles made the long journey back to their ruined city. Gradually they shook Jerusalem 'from the dust'[54] and it began to rise again.

The city upon which Jesus looked in AD 33, overflowing with the pilgrims of Passover, was greater than it had ever been before: just as Isaiah had said it would be. A colossal new Temple dominated Mount Moriah, its huge outer walls casting long shadows over the surrounding city and countryside. Yet Jesus was not convinced. He believed his people had lost sight of their promise to God, and had forgotten the lessons of exile. History was destined to repeat itself. Another apocalypse was on the way.

According to the Gospels Jesus entered Jerusalem riding on the foal of a donkey – the sign, according to prophecy, of the arrival of a king. His followers laid down palm leaves and their own cloaks before him, hailed him as the 'Son of David'[55], and sang that he was 'the King who comes in the name of the Lord!'[56] When others in the throng, troubled by these claims, urged Jesus to order his disciples to stop, he answered that, 'if these were silent, the stones would shout out'.[57] The Roman guards looked on with interest.

As they approached the city, the crowds grew thicker – hundreds of thousands were pouring down from the surrounding slopes and up from the lower town towards the Temple. The mass of pilgrims met below the southern wall, passed stalls offering food, drink and livestock for sacrifice[58], and funnelled into two giant, imposing gates. Moving through an underground gallery, they then climbed a monumental staircase bringing them back out into the light of a huge open courtyard, surrounded on all sides by towering, pillared porticoes. This was the Temple Mount.

It was a gathering to assault the senses. Everywhere, animals were being slaughtered for sacrifice, the smell of fresh blood and dung mingled with great waves of incense and the tang of roasting flesh. Discarded hides and carcasses were strewn across the courtyard floor. And straight ahead, soaring above the mass of people, was the new Temple of Jerusalem – the building at the centre of the world. It was covered on all sides by sheer plates of gold, and as the pilgrims emerged from the staircase, it caught the morning light and, according to Josephus, 'radiated so fiery a flash that persons straining to look at it were compelled to avert their eyes, as from the solar rays'.[59] This building was literally dazzling. The gold was mounted on Jerusalem stones polished 'purest white', so that to strangers approaching from a distance 'it appeared... like a snow-clad mountain.'[60] On its roof, function and ostentation combined: sharpened gold spikes prevented birds from perching on the Temple and fouling the glittering exterior.[61]

This colossal monument, one of the largest structures anywhere in the classical world, was the work of Herod, perhaps the most ambitious, cunning, violent – and disliked – king in the history of the Jewish people. Herod was a product of Rome. A friend of Mark Antony, he had been groomed for leadership since childhood, and was schooled in the military and administrative principles of the empire. He began his career as governor of Galilee, and then, in 37 BC, led a Roman army to recapture Jerusalem from a Persian invasion. As a reward for his success, he was named King of the Jews.[62]

Rumours of poisonings, betrayals, corruption and sexual scandal followed Herod's rise to power.[63] Yet, when it came to Jerusalem, no one could deny that the king had transformed the fabric of the city. Almost everything was remodelled along the principles of Greco-Roman architecture. A new grid layout was established, with wide, spacious streets, public squares, theatres, bathhouses and villas – all built in distinctive white stone. From a shattered ruin, Jerusalem had become, in the words of the Roman scholar Pliny the Elder, 'by far the most famous city of the East'.[64] Yet in 20 BC, over fifteen years after his reign had begun, there was still one final piece missing for Herod.

On the summit of Mount Moriah, visible above the whole city, stood a tired, faded and battle-scarred structure. This was the Temple of the Jews. It had been raised again half a millennium before, in the years immediately after the return from exile, on the same spot where Solomon's Temple had once stood.[65] And it was very much a product of a broken and impoverished people. When it was complete – in time for the Passover of 515 BC – some shouted for joy at the sight of it, but others, in particular the old men who remembered the first Temple, 'wept with a loud voice... so that the people could not distinguish the sound of the joyful shout from the sound of the people's weeping, for the people shouted so loudly that the sound was heard far away'.[66] The prophet Haggai similarly lamented the state of the structure, asking, 'Who is left among you that saw this house in its former glory? How does it look to you now? Is it not in your sight as nothing?'[67]

For an aesthete like Herod, this would not do. He wanted to take over the sacred site to create a building 'great enough to assure his eternal remembrance'.[68] Of course, he did not put it quite like that to the Jewish people. After first reminding them in a public speech that he had 'brought the Jewish nation to such a state of prosperity as it has never known before', he announced his intentions to rebuild the Temple. Here, he said, was the 'opportunity to restore this first archetype of piety to its former size'.[69] Regardless of its dilapidated state, there was dismay at the prospect of the Temple being pulled down. Its destruction five centuries before at the hands of Nebuchadnezzar had torn at the heart of the Jewish faith. Could they really risk levelling the house of God a second time? And what if, once it was gone, Herod proved unable or unwilling to complete his huge undertaking?

Herod was prepared for these objections, and employed all his skills of persuasion and rhetoric. He promised that work would not commence on demolishing the Temple until all the materials and craftsmen were in place to begin rebuilding. Whole forests of Lebanese cedar were felled, floated down the coast, and brought to the city. Massive ashlar stones were cut from the quarries of Jerusalem – the smallest weighing some 5 tons, with the largest over 12m long and 4m thick, and weighing some 400 tons.[70] A thousand wagons transported the vast blocks to Mount Kidron, where they were to be stacked into foundations dug all the way down to bedrock many metres below the surface. 10,000 workmen were assembled, and 1,000 priests were trained as carpenters and stonemasons, to ensure that only the sacred hands of the most pious Jews would construct the Temple.[71]

In Solomon's time, it was said that no hammering or chiselling had disturbed the peace of the construction site, so Herod ensured that all the massive stone building blocks could fit together without mortar or bolts. The glorious new Temple itself was completed within 18 months, but the vast edifice of the surrounding Temple Mount, with its towering colonnades, arcades and porticoes, remained under construction for nearly 50 years.[72] Abraham's hilltop became a colossal, artificial mountain, a block of truly monolithic architecture with a sacred building of pure gold at its centre. Josephus hailed this work as 'the greatest ever heard of by man.'[73]

Jesus was less impressed. His response to Herod's masterpiece was not awe, but anger. After arriving in the open central courtyard, he made his way with the Apostles beneath the vast canopy of the Royal Portico, a 30m-high, columned hallway that stretched along the entire length of the southern wall of the Temple Mount. This was the main meeting place where pilgrims gathered and where the pious came to preach, and it was packed full of yet more stalls selling animals for sacrifice: lambs, doves, even oxen for the most well-off. Against the back wall of the Portico were the long tables of the money changers – only the Hebrew 'holy shekel' could be used to make purchases or pay the Temple taxes, and it was here that all the other currencies of the empire were exchanged. Indeed, it is suggested by some that the modern word 'bank' comes from *banca*, the term for the bench of a money changer's table.[74]

Jesus was enraged by what he saw, crying out, 'Is it not written, "My house shall be called a house of prayer for all the nations"? But you have made it a den of robbers'.[75] He overturned the tables, sending shekels flying everywhere. It may have been righteous anger. It may have been a deliberate act of provocation. Jesus left in the midst of the commotion, but as he made his way out of the Temple, he repeated his prophecy to his disciples, and anyone else within earshot: 'Do you see these great buildings? Not one stone will be left here upon another; all will be thrown down.'[76] He went on to warn of an imminent apocalypse, with Jerusalem as its epicentre: 'Nation will rise against nation, and kingdom against kingdom, and there will be famines and earthquakes.'[77] This sermon on the 'end of days' may have excited the crowds, but it also caused serious alarm among the priests and the Roman administration. In the febrile atmosphere of Passover, Jesus's predictions seemed to them a dangerous incitement to riot, if not full-scale insurrection.

After a meal with his Apostles on the slopes of Mount Zion, Jesus walked down into the valley below Herod's Temple, to the olive groves of the Garden of Gethsemane. In the gathering dusk, he was met by an armed guard of Temple priests. Judas, one of the Apostles, approached Jesus and kissed his cheek. This was the signal for the guards to seize their man. Judas was paid for his betrayal in silver, while the other Apostles drew their swords for a futile and short-lived battle. As Jesus was taken, his followers were beaten back, and turned and fled into the darkness.[78]

The trial of Jesus took place in the Temple later that night. The high-priest Caiaphas asked Jesus if he had threatened to destroy the Temple. He gave no answer. Caiaphas then asked him if he was the Messiah, the Son of God. This time, Jesus did respond, saying, 'I am: and you will see the Son of man seated at the right hand of the power, and coming with the clouds of heaven.' In a triumphant fury, the high-priest tore the clothes from Jesus' body and turned to the crowd, saying, 'Why do we still need witnesses? You have heard his blasphemy! What is your decision?' They answered that he was guilty, and that his punishment must be death, by crucifixion.[79]

The next morning, Jesus, wearing a sign around his neck daubed with the slogan 'King of the Jews' and bearing a wooden crossbar on his back, was marched through the upper town of Jerusalem, out of the city gate, and up to the summit of a hill known as

Golgotha – the Place of the Skull. He was stripped naked and nailed to a cross through his forearms and ankles. Later that day, at around three o'clock in the afternoon, he died.[80]

In AD 638, a man arrived at the gates of Jerusalem, riding on a white camel. The man was very tall and broad – some described him as a giant – and he wore a 'soiled and torn' camel-hair tunic and the simple long white robes of a pilgrim.[81] He dismounted and stood waiting. The gates opened and Sophronius, Patriarch of Jerusalem and faithful servant of the Byzantine Empire, emerged clad in the bejewelled, golden robes of office. Sophronius handed the man the keys to Jerusalem. Then he turned and led the towering figure into the city.

The man's name was Omar. He was the 'Commander of the Believers': a vast army of Arab horsemen and cameleers who followed the teachings of a prophet called Mohammed. Omar had fought and prayed alongside Mohammed, who had died six years before, and he was one of the first converts to a new religion and nation known as Islam. In little more than two decades, this nation had grown from a nomadic rabble to conquer much of the Middle East, uniting the tribes of Arabia and routing the armies of the Persians and the Byzantines. Jerusalem was one of the last bastions of the Eastern Roman Empire, but with support routes cut off, it was isolated and alone. The city had no option but to surrender.

In a remarkable display of humility and respect, and to save further bloodshed, Omar agreed to come alone to accept the surrender of the city. Sophronius led him to the Church of the Holy Sepulchre, the most sacred Byzantine site in Jerusalem. According to the Patriarch, this had been built on top of the tomb of a man called Jesus, the Son of God, who had died at the hands of the Jews and Romans some six hundred years before. Yet after three days, this man had come alive again, and had ascended to heaven from the Mount of Olives, taking his place in paradise alongside his Holy Father. This church was not, however, what Omar wanted to see.

Instead, he ordered Sophronius to take him to 'the Mosque of David'.[82] They came to a gate set in a giant wall. Steps led upward, but huge piles of refuse blocked the entrance, even spilling out onto the surrounding streets. Omar made the Patriarch go ahead of him, and they had to crawl on their hands and knees up through the debris. They emerged onto a wide, empty plateau, high above the city. It was a picture of desolation: shattered stones were submerged beneath thick layers of dung, dirt and rubbish. Omar seemed shocked by the scene. Sophronius explained that this place had been abandoned deliberately.[83] The Holy Gospels told them that there would not be left on this site 'one stone... upon another; all will be thrown down.' Jesus had foretold destruction here, and his prophecy had come true. The sacred Temple of the Jews had been wiped from the face of the earth, and the architectural wonder built by King Herod had been left barren and ruined. To Sophronius and the people of Jerusalem, this structure was a monumental reminder of the failure and hubris of the Jewish religion.

The fall of the Temple had come in AD 70, less than thirty years after Jesus' death. For some two decades uprisings by the Judean people against their Roman overlords had grown increasingly common. This was a province characterised by insurrection. Religion was often the spark: heavy-handed Roman intervention in sacred Jewish rituals or sites spilling over into unrest and rioting. The tipping point came in AD 66, when Florus, the Roman procurator, seized sacred treasure from the Temple, claiming it was in lieu of unpaid tribute.[84] After a series of pitched battles in the streets of Jerusalem – including Jews fighting against Jews, the first signs of the civil war that would later engulf the city – the Roman garrison retreated to the fortress of Antonia within the Temple Mount, where they were overcome and massacred. For the next four years, bitter infighting blighted Jerusalem. Josephus called the city 'a raving beast', which 'at length preyed upon its own flesh'.[85] The Romans gradually fought to regain territory throughout the region, but they left the battle for Jerusalem till last. Finally, in AD 70, Titus, son of the new Emperor Vespasian, marched on the city with an army of 65,000 men.[86]

The resulting four-month siege was one of the most bloody and brutal that Jerusalem had ever known. Perhaps some six hundred thousand Jews were trapped inside[87] – the civil war had already devastated parts of the city and exhausted reserves of food. For the religious zealots among them, there could be no surrender: they would defend Jerusalem until their last breath. Many of the other citizens did not share this conviction, however, and attempted to escape by slipping past the encircling Roman army. Most were caught, and Titus ordered all prisoners to be crucified. Perhaps five hundred Jews were crucified each day.[88] The hillsides around Jerusalem became a forest of wooden crosses hung with the dead and dying – to look out from the city walls was to see a gruesome panorama of suffering. Starvation gripped the people as remorselessly as the Roman assault – Titus had ordered a new wall built around the entire city, a great noose of stone – and, as Josephus described, the 'famine enlarging its maw, devoured the people by household and families.' Streets were piled high with the 'corpses of the aged', while 'children and youths with swollen figures, roamed like phantoms through the market-places and collapsed wherever their doom overtook them'. Yet all those who perished, continued Josephus, did so with their 'eyes fixed on the Temple'.[89]

The Temple. The inevitable Roman advance and Jewish retreat took the battle to the very gates of the House of God. At dawn on 28 August[90], Titus ordered the storming of the sacred sanctuary of the Jewish faith. According to Josephus, the other generals argued that the Temple should be destroyed because it would always remain a focal point of rebellion. Titus, however, said he could not allow this to happen to 'so magnificent a work; for the loss would affect the Romans... as it would be an ornament to Empire if it stood'.[91] The ferocity of the battle was terrible. The Romans pushed the Jews back into the inner court of the Temple, and 'around the altar a pile of corpses was accumulating; down the steps of the sanctuary flowed a stream of blood, and the bodies of the victims killed above went sliding to the bottom'.[92]

The outer gates of the Temple had already been set on fire, and in the fury of battle, one legionary snatched a beam of burning wood, and tossed it into the golden window of the sanctuary. In Josephus' account, Titus gave furious orders for the blaze to be extinguished, but his men pretended not to hear, and threw more firebrands at the Temple walls.[93] Its fate was sealed. On the exact same day that Nebuchadnezzar had destroyed the first Temple some six centuries before, the holy sanctuary was again reduced to smouldering rubble. Josephus watched its death with horror. 'The roar of the flames streaming far and wide mingled with the groans of the falling victims... nothing more deafening or appalling could be conceived than that... You would indeed have thought the Temple hill was boiling over from its base, being everywhere one mass of flame.'[94]

In the aftermath, Roman engineers systematically dismantled everything that was left on the Temple Mount. The vast porticoes and columns were toppled – upended by levers and pulled down by ropes. Once all fragments of the buildings had been removed, the plateau of the Temple Mount was ploughed flat. All that remained were Herod's colossal outer walls[95], a giant stone platform topped by a bare wasteland. The rest of Jerusalem was similarly levelled. The aim, said Josephus, was 'to leave future visitors to the spot no ground for believing that it had ever been inhabited'.[96]

Gradually, however, people did come back. Local tribes resettled the city, and resentment at their past persecution grew. In AD 132, Jerusalem rebelled once again. Rome's response was devastating. The Emperor Hadrian ordered his most able general, Julius Severus, to 'crush, exhaust and exterminate' all rebels.[97] The Roman historian Cassius Dio reported that nearly a thousand villages were razed and nearly six hundred thousand men killed, while 'the number of those who perished from famine, disease and fire was past finding out'. In summary, he wrote, 'very few of them in fact survived.'[98] At Hadrian's command, the Jews were forbidden from ever returning to Judea or Jerusalem, and the city was rebuilt and renamed Aelia Capitolina. Aelia was repopulated from the surrounding provinces of the empire – mainly with Greek-speaking Syrians – and for a time a statue of Hadrian and a shrine to Jupiter were erected on the Temple Mount, right on top of the demolished Jewish sanctuary.[99]

Among the new citizens was a small religious sect, which still worshipped the memory of the man called Jesus. For this cult, the destruction of the Temple fulfilled a prophecy made by the Son of God. It was proof that their new religion, Christianity, was the true faith. Aelia Capitolina – Jerusalem – the site of the passion and the resurrection, was now *their* Holy City.

Omar had been told a wonderful story about Jerusalem by his friend and spiritual mentor Mohammed, a story that had become revered and repeated among all followers of Islam. As Mohammed slept by the Ka'aba, the sacred site at the heart of Mecca, the Archangel Gabriel came to his side and kicked him awake. Gabriel had come to take the prophet on a 'Night Journey'. Mounting a white steed with a human face and an eagle's wings[100] called Al Buraq, 'the Lightning', Mohammed flew at great speed above mountains and deserts, visited Mount Sinai and Bethlehem, before arriving finally at the 'distant shrine'. Below him was a city, and Al Buraq swooped down to land on a deserted platform raised up on high walls. There, waiting on an outcrop of rock, were the prophets who had appeared before Mohammed: Abraham, Moses and Jesus, and many other ancient apostles. He led all of these prophets in prayer, before ascending to heaven by a ladder of light.[101] When he returned to earth, and then to Mecca, Mohammed remembered clearly the commandment he had received from God: to show his piety and devotion, he was to pray five times a day.[102]

This miraculous journey had taken place just seventeen years before Omar arrived at the gates of Jerusalem. In that time, and since the Prophet's death, the significance of the city had only grown among the followers of Islam. As Omar walked the desolate platform of the Temple Mount, he recognised it as the 'distant shrine' that Mohammed had described to him. 'This is the place,' he said, and with his bare hands – the massive hands of a man who had been a wrestler in his youth[103] – he began to clear away the dirt and filth, filling his cloak with it and throwing it over Herod's walls into the valley below.

Once his army had entered the city, Omar set them to work cleansing the entire Mount, and as the rubbish and refuse were removed, they found Mohammed's rock, marked with an indentation where, it was said, the base of his ladder to heaven had melted the stone.[104]

At the southern end of the Temple Mount, on the site of the Royal Portico where Jesus had challenged the money changers, Omar built a large, simple wooden structure – the first mosque of Jerusalem. The Christian priest Arculf, returning from a pilgrimage to the city in AD 680, gives the only contemporary account of this building, describing how Omar had erected a crude 'oblong house of prayer... pieced together with upright planks and large beams over some ruined remains. It is said that the building can hold three thousand people'.[105] Omar was the latest in a long line of men to lead a conquering army into Jerusalem, yet his benevolence was remarkable. He allowed the Jews to return to the city after centuries of exile, and at the same time, granted Christians the freedom to worship at their holy sites.[106] The Temple Mount was sanctified as a sacred site of Mohammed – they called it the *al Haram al Sharif*, or Noble Sanctuary – and Jerusalem was named as the third most holy city of Islam, after Mecca and Medina. Judaism, Christianity, Islam: all three religions had descended from the same source, the patriarch Abraham. And now all three were united in the heart of the city. Omar had created the template for modern Jerusalem. It was a noble gesture, yet, perhaps inevitably, it sowed the seeds of future conflict.

Some three centuries later, the Islamic geographer Al-Muqaddasi gave a withering account of the people of the Holy City: 'Learned men are few, and the Christians numerous and... un-mannerly in the public places... Everywhere the Christians and the Jews have the upper hand, and the mosque is void of either congregation or assembly.'[107] Despite this, he still recognised Jerusalem as the 'most sublime of cities' and reserved special praise for the wondrous sight that had come to dominate its skyline – the Dome of the Rock.

'At the dawn,' wrote Al-Muqaddasi, 'when the light of the sun first strikes on the cupola, and the drum reflects his rays, then is this edifice a marvellous site to behold, and one such that in all of Islam I have never seen the equal; neither have I heard tell of aught built in pagan times that could rival in grace this Dome of the Rock.'[108] In AD 688, fifty years after Omar had erected his humble mosque, the new caliph of Islam, Abd al-Malik, had returned to the Temple Mount, and marked out the foundations of a building. Ropes were laid out in the form of a circle contained within an octagon.[109]

Builders and artists came to Jerusalem from across the lands of Islam. They took al-Malik's simple ground plan and crafted a central drum supported by eight exterior walls, which were covered with some 250 metres of beautifully ornate inscriptions. This calligraphic artwork encircled the entire building, and drew from a sacred Islamic text which al-Malik was still in the process of compiling: the Koran. On top of the drum, they built a vast golden dome, 20 metres in diameter and standing 30 metres high.[110] And beneath the dome, circled by a marble pavement and bathed in soft light from a series of windows, was the bare rock of Mohammed and Abraham.[111]

This was an immensely powerful and original statement of intent by a new religion. The first true work of Islamic architecture was a masterpiece. It was also intended to send out a pointed message to the Christians of Jerusalem. Far from 'crude', this Islamic shrine put the city's great Christian temple in the shade. From that moment on, up to the present day, Muslims have mocked the Church of the Holy Sepulchre, commissioned by Emperor Constantine in the fourth century, in comparison, referring to it as the *Kumamah* – the Dungheap.[112] Where the Christians had abandoned the Temple Mount, Islam had crowned it with a jewel of their Holy Empire. Their new structure utterly dominated the city – it defined Jerusalem, and it still does. It is the radiant icon that greets every arriving pilgrim or traveller. It is the building that marks the join between heaven and earth. Exactly whose heaven, and whose earth, however, is another question.

At noon on 11 December 1917, General Sir Edmund Allenby walked through the Jaffa Gate into the Old City of Jerusalem, and accepted the city's surrender.[113] The Foreign Office had stressed to Allenby the symbolic importance of entering on foot – the telegraphed message to the General read: 'STRONGLY SUGGEST DISMOUNTING!'[114] Beside the Gate there was a hole in the city wall, made in 1898 to allow Kaiser Wilhelm's motorcade to enter Jerusalem unhindered.[115] Allenby's gesture of humility – which echoed Omar's some twelve centuries before – was a calculated act of propaganda. The message: Britain and its Allies had come not to conquer, but to liberate. Jerusalem was to be free both from the corruption of the Ottomans and the rampant imperialism of the Germans.

Allenby's entrance appeared to have the desired effect, and reports described how the people of the city 'wept for joy' and 'priests were seen to embrace one another'.[116] T. E. Lawrence – of Arabia – was at Allenby's side as they walked into the city, and he described the entrance as 'the supreme moment of the war'.[117] The British Prime Minister, David Lloyd George, greeted the news with delight. In June that year, he had asked Allenby to deliver Jerusalem 'as a Christmas present for the British nation.'[118] The General had succeeded with a fortnight to spare, and Lloyd George had a keen appreciation of the worldwide significance of this feat: 'The most famous city in the world, after centuries of strife and vain struggle... has fallen into the hands of the British army, never to be restored to those who so successfully held it against the embattled hosts of Christendom. The name of every hamlet and hill occupied by the British army... thrills with sacred memories.'[119]

A growing crowd of soldiers and citizens followed Allenby to the steps below the Tower of David – an ancient citadel, rebuilt by the Turks in the sixteenth century – where he read out a proclamation to the 'inhabitants of Jerusalem the Blessed'. This statement, which had been crafted in London and telegraphed to Allenby three weeks before the capture of the city, was spoken first in English, and then in French, Arabic, Hebrew, Greek, Russian and Italian:

> 'Since your city is regarded with affection by adherents of three of the great religions of mankind, and its soil has been consecrated by the prayers and pilgrimages of multitudes of devout people of these three religions for many centuries, therefore do I make known to you that every sacred building, monument, Holy spot, shrine, traditional site, endowment, pious bequest, or customary place of prayer... will be maintained and protected according to the existing customs and beliefs of those to whose faiths they are sacred.'[120]

It was a wonderfully diplomatic speech, designed to avoid stirring any religious tension. For Lawrence, it seemed to hit the mark. 'Jerusalem cheered all of us mightily' he recalled.[121]

Yet there was still disquiet among the Arab population. In November 1917, a month after Allenby led his troops into Palestine, Foreign Secretary Lord Arthur James Balfour made public a letter to Lionel Walter Rothschild, a leading figure in the British Jewish community, which promised that 'His Majesty's Government views with favour the establishment in Palestine of a national home for the Jewish people, and will use its best endeavours to facilitate the achievements of this object'.[122]

Known as the 'Balfour Declaration', its contents came as a shock to the Arabs, who had fought alongside the British to overthrow the Ottoman regime – assuming that, once the battle was over, the land of Palestine would be theirs to claim.[123] Suspicion over British intentions was not helped by what Allenby was reported to have said as the Mayor handed him the keys to Jerusalem. Despite the diplomatic energy that had gone into the wording of proclamation, the General announced that, with the British capture of the Holy City, 'The Crusades have now ended'.[124] Whether it was spoken or not, this line was repeated widely among Arab circles, and was even recalled six decades later in a speech by the Egyptian president Anwar al-Sadat.[125]

'Crusade' was still an incendiary word in twentieth-century Jerusalem. In a city sustained and built on history, myth, religion and conflict, misplaced rhetoric can be deadly. The crusades were among the bloodiest episodes in Jerusalem's history – although there are many contenders for the title. And the word has come again, in our new century, to characterise the absolutist struggle between fanatical Christianity and Islam.

It began in November 1095, at a gathering in Clermont, where Pope Urban II delivered a sermon of such righteous zeal that it galvanised large tracts of Western Europe to raise armies and march on Jerusalem. Passions were inflamed by tales of Arabic obscenities, unmentionable blasphemies and threats to destroy the Church of the Holy Sepulchre, the Christian heart of the city. 'Wrest that land from the wicked race,' commanded Urban, 'and subject it to yourselves... Undertake this journey for the remission of your sins'. The battle cry of the Crusades was *Deus et volt* – 'God wills it'.[126] In the name of the Lord, any atrocity was permissible.[127]

All roads converged on the Holy Land. Groups of men came together to form a 'countless' army – attempts at actual figures by the chroniclers range from 600,000 to 60,000.[128] Once again, Jerusalem was under siege. And on 15 July 1099, the Temple Mount was again the scene of vicious slaughter. The Christian knight, Raymond of Aguilers recalled the carnage with sanctimonious pride:

> 'Wonderful sights were to be seen. Some of our men (and this was the more merciful) cut off the heads of their enemies; others shot them with arrows so that they fell from the towers; others tortured them longer by casting them into the flames. Piles of heads, hands and feet were to be seen in the streets of the city'.[129]

At the al-Aqsa mosque, first built by Omar four centuries before, 'men rode in blood up to their knees and bridle reins. Indeed it was a just and splendid judgement of God that this place should be filled with the blood of the unbelievers'.[130]

Thousands of Muslims were massacred within the walls of the mosque, and the Jews of the city were burnt alive in their synagogues. As the chronicler Fulcher of Chartres concluded, 'What more shall I relate? None were left alive, neither women nor children were spared'.[131] After the battle, soldiers climbed to the top of the golden Dome of the Rock and erected a giant cross. The Islamic shrine became *Templum Domini*, the Temple of Our Lord. Herod's Temple Mount, so long left empty by the Christian faith as a sign of the triumph of Jesus, became the sacred prize of Pope Urban II's holy war. Stones were once again raised 'one stone... upon another' and, for the first time, a Christian Temple stood on the heights above Jerusalem.

This rule would be short-lived. Once the crusader blood-lust had been sated, there was little appetite for staying in Jerusalem, and large numbers set off on the long journey home. Less than a century later, the great Muslim general Saladin led an army of Islam to reclaim the city, and the cross of the *Templum Domini* was toppled from its perch.[132]

The crusades may have been a brief, brutal punctuation mark in the history of Jerusalem, but they still exert a profound influence on the collective memory. A template was forever established for the battle between East and West, and a line drawn across the ruins of the Temple Mount. Here, fundamentalist 'holy war' and Islamic *jihad* collide. The Temple of Solomon. The Dome of the Rock. *Templum Domini.* They are three buildings and one building at the same time – a mystical, spiritual mirage. A faith hologram that changes shape depending on who you are, and how and where you look at it.

In 1841, the American scholar and geographer Edward Robinson published *Biblical Researches in Palestine,* an account of his travels in the Holy Land. During his time in Jerusalem, he recalled a strange and disquieting scene below the western wall of the Temple Mount.

> 'Two old men, Jews, sat there upon the ground, reading together in a book of Hebrew prayers... It is the nearest point in which they can venture to approach their ancient temple; and fortunately for them it is sheltered from observation by the narrowness of the lane and the dead walls around. Here, bowed in the dust, they may at least weep undisturbed over the fallen glory of their race; and bedew with their tears the soil, which so many thousands of their forefathers once moistened with their blood.'[133]

One hundred and twenty-six years later, it was a company of young, bloodstained Jewish soldiers who wept in the dust in this tiny lane. On 11 June 1967, less than a week after the end of the Six Day War, the Israeli Defence Force moved through the Magharib Quarter of the Old City – the tightly-packed Arab district that pressed right up against the Western Wall – and gave every resident just three hours to gather their possessions and leave. Once the quarter was empty, they began dynamiting the buildings, with bulldozers following to clear away the rubble: 135 homes were demolished and some 650 people evicted.[134] By March of the following year, the flattened district had been paved over. No longer would Jews have to file into a cramped, claustrophobic alleyway to pray. Instead, a wide plaza, big enough to hold thousands of worshippers, led up to the ancient stones of Herod's platform. A two-thousand-year-old ruined wall had become a national shrine.[135]

The summit of the Temple Mount remains out of bounds to orthodox Jews, however. Somewhere up there, among the Muslim mosques and shrines – perhaps even inside the Dome of the Rock – is the Holy of Holies. The Jewish Temple may have been destroyed, but the cube at its centre, the space for the divine presence on earth, remains. It would be the most extreme blasphemy for a Jew to walk, even inadvertently, into God's space.[136] It is much safer instead to line up against the outer wall of His temple to pray. And so, while Jerusalem is ruled once again by the 'kingdom' of Israel, the Temple Mount – the *al-Haram al-Sharif* – remains under the legal control of the Islamic authorities.

On 28 September 2000, the Israeli politician and future president Ariel Sharon walked the Temple Mount, surrounded by a guard of heavily armed police. He told the world's press that he came to the site 'bringing a message of peace' and as one who believes that 'Jews and Arabs can live together'.[137] How, he asked, could it be a 'provocation' to visit 'the holiest site in Judaism... it is the right of every Jew to visit the Temple Mount'.[138] Of course, Sharon knew very well that it was a 'provocation'. Jerusalem's Muslims, incensed by what they saw as a threat to their sacred Mosque and Dome, began to throw rocks from the summit of the Western Wall down onto the Jewish security forces and worshippers on the plaza below. The Temple Mount became a blur of Arab protesters, Israeli riot police, tear gas and rubber bullets. In the days that followed, anger turned into open revolt: this was the beginning of the 'Second Intifada', a Palestinian uprising against Israel that would see some four years of air-strikes, suicide bombings, violent demonstrations and thousands of military and civilian casualties.

Jerusalem's Magharib quarter (left of frame in front of the Wall) was bulldozed by the IDF in the same week that they seized the Temple Mount in 1967. © U.S. Library of Congress

There is a medical condition known as 'Jerusalem Syndrome': a religious psychosis that overcomes visitors to the Holy City,[139] In 1969, it prompted Denis Michael Rohan, an Australian sheep-shearer, to set fire to the al-Aqsa Mosque. At his trial, Rohan explained that he was God's 'chosen one', and that he had been tasked with building a new temple.[140] In 1982, an American-Israeli soldier from Baltimore, Allen Goodman, took an M-16 machine gun onto the Temple Mount, and began shooting indiscriminately.[141] He later claimed that he hoped to become 'King of the Jews by liberating this Holy Spot'.[142] In peace talks held by President Bill Clinton at Camp David in July 2000, the Palestinian leader Yasser Arafat declared that there had never been a Jewish Temple on the al-Haram al-Sharif, and that the holiness of the city for Jews was a modern invention.[143] At one stage in the negotiations, Clinton suggested dividing ownership of the Temple Mount not vertically but horizontally, creating a border between Israel and Palestine that would cut through the layers of architectural and archaeological history.[144] It appears that 'Jerusalem Syndrome' is highly contagious – it infects everyone from hapless tourists to world leaders.

Jerusalem is the centre of the world, and the Temple Mount is the centre of Jerusalem. To stand on its high, ancient walls is to experience the extreme vertigo of history. For many Jews, Christians and Muslims, this will be the site of the apocalypse. Like it or not – *believe it or not* – ancient prophecies of destruction are at the heart of world politics today. 'Jerusalem Syndrome' is a global religious pandemic: a fatal disease with no known cure. The modern world began on the Temple Mount. And that, we are often told, is where it will end.

Part Two

On the Unhappiness of Empires

It is a well-worn aphorism that every political career ends in failure. What is true of the individual – from Alexander or Caesar in antiquity, to Bush, Blair or Obama in more recent times – is also true of the collective. Empires are destined to fall. It is one of history's most common story-lines, a narrative that plays on constant repeat. But what of their buildings? Some are wiped out at the very beginning of the decline, marking the moment when the wheel starts to turn. Many more are brought down at the height of the fall, consumed by the bonfire of violence and chaos. Yet others struggle on, limping beyond the ends of the regimes that spawned them, experiencing slow deaths of vandalism and neglect, their bodies picked at and eroded over hundreds or even thousands of years. Few things undergo the sustained humiliation that can await buildings.

Shelley's famous poem *Ozymandias* captures the arrogance of the 'king of kings' who commands visitors to look around at his works – by now ruins – and 'despair'. The reader can't help but feel sorry for those 'colossal wrecks' as they decay on the 'lone and level sands': the shattered statues, porticoes and palaces. We do not find out what happened to Ozymandias: whether he met his end through a slit throat during a palace coup, or an unerring spear-point on the field of battle. Whatever his fate, we can be sure it was no match for the indignity suffered by his architecture. What better than a ruin, then, to speak on the unhappiness of empires?

6. THE RISE, DECLINE AND FALL OF THE COW PASTURE

The Forum of Rome – Italy
(Born 700 BC – Died AD 500)

7. THE LIBRARY OF BABEL

The Library of Alexandria – Egypt
(Born 300 BC – Died 48 BC)

8. ANARCHY'S THEATRE

The Hippodrome of Byzantium – Constantinople
(Born AD 330 – Died 1453)

9. THE CARPET OF THE WORLD

Madinat al-Zahra – Cordoba
(Born AD 936 – Died 1010)

Chapter Six

The Rise, Decline and Fall of the Cow Pasture

The Forum – Rome
(Born 700 BC – Died AD 500)

Towards the middle of the fifteenth century, the papal scribe and classical scholar Poggio Bracciolini made his way to the summit of Rome's Capitoline Hill.[1] At the hill's south-eastern corner was a sheer, 80-foot cliff known as the Tarpeian Rock. In ancient times this was the site reserved for the execution of the most nefarious criminals in the city. Murderers, perjurers, runaway slaves, and – worst of all – anyone guilty of betraying Rome, were taken to the cliff edge and thrown to their deaths.[2] This practice produced the Latin phrase *Arx Tarpeia Capitoli proxima* ('the Tarpeian Rock is close to the Capitol'[3]) – meaning that, regardless of honours or greatness achieved in the course of a life, a man's ruin could be swift and merciless. Here, in the heart of Rome, the concept of the 'fall from grace' was taken to a literal extreme.

Poggio had chosen an appropriate vantage point. As he wrote in his book *De varietate fortunae – On the Vicissitudes of Fortune* – he could scarcely believe the sight that greeted him from the Tarpeian Rock:

> 'The hill of the Capitol, on which we sit, was formerly the head of the Roman Empire, the citadel of the earth,

> the terror of kings; illustrated by the footsteps of so many triumphs, enriched with the spoils and tributes of so many nations. This spectacle of the world, how it is fallen! How changed! How defaced! The path of victory is obliterated by vines, and the benches of the senators are concealed by a dunghill.'[4]

Below him, at the foot of the cliff, was the space where the fate of the world had once been decided: the Forum. Surrounded by the temples of the gods, this was the most celebrated meeting place in history. Here, ancient Romans held public speeches and elections, criminal trials, triumphal processions, ritual sacrifices, gladiatorial contests and wild beast hunts. It was a central business and banking district, where anything could be bought and sold, from food and flowers to jewellery and sex.[5] It was the birthplace of the senate and the epicentre of Rome's revolutionary system of government – the city-state ruled by the will of its citizens. And over time it had become the stage for a titanic struggle between quasi-democracy and outright dictatorship, a fight that swallowed up a Republic and created an Empire.

What Poggio saw, however, was the palest echo of this former glory:

> 'The Forum of the Roman people, where they assembled to enact their laws and elect their magistrates, is now enclosed for the cultivation of pot-herbs, or thrown open for the reception of swine or buffaloes. The public and private edifices, that were founded for eternity, lie prostate, naked and broken, like the limbs of a mighty giant.'[6]

De varietate fortunae was written some nine hundred years after the fall of the Western Roman Empire. Yet Poggio's shock remained palpable: 'The temple is overthrown, the gold has been pillaged, the wheel of fortune has accomplished her revolution.'[7] For Poggio, the ruins of the Forum offered a nightmarish vision of a world without art, without culture and without knowledge. He was part of a growing movement known as 'humanism', which held that the learning of antiquity could expose and remedy the obscurity, ignorance and superstition of the medieval age. Poggio had already satirised the petty political concerns of some of the most powerful figures of the day – including the seven Popes under whom he had served – in a series of books including *On Greed*, *On Nobility*, and *On the Unhappiness of Princes*.[8] For decades, he had used his travels on papal business to search for rare manuscripts, discovering in the libraries of Italian, German, Swiss and French monasteries a massive haul of decaying and abandoned works from the classical world.[9] Among his finds were speeches by Cicero, the greatest orator of the Roman Republic; an epic account by Silicus Italicus of Rome's war with Carthage; a 7,400-line poem by the Greek philosopher Lucretius, entitled *On the Nature of Things*[10]; and *De Architectura* by Vitruvius, the only major study of the architecture to survive from classical times into the modern era.[11]

Poggio and others like him were piecing together the history of the ancient past from this fragmentary record of lost texts and manuscripts. At the same time, in the 'stupendous relics' of Rome, they could see the physical evidence of the refinement and supremacy of the classical world. These crumbling, abandoned structures had once been the stage for a bolder people who lived in a better time. Some two hundred years before the term was coined[12], Poggio was experiencing an acute *nostalgia* – from the Greek, meaning 'the ache or pain of homecoming'. As he looked out over the ruins of the Forum, he longed for the return of Rome's greatness.

On 18 March 44 BC[13], the body of Gaius Julius Caesar – the dictator in perpetuity of the Roman Republic – was borne through the city and laid upon an ivory couch on the Rostra, the raised speaker's platform at the head of the Forum.[14] Caesar had been assassinated three days earlier by a conspiracy involving some sixty senators, including Gaius Cassius and Marcus Brutus, two of the Republic's highest-ranking politicians.

With victory over his great rival Pompey in the Civil War of 49 to 45 BC, Caesar had removed his last obstacle to absolute power. Yet for the conspirators, this posed a fundamental threat to the true Roman way of life. The Republic had been established over four centuries earlier, the product of the city's triumph over tyranny. Yet Caesar had become something that was potentially even more dangerous than a tyrant: in the eastern provinces of the Republic, inspired by the general's remarkable deeds, people had begun to worship him as a living god. What would it mean for the senate, for freedom and for liberty, if Caesar were to become not only the supreme leader of Rome, but also the figurehead of a new, divine cult?

The murder was swift and vicious. Caesar was lured to a meeting of the senate, where he was surrounded by the crowd of conspirators and stabbed to death. Eventually he collapsed against the pedestal of a statue of Pompey, so that, as the historian Plutarch put it, 'one might have thought that Pompey himself was presiding over this act of vengeance against his enemy, who lay there at his feet, struggling convulsively under so many wounds'.[15] In the hysterical aftermath, the conspirators ran through the Forum in their blood-spattered togas, with their daggers held high, shouting out that they had 'destroyed a tyrant and king'.[16]

Rome was in a state of shock. Would Caesar's murder spark yet another period of civil strife, or had it been, as the plotters maintained, the only way to preserve freedom? The following day, Brutus and Cassius took to the Rostra in the Forum and addressed the crowd. They explained that they had been motivated not by hatred but by love of their country, and, according to the historian Appian, 'incited the people to act like their ancestors when they had overthrown the kings'.[17] This speech met with an ambiguous silence.[18] In the Senate, an amnesty was agreed between the conspirators and Caesar's supporters, led by his loyal friend and fellow consul Mark Antony. At the same time, it was decided that Caesar should have a public funeral. And this would be held, of course, in the symbolic centre of the Republic: the Forum.

Now it was Mark Antony's turn to occupy the Rostra. This

speaker's platform was as old as the Republic itself, first built at the end of the sixth century BC, and studded on its façade with the bronze prows of captured enemy ships.[19] It was a clear demonstration that in Rome, political power and military power were inseparable. The Rostra from which Mark Antony spoke, however, was not the original. In 46 BC, Caesar had built a new platform at the western end of the Forum. Much larger and more imposing than before, it was ascended by a curved staircase at the rear, and was set against the monumental backdrop of the Tabularium, the grandiose, three-storey state record office where the archives of the Republic were inscribed on bronze tablets.[20]

Mark Antony began by reading Caesar's will to the assembled crowd. First it emerged that Caesar had bequeathed his extensive personal gardens near the Tiber to the people of Rome, along with a gift of 75 denarii, to every male citizen living in the city. Then the audience was informed that he had named his great-nephew, the teenager Octavian, as his adoptive son and heir, with Decimus Brutus, one of the conspirators, as a secondary heir. The mood of the crowd began to turn.[21] They had been told that Caesar was a despot who cared only for himself, that he was a would-be tyrant who would destroy the hard-won customs and values of the Republic. Yet here, it seemed, was evidence of the deep-rooted public spirit of a man who, even in death, served Rome and cared for the well-being of its people.

Spurred on by cries of anger and lamentation from the crowd, Mark Antony began his speech. It was, he said, the people of Rome and the senate who had named Caesar as the 'father of his country', and who had acclaimed him as 'sacrosanct' and 'inviolate'. Caesar himself had never asked for these honours. Mark Antony wept over the body of his friend, chanting praise to Caesar as if he were a god, and reciting his victories in campaign after campaign. His voice was choked with emotion one minute, 'clarion-clear' the next.[22] The people were moved deeply by this performance, and – encouraged, perhaps, by a troop of actors Mark Antony had planted among them[23] – themselves began to wail, chant and sing. Mark Antony bent over Caesar's body and tore his clothes from him, then held them over the crowd on a spear point, so that they could see for themselves the stab holes and bloodstains. A wax effigy of Caesar was produced, showing each of the twenty-three wounds that, in the historian Appian's words, had been 'savagely inflicted on every part of the body and on the face'. Amid the tumult of wailing and angry cries, some heard the voice of Caesar himself naming each of his murderers in turn.[24]

Sensing the volatile mood of the crowd, the conspirators slipped away, either to barricade themselves in their homes or to flee the city altogether. Caesar's body was lifted up and carried to the Capitoline Hill, where the people intended to bury him in sacred ground alongside the gods of Rome. They were turned away by the priests, and so returned to the Forum, where they built a huge pyre. The seats, benches and tables used by the senate, courts and magistrates were smashed into pieces, and thrown onto the pile. Caesar's body was placed on top, and as the fire was lit, Mark Antony's actors, who were dressed in the various guises of Caesar – as warrior, general and politician – tore off their clothes and added them to the flames.[25] Veteran soldiers hurled their weapons and armour onto the blaze, while women tossed in their precious jewellery. Some took flaming brands and ran through the city, setting fire to the houses of the conspirators[26]; others stayed beside the pyre all night[27], watching it burn down until all that was left in the morning, covering the paved floor of the Forum, were ashes.

In death, Caesar became more than just a man. Rumours of his divinity continued to circulate among the people. According to Plutarch, a great comet shone in the sky above Rome for seven nights after the murder, while the sun was dimmed for a whole year, its 'orb... dull and pale', and its heat 'feeble and ineffective'.[28]

When the army of Cassius and Brutus was defeated at Philippi by the combined forces of Mark Antony, Octavian and the aristocratic general Marcus Lepidus – an alliance known as the Triumvirate – the two conspirators immediately took their own lives. Cassius stabbed himself with the same dagger that he had used to kill Caesar two years previously, while Brutus, haunted by a phantom figure, 'retired to a steep rocky place' and 'put his naked sword to his breast'.[29] It seemed that the gods had been angered by the murder of Caesar – the murder, perhaps, of one of their own.

In the aftermath, a series of bloody and brutal 'proscriptions' took place, a settling of scores that saw the execution of almost all of the conspirators and many of their political and military allies. Where Caesar had pursued a policy of clemency when it came to dealing with his enemies, his adoptive son Octavian showed no mercy. Most shocking, perhaps, was the death of Cicero, for decades the most eloquent voice in the senate, and the conscience of the Republic. Though he had not taken part in the assassination plot, Cicero had approved on moral grounds. He had also consistently baited Mark Antony, condemning his motives and mocking his limited intellect in fourteen published speeches known as the *Philippics.* It was no surprise when Cicero's name was added to a list of over 200 prominent 'enemies of the state'.[30] He was tracked down to his country villa near the sea, where his head and both his hands were hacked off and brought to Rome. Mark Antony fastened them to the ships' prows on the Rostra, the scene of so many of Cicero's memorable public speeches. As Plutarch wrote, 'it was a sight to make the Romans shudder'.[31]

For almost a decade and a half the Republic remained embroiled in civil war. Finally, in 31 BC, Octavian overcame his erstwhile ally Mark Antony, who had taken up with Caesar's former lover Cleopatra. The pair committed suicide rather than face the shame of returning to Rome as prisoners.[32] Like his father before him, Octavian had now become the sole ruler of the civilised world. This time, however, no conspiracy would prevent the ascent to ultimate power. The hated title of king was not mentioned. Instead the senate had taken to calling Octavian *Augustus*, meaning 'illustrious one', and *Princeps*, or 'first citizen'[33]; titles that could be seen as spiritual rather than political and conveniently obscured the true nature of Octavian's position.

Outwardly Octavian pursued a policy of 'restoration' of the values and ideals of the Republic, while at the same time annexing more and more power through a number of constitutional reforms. He pulled off this delicate balancing act with remarkable style, his public humility growing in direct proportion to his private control of the state.[34] The Republic had transformed itself, more or less willingly, into an Empire. Octavian, or rather *Augustus*, was the first ruler of an imperial dynasty that claimed to descend from the gods themselves.

In 29 BC, on the exact spot of Caesar's cremation in the Forum, Augustus completed the construction of a new temple. Called the Temple of Divus Julius, it honoured Caesar publicly as a god. Built almost entirely in marble, its central hall contained a massive statue of Caesar with a star set above his head[35]: a reference to the comet that appeared after his death and that was believed by the common people to have marked his soul taking its place among the spirits of the immortal gods. Privately, however, Augustus believed that the comet honoured him.[36] The Temple of Divus Julius was the first of a number of buildings that would transform completely the role and purpose of the Forum. As the centre of Republican political life, it had evolved organically over the centuries: it was both a busy civic space crowded with the buildings of administrative government, and a public meeting-place, market and shopping precinct. Most of the old buildings were made of tufa or travertine, porous cream and brown limestones quarried from the nearby Tiber valley. But now Augustus imported vast quantities of luxurious white marble from the hills of Carrara in Tuscany.[37] Later he would boast that he had found a city built of brick, and left one of marble.[38]

The Forum would become an architectural showcase for the cult of the divine emperor. Once Rome's Republic had once prayed to the gods for good fortune. Now its Empire was ruled by them.

In 27 BC, Titus Livius Patavinus, better known as Livy, published the first instalment of his colossal 142-volume history of Rome. This opening account began by chronicling the origins of his people, before sweeping through some four centuries of conflict and civil strife, to end with the cliff-hanger of the destruction and resurrection of the city after the Gallic invasion of 386 BC.[39] It was an epic tale indeed – and it arrived at the perfect time for the would-be emperor Augustus.

As he began his history, Livy reminded the Romans of their noble origins. 'If any nation deserves the privilege of claiming a divine ancestry,' he wrote, 'that nation is our own.'[40] This 'divine ancestry' was the Trojan warrior Aeneas, son of the goddess Venus. After the fall of his famous city, Aeneas and his men had endured years of wandering across the Mediterranean, finally to reach the shores of Italy having 'lost all they possessed except their ships and their swords'.[41] They had reached the end of their journey. After a series of wars, amnesties and alliances, Aeneas succeeded in creating a permanent home for the exiles of Troy. He was the first true hero of Rome.[42]

Aeneas had a son, Ascanius, also known as Iulus: it was from this name that the Julian clan, claimed to have descended.[43] Also from the same line were the twins Romulus and Remus, born out of a union between the virgin princess Rhea Silvia and the god Mars. Saved from drowning in the Tiber by a she-wolf, who suckled the infants at her teats, the twins were adopted by a shepherd and his wife, and brought up in a hut on the riverbank built from earth and reeds. In adulthood the twins would learn of their noble origins, but rather than inherit their rightful kingdom, they resolved instead to found a new city on the humble land that had always been their home. But the exact location of this city provoked a quarrel between the brothers: Romulus favoured the Palatine Hill, and Remus the Aventine. In the ensuing brawl, Remus was killed. Romulus had his way, and he named his new city after himself: Rome.[44]

Rome soon found itself at war with the kingdom of the Sabines, after Romulus ordered the kidnapping of their women to help boost his city's population. The decisive battle played out in the marshy ground between the Capitoline and the Palatine Hills. Amid the clamour of thrown spears and sword thrusts, the Sabine women came to plead with their husbands on one side, and their fathers on the other, to stop the bloodshed. After a tense silence 'the rival captains stepped forward to conclude a peace,' wrote Livy. 'Indeed, they went further: the two states were united under a single government, with Rome as the seat of power.'[45] Discourse and diplomacy had won the day, and the land between the two hills became the sacred centre of political life in the city. The Forum was born.

Romulus was succeeded by six kings, who grew more corrupt and tyrannical with every generation. The last of the rulers, Tarquin the Proud, was overthrown and exiled from the city in 510 BC, and Rome became a Republic. In place of a king, the Roman citizens elected two consuls, drawn from the aristocracy, who would serve for a year at a time.[46] These men in turn made appointments to the senate, a body that varied in size between 300 and 600 members, and was formed of 'experienced men' tasked with advising the consuls.[47]

Over time, the Forum's marshland was drained and paved, and developed as the seat of government and the senate. A series of temples was built around the open-air central courtyard.[48] In ancient Rome, politics and religion were almost inseparable: the senate met in the temple halls, and speeches were given from the ad-hoc platforms of their steps and porticoes.[49] At the east end of the Forum was the Temple of Vesta, a circular structure built in the image of Romulus' and Remus' hut of wattle and thatch.[50] It was attended by virgin priestesses known as vestals, and at its heart burned the eternal flame – the fire that had been brought from Troy[51] and which, if it ever went out, would signal the end Rome.

The fifth and final book of Livy's *Early History of Rome* portrayed a people in crisis. In 386 BC an army of Gauls had marched south down the valley of the Tiber, routed the Roman army, entered the city, and burned much of it to the ground. Camillus, a retired soldier and statesman, was called on to return to his people's aid, and was appointed dictator of Rome, a temporary role granting him autocratic powers for the duration of the crisis. After fighting off the invading army and reclaiming the city, Camillus stood on the Rostra among the scorched ruins of the Forum and addressed the senate. Many wanted to abandon Rome and migrate to the city of Veii, which had provided sanctuary during the conflict, but Camillus was scandalised by the prospect. 'Shall victory make Rome more desolate than defeat?' he asked. 'Those herdsmen long ago and that rabble of refugees, when there was nothing here but forest and swamp, made short work enough of building a new town – but we today, when the temples are still standing and the Capitol and Citadel intact, cannot bring ourselves to rebuild what the fires have destroyed! Shall we refuse as a nation to do what one of us would have done if his own house had burned down?'[52] He ended by reminding the crowd that, 'Not without reason did gods and men choose this spot for the site of our city.' Camillus's speech roused the senate to vote unanimously to stay. Rome would rise from the ashes.

In his introduction to *The Early History of Rome,* Livy claimed that the city of his time was not in physical, but rather moral and political ruin. Years of infighting and instability in the government had gone hand in hand with a growing decadence and the collapse of good values. 'The dark dawning of our modern day,' he wrote, resulted in Rome being riddled with 'vices' and unable to 'face the remedies needed to cure them.'[53] Livy was being deliberately provocative – and astute. He had tapped into widespread feelings of insecurity and introspection, and his book became a remarkable success.[54] Augustus, a keen student of history in general, saw clear parallels between his own situation and that of Camillus. Both men were patriots, both were dictators, both were faced with the very real prospect of the fall of Rome. Augustus resolved to return the city to its founding virtues. Strength and honour, gods and men – and men who were gods – would make it great once again.

The Forum was a building site throughout most of Augustus's reign. Central to his public mission of returning Rome to its traditional values was a vast programme of architectural improvements. In one single year, he claimed to have built or reconstructed eighty-two temples.[55] In the Forum, the temples of Saturn, Concord, and Castor and Pollux[56] were all overhauled and reconstituted in the majestic, monumentalist style that Augustus believed was worthy of the grandeur of Rome.

Not content with recasting the old Forum, Augustus also established a brand new one, in his own name, just north of the original. Built from scratch out of marble – what else? – it was dominated by a Temple to Mars, the avenging war-god, and it contained at its heart an avenue of statues of the conquering heroes of Rome, going all the way back to Romulus and Aeneas. As Augustus pronounced, 'he himself, and the rulers of later ages would be required to take the lives of these men as their model'.[57]

Augustus's successors strayed from this ideal to various degrees. Decadent, debauched and indeed insane as many of them were,[58] however, they all shared his desire to *build*.[59] Some copied him by establishing new *fora* of their own, but they all returned again and again to the original Forum, still the most symbolically significant piece of ground in the city. It became almost tradition for each new emperor to tinker with what was already there, to add their personal architectural stamps. They did so with little apparent concern for the coherence of the Forum as whole. Colossal new monuments were erected wherever there was free space – and often where there was not. The structures began to overlap and obscure each other in a chaotic jumble of imperial culture and history.

Triumphal arches were a popular choice. Augustus himself had erected a massive arch between the Temples of Divus Julius, and Castor and Pollux, and right in front of the Temple of Vesta. The aim of these structures was to impress and to intimidate: this was shock-and-awe architecture, a demonstration of power that could be exported across the world as the brand of Empire.[60] After the Arch of Augustus came the Arch of Titus, commemorating Rome's crushing defeat of the Jewish rebellion in AD 70. Constructed out of marble from Mount Pentelikon – the material used for the Parthenon in Athens – it was decorated with various scenes from Titus's life and death. One showed the emperor's ascension to heaven on the back of an imperial eagle. Another depicted a procession of victorious Roman legionnaires, marching in triumph through the Forum: on their shoulders they carried the spoils of the Jewish war, precious treasures taken from the obliterated Temple of Jerusalem – including the seven-branched candelabrum known as the menorah, one of the most sacred objects of the Jewish faith.[61] Here was desolation recast as celebration, along with a warning of the retribution that awaited any who dared disrupt the *pax romana*.

A century later, the Roman triumphal arch reached its climax, in a structure dedicated to the Emperor Septimius Severus. Crammed into the Forum, pressed right up against the Rostra, and completely obscuring the front of the Temple of Concordia, it honoured the victories of Severus and his two sons Caracalla and Geta over the Parthians.[62] Faced entirely in marble, with its inscriptions written in gilt bronze, it was adorned with delicate and extravagant friezes and topped by a huge bronze statue of an imperial chariot.[63] The arch was indeed a triumph – perhaps most of all of political purpose over practical function.

The beginning of the fourth century AD saw the ancient Forum's last great construction project. The Basilica Maxentius was one of the largest buildings ever erected by the Romans, a work of stunning ambition and technical innovation made possible by the invention of concrete – in the form of mortar mixed with slaked lime and crushed volcanic rock from Naples.[64] Begun in AD 307 by Maxentius, the last pagan emperor to choose Rome as his capital, it was completed by Constantine, the first Christian emperor. Dominating the western end of its magnificent great hall – higher than Westminster Abbey[65] – was a colossal marble statue of Constantine. This statue stood some thirty feet tall, with the head alone measuring over eight feet.[66] In form and scale it bore a striking resemblance to the icons of the gods sitting at the hearts of the pagan temples of Rome. Constantine may have been a convert to Christianity, but three centuries of the cult of the divine emperor were clearly hard to shake off.

By this time the Forum was an over-crowded mass of temples, halls, arches, columns and statues. The voices of the senate, which had once resounded among the stones, had been drowned out by the clamour of architects and artisans. This space at the centre of the city had become a monument to Empire – or perhaps museum would be more accurate. Although still a busy civic thoroughfare and an important business district, much of the life had gone out of the Forum. Political debate had departed, replaced by ever-multiplying memorials to the men who had presided over the move from Republic to dictatorship. Once the Forum had been all about the present and the future. Now it seemed to look backwards: to past glories and greatness, to leaders who ascended to the heavens as gods, to the mythical men who made the city. At the very height of Rome's power, there existed in the architecture of the Forum the subtle yet creeping symptoms of decline. Year by year, brick by brick and stone by stone, successive emperors were creating a graveyard.

In October 1764 the aspiring historian Edward Gibbon travelled to Rome for the first time. Gibbon had begun his studies at Magdalen College, Oxford at the age of fifteen, but was removed from the university by his father 'in despair' after converting to Catholicism, and sent to Lausanne to be re-educated by a Calvinist minister. Within a year he had renounced the Catholic faith, suspended his 'religious enquiries', and resolved instead to devote himself to classical and modern literature. After persuading his father that 'foreign travel completes the education of an English gentleman', he embarked on his Grand Tour of Europe.[67]

From the *salons* of Paris, Gibbon travelled to the ruins of Rome. As he later recalled in his memoirs, 'at the distance of twenty-five years I can neither forget nor express the strong emotions which agitated my mind as I first approached and entered the eternal City. After a sleepless night, I trod, with a lofty step, the ruins of the Forum; each memorable spot where Romulus stood, or Cicero spoke, or Caesar fell, was at once present to my eye; and several days of intoxication were lost or enjoyed before I could descend to a cool and minute investigation'.[68]

Like Poggio over three centuries earlier, Gibbon was transfixed by this scene of desolation. It was as he 'sat musing amidst the ruins of the Capitol while the barefooted friars were singing Vespers in the temple of Jupiter', that he was first struck by the 'idea of writing the decline and fall of the City'.[69] This idea would grow to absorb nearly two decades of Gibbon's life, and would result in one of the most ambitious and influential works of scholarship ever produced in the English language: the six-volume *History of the Decline and Fall of the Roman Empire.*

In recounting the 'memorable series of revolutions, which, in the course of about thirteen centuries, gradually undermined, and at length destroyed, the solid fabric of Roman greatness'[70], Gibbon presented a tragic narrative of the fallibility of liberty, civilisation and human nature. At the same time, he argued that the modern world – the world of the Enlightenment – presented man with a second chance. Here was the opportunity to learn from the lessons of the past, to pick up the torch of progress, and to carry forward the legacy of classical antiquity.

Gibbon described Rome at the beginning of the fifth century AD as a city which was home to around a million people and which revelled in unprecedented wealth and magnificence. Yet its pursuit of luxury had become its weakness. As the empire began to split into a Latin West and a Greek East, with Constantinople emerging as a rival capital, and as Christianity established itself as the dominant religion, control over the frontiers of the empire was slipping. It would not be long before someone grew bold enough to test the true resolve of Rome.

In AD 410, as Gibbon recounted, 'eleven hundred and sixty-three years after the foundation of Rome, the Imperial City, which had subdued and civilised so considerable a part of mankind, was delivered to the licentious fury of the tribes of Germany and Scythia.'[71] The barbarians were at the gates. Or rather, they had smashed the gates off their hinges. Over the course of six days, a ferocious army of Goths, aided by a slave uprising, took delicious joy in plundering the enormous reserves of treasure held within the city. Four decades later, in AD 455, it was the turn of the Vandals. For fifteen days they stripped Rome rapaciously of its gold, silver and bronze. Yet the city was not destroyed. Once they had been divested of their precious objects, metals and materials, the great works of civic architecture were left relatively unscathed.[72] The contemporary historian and priest Orosius may have claimed that 'the proud Forum of Rome, decorated with the statues of so many gods and heroes, was levelled in the dust by the stroke of lightning'[73], but the reality was rather less dramatic.

Nevertheless, by the end of the fifth century the population of Rome had dwindled to one hundred thousand. This time there would be no resurrection. What Camillus had feared after the Gallic invasion nine hundred years before – that Rome was to become 'a city deserted by gods and men'[74] – had come to pass. It was simple abandonment, a mass exodus. The glory of Rome moved to the east, and the great edifices of empire were left behind, their significance quickly forgotten by those that remained. 'A long period of distress and anarchy,' wrote Gibbon, 'in which empire, and arts, and riches, had migrated from the banks of the Tiber, was incapable of restoring or adorning the city; and as all that is human must retrograde if it do not advance, every successive age must have hastened the ruin of the works of antiquity'.[75] Or, as St Jerome put it as early as the fifth century, 'the gods adored by nations are now alone in their niches with the owls and the night birds. The gilded Capitol languishes in dust and all the temples of Rome are covered with spiders' webs'.[76]

While Gibbon was writing *The Decline and Fall,* the Italian artist and architect Giovanni Battista Piranesi was creating a remarkable visual tapestry of the remains of Rome. From the 1740s until his death in 1778, Piranesi produced a series of hundreds of etchings of the city.[77] Known as *Vedute* – or views – he declared that his work would 'endure for as long as there are men desirous of knowing all that has survived until our day of the ruins of the most famous city of the universe'.[78] Within the *Vedute* were twenty-five views of the Forum, captioned by Piranesi with the site's more commonplace, eighteenth-century name: The *Campo Vaccino.* The cow pasture.[79]

Like Gibbon, Piranesi wanted the greatness of the ancients

to inspire the people of his own day.[80] At the same time he was committed to portraying, in stark detail, just how diminished these monuments had become. The Arch of Titus was shown covered in moss and ivy, looking onto a pair of twisted trees, and with a ramshackle wooden gate at its foot. The Temple of Vespasian and the Arch of Septimius Severus were pictured buried up to their necks in layer after layer of accumulated debris, dirt and animal dung. Beneath the great, shattered arches of the Basilica of Maxentius, Piranesi had drawn a series of defeated-looking figures: pack horses next to a rickety cart; a foreman directing workers; a man and his donkey; a group of beggars huddled in the shadows. Most striking of all was a view of the eight remaining columns of the Temple of Saturn, now sitting alongside a row of shops and houses. Beyond some grazing cattle and stray dogs, a washing line hangs between two of the temple's marble uprights.[81] Piranesi's intention was not to mock the grand ambitions of the ancient Romans: his goal was rather to shame their coarse descendants.

'View from the centre of the Forum' by Giovanni Battista Piranesi. Here the columns of the temple of Castor and Pollux are topped by denuded stonework sprouting weeds.

These etchings are a vivid record of the accumulated indignities the Forum had endured since the fall of empire. In Gibbon's words, the once grand structures 'were disregarded by a people insensible to their use and beauty', and 'applied to every call of necessity of superstition'.[82] This process had begun as far back as the sixth century AD, when the new Christian 'emperors' of the city, holders of the holy office of Pope, ordered a number of the Forum's pagan temples and basilicas to be converted into churches. They also granted builders permission to pull down ancient columns and ceremonial statues to reuse their stones, or to burn their marble to make lime.[83] Between the ninth and fourteenth centuries, Rome was at its lowest ebb. Its papal leaders frequently lasted just weeks or even days before being ousted by an opposing faction. Their subsequent fates ranged from imprisonment to suffocation, stabbing, strangulation, and even, in one bizarre instance, being exhumed, robbed of luxury vestments, and tossed into the Tiber.[84]

In the twelfth century, with the Popes exiled, the population of Rome fell below thirty thousand, and rival warring families turned the city into a battleground for gangland squabbles. The monumental architecture of the Forum lent itself perfectly to adaptation for fortifications, and both the Arch of Titus and the Arch of Septimius Severus had towers and defensive structures erected crudely on top of them.[85] In the words of the nineteenth-century historian Ferdinand Gregorovius, the city became a 'forest of towers, rising in dark and threatening menace'.[86] By the time of the Renaissance, and despite the renewed interest in all things classical, the dismantling and destruction of the buildings continued. A section of the Forum was re-purposed as a quarry, and the site filled up with the brick cottages of the lime burners. In the mid-sixteenth century, the Basilica Julia and the Temples of Saturn, Vespasian and Vesta were all dismantled and their stone blocks recycled.[87] The Temple of Divius Julius, the memorial to Caesar the immortal god, was razed to the ground and its great quantities of marble reduced to lime and incorporated as mortar in St Peter's Basilica.[88] 'Nothing,' wrote the archaeologist Rodolfo Lanciani, 'would better illustrate the strange turns of fortune than the varied uses to which the marbles from ancient structures have been put in modern times'.[89]

Some respite came in the mid-seventeenth century. Pope Alexander VII was keen to return the Forum to its original function as a civic space, and in 1656 he ordered the planting of an avenue of elm trees running in a straight line between the Arch of Titus and the Arch of Septimius Severus.[90] For a time, either on foot or passing through by carriage, Romans could enjoy the ruins of their ancestors as the picturesque backdrop to a new public garden. By the late eighteenth century, the Forum was again inspiring dreams of greatness, its relics 'devoutly visited by a new race of pilgrims from the remote, and once savage, countries of the North', as Gibbon put it.[91] Men of the Enlightenment visited to wallow in the romance of ancient remains and to commune with the souls of the classical world. The Forum had become the ultimate, secular shrine to the lost glory of antiquity.

One of most passionate responses to the Forum came from Johann Wolfgang von Goethe, presiding genius of the European Romantic movement. He described the sensation of standing among the ruins as like being 'reborn', enthusing: 'All history is encamped about us and all history sets forth again from us. This does not apply only to Roman history, but to the history of the whole world. From here I can accompany the conquerors to the Weser and the Euphrates, or, if I prefer to stand and gape, I can wait in the Via Sacra for their triumphant return.'[92] Goethe would not have to wait long. New empires were on the march – and they would seek to reclaim from the Forum all the glories of ancient Rome.

On 27 and 28 July 1798, a cavalry guard and military band of the army of Napoleon Bonaparte led a procession of wagons laden with wooden crates through the streets of Paris.[93] Part of a programme of celebration known as the 'Fête de la Liberté', this convoy had travelled for months from Italy by sea, road, canal and river[94], and had arrived in the city a fortnight late.[95] Its slow, careful progress was due to the priceless cargo that was being transported: within the crates were some of the greatest and most celebrated art treasures in the world, from the paintings of the Renaissance masters to the sublime sculptures of antiquity. As the wagons passed through the Parisian crowd, a chant was struck up, 'Rome is no more in Rome. It is now in Paris'.[96] Most of the artworks were still hidden in their crates, so each wagon was helpfully decorated with a banner listing its contents.[97] On full public show at the very rear of the convoy, however, was the bust of Junius Brutus: a fourth-century BC bronze sculpture that depicted one of the very founders of the Roman Republic.[98]

Napoleon's triumphal procession eerily and deliberately echoed the depiction on the Arch of Titus in the Forum, of the Roman legionnaires as they carried away the treasures of Jerusalem after its conquest in AD 70. Following his invasion of the Dukedoms and Papal States of Italy in 1796, Napoleon had sought to legitimise his possession of these works of art through a series of 'contract-treaties' with the conquered territories.[99] Even so, the French made no apologies for the logic behind the appropriations. As a speech given at Fête de la Liberté explained, 'the fate of these productions of genius is to belong to the people who shine successively on earth by arms and by wisdom, and to follow always the wagons of the victors'.[100] Two years earlier, a petition signed by every prominent French artist – in anticipation of the treasures that were soon to be up for grabs – argued that, 'The French Republic, by its strength and superiority of its enlightenment and its artists, is the only country in the world which can give a safe home to these masterpieces'.[101] Since time immemorial, the accumulation of great art has accompanied the rise to empire. France now saw itself as the rightful heir to the legacy of ancient Rome.

The French had entered Rome unopposed on 10 February 1798. Napoleon's aim was to undermine the power of the Vatican, so he took great delight in hearing that, on the fifth day of the occupation, a group of Romans had held a ceremony in the Forum, planting a 'tree of liberty' in front of the Arch of Septimius Severus and declaring the formation of a new Roman Republic.[102] One of the city's newspapers reported of the Forum that, 'after centuries of decay and neglect, the site thus recovered its original civic function as a gathering place "for the people and the Senate when it became necessary to deliberate on the gravest concerns of the Republic"'.[103] The new regime was short-lived – it was overthrown by an invasion of Neapolitan forces at the end of 1799[104] – yet it heralded a remarkable change in the status of the Forum. It had already been rediscovered over the course of the previous several centuries as a cultural touchstone for artists, writers and poets. Now it was starting to regain its political significance.

Napoleon's armies returned to Rome in 1808, and in May 1809 the Papal States of Italy were formally incorporated into the French Empire, with Rome named as the second Imperial City.[105] Pope Pius VII was removed, and in his place a new 'king of Rome' was appointed: Napoleon François Charles Joseph Bonaparte, Napoleon's infant son from his second wife, the Austrian Archduchess Marie-Louise. A planned visit of the emperor and empress to Rome after their marriage in 1810 prompted a concerted excavation of the Forum, with workers digging up to ten feet down through the accumulated dirt and earth in an attempt to reach the original street level. In the end Napoleon did not come – indeed he never visited Rome in his life – but the work in the Forum did not go to waste. In June 1811, as part of an event to celebrate the birth of Napoleon II three months earlier, the newly uncovered monuments were lit up at night and displayed to a massed crowd.[106] The archaeology of ancient Rome had been appropriated, like the city's great artworks, to celebrate the greatness of a modern imperial dynasty.

A century or so later, Benito Mussolini marched on Rome, supported by 300,000 men 'organised and faithful'.[107] These men were the Voluntary Militia for National Security, a paramilitary faction better known as the *camicie nere* – the 'blackshirts'. Fearing civil war, King Victor Emmanuel III and his parliament handed power to Mussolini and his political allies. On 30 October 1922, Italy became a fascist state. Mussolini steadily set about transforming the role of democratically elected Prime Minister into Fascist *Duce.*[108] In this he was merely following in the footsteps of his ancient Roman hero Augustus. A republic would fall, he believed, so that a new, stronger empire could emerge.[109]

'Rome is our point of departure and reference,' said Mussolini in April 1922, adding that the ancient Romans had been 'not only warriors, but formidable builders.'[110] He soon became preoccupied with remaking the city in his own image of imperial greatness. 'Rome,' he declared in a speech on 21 April 1924, given from the Capitoline Hill overlooking the Forum, 'must not be only a modern city... it must be a city worthy of its glory and this glory must unceasingly renovate in order to hand down, as a heritage of the fascist era, to the generations to come'.[111] One of his first major projects was to drive a massive new road right through the centre of ancient Rome. The Via dell' Imperio – Empire Street – was a thirty-metre-wide, ceremonial highway running in a straight line from the Piazza Venezia to the Colosseum.[112] It passed directly over the *Fora* built by the Emperors Nerva and Trajan, and ran directly alongside to the original Forum.

Mussolini's aim was to provide an evocative backdrop to a grand avenue custom-built for military parades. He did not seem to care that this meant destroying 40,000 square metres of his historic city – and placing the surviving monuments of the Forum right next to a busy four-lane motorway.[113] In the ruined arches of the Forum's Basilica of Maxentius, which overlooked the new Via dell' Imperio, he erected five marble maps celebrating the victories of Rome from prehistory up to the present day. The last of the maps was installed in 1936, and featured the annexation of Ethiopia, one of the first conquests of Mussolini's fledgling 'empire'.[114]

On the evening of 3 May 1938, Mussolini had an opportunity to show off his new Rome to a worldwide audience. The international press had descended on the city to report on a state visit to Italy by the German Chancellor, Adolf Hitler. Fascism itself was on show, as the movement's two most prominent political leaders met in a city synonymous with empire. Hitler arrived by train into the newly built modernist structure of Ostiense Station in the south west of the city.

More than 20,000 flags had lined the tracks for his entire rail journey, split evenly between the Italian tricolour and the Nazi swastika, a symbol of the 'axis' between the two countries.[115] Hitler was taken from Ostiense by horse-drawn carriage to the king's residence in the Quirinal Palace. The ancient monuments that he rode past were illuminated by 45,000 electric lamps served by 100 miles of cabling.[116] As one spectator noted, Rome was 'transformed into a vast opera stage in which at night the Führer could admire a spectacle worthy of Nero'.[117] Towards the climax of the procession, Hitler travelled along the Via dell' Imperio itself, with the Forum on his left. The Colosseum was illuminated, with candles and red lamps placed in every archway. From the vantage point of Mussolini's brand new highway, this elaborate light-show bombarded Hitler's senses with a modernist vision of the ruined grandeur of imperial Rome. Fascism did not deal in subtlety.

The *Führer* was undoubtedly impressed. When he returned to Germany, he worked with his chief architect Albert Speer on the concept of the *Theorie von Ruinewert*, the 'Theory of Ruin Value'. Speer responded by producing a drawing of the viewing platform on the new Nazi Zeppelin Field, 'overgrown with ivy, its columns fallen, the walls crumbling here and there, but the outlines clearly still recognisable'.[118]

This romantic vision appealed greatly to Hitler. He dreamed of creating structures that, long after his death and the fall of his 'thousand-year' Third Reich, would 'speak to the conscience of a future Germany centuries from now'.[119] He ordered that steel and reinforced concrete should no longer be used for Nazi public buildings, and that architects must turn instead to the more durable materials of stone and marble. This, Speer confirmed, would result in structures, 'which even in a state of decay, after hundreds... or thousands of years would more or less resemble Roman models'.[120] When Hitler looked for artworks to adorn the Cabinet Room of Speer's new Chancellery Building in Berlin, his selection was revealing: two paintings of the overgrown ruins of the Forum by the eighteenth-century French artist Hubert Robert.[121] Once a symbol of political liberty, the Forum had become the romantic dream of a totalitarian empire.

The Forum today is a hard place to understand, harder to love. In his 1896 novel *Rome*, the French author Émile Zola wrote of the impact of archaeological investigation on the site. His description is as relevant today as it was a century ago. 'It was necessary to dig very deep – some fifty feet – to find the venerable Republican soil,' wrote Zola, so that 'all you see is a long, clean, livid trench, cleared of ivy and bramble, where the fragments of paving, the bases of columns, and the piles of foundations appear like bits of bone.'

For Zola, the scholastic obsession with finding out all that could be known about the Forum had left behind an archaeological carcass, its skeletal ruins picked clean by digging, brushing, scrubbing and polishing. For 'the mere passer-by, who is not a professional scholar,' Zola suggested, something had been lost: 'All he sees on this searched and scoured spot is a city's cemetery where old exhumed stones are whitening, and whence rises the intense sadness that envelops dead nations.'[122]

It may be small consolation to the modern visitor, confronted with a dusty valley filled with 'keep-out' fencing and scaffolding, pockmarked by holes and gouged by trenches, but there is something peculiarly appropriate about the current state of the Forum, as professional archaeologists lock horns with the general public and the city authorities.[123] From the start this has been a site characterised by conflict and confrontation. The battle-lines have changed over the millennia, but the adversarial spirit has remained. According to legend, the Forum was born out of a murderous fraternal quarrel and a fight over stolen women. After centuries of political debate it became the stage for an epic power struggle between democracy and dictatorship, republic and empire, paganism and Christianity. Its ruins have spoken to the soul of artists and tyrants, whispering to one of the tragic fall of liberty and civilisation, and of the romance of absolute power to the other.

As long as it remains the focus of discourse and discord, however, the Forum lives on. Whether political or spiritual, ideological or architectural, the promise of a good argument has always defined this broad rectangle of ground. It still enshrines – in its ruins, in its trenches, in its fragmentary foundations, and in all that is now lost – the eternal human capacity to disagree.

Chapter Seven

The Library of Babel

The Library of Alexandria – Egypt

(Born 300 BC – Died AD 650)

In 1960, four novels by the well-known English writer Lawrence Durrell were brought together in one volume and published as *The Alexandria Quartet*. Described by its author as 'an investigation of modern love'[1], it was set in the Egyptian city of Alexandria before and during the Second World War, and was largely based on Durrell's own experiences during his time there as a press attaché. The *Quartet* traced the personal lives of a number of key characters – seemingly based on real individuals, including Durrell's second wife[2] – from different, competing perspectives. He later claimed, however, that, out of all of the people portrayed and incidents featured, 'only the city is real'.[3]

Alexandria was the true hero of the book: an exotic, darkly seductive and sensuous city, fragrant of 'offal and drying mud, of carnations and jasmine, of animal sweat and clover'.[4] Durrell painted a picture of a cosmopolitan, Greco-Arab outpost, where East met West in a delicious collision of hotels, hashish cafés, colonial villas and squalid slums, all set between the blankness of the desert and the blue of the Mediterranean. Yet Durrell's Alexandria was far from a product of the twentieth century alone. Instead he called it a 'capital of memory', a place that still held on to the 'echoes of an extraordinary history'.[5] It was a remnant and a shadow of a much greater city, one born out of a dream two-and-a-half thousand years old.

In 331 BC, according to the Greek historian Plutarch, after successfully conquering Egypt, Alexander the Great received a vision in his sleep. A 'grey-haired man of venerable appearance'[6], told him of 'an island in the much-dashing sea in front of Egypt: Pharos is what men call it'.[7] Alexander believed that this visitation was the Greek poet Homer, communicating from beyond the grave. When he travelled to view Pharos, he declared it to be the perfect spot for a city: a city that would bear his name, and that would become a new capital of the ancient world.

With his architect Dinocrates, the young emperor paced out the plan of 'Alexandria', scattering barley meal in the sand to mark the locations of palaces, streets and buildings. The city was rectangular in shape and ordered in a grid system, with its length exactly double its width – a design said to be modelled on the *chlamys*, the woollen military cloak worn by Macedonian warriors.[8] A causeway was built between the mainland and the island of Pharos, spanning the sea from the vast royal palace complex that had emerged along the shoreline to create two huge, man-made harbours.

Fresh water was diverted from the mouth of the Nile, running along a twenty-mile-channel into a series of tunnels and great, vaulted cisterns carved out of the rock beneath the city.[9] At the tip of the island, marking the entrance to the port, was a colossal white marble tower: the Pharos – or lighthouse – of Alexandria.[10] At its top, 100 metres above the city, fires were lit and directed with mirrors of polished metal, creating a beacon visible, some said, over 300 miles out to sea.[11]

Little of this Alexandria remained in the city that so captivated Durrell. Certainly, little that could be seen and touched. Over the course of a thousand years, between around 300 and 1300 AD, a series of massive earthquakes, originating in a fault-line that ran from Sicily to Cairo, struck the Egyptian coast.[12] The harbour front dropped slowly closer and closer to the sea, before its great cluster of grand, ornate buildings started to topple into the water, eventually sinking beneath the waves.

In the mid-1990s, marine archaeologists rediscovered this ancient city in fragments lying scattered across the seabed of the modern port. They found hundreds of fallen columns and capitals, sphinxes sunk into the silt of the harbour floor alongside broken obelisks, and huge stone blocks covered in hieroglyphs and Greek inscriptions. The ruin of the great lighthouse was there too, still lying where it had crashed down into the water after an earthquake in the early fourteenth century.[13] Durrell had described it in the *Alexandria Quartet*, writing of the 'Ancient Pharos, whose shattered fragments still choke the shallows'; and one of his characters 'had once wanted to start a curio trade by selling fragments of the Pharos as paperweights.' The plan was to smash off the pieces with a hammer 'to deliver them to retailers all over the world'.[14] This was no idle whimsy. Nearly three decades after Durrell wrote his novel, people were doing just that with graffiti-dyed chunks of the Berlin Wall.

Although it was built on Egyptian soil, Alexandria was at first a determinedly Greek city, established as the main trading hub of an Empire stretching from the Mediterranean to eastern India. Over time, however, its atmosphere and its architecture became a blend of classical and oriental influences, a mishmash of styles reflecting both its diverse population and the individual tastes of a succession of increasingly self-indulgent – and corpulent – kings.[15] Yet what made the city truly unique was its role as a centre for learning and scholarship. Alexandria was built around a simple yet staggeringly ambitious idea: that of holding in one place all of the knowledge ever accumulated by man. A Great Library was established there to become the memory bank of the ancient world, filled with papyrus and parchment scrolls containing everything from poetry, drama and literature, to advanced treatises on mathematics, anatomy, geography, physics and astronomy.

The library became one of the original and most spectacular hostages to fortune in all of world history. The tenet 'knowledge is power' was its founding creed; yet if knowledge is power, it can also be threat, temptation, corruption and heresy. It was a sequence of natural disasters that saw the original city swallowed by the sea, but Alexandria's library had vanished long before. It was claimed neither by cataclysm nor by catastrophe, but by man.

The classical Greek playwrights had invented the concept of 'hubris', the fall that comes after overweening pride and ambition. Looking back across the millennia, there seems a terrible inevitability about the fate of the library at Alexandria. What other destiny could have awaited this first, universal archive – the store of all human intellectual achievement – than total destruction?

In 1996, as construction workers cleared a site in downtown Athens for the foundations of a new Museum of Modern Art, they found traces of a large structure sitting on the bedrock. A building had occupied this same spot some two-and-a-half thousand years earlier, when it was part of a wooded sanctuary outside the original city walls, on the banks of the River Ilissos. The excavation uncovered the remains of a gymnasium, a wrestling arena, changing rooms and baths. This had been a place for athletics and exercise, where the young men of Athens had trained to become soldiers and citizens. But it was more than just a centre for physical improvement. The archaeologists soon realised that they had found one of the most significant sites in all of western European intellectual culture, a site referred to continually by history's greatest philosophers: the Lyceum of Aristotle. The world's first university.[16]

As the dig continued, they uncovered the very chamber where Aristotle had lectured his students on logic, ethics, politics, economics, literature and science. It was only large enough to fit around ten people[17], but then Aristotle had never confined his teaching to the classroom. According to contemporary accounts, he ranged all over the grounds of the Lyceum, walking as he taught. His followers called his school the 'Peripatos', from the Greek meaning 'walkway', and they in turn became known as the 'Peripatetics'. His lecture notes were written down and incorporated into a small, private library, taking their place alongside a selection of prized scholarly books collected from his travels across the ancient world.[18]

Aristotle had established his school at the gymnasium around 335 BC.[19] For the previous eight years he had worked as personal physician and tutor to the son of Philip II of Macedon[20]: young Prince Alexander, before he became 'Great'. This was Aristotle's most famous pupil, although he also worked with two of Alexander's well-known friends – Ptolemy and Cassander.[21] Eventually relations between the teacher and his protégé broke down irrevocably. Alexander matured to manhood and came to the throne of Macedonia. As his power grew, and more and more territories fell to his army, he began to assume the role not just of a great leader – perhaps the greatest history had ever known – but also of a god.[22] Aristotle viewed this irrationality with a mixture of amusement and contempt.

Nevertheless, Aristotle had instilled in Alexander an enduring respect for education and scholarship.[23] It was the philosopher's teachings that inspired his student to envision Alexandria as the high watermark of Greek culture: a custom-built metropolis, designed according to purist principles. But Alexander died before he could begin work on his great project. In 323 BC, as he rested in his royal palace in Babylon, he succumbed either to malaria or poisoning. Some rather far-fetched, ancient gossip even linked Aristotle to an assassination plot.[24] In the end it was Ptolemy, Alexander's childhood accomplice, trusted general, and one-time fellow Aristotelian classmate, who would establish Alexandria as a world centre for the Greek arts.

At the heart of the city's palace complex, which stretched along the harbour front opposite the island of Pharos, Ptolemy founded two great institutions: a 'Shrine to the Muses' – a building known more commonly today as a *museum* – and a huge library.[25] To run the library, Ptolemy turned to a fellow disciple of Aristotle – Theophrastus, the new head of the Athenian Lyceum. Theophrastus declined the offer[26], but recommended instead one of his best students, Demetrius of Phalerum. For Demetrius, the timing could not have been better. In 317 BC, Cassander, the third of the young Macedonian pupils of Aristotle, had appointed Demetrius as ruler of Athens. For a decade Demetrius had tried to organise the city according to the high-minded political and philosophical ideas of his great teachers. The attempt was something of a disaster. By the end of his reign, the Athenians regarded him as little more than a tyrant whose lecture-hall theories were utterly ill-equipped to deal with governance in the real world. Overthrown and exiled from the city – on pain of death if he ever returned – Demetrius had been languishing back under the cloak of Cassander at his court in the Greek city of Thebes.[27] The opportunity of royal patronage to embark on another great intellectual endeavour – a safe distance from Athens – was too good to pass up.

One of the earliest surviving accounts to make specific mention of Alexandria's library comes in the middle of the second or third century BC (the actual dating is a matter of much debate)[28], written by Aristeas, a Jewish scholar who had come to live and work in the city. In a letter to his brother Philocrates, he appears to detail both the extraordinary progress made by Demetrius after being put in charge of the institution, and the vast scope of the task set by Ptolemy:

> '[Demetrius] was assigned large sums of money with a view to collecting, if possible, all the books in the world; and by arranging purchases and transcriptions he carried the king's design to completion as far as he was able. When he was asked, in my presence, about how many thousands of books were already collected, he replied: "above two hundred thousand my king; and in a short while I shall exert every effort for the remainder, to round out the number of half a million".'[29]

Aristeas also recounts his own involvement at the library, along with seventy-one other Jewish scholars, in one of the most significant projects of ancient history: translating into Greek the writings that would later form the Christian Old Testament.[30]

Alexandria's library was not the first the world had ever known. Attempts had been made to collect and preserve writing almost from the moment that it had been invented. The Mesopotamians, for instance, had established a number of royal libraries; Egyptian priests had managed great archives of diplomatic correspondence written on scrolls or tablets; and the Assyrian King Ashurbanipal had kept a huge collection of works inscribed in baked clay, which included the Epic of Gilgamesh, the world's earliest known work of literature. Yet nothing had come close to the ambition of Alexandria. Conceived by the students of Aristotle[31], now among the most influential figures in the western world, it combined philosophical and intellectual purity with swaggering imperial might. The modest model of the Athenian Lyceum and its private library was re-imagined on a gargantuan scale: as if the voracious quest for 'more worlds' in Alexander's reign had been replaced by an equally urgent search for knowledge. In both cases, however, the objectives were clear: prestige and power. As humanity's intellectual capital, Alexandria could stand proud above every other city on earth.

Like today, most libraries in the ancient world grew through acquisitions, gifts, bequests and loans – as well as, of course, from the writing and depositing of entirely new texts. In Alexandria, however, where the goal was to gather and catalogue every book ever written, the collections strategy was more extreme. The Ptolemy dynasty instituted a law that any book brought into the city had to be passed immediately to the library's scribes for copying. More often than not, the original was kept and the copy returned to its owner.[32] The thousands of ships docking in the city's three inter-connected deep-water harbours were searched routinely, and any texts not already declared and unloaded onto the quay-sides were seized and confiscated.

So many books were added to the library through this method, that they received their own categorisation: a label attached to each parchment that read 'from the ships'.[33] Agents were employed to travel to book markets across the Mediterranean in search of rare and original works. In the third century BC, Ptolemy III sent emissaries to all the kings and leaders in the known world, asking to borrow their books for copying. When the Athenians lent him the master copies of the works of the great Greek tragedians Aeschylus, Euripides and Sophocles, the king kept the originals and sent the fresh copies back across the sea[34], regarding his forfeited deposit of fifteen talents[35] as a small price to pay for so precious a set of first editions.

The shelves – or *theke*[36] – of the library filled up at an incredible rate. At the same time, the Ptolemies worked jealously to establish a monopoly on the practice of collecting and curating information. When a rival library was established at Pergamum in present-day Turkey, they banned the export of Egyptian papyrus, an attempt to cut off at source the 'oxygen' for the creation and copying of books.[37] The Pergamum library struggled on, with their scribes forced to work on parchments made from animal skins.[38] As the reputation of Alexandria grew, its combination of reference works, scholarship and research began to reach critical mass. Academics flocked to the city on the promise of free board and lodging in the opulent royal quarter, as well as exemption from taxes, funding for study, and of course access to the library. It became an irresistible magnet for the great minds of the ancient world. They could flourish under the patronage of their Greek kings, and devote their lives to nothing but the pursuit of knowledge.[39] The dream of the Ptolemaic rulers was crystallising into an ever more potent reality: as the intelligentsia flooded the city, the kings came to hold dominion over the Empire of the Mind.

Towards the end of the second century BC, the scholar Athenaeus described the fame the library had achieved in the ancient world. 'What reason is there for me even to speak of the number of books, the establishment of libraries, and the collection in the Museum,' he wrote, 'considering how they are all the memories of everyone?'[40] Yet in his account Athenaeus also appeared to hint at the drawbacks of accumulating such a vast repository of data: too much raw, unprocessed knowledge can be little different to no knowledge at all.

The Roman architect and engineer Vitruvius' description of the life of Aristophanes of Byzantium, who was Alexandria's head librarian at the start of the second century BC, stood as a similar warning of the dangers of bibliomania: 'Every day he did nothing other than read and reread all the books of the Library, for the whole day, examining and reading through the order in which they were shelved.'[41] If he was not careful, the librarian could be swallowed up by his own library.

It became clear that the scale of the Alexandrian enterprise presented a new and unique challenge. Once you had brought all of the works of man under one roof, how could you then go about finding information on just *one* specific topic? The answer was to invent an entirely new system for identifying, registering and locating texts. This monumental task fell to the critic, poet and scholar Callimachus of Cyrene, who devised a system called the *Pinakes* – literally, the 'Tables' – which compressed and categorised any given book into an abbreviated shorthand.

The *Pinakes* divided texts by genre and subsection, ordered authors alphabetically, offered potted biographies and lists of their other works, included titles and opening words, and provided estimates of the extent of each individual work by number of lines.[42] It was the creation of an archive within an archive, the key that unlocked the library's vast data bank. Callimachus changed forever how we engage with writing. Massive works were reduced to basic ciphers, signposts inviting a scholar to read on, or move on. All of a sudden, books were defined by their catalogue entries, translated into a new grammar of genres, titles and line-counts – the universal language of the index.

If some were dismayed by the implications – in particular by the subjectivity inherent in the summarising process – without the *Pinakes*, the library would have been unusable. Callimachus' innovation transformed Alexandria, and remains the basis for the cataloguing and bibliographic system we use today. For the first time, scholars could access information on a huge range of diverse subjects, and consult, process and synthesise data all at once. The results were sensational.

As early as 235 BC, the geographer and mathematician,

Eratosthenes of Cyrene was proposing not only that the earth was round – in an age when almost all believed it was flat, with an edge off which the unwary could drop – but had also calculated its circumference and diameter (the former to within 200 miles of its actual size, the latter to within 50 miles). He was also able to conclude that all the oceans were connected, and was the first man in history to suggest the possibility of circumnavigating the globe. But scholarship at Alexandria was not confined to exploring the extent and properties of our own world. Men like Timocharis, Hipparchus, Aristyllus and Claudius Ptolemaeus created maps of constellations and catalogued thousands of stars. Nearly two millennia before Copernicus, Aristarchus of Samos put forward the theory that the sun was the centre of the universe, and that the earth and all the other planets in the solar system revolved around it in a circle.[43]

In the dissection rooms of the Museum, huge advances were made in medical science, aided by the Ptolemies' willingness to offer up dead bodies for study. Chillingly, it was also rumoured that condemned criminals were supplied 'out of prison by the Kings'[44], to be subjected to the horrors of vivisection. Herophlius' study of the brain at Alexandria led to the discovery of the central nervous system and the role of the veins in blood circulation, proposing, for the first time, that the brain, and not the heart, housed the human mind. His younger colleague Erasistratus, with whom Herophilos founded a school of anatomy, carried on this ground-breaking work[45], mapping all of the body's arteries, identifying the respiratory function of the lungs, and exploring the digestive system to conclude, among other things, that the feeling of hunger stemmed from an empty stomach.

In the early third century BC, the mathematical genius Euclid wrote the *Elements* at Alexandria, a series of proofs and axioms drawn together in a single, logical treatise. It was the founding work of mathematics and geometry, the definitive reference book enabling every future scholar to apply universal theories to myriad practical applications.[46] As a result, engineering and physics flourished in the city. It was here, for instance, that Archimedes invented his enduring 'screw' water-pump[47], and experienced his famous '*Eureka!*' moment to create calculus, his methodology for working out areas and volumes. But the many great advances were not confined to endless rolls of parchment and lines of shelving. Over time, this feverish spirit of discovery and invention spilled out of the halls of learning to transform the city itself.

Alexandria became the setting for awe-inspiring wonders. Operated by running water, mechanical birds sang and whistled from the tops of trees and fountains. Using compressed air, statues would blow trumpets, raise wine-skins to their lips, or shoot arrows. Temple doors would open and close automatically, controlled by the lighting and extinguishing of fires. The city's wide, central avenue was lit at night by automatic, air-powered street-lamps burning olive oil.[48] These devices came from the mind of Hero, a native of Alexandria in the first century AD, and one of the most prolific innovators of the ancient world. The founding father of hydraulics, he explored in his master-work *Pneumatica* how 'by the union of air, earth, fire and water, and the concurrence of three or four elementary principles, various combinations are effected, some of which supply the most pressing wants of human life, others produce amazement and alarm'.[49]

Hero's box of tricks also included the coin-operated drink-dispenser – 'a sacrificial vessel which flows only when money is introduced'[50] – and the syringe. In his construction of a short play performed by automata, controlled by weights winding ropes and strings back and forth around an axle, he is credited with building the very first programmable robot.[51] Most remarkable of all, however, was what he named the 'Aeolipile'[52], after Aeolus, the Greek God of the air and winds. A sphere held above a heated, water-filled cauldron was made to revolve perpetually under the power of pressurised steam. Hero intended this as a simple amusement, an intriguing toy that proved a theory.[53] What he had in fact created was the world's first steam engine and turbine, the same 'motor' for the Industrial Revolution, sixteen centuries later.

Looking back now, the imagination is sent reeling by the possibilities. Imagination, of course, is almost all that we have left. At some point in ancient history, we know that the library and its priceless contents were destroyed, most likely burned to ashes. A vast tract of the collective memory and accomplishments of classical human civilisation and culture was wiped out. What we do not know, at least for certain, is who was responsible.

Historians ever since have told and retold the story as a persistent, haunting and unprecedented narrative of loss. At the same time, they have pored over the fragmentary evidence in their search for a culprit, embarking on a politically charged manhunt to find and prosecute whoever consigned the library to its terrible fate.

In the autumn of 48 BC, the Roman General – and soon to be dictator – Julius Caesar looked out from the palace quarter of Alexandria over the vast, sweeping harbour to the Mediterranean Sea, and reflected on how quickly man's fortunes could turn. When he had arrived in the city several weeks earlier, he had been presented by the local authorities with the signet ring and severed head of his great rival, Pompey. Caesar wept at the sight of the ring, and was too distraught even to look at the head.[54] Pompey and Caesar, the two great Titans of Rome, had fought out a vast and sprawling civil war that would ultimately see their Republic transformed into an Empire. Pompey's demise, as victim of a crude assassination plot after he landed in Alexandria three days ahead of a pursuing Caesar, had been a tawdry end to such an epic conflict.

The murder, it seemed, was an attempt by the Alexandrians to demonstrate their allegiance to Caesar. Battle-weary and exhausted, and with sailing impossible due to the prevailing winds, Caesar decided to land his troops in the harbour and take up temporary residence in the royal palace. He marched with his legionnaires through the streets, carrying at the head of their procession a *fasces* – a bundle of rods containing an axe – signifying the military might and authority of Rome.[55] The gesture backfired, quite spectacularly. Roman soldiers were attacked and killed in the streets by angry mobs, and soon

Caesar and his men found themselves holed up in the palace, their small fleet blockaded in the harbour, and the city besieged by an army of 20,000 men[56] belonging to the teenage King Ptolemy XIII. Egypt, it transpired, was undergoing a civil war of its own. Caesar had inadvertently found himself at the centre of an ongoing and bloody battle for succession. And things were about to get even more complicated.

One evening, a twenty-year-old princess, the older sister of Ptolemy XIII, landed a small boat near Alexandria's royal palace. In the gathering dusk, she was smuggled by her servant Appollodorus into Caesar's chamber, her body hidden lengthways in a thick roll of bedding. She had come to plead for Caesar's support and for his help to wrest control of Egypt away from her younger brother. Her name was Cleopatra. At around the same time, Caesar suspected that the eunuch Pothinus – his palace host and Ptolemy XIII's obsequious regent – was plotting against him. In the circumstances, it is hardly surprising that he had taken to sitting up whole nights with his soldiers drinking.[57]

Alexandria had become a war zone. Caesar's men fought pitched battles in the streets as they struggled to hold out in the palace compound. In one skirmish, Ptolemy's army attempted to break through the Roman lines to take complete control of the harbour and all of its warships. As Caesar later recounted in his book *Commentaries on the Civil Wars* – writing in the third person – he knew it would spell catastrophe if he allowed his ships to fall into enemy hands: 'If they made themselves masters of these, Caesar being deprived of his fleet, they would have the command of the port and whole sea, and could prevent him from procuring provisions and auxiliaries.' In desperation, he ordered an action at once extreme and tactically masterful. 'Caesar gained the day,' he wrote, 'and set fire to all those ships, and to others which were in the docks, because he could not guard so many places with so small a force.'[58] If he could not hold the harbour, then no one would. Full of self-admiration for the success of his ploy, Caesar moved briskly on to detail the next episode in the siege.

Over time, however, other writers and scholars kept coming back to this incident, scrutinising its consequences in ever more vivid detail. Around a century later, the great Roman poet Lucan published an epic verse on the civil wars, called the *Pharsalia.* According to his account, Caesar, 'so great in his firmness of mind... commands that firebrands dipped in pitchy fat be hurled against the vessels linked together.' While at first the fire raced across the fleet, till 'the top most yard-arms caught alight', Lucan writes that 'not on ships alone did fire settle; but the dwellings which were near the sea caught fire from its far-reaching heat... and the flame, struck by a whirlwind, ran through the dwellings as swiftly as a meteor often races with its trail in the ether.' Such, it seemed, was the extent of the blaze, 'that destruction for a little time recalled the people from the besieged palace to help the city'.[59]

While Lucan did not dwell on which buildings were caught up in the conflagration, his contemporary, the philosopher Seneca, allegedly basing his story on a mysteriously lost account of the conflict, written at the time by the great historian Livy[60], was unequivocal. '40,000 of the books of Alexandria burned,'[61] he wrote. It was the first time that any explicit link had been made between Caesar's fire and the destruction of the library. While the number of books mentioned seems a small portion of Alexandria's vast collection, it has been suggested that this figure is a mistranslation from the original Latin, and should read 400,000.[62] Regardless of the numbers, later writers seized on the detail and elaborated on the impact. Most influential of all was Plutarch. In his *Life of Caesar*, written at the end of the first century AD, he described the moment in the Alexandrian siege when Caesar's enemies 'tried to intercept his communications by sea and he was forced to deal with this danger by setting fire to the ships in the docks. This was the fire which, starting from the dockyards, destroyed the great library'.[63] A century on, and the Roman historian, Aulus Gellius reported that 'an enormous quantity of books, nearly seven hundred thousand volumes... burned during the sack of the city in our first war in Alexandria'.[64]

Lucan's insinuating spark had, over the centuries, burst into an inferno of scholarly condemnation. There was, it seemed, quite literally, no smoke without fire. Julius Caesar stood accused of perpetrating the greatest act of cultural vandalism in the entire history of the ancient world. As time passed, however, he would not be alone.

In March of AD 415, during the celebration of Lent, a young woman called Hypatia was travelling by chariot through the streets of Alexandria. Hypatia was the daughter of Theon, perhaps the greatest mathematician of the age, and a keen student of the great works of the now-distant classical world. At the beginning of the fifth century, she began teaching the philosophy of Aristotle and Plato to the people of Alexandria[65], and as the contemporary historian, Socrates Scholasticus put it, she had 'made such attainments in literature and science,' that many students 'came from a distance to receive her instructions'.[66] As her fame and her reputation grew – she was said to be revered not just for her wisdom, but also for her beauty and virtue – she began to attract the attention of the city's religious authorities, and became implicated in a political power struggle between Orestes, the governor of Alexandria, and Cyril, the Christian Bishop.[67]

For years, religious disputes between the city's Christians and Jews had been escalating into increasingly bloody riots, and a group of fanatical monks, eager to fight for their holy cause, had descended on Alexandria from their sanctuary in the remote mountains of the Nitrian desert. Orestes had often come to Hypatia to seek council, and a rumour spread that she was responsible for turning the governor away from the Christian faith. According to Bishop John of Niku, writing around AD 650, Hypatia was 'a pagan... devoted at all times to magic', who had 'beguiled many people... And the governor of the city honoured her exceedingly; for she had beguiled him through her magic'. For Niku, this woman's famed knowledge of philosophy and mathematics only confirmed her 'Satanic wiles'.[68]

Drunk on puritanical fury, a group of the Nitrian monks, led, ironically, by a man called Peter 'the reader', ambushed Hypatia in her chariot, pulled her down from her carriage to strip her naked, and then dragged her through the streets to the Caesareum, a nearby church. There the mob used oyster shells and roof tiles to scrape her skin from her body[69], before they tore her limbs apart, and carried them outside the city walls to burn them to cinders.[70] For Niku, the brutal murder of Hypatia marked a triumphant, final end to pagan worship and idolatry in the city.[71] Scholasticus, on the other hand, despaired that 'nothing could be farther from the spirit of Christianity'.[72] What seemed abundantly clear was that the city's great tradition of learning and scholarship – its very founding principle – was no more. It was not one great mind that died with Hypatia. It was all intellectual life in Alexandria.[73]

There had been a horrible inevitability to this. From AD 378 onwards, the Roman Emperor Theodosius, the last sole ruler of the empire before it split into East and West, announced a series of decrees ordering the disbanding, dismantling, and ultimately the destruction of all pagan temples. Christianity became the official religion of the Romans, and there was a zealous desire to sweep away every impious and heretical trace of the old gods. First, the eternal fire in the pagan Temple of Vesta in the Forum of Rome was extinguished, and as it flickered out, persecution spread across the empire.[74]

In Alexandria, a man called Theophilus, the city's Christian patriarch and Bishop, sparked a religious war as he campaigned to eradicate the ancient faiths. The last stand for the city's pagan followers came in AD 391 at the Serapeion, the great temple fortress built to honour the Greco-Egyptian God Serapis – a deity who had been invented some seven-and-a-half centuries earlier by Ptolemy to help *unify* the people of his kingdom. Although the pagans taunted their Christian adversaries by hoisting crucified prisoners up onto the Serapeion's walls[75], they were vastly outnumbered, and their fleeting resistance served only to further heighten the atmosphere of destructive fervour. As the temple fell, the great statue of Serapis was smashed down and kicked through the streets, before being thrown onto one of many great fires set burning in every precinct of Alexandria.[76] It joined countless other profane objects and artefacts depicting the ancient gods and goddesses.

Something else may also have been fuelling the flames, however: the hundreds of thousands of scrolls of the city's famous library. According to Edward Gibbon, the author of the landmark work *The History of the Decline and Fall of the Roman Empire,* in the rioting, 'the valuable library of Alexandria was pillaged or destroyed; and, near twenty years afterwards, the appearance of the empty shelves excited the regret and the indignation of every spectator, whose mind was not totally darkened by religious prejudice'.[77] Gibbon's narrative set Roman Christianity against Greek intellectualism, piety against enlightened thought. Science was tainted as a pagan pursuit, and an enemy of faith. The library, as with many others throughout the empire, was seen as a living archive of heresy, and just like the old temples, it had to be destroyed. 'The compositions of ancient genius' wrote Gibbon, were heaped onto the bonfires, where they 'irretrievably perished'.[78]

Two centuries later, however, the library had mysteriously and miraculously come back to life – Gibbon's empty shelves were once again filled with scrolls and parchments. Unfortunately, this bibliographical resurrection was less reality, more narrative device: a means of introducing yet another villain into the mythology of Alexandria. In the early years of the seventh century AD, a new power had emerged from the deserts of the Middle East: a rapidly swelling group of Arab nomads following the teachings of Mohammed. This was the beginning of the Muslim Empire.

By AD 640, the armies of Islam had conquered Persia, Syria and Palestine, and had advanced through Egypt to lay siege to Alexandria. The city was one of the last major footholds of the Byzantine Empire in Africa. Heavily fortified, its subterranean cisterns full of fresh Nile water, and its grain stores abundant, it was prepared for a war of attrition. It took fourteen months for the Muslim general Amr ibn al-As to break down the will and the spirit of the defenders[79], much to the displeasure of the impatient Caliph Omar, Islam's spiritual leader. Finally, on 29 September AD 641, the city surrendered. As the Arabs rushed through the streets in celebration, they found a city largely emptied of its inhabitants: many had already fled by boat to Cyprus, Rhodes and the Byzantine capital, Constantinople.[80]

Writing five centuries after the siege, the Muslim historian Ibn

Al-Qifti[81], described how a victorious Amr talked with an Alexandrian priest, John the Grammarian, and learned of a priceless collection of 54,000 books[82] kept within a library in the city. A faithful and conscientious lieutenant, Amr wrote to his leader Omar to ask him what he should do with the books. The response was a study in the warped logic of fanaticism. 'If these writings of the Greeks agree with the book of God,' said Omar, 'they are useless and need not be preserved; if they disagree, they are pernicious, and ought to be destroyed'.[83] According to Al-Qifti, Amr obeyed without question. The vast rolls of paper and parchments were divided out among the city's four thousand bathhouses, where they were burnt to heat the water. There were so many books it was said, that they kept the baths of Alexandria warm for over six months.[84]

And so Alexandria's library, and its disappearance, remains one of the greatest enigmas of ancient history. It could have contained everything. And, just as conceivably, it could have contained nothing. Its books were collateral damage in the civil war that turned the Roman Republic into an Empire. They were the victims of a Christian crusade against pagan learning. They fell foul of the absolutist policies of early Islamic fundamentalism. Each theory is put forward by one group of historians, only to be demolished by another.[85]

Some say, for instance, that Caesar's fire merely destroyed a warehouse filled with scrolls and parchments recently unloaded from the harbour.[86] The story of fourth-century Christian vandalism is attacked as a misinterpretation or a deliberate manipulation of the sources to serve an anti-religious agenda on the part of enlightenment scholars like Edward Gibbon.[87] And Ibn Al-Qifti's account is exposed as a myth written out of political expediency: as libraries across the twelfth-century Muslim world were dispersed and auctioned off to pay debts, Al-Qifti created the legend of the bathhouse fires to stress that it was less of a crime to sell books than to burn them.[88] In the end, no one was responsible for the library's destruction. That always happened sometime else, at the hands of someone else. Perhaps, suggest the whispers, it had never really existed in the first place.

Except now, it certainly does exist. On a peninsula overlooking Alexandria's eastern port and facing out to the Mediterranean Sea, a giant disc has emerged, sloping up out of the harbour front. According to one of its architects, Christoph Kapeller of the Norwegian practice Snøhetta, this structure is intended to appear 'familiar and alien, ancient and contemporary, glittering and shining like a polished mirror in the morning, gray and huge like Moby Dick in the afternoon light – a timeless structure'.[89] It is the Bibliotheca Alexandrina, the modern incarnation of the city's ancient library. It is also the world's first globally sponsored archive, created under the auspices of UNESCO, the United Nations' cultural body, as a 'vital link in a living tradition' stretching all the way back to Aristotle's Athenian Lyceum.[90]

Relief mural on the facade of the modern Bibliotheca Alexandrina

Beneath the windows of the Bibliotheca's tilted, circular roof, which looks disarmingly like a giant microchip[91], is the largest reading room ever built, with shelf-space to accommodate 8 million books. Opened in 2002, and constructed at a cost of over $200 million[92], the building also houses a conference centre, four museums, four art galleries, a conservation laboratory and a planetarium.[93] For Moshen Zahran, the Bibliotheca's former director, the aim is not to revive Alexandria's former library, but to revive instead the purity of the idea that lay behind it – the relentless pursuit of knowledge. 'The old library encouraged the public to debate, create and invent,' he said. 'The new library is carrying that legacy forward'.[94]

The most striking demonstration of this ambition, however, can be found not in the Bibliotheca's growing collection of books, but in an underground room filled with row after row of computers. There are nearly two thousand, all working continuously in an attempt to store, in one vast digital data-bank, every web page of every single website that has ever existed. This is the so-called Internet Archive. Yet, in the best tradition of the ancient Ptolemies, it is also a copy.[95]

This version of the Internet Archive was gifted to the Bibliotheca to act as a backup to the original, based over 7,000 miles away in a neoclassical former church building in San Francisco. According to the Archive's co-founder, Brewster Kahle, a graduate of the Massachusetts Institute of Technology, the specific goal was to create the 'Library of Alexandria 2.0'.[96] Or, as Rick Pellinger, the president of the Archive's board put it, echoing Ptolemy I from two and a half thousand years previously, 'our mission is universal access to all information all of the time. We are the web's memory'.[97] The Archive now holds over 440 billion web pages dating back to the birth of the internet in 1996, with billions more added every single month.[98] Using a device called the 'way-back machine', the web can be displayed just as it looked on any given date over the last two decades.

In October 2012, the Archive's staff celebrated the database reaching 10 petabytes in size: equivalent to a staggering 10 billion books.[99] This is the true successor to Alexandria's ancient library. While the Bibliotheca is an admirable work of symbolic architecture, an optimistic memorial, celebrating a long-distant cultural heritage, the Archive is a modern data repository of almost unimaginable size and complexity. The digital fabric of the web can be more fragile and fleeting than any physical object – as anyone who has ever experienced the sheer existential terror of a failed hard-drive will know. Yet, as the administrators – or rather 'librarians' – of the Archive admit, they may only really be able to capture a tenth of the internet's total output at any one time. 'We know we'll never get it all. The web by its nature is infinite'.[100]

Even if the Archive did succeed, what would it actually mean to have access to the greatest ever accumulation of human knowledge and memory? In 1941, the Argentinian author Jorge Louis Borges wrote a short story called *The Library of Babel.* 'The universe (which others call the library),' he began, 'is composed of an indefinite, and perhaps infinite number of hexagonal galleries.' Within these galleries could be found every book that could possibly exist: the product of every conceivable combination of the characters making up every known alphabet, ranging from books written all in just one letter, to landmark treatises on science, or the greatest works of literature. 'When it was proclaimed that the Library contained all books,' wrote Borges, 'the first impression was one of extravagant happiness. All men felt themselves to be masters of an intact and secret treasure. There was no personal or world problem whose solution did not exist in some hexagon.'[101]

Yet the irony of this über-library was that the *possibility* of any book having been written did not have any bearing on the *probability* of finding it. This vast archive was neither curated nor critiqued, and expert accounts would be shelved side by side with imperfect or nonsensical ones. Universal knowledge, in Borges' library, simply meant too much information.[102] 'On some shelf in some hexagon,' he speculated, 'there must exist a book which is the formula and perfect compendium *of all the rest*.' And whoever found that book, would be God.[103]

The new librarians of the Internet Archive may already be working with a volume of data that approaches Borges' surrealist vision. They operate on a three-month cycle, capturing and storing the world's top one million sites, and following the links embedded in those sites to other sites and web pages, which are also archived. Information proliferates on top of information, and then, once the three months are up, the process begins again from scratch – because the list of the top one million is changing all the time.[104] Just as Borges writes, 'those who judge it to be limited, postulate that in remote places the corridors and stairways and hexagons can conceivably come to an end – which is absurd'.[105]

As the Archive tackles the immense challenge of simply *recording* the web, the creation of new content continues at a remarkable pace. In July 2008, some 600 people from 47 countries around the world came together at a conference held at the Bibliotheca Alexandria.[106] They belonged to an online community now numbering over 50 million users, and they were meeting to discuss their ongoing mission: to write a complete online encyclopaedia from scratch. The name of this project is, of course, Wikipedia. When first established as a non-profit charity on 15 January 2001 – the 'wiki' is taken from the Hawaiian word for 'quick' – its stated aim was to realise a website where content could be not just viewed, but created and edited, by anyone. The goal was to reach 100,000 pages.[107] The subsequent success of Wikipedia has been one of the revelations of the internet. At the beginning of 2015, there were over 34 million articles in 288 languages – including over 4.6 million in English – which have all been written collaboratively by volunteers.[108]

The vast reading room of the modern Bibliotheca Alexandrina
© Dennis G. Jarvis, 1994

The 2008 conference at the Bibliotheca was attended by the most ardent and prolific 'Wikipedians' as a spiritual homecoming. They see themselves, quite explicitly, as the inheritors of the legacy of Alexandria's Great Library. There is now a web page, running in real time, which counts up the total number of edits which have taken place in the history of Wikipedia. This has already passed 2.3 billion. A slogan beneath the counter announces 'All human knowledge – there is a deadline'.[109] The deadline, we are told, is always 'now', before it is too late. Linked to the web page is an engraving of the ancient Library of Alexandria, with a caption explaining that it was 'one of many destroyed libraries in antiquity, lost long before Wikipedia had a chance to save their contents.'[110] It is a self-sustaining, self-regulating and self-perpetuating entity. Each article has the potential to spawn a hundred or a thousand more articles. Every definition needs its own definition. It is a process conceivably without end. There is even a web page which asks what number of Wikipedia articles is required to encompass all of human knowledge. 96 million is the estimated answer.[111] It is a figure of wonderfully arbitrary precision which, to follow Borges, is also absurd.

Amid this twenty-first century culture of information overload, it is interesting to recall a number of provocative writers from the past – from historians to dramatists – who appeared actually to welcome the destruction of Alexandria's ancient library.[112] The Roman historian, Seneca would not 'praise the library as the most noble monument to the wealth of kings', because there was, 'no 'good taste' or 'solicitude' about it, only learned luxury'.[113] The sixteenth-century humanist, Louis LeRoy, cautioned that if everything that had ever been written had survived down the ages, then there would be no space in the world save for that which was taken up by books. 'We should have no other movables in our house but books: we should be constrained to go, sit and lie upon books. And yet there are so many, and are made from day to day, that the age of man could not suffice to read'.[114]

While Edward Gibbon mourned the Alexandria library's loss in an earlier account in his *Decline and Fall*, in a later volume he wrote that, 'a philosopher may allow with a smile,' that the loss was, 'ultimately devoted to the benefit of mankind' as no 'important truth' or 'useful discovery in art or nature, has been snatched away from the curiosity of modern ages'.[115] In the 1901 play *Caesar and Cleopatra*, George Bernard Shaw imagined the following exchange between Caesar and a character called Theodotus, the tutor of Ptolemy, who rushed in to the palace to exclaim that a harbour fire had spread to the library:

> *Theodotus:* What is burning there is the memory of mankind.
> *Caesar:* A shameful memory. Let it burn.
> *Theodotus (wildly)*: Will you destroy the past?
> *Caesar:* Aye, and build the future with its ruins.[116]

The implication is that an obsessive preoccupation with what has gone before can hold back knowledge and creativity in the present. Yet there is also a deliberate lightness, noticeable in particular in Gibbon's 'smile' and Shaw's comedic dramatisation of historical events. In presenting the destruction of Alexandria as a mere setback on the inexorable march of human progress, these writers seem to take for granted that a lesson has been learned and that no similar event on such a scale could ever happen again.

It is a dangerous assumption. As a vast amount of content is now 'born digital', and the average lifespan of a web page is said to be just 75 days.[117] Total loss is the most common outcome.[118] The result is the prospect of a 'digital dark age'[119] where the glut of information, and the inability to record it all, equates to a collective amnesia. It is here that a warning echo resounds across the millennia from the fate of Alexandria's ancient library.

Yet perhaps there is also an alternative outcome. As Borges speculates at the end of his story, 'the human species – the unique species – is about to be extinguished, but the Library will endure: illuminated, solitary, infinite, perfectly motionless, equipped with precious volumes, useless, incorruptible, secret'.[120] What if, in the future, we are the ones who are lost, while, in some endless and inaccessible data repository, all our accumulated knowledge lives on?

Chapter Eight

Anarchy's Theatre

The Hippodrome of Constantinople (Born AD 200 – Died 1500 AD)

In the sixth century AD, the streets of Constantinople were not a safe place to be. 'Constant fear made everyone expect that death was just round the corner,' wrote the Byzantine historian Procopius. 'Even before sunset they hurried back home and got under cover.'[1] Gangs of young men roamed the city. At first they confined themselves to robbing and murdering under cover of darkness. But, as their crimes went unpunished, they became bolder. They began to steal in broad daylight, and no longer in narrow alleys, but openly in the public squares. They committed acts of violence and vandalism for fun, assembling in rowdy groups for tests of strength and brutality. These included placing wagers on being able to kill any unfortunate passer-by with a single, unarmed blow. Laws and contracts were ignored, and creditors were forced to write off debts. Instances of rape were endemic, with young wives and boys in particular danger. In the rare event that a case ever made it to trial, no magistrate would deliver a guilty verdict for fear of reprisals.[2]

Membership of the gangs crossed the social hierarchies; the only common factor was youth. Sons of artisans caroused in the streets with the sons of noblemen. They were not difficult to spot, adopting outlandish hairstyles and clothing. They grew their beards and moustaches as long as possible, shaving the tops of their heads but allowing their hair at the back to fall down in long, tangled masses like the 'Huns', the warrior tribesmen of the Eurasian steppes – a style known more commonly today as a 'mullet'. Their clothes were deliberately, and almost comically, luxurious, as if to make a mockery of the citizens they terrorised. Their tunics were bound tight at the wrists and waists, but then the arms ballooned outwards with fabric, before they were cinched in again at the shoulders, giving the impression of cartoonishly well-muscled physiques. Most important of all was the colour of their dress. There were two gangs and they were bitter rivals: the Greens and the Blues.[3]

Some put the divisions between them down to political and religious differences, but this was to overcomplicate. It was no secret that the origins of the gangs – or 'factions', as they were known – could be traced to a huge amphitheatre built of stone and wood that dominated the centre of Constantinople. Here chariots of the Greens and Blues raced against each other over the circus sands in front of some 100,000 spectators, including the emperor himself. The factions represented the most fanatical and vociferous sections of the crowd, the supporters whose passion for their favoured colour had morphed into all-consuming obsession. This was the bond that brought young men of all creeds and stations together, from the highest to the lowest. To be a Green or a Blue was to revel in the spirit of competition inside the arena – and, increasingly, to glory in acts of 'ultra violence'[4] outside it. The sport of chariot racing was taking over Constantinople, and the stakes riding on the colour of a shirt were getting higher and higher.

Indeed for a time it seemed that the fate of the city, and even of the empire, could be decided among the sweat, blood, sand and fury of the Hippodrome.

For the first hundred years of its life, the Hippodrome remained only half-built, a construction site prematurely abandoned to become an instant ruin. In this state, it was quite at home in its immediate surroundings. Before Constantinople became Constantinople, it was known as Byzantium, and by the end of the second century AD, it was a city left derelict and devastated by civil war.

In AD 193 the Roman Emperor Septimius Severus had taken a vast force eastwards to quell a bid for power by the general of the Syrian legions – and rival emperor – Pescennius Niger. From his new headquarters at Byzantium, Niger watched as the armies of Western Rome approached by land and sea.[5] The city was, however, well prepared for siege. Byzantium was built on high ground, occupying the triangular promontory whose narrow point stretches out into the Sea of Marmara – the last extremity of the continent of Europe.[6] Its entire north-eastern edge was formed by the deep-water inlet known as the Golden Horn. To reach the city in its enclosed sea, ships had to pass through either the narrow channels of the Bosphorus to the east or the Dardanelles to the west. The Bosphorus in particular made navigation difficult for any war fleet, with its strong currents rushing out into the Mediterranean and pushing ships relentlessly towards the rocks of the headland.[7]

If nature had endowed Byzantium with formidable defences, these had been bolstered in a variety of ways. Great walls, built of massive, squared stones fastened together with bronze plates, surrounded the city on its peninsula. In the sea, long chains, strung from the breakwaters across the entrance to the Golden Horn, could be raised in times of trouble to make access to the harbours impossible. Seven towers, taller than all the rest, had been built as giant 'echo chambers', able to circulate warnings of danger around the city from one tower to the next at great speed. The famous engineer, Priscus, a native of Byzantium, had designed a range of ingenious siege defences. Some could throw rocks, spears and wooden beams at advancing forces; others dropped huge hooks into the sea to catch hold of enemy ships and tear them out of the water.[8]

The Roman historian Cassius Dio recounted how the city held out for three years against 'the armaments of practically the whole world'[9], long after the severed head of Niger, who had been captured trying to escape to Parthia, was displayed in full view of the city gates. In the end, rather than succumbing to the strength of any military onslaught, Byzantium was conquered by hunger. In AD 196, the famine-stricken city surrendered. Severus took swift revenge for its loyalty to the pretender emperor. Every magistrate and soldier was killed, and the famous impregnable walls were entirely demolished. Severus first 'deprived the city of its independence and its proud position as a state... treating it like a village,' wrote Cassius Dio, then 'visited every insult upon it'. The emperor was soon criticised, however, for eroding one of the most strategically important outposts of the Roman Empire – a bridge between Europe and Asia, and a bulwark against the barbarians to the east.[10]

Rebuilding work began at the start of the third century. In particular Severus ordered the construction, high on the hillside overlooking the sea, of the Hippodrome. This had come to be viewed as one of the most essential of all Roman civic buildings. Around the middle of the second century AD, the poet Juvenal had satirised the simplistic desires of the common people with the famous phrase *panem et circenses*[11] – bread and circuses. This, he concluded contemptuously, was what the political dream of Rome had been reduced to: citizens who cared only for food and entertainment. Juvenal's judgement was damning, yet it also appeared to be true. Indeed, the need to provide 'bread and circuses' had become a keystone of imperial foreign policy.

Throughout the far-flung territories of the empire, circuses or hippodromes, large and small, could be found at any significant settlement, from Western Europe to Asia and Africa. The games and entertainments they hosted were both a distraction and a unifying social event.[12] In Byzantium, the city he had reduced to ruin, Severus embarked upon a hippodrome of such size and ambition that it was rivalled in scale by only one other sporting arena: the original hippodrome, the Circus Maximus of Rome. When he died in AD 211, however, work shuddered to a halt. Only fragments of the grandstands and the sweeping curved end of the track – known as the *sphendone,* from the Greek for 'sling'[13] – had been completed.[14] It would be over a century before the circus really came to town.

On 11 May AD 330, Byzantium was dedicated as 'New Rome', and the empire's new capital was officially born.[15] Lavish ceremonies were held to celebrate the founding of the city. Every urban festival lays claim to special significance, but in this case the hype was justified. This day – a Monday[16] – marks one of the pivotal moments in history: the first in a cascade of events that would shape the modern world.

The man who founded the new capital, and from whom it would take its name, was born in the Balkans in the second half of the third century AD. Constantine was the son of Flavius Constantius, who held the position of *Caesar*. The Emperor Diocletian had created a new system of rule known as the Tetrarchy, splitting Rome into four parts, with two ruled by an *Augustus,* and two by their deputies, the *Caesars*. Diocletian had responsibility for Asia and the East; Maximian controlled Italy and Africa; Galerius was stationed in the area around the Danube; and Constantius held power in Gaul, Spain and Britain.[17] In AD 305, as Constantius was about to launch a major military campaign in Britain, Diocletian and Maximian stepped down as joint emperors, and passed their titles on to their *Caesars*. Constantine travelled to join up with his father, and together the newly fledged *Augustus* and his son led their legions northwards, beyond the frontier of Hadrian's Wall, to confront the wild and mysterious Picts.[18]

When Constantius died of illness at York in AD 306, his armies proclaimed his son Constantine as *Augustus* – Emperor of the West[19] – but as so often at the summit of Roman politics, dissension and counter-claims led to civil war. In the ensuing struggle for power, Constantine out-thought, out-fought and out-lasted all rivals. The decisive moment of his victory in the west came in AD 312, at the battle of Milvian Bridge, just outside the walls of Rome. Before the battle, the story goes, a great cross in the sky[20] appeared to Constantine. He interpreted this vision as a sign that his campaign had the support of the God of the Christians. When he entered Rome to be acclaimed by the people, Constantine did not, as tradition dictated, thank the pagan gods at the Altar of Victory in the Senate House. Romans had always attributed their successes on the world stage to the favours of the gods, but Constantine, it seemed, had found a new religion and a new god to lead him to glory. Of course, a changing of the heavenly guard also required a fundamental shift back on earth. Christianity was on its way to becoming the official religion of the Roman Empire.

While Constantine had managed to take the west by military force, the East remained in the hands of a second emperor – Licinius. The two men met at Milan in AD 313 to acknowledge each other's sovereignty, and to agree a so-called 'Edict of Toleration', granting the right of free worship to all religions across the empire. It was the first time in the history of Rome that the Christian faith had been given full official recognition and legal protection.[21]

The truce between the two men did not last long. Constantine marched against Licinius in AD 314, on the pretext that he was snuffing out an attempted political coup by an eastern general. There followed eight years of simmering tension, before Constantine made his move. In AD 323 he advanced eastwards once again, defeating Licinius in a series of battles culminating in a siege of Byzantium. Licinius was married to Constantine's sister, Constantia, and she interceded with her brother on her husband's behalf, hoping to secure a pardon in exchange for surrender. Constantine agreed, giving Licinius a posting in Thessalonica. He then promptly had him assassinated.[22]

Constantine had made the Roman Empire whole again. Yet he could muster little affection for its illustrious capital. He had not grown up a product of the city of Rome, and when he spent time there, he detected among its many ancient pagan statues and temples, and in the careless decadence of its people, the unmistakable whiff of decay.[23] Rome, he concluded, was no longer the future. That lay to the east, where the trade routes of Europe, Asia and Africa converged, and where the resurgent Persian Empire needed to be kept in check. The centre of the world had shifted away from Italy, towards the place guarding the passage between the Black Sea and the Aegean, a gateway between worlds: Byzantium.

The political, military and economic reasons for choosing the city on the Bosphorus as the new Rome were clear. Yet Constantine was conscious that the great cities of history all had a mythical or spiritual origin story. To serve this purpose, he told of a dream that had come to him as he slept at Byzantium. An old maid had appeared to him, wizened with age, yet at his touch she was transformed into a beautiful young woman. It was a sign, he claimed, that the rebuilding of the city was the will of heaven.[24]

To set the perimeter of his new capital, Constantine walked out with a spear far beyond the existing boundaries of Byzantium, marking the lien of the new city walls. As he continued outwards, his advisors began to express their concerns at the great size of the city their emperor was planning. His response was that God was the city's planner, and he with his spear merely the draughtsman. 'I shall advance,' he told them, 'until he who comes before me comes to a stop.'[25]

Constantinople – the 'City of Constantine' – used fragments of the empire's pagan past to help celebrate its Christian future. Its architects, somewhat tenuously, identified seven summits to match the seven hills of the 'Old' Rome, and they filled its grand new squares and public spaces with statues and sculptures imported from across the Roman world. In Constantine's Forum there was a 100-foot marble column transported from Heliopolis in Egypt, and on its summit was placed a bronze statue of Apollo, its head recast in the image of the emperor wearing a crown of the rays of the sun, a sceptre added to one hand, and a globe to the other.[26] Inside this outwardly pagan column, however, were said to be a number of precious Christian relics: the axe Noah used to build his Ark, the baskets Jesus passed out when feeding the five thousand, and an alabaster jar of ointment that had once belonged to Mary Magdalene.[27]

To emphasise that this was the new centre of the world, the city had is own *Milion*, or 'first milestone', the symbolic point from which all distances in the empire were measured. This was a deliberate move to replace the *Milliarium Aureum,* the bronze monument erected by Augustus in 20 BC to signify that all roads led to Rome. Constantinople's *Milion* comprised four large triumphal arches, set in a square to support a great central dome. On top of this dome was placed the most sacred object of the whole Christian faith. This artefact, brought from Jerusalem by Constantine's mother, the Empress

Helena, was the 'True Cross' itself, the crucifix that had borne the body of Jesus Christ.[28]

Constantine strove to create a city dominated by Christianity, recasting symbols of pagan worship as works of civic art and commissioning a series of churches dedicated to the peace, love and wisdom of God. But he was not prepared to let go of all the old ways of the empire. He built a grand new Senate House, the symbolic seat of government ever since the days of the Republic. It was the first time that a senatorial building had ever been constructed outside of Rome. Noble political families were lured to the east with the promise of opulent palaces, villas and extensive estates. At the same time, Constantinople's distance from traditional Roman society, with its deep-grained snobbery and nepotism, created opportunities for ambitious citizens from across the imperial world to advance through the ranks on the basis of talent rather than name.

Perhaps the most powerful incentive to all settlers was the promise of free grain to anyone who built a house within the city walls.[29] Constantine was well aware, however, that grain was only half of the equation for a happy population. To cater for the other half, he oversaw the completion of the vast structure of the Hippodrome[30], some 130 years after work on it had begun. The emperor may have found a new God, but he was not prepared to do without bread and circuses. On the day of the city's inauguration in AD 330, the sparkling new Hippodrome was the venue for the climax of the celebrations.[31] And to run the show, Constantine imported the best entertainers and chariot racers in the empire. The Greens and the Blues were on their way to Constantinople.

Before there were Greens and Blues, there were Reds and Whites. The mysterious origins of the colours – and the factions that grew to support them – appeared to date back to the founding of Rome in the eighth century BC. The sport of chariot racing, it was said, played a major role in the first days of the city. According to Livy, writing in his landmark work *The Early History of Rome,* Romulus himself organised a lavish festival in honour of Neptune, patron of horses, inviting all people from the surrounding lands to come and enjoy the hospitality and spectacle of Rome.

The natural amphitheatre between the Aventine and Palatine Hills became the setting for a series of chariot races that so enraptured the crowds that 'nobody had eyes or thoughts for anything else'.[32] This was just as Romulus had planned. Almost from the moment that it was established, Rome's future had been threatened by a chronic lack of wives for its predominantly male population. The entertainments were a deliberate distraction. At a given signal, the city's men burst through the crowds and seized all the unmarried young women.[33]

This site, with its queasy back-story of racing, abduction and rape, would later become the Circus Maximus. According to Livy, in the sixth century BC, Tarquinius Priscus, the fifth king of Rome, needed a venue for public games to celebrate his victory over the Latins. The flat ground of the valley floor was drained and wooden stands – or 'decks' as they were called – were erected on props that raised them some twelve feet high.[34] It was a humble beginning for what would become one of the grandest and most important structures in all of Rome. Over the centuries the circus evolved into a vast stadium of stone and marble, surrounded by an arcade of wooden shops known as *tabernae*, with seating for over 150,000 spectators, and the opportunity for another 100,000 to view the games from vantage points on the surrounding hillsides.

The circus was the Roman world in miniature. The sands of the arena were the earth; the central barrier, or *spina,* around which the chariots raced and which was often filled with water, was the sea; and the giant obelisk erected half-way between the turning posts, or *metae,* connected the circus to the sky. Chariots raced each other over seven laps, representing the days of the week; there were 24 races for the 24 hours of the day, and 12 starting blocks for the 12 months of the year.[35] The circular track was symbolic of the annual cycle of rebirth and renewal, and the four teams corresponded to the four seasons. Here, it seems, is the origin of the colours: the Reds were the sun and the summer; the Whites were the snows of winter; the Greens the verdant shoots of spring; and the Blues the cooling shades of autumn.[36] Every section of society was represented in the circus, from the emperor and the senate, down to the lowliest *pleb*; and every one of them, without exception, had a favourite colour.

Towards the end of the first century AD, the lawyer, magistrate and author Pliny the Younger expressed an intellectual's bemusement at the enduring appeal of the games. 'It amazes me that thousands and thousands of grown men should be like children, wanting to look at horses running and men standing on chariots over and over again,' he wrote. 'If it was the speed of the horses or the skill of the drivers that attracted them, there would be some sense in it – but in fact it is simply the colour. That is what they back and that is what fascinates them. Suppose halfway through the race the drivers were to change their colours, then the supporters' backing will change too and in a second they will abandon the drivers and horses whose names they shout as they recognize them from afar. Such is the overpowering influence of a single worthless shirt.'[37] This forensic, lawyerly analysis of the absurdity of all sporting fandom is witheringly accurate. And of course, it completely misses the point. What centuries of racing and competition had created was the delicious and addictive tribalism of belonging. The fate of the colours in the arena was intimately bound up with the self-worth of the supporters. One part of the city would always leave the circus in elation, the other in despair. Chariot racing wasn't life and death. It was much more important than that.

Supporters of the Greens and the Blues were known to take their obsession to extremes. In the second century AD, the philosopher Galen witnessed with astonishment fans smelling the dung of their team's horses to check that the animals were on the right diet.[38] Others would throw into the arena inscriptions carved in lead, wood or stone, known as curse tablets; these called on evil forces to bring misfortune, injury or death on opposing horses or racers.[39]

The emperors themselves were not immune to the fanaticism of the factions. Nero would wear a green cloak to the circus, decorate the grandstands in green cloth, and fill the arena floor with pebbles and dust from chrysocolla, a green mineral rock normally used to solder gold.[40] Caligula was also a supporter of the Greens, and, according to Cassius Dio, it was not unknown for him to poison horses and charioteers belonging to rival teams. Other Green emperors included Domitian, Verus and Commodus, while the Blues counted Vitellius and Caracalla among their patrons. Imperial favour always seemed to fall on one or other of these two factions: by the time of the empire the Reds and Whites appeared to have been reduced to also-rans.[41]

As Republic transmuted into Empire, the circus started to assume a peculiar political role. Emperors were expected to attend the games – and as much out of duty as for pleasure. Those who did not were roundly criticised and even accused of disloyalty and dishonour.[42] Paradoxically, in a dictatorship the best way to maintain power proved to be through popularity. The circus gave the people – hundreds of thousands of them all at once – a personal audience with their 'first citizen'. Huge crowds would sing or chant an emperor's name in praise. But they would also question him on policies that concerned them, most commonly the price of corn or high taxes.[43] And inevitably given the huge size of the gathering, things could descend quite rapidly into agitation and disorder.

Writing in AD 41, the Jewish-Roman historian Josephus gave an account of events in the circus just weeks before the murder of Caligula. 'At this time occurred the chariot races. This is a kind of spectator sport to which the Romans are fanatically devoted. They gather enthusiastically in the circus and there the assembled throngs make requests of the emperors according to their own pleasure.' Emperors who granted the wishes of the circus crowd, he continued, were very popular.[44] In this instance, however, Caligula was not prepared to cooperate. Refusing the calls from the crowd to reduce taxes, Josephus describes how Caligula 'had no patience with them, and when they shouted louder and louder, he dispatched agents among them in all directions with orders to arrest any who shouted, to bring them forward at once and to put them to death... The number of those executed in such summary fashion was very large.'[45]

Cassius Dio was another who observed the attitude of Caligula to the circus crowd. He concluded that, 'with an angry ruler on one side and a hostile people on the other' there could be only one winner: the emperor.[46] This may have been true in the short term. But ultimately, losing the support of the mob was the quickest way to meet the assassin's knife. What might at first appear a potent demonstration of absolute power can also be seen by the regime's enemies as an open invitation to strike. Within weeks of this incident, Caligula was overthrown and murdered.[47]

Other emperors were more inclined to heed the will of their citizens. In AD 19, after a public outcry, Tiberius announced to the circus his intention to fix corn prices. On another occasion he was taken to account for having removed a favourite statue from the baths of Agrippa and set it up in his own home. At the first chance they had, the crowd in the circus requested that he put it back.[48] In AD 58, Nero was so agitated by a protest against tax collectors that he resolved to overhaul the whole revenue system.[49] According to Pliny the Younger, Trajan was so enthusiastic about this public forum that 'requests were granted, unspoken wishes were anticipated, and he did not hesitate to press us urgently to make fresh demands'.[50]

The dialogue between the crowd and the emperor had grown into an almost ritual performance, an extension of the entertainments that played out on the arena sands. As a result, it gradually fell to the most passionate and vocal of the circus fans to lead the cheer for or against imperial policy. Through sheer fanatical exuberance, Rome's chariot racing 'ultras' – the fans of the Greens and Blues – became the political mouthpiece of the people.

The Hippodrome of Constantinople, like every other arena throughout the empire, took the Circus Maximus of Rome as its template, but it was no replica. For one thing, it was built on a hillside, rather than on the level ground of a valley floor. To ensure that its racecourse was completely flat, its southern end – the great curved semi-circle of the *sphendone* – was supported by a series of massive arched stone vaults, which dropped below the level of the arena and squared off the land as it sloped down sharply towards the sea.[51] The Hippodrome itself was over 1,500 feet long, and was surrounded by an arcade of columns, an internal tunnel allowing spectators to enter from the city, make their way to their reserved section, and then emerge into the arena.[52] Some forty tiers[53] of stone and wooden seating stretched out in a U-shape around the track, broken only at the northern end, where the chariots entered through twelve starting gates taking the form of a series of large triumphal arches.

On top of these gates were copper and bronze sculptures of *quadrigae*: chariots drawn by four horses, just like the chariots that raced around the Hippodrome sands.[54] At least one of these *quadrigae* was said to be the work of the Greek master-sculptor Lysippos, one of a number of pieces produced for Alexander the Great in the fourth century BC. The story went that it was seized from the Greeks by the Romans as a spoil of war and was installed in the Campus Martius by Augustus at the beginning of the first century AD. Three centuries later it caught the eye of Constantine – and joined a great haul of antiquities transported from Rome to Constantinople.

This trend continued in the *spina,* the central barrier of the racetrack, where at least two-dozen ancient monuments had been transplanted from across the empire.[55] There was the Serpent Column: a bronze sculpture of three intertwined snakes that had once formed a support for a golden tripod in the sanctuary of Apollo at Delphi. Hercules was depicted in two giant bronze statues: one captured him wrestling with the fabled Nemean Lion, and the other showed him collapsing in exhaustion after completing the cleaning of the Augean stables. This latter statue, also thought to be the work of Lysippos, was sixty feet tall and had once adorned the Capitoline Hill in Rome, until Constantine removed it at the beginning of the fourth century AD.[56] There were exquisite representations of Helen of Troy and the Greek gods, Zeus, Artemis, Juno and Minerva, along with a series of exotic, sometimes fantastical animals, from lions, crocodiles and hyenas, to sphinxes and dragons.[57]

There was also a conscious effort to represent the great figures of 'old' Rome on the *spina*. A she-wolf, with the twins Romulus and Remus suckling at her teats, and the demi-god horsemen Castor and Pollux, represented the empire's earliest beginnings. Julius Caesar and the Emperors Augustus and Diocletian stood atop great marble columns alongside one of the defining images of Roman triumph: the imperial eagle grasping a snake in its claws.[58] In direct reference to the Circus Maximus, a giant obelisk of pink granite was erected at the midpoint of the *spina*. Constructed by Pharaoh Thutmosis III around 1490 BC, this obelisk was one of two taken from the Temple of Amon in Thebes, to be installed in the Hippodrome in AD 390 by the Emperor Theodosius, who set it on top of a square marble pedestal.[59] This new base was adorned with a series of sculptures, first showing the obelisk being raised upright on the *spina*, and then capturing a chariot race in action, with Theodosius pictured handing out laurels to the winners.

This contemporary embellishment was typical of the way monuments were treated in the arena. The sculptures and statuary were constantly being added to by works depicting the present imperial family – and even, on occasion, famous Hippodrome competitors. A particular favourite was Porphyrios, the greatest chariot racer of all. A least two statues were erected on the *spina* in celebration of his remarkable achievements on the track.[60] Porphyrios was one of very few who crossed the divide between the Greens and the Blues, switching his allegiance back and forth in order to demonstrate that his skill and superiority could prevail no matter which colour he wore or whose horses he raced.[61]

Just as elsewhere in Constantinople, the *spina's* display of pagan iconography – at the heart of a now ostensibly Christian city – was a calculated act. In effect, these monuments were stripped of their religious provenance, and displayed as amusing relics of the old faiths. As the Christian historian Eusebius put it in his fourth-century *Life of Constantine*, the Hippodrome was 'filled with brazen statues of the most exquisite workmanship, which had been dedicated in every province, and which the deluded victims of superstition had long vainly honoured as gods with numberless victims and burnt sacrifices.' Now, however, the 'emperor held up the very objects of their worship to be the ridicule and sport of all beholders'.[62] Arranged like trophies in the centre of the arena, they were symbols not only of conquered peoples, but also of conquered faiths.

Not everyone could let go of their superstitions quite so easily. Some believed the statues were evil to their core, and that within their shells ancient demons were encased. One myth held that the face of the man who would ultimately destroy Constantinople was depicted on the underside of one of Pegasus's hoofs.[63] Hundreds of years after the Hippodrome was built, the medieval historian Niketas related the bizarre story of Euphrosyne, wife of the Emperor Alexios III, who had the giant bronze statue of Hercules flogged in an attempt either to punish or to appease the old gods.[64]

The *spina* monuments emphasised that the Hippodrome was not just an arena for sporting occasions. This was the ceremonial centre of the city, the stage for every major political or celebratory event. For centuries, the seating around the curve of the *sphendone* was used for the most popular public spectacle after chariot racing – execution. A variety of gruesome methods was used to dispatch enemies of the state, from decapitation and mutilation to burning alive and, in the case of the unfortunate Emperor Andronicus, being strung upside down between two pillars and methodically butchered.[65]

For better or for worse, the fate of the ruling elite was tied intimately to the circus. Indeed, so close was this relationship that the vast imperial palace was built adjoining the eastern grandstand, and a passage led directly between it and the arena. A wall of sound would greet the emperor on race day: the chatter, shouts and chanting of the Constantinople faithful. His box –the *kathisma* – was built out of gleaming marble and was set looking over the midpoint of the track, halfway between the starting gates and the *sphendone*. The emperor took his seat among a host of attendant officials, priests and *magisters*, and, when he looked out over the *spina* to the opposite grandstand, he saw two bright, seething blocks of colour.[66] The Greens and the Blues stared straight back at him.

In the first decade of the sixth century AD, three young sisters walked through the grandstands of the Hippodrome towards a group of Green chariot racers and entertainers. The girls' mother, an acrobat and actress, had placed wreaths on the girls' heads, given them flowers to hold, and directed them to appeal to the employers of their recently deceased father – the Greens. The three daughters were Comito, the eldest at six years old, Theodora and Anastasia. Their father had been the Greens' Master of the Bears. Their mother had recently remarried, and she hoped that the faction could be prevailed upon to appoint her new husband as animal trainer. Although stage-managed astutely, the appeal was unsuccessful. The Dancing Master of the Greens had already been bribed to remove the mother and her husband from their roles. The three girls' solemn entreaties from the circus sidelines were ignored.

At least, they were ignored by the Greens. The Blues had been watching the scene with interest, and they saw the opportunity, on the great public stage of the circus, to show compassion where their opponents had shown none. By coincidence their own Master of the Bears had just died, and so they were able to offer the mother, her new husband and the three daughters, the security of their patronage. They became part of a new family and they pledged a new allegiance. No longer were they Greens. From now on, they were *Blues*.[67]

If the middle daughter, Theodora, had looked up above the sands towards the imperial box, she would have seen her future. This lowly circus girl would one day take her place in the *kathisma* as Empress. And as she surveyed the cheering grandstands before her, she would remember the Greens who had abandoned her, and the Blues who had taken her in.

Around the mid-point of the sixth century AD, Procopius of Caesarea, adviser to the general Belisarius, wrote three compelling works of history. The first, which was begun around AD 545 and finally completed eight volumes later in AD 553, was *The History of the Wars.*

This was an account of the Byzantine Emperor Justinian's campaign to re-conquer the western half of the Roman Empire: territories now under barbarian rule, stretching from North Africa, through Italy and Rome itself, and on to the Iberian Peninsula. The final work was known simply as *Buildings*, and it described, in great detail and with fulsome praise, the many wondrous construction projects undertaken by Justinian during his reign – including the cathedral church of St Sophia in Constantinople, one of the most spectacular, original and ambitious examples of religious architecture the world had ever seen.[68]

Between these two works, however, Procopius had written something different, something unique. It went under several titles – *Anecdota*, *Unpublished Writings*, or, most enticing of all, *The Secret History*. Procopius never intended for it to be published during his lifetime: 'it is impossible,' he wrote in the introduction, 'either to avoid detection by swarms of spies or if caught to escape death in its most agonising form.' In his official works he glorified the life and achievements of the political elite. But in this illicit manuscript he promised to tell the real story, 'the events hitherto passed over in silence'. In particular he wanted to expose the blackness at the very heart of Byzantium, an insidious and tyrannical evil which threatened the very fate of civilisation. *The Secret History,* so Procopius promised in his opening lines, would reveal 'all the wicked deeds' committed by the Emperor Justinian and his wife, the Empress Theodora.[69]

It is Procopius who recounts the story of Theodora in the circus as a little girl. Taken in isolation, it makes for a poignant tale. Yet it is merely a precursor to one of the most sustained, vitriolic and viciously gossipy character assassinations ever put down on paper. Once Theodora and her sisters had joined up with their new benefactors the Blues, their mother put them to work on the stage. What this also meant, according to Procopius, was a life of prostitution. Theodora first carried the bench for her elder sister Comito to sit on while waiting for prospective clients – until she, too, was old enough, and 'sold her youth to passers-by, working with nearly her entire body'. By day she was a theatre performer with excellent comic timing, and prepared to perform fully nude; by night she was the star attraction at Constantinople's most exclusive orgies, with a reputation for insatiable lust. 'She would lie with all her fellow diners the whole night through,' wrote Procopius, 'and when she had worn them all out she would turn to their servants, as many as thirty on occasion, and copulate with every one of them.'

Such was Theodora's appetite, Procopius claimed, that she would bemoan that 'nature had not made the holes in her nipples larger so that she could devise another variety of intercourse there'. In the theatre, she contrived an act that drew on her famous talents for flamboyant lasciviousness. Lying on the floor, she would have stage-hands 'sprinkle barley grains over her private parts', whereupon trained geese would 'pick them off with their beaks one by one and swallow them'.[70]

For a time Theodora left Constantinople, travelling to Libya as the mistress of a high-ranking government official. The relationship soon turned sour, however, and she was kicked out into the street. Her only option was to return to the profession that had sustained her since childhood, 'making her body the tool of her illegal trade'.[71] Travelling first to Alexandria, she then worked her way eastwards from city to city, until at last she returned to Constantinople. Somewhere along the way, she claimed to have found God. And once back in the imperial capital, she found something even more useful than that. It was the Holy Grail for a former courtesan looking to go straight – the attention of the most powerful man in the world: Justinian. After the death of Justinian's mother, the Empress Lupicina, who was bitterly opposed to her son's choice of partner, the pair were married in the church of St Sophia in AD 525. As far as Procopius was concerned, Justinian's union with a woman 'double-dyed with every kind of horrible pollution and guilty over and over again of infanticide by wilful abortion'[72] was damning evidence of his moral sickness.

On 4 April AD 527, with the Emperor Justin on his death bed and relieved of his duties due to extreme senility, Justinian and Theodora were crowned co-emperor and empress of Rome. Behind this event Procopius saw the terrifying shadow of the Antichrist. Politicians and courtiers who had once watched Theodora perform her lewd acts in the theatre suddenly fell at her feet as if she were a goddess.[73] What they could not see, lamented Procopius, was that Justinian and his wife were not human, but 'a pair of blood-thirsty demons... plotting together to find the easiest and swiftest means of destroying all men and all their works.'[74]

There was no doubt that chaos and anarchy were brewing in the streets of Constantinople. Theodora had been a passionate supporter of the Blues since the betrayal of her family by the Greens in childhood. Justinian was a long time patron of the Blues. He had run with the partisans during a misspent youth, and later used them as petty enforcers, discreetly deploying their wanton thuggery to achieve political gain. It was even rumoured that their mutual affection for the Blues was what had first brought the emperor and empress together.

With Justinian and Theodora on the throne, the Blues spread throughout the infrastructure of the state. Crime was on the rise – robbery, vandalism, assault, rape and murder – yet if those responsible wore blue livery, the law looked the other way. At first supporters of the Greens were singled out for mistreatment, but soon indiscriminate violence and disorder spiralled out of control. The emperor and empress continued to 'openly spur on the Blues'. The result, wrote Procopius, was that 'the entire Roman Empire was shaken to the foundations as if an earthquake or deluge had struck it, as if every city had fallen to the enemy. For everywhere there was utter chaos.'[75]

Constantinople was on the brink. The Hippodrome would push the city over the edge.

On 13 January AD 532 Justinian took his seat in the *kathisma* and announced the opening of the games.[76] From the moment of his arrival in the Hippodrome, it was clear that there was something wrong. Angry chants and vitriolic insults were commonplace in the arena. But they normally passed back and forth between the factions, a constant push and pull centred on the vast blocks of segregated seating for the Blues and the Greens. The open dialogue between the emperor and the factions – passed down from the Circus Maximus in Rome – was still a central tradition of the arena, but it had come to follow a rigid, formalised structure.[77] These protocols were being ignored completely. Justinian was assailed by shouts and cries from every corner of the Hippodrome – a raucous barracking that shook the tiers of the grandstands. The emperor suddenly felt very exposed and isolated in his marble box.

For some time the atmosphere in the Hippodrome had been growing increasingly rancorous. At a previous race meeting the dialogue between the Greens and the emperor had broken down almost irreparably. What had begun as a series of respectful entreaties to Justinian for fairness – appended by chants wishing the emperor the longest of lives – descended into an ugly slanging match.

'We are poor, we are innocent, we are injured, we dare not pass through the streets,' the Greens had begun. 'A general persecution is exercised against our name and colour. Let us die O Emperor, but let us die by your command and for your service.'[78] Justinian remained unmoved, refusing to admit any favouritism towards the Blues. The Greens grew more desperate, accusing their ruler of oppression and of a failure to follow the laws of the empire. An increasingly irritated Justinian, speaking through his *mandator*, or herald, continued to ignore the substance of the complaints, suggesting instead that the Greens were not the victims, but rather the perpetrators, of criminal behaviour. Here the dialogue took a turn for the worse. The Greens informed their emperor that they wished his father had never been born, because he had produced a son who was a blasphemer, a tyrant and a murderer. 'Do you despise your lives?' thundered an incredulous Justinian. The Greens answered with their feet. To the delighted catcalls of the Blues, they walked out of the Hippodrome *en masse*.[79]

Disorder and riots were beginning to plague Constantinople. After a series of particularly violent clashes in the streets between Greens and Blues, seven members of each faction were arrested and sentenced to death. On this occasion, perhaps stung into action by the exchange in the circus, Justinian was not prepared to ignore the wrongdoings of his favoured colour. Five of the criminals were executed, but the final two enjoyed a last-minute reprieve. As the nooses were tightened around their necks, the entire gallows upon which they stood collapsed. The watching crowd saw this as an omen from God that the men's lives should be spared, and they were given sanctuary by a chapter of monks in the church of St Laurence. Most significant of all: one survivor was a Blue, and the other a Green.[80]

This failed execution had taken place just three days before the games in the Hippodrome.[81] Justinian himself may have come to watch the chariot races. But for once, he was on his own. Every other person in the arena was there to hear the emperor pardon the two faction members. For twenty-one races, the crowd kept up their hectoring cries towards the imperial box. Justinian met the calls with a resolute silence. Then, during the 22nd race, something remarkable happened.[82] As one, the whole Hippodrome began to chant, over and over, the famous watchword of the arena: *Nika!*[83] – translated variously as *win*, *vanquish* or *conquer*. The Blues and Greens had set aside their fundamental differences for a common cause.

For the Greens, the emperor's refusal to agree a pardon was further proof that they were being singled out for cruel and unjust treatment. For the Blues, it seemed a betrayal after so many years of loyal servitude to Justinian. As the chants of '*Nika! Nika!*' resounded ever more forcefully in the stone bowl of the circus, the emperor and his entourage made a hasty exit from the *kathisma,* disappearing down the tunnel into the relative safety of the imperial palace. Behind them, the Hippodrome became the epicentre of a vast, rampaging riot.[84]

The people streamed out of the arena and set about looting and vandalising the central district of the richest city in the world. They assaulted the palace of the Prefect, killing all his guards and freeing the inmates of the adjoining prison, before setting fire to both buildings.[85] Isolated acts of arson were spreading through Constantinople to create a dangerous conflagration. Architectural masterpieces from the time of Constantine were reduced to smouldering rubble. Churches all over the city, including the St Sophia, were in flames; the wonderful

Baths of Zeuxippus and the august Senate House were burnt to the ground; hospices were consumed with their ailing patients still inside; and even sections of Justinian's vast imperial palace were set alight. The Forum of Constantine, along with its great statues in bronze and gold, was shattered into pieces, and its precious metals were either stolen, or melted away to nothing in the ferocity of the blaze.[86]

On the second day of the riot, Justinian attempted to re-open the games. The people responded by setting fire to a section of the Hippodrome.[87] *Panem et circenses* were not going to placate the mob this time. Amid the chaos, the disturbances took on an increasingly political hue. The original goal of pardoning the two condemned Greens and Blues had been forgotten. Instead – perhaps directed by some dissident senators within the imperial government – the rioters returned to the Hippodrome to demand the dismissal of the Ministers of Justice and Finance, Tribonian and John of Cappadocia.[88]

While Tribonian was blamed for the lawlessness that had pervaded Constantinople, the real hatred of the people was reserved for John of Cappadocia – the tax man who bled citizens dry with patrician public policies, yet who lived a private life of excess and indulgence. 'He flung himself completely into the sordid life of a drunken scoundrel,' wrote Procopius, continuing:

> 'For up to the time of lunch each day he would plunder the property of his subjects, and for the rest of the day occupy himself with drinking and with wanton deeds of lust. And he was utterly unable to control himself, for he ate food until he vomited, and he was always ready to steal money and more ready to bring it out and spend it.'[89]

Against the backdrop of the smoking city, Justinian returned to the Hippodrome to meet the people. He agreed to sack the two ministers, then confessed his faults as a ruler, swearing on the Holy Gospels that he would pardon all citizens if they stopped rioting.[90] It appeared, however, that things had already progressed too far. Terrified by a mob revelling in their new-found power, the emperor retreated to his

Tower of Babel' by Pieter Bruegel the Elder, 1563. In Bruegel's painting, architecture is the ultimate metaphor for man's conceit and hubris. *Kunsthistorisches Museum,* Vienna.

1 October 2009. A US Army Black Hawk helicopter takes off from Tallil Air Base in Iraq to fly ast the ruins of the remaining tier of the Ziggurat of Ur, as reconstructed by Saddam Hussein. © Everett / REX Shutterstock

Arthur Evans's brightly painted concrete 'reconstitution' of the north portico of the Palace of Kin
Minos at Knossos, Crete.

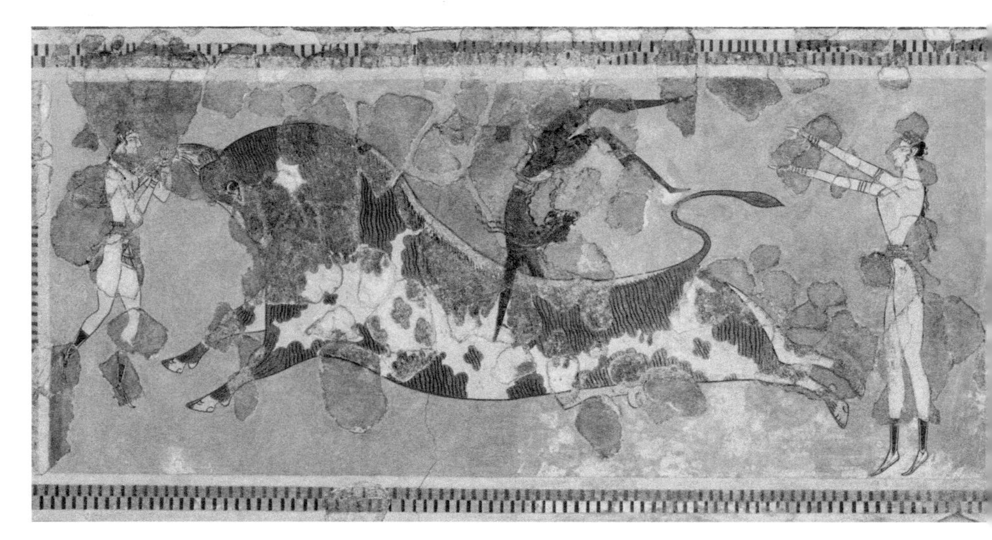

The extensively restored bull-leaping fresco at Knossos: the darker spots are the remnants of th
original c1500 BC Minoan artwork unearthed by Evans. The rest is the work of Émile Gilliéro
père in 1906-7.

The ruins near the summit of the citadel of Mycenae, in the mountains of the Peloponnese.

The golden death mask of Agamemnon?

An armed tourist guide walks on the cliffs overlooking the site of Amarna in Egypt. It was here, on the banks of the Nile, that Akhenaten built his short-lived 'sun city'. © Kenneth Garrett

The restored Queen Nefertiti bust in the *Neues Museum*, Berlin. The bust was rediscovered at Amarna in 1912, still buried where it had fallen from a termite-ridden shelf thousands of years before.

'The Destruction of the Temple in Jerusalem' (1867) by Francesco Hayez. Hayez based his painting on the account by Josephus of the architecture of the Temple, and the Roman siege and sack of Jerusalem. Courtesy of *Galleria d'Arte Moderna*, Venice.

The Temple Mount – or *al-Haram al-Sharif* – topped by the golden Dome of the Rock, as seen from the direction of the Mount of Olives.

Ancient ruins became part of the fascist pageantry of Adolf Hitler's meeting with Benito Mussolini in Rome on 3 May 1938. Drawing by Achille Beltrame (1871-1945) in the Italian weekly newspaper *La Domenica del Corriere*, 1938. By permission of De Agostini Picture Library.

'Napoleon's Army Enters Rome, 15 February 1798' by Hippolyte Lecomte (1781-1857)

The underwater remains of ancient Alexandria © Stephane Compoint

The Great Fire of London, with Ludgate Hill and Old St Paul's in the background, c.1670. Artist unkown. Paul Mellon Collection.

palace, and began making panicked preparations to flee the city. At the same time, he ejected from his court Hypatius and Pompey, the nephews of the former Emperor Anastasius, fearing the two brothers were part of a plot to depose and assassinate him.[91]

Ships waited ready, moored to the garden stairs at the rear of the palace, with orders to take the imperial court and its greatest treasures away across the Bosphorus. Justinian's courage had clearly failed. His wife's, on the other hand, had not. Theodora, displaying the pluck of the street child who had long ago resolved never to take a backward step, announced that she would rather face death than give up her hard-won position as Empress.

'The present time, above all others, is inopportune for flight, even though it bring safety,' she told the emperor and his council:

> 'For while it is impossible for a man who has seen the light not also to die, for one who has been an Emperor it is unendurable to be a fugitive. May I never be separated from this purple, and may I not live that day on which those who meet me shall not address me as mistress. If, now, it is your wish to save yourself, O Emperor, there is no difficulty. For we have much money, and there is the sea, here the boats. However consider whether it will not come about after you have been saved that you would gladly exchange that safety for death. For as for myself, I approve a certain ancient saying that royalty is a good burial-shroud.'[92]

As always, Justinian bowed to the will of his wife. Rather than escape, the new plan was to muster the remaining loyalists within the imperial armies, and send them out to fight. Meanwhile, the mob had learned of the dismissal of Hypatius and Pompey, and were scouring the city in search of the two brothers. Hypatius was found first. He was carried high above the crowd and taken to the Hippodrome. There, he was installed on the imperial throne in the *kathisma* and, in the absence of a crown, a golden necklace was brought out from the crowd and placed on his head.[93] The people had chosen a new emperor. With growing excitement, they called on Hypatius to lead them into the palace, where they would depose Justinian by force.[94]

This unofficial coronation ceremony had, however, played directly into the hands of the imperial forces. Almost all the rioters were gathered in one place – milling around on the circus floor. Justinian's two loyal generals, Belisarius and Mundus, commanded some 3,000 veterans, battle-hardened from recent campaigns against Persia.[95] They picked their way through the broken ruins of the city centre to take up positions at opposite ends of the Hippodrome. Among the crowd, loyal members of the Blues declared themselves ready once again to show their support for Justinian by turning on their temporary allies, the Greens.[96] A messenger reported that, with every passing minute, Hypatius 'sat more confidently in the imperial box'. On hearing this, the emperor gave the order to attack.[97]

What followed was less a battle than a massacre. Many of the rioters were unarmed, all exits from the Hippodrome were blocked, and the mob had no time to order its ranks to meet the onslaught. Within minutes the arena sands were saturated with blood. Fierce fighting gave way to methodical slaughter. Bodies were piled upon bodies, and by the time the carnage had come to an end, some 30,000 people lay dead[98] – almost a tenth of the entire population of Constantinople.[99] Hypatius and his brother were thrown at Justinian's feet and accused of treason. They pleaded that the rioters had captured them under duress, and the emperor, whose need to be liked bred a tendency to mercy, was on the point of awarding a pardon. Once again, Theodora stepped in. If her husband let the brothers live, she told him, there would always be the danger they could be used again as figureheads of rebellion. The next day Hypatius and Pompey were executed in private, and their bodies thrown into the sea.[100]

Other bodies were rather harder to dispose of – namely the tens of thousands rotting in the arena. The games, the tinderbox of insurrection, were suspended for several years, and the Hippodrome, which had been variously damaged during the rioting, underwent gradual repair and reconstruction. A persistent, macabre rumour held that the new marble tiers of the grandstands gained some unconventional foundations. The Hippodrome, if you believed the whispered gossip, was now a 'vast charnel-house' rebuilt out of the bones of the Nika rioters.[101]

In April 1204, Robert de Clari, a Frankish knight of the Fourth Crusade, described with wonder the Hippodrome of Constantinople:

> 'That place was a full crossbow shot and half in length, and about one in breadth... Round this open space were thirty or forty tiers of stairs, where the Greeks went up to see the games; and there were lodges there, very magnificent and very noble, where sat the Emperor and the Empress... together with other nobles and ladies.'

What transfixed de Clari most of all was the statuary of the *spina*: 'on top of this wall were statues of men and of women, of horses, and oxen, and camels, and bears and lions and all manner of other beasts, cast in copper.' These, he continued, 'were so cunningly wrought and so naturally shaped' that no living craftsman could come close to matching their fine detail and exquisite beauty.[102]

De Clari's presence in Constantinople in the spring of 1204 was the result of the bizarre sequence of events known as the Fourth Crusade. In 1198, Innocent III had gained the papal throne. One of his first actions had been to announce the need for another mission against the Muslims to the east – specifically to the Holy Land, where Jerusalem itself was in the hands of the pagans. The plan was for the crusaders to travel first by sea to Alexandria, then to advance by land through Egypt into Palestine.[103]

An enormous fleet was required to transport the army. The Republic of Venice, always with a nose for business, saw an opportunity. They would build the ships for a discounted fee – payable on delivery – on condition that they receive half the spoils of the holy war. But when the crusader army assembled in Venice in June 1202, it was less than a third of the anticipated size. With such a paltry force, the knights would never be able to pay Venice for the fleet.[104]

The Doge, Enrico Dandolo, realised that he had a powerful asset at his disposal. He struck a deal with the crusaders. He would write off what was owed, on condition that they accompany him to lay siege to the city of Zara – Zadar in present day Croatia – which had rebelled against Venetian rule and was under the protection of both the King of Hungary and the Pope. They set sail on 8 November 1202, and within a week, the city had fallen. The attack so infuriated Innocent III, however, that he excommunicated his entire crusade. He later relented, absolving everyone – apart from the Venetians. It was a chaotic start to a mission supposedly bound for the Holy Land, and it would grow even stranger. Prince Alexius, the exiled nephew of the Byzantine Emperor Alexius III, contacted Dandolo and the leaders of the crusade as they wintered their fleet at Zara. He offered them 200,000 silver marks to help him claim his rightful place on the imperial throne.[105] The Doge himself, now in his eighties and almost completely blind, agreed to lead the offensive. He had represented Venetian interests in Constantinople in the 1180s, had no love for the Byzantines, and clearly could not resist one last adventure.

In June 1203, the fleet arrived and began to surround the city. Within weeks the siege began, and days later the city's defences were breached. Remarkably, the sightless Dandolo was the first Venetian to jump from his ship to plant the standard of the Venice in the ground of Constantinople.[106] On 1 August 1203 Alexius IV was crowned emperor. When he checked the imperial coffers, however, the new ruler was horrified to discover that he could not pay the crusaders their promised reward. After months of stalling, Alexius was finally deposed and murdered by his own people. The new emperor, Alexius V, announced that the Bzyantines would not pay the 200,000 marks, since his predecessor had had no right to make any deal in the first place.

Without the money, the crusaders could not clear their debt to Venice – unless, Dandolo suggested, they sack the city. No one except the Doge wanted another war. But war had become inevitable.[107] On 9 April 1204 Constantinople was attacked once again by combined crusader and Venetian forces. Before the offensive, Dandolo drew up yet another agreement – carefully agreeing a split of the city's spoils.[108]

The devastation was terrible. The medieval chronicler Niketas Choniates, who witnessed the carnage, wrote of how 'Constantine's fair city, the common delight and boast of all nations, was laid waste by fire and blackened by soot, taken and emptied of all wealth, public and private, as well as that which was consecrated to God.' Everything was up for grabs. 'These haters of the beautiful,' continued Niketas, 'did not allow the statues standing in the Hippodrome and other marvellous works of art to escape destruction'.[109]

De Clari's fellow knights may have shared his amazement at the sublime artworks of the *spina*, but if they did, their wonder did not last long. Hundreds of bronze statues were melted down 'into worthless copper coins'. Niketas recalls with particular vividness the looters toppling the colossal statue of Hercules: the loop of one of the ropes used to pull it to ground, which was fastened around the hero's thumb, was the size of a man's belt.[110] Years of neglect had left the structure of the Hippodrome somewhat down-at-heel, but it had still been in regular use for games and chariot-racing at the beginning of the thirteenth century. The crusaders left it in ruins – and in the process destroyed one of the most fabulous collections of antiquities ever assembled.[111]

The *quadriga* of Constantinople's Hippodrome, now in the Basilica San Marco in Venice. © Wikicommons

Some fragments survived. Unlike the Franks, the Venetians were not blinded by the need for money, and brought a more refined eye to their looting.[112] Statues and sculptures were removed intact from their columns and pedestals, to be packaged and returned as victory totems.[113] Greatest of all were the four horses taken from above the Hippodrome starting gates: the *quadriga* fashioned by Lysippos in the fourth century BC. The horses had travelled from Greece to Rome to Constantinople – and now they were on their way to Venice. Once there, they were installed above the main portal of the western façade of St Mark's Basilica, as if about to charge out across the city's great central piazza.[114]

The horses' travels were not yet over. Almost six centuries later, Napoleon Bonaparte marched into Italy at the head of a conquering army. As he advanced through Europe, he ensured that the continent's finest art treasures were gathered up in his wake, to be transported to Paris as trophies. For some two decades the *quadriga* occupied the summit of a Parisian triumphal arch. After Napoleon's final defeat at the Battle of Waterloo, the Austrian emperor ordered the return of the horses to Venice, where they remain today – though not in their original position.[115] The four steeds that rear up on the balcony of St Mark's are replicas: the originals are stabled inside the basilica's museum, where they are protected from the threats of time, decay, pollution, and theft.[116] Given their track record, however, it would be foolish to suggest that their long journey is finally at an end...

In the late afternoon of 29 May 1453, the twenty-one-year-old Ottoman Sultan Mehmet II rode triumphantly towards the city of Constantinople.[117] He first passed through its great outer walls, which had been shattered by a relentless barrage from a gigantic, twenty-seven-foot-long bronze cannon[118], and picked his way through streets painted red by the blood of dead Muslims and Christians. The battle was over, the looting had begun, and the lives of the people of Constantinople were forfeit. They were now at the mercy of the Ottoman ruler. Surrounded by his imams, his viziers, and his colossal bodyguards, the Sultan arrived at the great domed cathedral of St Sophia, the masterpiece created by Justinian nine centuries earlier in the aftermath of the *Nika* riots. No more, he proclaimed, would the Christian mysteries be celebrated on the great altar: now and for evermore, this house of God would be a mosque. Icons and crosses were torn down, and mosaics stripped from the walls. That very evening, the Sultan's *muezzin* climbed to the summit of St Sophia's highest turret, and the Muslim call to prayer drifted out over the city.[119]

From St Sophia, Mehmet made his way to the city's old Palace, the vast structure built by Constantine in the fourth century. This one-time architectural jewel of 'New Rome', with its elaborate complex of buildings, pavilions, gardens, vaults and harbours descending down a steep, terraced hillside to the shoreline of the Sea of Marmara, was in ruins. It was not, however, the Muslim siege that had caused this destruction. In the eleventh century, the Emperor Alexios I had moved the imperial residence to a new palace at Blachernae. The old palace continued to be used for ceremonial and administrative purposes, but its lustre faded fast. During the sack of Constantinople by the knights of the Fourth Crusade, it was looted, plundered and vandalised, and a half-burnt-out shell was left behind.[120] There was no money either to repair or demolish what remained, and so it was left empty on its hill overlooking the city and the sea. Towards the end of the thirteenth century, adding insult to injury, Emperor Baldwin II had removed many of the palace's lead roofs, selling them on in a desperate bid to supplement the imperial coffers.[121]

Fourteen hundred years after it was founded by Augustus, the Roman Empire had shrunk to a tiny circle of land surrounding the city of Constantinople. The mouldering ruin of the palace had become a living relic of fallen glory, and a mirror for the slow but inexorable decline of Byzantium and Rome. As Mehmet walked among its roofless rooms and empty, dusty corridors, he is said to have recited two lines by the Persian poet Saadi:

The spider weaves the curtains in the palace of the Caesars
The owl calls the watches in the towers of Afrasiyab[122]

Remarkably, even at the moment of his greatest victory, the young Sultan found time to reflect on the hubristic end that awaits all empires.

Mehmet also came to inspect the Hippodrome. Like the palace, it had been left in near ruin since the thirteenth century. There had been no more chariot races, and no more Greens or Blues. Knights had used the sands to stage occasional jousting tournaments, but the surrounding grandstands were crumbling away.[123] As the Sultan entered the arena, he was drawn immediately to the bronze statue of the three intertwined serpents, first erected in the sacred Greek shrine of Delphi nearly two millennia before. He brought out his battle-axe, and shattered the lower jaw from one of the three heads.[124] It was in part a display of strength, and in part a symbolic act. The icons and talismans of the old order had lost their power. Mehmet could sense a tectonic shift in the plates of history. He knew he was at the vanguard of the modern world.

William Hogarth's 1723 etching titled 'a procession through the Hippodrome'. At the centre of the picture can be seen the obelisk of Theodosius and the serpents of Delphi.

The obelisk of Theodosius and, far right, the serpents of Delphi pictured in 1922 at the centre of the former site of the Hippodrome.

The Hippodrome became the *Atmeidan*, a long rectangle of flat ground that the Sultans used to exercise their horses.[125] Over the centuries, the colonnades and tiers of stone seating were pulled down, and the curve of the *sphendone* was demolished, although fragments of its deep vaults, built down into the hillside, still remain. In the late nineteenth century, Joseph Antoine Bouvard, inspector-general of the Architectural Department of the City of Paris, was commissioned by the Ottoman Empire to redesign the urban fabric of Constantinople. A key part of Bouvard's plan was to turn the flat expanse of the Hippodrome into a French garden, a public space drawing inspiration from the central boulevard of the Place de la Concorde in Paris. Two parallel rows of trees were planted to frame a central walkway formed from a small collection of ancient monuments. These were the last remnants of the *spina*: the obelisk of Theodosius; a second, smaller obelisk, installed in the tenth century by Emperor Constantine Porphyrogenitus; and the stumpy, broken base of the Serpent Column.[126]

This park and its monuments remain in Istanbul today. Walk among the trees and pavement stones, and it is hard to imagine the great arena that once surrounded the gardens and rose high above the city. The thunder of hooves and the roar of the crowd have been replaced by birdsong and the soft, slow, relentless pad of tourist feet.

Chapter Nine

The Carpet of the World

Madinat al-Zahra, Cordoba – Spain
(Born AD 936 – Died AD 1010)

Towards the end of the eleventh century, Mohammad al-Mu'tamid, the Islamic ruler of the kingdom of Seville, travelled with his courtiers to a great ruin at the foot of the dark mountains of the Sierra Morena, five miles west of Cordoba. The party entered a city which had been devastated by war and fire: its walls and gates toppled, its roofs open to the sky, its gardens wild and overgrown. The remains of the city's buildings rose up the mountainside in three massive stepped terraces, and with each level the scale, ambition and grandeur of the shattered architecture increased. Al-Mu'tamid was a patron of the arts with a romantic soul: he was said to have married one of his wives because she had managed to finish a problematic verse of his poetry.[1] The story of his visit to the ruins was recounted by the scholar Ibn Khaqan in *The Collars of Gold*, an anthology of the lives and works of the greatest writers and artists of Muslim Spain.

'They wandered from palace to palace, hacking away at the branches and brambles,' wrote Ibn Khaqan.

> 'They climbed to the topmost rooms, exchanging cups of wine among those high terraces until they arrived finally in the garden after having examined the ruins closely, their view increasing in increments as they went.

> In the garden they settled themselves on springtime carpets striped with white flowers and bordered with streams and water channels... overlooked by the ruins of those halls which, like bereaved mothers, mourn the devastation and the end of the joyful gatherings, now that the lizard plays among the stones and croaks on the walls. Nothing remained except holes and stones: the pavilions had collapsed and youth had become old age, as occasionally iron becomes soft and that which is new rots. All the while they drank cups of wine and wandered about, both enjoying themselves and yet pausing for reflection.'[2]

Al-Mu'tamid and his party picnicked in the abandoned city, and rested in the shells of the buildings that, so quickly, had been reclaimed by nature. From the raised slopes of the mountainside, they watched as the sun travelled from east to west over the Cordoban plains and the valley of the Guadalquivir River. Al-Mu'tamid experienced the ruins as a poignant entertainment – inspiration, perhaps, for some new poem. And what inspiration. Travellers came from all over the Muslim – and the Christian – world to visit a place that had taken on almost mythical significance.[3] It had once been, the stories said, the greatest city on earth, full of palaces and gardens of unequalled splendour. At the end of the twelfth century, the poet Ibn al-Arabi explored the site and, overcome by a sense of loss, composed a paean to a vanished world:

> Halls alongside of playgrounds gleam,
>   But they have no occupants and they are in ruins.
> Birds are lamenting in them from every side,
>   At times they are silent, at other times cooing.
> I addressed one of the wingborn singers,
>   Who was sad at heart and a-quiver.
> 'For what do you lament so plaintively' I asked,
>   And it answered, 'For an age that is gone forever.'[4]

For Muslims in particular, the desolation of the city was shocking. These were not ancient remains. Al-Mu'tamid's visit came a mere fifty years after the site had been reduced to ruins, and just a century after it had been built. For the briefest of periods, paradise flourished, and then just as quickly, it was gone again. As the historian Ibn Hayyan wrote:'With the ruin, the carpet of the world was folded up'.[5] The Madinat al-Zahra – 'the brilliant city'[6] – had been paradise on earth. Now its beauty would never return.

In April AD 711, a fleet of Muslim warriors rowed through the night from the African port of Cueta towards the southern tip of the Iberian Peninsula. At the head of this army, which was made up of 7,000 Arab and Berber tribesmen, was the general Tariq ibn Ziyad. The Islamic invasion of Western Europe had begun. At the place where they first came ashore, there was a great plug of volcanic rock, and they named it in honour of their devout and pious leader. It was Tariq's Mountain – in Arabic, the *Jabal al-Tariq*. Gibraltar.[7]

Driven by the righteous zeal of their young religion, and by the momentum of conquest, this advance army outperformed even its own expectations. Tariq swept over the peninsula, often meeting no resistance. And where he did, he led his men to victory after victory. The Muslim chroniclers recorded the campaign as an epic tale with Tariq as the hero, yet the truth was not always so glorious. Much of the landscape through which they marched had been ravaged by plague, famine and drought. Up until the fifth century, this had been the Roman province of Baetica. When it collapsed along with the rest of the Western Empire, tribes from the north crossed the Pyrenees to pick over the bones of the Roman carcass. The Visigoths gradually saw off their 'barbarian' rivals, and settled on the *Meseta* – the high plains of Castile – taking the central city of Toledo as their capital.[8] When Tariq arrived three centuries later, this kingdom was in disarray, embroiled in civil war and civil insurrection. Many inhabitants saw the Muslims not as conquerors, but as saviours.[9]

Nothing, it seemed, could halt the spread of Islam. In less than a century, the religious empire created by Mohammed – an Arab camel-driver turned prophet – had emerged from the Middle East to claim territories stretching from the borders of India to the Pillars of Hercules. Islam meant 'submission', and the Iberian Peninsula was just the latest in a long line of lands to submit. The Muslims named it *al-Andalus*, perhaps from the Visigothic *landahlauts*, meaning 'allotted territory'[10], or perhaps simply to refer to it as the Atlantic region of their domain.[11] This new, eastern province was ruled from Damascus by the *caliph* – the 'successor' of the Prophet, the 'Commander of the Faith', and the sole leader of the Muslim Empire. At the beginning of the eighth century, the caliphs came from the Umayyad dynasty, a family tracing its line back to the Quraysh, the tribe to which Mohammed had belonged. All this changed, however, in AD 750. The Abbasid family, who believed they had a more legitimate claim to Islamic rule as descendants of the Prophet's paternal uncle, staged a brutal coup.[12] In cities and palaces throughout the empire, Umayyads were assassinated.

One young prince, Abd al-Rahman, the grandson of the Caliph Hisham, managed to escape the purge, fleeing from Syria across North Africa in the company of his loyal slave, Badr. Abbasid agents were despatched to hunt him down. He continued westwards, relying on the support of Berber tribes loyal to his Berber mother. At last, after five years on the run, al-Rahman crossed the Straits of Gibraltar and landed in Europe for the first time.[13] Within a year, he had assembled an army loyal to the Umayyads and had fought to take control of the entire Iberian Peninsula. Sealing his victory at Cordoba, the old Roman capital, he proclaimed himself *emir* of al-Andalus in AD 756.[14] From that moment on, the former prince of Damascus set about building a new kingdom in exile.

In AD 822, the musician, poet and polymath known as Ziryab arrived at the court of Abd al-Rahman II, the fourth Umayyad emir of Cordoba.

A mixed-race African-Arab most famous for his beautiful singing voice – Ziryab was a nickname, from the Arabic for 'blackbird'[15] – he had travelled from kingdom to kingdom across the Muslim world on his way to al-Andalus. A man of cosmopolitan tastes and a model of sophistication, his presence at court was something of a revelation.[16]

The Umayyads pretended that they only looked back across the Mediterranean to Africa in anticipation of the day when they would overcome their Abbasid usurpers. But they were not fooling anybody. Al-Andalus had fluctuated between stability and periods of fierce, though often isolated, rebellion. In the north, the Christian kingdoms of Asturias-Leon, Castile, Navarre, Aragon and Catalonia had established a foothold on the peninsula, and a holy war was underway along the al-Andalusian border.[17] The Umayyads were too busy holding on to what they had to even contemplate a bid to reclaim the empire.

Their kingdom was an anomaly in the Muslim world. Rulers had a degree of independence, but the foundations of Islamic government were religious. Authority came from the laws of God, set down by the Prophet Mohammed in the Koran; it was the duty of the caliphs, his successors on earth, to enforce them. In al-Andalus, they still commemorated the name of the Abbasid caliph in public prayer. The Abbasids, who had moved the Muslim capital from Damascus to Baghdad, may have had no practical power on the peninsula, but they still exerted a hold over their bitter rivals.[18] The Umayyads could not help but take a gnawing, almost obsessive, interest in the lives, tastes and fashions of the regime that had supplanted them.

Ziryab had once been a prized member of the court of the Abbasid Caliph al-Mahdi, until a quarrel with his music master forced him to leave Baghdad.[19] Abd al-Rahman, the emir, was delighted to secure such a famous talent for al-Andalus, and soon, many other artists, poets and scholars were following his trail to Cordoba. In music, one of Ziryab's greatest innovations was to add an extra string to the traditional Arab instrument known as the *oud*, and to replace the wooden plectrum for strumming with the quill feather or talon of an eagle (for some music historians, this moment marks the origin point of rock and roll).[20] He was said to know over 10,000 songs[21], and al-Rahman was so captivated by Ziryab's voice that he declared he could listen to no other singer.

There was more to Ziryab, though, than his music. He brought to al-Andalus the arts of elegant living developed at the Abbasid court: fashions in dress, food and hygiene direct from Baghdad. Men began to cut their hair short, baring the neck and ears, and dying their beards with henna. Meals were transformed into grand events, performances that followed a carefully chosen sequence of courses. Fragrances and perfumes were introduced, along with the idea that deodorants and scents like ambergris, musk and camphor had medicinal properties.[22] Perhaps most significant of all, however, were the tales Ziryab told al-Rahman of the great palaces of the Abbasids.[23] The kings of Islam were living in buildings of such splendour that their like had never been seen before – outside of paradise, at least. Their cities were unsurpassed either in size or magnificence. The Abbasid buildings, along with their creators, were becoming as much myth as reality.

Just under a century later, in AD 912, the great-great grandson of Abd al-Rahman II – Abd al-Rahman III – was crowned Emir of al-Andalus. From a very early age he had been groomed for power: his grandfather, Abd Allah had named al-Rahman successor ahead of his own son, Muhammad. Al-Rahman was of mixed race: the son of a Christian slave and concubine, and the grandson of a Basque princess. He had white skin, fair hair and dark blue eyes – a handsome figure according to contemporary accounts – and when he came to the throne, aged just twenty-one[24], he was already respected at the highest level by government and military officials for his intelligence and courage.[25] His choice of name was significant, intended to signal a new age of prosperity for al-Andalus by recalling the great leaders of the past. The first al-Rahman had founded the kingdom after his escape from Africa, uniting the warring factions of the Iberian peninsula. The second had established culture, science and scholarship as the pillars of the Umayyad court. The third had an even greater goal.

Over the first twenty years of his rule, al-Rahman III worked tirelessly to bring together the dissident factions and tribes of al-Andalus. He offered pardons to any rebels who rejoined the fold, and guaranteed free rights of worship to Jews and Christians alongside Muslims. The emir's own mixed parentage helped defuse racial tensions within the kingdom, and he pledged that anyone, regardless of their background or origin, would have the chance to rise to prominence in his service.

Meanwhile he subdued the Christian states in the north. Treaties allowed them to cling on to their lands, but only thanks to the benevolence of al-Rahman.[26] Cordoba, the capital of al-Andalus, grew to become one of the largest cities in the world. With a population of over a quarter of a million, its size was rivalled only by Baghdad and Constantinople.[27] The people began to discern an almost messianic quality in their young emir, as if his success were propelled by a divine will. The court poet, Ibn Abd Rabbihi, compared him to King Solomon and Alexander the Great, and wrote of how he lifted 'the obscure coverings of darkness' from al-Andalus, with 'a light putting heaven and earth next to each other'.[28]

On Friday 16 January AD 929, the day that marked the beginning of the month-long pilgrimage to Mecca, al-Rahman claimed his destiny.[29] After nearly two hundred years in the wilderness, the ancient rights of his family were reasserted. Al-Rahman was proclaimed the leader of the entire Muslim faith: the one caliph, the *amir al-munimin,* the Prince of all Believers. It was an act of thundering political and spiritual intent, announcing to the world that the true capital of Islam lay not in Baghdad with the Abbasids, but in Cordoba, at the court of the Umayyads.

As al-Rahman wrote in his instructions to his governors, 'because the most high God... has shown his preference for us... and has extended our fame throughout the world and exalted our authority... we have decided that we should be addressed by the title Prince of Believers'.[30] Twenty years previously, in AD 909, the Fatimid dynasty of North Africa had also claimed the right to the caliphate, in another direct challenge to the Abbasids. Al-Rahman delivered a pointed message to his two rivals, reminding them that the Umayyads had been there first: 'Anyone, other than ourselves, who uses [the title], does so improperly and is an intruder and arrogates to himself a title that he does not merit.'[31] In the course of just two decades, the great empire of Islam had split in three.

As caliph, al-Rahman was raised above the level of ordinary mortals. He was God's agent on earth, and could no longer be as accessible – or even visible – to his subjects as he had been before. It was required that mystery should shroud the Prince of Believers, that a curtain of obscurity should hide his life from outside eyes. He needed to distance himself from the bustle of Cordoba's city, and relocate to a new, custom-built palace, a refuge that represented the magnificence of his kingdom.[32] Architecture was the means that could raise al-Andalus above its rivals, and demonstrate its position as the true centre of the Muslim world.

The task al-Rahman faced was a daunting one. Palaces held a special place in Islamic mythology. Stories of their greatness had existed long before the *nouveau riche* excesses of the Abbasids. Arab folklore was filled with accounts of wondrous cities, and of the impiety and hubris that often led to their downfall. Poets and minstrels, men like Ziryab, told and retold these fables, embellishing them over the centuries, adapting them to the tastes of their audiences, often merging fact and fiction. Real historical figures and places blurred into fantastical narratives.[33] By the ninth century, many of these stories had made their way into one of the most famous works of Islamic literature, the *Katih Hadith Alf Layla – The Book of the Tale of One Thousand Nights*. Drawing heavily from Persian and Indian origins, the compilation evolved into the *Thousand and One Nights.* This was a great 'sea of stories' connected by the narrative device of a concubine named Shahrazad, who fends off her execution by King Shahriyar by telling him tales each evening that remain unfinished by the break of dawn. Each story leads immediately to another, and a rapt Shahriyar is kept entertained for a thousand and one nights, until he finally decides to spare his concubine's life.[34]

One of the oldest of these stories – that of Iram, City of the Columns – acted as both a dire warning and a template for the architectural ambitions of the caliphs.[35] The version in the *Thousand and One Nights* begins with a herder searching the deserts of Yemen for a stray she-camel. In the course of his wanderings, he comes across a huge city with colossal palaces of gold and silver bricks, where gemstones and pearls pave the streets and the soil is musk, ambergris and saffron. The herder explores the whole city, climbing to its highest towers, but can find no sign of any people. Scooping up what gems he can carry as proof of the city's existence, he leaves and returns to his own land to tell of his discovery. News reaches the Caliph Mu'awiya ibn Abi Sufyan, and the herder is summoned before the court. After inspecting the herder's treasures, the caliph calls on his advisor, Ka'b al-Ahbar to ask if he has ever heard of such a place. Ka'b replies that he has, and that this must be 'Iram, City of the Columns, whose match was never found in any other land'.[36]

Iram was built by Shaddad, the ruler of the whole world, who had come across a description in an ancient book of the palaces and gardens of paradise. 'Go to the best and broadest stretch of open country on earth and build me a city of gold and silver there,' he told his advisors. 'Its pebbles are to be chrysolites; it is to be filled with palaces whose upper stories must be filled with chambers. Under these palaces, in the lanes and streets, there are to be trees producing varieties of ripe fruits with streams running beneath them through conduits of gold and silver.'[37] Shaddad commanded the rulers of every district to gather and send him all the precious stones in their lands, even if they were buried far below the earth or found deep beneath the sea. He assembled the greatest architects and craftsmen and sent them to scour the entire world for the perfect site: 'a wide plain of clear country, without hills or mountains,' with 'gushing springs and flowing streams'.[38]

For three centuries they worked to build this magnificent city.

When they had finished, Shaddad asked for one final addition: a fortress to tower above the other buildings, surrounded by a thousand palaces raised up on a thousand columns, one for each of the kings of the world. After another twenty years, Iram was finally complete, and Shaddad and his court set off on a great procession to their new home. They would never reach their destination.

As the city came into sight on the horizon, God let out an angry cry from heaven – a noise so terrible that it killed Shaddad and all his people. Iram was left standing, but all roads to it were hidden, so that it was lost to human eyes, until the day it was chanced upon by the humble camel herder. Shaddad had dared to compete with God as a creator, and he had been punished for his arrogance.[39]

Another similar story in the *Thousand and One Nights* told of the City of Brass. Musa ibn Nusair – who was the governor of North Africa at the time of the Muslim invasion of Spain[40] – was said to have set out on a quest to find brass bottles containing the legendary *jinnis*. He eventually came to a city of awesome size and majesty, surrounded by a colossal, unbroken wall as large as a mountain ridge. After much trial and error, which claimed the lives of a number of his men, Musa managed to enter this City of Brass. Unlike Iram, which never had a human inhabitant, this place had once been full of life. Yet all Musa found was death: the bodies of citizens littered the streets. 'Traders could be seen dead in their booths with their flesh desiccated and their bones crumbled away' he recounted, while in the silk and jewellers' markets there were 'owners lying dead on leather mats but looking as though they were just about to speak', and money-changers laid out 'on carpets of silks of various kinds, with their booths filled with gold and silver'.[41] Under a great palace dome of red gold, they came upon a princess lying on a couch studded with pearls, gems and sapphires, who wore a crown of red gold, and appeared to be watching Musa and his men. They soon discovered that this was a trick: her eyes had been coated in quicksilver after death, to give the illusion that they were twinkling. On a gold tablet, Musa read the fate of the city:

> Look at those who once adorned their homes,

But then went to their graves to account for what they did.
They built, to no avail; they stored up wealth,
But this wealth did not save them when their time had come.

…

When they were buried, a voice was heard to cry:
'Where are your thrones, your crowns and all your robes?
Where are the faces that were veiled away,
Protected by the curtains and the drapes?'
The grave has a clear answer for the questioners:
'The roses are no longer on their cheeks.
For many days they ate and drank their wine,
But after their fine foods, they too were eaten.'[42]

Famine had consumed the City of Brass. All the people's great wealth could not save them. At last, resigned to their fate, they brought all their goods and treasures out into the streets, sealed the city gates from the inside, and surrendered themselves to God's punishment. The tablet ended by recommending that any 'who come to this place and see us should learn not to be deceived by the world and its vanities'. Weeping at the fate of the city, Musa concluded that 'piety is our chief duty'.[43]

The message of these stories appears unequivocal: to build too boldly and with too much ambition is both folly and sacrilege. This was not, however, the interpretation favoured by the Abbasids.[44] Towards the end of the eighth century, the Caliph al-Mansur commissioned the construction of a palace-city in Baghdad that might have come straight from the pages of the *Thousand and One Nights*. The city was a perfect circle – known as the Round City, or the City of Peace – with its eight-kilometre-long outer wall incorporating four equidistant gates topped by large domes at the north-west, north-east, south-west and south-east points.

There were four more concentric, circular walls inside the main wall, with every element of the urban architecture designed to exalt the status of al-Mansur. Like the spokes of a wheel, all roads both led to the centre of the city, and, theoretically, spread out beyond it to circle the globe. At its centre, which was also, symbolically, the centre of the world, was the caliph's palace, a great, double dome, with an elevated throne room allowing al-Mansur to gaze out in every direction across his empire.[45] The caliph deliberately copied the approach of King Shaddad in the fable of Iram. He issued a written demand to kingdoms across the world that they 'should send him all those who knew anything about construction'; in response 'there arrived one hundred thousand various artisans and labourers'.[46] In the ninth century, the Abbasids removed themselves still further from the general population, constructing monumental palace complexes outside Baghdad in the landscape of Samarra. There the caliph could be kept concealed within a labyrinth of courtyards, halls, chambers and gardens. Everywhere there was luxury and the finest materials, with access to the spiritual leader of Islam controlled by the confining architecture.[47]

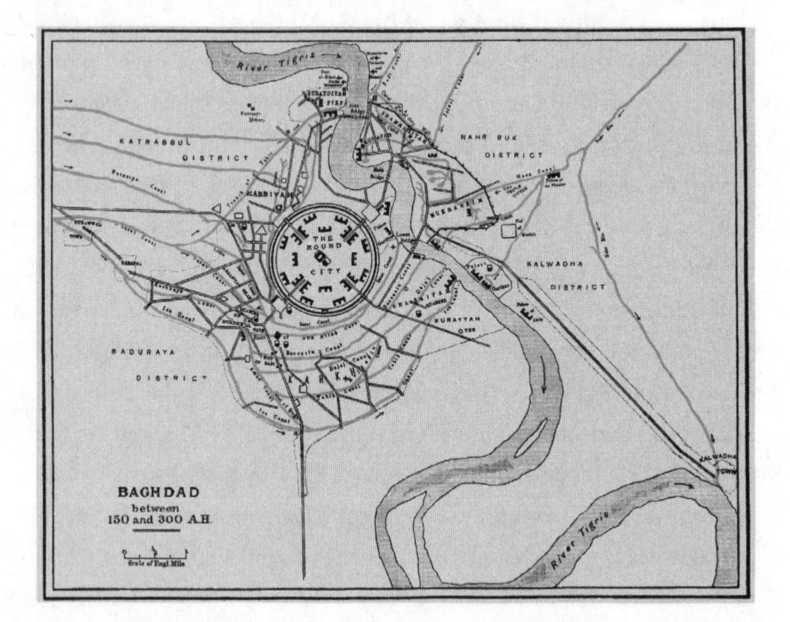

Map of the Round City of Baghdad between AD 767 and 912, from *The Caliphate: Its Rise, Decline, and Fall* by William Muir

To build from scratch was to demonstrate mastery of both people and landscapes. That it also strayed perilously close to assuming the role of God did not appear to matter to the Abbasid caliphs. Instead, overseeing great construction projects had become a rite of passage for those who came to power. 'Now I know that I am a king,' said the ninth-century Abbasid Caliph al-Mutawakkil, 'for I have built myself a city and live in it.'[48]

Al-Rahman knew that the only way the embryonic Umayyad caliphate could compete with the grandiose appeal of the Abbasids – not to mention the legendary rulers of Arab folklore – was to indulge in some myth-making of his own. The poets and chroniclers of al-Andalus colluded in the process, producing exaggerated accounts and commemorative verses merging literary tropes of palace construction with historical fact.

There was a tried and tested formula they could follow. First, the new city needed an origin story, which duly emerged as a romantic tale of love and pious charity. It was said that a wealthy concubine in al-Rahman's harem died, and left behind a large bequest to pay for the return of Muslim prisoners held in foreign lands. No such hostages could be found, however, and so another concubine – al-Zahra, a favourite of al-Rahman – convinced the caliph to use the money to build a new city instead. She also suggested that he name it after her, calling it the Madinat al-Zahra.[49] In this, there was the echo of one of the earliest and best-known origin myths – that of the Persian King Parviz and his lover Shirin. To honour Shirin as the most beautiful woman in the world, Parviz was said to have built the greatest palace in the world.[50]

The next step was the search. Like King Shaddad, al-Rahman's mission was to scour the world for virgin earth to build upon. Conveniently he found this just to the west of Cordoba, on a gentle mountain slope above a verdant, irrigated landscape. Next was the requirement to collect the most precious materials from the four corners of the world, and to secure the services of the greatest architects and craftsmen alive. According to the historian al-Maqqari, over 4,000 marble columns were gathered, including 1,000 from Tunisia, 140 from Byzantium, 19 from the kingdom of the Franks, with the rest sent by cities from Rome to Seville. Artisans, engineers and mathematicians came from Baghdad and Constantinople to oversee the planning, and vast numbers of paid and slave labourers were assembled: sources suggest there were some 12,000 available for daily labour, as well as 1,500 beasts of burden.[51]

At last Al-Rahman was ready. Construction of the Madinat al-Zahra began on 19 November AD 936[52], and continued for the next 40 years.[53] The city was a kilometre and a half wide, and three-quarters of a kilometre long – the shape of the ideal rectangle formed by a double square.[54] The mountain setting was an integral facet of the design, with the city divided into three great terraces, each one cut higher up the slope than the last. As the historian al-Himyari described:

> 'It is a city with stepped constructions, one precinct on top of another so that the ground floor of the upper level is on a level with the roofs of the level below. Each one of its parts is separately walled. On the upper level are the palaces, beautiful beyond description. On the middle level are the gardens and orchards; and on the lower level are the houses and the congregational mosque'.[55]

Buildings were arranged according to a rigorous hierarchy: the higher up they were positioned, the more important they were in the life of the city. There was nothing organic or accidental about this layout. Everything was the result of meticulous planning. The difference in height from the city's base to its summit was 70 metres, and the three discrete terraces were linked by passageways, stairs and ramps. For those privileged enough to be granted an audience with the caliph, the route to the top involved an ascent through a maze of reception halls, gardens, avenues, walkways and antechambers. Indeed, the whole city was framed with this idea in mind. Travellers approached from the south from the valley of the Guadalquivir, along a main road built to connect the city to Cordoba and the rest of al-Andalus.[56] Facing the visitor were Madinat al-Zahra's high walls, which obscured much of the splendour that lay within, creating an air of mystery and emphasising the separation of the caliph from his people. Yet everywhere there were tantalising glimpses of great buildings and gardens, and the eye was drawn continually higher, to the wondrous palace that crowned the city.

Madinat al-Zahra was, however, in no way purely ornamental, or a mere royal retreat. It was a palace city: a self-contained and self-sufficient urban environment, with markets, housing, mosques and baths. The water supply came from the mountains. A ruined Roman aqueduct was reconstructed and redirected to feed a stone reservoir and a system of pipes and sewers. As the city took shape, the caliph's government and administrative offices moved away from Cordoba and into their new home. There was a police chief and a prison, military barracks, a mint, artisans' quarter and storehouses for grain, olive oil, butter and other essentials. The city's central mosque was built on the lowest level, but was positioned directly below the second terrace, which meant that ordinary citizens could enter from the ground, whereas the nobility had access over a bridge from the garden above, crossing into the mosque roof. Here again, the placement of the building and the careful use of height were employed explicitly to reinforce social status.[57]

The city's gardens were constructed on a vast scale, with at least one on each terrace. The garden on the second level was Madinat al-Zahra's main outdoor ceremonial space. It was overlooked by a grand reception hall, with an ornate facade of marble pillars supporting half-moon arches. It was here that the caliph would sit on a raised throne to receive visiting dignitaries and foreign ambassadors. His view over the terrace took in a pavilion directly opposite, which sat surrounded by wide, shallow pools, creating the illusion that the building floated on the water.[58] The pools themselves were stocked with huge numbers of fish, which were fed with 8,000 loaves of bread each day.[59]

On another level was the city zoo, filled with exotic animals – lions, gazelles, ostriches and camels – gifted to the caliph by his African allies, and including a giant aviary, where colourful birds of paradise were kept from flying away by netted awnings.[60] There was one last garden, on the highest terrace. Much smaller than the rest, it was designed in the traditional Islamic style as an entirely enclosed, private space, screened from the outside by high walls. Filled with the most beautiful plants and flowers, which were set among elaborate water-features, this was an intimate refuge to be used only by the caliph, his family and the very highest-ranking officials.[61]

The level of detail and ornamentation throughout the city was astounding, from wall murals depicting scenes of bountiful nature, to intricately-carved wooden balconies, stairs, roofs and ceilings, and row after row of exquisitely crafted bookshelves for the caliph's massive library.[62] Yet the greatest sight was reserved for just a select few: the great hall of the caliph's palace. The hall lay beyond a reception room dominated by a large green marble basin – a gift from the city of Constantinople. The basin was surrounded by twelve golden animal statues, including a lion, a crocodile, a snake, a giraffe, an elephant and an eagle, studded with jewels and pearls, which shot water out of their mouths.[63]

It was here, at the pinnacle of the city, that al-Rahman had saved the best for last. His hall was supported by eight arches of ebony and ivory inlaid with gold and gemstones. The ceiling was entirely of gold, and the walls were composed of marble of every imaginable colour. A giant pearl, a present to al-Rahman from Leo, emperor of Byzantium, hung down from the roof. Most remarkable of all, in the middle was a large pool of mercury. When the sun shone into this hall, according al-Maqqari, 'its rays rebounded off the roofs and walls, the hall sparkled with light, and confounded all vision.' As a special trick to impress his visitors, al-Rahman would order one of his slaves to make the mercury in the pool vibrate, 'whereupon in the chamber there would appear a flash like that of lightning bolts that would fill their hearts with fear'.[64]

It was only the most prestigious visitors who reached the hall, as the spectacular end of a long ceremonial procession. The chroniclers of al-Andalus record how, on certain occasions, the entire road from Cordoba to Madinat al-Zahra was lined with double rows of soldiers holding silk flags. After passing through this honour guard, guests entered the city, ascended its three levels, and at last arrived into the astounding glory of the great hall.[65] It was no surprise that, as al-Maqqari wrote, 'there was nobody, absolutely nobody', who entered Madinat al-Zahra 'from the furthest lands, from the most diverse faiths, be it a king, an emissary or trader, that did not wholeheartedly conclude that they had never seen the like, and further still, they had never heard of anybody speak of something similar, nor had it even occurred to them'.[66]

It was a fundamental design principle of the city to lead the viewer and visitor ever inward and upward, controlling where they went and what they saw, until finally they reached the caliph, who, said al-Maqqari, awaited on his throne 'in a most solemn, brilliant, majestic and impressive manner'.[67] Yet there were other times, when the pomp and pageantry was over, that this architectural function was reversed. In the cool of dusk perhaps, with the heat of the sun dropping below the western horizon, al-Rahman could stand on his highest palace *mirador* – meaning 'place for looking' – and take in the panoramic views. In Madinat al-Zahra, vision and elevation were a privilege of status. Only the caliph, God's right hand man, was permitted to experience the sweep and extent of the landscape beyond the city. The carpet of al-Andalus – of the world – rolled out before him. To see was to own, and to rule.[68]

Towards the end of the tenth century, a young man walked alone in the halls, corridors and gardens of the highest palace of Madinat al-Zahra. He spent much of his time in silent contemplation in the small, walled garden. If he was aware at all that the city below him was steadily emptying of people, then he did not seem to care. The great celebrations, festivals and ceremonies which he remembered as a young boy no longer filled the garden terraces and the grand rooms with noise and colour. Where musicians, poets and scholars had once played, sung, laughed and argued long into the night, now there was only silence, apart from the gentle hum of bird call.

The architecture of the city had always been intended to keep the king one step removed from his people. Now it appeared that it could also be used for a more sinister purpose. The young man was Hisham II, the grandson of al-Rahman and the son of Hakam II. He had become caliph at just ten years old, after the death of his father in AD 976. And at that moment began the process of transforming the Madinat al-Zahra from a palace capital into the world's most luxurious prison.[69]

Abd al-Rahman III died on 15 October AD 961, at the age of seventy.[70] His son, Hakam II, was already in middle age when he came to the throne. For the next fifteen years al-Andalus enjoyed a period of peace and tranquillity, untroubled by the Christian kingdoms to the north, while also reclaiming Umayyad lands to the south in Morocco after the Fatimids moved their capital to Cairo.[71] Hakam was a lover of books and scholarship[72], and like his great-great-great grandfather, Abd al-Rahman II, opened up his court to writers and artists from across the world. He had only two sons, both with a Christian concubine called Subh. The first died in childhood, and the second was Hisham, the sole heir to al-Andalus.[73]

When Hakam died, a plan was set in motion by a cabal of high-ranking government officials to prevent Hisham from inheriting the kingdom. The ten-year-old prince had, however, a protector and advisor called Ibn Abi Amir. A former inspector of the royal mint and chief of police, he became known as al-Mansur, 'the victorious', after having distinguished himself as commander of the African armies in suppressing rebellion in Morocco.[74] Al-Mansur snuffed out the conspiracy, and was rewarded in turn with the title of *hijab* – first minister and head counsellor of the state. Before his appointment in Africa al-Mansur had had no military experience, but now he proved a charismatic general, aggressively expanding the borders of al-Andalus, and recruiting many new Berber tribesmen and Christian mercenaries to his cause. Though he continued the policies of religious tolerance instituted by al-Rahman and Hakam, there were early signs that he was also a shrewd, ruthlessly ambitious politician. In an attempt to gain the support of Cordoba's religious hard-liners, he made a public display of disposing of the great library of Hakam, burning many books of science and scholarship for their sacrilegious content.[75]

As Hisham grew older, there were no signs that the young caliph was being readied to take up the reins of power. Quite the opposite, in fact. In AD 996, he endorsed al-Mansur's bid to make the position of *hijab* hereditary. The role of caliph was being reduced to little more than a figurehead, while a new dynasty – the Amirids of al-Mansur – was emerging at the heart of government.[76]

Towards the end of his life, Hisham's father Hakam had started putting plans in place for a new palace city of his own. This scheme, which had been left, literally, on the drawing board, was resurrected by al-Mansur.[77] As the historian al-Himyari wrote, al-Mansur 'elevated himself almost to the level of kings in planning a palace where he, his family, and his followers would reside, where the seat of government would be fixed and the administration of the political organisation carried out, where he would gather his guards and staff and assemble tradesmen'.[78]

The new city was known, rather confusingly, as the Madinat al-Zahira, and it was built on the bank of the Guadalquivir River, to the south-east of Cordoba. Once again the ritual of palace construction was played out, with al-Mansur summoning the finest materials and artisans from across the world. The *hijab*'s palace glimmered in gold and silver, and was festooned with gemstones and lapis lazuli. It soon became the new location for entertaining foreign dignitaries, and al-Mansur proved adept at staging stupendous displays of ostentation. On one occasion he ordered that nuggets of gold be inserted in the morning into closed water lilies floating in a large pool in the palace gardens. As the day progressed, and the lilies opened in the sunlight, al-Mansur's guests were tricked into believing that, in al-Andalus, even the pollen was made of gold.[79]

All eyes in Cordoba turned away from Madinat al-Zahra and towards al-Mansur's new city. 'Once the seat of power was transferred to the palace of al-Zahira, the Caliph was left alone,' wrote al-Himyari. He was 'ignored as a nonentity, forgotten, his door closed and his person hidden from the public eye... and soon it got to the point where no one even knew the Caliph any longer'.[80] Madinat al-Zahra was almost completely deserted, a remote, gilded cage for a caliph who passed his days in contented confinement.

Al-Mansur died in 1002, and, as had been decreed, his son Abd al-Malik stepped into the role of *hijab*. Al-Malik died just seven years later, at the age of thirty-three. Some Islamic chroniclers suspected his successor – his younger brother Sanjul – of having poisoned him.[81] Sanjul was arrogant, impulsive and ambitious, and he took the step that his father and brother had always avoided: he convinced the caliph to nominate him as his heir. Certain that he had now succeeded in supplanting the Umayyad dynasty with the Amirids, Sanjul embarked on a military campaign to the Christian north. The moment he left, the Arab aristocracy, shocked by this act of sacrilege, joined up with members of the Umayyad family to lead an uprising. Hisham abdicated and was replaced as caliph by Muhammad II, a great-grandson of Abd al-Rahman III. On 16 February 1009, Muhammad's forces sacked al-Mansur's city of Madinat al-Zahira. The *fitna*, the civil war that would destroy al-Andalus, had begun.[82]

News of the revolt reached Sanjul in the city of Toledo. As he prepared to return to Cordoba, he was betrayed by his own troops, taken prisoner, and crucified at the gates of the royal palace. The kingdom was split in two, between Umayyad loyalists and the Berber incomers, who remained fiercely loyal to the family of their former general, al-Mansur. Both sides also sought alliances with the Christian kingdoms. Much of the fighting centred on Cordoba, as the capital of al-Andalus. The city changed hands several times, smashed back and forth by successive waves of conflict.[83] For a time, Madinat al-Zahra's remote location in the foothills of the Sierra Morena helped it avoid the devastation. Finally, however, on 4 November 1010, Berber rebels, having pillaged their way westwards along the Guadalquivir valley, entered the palace-city, stripped it of its fabulous materials, and burned it to the ground.[84]

The people of the Muslim Empire had never really seen ruins before. Of course, they had come across remains left behind by older civilisations – like the Persians, the Egyptians and the Romans – but these were treated as mere foundations to use in the construction of their new order. The great shattered fragments of the past held no fears for them. How could they? It was clear that the decline of the decadent West was fated, in order to allow the rise of the nation of Islam in the East. All that changed, however, with the devastation of Madinat al-Zahra. For many Muslims, to visit these ruins was to confront for the first time the fragility and mortality of their own civilisation.[85] Al-Rahman's palace had taken four decades to build, and yet all that majesty had been undone in just one day. So it could be for an empire.

The restored and partially reconstructed great portico of the Madinat al-Zahra © Daniel Villafruela

A creeping fatalism emerged among the people of al-Andalus, as if the death of Madinat al-Zahra was a portent and a warning of some more universal doom. The polymath, Ibn Hazm, who grew up in Cordoba and became a prominent figure among the Amirid court, fled to a family estate in Seville during the civil war. When he asked for news of his former home, he was told that, of the city's many great buildings, almost nothing was left. 'It was as though the graceful palaces and embellished chambers that were as radiant as the sun... now that ruin and utter destruction was all around, were as the gaping mouths of wild predators announcing the annihilation of the world'.[86] In the darkness of the empty, broken halls, Hazm saw the terror of the abyss, and the beginning of the end.

Others, however, with the benefit of hindsight, were not so surprised. Had not the old folk tales – the stories of Iram and the City of Brass – warned what would happen once pride overcame piety? As the writer Ibn Shuhayd wrote of the remains of Madinat al-Zahra: 'I was sadly affected by the death which has befallen you. But was it not divine justice, since, during your life, you were so endlessly proud of your own splendour?'[87] Al-Maqqari recounted a story of a visit of a holy man to al-Rahman's city. The man remarked on how every house in the land had contributed to the palace's 'ornament and perfection'. Yet he also delivered a dire prediction of ruin. One day, he said, the process would go into reverse. Madinat al-Zahra would be dismantled, and the materials once used in its construction would be taken away and scattered across the land.[88] What everyone appeared to agree on, however, was that there was no going back, no returning to the way things had been. As the Almerian poet al-Sumaysir wrote:

> I stopped at al-Zahra weeping, looking at it
>   I lamented its slow decay
> And I said, "O Zahra, come back." And she responded,
>   "Who can return from death?"[89]

In death, however, Madinat al-Zahra's significance was perhaps even greater than it had been in life. It crossed over into the realm of myth, taking on the role of a dream palace, a mirage in the Cordoban mountains. Its existence had been so brief that some began to wonder if it had ever really been there at all. The philosopher poet Ibn Zaydun arrived to commune with the ruins and recalled how, in better times, he had met his former mistress, the poetess Wallada, in the beautiful palace gardens. 'I remembered you in al-Zahra,' he wrote. But al-Zahra, just like his love, was gone, and perhaps he had only ever imagined it.[90]

Just twenty years after Madinat al-Zahra was destroyed, Abd al-Hazm Ibn Jahwar, the new ruler of the independent kingdom of Cordoba, visited the site. He was inspired to write a short verse treating the palace as if it was already something from a fable:

> One day I asked the house of those who had passed on,
> "Where are your inhabitants to us so dear?"
> They replied, "They lived here for a short while,
> Then they went way, but I know not where."[91]

Just as al-Maqqari's holy man had prophesied, Madinat al-Zahra was taken apart piece by piece. It became a quarry filled with precious stonework, and its thousands of columns and capitals were removed, reappearing in palaces throughout Spain, and even as far afield as Morocco. Soon little of any value was left, and nature had come to dominate the ruins. Unchecked, the gardens rapidly consume the walls and terraces. The condition of the site mirrored the decline of the Muslim Empire in Spain. In 1031, the title of caliph was abolished, and the Umayyad dynasty finally collapsed. Al-Andalus ceased to exist as a unified kingdom, and the peninsula broke up into a series of small, independent states known as *taifas.*

By the middle of the eleventh century, there were some twenty-three *taifas*. Split along ethnic and tribal lines, they became embroiled in near incessant war. Gradually the smaller states were swallowed up by the larger ones.[92] Yet all the time the Christian kingdoms in the north were growing in strength and confidence. In 1085, Alfonso VI, king of Leon, seized the city of Toledo. It was the first great blow of the *reconquista*: the Christian campaign to 'recover what was taken from them' and win back the Iberian Peninsula by force.[93]

When Cordoba fell to King Ferdinand III of Castile on 29 June 1236[94], Madinat al-Zahra was reduced to the faintest of memories. Plaintive Muslim songs of loss and longing still spoke of a great city in the mountains, but precisely what it was and where it had been were no longer clear. By the fifteenth century, the ruins were known as *Cordoba la Vieja* – Old Cordoba – and the land around the palace had been granted to the monks of San Jeronimo. They dragged marble and ashlar blocks from the city up the mountainside to use in the construction of a monastery.[95]

In 1492, Boabdil of Granada, the last Muslim ruler in Spain, surrendered the Alhambra Palace to the armies of Ferdinand, king of Aragon, and Isabella, queen of Castile.[96] After eight centuries of dominance, Islam had at last succumbed to the *reconquista*. In the lonely foothills of Cordoba, Madinat al-Zahra was forgotten, and those who did stumble over its low stones thought they had found a Roman settlement.

Perhaps Abd al-Rahman had known from the start that his palace could not last. Yet, as he said to his *qadi* – his spiritual advisor – 'if over it wafts the breeze of memory and nostalgic yearning, and tender tears water it, then it will not fade.'[97] For a time, all was still in the valley of the Guadalquivir. Then, around the middle of the nineteenth century, accounts of a lost wonder began to emerge in the rediscovered works of the historians of al-Andalus. Archaeologists soon followed. Al-Rahman's 'breeze of memory' had returned. And it brought with it the whisperings of a tantalising story, half-truth, half-myth. The Madinat al-Zahra is alive again, if only a little. It is a memory palace; a poem; a tale of splendour and pride. A ruin.

Part Three

The King is Dead, Long Live the King!

We build to remember. We also build to forget. Aristotle's concept of the *tabula rasa* – the 'blank slate' – has found particular resonance in the sphere of architecture. Countless buildings and cities have been 'levelled' over the course of history, whether by cataclysmic accident or belligerent design. The question has always been – what to do in the aftermath? Should a structure be recreated just as it was, a replica rising from the rubble or ashes? Or should something new emerge, something grander, bolder and more ambitious, something that so far overshadows its predecessor that it slips from memory? What also of those structures which owe their existence to a single, specific cause – the charisma of a great emperor, for instance, or the proximity of a precious resource? Once the original connection is broken, they often fade so completely from the collective consciousness that it is as if they never existed at all. Finally, there are the buildings that are changed radically in the process of their destruction, transformed by history into their opposites: a remote, near-inaccessible hideout becomes the most-visited poster site of lost civilisation, or a symbol of state oppression is reborn as an icon of democratic freedom.

10. 'LONDON WAS, BUT IS NO MORE'

Old St Paul's Cathedral – London
(Born 1087 – Died 1666)

11. THE TENT AT THE CENTRE OF THE WORLD

Karakorum – Mongolia (Born 1220 – Died 1388)

12. THE HOUSE OF DIAMONDS

The Fortress of Golconda – Hyderabad, India
(Born 1300 – Died 1700)

13. LIBERTÉ FOR SALE

The Bastille – Paris (Born 1356 – Died 1789)

14. VIRTUAL CITY

Vilcabamba – Peru (Born 1539 – Died 1572)

Chapter Ten

'London Was, But Is No More'

Old St Paul's Cathedral – London (Born 1087 AD – Died 1666 AD)

In 1638, Wenceslaus Hollar, a draughtsman, water-colourist and etcher from Prague in the kingdom of Bohemia, climbed to the roof of the tower of the church of St Saviour in Southwark on the south bank of the River Thames, and began work on a series of sketches of London.[1] St Saviour was the highest vantage point with views to the north. Set within a strip of land known as Bankside, the church and its surrounding streets and houses were at that time not considered part of the city[2], kept at a distance by the metaphorical arm's length of London Bridge. Rather, this was a district with a reputation for immorality and unseemliness.

It was a magnet for pleasure-seekers. People flocked south of the river to be entertained, whether by the plays of Shakespeare in the Globe and Swan theatres, or by the popular spectacle of bear-baiting. The streets were full of taverns and guest-houses. Brothels were often set right up against the river, allowing customers to step off their ferry boats, conclude their business, and step right back on again to be rowed back to the city. Even before the late fourteenth century, when Geoffrey Chaucer used the Tabard Inn in Southwark as the point of departure for the pilgrims of *The Canterbury Tales*, this had been a place to pass through. Not, if you could help it, a place to live.

Hollar was one of a coterie of talented artists enjoying the patronage of Lord Thomas Howard, the twenty-first Earl of Arundel.[3] The earl was a prominent figure in the court of Charles I, revered among his peers as a gentleman of the highest taste and refinement. With the support of the king, and accompanied by his friend and protégé Inigo Jones, who became England's 'first architect', Arundel travelled across the continent, bringing the artistic sensibilities – and the physical artworks – of Renaissance Europe back to England.[4] He commissioned portraits by the Flemish masters Rubens and Van Dyck, and amassed at Arundel House, his London home on the Strand, a collection of some of the finest artworks in history, from the drawings of Da Vinci, Leonardo and Holbein to the paintings of Titian, Raphael and Bruegel.[5] The earl had met Hollar in Cologne in April 1636, and employed him to accompany his party on their journey down the Rhine, and make sketch drawings of the landscapes along the way. Impressed with how Hollar 'drawes and eches printes in strong water quickely, and with a pretty spirit'[6] he invited him to travel on to London, where he tasked him with recording the many items in his art collection for inclusion in one great catalogue.[7]

Hollar was given lodgings within Arundel House, and for the next six years, he lived a sheltered existence full of artistic freedom. A favourite of the household, he not only worked for the earl, but also received commissions from a number of other prominent London figures, including the early print-maker and publisher Peter Stent. Through Arundel he gained introductions to the royal court, and may even have taught drawing to the young Princes – the future King Charles II and King James II.[8] He walked the streets of London tirelessly, bringing both an artist's and an outsider's eye to bear on the city. Having first arrived at Arundel House by barge along the Thames, and after a time living on its banks, he came to see the river as London's soul and its defining characteristic. In his sketches from the roof of the church of St Saviour, it was the river that came to dominate, sweeping past Whitehall to open up as a great glistening expanse passing Southwark and running beneath London Bridge, before twisting away again into the distance, heading eastwards to Gravesend.

In 1647, Hollar transformed his sketches into an etching on six plates, which, when assembled and printed together, created a panorama nearly three metres wide. The work was titled *Long View of London from Bankside.* Although not a completely accurate representation – Hollar assumes a viewpoint much higher than the tower of St Saviour, and he flattens out the bends of the Thames – his image remains the definitive depiction of the still medieval city. It is also, arguably, the greatest view of London ever created.

The level of detail is astonishing. The painstaking etcher's technique involved creating a plate by drawing lines with a fine needle on a copper surface covered with a waxy substance, dipping the marked copper in acid, and then using the finished impressions in a printing press.[9] The technique allowed for subtle variations in light and texture, and was perfect for capturing the essence of London. In the *Long View* Hollar depicts a sprawling city with no real streets. Buildings are packed tight, thrust against each other in a bewildering mass of overlapping wooden roofs and façades. The only signs of passageways are the glimpses of shadowy canyons running between rows of gable ends. Peculiarly, there is almost a total absence of people in the city itself, and yet the picture is strikingly vibrant and dynamic. This is the genius of Hollar's panorama. The massed anthill of the city clusters around the Thames, and it is in the river that life can be found.

To the west of London Bridge, ferryboats pass up, down and across the water, dodging between large merchant barges and eel ships. To the east, a great flotilla of three-masted galleons passes the Tower of London, each ship with its bowsprit facing out towards the sea. All movement is centred on the water and the wharves, with river-front sites and buildings marked on the etching in Hollar's own hand: 'Fishmongers Hall', 'The Old Swan' pub, 'The 3 Cranes', 'Queen Hythe', 'Baynards Castle' and 'Blackfreyars'.

Rising above the city and overlooking the Thames, there is, however, one building that dwarves all others. Its huge, Gothic bulk dominates everything that surrounds it, and it sits high over London, as if Hollar sees it as the city's crown. Look closer, however, and it is obvious that this crown is tarnished. Most notably, its central tower ends in an unfortunate stump. A spire once rose up from the stump, reaching 489 feet in height, but it was destroyed by a bolt of lightning in 1561, and never rebuilt.[10]

At the time when Hollar was drawing the *Long View,* this building was already a shabby reflection of its former self, crumbling at the seams, groaning under the weight of its own structural irregularities, and from the blows of history. Some were even wondering whether it should be pulled down, and rebuilt from scratch. In his etching Hollar had written a name above the denuded tower: 'S Paulws Church'. Or, as we would know it better today, St Paul's Cathedral.

St Paul's had become a crumbling monument to the scarred psyche of a troubled city and a divided nation. And it had less than twenty years left to live.

Before St Paul's was a Cathedral, it was a church. Before it was a church, some say, it was a great pagan temple.[11]

The first people to erect any significant buildings on Ludgate Hill were the Romans. Around the mid-point of the first century AD, they bridged the Thames with a wooden crossing, and established a settlement that was part military camp and part supply centre. Just a decade after it was founded, *Londinium,* as this settlement was called, was reduced to ashes by the tribal armies of Queen Boudicca. The evidence of this first fire can be found in the earth below the modern city – a thin red line made up of the burnt remains of clay and wood.[12]

It did not take long, however, for the Romans to return, and for London to grow further. By the second century AD, it had become the capital of the province of *Britannia.* The centrepiece of the city was a forum and an enormous basilica, said to be larger even than St Paul's today.[13] Sixteen feet below the present pavement level, a Roman road once led east to west from Ludgate – one of six gates in London's original city wall – to modern Watling Street[14], passing right across the site of St Paul's. When the remains of large quantities of cattle bones and stag horns were dug out of the Cathedral grounds in the fourteenth century, they were attributed to a Roman temple.[15] What else could they have been, it was argued, apart from the remnants of countless sacrifices to Diana, goddess of the hunt? Despite a lack of archaeological evidence, this myth has persisted, attributing to Ludgate Hill a near unbroken history of religious worship moving from paganism to Christianity over the course of two millennia.[16]

Perhaps there is truth in this myth. When the Roman Empire collapsed, London did not fall. Some buildings may have declined and decayed, but many simply adapted. The purpose of individual sites in London has a tendency to pass down the generations, even surviving the total destruction of the physical structures that occupy them. A few hundred yards to the north-west of St Paul's for instance, beneath modern Guildhall, the remains of the largest Roman amphitheatre in Britannia have been discovered – two civic centres, separated by millennia.[17] So as Roman power ebbed, London continued to do what it did best – carry on. Rulers, kings and gods might come and go, but people and commerce, flowing in relentlessly on the river, remained.

In the fourteenth century, an anonymous author wrote a poem exploring this very idea of urban continuity. Titled *St Erkenwald,* it survives in a single copy made in 1477, now held in the British Library. According to historical accounts, in AD 675 a monk called Erkenwald became the first true Bishop of London, with St Paul's as his seat.[18] This original church had been built seven decades earlier, in AD 604, by the Saxon King Ethelbert, as a place for the Christian missionary Mellitus to hold his London sermons.[19] Mellitus, and other monks like him, were part of the second wave of a religious invasion of Britain. In AD 595, Pope Gregory the Great sent Augustine, a Benedictine prior, from Rome to Canterbury to convert Ethelbert from paganism. The mission met with such rapid success that by AD 597 Augustine had been appointed as the first Archbishop of Canterbury, and became, in effect, the founder of the English Church. Many more monks followed, establishing monasteries on British soil, and, with the support and patronage of the king, spreading the Christian gospel throughout the land.[20]

The poem *St Erkenwald* begins with a summary of this great Saxon conversion, but makes London the centre of the story. It calls the city 'New Troy': there was a medieval fixation with the legend that London and Britain had been founded by Brutus, a descendant of the Trojan warrior Aeneas, who escaped the destruction of his legendary city to settle on the Italian peninsula and become the father of the Roman people.[22] London, claims the poem, has always been the 'metropolis' and largest settlement in the land. It tells of how Augustine and his monks worked their way through the city, replacing blasphemous idols with icons of the saints, turning pagan temples into churches, and renaming them according to the gospels: Apollo's became St Peter's, Jupiter's became James', and Juno's became Jesus'.[23] On the site of St Paul's however, was the largest of all the Saxons' temples, dedicated to a god so terrible the poem will not even mention its name. Here, re-consecration was not enough. Instead, 'the temple was knocked down and beaten down again, anew – a noble enterprise for the occasion, and called the New Work'.[24] This 'New Work' was St Paul's.

While Bishop Erkenwald is overseeing the construction of the church, a discovery is made deep in the building's ancient foundations. The poem tells of a 'marvellous' tomb, crafted exquisitely out of grey marble, decorated with carvings of fearsome-looking gargoyles, and covered in gold writing in an unknown and indecipherable language. When the tomb is opened, it reveals an interior painted in gold, and a body wrapped in expensive royal garments – a gown of gold and pearls, and a fur mantle – wearing a crown and holding a sceptre. This corpse shows no signs of decay, yet it defies identification.[24] Everyone from the Cathedral clerks to the ordinary citizens of London searches for some record of this man, but they find nothing. Yet surely, they tell themselves, 'such a man would have stayed in memory for a long time... it is astonishing that no man can say that he knew him'.[25]

At the time of the discovery, Erkenwald is visiting an abbey in Essex. On hearing the news he rushes back to St Paul's. There, with seemingly the entire city in attendance, he performs mass, and then approaches the corpse, commanding it, by the power of God, to speak. Miraculously, the corpse obeys, and, 'when he in the stone coffin spoke thus, there arose no people in all the world, nor any noise, but all stood as still as the stone and listened, seized by great wonder, and very many wept'.[26] For once the incessant clamour of the city is silenced, as it comes face to face with its past. The corpse explains that he was a judge appointed by a pagan prince, and that he himself followed a pagan faith. He performed good and just works for over forty years, and when he died the whole city mourned him and buried him in this noble tomb. 'How long I have lain here is from a time forgotten,' he says, 'it is too much for any man to give it length'.[27]

The onlookers know instinctively that this judge is a Londoner, one of their own. Accounting for his appearance, he explains that he has not decayed because he has remained in Limbo – a righteous pagan stranded outside of the afterlife because he never knew the ways of God and Heaven. On hearing the judge's story, Erkenwald weeps, and one of his tears falls on the face of the corpse. 'The tears of thine eyes have become my baptism,' cries the judge, 'my soul even now is seated at the Table... where sup the faithful'.[28] At this his body crumbles instantly to dust. 'All the beauty of the body was black as the mould... for as soon as the soul was seized in bliss, corrupt was the embrace that covered the bones'.[29] At the poem's end, everyone exits St Paul's in a great, joyful procession, 'and all the bells in London town burst forth at once'.[30]

St Erkenwald is about reclaiming and legitimising a difficult, sometimes forgotten past. For the Christian Londoners in the poem, the inconvenient truth is that their city's most important and sacred building, St Paul's, stands on the exact spot once occupied by an older, idolatrous religion. The judge helps set the collective civic mind at rest. His miraculous voice, travelling from an ancient world, assures them that, had he known of Jesus and God, he would have followed him faithfully. All at once, the city's pagan past is given a Christian foundation.[31]

In the poem, art is imitating life. The real Erkenwald died on 30 April AD 693.[32] After he was buried in the nave of St Paul's, his tomb became the greatest and most famous shrine in London, and he was named as the city's patron saint.[33] In AD 962, and then again in 1087, the original Saxon church was attacked by two fires.[34] The second ravaged London, and all that survived of St Paul's was St Erkenwald's centuries-old tomb.[35] In the fourteenth century, at the exact time the poem was written, his remains were moved to an even greater shrine in the rebuilt cathedral, and covered in jewels and precious gifts. Three goldsmiths spent a year on its decoration. In effect, St Erkenwald *is* the pagan judge of the poem: a figure from ancient London, interred in St Paul's in his own arcane tomb of gold.

With this in mind, it is possible to see a more satirical message hidden within the work. The key comes with the judge's body crumbling to dust in the moment of his baptism. The implication is that we change history to suit our modern sensibilities, in the process denying or even destroying the physical, objective evidence of the past.[36] It is a prophetic message. Unknowingly, the fourteenth-century poem anticipates a devastating religious war to come. Two hundred years after *St Erkenwald* was written, the fabric of both St Paul's, and the whole of Western Christianity, would be torn apart.

In the immediate aftermath of the 1087 fire, a new cathedral began to emerge from the burnt-out shell of the old church. Just months before his death in September of that year, William the Conqueror granted the use of building materials 'out of the ruins of that strong castle, then called the Palatine Tower, which stood on the west part of the City, towards the little River of Fleet'[37], near the site of modern day Fleet Street. Despite this promising start, progress was slow. The Bishop of London, Maurice, was responsible for the design and construction of the cathedral, but he does not seem to have been the most pious or conscientious of men. After twenty years all he had succeeded in building were the foundations. Nevertheless, there was no denying the ambition of his ground plan for the new structure. St Paul's, if it was ever finished, would be one of the largest Christian buildings in Europe; at nearly 600 feet in length it would be 60 feet longer than its rival at Winchester.

Maurice's successor, Richard de Belmeis, brought both more energy and more of the episcopate's finances – with which the previous Bishop had been reluctant to part – to bear on the work, and gradually the cathedral began to take shape. Belmeis received generous support from Henry I, who provided him with stone and waived the toll for any materials brought to the construction site along the River Fleet. In recognition of Belmeis' dedication to the cause, the king also granted St Paul's the rights to any fish caught in the Thames or the Fleet in the vicinity of the new cathedral, along with a share in all venison hunted in the County of Essex. Another twenty years of work passed under the Belmeis' stewardship, but still the cathedral was not finished. The Bishop died in 1129 AD with St Paul's little more than half built. He did, however, leave one lasting legacy: the school he founded on the site, which has endured in one form or another right up to the present day.

Once again, fire, that recurrent motif in the life of St Paul's, came to claim the cathedral. According to the chroniclers Matthew Paris and Matthew of Westminster, in 1136 AD St Paul's 'had great hurt by a dreadful fire... which began at London Bridge and raged as far as the Church of the Danes'. So great was this 'hurt' that the building was completely destroyed, according to the two monks.[38] Other sources suggest that this was an exaggeration[39], but there is no doubt that the fire had a serious impact on the reconstruction. Patrons had to be sought and money raised before the builders could get back to work. By around 1175 most of the fabric of the cathedral was in place, with a roofed nave and choir giving St Paul's a functional core. Work continued on its tower, which was completed in 1221. At around 460 to 489 feet high, it was probably the tallest structure in all of Europe at that time. Indeed, no building in London would exceed this height until the second half of the twentieth century.[40]

Almost a century and a half had passed since construction had begun – a century and a half of changing tastes and fashions. These were written across the fabric of the cathedral in a haphazard mix of architectural styles. Throughout the building, blunt and heavy Norman structures sat alongside English Gothic flourishes – pointed arches and delicate, clustered pillars. A unified style was anathema to St Paul's. In this the building reflected its city and its people.

The fitful building process did not improve the cathedral's general structural integrity. In 1255 the Bishop of London launched an appeal to 'save' the newly-completed St Paul's because it had, he said, over time been 'so shattered by tempests'[41] that its roof and tower were on the verge of collapse. Towards the end of the thirteenth century, and into the fourteenth, St Paul's was shored up by a series of repairs and extensions, which became known collectively as the 'New Work' – the very term used by the poem *St Erkenwald* to describe the seventh-century construction of the cathedral.[42] The choir was rebuilt, a wide pavement of marble laid around the outside of the building, and the spire was taken down. In its place was erected 'a new Cross, with a pommel large enough to contain ten bushels of corn'[43], which rose up from a reinforced, Gothic tower of stone.

The long history of St Paul's, leading back beyond St Erkenwald into a mythic pagan past, along with its numerous and very visible travails, granted the cathedral a special place in the affections of Londoners. Built and rebuilt, over and over, out of funds drawn from public and private sources, it belonged, in a sense, to every citizen. Its function extended far beyond its primary purpose as a place for spiritual worship, its great, dark and bulky gravity seeming to draw in city life in all its varied colours and hues. In 1285, on the orders of Edward I, St Paul's was enclosed by a substantial wall, with guarded gates that were closed at night, because 'by the lurking of thieves, and other bad people, in the night time, within the precinct of the Church Yard... robberies, homicides, and fornications had been committed herein'.[44] In Saxon times, civic gatherings, known as *folkmoots*, had taken place on a large green to the east of the St Paul's.[45] Now these public assemblies continued within the cathedral grounds. At the ringing of the great cathedral bell, people would come to meet before a covered pulpit set over a series of stone steps, and topped by a crucifix.

This was known as 'Paul's Cross' and it was the site, in 1259, where Henry III chose to issue his order that every Londoner must swear allegiance to the king of England and his heirs. Papal bulls and the sentencing of notorious criminals were also announced from the Cross, and it became the central hub from which both official news and scurrilous gossip spread throughout the city.[46] Traders and merchants were attracted by the crowds. From the fourteenth century, stalls appeared every day in the churchyard, even inside the nave of St Paul's itself. Scriveners in particular set up shop within the cathedral, and all of London came to them to write or notarise contracts and documents.[47]

As well as playing a central role in the everyday life of the city, St Paul's was called upon to host grand ceremonies. In 1184, the Archbishop of Cologne and the Count of Flanders came to London on a religious visit. They were received by a city revelling in pageantry, covered in decorations, with dancers lining the streets, and were led in a long procession over London Bridge to St Paul's. Similarly, in 1194, when Richard I, who had been imprisoned for two years while journeying back from the Crusades, finally made it home to England, his return was honoured with an extravagant march through the city to the cathedral. Richard II, Henry VI and Henry VII lay there in state before their funerals.[48] St Paul's was becoming the theatre of all London life, frequented by everyone from market traders and pickpockets to the highest-born royalty, alive or dead.

It was perhaps inevitable, then, that the cathedral would stage the first of a series of events that would see England lurch, over a century and a half, towards religious revolution, civil war, and the execution of its king.

On Sunday 14 November 1501 – St Erkenwald's day – the Prince and Princess of Wales were married in St Paul's Cathedral.[49] Then as now, few occasions generated such levels of hype and hysteria as a royal wedding. Scaffoldings were erected throughout the city, running from Gracechurch Street to St Paul's, and hung with the finest satins, silks and velvets of silver and gold. The sixteenth-century chronicler Edward Hall wrote of the 'musical instruments which sounded with heavenly notes on every side of the street', and of the 'costly apparel, both of goldsmiths work and embroidery, the rich jewels, the massy chains, the stirring horses'.[50] He described citizens standing on the scaffoldings in their finest colourful clothes and expensive furs, while the Mayor of London and his retinue sat on horseback, clad in velvets, golden chains and – it being the fashion to perfume clothes – their most 'odiferous scarlets'.[51]

Running through the centre of St Paul's, from the west doors to the steps leading into the choir, was a custom-built wooden walkway, elevated six feet off the ground, and almost 600 feet in length. The walkway was covered in red worsted cloth, secured by golden nails. At its halfway point was a stage, raised even higher by a series of steps, where the wedding would take place in full view of the large crowd crammed into the cathedral. Both the prince and princess wore white satin, and Hall described them as 'both lusty and amorous, he of the age of fifteen and more, and she of the age of eighteen or thereabouts'.[52] The groom was Arthur, eldest son of the Tudor King Henry VII, and his bride was Catherine, daughter of the indomitable Spanish power couple, King Ferdinand of Aragon and Queen Isabella of Castile. At the end of the ceremony, as had been prearranged, Arthur's younger brother Henry, the Duke of York, who, even at the age of nine, was a tall and striking-looking, took the hand of the new Princess of Wales and walked her back along the wooden walkway and out of the cathedral's main doors, to a crescendo of music and cheers.

That night saw a feast so great that Hall felt incapable of describing it, saying only that it was 'not so sumptuous as populous, nor yet so populous as delicate, nor so delicate as of all things abundant.' Afterwards, the prince and princess 'were brought and joined together in one bed naked, and there did that act which to the performance and full consummation of matrimony was most requisite and expedient'.[53]

The next morning, Arthur called to his servants for drink, remarking that he was so thirsty because 'I have this night been in Spain, which is a hot region, and that journey maketh me so dry'.[54] It was just the sort of crude boast one might expect of a 'lusty', teenage prince. But was it true? The fate of the English nation would turn on this question.

Arthur died, probably of consumption, five months after the wedding. His younger brother did not, however, forget the experience of walking the Spanish princess down the aisle of St Paul's. Eight years later, at the age of seventeen years and ten months, Prince Henry became King Henry VIII. And for his queen, he chose Catherine, the widow of his dead brother. Contrary to Arthur's wedding-night boasts, Catherine and her governess Dona Elvira insisted that the original marriage had never been consummated. Nevertheless, both the English and Spanish crowns proceeded on the basis that there had been a physical union, and sought a dispensation from the Pope for an annulment. Once this was granted, Henry and Catherine were free to wed.

Two decades later, with the queen in her early forties, and with no male heir to the throne, Henry was growing restless. Desperate to marry his would-be lover, Anne Boleyn, he returned to the Pope, this time to seek the annulment of his own marriage, citing the words of Leviticus: 'If a man shall take his brother's wife, it is an impurity: he hath uncovered his brother's nakedness: they shall be childless'.[55]

The backdrop to this royal soap opera was a religious schism – known as the Reformation – that had struck at the heart of Western Christianity. On 31 October 1517, a German cleric called Martin Luther nailed to the door of the cathedral of Wittenberg an inflammatory objection, in ninety-five *Theses,* to the corruption that he believed was endemic in the Catholic Church. At first, Henry spoke out against Luther's ideas, which formed the basis for the new doctrine of Protestantism, earning himself Papal favour and the title 'Defender of the Faith'.

As time passed, however, the king's attempts to prove the illegality of his marriage to Catherine were sparking increasingly intense political and theological arguments across the continent. Henry's closest advisor Thomas Cromwell, and the Archbishop of Canterbury Thomas Cranmer, convinced him that a total break from Rome was the only way to untangle the messy circumstances of his personal life. Although Henry remained a Catholic, he was excommunicated by the Pope, and effectively became the figurehead for Protestant reform in England. In 1540, Henry decreed that all property held by the Catholic Church should be surrendered to the crown. Lands were seized and sold on to raise money for the royal coffers. In keeping with the more puritan aesthetic and ideals of Protestantism, the shrines, icons and altars which adorned ecclesiastical buildings were torn down, and in many cases destroyed. The monasteries, which had brought the Christian faith to England, were dissolved, and many were left to go to ruin.

On several occasions during the 1520s, St Paul's had been the venue for mass burnings of Protestant books and pamphlets. By the late 1530s, however, the position was reversed. Now preachers gathered at St Paul's Cross to denounce the Pope and the 'magic' and 'mystery' of Catholicism. In February 1538, in a ceremony rich in symbolism, the rood screen of Boxley Abbey in Kent – whose centrepiece was a sculpture of Jesus with eyes that moved thanks to hidden wires – was brought to St Paul's, smashed to pieces and thrown on a bonfire in the centre of the churchyard.[56] As they demonstrated to the watching crowd the rood's secret mechanism, which the Boxley monks had presented as a miracle, the Protestant supporters proclaimed that they had exposed another instance of Catholic dishonesty.

Rather than burning and banning books, the king now promoted public access to the holy text, on condition that it be read 'meekly, humbly, and reverently, for their instruction, edification and amendment'.[57] Any church that did not make copies of the Bible available in both Latin and English was subject to a severe financial penalty. In St Paul's, six copies were chained to separate pillars.[58]

During the reign of Edward VI – Henry VIII's only son from his third wife Jane Seymour – the architectural ornamentation of St Paul's came under sustained attack. Edward sent commissioners to the cathedral, and tasked them with overseeing a programme of 'iconoclasm', entailing the removal or destruction of every symbol of the Catholic faith they could find inside the building. The cathedral's great rood screen was pulled down and broken up, interior chapels, altars and reredos screens were destroyed, and the substantial Becket Chapel in the north cloister, along with its famous wall mural of the 'Dance of Death', was flattened and turned into a garden. This last act was perpetrated by the Lord Protector, the Duke of Somerset, who used the cathedral stones for a new home he was building on the Strand – a certain Somerset House.[59]

With much of the religious texture removed from St Paul's, the building became less of a church and more of colossal market and meeting place. On 5 August 1554, the Lord Mayor of London issued a proclamation bemoaning the tendency of the people 'to make the common carriage of great vessels full of ale and beer, great baskets full of bread, fish, bundles of stuff and other gross wares through the Cathedral Church of St Paul', and emphasised that those 'leading the horses, mules, or other beasts through the same unreverently', did so 'to the great dishonour and displeasure of Almighty God, and the great grief also and offence of all good and well-disposed persons'.[60] The Mayor declared all these practices forbidden – on penalty of imprisonment – yet the edict was largely ignored.

Despite these major political and religious upheavals, the greatest damage to St Paul's in the sixteenth century was caused not by men, but by God. In his book *Annals of St Paul's Cathedral,* Dean Millman describes how, in 1561, 'a terrific storm burst over London', and 'lightning was seen to flash into an aperture in the steeple of the Cathedral'. Because the steeple was made of wood covered with lead, 'the fire burned downwards for four hours with irresistible force, the bells melted, the timber blazed, the stones crumbled and fell. The lead flowed down in sheets of flame... the fire ran along the roof, east, west, north and south, which fell in, filling the whole church with a mass of ruin'.[61]

On both sides of the religious divide, this incident was seen as a demonstration of heavenly wrath. For Catholics, it was a divine judgement on the desecration of the city's holiest temple; for the Protestants, God's hint that reform had not gone far or fast enough. Nevertheless, all London society joined together to restore the fabric of the cathedral. Queen Elizabeth I ordered a thousand loads of timber be taken from her forests to help with the rebuilding work, while the Bishop of London and the Dean of St Paul's added their own money to the substantial sums raised from a public appeal to fund the repairs.[62] Within five years new roofs of timber and lead covered the cathedral, but the great spire on top of the central tower would never be rebuilt.

Very soon the patched-up St Paul's was reprising its role as the centre of all London life, and life in general. While still used as the setting for great national ceremonies – in 1588, Elizabeth and all the English nobility gathered in the cathedral for a sermon to give thanks for the defeat of the Spanish Armada[63] – increasingly, St Paul's was becoming a secular meeting-place for every class and creed of London citizen.

The main aisle of the cathedral was dubbed 'Paul's Walk', and, like the Forums in ancient Roman cities, it was the hub for all news, politics, business, and public and private affairs. The seventeenth-century essayist, Francis Osborne wrote of how it was 'the fashion of those times... for the principal gentry, lords, courtiers, and men of all professions not merely mechanic, to meet in Paul's Church by eleven and walk in the middle aisle till twelve, and after dinner from three to six, during which times some discoursed on business, others of news'.[64]

In his 1628 work *Microcosmography,* Bishop John Earle went even further, describing Paul's Walk as:

> 'the land's epitome, or you may call it the lesser isle of Great Britain. It is more than this – the whole world's map, which you may discern in its perfectest motion, jostling and turning. It is a heap of stones and men, with a vast confusion of languages; and were the steeple not sanctified, nothing like Babel. The noise in it is like that

> of bees, a strange humming or buzz mixed of walking, tongues and feet; it is a kind of still roar or loud whisper. It is the great exchange of all discourse, and no business whatsoever but is here stirring and afoot... It is the general mint of lies, which are here, like the legends of popery, first coined and stamped in the church. All inventions are emptied here, and not a few pockets. The best sign of a temple in it is that it is the thieves' sanctuary, which rob more safely in the crowd than in the wilderness... It is the other expense of the day after plays and tavern, and men still have some oaths left to swear here'.[65]

Not surprisingly, as a major focal point for life in Elizabethan London, it came to the attention of the leading dramatists of the day. In the 1598 play *Englishmen for My Money*, William Haughton described St Paul's as an 'open house' filled with a 'great store of company that do nothing but go up and down, and go up and down, and make a grumbling together'.[66] Ben Jonson's satirical play of the same year, *Every Man out of His Humour,* opens its third act in St Paul's Walk. On being asked why he is there, the character Shift replies, 'I have been taking an ounce of tobacco here, with a gentleman, and I am come to spit private in Paul's'. He then suggests to his compatriot that they walk in 'Meditteraneo' – the middle aisle.[67]

In *Henry IV, Part II*, Shakespeare similarly refers to the cathedral as a place to do business: it is in St Paul's that Falstaff 'buys' the services of the drunkard captain Bardolph. Shakespeare had a professional interest in the cathedral: in 1599, the new choirmaster of St Paul's reformed the Paul's Boys' company of child actors, and began staging plays in the churchyard. By advertising 'private' shows open to just a few hundred spectators, the Boys could operate without a license from the Master of the Revels, allowing them to stage more daring performances, supported by more influential backers. Shakespeare viewed the position of this company with envy.[68] St Paul's provided him with a dramatic backdrop for one of his most famous plays: *Julius*

Caesar has as its pivotal moment two speeches given in turn at Caesar's funeral by Brutus and Mark Antony. According to the historical accounts the two men stood on the famous orator's platform known as the Rostra, at the heart of the Forum of Rome. Shakespeare, however, describes them as delivering their lines from a 'pulpit'. Rather than Caesar's ancient city, he is describing for his Elizabethan audience Paul's Cross – for hundreds of years the most important public meeting place in London.[69]

The increasing popularity of drama did not go unnoticed by the more extreme advocates of the Protestant Reformation. As early as 1578, the Puritan clergyman John Stockwood complained, 'Will not a filthy play, with the blast of a trumpet, sooner call thither a thousand, than an hour's tolling of a bell, bring to the sermon a hundred?'[70]

There was a sense that, in stripping away both the ritual and physical fabric of Catholicism, a vacuum had been left in St Paul's. And rather than be filled with puritan thoughts of God, it was being invaded by the teeming multitudes of city life, in a way that recalled a millennia-distant pagan past. The empty alcoves, cloisters and chapels of St Paul's became storerooms for goods and lumber, and workshops for glaziers and carpenters, whose 'knocking and noise' frequently disturbed church services.[71] Merchants' booths were erected against the outer walls of the cathedral, selling tobacco and freshly-baked pies; bell-ringers ran a sideline offering tours to the top of the tower for a small fee. From the summit customers entertained themselves by shouting out across the city or even throwing stones at passers-by below. In 1569 the West Door of St Paul's became the venue for the drawing of the first recorded lottery in England. And in 1630, in what may have seemed the final indignity, the Dean of St Paul's let out the cathedral vault to the Green Dragon public house, for use as a wine cellar.[72]

On 27 August 1666, John Evelyn, one of the foremost intellectuals and diarists of seventeenth-century England, and Christopher Wren, an aspiring young architect, went to St Paul's 'to survey the general decays of that ancient and venerable Church, and to set down in writing the particulars of what was to be done, with the charge thereof, giving our opinion from article to article'.[73] Their task, as directed by King Charles II, was to 'consider a model for the new building, or (if it might be) repairing the steeple, which was most decayed'.[74]

Wren had already produced his own report on St Paul's, submitted on 1 May 1666.[75] In Evelyn he had found a willing and influential supporter. Wren's report began with a summary of the various competing opinions over the way forward for the cathedral. 'Among the propositions that may be made to your Lordships concerning the repair of St Paul's,' he wrote, 'some may possibly aim at too great magnificence... Others again may fall so low as to think of piecing up the old fabric, here with stone, there with brick, and cover all faults with a coat of plaster, leaving it still to posterity as a further object of charity.'[76]

In his forensic assessment of the building's creaking structural integrity, Wren sought to demonstrate to the king and his advisors both his passion for the task at hand, and the depth of his architectural skill. He identified instantly that the roof was too heavy for its supporting walls and pillars, some of which were already bent outwards a considerable distance, as they were filled with 'nothing but a core of small rubbish-stone, and much mortar, which easily crushes and yields to the weight'.[77] He could see that new arches had been erected in an attempt to shore up the roof, but described their installation as a 'deformity'. His provocative conclusion was that St Paul's was 'ill designed and ill built from the beginning'.[78] Yet it was not totally lost. And in urging substantial reconstruction, Wren was proposing, quite deliberately, a building project that could act as a potent symbol for the rebirth of a modern nation, healing the divisions after a century of trouble.

Once again, St Paul's had worn England's turbulent history on its sleeve – or rather, on its decaying and mouldering stonework. In 1625, Charles I, the son of James I of England and James VI of Scotland, came to the throne. Tensions had mounted throughout his reign. Parliamentarians objected to the king's authoritarian style of rule, while some of the more radical Protestants among the population began to suspect Charles of being at the centre of a plot to undo the Reformation and restore the Catholic faith. By 1641, widespread discontent had begun to spill over into revolution. London, the home of parliament, was where it began.

As England's capital prepared to stand against its king, trenches were dug and barricades built to defend Westminster and the City of London from Cavalier attack.[79] Behind the defences, no building was sacrosanct – least of all the cathedral. Despite its steady decline as a place of worship, St Paul's remained a symbol of royal rule and the establishment. In the 1630s Charles I had commissioned his favourite architect, Inigo Jones, to revamp the dark Gothic mass of St Paul's. In direct imitation of the basilicas of antiquity, which he had studied on a 'Grand Tour' of Europe, Jones had designed a façade of Corinthian columns supporting a row of classical statues depicting key figures in the royal family, set between two flanking towers. Clad in bright white Portland stone, it crash-landed a shining vision of an entirely new style of architecture into the heart of old England. To the feverish eyes of the Puritans, this supplied further evidence – if evidence were needed – of the king's obsession with Rome and, by extension, popery. Jones had been planning further alterations, and much of the building was covered in scaffolding as civil war broke out.[80]

Over the next decade, as the nineteenth-century Dean of St Paul's Henry Hart Milman put it, 'with Puritanism in the ascendant, St Paul's became a vast useless pile'.[81] Although the cathedral was not destroyed 'for it would have been a work of cost and labour to destroy it', it was 'left to chance, exposed at least to neglect, too often to wanton mischief'.[82] The parliamentarian leader, Oliver Cromwell, was one of the chief tormentors of St Paul's. As marble flooring was torn up and lead stripped from the roof – both sold to raise funds for the war – the voices of Puritan preachers filled the echoing spaces of the cathedral. One end of the building was turned into a sawmill, while Cromwell's 'New Model Army', his innovative, highly professional 'people's' military, requisitioned the rest of the building for use as a barracks and stables.[83]

This mistreatment of the building was deliberately disrespectful, a sign of just how far the revolutionaries were prepared to go.

On 30 January 1649, Charles I was beheaded in front of a massed crowd gathered outside the Banqueting House of the Palace of Whitehall. This vast neoclassical building had been designed two decades before for the king's father James I, by none other than Inigo Jones.[84] The civil war left St Paul's a wrecked and empty shell. Despite Cromwell's provocative suggestion that it be converted into a Jewish synagogue[85], for the next ten years it remained a semi-derelict barracks. It was only after Cromwell's death in 1658, and the failed rule of his son and successor Richard as Lord Protector, that any hope of salvation emerged.[86] In May 1660, the exiled son and heir of the executed king returned to English shores, making a triumphant entry into London. Just under a year later, on 23 April 1661, he was crowned Charles II.

The new king was faced with a country in a parlous state of division and shock. Just two months before Charles's coronation, a small force of radical Puritans had mounted a counter-revolution, barricading themselves within the churchyard of St Paul's.[87] After several days of intense fighting, the dissidents were all shot and killed. No matter how diminished it had become, both the Royalists and the Republicans knew that the cathedral still *mattered*.

It was with this sentiment in mind that Charles II ordered a Royal Commission on 18 April 1663 to explore what could be done to repair and restore St Paul's.[88] Even during the years of fury and fanaticism that characterised the civil war and its aftermath, some had championed the cause of the cathedral. In 1655, the Reverend Thomas Fuller, in his work *The Church History of Britain,* remarked that the cathedral 'formerly approached with due reverence, is now entered with just fear – of falling on those under it'.[89] Between 1656 and 1658, the prominent historian and antiquarian William Dugdale, drew on confiscated church records and myriad historical documents to write *The History of St Paul's Cathedral in London.* His book was at once a chronology of the building's development from earliest times up to his own day, and an impassioned plea to preserve St Paul's as an icon of the nation.[90] This sentiment was echoed by the man employed by Dugdale to illustrate his history: Wenceslaus Hollar. The Bohemian etcher had fled London to Antwerp during the worst years of the civil war, not least because his former patron, Lord Arundel, was a close confidant of Charles I and one of the most prominent Catholic noblemen in England. Hollar had returned in 1652, again making his living from artistic commissions.[91] Under one of the most striking of the many etchings he produced for Dugdale's book – a masterpiece of light and shadow showing a perspective view looking down the cathedral's great medieval nave – he inscribed a portentous message: 'Wenceslaus Hollar, daily expecting the collapse of this church, of which he is the drawer and long-term admirer, thus preserves its memory.'[92]

Wenceslaus Hollar's 1656 etching of the nave of St Paul's, popularly known as 'Paul's Walk'

Christopher Wren was rather less concerned with preserving the memory of St Paul's than with gradually, yet comprehensively, altering its architectural DNA. Following the portico built by Inigo Jones, which he described as 'an entire and excellent piece', he proposed 'cutting off the inner corners of the cross to reduce this middle part into a spacious dome or rotunda, with a cupola or hemispherical roof, and upon the cupola, a lantern with a spring top, to rise proportionably'. With this innovation, he predicted, 'the church will be rendered spacious in the middle, which may be a very proper place for a vast auditory'.[93]

Unsurprisingly, not everyone agreed with Wren's assessment, in particular Roger Pratt, an older and more senior architect appointed by the Royal Commission into St Paul's, and also present to survey the cathedral on 27 August 1666.[94] Evelyn's judgement carried considerable weight, however, and as was clear from his diary, he had become an eager convert to Wren's vision. 'When we came to the steeple, it was deliberated whether it were not well enough to repair it only upon its old foundation,' he wrote. After much discussion, this idea was 'totally rejected' in favour of a new foundation which would support 'a noble cupola, a form of church building not as yet known in England, but of wonderful grace'.[95]

For Evelyn, the matter was settled: 'We offered to bring in a plan and estimate, which, after much contest, was... assented to... This concluded, we drew all up in writing'.[96] Wren, it seemed, had won the contest of wills over the future of St Paul's. The old Gothic cathedral would emerge from its puritan chrysalis as a grandiose homage to the ancient world. A great dome was set to rise above London.

On 2 September 1666, less than a week after the meeting at St Paul's, John Evelyn's diary entry opens with a shocking sentence: 'This fatal night about ten, began that deplorable fire, near Fish Street in London'.[97] Evelyn described how, after finishing his prayers and dinner at his home, he went with his wife and son by coach to Southwark, and was astonished by the sight of 'the whole city in dreadful flames near the waterside'. The next morning, after a night 'which was as light as day for 10 miles round about after a dreadful manner'[98], Evelyn returned on foot to the same spot to survey the extent of the blaze. He saw the whole north bank of the city burning – Cheapside, Tower Street, Fenchurch Street, Gracious Street – and even thought he could discern the fire taking hold of St Paul's.

At the same time, across the Thames on the other side of the city, Samuel Pepys, a naval administrator and committed diarist, who lived just eight streets east of Fish Street, climbed to the top of the Tower of London to assess the danger, to the city and to his own home. 'There I did see the houses at that end of the bridge all on fire,' wrote Pepys, 'and an infinite great fire on this and the other end of the bridge. So with my heart full of trouble, I down to the water-side, and there got a boat and through the bridge, and there saw a lamentable fire'.[99] Pepys recorded the terrible panic of Londoners throwing their goods into boats, or just into the river itself, as they attempted to flee. He even noticed the pigeons in the skies above. They flapped around their burning nests in the rafters of the city's houses, and when some came too close to the fire, or had their wings singed by sparks, he watched as they dropped helpless into the flames.[100]

Old St Paul's consumed by the Great Fire, by Wenceslaus Hollar. The legend at the top can be translated as 'even the ruins perished' and was intended as a reference to the legendary city of Troy.

As Thomas Vincent described in his 1667 account of the fire, entitled *God's terrible voice in the city*, the starting point was a baker's house in Pudding Lane, 'in the depth and dead of the night, when most doors and fences were locked up in the city'. Once the first flames had caught hold, Vincent wrote of how the fire, 'like a mighty giant refreshed with wine', awoke and 'made havoc' as it ran 'with great noise and violence through Thames Street westward; where having such combustible matter in its teeth, and such a fierce wind upon its back, it prevails with little resistance'.[101]

On 3 September, Evelyn wrote that 'all the sky were of a fiery aspect, like the top of a burning oven', and described 'above ten thousand houses all in one flame, the noise and crackling and thunder of the impetuous flames, the shrieking of women and children, the fall of towers, houses and churches... like a hideous storm, and the air all about so hot and inflamed'.[102] Pepys, for his part, had taken up a position in a 'little alehouse' in Bankside, opposite the Three Cranes. 'We stayed till, it being darkish, we saw the fire only as one entire arch of fire from this to the other side of the bridge,' he wrote. 'It made me weep to see it' and, as he watched 'the cracking of houses at their ruin'[103], he hurried home to begin packing up his own belongings and evacuate his family.

The next day, Evelyn attempted to ride on horseback to the western front of the fire – in the vicinity of St Paul's. There he saw Fleet Street, the Old Bailey, Ludgate Hill, Warwick Lane, and Watling Street 'now flaming and most of it reduced to ashes', and above the roofs of the burning houses 'the stones of St Paul's flew like grenades, the lead melting down the streets in a stream, and the very pavements of them glowing with fiery redness, so as nor horse nor man was able to tread on them'.[104] Pepys recorded the fate of the building with a weary brevity: 'Paul's is burned, and all Cheapside'.[105]

On 7 September, with the fire finally dowsed, both Evelyn and Pepys made their way through the city to St Paul's. Pepys rose at 5 o'clock in the morning, and travelled up the Thames by boat to land at Paul's Wharf. As he walked into the midst of the disaster area, he 'saw all the town burned, and a miserable sight of Paul's church, with all the roofs fallen'. He was soon, however, turning his restless mind back to business – writing that there was 'the growth of the city again to be foreseen.'[106]

Evelyn, a committed aesthete, lingered longer over the charred ruins of the old cathedral. Fighting his way towards the site through mounds of smouldering debris, sweating profusely from the heat and burning the soles of his shoes on the dying embers of the fire, he was

> 'infinitely concerned to find that goodly church St Paul's now a sad ruin, and that beautiful portico (for structure comparable to any in Europe, as not long before repaired by the late king) now rent in pieces, flakes of vast stone split asunder, and nothing remaining entire but the inscription in the architrave saying by whom it was built, had not one letter of it defaced'.[107]

Evelyn described the building's huge Portland stones 'calcinated' by the heat, the 'six acres' of lead roof totally melted, and the shattered remains of columns, archways and capitals, many of which appeared to have exploded in the heat. In a bizarre echo of the poem *St Erkenwald,* one tomb in the roofless nave stood without its lid, but otherwise intact.

Lying inside was the body of Robert Braybrooke, a fourteenth-century Bishop of London. The fire had baked his skin hard, but his shock of red hair was still visible. 'Thus lay in ashes that most venerable church, one of the most ancient pieces of early piety in the Christian world,' wrote Evelyn.[108] As he lifted his eyes away from St Paul's, he saw other shocked and listless Londoners picking their way through the ruins 'like men in some distant, dismal desert, or rather in some great city, laid waste by an impetuous and cruel enemy'. For a classicist like Evelyn, it called to mind nothing less than the devastation suffered by ancient Troy. 'London was,' he wrote, paraphrasing Virgil's *Aeneid,* 'but is no more'.[109]

On 26 October 1708, Christopher Wren's son was raised by crane some 365 feet above the streets of London, to place the final stone of the new St Paul's Cathedral on the lantern at the very summit of the building. The younger Wren, who was also named Christopher, had been born in 1675 – the same year that the foundation stone of the building was laid. The elder Wren had just turned seventy-six. He watched his son ascend the superstructure from the safety of the churchyard below. With this last piece slotted into place, St Paul's became the first English cathedral to be completed within the lifetime of its original designer.[110]

Wren's initial vision for the building had evolved and matured in the years after the Great Fire, but it retained its unifying central device. At last, London's skyline had its great, classical dome. Clad in radiant copper, it was visible from as far away as the Essex coast to the east, and Windsor to the west.[111] That was, of course, on those rare occasions when fog and pollution did not obscure the spectacle. 'Our air being frequently hazy prevents those distant views,' bemoaned Wren, 'except when the sun shines out, after a shower of rain has washed down the clouds of sea-coal smoke that hang over the city from so many thousand fires kindled every morning'.[112]

The work to replace the gutted shell of Old St Paul's had been slow, with a number of false starts. In September 1668, Samuel Pepys wrote in his diary of a visit to St Paul's. Two years had passed since the fire, but in his account, it could have been just two days. He described the 'hideous sight of the walls of the church ready to fall' and confessed to being 'in fear as long as [he] was in it'.[113] Apart from clearing the debris from the church floor, almost nothing had been done. 'It is pretty here to see how the late church was but a case wrought over the old church,' observed Pepys, 'for you may see the very old pillars standing whole within the walls of this.'[114]

Despite Wren's observations in his 1666 report on the dreadful state of the cathedral's structure, some of these 'old pillars' and piers had survived the disaster and remained so strong that they could only be brought down by a combination of explosives and battering rams. By 1669, thousands of cartloads of debris were being transported down

Ludgate Hill and taken away by barge along the Thames.[115] 'Architecture aims at Eternity,'[116] Wren wrote in his early thirties. As he removed the last traces of Old St Paul's to provide a clean slate for his new building, one wonders if he paused to consider the irony of this pronouncement. Picking through the ashes and scarred bones of the old – in the case of St Paul's, a cycle of destruction and reconstruction going back to Roman times – was surely to come face-to-face with man's endless capacity for hubris.

During the Second World War, with London subjected to night after night of Luftwaffe bombing raids, St Paul's became a symbol of resolve, resilience and hope – all the more reason, of course, for the German air force to seek to destroy it. Winston Churchill ordered that 'the cathedral must be preserved at all costs'[117], and patrols monitored the building around the clock, with fire crews posted in the immediate vicinity and on constant standby.

Keeping watch over St Paul's during the Battle of Britain
© U.S. National Archives and Records Administration

On the night of 29 September 1940, almost exactly 274 years to the day since London's Great Fire, an incendiary bomb scored a direct hit on the dome of St Paul's. Just as it had done centuries before, the lead in the roof began to melt with the heat, and pour down into the space below. As he watched the devastation across the city, the war correspondent Ernie Pyle wrote, in a chilling echo of Pepys and Evelyn, of how 'flames seemed to whip hundreds of feet into the air. Pinkish-white smoke ballooned upward in a great cloud, and out of this cloud there took shape – so faintly at first that we weren't sure we saw correctly – the gigantic dome and spires of St Paul's Cathedral.' Once again, the life of St Paul's was in the balance. 'It stood there in its enormous proportions – growing slowly clearer and clearer, the way objects take shape at dawn. It was like a picture of some miraculous figure that appears before peace-hungry soldiers on a battlefield... St. Paul's was surrounded by fire, but it came through.'[118]

Wren was lucky. 'Eternity' remains within his grasp – for now.

Chapter Eleven

Journey to the Tent at the Centre of the World

Karakorum – Orkhon Valley, Mongolia
(Born 1220 – Died 1388)

In the late summer of 1251, Ala al-din Ata-Malik Juvaini, a Persian government official and historian, began the long journey to the capital of the world.[1] He set off eastwards from the town of Merv, one of many staging posts on the 4,000-mile-long Silk Road, the trade route linking Europe and Africa with Asia. The road led to Bukhara and Samarkand, then beyond to the dunes of the Taklamakan desert, and the dark sands and gravel of the Gobi desert. To the south lay the Himalayas; to the north was the Altai Mountain range. In between, there was a high, wide plateau of bare – or, if the rains came in the summer months, lush – grassland steppes.

By the time Juvaini and his party reached the city of Talas, in modern day Kyrgyzstan, the heavy winter snowfalls had made the journey onwards almost impossible. 'That winter was long and drawn out and the chill of the air and violence of the cold were such that all of the climes were like the lands of snow,' recalled Juvaini. In a message to his father he described, in a few lines of poetry, how 'the wind has pitched over our heads tents of snow without ropes or poles/ Its arrows penetrate our clothes like an arrow shot by a person of great strength'.[2]

Despite the extreme weather, they pressed onwards. Finally, on 2 May 1252, after almost a year of travelling, Juvaini arrived at his goal – a city set in the middle of an open steppe in the valley of the Orkhon River, on the edge of the Khantai Mountains. The flat grasslands around the city were filled with multicoloured domes of all shapes and sizes: fur- and felt-lined tents called *gers*. At the centre of this *ger* encampment was a substantial rectangular wall, with four gates built at the midpoint of each side. 'One for the passage of the World-Ruling Emperor,' wrote Juvaini, 'another for his children and kinsmen, another again for the prince, and a fourth for the entrance and egress of the populace.'[3] The wall was built of black stones – 'kara' and 'korum', in the language of the steppe-people – and this gave the city its name. Karakorum.[4]

Juvaini described how architects and craftsmen from China had 'reared up a castle' inside the black wall, with four entrances to match the four gates of the city. The walls of this castle were covered with painted pictures, and inside, at the top of three flights of steps, was a great throne. The emperor, he said, would come to this place in the early spring and, 'as the bounty of the rain reached both herbs and trees'[5], would feast for a month. The palace contained a series of giant gold and silver vats, filled with alcohol during the celebrations, and so heavy that they had to be carried into the midst of the festivities on the backs of camels and elephants. Naturally, all the utensils at these feasts were of gold and silver, and lined with jewels.[6]

As spring began to turn to summer, the royal court moved out of the city, to another palace, a day's journey away. This had been built by Muslim architects, and was a towering structure of tiles and bricks decorated throughout with colourful, jewel-encrusted embroideries and exquisite woven carpets. In front of the palace, the emperor had commanded the construction of a large lake, where 'many water fowls used to gather'. From the palace terrace, he watched as his falconers hunted the water fowl, and 'afterwards would give himself up to the joys of drinking and spread the carpet of bounty, which was never rolled up'.[7]

As the seasons passed, the royal court moved on again, this time to the mountains, to a Chinese-built pavilion made of latticed wood, its light, spacious rooms hung with white felt and golden cloth. At the height of summer, this highland retreat offered cool breezes and waters, and verdant grasses.[8] The emperor would stay until the first snows, and then, near the end of autumn, travel on to his winter residence, 100 miles to the south, near the fringes of the Gobi desert.[9]

This was a land of harsh and fluctuating weather conditions. The summer could bring temperatures as high as forty degrees centigrade, and periods of unbroken sun that turned the undulating green of the steppes and the colourful blossoms of the wild flowers into a scorched wasteland. In October, bitter north winds blew in from Siberia and the Arctic Circle, carrying prolonged snowstorms. By November, every lake and river was frozen solid. The cold was unrelenting, dropping to forty degrees below zero.[10] During this time, the emperor remained in his winter palace. Having stockpiled food, drink and fuel, he would 'make merry for three months' until the thaws began.[11] The imperial court enjoyed a nomadic existence, migrating with the seasons, but Karakorum was always at the centre, a constant stop-off as the emperor criss-crossed his domain.

Juvaini remained in Karakorum for just over a year, witnessing these comings and goings first-hand before he journeyed back to the west in the late summer of 1253. It was during this stay that he resolved to write an account of the people who had made these steppes and this landscape their home.[12] He focussed on one man in particular, called Temujin, who had united the region's many nomadic tribes and led them from obscurity to imperial pre-eminence. This man had died two-and-a-half decades before Juvaini's arduous trek to Karakorum, but his legacy was remarkable: the creation of the single largest continuous land empire the world had ever seen.[13] Today, this territory of over 12 million square miles would contain over half of the earth's population.

As was the tradition of his people, Temujin had been buried in secret, in an unmarked grave.[14] His soul however, lived on, in an object known as a *sulde*, or 'spirit banner', a spear shaft tied at one end with strands of hair taken from a warrior's best stallions. Remaining always in the open air, blown by the winds of the steppe and drawing strength from the 'Eternal Blue Sky', the *sulde* gave a man his power in life. It also offered protection in death. Temujin, uniquely, had two spirit banners, one made from white stallions to be displayed in peacetime, and another from black stallions, to be carried to war.[15]

Juvaini would have seen both of these sacred objects, twisting in the breeze, during his year in Karakorum. He was, himself, a conquered subject of this nomad empire, and he was fascinated by the speed and scale of its growth. By 1260, not long after he had been appointed governor of Baghdad – this one-time capital of its own Islamic empire now took its orders from Karakorum – Juvaini's book was nearing completion. After a decade of work, conducted 'in the course of distant journeys', when 'this present writer... snatches an hour or two, when the caravan halts, and writes down these histories', he was ready to publish.[16] In his narrative, he referred to Temujin by the ceremonial title that has echoed down the centuries. The hero of Juvaini's *History of the World Conqueror* was the 'Universal Ruler'.[17] In the language of the central Asian steppes, this translated as *Genghis Khan*.

In 1866, Pyotr Ivanovich Kafarov, a Russian Orthodox friar based in China, published in the journal of the *Works of the Members of the Russian Religious Mission in Peking* a translation of a very old hand-written manuscript.[18] The title he gave his work was *An Old Mongolian Story about Genghis Khan*.

The provenance of this manuscript is horribly complex. Various translations and adaptations had been made over the course of some five centuries. Many were lost or destroyed, but some survived. Of the first, master document, however, there is no trace. What Kafarov – better known by his official title the Archmandrite Palladii – had discovered was a Chinese abridgement of a Mongolian text, which had been reproduced in Chinese characters that represented the phonetic value of the sounds of the original Mongolian words.[19] This first, painstaking translation, which was re-scribed an unknown number of times, had been made in Peking in the fourteenth century.[20] The original document was another century older, completed, according to some of its final lines, at the *yeke qurilta* – the 'Great Assembly' – which took place on the central Mongolian steppe by the Kerulen River in the Year of the Rat. Much heated scholarly debate has contested exactly *which* Year of the Rat this refers to: it could be one of several recurring on a twelve-year cycle. The most likely candidate appears to be 1228, and the *qurilta* which, the year after Genghis Khan's death, saw the selection of his third son, Ogodei as his successor.[21] The original manuscript had no title, and so was known by its very first line: *The origins of Genghis Khan*. The Chinese, however, proposed a more enigmatic appellation, and today we call the work *The Secret History of the Mongols*.[22]

Up to the thirteenth century, the nomadic peoples of the steppes, now known collectively as Mongolians, were almost completely illiterate.[23] It was Genghis Khan who helped to introduce writing, borrowing a script which was a variation of the Turkic language used by the Uighur tribes of northern China.[24] This meant that the first ever recorded history of Mongolia and the Mongol Empire was also the history of Genghis Khan himself. The opening of the *Secret History* is a classic origin story – a narrative intended to provide a unifying myth for a new nation. 'At the beginning,' it tells us, 'there was a blue-gray wolf' whose destiny had been set in heaven, and his wife, a 'fallow doe', who travelled across a great lake to the source of the Onon River, in the shadow of the mountain Burkhan Khaldun. There, the deer gave birth to a human son: Batachikhan, the earliest ancestor of Genghis Khan and the Mongol people.[25]

The account proceeds rapidly through a list of descendants, including 'Alan the Fair' and 'Bondochar the Fool', before arriving at the twelfth century and the birth of Temujin, who is described portentously as emerging from the womb clutching in his right hand a blood clot the size of a knucklebone.[26]

The dramatic story of Temujin's childhood follows – *Young Genghis*, if you like – as he becomes the supreme ruler of the tribes of

Mongolia. We read how Temujin's father Yesugei kidnaps his mother Hoelun, and takes her to his tribal lands by the Onon River in the dense northern forests, where Mongolia meets Siberia. Hoelun is Yesugei's second wife, and Temujin is the eldest son of his second family. When Yesugei dies after being poisoned during a visit to a rival tribe, his two widows and their children are judged to be too great a burden, and are cast out.

With winter approaching, exile is nothing less than a death sentence. Temujin is just ten years old. Somehow, however, Hoelun keeps herself and her children alive. Covering her head against the cold and 'tying tightly her belt to shorten her skirt', she runs up and down the Onon valley gathering fallen apples and cherries, foraging for wild garlic, leek and onion, and dropping hooks into the river to catch meagre salmon and 'fingerlings'.[27]

The *Secret History* then recounts the pivotal moment in Temujin's early life – the incident that first demonstrates his driving will to power. The strict hierarchy of the Mongolian tribes dictated that the eldest male was the head of the family; accordingly, after the death of Yesugei, authority passes down to Begter, Temujin's half-brother. As the boys grow older, however, squabbles start to break out during hunting expeditions. Tensions finally boil over when Begter snatches away a lark shot by Temujin, then steals a fish he has caught.

Temujin's response is remarkable – and somewhat chilling. He complains about Begter to his mother, but she admonishes him for his selfish inability to put the family's needs above his own desires. Temujin realises that Begter will always stand in his way. He takes up his bow and sets off into the steppe with his younger brother Khasar. As the sun sets, the two boys stalk Begter to a hillock, where he sits guarding the family horses. Begter refuses to fight his brothers, echoing Hoelun's injunction that they should all pull together against their outside enemies. The brothers ignore him – Khasar shoots him from the front, and Temujin from the back – and leave him, according to tradition, to rot away on the spot where he has died.[28]

When her sons return to the *ger*, Hoelun understands immediately from their faces what they have done. Her response in the *Secret*

History is a furious monologue, during which she compares the two boys to the most remorseless of predators: lions, tigers, pythons, jackals, wolves and falcons, and a 'Mandarin duck who eats his own chicks'. At last, exhausted, she tells them that the family now have 'no friends but [their own] shadow'.[29] She is wrong, however, to suggest that Temujin has behaved without thought. This murder was a calculated act, and the template for every battle for leadership he would face in the future.[30]

When the local tribal elders hear of this crime, they hunt Temujin down to punish him for the killing. He is captured at the beginning of summer, taken to the main tribal camp, and forced to spend his days in a *cangue*, a heavy wooden board adapted from a yoke used for oxen, which was worn around the neck and which bound the hands. After a month of humiliating imprisonment, Temujin uses the distraction of a great, very drunken feast held on the banks of the Onon to escape, jumping into the river and using the *cangue* to float downstream on the current. When search parties are sent out to look for him, he is discovered hiding in the reed beds by a member of a family he has befriended during his time in the camp. Rather than give him up, this man instead proposes to help him, 'because you are so clever, and because there is fire in your eyes, there is light in your face'.[31]

This is the turning point in Temujin's fortunes. Although an outlaw on the run, he soon gains the support of a powerful patron – Torghil, a compatriot of his late father, and ruler of some of the most fertile steppes in the central Mongolian valley of the Orkhon River. The story of his escape from the *cangue* has shown that there is something special about Temujin – a charisma that inspires devotion, and crosses blood ties and family boundaries.

Soon Temujin is leading Torghil's armies against the rival factions of Mongolia. Having wiped out the tribe which kidnapped his own wife, Borte, he proceeds to mount campaigns over increasingly wider territories.[32] A supreme military strategist – perhaps, it is said, because in his childhood he had learnt the arts of both the ruthless hunters of the mountain forests and the ordered herdsmen of the steppes – he wins victory after victory.

It is only a matter of time before Temujin comes into conflict with his patron-turned-surrogate-father, Torghil.[33] With the support of the shamans, who tell the people that Temujin has a heavenly mandate to rule the steppes[34], he mounts a final, decisive bid for power. At a *qurilta* in 1206, with all rivals overcome, he is given the title 'Genghis Khan'.[35]

Temujin was thirty-nine years old. He had created a new nation through sheer force of personality, and he was its sole leader. But what, he wondered, lay across the deserts and over the mountains? Who were his rivals in the lands beyond the steppes? Who was the ruler of the world?

At the start of the thirteenth century, almost no one outside East Asia had heard of the Mongols. Yet within a few decades the panicked scribes of the Christian west had identified them as the number one threat to medieval civilisation. Around 1238[36], a Benedictine friar called Matthew Paris, based almost 7,000 kilometres west of Karakorum at St Albans Abbey in Hertfordshire, wrote in his *Chronica Majora* of 'an immense horde of a detestable race of Satan' which had 'burst forth from their mountain-bound regions' and passed through rocks 'like demons'.[37]

These men, whom Paris termed Tartars – after *Tartarus*, the Greek name for the lowest rung of Hell – were 'inhuman and of the nature of beasts, rather to be called monsters than men, thirsting after and drinking blood, and tearing and devouring the flesh of dogs and human beings.'[38] He described the Mongols as clothed in the skins of bulls, 'short in stature and thickset, compact in their bodies, and of great strength; invincible in battle, indefatigable in labour', and recounted how, by burning down woodland and pulling down castles, razing cities to the ground and massacring citizens, they had 'ravaged the eastern countries with lamentable destruction, spreading fire and slaughter wherever they went'.[39] In a wonderfully English aside, he also noted that the Mongol threat had ruined that year's foreign trade of herring out of Yarmouth.[40]

It was only after invading the lands occupied by the Mongols' closest relatives and rivals, the Chinese, that Genghis Khan had made his move westwards. In 1209, three years after his enthronement, his armies had struck out from the steppe to attack the Tanguts of Hsi-Hsia, the westernmost kingdom of China. This was a 'practice run' at a small, isolated state.[41] Two years later, the Mongols were ready for a major campaign. They crossed the Gobi desert and carved their way into the heart of the Chin empire. By 1215 they had broken through the famous Great Wall, laying waste to the Chin capital Chung-tu on the Yellow River.[42]

Some historians view Genghis Khan as the inventor of the *blitzkrieg* – the 'lightning war' made infamous in the twentieth century by the military commanders of Nazi Germany.[43] His horseback armies moved at unprecedented speed and were comfortable living in temporary encampments: they were nomads, after all. They could shift their point of attack at any time, and fight on multiple fronts.

Yet Genghis Khan's relentless belligerence was as much about maintaining internal order among a restless population as it was about conquest.[44] Even as the war against the Chin empire dragged on, he began to turn his attention to the west – towards the Muslim kingdoms of the Middle East and the European states of Latin Christendom. It was perhaps inevitable. The Mongol Empire was powered by momentum. The idea of putting down permanent roots was alien to the steppe peoples, and thought to lead to decadence and immorality.

Although Genghis Khan established a fixed imperial capital at Karakorum[45] in around 1220, his vision for the city would not have been recognised by any western emperor. He conceived of Karakorum as a gathering place, a nomad city that could appear one minute and disappear the next. When the court came together, or if a *qurilta* had to be called, then the city would briefly become a riot of *gers*, a tented city spreading across the plain. The site was a touchstone, a permanent foundation for an urban mirage. It was the perfect symbolic centre for a people who existed on the hoof.[46]

Karakorum was situated on the main east-west route through central Mongolia. Close to the Orkhon River, its surrounding landscape was fertile and suitable for farming and livestock, and it lay near enough to the Silk Road to be valuable as a new centre for trade and commerce. The site also held significance as the homeland of the ancestors of Genghis Khan's tribe, even boasting the ruins of a settlement established many centuries before by an ancient steppe kingdom.[47] For a ruler attempting to bind together an infant nation, there was huge value in choosing a location that spoke of a shared historical and mythological past.

When Genghis Khan died in 1227, his successor – his third son Ogodei – set about realising his own, very different vision for Karakorum. Drawing on the vast wealth acquired by the Mongols through their many conquests, and employing skilled Chinese and Muslim architects and craftsmen taken as prisoners of war, Ogodei embarked on a series of lavish construction projects.[48] The floor-plan for his palace at Karakorum had a peculiarly Mongolian beginning: each wing was measured out as the length of a bowshot.[49] Yet at its centre was something unique: a tall palace-tower, the like of which had never been seen before on the steppes.[50] To reinforce the sense of an fixed urban environment within a nomadic landscape, he had the whole royal complex surrounded by an 8m-high boundary wall[51] 2.5 kilometres long by 1.5 kilometres wide.[52]

Ogodei had not abandoned completely the ways of his people. Rather he was overseeing a creative architectural response to the nomad lifestyle. It was Ogodei who ordered the construction of the seasonal palaces that Juvaini described during his stay in Karakorum between 1252 and 1253.[53] Yet even after the construction of these elaborate towers and pavilions, the 'Great Khans' – as the successors to Temujin were known – often stayed in a large royal *ger* pitched behind the palace walls, using the permanent physical structures of the city only for ceremonial occasions like ambassadorial visits or festive celebrations.[54] The majority of the permanent residents of Karakorum were not indigenous Mongols, but men and women from the various foreign nations absorbed by the empire. These included skilled artisans, but most of all clerks, scribes and translators. Karakorum became a bureaucratic and administrative centre, a multicultural, multi-lingual hub processing the vast amounts of official correspondence required to manage the affairs of the vast Mongolian territories.[55]

One such government scribe living in Karakorum embarked on a sequel to *The Secret History of the Mongols.* The *Altan Debter* – the 'Golden Book' – took up the story from the death of Genghis Khan. No trace of this chronicle remains today, but we have an insight into its contents through the thirteenth-century Persian physician and historian, Rashid al-Din. His work *The Successors of Genghis Khan* was drawn directly from the official Mongol history, and, although he was never allowed to see the sacred document, which was reserved for the eyes of the highest native nobles and princes, its narrative was conveyed to him by specially appointed intermediaries. The result was not just a detailed survey of Eurasia under the *Pax Mongolica*, but also a series of intimate portraits of the Great Khans – the most powerful men in the world.[56]

The account of the life of Ogodei is particularly rich in detail. We are told that the Khan's name meant 'ascent to the top', and that Ogodei was 'famous for his intelligence, ability, judgement, council, firmness, dignity and justice' – but also that he was 'pleasure-loving and a wine-bibber', and that his father Genghis Khan 'used to rebuke and admonish him on that account'. The description continues in this vein:

> '[The Khan] concerned himself with pleasure and merrymaking, moving happily and joyously from summer to winter residences and from winter to summer residences, constantly employed in the gratification of all manner of pleasures in the company of beauteous ladies and moon-faced mistresses and on all occasions turning his august mind to the diffusion of justice and beneficence, the removal of tyranny and oppression, the restoration of the lands and provinces, and the creation and construction of all manner of buildings.'[57]

In a series of amusing vignettes, Rashid al-Din set out Ogodei's plan for turning his new capital into an essential destination for Silk Road trading caravans: he would pay vastly inflated prices for any goods passing through Karakorum. 'When the fame of his bounty and beneficence had been spread throughout the world,' he wrote, 'merchants made their way to his court from every side.' Ogodei 'would sit, every day, after he had finished his meal, on a chair outside his court, where every kind of merchandise that is to be found in the world was heaped up in piles.' He would then 'command their wares to be bought, whether good or bad... And it usually happened he would give them away without having looked at them'.[58]

His advisors continually expressed their astonishment at this profligacy, yet Ogodei was unmoved. He asked them if anything in the world could endure forever, and when they said there was nothing, he replied that they were wrong: 'Good repute and fair fame will endure forever'.[59] The Great Khan was under no illusions about just how remote Karakorum and Mongolia were from the rest of the world. In fact, he revelled in the power and influence of his empire – that it compelled people to make the arduous trek across the steppes. As he remarked to his officials after he had paid a foreign trader another colossal sum, it was only right to reward the man who because 'of our fame... has traversed many mountains and plains and experienced heat and cold'.[60]

There was more than just whimsy to Ogodei's economic strategy. The establishment of Karakorum as a commercial hub helped the Mongol Empire to institute free trade throughout its borders. Punitive taxation systems were abolished, standardised weights and measures introduced, and a system of paper money devised. The road networks were essential to the flow of goods, and imperial troops patrolled the major routes to ward off bandits and robbers.[61]

Ogodei's approach was very different to that of his father, Genghis Khan. Unlike the founder of the empire, Ogodei preferred to remain at his seasonal palaces in the Mongol homeland rather than lead the charge at the head of his armies. One of his closest confidants, Yeh-lu Ch'u-ts'ai, who had also been a favoured advisor to Genghis, had told him that, while an empire could be conquered on horseback, it could not be ruled *from* horseback.[62] Ogodei was a pragmatist, and he embraced the logic of this counsel. At the same time, with strategic control of the military delegated to his best generals, his empire continued to expand at a remarkable rate.[63] In the east, the Mongols finally destroyed the last strongholds of the Chin, conquered Korea, and prepared for an assault on the Sung empire of southern China. To the west, Armenia, Persia and Mesopotamia had already fallen, and incursions were beginning into the heart of Europe.

In December 1240, Kiev was captured and destroyed, and in 1241 the Mongols swept through Poland and Hungary, advancing as far as the walls of Vienna.[64] In March of 1242[65], however, reports reached the western front that the Great Khan had died – the victim, it was said, of his propensity for the celebratory consumption of enormous quantities of alcohol.[66] The campaigning stopped almost instantly, and the entire Mongol hierarchy descended on Karakorum to elect a new leader.

Ogodei was succeeded by his young son Guyuk, but until he came of age, it was his mother, the Great Khan's widow, who assumed control. In the event, Guyuk did not ascend the throne until 1246, and even then, his reign lasted just two years. In 1248 he died in mysterious circumstances (perhaps poisoning[67], perhaps gout and alcoholism[68]) sending the Mongol Empire into another bout of internal strife. After a fierce power struggle, the *qurilta* of 1 July 1251[69] announced Mongke, the son of Genghis Khan's youngest son Tului, as Great Khan. This appointment caused considerable division, and led to the purge of hundreds of Mongol nobles and officials.[70] Once the political blood-letting was over, Mongke restored unity to Mongolia, but he was fated to be the last Great Khan, and the last sole imperial ruler. Just two generations after its foundation, the vast Mongol Empire was cracking apart.

In May 1253, at almost the exact moment Ata-Malik Juvaini was leaving Karakorum, another traveller was crossing the Black Sea from Constantinople, bound for the lands of the Mongols.[71] The destination of the Flemish-born translator and missionary, William of Rubruck was the court of Sartaq, ruler of the north-western province, or *khanate*, of the Mongol Empire, and great grandson of Genghis Khan. Sartaq's territory included almost all of Eastern Europe between the Urals and the Danube, and continued south to the Caucasus Mountains. There it met the border of another khanate, which in turn controlled the Middle East, running from the Mediterranean coast, around the southern half of the Caspian Sea, and beyond the Persian Gulf to the mountains of Afghanistan.

Rubruck had received reports that a group of German Christians had been taken prisoner and transported to the Central Asian city of Talas to work as slaves for a Mongolian prince. He had also heard that Sartaq himself had recently converted to Christianity.[72] Friars of Rubruck's Franciscan order dedicated their lives to preaching the gospel among the heathens, and in Sartaq's khanate Rubruck saw an enticing opportunity to spread the word of God.

Despite his protestations to the contrary, however, Rubruck was more than a humble pilgrim. He carried with him letters from his king, Louis IX of France, and from his spiritual leader, Pope Baldwin II. To the many officials and governors he encountered on his journey, he appeared at once a holy man, an ambassador, an envoy, and perhaps even a spy. Whether by accident or design, Rubruck's ambiguous status saw him penetrate deeper and deeper into Mongol lands. His mercy mission turned into a two-and-a-half-year, 7,000-mile odyssey to the heart of the empire, and earned him an audience with Mongke Khan, the king of the world, in the palace capital of Karakorum.[73]

Rubruck and his party set off overland from the northern coast of the Black Sea at the beginning of June. Travelling on horseback, and accompanied by four covered wagons pulled by oxen, they ascended the 'lofty promontories along the sea coast'. From this high vantage point they could see to the north a 'fine forest on a plateau'[74], and beyond that a vast plain.

Three days after leaving the sea, Rubruck encountered the Mongols for the first time. 'When I came among them,' he wrote, 'I really felt as if I were entering some other world'.[75] The journey onwards to Sartaq's encampment took another two months. In all that time Rubruck and his party 'never slept in a house or a tent, but always in the open air or underneath our wagons'; nor did they see 'a town or any trace of a building where a town might have existed'.[76] By the end of July they reached the ferry crossing of the River Tanais, today known as the River Don, which flows into the Sea of Azov, but in a misunderstanding over the terms of the charter, found themselves on the far bank without their horses, oxen and wagons.[77] When they finally gained an audience with Sartaq, it marked the beginning of a series of diplomatic misunderstandings that propelled Rubruck and his party onwards into the Mongol heartlands. After briefly examining their possessions, including the letter from Louis IX, Sartaq dismissed the friar. The next day, Rubruck's party were informed that they were to be escorted to the court of Batu, Sartaq's father, the grandson of Genghis Khan and cousin of Mongke, and the ruler of the entire western half of the Mongol Empire.[78]

Batu's camp migrated with the seasons up and down the course of the eastern bank of the Volga. To reach it, Rubruck passed beyond the Iron Gate of Alexander the Great, built by the Macedonian king to keep the barbarians from crossing into Persia, and into a country which, according to rumours, 'contained dogs so large and ferocious that they attack bulls and kill lions'.[79] There, he experienced his first sight of one of the Mongols' vast nomad cities. 'On sighting Batu's camp, I was struck with awe,' wrote Rubruck. He describes a settlement with 'the appearance of a large city stretching out far lengthways and with inhabitants scattered around in every direction for a distance of three or four leagues'. The path immediately to the south of Batu's large central *ger* was kept clear, 'but to the right and left they spread themselves out as far as they like within the limitations imposed by the terrain'.[80]

Brought before Batu, who sat on a golden throne in the centre of his *ger*, Rubruck explained: 'I came to your son because we heard he was a Christian and brought him a letter from my lord the King of the French. He sent me here to you'.[81] Batu responded by asking Rubruck his name, and that of his king, and also with whom the French were at war. The two men then shared a drink of *comos* – fermented mare's milk – before Rubruck was dismissed. For six weeks the party were largely ignored within the camp, and provided with only the most meagre portions of food and drink[82], until finally, a man approached Rubruck and told him, 'I am to take you to Mongke Khan.'

This guide, a Mongol nobleman, appeared less than enthusiastic about his appointed task. 'It is a four-month journey,' he told Rubruck, 'and the cold there is so intense that rocks and trees split apart with the frost... If you prove unable to bear it, I shall abandon you on the way.' The friar and his party were provided with sheepskin coats and trousers, and boots and hoods of thick fur. On 16 September, with winter fast approaching, they set out for Mongke's court.[83]

'There is no counting the times we were famished, thirsty, frozen and exhausted,' wrote Rubruck. His party were given food only in the evenings – shoulder and ribs of mutton – with broth to drink at certain points throughout the day. 'Sometimes we were obliged to eat meat that was only half-cooked or practically raw, since we lacked fuel for a fire'.[84]

Despite the hardships, relations between Rubruck and his guide improved. By December, having crossed a series of high, windswept plains and skirted north of the imposing Qara Tau mountains, the party advanced into the snow-clad Tarabaghatai range, five hundred miles to the west of Karakorum. Ahead of them, the guide told Rubruck, was a pass where 'it was usual for demons suddenly to carry men off and nobody knew what became of them'. The friar offered to lead the party onwards, chanting *Credo in unum Deum* – 'I believe in one God' – until they had navigated the route unharmed. With this act Rubruck identified himself as a holy man, akin to a Mongol shaman, who could protect his companions from the supernatural. He wrote out the *Credo* for his guide on paper, and from then on the Mongol wore it around his neck as a talisman to ward off evil.[85]

On 26 December, the party 'came into a plain as broad as the sea and so flat that not the smallest rise was visible'. The following day, they reached the winter palace of Mongke Khan.[86] Just a few weeks earlier, Rubruck had endured a disquieting encounter with a passing Mongolian official. It appeared that the friar's epic journey had been prompted by a fundamental misunderstanding. Batu's translators had interpreted the letter from King Louis IX as a request for military assistance against the Muslims of the Holy Land. Batu had even dispatched his own letter to Mongke to explain that this was why he had sent the Frenchman to the imperial court.[87]

Full of trepidation, Rubruck was brought before the Great Khan. Mongke's winter throne room was covered in gold cloth, with a fire burning at its centre. The Khan sat reclined on a couch wearing spotted and glossy furs of otter skin. Rubruck, Mongke and both of their interpreters drank rice wine together. At first Mongke paid little attention to the friar, and instead became preoccupied with a number of falcons and birds of prey that courtiers brought before him to inspect. As time passed, Rubruck noticed that his interpreter was quite drunk on the rice wine.

At last Mongke ordered the friar to kneel before him and speak. Rubruck explained the purpose of his mission, his journey to Sartaq, the letter he carried from the king of France, and his audience with Batu. At this point, it appeared that everyone apart from Rubruck was feeling the effects of the alcohol, including Mongke. The interpreters were slurring their words, and Rubruck could no longer make out what they were saying. After a few minutes the friar was dismissed and began to return, bemused, to his lodgings. Slowly his interpreter managed to convey what had happened during the meeting. 'Mongke takes pity on you and gives you leave to stay here for two months,' he explained, 'by which time the severe cold will be over. He informs you that ten days from here lies a fine city called Karakorum, and if you wish to go there he will have you provided with what you need.'[88]

When William of Rubruck entered the city of Karakorum on the afternoon of 5 April 1254 – Palm Sunday – his first impression was not favourable. 'Excepting the Khan's palace,' he wrote, the city 'is not as fine as the town of St Denis'. He was struck by the noise, colour and clamour of the bazaars. At each of the city's four gates, he noted, discrete goods were offered for sale and trade. At the eastern entrance was grain; at the western sheep and goats; at the southern cattle and wagons; and at the northern the most prized of Mongolian possessions – horses.

Without question, the focal point of the city was the palace. It was enclosed by a brick wall 'just as are the priories of our own monks', and, to the friar, what it most resembled was 'a church, with a middle nave and two sides, beyond two rows of pillars and three doors on the south side'. It was in this palace, he continued, that Mongke held 'drinking sessions twice a year, once at Easter when he passes by there, and once in the summer when he is on his way back'.[89] Mongke's predecessor Ogodei had relied on Chinese and Muslim artisans to help develop his city. The new Khan drew instead on the artistic and architectural skills of the most recently conquered subjects to join the Mongol Empire: Europeans.

In the courtyard, just beyond the entrance to the palace, Rubruck encountered Karakorum's most remarkable monument: a giant tree sculpted entirely from silver. It rose up from a base of silver roots surrounded by four silver lions, and was as tall as the palace, with its branches reaching out to touch the adjoining roof beams. All the branches, leaves and fruit hanging from the tree were also made of the most delicately fashioned silver. As if this were not impressive enough, the sculpture also housed a system of internal, pneumatic pipes, allowing it to operate as an elaborate drinks dispenser. The trunk of the tree was fitted with four separate tubes, each encircled by golden serpents, leading upwards before curving down again to rest above four silver vessels. At the very top of the sculpture was an angel cast in silver, holding a trumpet. Using compressed air, this angel could be made to bring the trumpet to its lips, and sound a fanfare. This was the cue for the pipes to pour their liquids into the vessels below. *Comos* gushed from one tube, and mead from another; a third produced rice wine; and the fourth, rice ale. During festivities, the tree became an alcohol fountain, working non-stop to fill up the vessels, while servants rushed back and forth with trays of drinks between the courtyard and the palace.[90]

The tree was the work of William Bouchier, a Parisian gold and silversmith taken prisoner in Belgrade when the Mongols overran Eastern Europe. Bouchier had 'belonged' originally to Sorkhokhtani, Mongke's mother and the daughter-in-law of Genghis Khan, for whom he produced religious jewellery, including a series of ornate Christian crosses.[91] When Mongke learned of the silversmith's skills as a craftsman, he commissioned him, along with fifty of his countrymen, to produce a great artwork for his palace. The sculpture was intended to represent Karakorum as the centre of the universe. The silver tree grew up from the treeless expanse of the steppes, spreading its branches in all directions – just as the Mongol Empire had emerged from nothing to conquer the world.

The friar, of course, was more interested in the religious life of the city. On first entering Karakorum, he had been met by a procession of monks from the capital's Christian community. As they walked, holding a banner marked with the cross above their heads, to the city's one church to celebrate Mass, Rubruck counted two mosques and 'twelve idol temples belonging to different peoples'.[92] While holy wars raged throughout much of the rest of the world, the Mongolian capital appeared to be an oasis of tolerance, where all worship was permitted free of persecution. Muslims, Christians, Buddhists and Jews, from a wide variety of nationalities and ethnicities, coexisted peacefully.

The Mongolians traditionally followed a shamanistic religion, which observed the rhythms of nature, the earth and the sky, and was largely preoccupied with ancestor worship. They did, however, also believe in a single god in Heaven. Unusually, they did not see their own rituals and faith as incompatible with others'.[93] Indeed, their attitude to towards religion in general was a mixture of curiosity and a wary, intellectual scepticism. Those, like Rubruck, who arrived at the imperial court to preach, were often interrogated as to exactly how they had come into possession of their spiritual knowledge.

On 24 May, five months after his first meeting with the Great Khan in his winter palace, Rubruck was brought before Mongke's chief secretary and a group of clerics and courtiers. When he was asked the purpose of his visit, and what he would like to say to Mongke, his response was: 'all I should utter is the words of God, if he were willing to hear them'. Rubruck was pressed on exactly what these words were. After quoting verses from Luke and Matthew, and explaining that those who loved God kept his commandments, he was confronted by the Muslim and Buddhist representatives of the court. 'Have you been in Heaven that you know the commandments of God?' they asked the friar. 'Do you mean that Mongke Khan does not observe God's command?' they continued. After these exchanges, the Khan's secretary relayed the details of the conversation to his master.

The following day, Rubruck and the other clerics received a message from Mongke: 'Here you are, Christians, Muslims and Buddhists, and each one of you claims that his religion is superior and that his writings or books contain more truth.' The Great Khan ordered that a debate be held between the competing religions, and its arguments written down, so that he could judge for himself where the truth lay.[94]

The result was one of the most bizarre theological contests in history. It began with the Christians and Muslims forming an alliance to argue against the Buddhists. Rubruck took the floor as the spokesperson for his team, and opened the debate. Topics ranged from defining the nature of God and the origins of good and evil, to whether there was one God or many, and if there were just one, whether He could truly be all-powerful. Not surprisingly, Rubruck's account shows him outmanoeuvring his opponents at every turn, exposing their fragile heathen beliefs. The debaters drank *comos* between every round, and the intellectual rigour of the contest steadily deteriorated. It ended, Rubruck tells us, with the Christians and Muslims singing together in loud voices 'while the Buddhists remained silent', after which 'everyone drank heavily'.[95]

On 31 May, Rubruck was granted his second and last audience with the Great Khan. After a brief religious discussion, Mongke said to the friar, 'You have stayed here a long time; it is my wish that you go back.' He asked Rubruck to take with him a letter to his king, Louis IX. The Khan first composed the message, before it was translated through an interpreter for the friar to transcribe.

At the end of July 1254, Rubruck left Karakorum. Over a year later, on 15 August 1255, he arrived in Tripoli. From there he moved on to a convent in the crusader city of Acre in Palestine, and began to 'put in writing' for Louis IX, 'everything I saw among the Mongols'. The result is one of the most detailed and intimate insights into the life of the Great Khan and his empire. As a religious mission, of course, Rubruck's journey had been an abject failure. The friar had been treated with mingled scepticism and amusement by those he met on his journey, and his attempts to spread the Gospel had been hampered at every turn by inadequate or uninterested interpreters. He lamented, on leaving the Mongolian capital, that he had 'baptised there a total of six souls'.[96]

As for Mongke Khan's letter to Louis IX, it began by explaining that, just as there was one God in Heaven, there was also one ruler on earth: Genghis Khan and his descendants. Those who accepted the truth of this would see the entire world 'from the sun's rising to its setting... become one in joy and peace'. For nations that did not, however, there was a message of warning. Some may say to themselves, Mongke continued, that 'our country is far away, our mountains are strong, our sea is broad' and, relying on this, decide to make war on the Mongol territories. If they believed that they had any chance of victory, he warned them that they were mistaken: 'He who has made easy what was hard, and brought near what was distant, the everlasting God – He knows'.[97]

Around 1271, less than two decades after Rubruck's journey, three Venetian merchants set out from Palestine on a mission, part diplomatic and part commercial, to visit the new Great Khan of the Mongol Empire. The Venetians were two brothers, Niccolo and Maffeo Polo, and Niccolo's seventeen-year-old son – Marco.[98] Like Juvaini and Rubruck before them, they embarked on the arduous overland journey through the Middle East and into the mountains and plains of Central Asia. Marco described reaching a city called Etzina, on the northern fringe of a sand desert: 'In this city the traveller must take in a forty days' stock of provisions,' he wrote, 'for, when he leaves Etzina for the north, he has forty days' journey ahead of him across a desert without house or inn, where nobody lives.'[99] Beyond the desert lay Karakorum. Marco described a city 'three miles in circumference, surrounded by a strong rampart of earth, because stones are scarce here' – but he said no more about the place.[100] It is likely that he did not even visit the city, because Karakorum was no longer the home of the empire.[101] To reach that, the Polos had even further to travel – over the Mongolian steppes and into the lands of China, where a king called Kubilai Khan awaited them.

Mongke's death in 1259 had been the catalyst for the rapid break-up of the Mongol Empire. In the west, Mongke's brother Hulegu controlled almost all of the lands of Islam, including Persia, Mesopotamia, Egypt and Anatolia. Just a year before, he had crowned his triumph by capturing the great Muslim capital of Baghdad. In Eastern Europe, in the Slavic territory to the north of the Black Sea and surrounding the Caspian Sea, Berke Khan, the grandson of Genghis Khan, ruled as the leader of a branch of the Mongolian dynasty that called itself the 'Golden Horde'. In the east, Kubilai, another of Mongke's brothers, had been engaged in a long conflict with the Sung empire of southern China. And back in the homeland of Karakorum, there was Mongke's youngest brother, Arik Boke.[102]

With tensions mounting, Hulegu and Berke were eager to consolidate power in their own kingdoms, and opted not to venture back to the steppes to fight over the succession of a clearly fractured empire.[103] Arik Boke and Kubilai each held separate *quriltas*, where each proclaimed himself Great Khan. Arik's *qurilta* took place in the traditional location of Karakorum, and was attended by representatives of most of the Mongolian nobility. Kubilai held his ceremony, which was attended by almost no one except his own followers, at a city called Shang-tu, better known today as Xanadu.[104]

Inevitably, civil war broke out in the east between Arik and Kubilai. The younger brother's claim to the throne may have been stronger, but his strategic and military position was not. Kubilai could draw on both his own Mongol forces and the vast – and loyal – armies of the conquered kingdoms of China. Karakorum relied on the flow of produce from the east, and it was easy for Kubilai to cut the supply of food and livestock.[105] There was only one possible outcome.

Kubilai's armies drove Arik from Karakorum, and although the city was briefly retaken in 1261, resistance could not last. In 1264, Arik admitted defeat, and travelled to Xanadu to surrender to his brother in person.[106] Kubilai assumed the title of Great Khan, and the city of Karakorum was reduced almost instantly from a capital city to a remote outpost. For three decades it had been the unlikely centre of the world, but now the focus shifted east, where Kubilai had not only pronounced himself Great Khan – he had also established himself as the figurehead of a new Chinese royal family. He was the first emperor of the 'Yuan' dynasty.[107]

It was into this strange and exotic empire that the Polos arrived. Thanks to the poet Samuel Taylor Coleridge (as well as the 1970s prog-rock trio Rush and a 1980s film starring Olivia Newton John) Xanadu has been immortalised in the popular imagination as an oriental paradise, site of the famous 'pleasure dome'.[108] Marco Polo describes a palace of marble and golden halls, surrounded by sixteen miles of verdant parkland filled with springs, streams and lawns. 'Into this park there is no entry except by way of the palace,' wrote Marco, and 'here the Great Khan keeps game animals of all sorts, such as hart, stag and roebuck'.[109]

Yet, for all its magnificence and luxury, Xanadu was not where Kubilai made his capital. For a new emperor looking to win the favour of his Chinese subjects, there was too much of the steppe and the nomadic life about Xanadu, situated in the borderlands between Mongolia and China. Kubilai kept it as a summer retreat and hunting ground[110], looking even further east, to the delta of the Yellow River, for the site of his imperial capital. He settled on Chung-tu, the former centre of the Chin empire, which Genghis Khan had sacked and destroyed in 1215. The Chinese called this new capital Daidu, the 'Great Capital'.[111] Kubilai called it Khanbalik, the City of the Khan.[112]

Marco described a square wall at the centre of Khanbalik, its sides a mile in length, 'all white-washed and battlemented', with palaces of great beauty and splendour at each corner. A series of further walls, with more palaces, continued inwards, until they reached the Great Khan's Palace, which Marco, not prone to understatement, called 'the largest that was ever seen'.[113] Its walls and chambers were 'all covered with gold and silver and decorated with pictures of dragons and birds and horsemen and various breeds of beasts and scenes of battle', and it contained a hall 'so vast and so wide that a meal might well be served for more than 6,000 men.'

Polo also mentions a 'very fine piece of furniture of great size and splendour... elaborately carved with figures of animals' which dispensed different drinks into a series of large vessels.[114] The similarity between this device and Boucher's silver tree may not be coincidental. After the capture of Karakorum, it is possible that Kubilai had the great sculpture dismantled and transported to his new capital.[115] Within the Khan's Palace, there was also a walled compound which only Mongolians were permitted to enter. On prairie grass replanted from the steppes, horses roamed free among a miniature *ger* encampment. Here, amidst a city of stupendous opulence, the Khan and his family could still live as artificial nomads.[116]

However Kubilai behaved behind closed doors – or, rather, high walls – in front of his subjects he made every effort to appear Chinese. By blurring the boundaries between Mongolia and China, and implying that the two peoples were one and the same, he sought to create a permanent legitimacy for his new 'Yuan' dynasty.[117] This plan relied, however, on his successors embracing a similar policy of ethnic integration. Instead, after Kubilai's death in 1294, a series of short-lived Khans swung back and forth between Chinese integration and reasserting their – as they saw it, inherently superior – Mongolian heritage.[118]

Some three decades into the fourteenth century, a mysterious and fatal disease, which subjected sufferers to fever, vomiting and grotesque seeping growths known as *buboes*, spread from southern China, travelling rapidly along the trade routes into Europe and Africa. It was the beginning of the 'Black Death'.[119] This global pandemic had devastating consequences for world trade, and weakened the Yuan dynasty just as popular uprisings were flaring in the southern provinces. By the middle of the century, these isolated insurrections had united into a full rebellion.

A vast army advanced steadily northwards, until in 1368 it reached Khanbalik, and razed it to the ground.[120] To celebrate this victory, the leader of the rebels, Zhu Yuanzhang, proclaimed the beginning of a new imperial era – the Ming dynasty.[121] Forty years later, a new city would emerge right on top of Kubilai's old capital. The Ming imperial palace would come to be known as the Forbidden City. And the vast settlement that grew up around it was called Peking – modern day Beijing.[122]

The Mongolia Yuans fled first for Xanadu, and then back across the mountains to the steppe lands. In 1388, the armies of the Ming dynasty pursued their former masters all the way to the plains of Karakorum. There, they surrounded the old Mongolian capital, overthrew its defences, and reduced it to rubble.[123]

A folk legend tells of one escapee from the city of Karakorum: an imperial stone tortoise.[124] The Mongolians had chosen the tortoise to symbolise eternity – an ironic choice, perhaps, for an empire that burned so brightly and then was gone. Today the Soviet-built town of Kharkhorin occupies the site of old Karakorum. It is a dull settlement dominated by a giant flour factory and a power station, but on the fringes of this cluster of rusting modern buildings, overlooking the bare grasslands, a stone tortoise still remains – a last fragment of the vanished city. It is an odd yet popular tourist attraction. A tradition has emerged of leaving small rocks or pebbles on the back of its sculpted shell, and of tying colourful Buddhist prayer scarves to its stonework. In thousands of identikit travellers' photographs, it stares glumly into the camera, its scarves flapping in the incessant winds.

For six decades of the 20th century, with Mongolia effectively a province of the Soviet Union, Genghis Khan was taboo: 700 years after his death, he was still considered a dangerous figure by the Moscow party elite. For a time there was even a ban on mentioning his name, for fear that it would stir Mongolian nationalism.[125] His home province was designated a 'Highly Restricted Area', the only main road into the region blocked by a tank base and a MiG air base.[126]

In the 1990s Mongolia emerged from the Soviet shadow, and as the country attempted to reinvent itself as free-market democracy, Genghis Khan suddenly became big business. Today his likeness can be found on everything from beer bottles, cigarette packets and energy drinks, to hotels, banks and even the Mongolian currency.[127] Students attend Genghis Khan University, and visitors fly into Genghis Khan International Airport. Perhaps the most remarkable appropriation of his likeness rose up in 2008, on the banks of the Tuul River 30 miles east of the capital Ulan Bator. Even from a great distance, it can be seen rising above the surrounding grasslands – a 40-metre-tall statue of Genghis Khan on horseback, clad in 250 tons of stainless steel. The statue sits on top of a neoclassical visitors' centre, a circular stone building surrounded by 36 columns to represent the 36 Khans of the Mongol Empire.[128]

'Rising above the grasslands': the 2008 stainless steel statue of Genghis Khan on horseback. © Henry Korell, 2011

Inside the building a lift rises up through the statue, emerging where Genghis Khan's crotch meets his saddle. From there, visitors walk out into the open air, and are faced with a wide staircase rising up the mane on the back of the horse's neck. At the top of the staircase, they can look in one direction for hundreds of miles over the plains, towards the distant mountains and the Great Khan's birthplace. From the other side the giant face of Genghis Khan stares straight down at them. It is one of the most impressive – if overblown – monuments to a historical figure ever constructed.

In 2004, the Mongolian Prime Minister Tsakhiagii Elbegdorj launched a plan to reinvent his nation. 'In 2006 we will be celebrating the eight-hundredth anniversary of the Mongol Empire which was established by Genghis Khan,' he proclaimed. His great scheme was to move the capital city from Ulan Bator to Karakorum: 'We hope to create out of Karakorum a city which will be a model community in Mongolia.' A new international airport was planned, along with hotels, a high-tech business park, and casinos alongside important cultural heritage sites. 'We would like to make it a small administration city, a city of universities and new knowledge,' continued the Prime Minister.[129] Not long after announcing these plans Elbegdorj was voted out, but in July 2013 he was returned to power. Meanwhile, Karakorum waits in the wilderness. Perhaps it will take its chance to return to the world stage. Or perhaps it will remain a rest-stop on the tourist trail, a ramshackle city of 'authentic' *gers* filled with western backpackers, looked over by a single, morose, stone tortoise.

Chapter Twelve

The House of Diamonds

The Fortress of Golconda – Hyderabad, India
(Born 1300 – Died 1700)

Hast thou from the caves of Golconda, a gem

Pure as the ice drop that froze on the mountain?

Bright as the humming-bird's green diadem,

When it flutters in sun-beams that shine through a fountain?

On Receiving a Curious Shell and a Copy of Verses,
John Keats, 1817[1]

In the early morning of 21 September 1687[2], Abul Hassan, the eighth and last ruler of the Qutb Shahi dynasty, dressed himself in the jewelled splendour of his royal robes, sat down for his breakfast in the throne room of the reputedly impregnable hilltop fortress of Golconda, and prepared to surrender. Four hundred feet below, Hassan's treacherous general Abdullah Khan had opened one of the fort's gates to the forces of Aurangzeb, the sixth Mughal emperor of India. After eight months, the siege of Golconda – and the resistance of one of the last independent kingdoms of the southern subcontinent – was about to come to an end.

At the summit of the fortress, beside the royal palace, was the hall of justice: a flat-roofed building topped by a stone throne reached by ten steps. From this elevated seat, generations of Qutb Shahi kings had looked out across the lands of Golconda over the flat floodplain of the Musi River.[3] Around a mile and a half to the north – 'about two musket-shot from the Castle'[4], as the seventeenth-century French traveller Jean de Thévenot put it – were the royal tombs: a line of ornate granite cubes and oblongs set on raised terraces within beautiful gardens, decorated by arcades of pointed arches, and crowned by enormous domes. There were eight tombs for the eight Qutb Shahi kings, although one was only half-built. As per tradition, Hassan was overseeing the construction of his own mausoleum.

In January 1687, Hassan had watched from his elevated throne as the vast Mughal army gathered.[5] The Italian merchant traveller Gemelli Careri described the imperial war camp as a 'moving city'. The tents of the emperor, his princes and his harem took up three square miles alone, with a fortified perimeter of palisades, ditches and gun emplacements. Surrounding the royal enclosure were accommodations for 100,000 foot-soldiers and 60,000 cavalry, and an entourage of over 500,000 servants and followers. To carry the baggage, the camp required 50,000 camels and 3,000 elephants. Its size was so great that it had its own internal economy, and was filled with 250 markets and bazaars. Careri estimated its total area at thirty square miles.[6]

Hassan had already abandoned the town of Bhangnagar, situated three miles across the plain from Golconda, to the Mughal host. He made a series of increasingly desperate diplomatic pleas, but Aurangzeb was implacable. 'The evil deeds of this wicked man' said the Mughal emperor of Hassan,

> 'pass the bounds of writing... He has given the reins of government into the hands of vile tyrannical infidels; oppressed the holy men of Islam; and abandoned himself to reckless debauchery and vice, indulging in drunkenness and lewdness day and night. He makes no distinction between infidelity and Islam, tyranny and

> justice, depravity and devotion... In all this insolence and vice and depravity, he has shown no shame for his infamous offences, and no hope of amendment in this world or the next'.[7]

Aurangzeb presented his campaign into the kingdoms of southern India – the region known as the Deccan – as a religious crusade. Certainly, his reputation was as a ruler of unimpeachable piety, spending 'whole nights in the palace mosque' in 'the company of devout men'.[8] From his early youth, it was said, he had 'abstained from forbidden food and practices' and did 'nothing that is not pure and lawful'.[9] At Golconda, however, there was more at stake than territory or righteousness. This sentinel fortress was the origin and the centre of the world diamond trade. Its capture would make Aurangzeb the richest man on earth.

The earliest known written account of diamonds comes in a Sanskrit text dating from the fourth century BC.[10] Famed as the 'jewel above all others' and named *Vajra* – Sanskrit for 'thunderbolt' – diamonds were believed to be magical stones, gifts from the gods.[11] *On Stones,* an Arabic manuscript from the ninth century AD, itself claiming to be a translation of a Greek work attributed to Aristotle, tells of a place called the 'Valley of the Diamonds'. It was said that, after conquering Persia and crossing into India, Alexander the Great, Aristotle's most famous pupil, was the one man to have ever reached this valley, the only source of diamonds in the world.[12]

In the thirteenth century, the Persian astronomer and geographer al-Kazwini took up the tale, describing the valley as, 'connected with the land Hind. The glance cannot penetrate to its greatest depths and serpents are found there, the like of which no man hath seen, and upon which no man can gaze without dying'.[13] Alexander, he wrote, ordered his men to polish their shields before they arrived at the valley. 'When the serpents approached,' al-Kazwini went on, 'their glance fell upon their own image in the mirror, and this caused their death'.[14] Alexander's next challenge was to recover the diamonds. His solution was to throw raw meat down into the valley floor: the flesh stuck to the diamonds, and birds of prey dived down to take the bait. Alexander's men then followed the birds to their nests, frightened them away, and took the stones.[15]

Another version of this story appeared in that great work of Arab folklore, the *Thousand and One Nights*. Stranded and alone on a wild and seemingly deserted island, Sinbad chanced upon a 'broad and deep valley' with soil made of diamonds, 'the hard and compact stone that is used for boring holes in metals, gems, porcelain and onyx'.[16] To escape the valley, at the bottom of a 'vast and unscalable mountain that towered so high into the sky that its summit was invisible', Sinbad strapped himself to a sheep which appeared to have fallen to its death, and was carried away, along with the carcass, by a giant eagle.[17]

Deposited at the eagle's nest, he cut himself loose and was preparing to make his escape, when 'there came a loud shout from behind... together with the noise of sticks striking against rocks'.[18] Sinbad came face to face with a diamond trader using the same ingenious trick pioneered by Alexander. The trader was crestfallen that no diamonds had attached themselves to the sheep – until Sinbad emptied his pockets, which were full of the precious stones.

Gradually, this entertaining myth began to give way to something closer to reality. In his thirteenth-century travelogue, the Venetian merchant Marco Polo described his journey through India on the way to China and the court of Kubilai Khan. Not far north of the tip of the Indian peninsula, he wrote, was a 'kingdom ruled by a queen, who is a very wise woman'.[19]

At the time of Polo's adventures, which began in 1271, there was indeed a land in the Deccan plateau of central southern India, ruled by a Hindu queen called Rani Rudrama Devi, of the Kakatiya dynasty. 'This kingdom produces diamonds,' wrote Polo, and contains 'many mountains in which the diamonds are found.'[20] He went on to describe how seasonal rainwater would rush through these mountains, scouring their gorges and caverns. In summer, once the water had evaporated, the diamonds were 'found in plenty'. Polo could not resist, however, repeating the old legend of the snakes, the eagles and the raw flesh, which, he claimed, remained the only way of retrieving the stones from the 'deep valley so walled in by precipitous cliffs that no one can enter it'.[21] Even this, however, has some basis in fact. It was a Hindu custom for sheep or cattle to be sacrificed whenever a new mine was opened. The meat would be left as an offering to the gods, but was often snatched away by birds of prey.[22]

Polo was justified in claiming that 'in all the world diamonds are found nowhere else except in this kingdom alone'.[23] There were small deposits in Borneo, but India was the sole significant source of the world's diamonds. This remained the case from antiquity right up until the discovery of the stones in Brazil in the eighteenth century.[24] Indeed, at the beginning of the thirteenth century, diamonds were almost unknown in the lands of Christendom. Instead, Polo wrote, 'they are exported to the Great Khan and to the kings and noblemen of these various regions and realms. For it is they who have the wealth to buy all the costliest stones'.[25]

Golconda, of course, had its own origin myth. In the early years of the sixteenth century, Quli, the first king of the Qutb Shahi dynasty, was 'seeking out for a place where he might build a strong castle'.[26] He chanced upon a shepherd boy, who led him through dense woods to a tall hill rising above the plain. Quli found the place 'very proper for his design'[27], and thereafter called it 'Golconda', a compound of the local Telegu words 'golla', meaning a shepherd, and 'konda', a hill.[28] What this Qutb Shahi legend ignored, no doubt deliberately, was another account suggesting that the history of the fort went back to the end of the twelfth century. This older story also involved a shepherd, but this time, while he was herding his animals over the hill, he found a holy idol. When 'Dev Rai', the first king of the Kakatiya dynasty, heard of the discovery, he ordered the construction of a mud fort on the spot, to honour the location's sacred properties.[29]

Golconda's transition from ceremonial site to defensive bastion began in the fourteenth century. In the face of aggressive expansion southwards by the Muslim sultans of Delhi, the Kakatiyas established a series of militarised, hilltop fortifications throughout the Deccan. Golconda became a key component of the kingdom's defences. It was at this time that the massive walls of the *Bala Hisar* – the 'lofty citadel' – were built to encircle the summit of Golconda. Giant blocks of granite were hewn into squares and rectangles, and fitted together without mortar. The builders incorporated natural features – large rocky outcrops and boulders – into their design, with the walls seeming to merge with and rise out of the hillside.[30]

The ruined walls of Golconda today © Wikipedia Commons

In the end, however, none of these measures could halt the march of the Islamic armies. The first written record of Golconda comes in the work of the Persian historian Ferishta, who chronicled the early Muslim conquests of India. And in 1363 the fort is mentioned in a treaty ceding Golconda to Muhammad Shah, the first king of the Bahmani dynasty, which had broken away from the Delhi Sultanate to take control of the Deccan region.[31]

The Bahmanis ruled for a century and a half, until a bitter war of succession saw them splinter into five separate, independent kingdoms: Bijapur, Ahmednagar, Bidar, Berar, and Golconda. The agent of Golconda's independence was Quli Qutb Shahi. A Persian born in the village of Hamadan in the mid-fifteenth century, Quli claimed ancestry from Noah[32], and had been forced to flee his homeland as a political refugee when a rival dynasty seized power.

Along with many other Persian immigrants, Quli found favour and advancement at the Bahmani court, impressing as a warrior and military strategist. By the end of the fifteenth century, he had been appointed governor of the province of Teligana, which included the territories around Golconda. In 1501, he moved his capital to the fortress of Golconda, and strengthened the site with a series of walls punctuated by imposing gateways, which spread out to encircle the lower slopes of the hillside.[33] Quli remained loyal to his Bahmani masters for longer than the other breakaway kingdoms of the Deccan. Yet, by 1518, with the old empire in disarray, independence was inevitable.[34]

The Muslim state of Golconda under 'Sultan' Quli Qutb Shahi was remarkably diverse. Hindu and Islamic art, architecture and literature mingled and flourished, supplemented by influences brought to the royal court from across the Middle East, Central Asia and Africa, in particular in music, dress, cuisine and technology.[35] Quli wisely opted to integrate the customs of the new dynasty – the Qutb Shahis – with ancient Kakatiya past and traditions, rather than impose an alien Persian identity on the region.[36]

At the same time, Golconda began a gradual conversion into an imperial palace-fortress, complete with mansions for the royal family and prominent noblemen, bazaars, baths, and the new kingdom's first great religious building, the Jami mosque. Ferishta described Sultan Quli as 'a chief of great abilities'[37], but also recorded his ignominious end. While praying in his mosque in 1543, reputedly at the advanced age of ninety-nine, he was 'assassinated by a Turkish slave, supposed to have been bribed by Quli's son and successor'.[38] This treacherous heir, Quli's eldest son Jamshid, ruled for seven years, until his death in 1550. Jamshid had ensured that his own, seven-year-old son would inherit the throne, but this minority lasted just six months. Ibrahim, another of Quli's sons, returned from exile in the southern kingdom of Vijayanagra to claim his birthright.[39]

'Ibrahim was a wise and politic Prince,' wrote Ferishta, 'fond of the pleasures of the table, but neglected not business for luxury.'[40] He continued the work of his father in expanding the walls of Golconda, and built further structures both inside and outside the fort, championing an eclectic artistic style, with gates and walls adorned with relief sculptures, paintings of lions, elephants, peacocks, geese and oxen.[41] As well as transforming the physical fabric of Golconda, Ibrahim was determined to assert its imperial legitimacy. He used his armies to ensure that 'merchants and travellers could journey night and day, without going in caravans, in perfect security'[42] throughout his lands.

The Sultan had an international outlook, and grand ambitions. He was the first of the Qutb Shahi kings to mint coins in his own name. All races, religions and nationalities were welcome at his court, and he acquired 'weight and respect'[43], and a growing political reputation. Traders journeyed from across Asia and the Middle East to enjoy the hospitality of Ibrahim's Golconda. It did not take long for tales of this exotic hilltop city far beyond the Indus valley to reach Europe. Most compelling were the accounts of exactly what was being bought and sold in Golconda – the source of the kingdom's extravagant wealth. Diamonds.

In 1642, the French merchant Jean-Baptiste Tavernier arrived at Golconda for the first time. Tavernier had been born in Paris in 1605. His father Gabriel, a Dutch geographer and cartographer, had fled Antwerp in 1575 to avoid religious persecution as a Protestant.[44] 'Many learned men' came to visit Gabriel to speak about 'geographical matters'. The young Tavernier, listening to their conversations, surrounded by maps at which 'he could not then tire of gazing'[45], resolved to visit the places which his father had only drawn. 'I came into the world with a desire to travel,' he wrote in his memoirs.[46]

He set about fulfilling this desire at the age of fifteen, and by twenty-two had 'seen the best parts of Europe'.[47] In 1631, Tavernier made his first major voyage east, to Constantinople and Persia. Inevitably, this fuelled his enthusiasm to go even further.

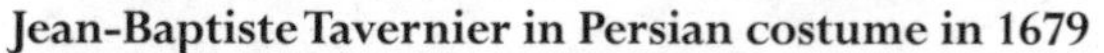

Jean-Baptiste Tavernier in Persian costume in 1679

Tavernier had one other passion – gemstones. 'The diamond is the most precious of all stones,' he wrote, 'and it is the article of trade to which I am most devoted.'[48] To give purpose to his wanderings, he 'resolved to visit all the mines, and one of the two rivers where diamonds were found.'[49] He had heard the legends of the 'valley of the diamonds', but dismissed them as scare-stories. 'As the fear of dangers has never restrained me in any of my journeys,' he wrote, 'the terrible picture that was drawn of these mines, situated in barbarous countries to which one could not travel except by the most dangerous routes, served neither to terrify me nor turn me from my intention.'[50]

Tavernier found his diamond mines in the mountains, five to seven days' distance from Golconda. 'All round the place where the diamonds are found the soil is sandy, and full of rocks and jungle'[51] he wrote. The rocks were riddled with veins around a finger in width, into which the miners would thrust small irons with crooked ends, to draw them out. Tavernier then described, with a sense of horror, how they would break the rocks open with a 'heavy iron crowbar', and search for diamonds among the pieces. 'The evil,' lamented Tavernier, 'is that it fractures the diamonds and gives rise to flaws.'[52]

Another mine, identified by Tavernier by the name 'Kollur', was said to have been opened after a peasant unearthed a 25-carat stone while digging in a piece of surface soil. There, he wrote, 'they still find large stones in greater abundance than at any other mine.'[53] Stones between 10 and 40 carats were common, and sometimes diamonds of unprecedented size were found. Kollur, related Tavernier, was the source of the 756-carat diamond owned by Shah Jahan, the Mughal emperor and father of Aurangzeb, for a long time the largest stone ever recorded. During his visit to the mine, he saw some 60,000 men, women and children burrowing into the earth.[54]

Superstition still played a major role in the mining process. Tavernier described how families would place a stone idol in front of the area they were about to search, daub their heads with a paste of saffron and gum to which they would attach grains of rice, and then sit down in ranks to eat. Only once dinner was finished, would the relentless digging and sifting begin.[55]

When Tavernier arrived in Golconda in the mid-seventeenth century, it had become more than just an opulent and imposing hilltop retreat. In 1589, Ibrahim's successor, Muhammad Qutb Shahi had founded an un-walled city several miles across the plain from the fort. Tavernier called it Bhagnagar – the 'Fortunate City' – and said it had been named by Muhammad after a favourite mistress.[56] Others treated it as an extension of the fort, and simply called it Golconda.

Tavernier described the city as 'well built and well opened out, and there are many fine large streets in it', but bemoaned the lack of paving, which left the town full of sand and dust, and 'very inconvenient' in the summer months.[57]

Over the Musi River, crossed by a grand stone bridge which Tavernier considered as beautiful as the Pont Neuf in Paris[58], was a large suburb called Aurangabad. It was here that the merchants, brokers, craftsmen and common people lived, with the fortress and the rest of the town reserved for the nobility and the royal court. From 10 o'clock in the morning until 5 o'clock in the evening, local merchants and brokers came into the town to meet with foreign traders, 'after which,' Tavernier recounted, 'they return home to sleep'.[59] Some, however, found other entertainments. The Frenchman estimated that the town's prostitute population was in the region of 20,000. 'In the cool of the evening you see them before the doors of their houses, which are for the most part small huts, and when the night comes they place at the doors a candle or lighted lamp for a signal. It is then also that the shops where they sell *tari* are opened. This is a drink obtained from a tree, and it is as sweet as our new wines.' Beyond the suburb of Aurangzeb, looming above the plain, was the fort where, Tavernier said, 'the king keeps his treasure'.[60]

Tavernier's fellow Parisian, Jean de Thévenot, a geographer, natural scientist and explorer, travelled to Golconda in March 1673. He described the fort as a 'hill that rises like a sugar-loaf in the middle of the castle, which has the king's palace all round upon the sides of it'.[61] By the late seventeenth century, the fortress was an imposing sight. It was enclosed by a three-mile-long granite wall, studded with 87 bastions, and surrounded by deep ditches full of water.[62] It was really three forts in one: eight gates led inside from its outer wall, to another battlemented wall, which circled the base of the hill.

Halfway up the hill was the *Bala Hisar*, the citadel and royal palace, and the oldest part of the fort. Cannons bristled everywhere from gaps in the stonework, their elevated positions giving them unbroken lines of sight over the plain. 'Though there be several gates into this castle,' wrote de Thévenot, 'two only are kept open, and as we entered we... went through a very narrow place between two towers, which turning and winding, leads to a great gate guarded by Indians sitting on seats of stone with their swords by them'.[63]

The gates were made of heavy teak, studded with spikes to repel attacks by war elephants. The guards would refuse entry to anyone without permission from the governor or an officer of the king. Once inside, de Thévenot noted instantly the number of busy jewellers and artisans. They lived there for free, he was told, on the condition that they attended to all of the king's most important diamonds, and did not 'tell any what work they are about'. As he walked through the streets of the fortress, he saw innumerable workshops where sapphires were cut with bows of wire, and diamonds were polished, sawed and cleaved in two. Precious stones were so abundant that the workers needed no other employer than their king.[64]

The results of all this craftsmanship were on display in the crown jewels of Abul Hassan. De Thévenot described the king wearing a crowned turban, studded with 'a jewel almost a foot long, which is said to be of inestimable value'.[65] The crown was formed of rows of diamonds each three or four inches in diameter, and was topped by a branch shaped like a palm tree, with the palm leaves made of pearls. Yet more diamonds, rubies and pearls dangled from the sides of the crown. 'In short,' wrote de Thévenot, 'that king hath many other considerable pieces of great value in his treasury, and it is not to be doubted, but that he surpasses all the kings of the *Indies,* in precious stones; and if there were merchants (who would give him their worth), he would have prodigious sums of money'.[66]

Muhiuddin Muhammad Aurangzeb proclaimed himself emperor of the Mughals in a hurried ceremony held in the garden of Shalimar, just outside Delhi, in July 1658.[67] His self-appointed title was *Alamgir Padshah Ghazi*: 'Conqueror of the Universe'.[68] This name came from an engraving on the imperial sword of his father, Shah Jahan.[69] A month earlier, Aurangzeb had placed the ailing Shah under house arrest in the fort of Agra, declared him incompetent to rule, and taken his imperial sword for himself.[70]

It was a key moment in the endgame of a typically brutal war of succession. Shah Jahan had four sons: Dara, Aurangzeb, Shuja and Murad. Aurangzeb was the second oldest, and his mother was Mumtaz Mahal, the favoured wife of the emperor, whose tragic death had inspired the construction of the world's most famous and extravagant tomb: the Taj Mahal.[71]

In September 1657, Shah Jahan became so ill that he seemed close to death. He named his eldest son Dara as his successor, but in practice this was simply an invitation to the other three heirs to mobilise for civil war.[72] The Mughals had no law of succession. Struggles for the crown took on a Darwinian aspect – only the strongest survived. When it came to military expertise, leadership and tenacity, Aurangzeb had no match.

At the age of twenty-four, the prince had renounced his imperial duties to travel to the wild mountains of the Western Ghats in order to live as an ascetic holy man.[73] This decision met with the fury of Shah Jahan, who stripped his son of his wealth, estates and his rank, and the amusement of other family members. His eldest brother Dara referred wryly to Aurangzeb as 'that saint'.[74] After a year of solitude, he returned to the world, and was reinstated as a viceroy and general. Then, in 1647, his father gave him the command that would turn him from a pious prince into an emperor-in-waiting. Aurangzeb was sent to what was – and perhaps remains – the world's most challenging theatre of war: Afghanistan.[75]

As he battled the ferocious hilltop tribes, Persian invasions from the west, and the brutal extremes of the weather, Aurangzeb displayed great fortitude. In one skirmish, he even dismounted from his horse while under fire in order to observe the evening prayer,[76] prompting the king of his enemies to exclaim, 'To fight with such a man is self-destruction!'[77] This seemingly unnatural courage, a by-product of his unwavering faith, made a deep impression on his fellow generals and troops. When the fight for the throne began, he could command the loyalty of the most accomplished units in the imperial army.[78]

Aurangzeb's tactic in the civil war was to pick off his brothers one by one. First, Dara's forces were hounded further and further northwards, until the prince was forced to flee with his family to Afghanistan through the Bolan Pass. Dara's wife died of dysentery on the journey and, when he sought refuge with the Afghan Malik Jivan of Dadar, he was promptly arrested and returned to Aurangzeb. He was paraded through the streets of Delhi as a prisoner, an event witnessed by François Bernier, a French physician working at the imperial court, who described 'men, women and children wailing as if some mighty calamity had happened to themselves'.[79] He was then put on trial, found guilty of being an 'ally of the infidels' and, on 15 September 1659, executed.[80]

Shuja was then chased eastwards in a series of running battles, retreating first through the Deccan, then Bengal, before, in May 1660, reaching the lands of modern day Myanmar. There he was last seen heading into the Arakan mountains, with his wife and three remaining followers. No record exists of his fate after that.[81] Finally, there was the youngest of Shah Jahan's sons, Murad. Aurangzeb had formed an alliance with Murad at the outset of the civil war, based on an agreed future division of the empire. With Dara and Shuja gone, however, Aurangzeb resurrected an old charge of murder against his last surviving brother. Murad was brought to trial and executed in December 1661.[82]

Aurangzeb's fratricidal campaign had won him the largest Islamic empire in Indian history, but for the 'Conqueror of the Universe' this was not enough. Before launching further military ventures, though, he was determined to cleanse the moral impurity within his own borders. He suppressed the popular vices of drinking and gambling, and withdrew patronage for the 'decadent' practices that polluted his royal courts. Artists, musicians and architects were all sent packing.[83]

Aurangzeb also revoked the religious tolerance practised by his predecessors. In 1670 he issued an order for all non-Islamic schools and temples to be destroyed and for their jewelled idols to be buried under the steps of a new mosque being built at Agra – so that, as the official records of his empire, the *Maasir-i-Alamgiri*, put it[84], they were 'continually trodden upon' by the true believers. A decade later, in 1679, he imposed a tax on the followers of other religions[85], and when the Hindus of Delhi rose in protest at the gates of Aurangzeb's riverside palace, the emperor's response was uncompromising. 'The elephants were brought out and charged the mob,' recounted the contemporary Mughal historian Khafi Khan, 'and many people were trodden to death'.[86] So strict were Aurangzeb's politics that 1681 saw his fourth and favourite son, Prince Akbar, defect to the Hindu cause, and attempt to seize the throne. This religious and military coup soon faltered, and Akbar escaped into the western regions of the Deccan, seeking refuge in the Hindu kingdom of the Marathas. From there, he travelled by ship to Persia, where he spent the rest of his life trying, in vain, to raise an army to return to India and supplant his father.[87]

The willingness of the Deccan kingdoms to shelter the treacherous Akbar now turned the emperor's attention southwards. It had become his ardent desire, bordering on obsession, to conquer the region's remaining independent Muslim kingdoms, which followed a 'heretical' Shia sect of Islam. From there he could push on to the west to eradicate the growing threat of the Hindu Marathas.[88]

In 1656, Aurangzeb had, on a flimsy pretext, laid siege to Golconda. In a letter to his father, he had set out his ardent admiration for the kingdom. 'What shall I write about the beauty of this country – its abundance of water and population, its good air, and its extensive cultivation?'[89] It was a travesty that it remained in the possession of Abdullah Qutb Shahi: 'Such a money-yielding country, unmatched by the Imperial dominions,' he wrote, 'has fallen into this wretch's hands.'[90] But Aurangzeb's arguments and entreaties did not sway Shah Jahan. The prince was ordered to withdraw and the siege lifted, though Golconda was forced to submit to a variety of political and financial concessions. A year later, Shah Jahan's illness plunged the Mughal Empire into civil war.

Golconda enjoyed three decades of respite and, despite the imperial sanctions, relative peace and prosperity. It was, however, borrowed time. Aurangzeb was returning to the Deccan.

When Abul Hassan learned of the approach of Aurangzeb's vast army he 'shut himself up' in his fortress and 'remained bewildered, with his face to the wall, like a picture, lips despairing of laughter, eyes full of tears, head vacant of sense, tongue speechless.'[91] The king of Golconda sent a series of messages to the emperor, promising great tributes of money and jewels. According to the official account in the *Maasir-i-Alamgiri,* 'the only reply given to him was the sword.'[92] On 28 January 1687, the Mughal army mounted their first assault. Hassan's forces, which had assembled at the base of Golconda 'like swarms of ants and flies around a carrion', were rapidly driven back behind the fortress walls – 'the wind came and the gnats fled'.[93] Emboldened by this success, the veteran Mughal general, Qalich Khan, charged forward and attempted to storm the gates single-handed. He was hit in the shoulder by a bullet, and was rescued and carried away on horseback to be attended to by the surgeons of the imperial camp. As splinters of bone were pulled from the wound, Qalich sat calmly sipping coffee. Gesturing to his doctor, he was heard to remark, 'I have got an excellent tailor.' He died three days later.[94]

This first skirmish set the tone for a protracted siege. Imperial offensives continually broke against the walls of Golconda, repelled by the strength of the fortress, and its fearsome artillery. 'Guns, muskets and rockets were fired incessantly day and night from the fort, which seemed as if it were made of fire.'[95] Aurangzeb's army crept forward, digging trenches that zigzagged towards Golconda. Subjected to constant bombardment, and the frequent sallies of Hassan's cavalry, the Mughal engineers and troops suffered terrible losses. The imperial forces tried to reply in kind, directing their fire-power at the fortress walls, but their barrage met with little success. The Italian traveller Gemelli Careri described three Mughal cannons 'of such a prodigious bigness, that each of them was drawn by 500 elephants and 200 oxen'.[96] Even these, however, failed to punch holes in Golconda's stonework.

By March the imperial trenches had reached the moat surrounding the fortress. Sacks were filled with cotton and earth, and thrown into the water. The first sack was sown together by Aurangzeb himself, and dedicated with a victory prayer. After another month of struggle, the moat was almost full, and Golconda was close enough to touch. On 16 May, the Mughal commander-in-chief Firuz Jang attempted to scale the walls to take the fort by stealth. Hidden by darkness, he led a small detachment to a bastion where the sentries appeared either to be asleep or to have left their posts. A ladder was laid against the wall, and two men sent climbing up to the ramparts. At the top, they were confronted by a stray dog, no doubt looking for a route down, attracted by the many rotting corpses piled up in the moat below.[97] The dog began to bark at the intruders, and the noise brought the fortress guards. The Mughals were killed, and their ladders thrown down. When Hassan heard of the incident, he ordered the dog be fitted with a collar set with jewels, and dressed in a golden coat.[98]

It was clear to Aurangzeb and his generals that brute strength would not work. 'Owing to the shower of musket bullets, rockets, chain shot and bombs,' reported the *Maasir-i-Alamgiri,* 'the men could not advance one inch... without being slain or wounded'.[99] For months, however, a detachment of imperial troops had been working day and night on a secret plan. By the end of June, they were ready. The Mughals had extended their siege trenches by tunnelling underground, creating mines that led to three chambers excavated directly below the bastions of Golconda's outer wall. The chambers were filled with gunpowder. At dawn on 20 June, massed ranks of the imperial army charged the sections of the wall positioned directly above the explosives. The aim was to draw as many of Golconda's defenders as possible to the bastions to maximise the casualties, with the Mughal forces then storming through the breach created by the blast. As the troops broke cover and rushed from their trenches, the signal was given for the first fuse to be lit. Aurangzeb himself was present at the front alongside Firuz Jang, sensing the moment of victory. The emperor watched as a huge explosion tore through the ground at the base of the fortress.[100]

When the smoke, dust and debris cleared, the wall was still standing. The Mughal offensive, on the other hand, had been devastated. 'In the twinkle of an eye, the flying splinters killed 1,100 imperialists'.[101]

Bodies were littered around the perimeter of a huge crater, and 'great wailings and complaints arose from the troops'[102] still alive. The force of the blast had been directed outwards, away from the wall and directly into the advancing army. Taking advantage of the chaos and confusion, the Golcondans poured out of the fort to seize the Mughal trenches. According to Firuz Jang's predetermined plan, the second fuse was lit. This time, part of a bastion was caught up in the explosion, but the effect was no less calamitous for the imperial troops. Huge blocks of granite masonry came crashing down on the attackers, killing another thousand men.

A tropical storm now burst over Golconda: 'Wind and rain arose and obstructed the progress of the assailants, and they were forced to fall back drenched.'[103] Amid the torrential downpour, the fortress garrison 'made a sally, took possession of the trenches, spiked the heavy guns, and carried away all that was portable.'[104] In particular, they gathered up the many thousands of cotton bags and wooden logs from the moat, and used them to repair the small breach in the wall caused by the second explosion. The imperial army struggled in vain to retake the lost ground, but at sunset they were forced to retreat to their camp.

The next morning, when Firuz Jang ordered the firing of the third mine, nothing happened. The Mughals soon discovered that they had been outwitted by Hassan's men. Having learned of the plan from deserters in the imperial camp, the Golcondans had begun digging mines of their own. The night before the assault they had broken into the Mughal tunnels, removed all the gunpowder from the third chamber, and part-filled the other two with water, thereby ensuring that the explosions were directed away from the fortress walls.[105]

Meanwhile the siege showed no signs of ending. In June and July, monsoon rain and thunderstorms settled over the Golconda plain. The Mughal trenches filled up with water, and their gun emplacements were swept away by treacherous mud-slides. Even worse for Aurangzeb's forces, the conflict had disrupted the work of the region's farmers, and the rain had submerged the unsown fields beneath wide tracts of flood-water. The war camp was starving, and there was no way for supplies to get through.

As they looked on, Golconda's defenders saved their bullets – famine was devastating the imperial army for them. 'At night piles of the dead were formed around the emperor's quarters,' reported the *Maasir-i-Alamgiri*. 'Sweepers dragged them and flung them on the bank of the river from sunrise to sunset... The incessant rain melted away the flesh and the skin... After some months, when the rains ceased, the white ridges of bones looked from a distance like hillocks of snow.'[106]

Hassan offered the imperial army grain in return for lifting the siege. At the same time, in a petition to Aurangzeb, he pledged to remain in Golconda as a 'vassal paying tribute'. The land, he said, would then 'be more profitable to the emperor than if he annexes it and governs it by a viceroy'.[107] This was, however, to underestimate the Mughal ruler's crusading zeal. Aurangzeb's response left no doubt that, no matter how long it took, the siege would only end one way. 'If Abul Hassan is really submissive to me, as he professes to be, let him come with his arms tied together and a rope round his neck, like a sentenced felon.'[108] The emperor ordered another 50,000 sacks to be delivered to his camp to refill the moat. At the same time, a 'fort' of mud and wood was built to encircle Golconda.[109] For the defenders, there was a chilling symbolism to this act. For months their great granite walls had kept the Mughals out. Now the enemy was building a barrier to keep them *in*.

'Various other plans were tried,' wrote the *Maasir-i-Alamgiri,* and 'immense wealth was spent.'[110] In the end, the money proved decisive. Golconda's fall could not, it seemed, be won by force. But it could be bought. Abul Hassan had placed two generals in charge of the defence of the fortress – Abdur Razzak and Abdullah Khan. Both men had been bombarded by Aurangzeb with promises of wealth, estates and titles if they defected to the Mughal cause. Abdur Razzak had even shown one letter to his troops, and torn it to pieces in front of them. Abdullah Khan's loyalty, however, did not run so deep. An Afghan mercenary who had also once served with the Mughals, he elected to follow the path of self-preservation. Late in the night of 21 September, he opened a side gate to a detachment of imperial troops. Once this entry point was secured, they moved to open the main gate to allow the rest of the army to advance into the fort.[111]

Golconda, it seemed, was lost. Yet one man was not prepared to admit defeat. Abdur Razzak charged into the advancing Mughals on horseback, fighting them all the way to the summit of Golconda and the gates of the *Bala Hisar.* Covered in seventy wounds, with his forehead slashed open and one eye useless, Abdur Razzak was carried senseless from the battle by his horse, itself dying from loss of blood, and was found the next day, lying under a coconut tree, still clinging to life.[112] Learning of this display of valour and loyalty, Aurangzeb sent his best surgeons to attend to the general. After sixteen days, Abdur Razzak regained consciousness and was offered both wealth and a high-ranking position in the imperial army. 'No man who had eaten the salt of Abul Hassan,' responded Abdur Razzak, 'could enter the service of Aurangzeb.'[113]

Abul Hassan received the Mughal forces in his throne room as he sat down for an early breakfast. The enemy were led by Aurangzeb's son, Prince Azam, and Hassan greeted them with a calm 'good morning'[114], before inviting them to dine with him. Once the meal was over, Hassan mounted his horse, and rode out of Golconda for the last time, to meet his fate. He was taken first to the prince's tent, and then brought before Aurangzeb himself. There, 'he fell under the Emperor's gracious indifference instead of wrath'.[115] Within days he began the journey to Daulatabad, another hilltop fortress several days to the north-west. This would be his home, and his prison, for the rest of his life.

It is part of the allure and the mythology of diamonds that they can bring bad luck to those who possess them. Yet this is, of course, nonsense. How can a mere rock, even one formed over billions of years by the intense heat and pressure of the earth's crust, have any influence on the course of a human life? And yet...

Since the moment of their first discovery, humans have attached great worth and importance to diamonds. For those seeking wealth and power, and the trappings that come with them, they have a singular capacity to consume and obsess. Is it any surprise, then, that the later history of Golconda's diamond fortress – and of those who ruled it, travelled to it, coveted it and fought over it – is so conspicuously littered with misfortune?

Jean-Baptiste Tavernier boasted in his memoirs that he was the first European to open the route to Golconda's diamond mines – which were, he reminded his readers, 'the only places in the world where the diamond is found'.[116] During his travels, he had the opportunity to handle and purchase a remarkable number of stones, and even dedicated an entire chapter of his book to 'the largest and most beautiful diamonds and rubies which the author has seen in Europe and Asia'.[117] In November 1665, Tavernier was received by Aurangzeb at his royal court, where the emperor showed him his collection of jewels. Four eunuchs carried them into the throne room on two large wooden trays lacquered with gold leaf. The stones sat on beds of brocaded green and red velvet.[118]

The first stone he was shown was the 'Great Mogul', the giant diamond reputed to have come from the Kollur mine Tavernier had visited in the 1640s. The stone was, however, much diminished from its astonishing original size of 756 carats. Tavernier learned that a Venetian by the name of Hortensio Borgio had cut the diamond – so poorly that the emperor fined him 10,000 rupees – reducing substantially its size and weight. Even so, the stone, 'a round rose, very high at one side' was still 268 carats.[119]

Tavernier handled diamond after diamond, describing them as being 'of first-class water, clean and of good form, and the most beautiful ever found'.[120] Aurangzeb also showed him the Mughal dynasty's famous 'Peacock Throne'. Tavernier described a golden platform, some six feet long and four feet wide, with supports reaching up to a domed canopy. In form, it was more like a four-poster bed than a throne, and it was studded with hundreds, perhaps thousands, of diamonds, pearls, rubies and emeralds. Although Tavernier placed a value on it – a rather arbitrary 160 million livres[121] – its true worth was inestimable.

In 1668, Tavernier was back in Paris. The fame of his travels had spread, and soon after his return, he received an invitation to the royal court of Louis XIV.[122] Of course, he took his finest diamonds with him. The king was entranced by the stones, and bought a significant number from Tavernier. The most famous was the 'French Blue', better known today as the 'Hope', a 112-carat grey-blue diamond from the Kollur mine. In 1678 it was re-cut by the royal jeweller to a 67-carat heart shape and set in a gold neck ribbon, which the king wore to state ceremonies.[123] Tavernier received a handsome sum of money for the stones, along with a title. In 1676, he published his memoirs, *The Six Voyages of Jean-Baptiste Tavernier, through Turkey, into Persia and the East-Indies,* and, although he still travelled on occasion, settled comfortably into his new role as the 'Baron of Aubonne'.[124]

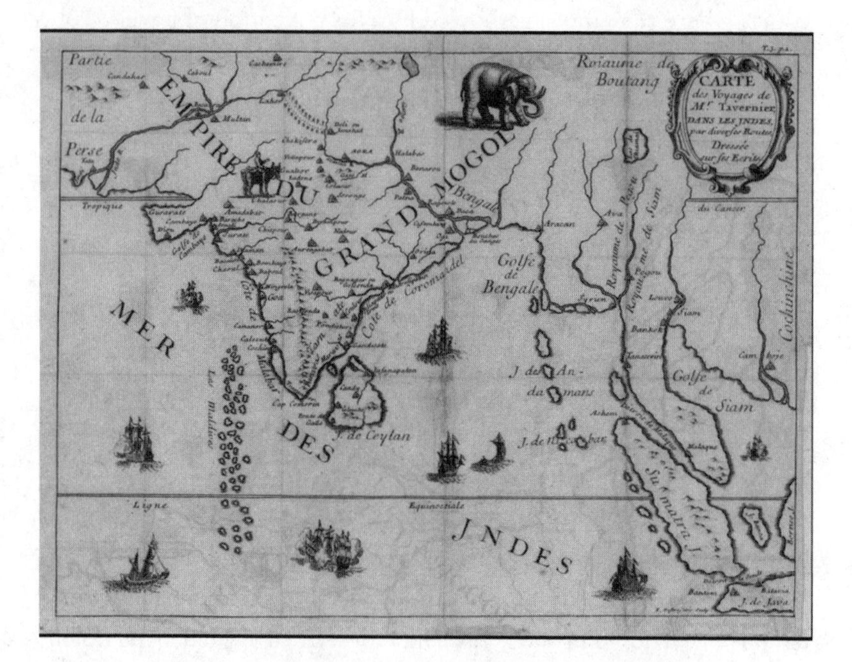

Map showing Tavernier's travels in the Mughal Empire

Something, however, came to interrupt this idyllic retirement. In 1685, Tavernier sold off the land and barony of Aubonne. A year later, on 13 January 1686, the archives of the Bastille, France's most notorious state prison, record the incarceration of a 'J. B. Tavernier'. We do not know if this was the famed diamond merchant, or another man of the same, not uncommon name.[125] We do know that around this time Tavernier went into business with his nephew Pierre, the son of a gold merchant. Some sources suggest that Pierre took a large portion of his uncle's fortune with him to Persia to contract a business deal, and never returned.

In 1687, now in his eighties, Tavernier set off on his seventh 'voyage' east. Perhaps this was an attempt to recover his losses. There are indications that he passed through Copenhagen in 1688 or 1689 – then nothing. It would be another two hundred years before his fate was discovered. In 1876, a grave was found in an old Protestant cemetery on the outskirts of Moscow. Tavernier's full name was still legible on the headstone, but time and the elements had erased half of the date. Only the first two digits – 16 – remained.[126]

The fall of Golconda was to be Aurangzeb's last great triumph. His vast empire stretched from Kabul to Bengal, and down as far as Cape Comorin at the very tip of the southern Indian peninsula. There remained, however, one last pocket of stubborn resistance: the Hindu Marathas of the wild country of the western Deccan. For the next twenty years, Aurangzeb would remain in this region, engaged in a futile attempt to subdue a people who thrived on rebellion.[127]

The Marathas were experts in guerrilla warfare. They would staunchly defend one hilltop fort, only to disappear suddenly into the wilderness. As the massive Mughal camp slowly mobilised to give chase, the Marathas would hit supply caravans and steal the imperial elephants, horses and camels. Aurangzeb was chasing shadows. By 'hard fighting and by the expenditure of the vast treasure accumulated', the Mughals had succeeded in occupying the 'wretched country' of the Marathas, and 'had subdued their lofty forts, and had driven them from house and home.'[128] It was not enough, though, to subdue the people. 'Still their daring increased,'[129] wrote the Mughal historian, Khafi Khan. The implacable will of Aurangzeb had met its match in the unyielding belligerence of the Marathas. The war could have no end, and no winner.

The years of conflict took their toll on Aurangzeb. They also drained the imperial treasury. In the late seventeenth century, Gemelli Careri had attempted to assess the wealth of Aurangzeb's empire. The most conservative estimate he had heard was of '330 millions' – of what currency he did not make clear. At the other end of the scale were those who judged it 'infinite'.[130] The Maratha campaign proved that there was an end to Aurangzeb's riches. His all-consuming obsession with the Deccan, and his two-decade absence from the royal seat of Delhi, had left the empire in disarray and the coffers empty.

In 1704, another European traveller, Niccolao Manucci, met Aurangzeb at his war camp. 'Most of the time he sits doubled up, his head drooping,' wrote Manucci. 'When his officers submit a petition, or make a report to him of any occurrence, he raises his head and straightens his back. He gives them such an answer as leaves no opening for reply... But those who are at a distance pay very little attention to his orders.'[131]

The emperor knew he was nearing the end of his life. 'My back is bent with weakness, and I have lost the power of motion,' he wrote in a letter to his favourite son Kambaksh, the only son he had not imprisoned or accused of treason. 'The breath which rose has gone and has left not even hope behind it. I have committed numerous crimes and I know not with what punishments I may be seized... I am going. Whatever good or evil I have done, it was for you.'[132] On 4 March 1707, at the age of eighty-nine, and after concluding his morning prayers, he died. His last command was for his courtiers to 'carry this creature of dust to the nearest burial place, and lay him in the earth with no useless coffin.'[133] According to his wishes, Aurangzeb was wrapped in a canvas shroud and placed in a humble tomb in the village of Rauza, near Daulatabad.[134]

With Aurangzeb gone, the Mughal Empire collapsed into civil war. This was nothing new, but this time, as the years passed, no figure emerged with the will or strength of character to unite India's fractured provinces. The Marathas grew in power, and began to expand outwards. To the north and the west, the Mughals were overcome by Persian and Afghan aggression. In 1739, the imperial capital of Delhi was sacked by the Persian king, Nadir Shah. 'The streets were strewn with corpses like a garden with dead leaves,' lamented a contemporary historian. 'The city was reduced to ashes and looked like a burnt plain'.[135]

The last and greatest of the Mughal treasures were carried away to the west, including all the diamonds Tavernier had handled, and the famous 'Peacock Throne' itself.[136] The empire limped on, a dismal parody of its former greatness. In September 1803, Lord Lake, Commander of the British Armies in India, entered Delhi,[137] where the Marathas had retained Shah Alam, the eighteenth emperor of the Mughal dynasty, as a puppet king. Lake found a blind and raving old man sitting under a tattered canopy. This pitiful figure was the Shah. His eyes had been removed as a punishment for his failure to reveal the whereabouts of the fabled treasures of his predecessors[138] – treasures which had evaporated centuries before. This was Aurangzeb's legacy: an emperor reduced to a blind beggar.

The Imperial Gazetteer of India, the British Empire's comprehensive survey of its territories in the subcontinent, was first published in nine volumes in 1881. The entry for Golconda described a fort 'situated on a rocky ridge of granite' ringed by 'many enclosures'.[139] Along its walls, the surveyors found large numbers of cannons marked with Persian inscriptions, a moat 'choked with rubbish', and inside, 'scattered everywhere', the 'ruins of numerous palaces, mosques, dwellings'. To the north, they recorded the 'summits of the enormous and massive mausolea of the ancient kings.' The tombs of the Qutb Shahis were set in 'an arid, rocky desert', and it was only, the surveyors surmised, 'the great solidity of their walls' that had preserved them from utter destruction.[140] They also recorded that the ruins of Golconda had been put to a new use, as an occasional state prison. The description in the

Gazetteer ended on a dismissive note: 'The diamonds of Golconda have obtained great celebrity throughout the world; but they were merely cut and polished here'.[141]

Today, the fortress sits surrounded by the urban sprawl of Hyderabad, the fourth most populous city in India. Tourists climb among Golconda's fallen buildings, and walk its still sturdy walls. Clap your hands at the right place at the bottom of the fort, say the guides, and, thanks to an ingenious architectural device, the sound will carry all the way to the top.[142] It was, perhaps, this same device that had warned Abul Hassan of his imminent capture by the Mughal army.

Golconda is now an empty shell. It has been abandoned and neglected, reoccupied, and then abandoned again, over the three-and-a-half centuries since its fall. The stones that remain today are not the ones that send merchants around the world or armies to war. Those stones – the *other* stones – have gone.

Diamonds are survivors. They are the hardest naturally occurring materials, built to last at a molecular level. Time is different for them. Diamonds can be anywhere from one billion to three billion years old.[143] Or, to put it another way, a diamond can have existed for up to three-quarters of the earth's entire lifespan. In comparison, a human life – or indeed the life of a building – is so fleeting as to be invisible. Perhaps that is why we are irresistibly drawn to diamonds. They are held to represent the greatest gift one person can give to another: a symbol of eternity, of eternal love.

When Delhi was sacked in 1739, the tremendous spoils carried back to Persia included a diamond so entrancing to the Persian King Nadir Shah that, when he first saw it, he exclaimed 'Koh-i-Noor!' – Arabic for 'Mountain of Light'. The history of the Koh-i-Noor is a matter of considerable debate. A product of the Golconda mines, some believe the stone was embedded in the Peacock Throne, and later removed by Nadir Shah. Others say it is the stone formerly known as the 'Great Mogul' diamond, viewed by Tavernier in 1665.[144]

Nadir Shah was murdered in 1747. For a century the Koh-i-Noor passed from one ruler to the next. Deposed kings were tortured to reveal its whereabouts; imprisoned princes hid it in the cracks in the walls of their bare cells. It moved from Persia to Kabul, then made its way back to India. In 1849, as the region of the Punjab was annexed by the British Empire, it was ceded by treaty to Queen Victoria. By this point the diamond, which may once have weighed 756 carats, was reduced to 186. In 1851, it was put on display as one of the main attractions of the Great Exhibition, and then, in 1852 it was re-cut by a Dutchman named Voorsanger, of the famous Costar company of Amsterdam.[145] Now 105 carats, it was set in a brooch worn by Queen Victoria. Over the years, it was remounted in the crowns of Queen Alexandra, Queen Mary, and, most recently, Queen Elizabeth, the Queen Mother.

The Koh-i-Noor is currently on display in the Jewel House of the Tower of London. Every day thousands of tourists roll sedately past on a special conveyor belt, staring. The Koh-i-Noor stares right back. It doesn't see the people, or the building in which it is kept, or the city that surrounds them all. It looks straight through them, to a distant horizon. If diamonds are cursed, as the legends say, then it is the curse of longevity. They live to see everything else die: people, buildings, nations, civilisations, species. They are fated to outlast the world.

Chapter Thirteen

Liberté for Sale

The Bastille – Paris (Born 1356 – Died 1789)

On the night of 25 February 1756, at No. 232, Rue Saint-Antoine, Paris, the prisoner Jean-Henri Masers de Latude and his young accomplice D'Alegre climbed up the inside of the chimney in their cell, forced open an iron grate at the top, and emerged onto the roof of a tall stone tower. The ascent had been arduous enough – Latude almost suffocated from the soot, and his arms and legs were bleeding profusely from scrapes and cuts – yet this was only the first step in their bid for freedom.[1] From the tower – one of eight punctuating the walls of a hexagonal fortress – to the wide ditch below, was a drop of eighty feet.[2] From the ditch back up to the outer parapet was a wall at least twenty feet in height, overlooked by sentries patrolling the ramparts of the prison.[3]

The two cell-mates had been preparing for this moment for six months. They had manufactured a rope ladder from strips of thread silk torn from their supplies of shirts, bed sheets, napkins, stockings and nightcaps, with rungs whittled from the meagre portions of firewood they had been given to see them through the winter. The ladder, which eventually stretched to three hundred and sixty feet, was hidden away each night beneath the floor of their cell.[4]

Latude was first to descend to the ditch, which was filled with over four feet of water after the Seine had burst its banks. With one end of the ladder fastened to a cannon, he climbed down from the overhang of the battlements of *La Tour du Trésor* – the Tower of the Treasure – swinging out into the air with every step. To muffle the sound of the rungs rattling against the stone, the two prisoners had fashioned coverings for the wood from the linings of their morning gowns and waistcoats. With Latude safely at the foot of the tower, D'Alegre lowered a leather *portmanteau* packed with a change of clothes, and a bottle of whisky to keep them warm[5], and then followed his friend down the ladder. Ice floated on the surface of the freezing water of the ditch, and there was no sign of the rain they had hoped might drive the guards indoors. Above them, patrols still marched the walkways of the outer wall, making climbing it without detection impossible. Latude realised that their only chance of escape was now not over the wall, but through it.

As silently as they could, they picked a section and began to work the bricks out one by one, every so often ducking their heads beneath the water to hide from the lantern lights of the guards. After nine hours, they had made a hole large enough to fit a man. Latude squeezed into the darkness, felt the clear air at the far side, and tumbled straight into the ten-foot-deep water of an aqueduct crossing the Rue Saint-Antoine. D'Alegre was right behind. In their first moments of freedom, these two numbed and exhausted men were in serious danger of drowning.[6]

As a nearby clock struck five in the morning, they hauled themselves, soaked and shivering out onto the roadside, helped each other into their change of clothes from the *portmanteau*, and hailed a hackney coach. Latude knew a tailor who lived in Saint-Germain, a man called Ronit from his home region of the Languedoc. Ronit would hide the pair of fugitives until they could flee from Paris to the Low Countries.[7] Against all the odds, the audacious plan had succeeded. Latude and D'Alegre had escaped from the most feared prison in France, an 'abyss' into which citizens vanished, only matched in its tortures and privations by 'the infernal regions'[8] – the Bastille.

The Bastille was a building with a singularly bad reputation. By the beginning of the eighteenth century, it was the stuff of nightmares for the ordinary citizens of Paris: a bogeyman in stone; an oppressive, Gothic prison visible across the city, and towering over the suburb of Saint-Antoine. People avoided it, or pulled their coats tighter around their bodies as they hurried past its high walls.[9] Yet in the pamphlets of the underground press, it was caricatured and mocked, portrayed as a brutish enforcer of the monarchy.[10] The conservatives in the French government believed they had established an unshakeable monument to state power at the heart of Paris. Certainly, they had created an icon. But would it be an icon of the *ancien regime*, or of the revolution?

The Bastille's life began in the mid-fourteenth century. The Hundred Years' War had placed Paris under direct threat from the English, and in 1356 Etienne Marcel, Provost of the city's merchants, expanded and bolstered the city walls, and constructed two large, fortified gateways – 'bastilles' – as entry points. One protected the Porte Saint-Denis to the north, the other the Porte Saint-Antoine in the east.[11] Marcel was a leading figure of the French bourgeoisie, and a proto-revolutionary. He would try to reform the monarchy and replace it with governance by the merchant class, but he moved too far and too fast even for his own supporters. In July 1358, as he attempted to provide passage into the city for the armies of the kingdom of Navarre, Marcel was killed by an axe wound to the head. He died in the shadow of his own new gate at the Porte Saint-Antoine.[12] Right from the start, the stones of the Bastille were linked with civil unrest.

Ten years later, Charles V, still terrified by the volatility of his subjects, and increasingly concerned about an English offensive, ordered Hugues Aubriot, the new Provost of Paris, to turn Marcel's gate into a much larger defensive structure.[13] By the mid-1380s, the 'bastille' of the Porte Saint-Antoine had been transformed into a looming fortress of eight towers linked by a 10-foot-thick curtain wall, surrounded by ditches and accessed by four sets of drawbridges. Built into the foundations of six of the towers were the underground *cachots,* a network of dark, sewer-like dungeons.[14] At the start of the fifteenth century, the building was still regarded as a powerful and reassuring symbol of security for Parisians – no longer just *a* 'bastille', but *the* Bastille. As with his predecessor Marcel, Aubriot's fate was tied to his building. After the death of Charles V in 1380, which left a 12-year-old Charles VI on the throne, Aubriot became a target for his enemies in the French intelligentsia, and was tried on charges of heresy – specifically for engaging in sexual acts with Jewish women. Found guilty, the creator of the Bastille became its first prisoner.[15]

By the time Charles VI reached adulthood, the fortress had reached its final shape and size, yet its purpose was in flux.[16] At first the shift was subtle and irregular. The stout structure in the suburb of Saint-Antoine still sent out a potent message about the defence of the city and the realm. Over time, however, this message became confused. Increasingly, it was less concerned with external aggressors, and more preoccupied by the enemy within. Alleged conspirators against the crown and religious activists accused of heresy began to disappear behind the Bastille's stone walls. Little by little, the skies above the fortress were darkened by a pall of secrecy.

In the first half of the seventeenth century, one man did more than any other to alter the building's purpose and reputation forever: Armand-Jean du Plessis, better known as Cardinal Richelieu.[17] A Parisian by birth, the third and youngest son of a soldier and courtier[18], Richelieu would become one of the most influential men in the history of French politics. His father had died in the religious wars when he was just five years old, and at nine he was sent to the College of Navarre to study the classical 'humanities'. Earmarked for a career in the military, he was enrolled in the officer academy of Antoine du Pluvinel[19], where he proved skilled in horseback riding, handling weapons and dancing[20], before his mother diverted his future into the clergy.

A voracious student, Richelieu's ascent was rapid. Nominated as Bishop of Lucon by Henry IV in 1606, before he had reached the official age, he travelled to Rome and received a special Papal dispensation to take up the post. In 1616 he was made Secretary of State, by 1622 he had been granted the title of Cardinal by Pope Gregory XV, and in 1624 – aged thirty-eight – he was named by Louis XIII as his Chief Minister.[21]

Richelieu was an arch reformer, and his goal was to achieve the centralisation of power in France. Sweeping away what he saw as the petty interests of the nobility and the feudal political structure, he subordinated the needs of everyone, from aristocracy to clergy, to the state.[22] He adapted the philosophy of horsemanship he had learned at the officer academy to that of government: always remain in control, break the strongest spirit, display unwavering authority.[23] Three hundred years later, Henry Kissinger would assert, 'Few statesmen can claim a greater impact on history. Richelieu was the father of the modern state system.'[24] A ruthless pragmatist, Richelieu held that, if power was exercised through rational thought, it must, by extension, be the will of God. 'The natural light of thought,' he wrote, 'makes it obvious to anyone that man, having been created reasonable, is bound to act using this power.'[25] Cardinal de Retz, a contemporary of Richelieu, took the analogy further: 'He struck down humans like lightning rather than governing them.'[26]

Richelieu employed the Bastille as a key piece in his game of realpolitik and power. Using *lettres de cachet* – warrants issued under the authority of the king – he detained, without judicial process, those suspected of being 'enemies of the state'.[27] Anyone who stood in Richelieu's way qualified for this title: aristocratic conspirators; Protestant agitators; satirists who criticised the regime and the king; writers whose works were thought likely to incite public disorder.[28] The *lettre de cachet* was an anachronism derived from the legal system of imperial Rome – specifically the maxim, *Rex solutus est a legibus:* 'the king is released from law'.[29] Citizens were seized and detained as the king pleased, by the will of God as expressed through his envoy on earth, none other, of course, than Richelieu. The Cardinal's network of spies hunted down dissidents, and the Bastille took them in, filling its cells with anyone suspected of sedition.[30] The fortress had turned into a prison.

As the seventeenth century ended, forbidding rumour shrouded the Bastille. It was just too prominent a landmark to be ignored: what really happened behind its walls was a matter of suspicion and fevered speculation. The literature of the French underground portrayed the building as a spectre whose purpose was to frighten fellow citizens at night. In 1668 the pamphlet *Scandalous chronicle, or ridiculous Paris* described the Bastille as a place which made 'everyone tremble'.[31] The fate of its author, a libertine named Claude Le Petit, was itself a cautionary tale. *Scandalous chronicle* was published posthumously: six years before, Le Petit had been burnt at the stake for writing a pornographic novel.[32] Putting quill to paper was a dangerous enterprise in France in the seventeenth and eighteenth centuries.

Yet it was literature that would furnish the Bastille with its most famous prisoners. These 'men of letters' would lift the fortress out of the mundane and into the realm of the mythic. Vivid accounts began to emerge of life as an inmate. Stories of suffering, torture and mental torment scandalized and thrilled the public in equal measure, confirming their worst fears about the prison and the regime behind it. The veracity of these tales mattered little: the Bastille was the perfect setting for the Romantic narrative: a gothic cage to entrap liberty, humanity and individuality. The cage itself, that stocky mass of medieval walls and towers, was despotism translated into physical form, the architecture of secrecy and suppression.

The model for the Bastille 'misery memoir' was established by Constantine de Renneville, a French Protestant who, on his return to Paris after a period working as a tax official in the Netherlands, was implicated as a Dutch spy. He was imprisoned in the Bastille for eleven years, from 1702 to 1713, and on his release moved in exile to London. There, supported by a pension from King George I, he penned an explicit exposé of the regime inside the fortress.[33] Published in 1715, *The French Inquisition: or, the History of the Bastille in Paris, the State Prison in France* painted a terrifying picture of unlawful incarceration and the arbitrary abuse of power. 'What have I not seen

The morose stone tortoise of Karakorum © Dean Conger / Corbis

The ruins of the fortress of Golconda – now set in the midst of Hyderabad, the fourth most populous city in India. © Bridgeman Images, 2007

Napoleon's Bastille Elephant: watercolour by the elephant's architect Jean-Antoine Alavoine (1776-1834). Louvre Museum, Paris.

Charlie Hebdo Rally at the Place de la Bastille, 11 January 2015 © Stephane Cardinale / Corbis

The acme of the sublime ruin – Machu Picchu with the cloud-topped peak of Huayna Picchu behind. Photograph © Martin St Amant

The ruins of a modern Panopticon? Empty cells surround a central tower in one of the prison blocks of the Presidio Modelo on the Isle of the Pines, Cuba

loon pictured in 2014. The public park built on the site of the former Walled City is viewed here from op floor of a new shopping mall. In the foreground is photographer Patrick Zachmann's image of the Valled City in its heyday, from the book *W. or the Eye of a Long-nose.* © Patrick Zachmann / Magnum

A graveyard for fragments of the Berlin Wall at Teltow, Germany. © Sean Gallup / Getty Images

The pointed trident arches at the foot of the twin towers: designed by Minoru Yamasaki as a modernist representation of traditional Islamic architecture.

The twin towers cast their long shadows over Manhattan. © Visions of America / Getty Images

in that mansion of horror, during the space of above eleven years that I was there?' he wrote.

> 'I have seen guilt triumph over virtue, and trample upon innocence, avarice gorge itself with the blood of the unfortunate... I have seen dragged into dreadful and stinking dungeons, persons of quality, God's ministers, Abbots, Priests, religious men, persons venerable for their age, virtuous ladies, young maidens, and small children, without any other cause than to feed the insatiable avarice of a barbarous Governor.'[34]

Renneville recounts the chilling advice carved into the window-ledge of his cell by an Italian prince, advocating poisoning or hanging oneself as the only means of escape. He describes the harrowing experience of being held in irons in the subterranean *cachots*, next to the rag-bound skeletons of a mass grave.[35] Renneville's book lifted the Bastille's veil of secrecy in the most shocking fashion.

The degrees of exaggeration – or artistic licence – in these memoirs varied from author to author, but all stuck to the same formula: wrongful imprisonment; warrants issued by *lettres de cachet* secured by powerful rivals or enemies; arrests carried out under the cloak of deception; the secrecy of confinement; the poverty of living arrangements; and the arbitrary and spiteful rule of the prison governor.[36]

Renneville's success caught the attention of other writers, who started to recognise that their suffering might have a compensation – fame. Among them was Andre Morellet . The Enlightenment economist, abbot and philosopher had spent a short time in the Bastille after being accused of libel, and later wrote of the experience, perhaps with tongue in cheek: 'I saw literary glory illuminate the walls of my prison. Once persecuted I would be better known... and those six months of the Bastille would be an excellent recommendation and infallibly make my fortune.'[37]

In fact conditions for many of the Bastille's inmates were markedly better than in most other prisons of the time, and indeed their relative luxury may surprise our modern sensibilities.[38] By the time of Louis XVI, the majority of prisoners were held in spacious, sixteen-foot-wide octagonal cells, positioned in the middle levels of the fortress towers. Each cell had a four-poster bed lined with green curtains, as well as tables, chairs, a stove and a chimney. Prisoners were often allowed to bring in their own possessions.[39] In the case of the Marquis de Sade, held in the Bastille until the week before it was stormed[40], these included a wardrobe stocked with shirts, silk breeches, dressing gowns, hats, coats and boots, and a library of 133 volumes, including Hume's histories and Homer's *Iliad*.[41]

Breakfast in the Bastille was served at seven, lunch at eleven, and dinner at six in the evening. The typical menu for the midday repast was soup, an entrée and a meat course of mutton, pork, sausage or veal, washed down with a bottle of wine. Supper consisted of two dishes, one of which was meat, often roast chicken or calf's liver.[42] Seafood options included pike, sole, trout, prawns and even oysters.[43] De Sade was not impressed: 'They are clearly starving me to death here,' he wrote to his wife Renée in 1784.[44] He supplemented prison fare by ordering in pâtés, terrines, and jams, as well as the chocolates that he was 'accustomed to get from [his] regular shop'; he was provided with fresh flowers every week, and was served strawberries every day.[45] These purchases were on top of those that had already been made out of the budget allotted by the king to the prison governor for the care of the prisoners: three livres a day for commoners, five for tradesmen, ten for the middle class, and fifteen for high-ranking officials.[46] The heftiest stipend of all, however, was reserved for literary and cultural prisoners like the Marquis: nineteen livres a day.[47]

The reality of life in the Bastille may have been moving away from its murky past, but the myths grew more elaborate, the horror stories more compelling. In 1719, the Abbé Bucquoy, a cleric arrested in 1707 as a salt-smuggler and spy, published *The Hell of the Living, or the Bastille in Paris*, a record of his time in the fortress, which spoke of secret torture chambers and 'death cells' in the *La Chapelle* tower.[48]

Even more potent was a story written in 1751 by the father-figure of the French Enlightenment, Voltaire, in *The Age of Louis XIV*. In 1717,

Voltaire, then an aspiring writer going by the name of Arouet, had been imprisoned in the Bastille for eleven months for writing pornographic poetry about the Prince Regent and his daughter.[49] Voltaire's remarkable account was not about his own incarceration. Instead it concerned one who had come before him, a prisoner who wore 'a mask, the lower half of which had steel springs, which allowed him to eat while the mask was on his face. Orders were given to kill him if he uncovered himself... This unknown personage was taken to the Bastille where he was lodged as comfortably as it was possible to be... Nothing that he asked for was refused. His predominant taste was for linen of extreme fineness, and for lace... His table was profusely served... This unknown individual died in 1703, and was buried at night.'[50]

An 18th-century engraving of the Man in the Iron Mask
Photo © Liszt Collection / Bridgeman Images

The source material for this passage was a blend of rumour and hearsay relating to a mysterious prisoner who had entered to the fortress in 1698, and died of illness five years later, at around the age of forty-five.[51] With the imprimatur of Voltaire, it grew into one of the most enduring myths of the despotic, even demonic, forces at work in the Bastille. 'The Man in the Iron Mask'[52] was a piece of gothic-horror genius, with gleeful public speculation – prompted by Voltaire himself in his later writings – even going so far as to suggest that the anonymous inmate had been the illegitimate elder brother, or else the identical twin, of Louis XIV.[53] The symbolism was powerful: a man's identity erased by iron, his sense of self imprisoned, and all to hide a secret cutting to the heart of a corrupt regime. 'The Man in the Iron Mask' was taken up as the poster-boy of the anti-Bastille movement, an iconic martyr for those seeking a new France. The faceless man became the face of the Bastille.

By the 1780s, the fortress was in crisis, hated by the citizens of Paris and increasingly seen as an embarrassment by the ministers of the *ancien regime*.[54] This would be the last decade of the Bastille's life. If Paris was a powder keg of revolution, then all fuses led to the Rue Saint-Antoine. The bourgeoisie, the so-called 'Third Estate' of France, were uniting behind a simple, yet potentially world-changing idea, a product of the philosophy of the Enlightenment. This idea held that, as the power of reason was common to all men, it followed that all men were therefore equal, and should be treated as such under the law. Every citizen, irrespective of birth, should have the same rights and duties in relation to the state. These rights should be enshrined in a binding social contract between an individual and his country – a constitution – guaranteeing liberty, property, security and freedom from oppression.[55]

There were pockets of Enlightenment thinkers throughout eighteenth-century Europe, but the movement's spiritual home, thanks to the likes of Voltaire, Rousseau, Diderot and Montesquieu, was

France.[56] And its manifesto spread like – as many of its hard-line monarchist opponents must have seen it – a virus or a plague, a contagion born of the pen and the printing press, carried and passed on by the pamphleteer.

Yet an idea is not enough, particularly when it proposes so radical a change to the fabric of society and the course of history. Action is also needed. And two men, whose Bastille stories became common revolutionary currency in the 1780s, provided exactly that.

On 27 September 1780, Simon-Nicolas-Henri Linguet, a lawyer-turned-journalist and the author of the influential journal *Annales Politiques*, was arrested in Paris and taken to the Bastille. For some time, Linguet had been writing his journal from the safety of England, but had been lured back to France on the express assurance that he would be able to work free from government persecution.[57] Almost immediately on his return, a *lettre de cachet*, issued on behalf of the Maréchal Duras, an especially piqued victim of Linguet's pen, dispatched him to the state prison.

He would remain there for twenty-one months, until his release on 19 May 1782.[58] Linguet was a dangerous enemy for the Bastille to make at a dangerous time. It took him just over six months to prepare his revenge. In January 1783, he published the wonderfully titled *Memoirs of the Bastille: Containing a full exposition of the mysterious policy and despotic oppression of the French Government, in the Interior Administration of that State-Prison, interspersed with a Variety of Curious Anecdotes.* This would become the most popular and widely reproduced indictment of the fortress ever written.

The book bristled with the righteous ire of the wrongfully imprisoned, like all the anti-Bastille literature before it. What set it apart was its forensic dissection of the ideology behind the fortress. The lawyer in Linguet took the idea that had inflamed the passions of the French bourgeoisie and applied it to the arbitrary and inhumane mechanisms at work in the Bastille. Where others had recited litanies of physical abuse and privation, Linguet focussed in particular on the 'tortures... of the mind' caused by the prison[59], depicting the Bastille as the arch-enemy of the Enlightenment, as it defied all law and reason.

'I am no longer at the Bastille,' wrote Linguet in the introduction to his book. 'It is necessary to prove that I never deserved to be there. It is necessary to do more: to demonstrate that none have ever deserved it: the innocent, because they are innocent; the guilty, because they ought not be convicted, judged and punished, but according to the laws, and because at the Bastille none of the laws are observed, or rather they are all violated.'[60]

Linguet's memoir reads as the definitive, closing statement in a dazzling prosecution case against the Bastille. He exposed the perversity of a nation where ordinary people clamoured in vain for equality, but where the one place it could actually be found was behind the walls of an infamous prison. 'The Bastille, like death, brings an equality to all whom it swallows up,' he wrote. From 'sacrilegious villain' to 'undaunted patriot', all are 'overwhelmed alike in uniform darkness' and 'detached from all the rest of mankind; farther removed from his relations, from justice, than if he had been transferred into another planet'.[61]

For Linguet, the equality the Bastille offered was one where understanding was stripped away, identity erased and rationality confounded. It was the equality of oblivion. Writing in 1862, Fyodor Dostoevsky proposed famously that the best way to judge the degree of civilisation in a society was by entering its prisons.[62] In France in the 1780s, Linguet had already made this message clear. If the bourgeoisie were not careful, if they did not act, then they would all endure grimly, as equals, a life without hope and freedom. Linguet emphasised, as never before, that the fortress was a symbol of everything corrupt and malevolent in the organs of state. 'The Bastilles of France,' he wrote, 'have devoured, are daily devouring, men of all ranks, and of all nations.'[63]

One man had, like Jonah, been languishing in the belly of the beast for over three decades. Giving himself the title of 'Chevalier', he was the illegitimate union of a laundress from Montagnac and an impoverished Count. Originally named Danry – a compression of Jean-Henri – he had assumed the noble title of the father who had never acknowledged him: the Marquis de Latude.[64] This was the very man who had escaped the Bastille in the most daring fashion on a February night in 1756. Yet, apart from a few fleeting months on the run, he would spend the following twenty-eight years of his life in jail.

The opening acts of Latude's Bastille story carry more than a whiff of farce. After serving as a surgeon and barber in the army (the two professions being interchangeable at the time), he came to Paris in 1748, and devised a hare-brained scheme to find fortune and favour among the royal court. His plan was to foil an assassination plot against the king's mistress, the Marquise de Pompadour. A noble cause, perhaps. Except that Latude had manufactured the plot himself after overhearing two men criticising the Marquise while walking in the garden of the Tuileries.[65] He sent a poison letter (in fact containing a harmless powder) to his mark, and then obtained an audience with her at Versailles to warn her of the danger. Before he could leave, however, he was tricked into providing a sample of his own handwriting. When this was compared to the script on the letter, it was immediately clear that saviour and conspirator were one.

Within days Latude was making his first acquaintance with the Bastille.[66] After a few months, he was transferred to the prison of Vincennes. He duly escaped, making his way through fields and vineyards to a safe-house in Paris. From there, he wrote to the king for clemency – including on his memorandum a return address. Latude was back in the Bastille in a matter of hours.[67]

He would remain in the fortress for another five years, many of them confined to the underground *cachots*, before his spectacular escape with D'Alegre. After temporarily hiding out with Latude's tailor friend in Saint-Germain, the two men split up to make their way separately from France to Belgium. D'Alegre was recaptured at the pair's planned rendezvous point at the *Hotel du Coffi* in Brussels, whereupon Latude fled on to Antwerp and Amsterdam, but the 'exempts' – the Interpol of its time – were hot on his trail. Just three months after his escape he would be apprehended in the Dutch capital.[68] Back in Paris, the mouth of the Bastille opened for Latude once again.

After another escape and recapture in 1765[69], Latude's picaresque adventures took a macabre turn. Abandoned in the dungeons with only the rats as his companions – his 'family' as he came to call them

– he passed the time playing music on a flute fashioned from a strip of elder found in his bedding straw, and writing a tactical treatise on the *halberdiers* of the French army. He used flattened bread as his paper, carp bones as his pens, and his own blood as ink.[70]

In 1782, a young knitwear trader and vendor of pamphlets found a package marked with an unreadable address dropped on the streets of Paris.[71] It contained a letter, intended for the king, from 'Masers de Latude, prisoner during thirty-two years at the Bastille, at Vincennes and at the Bicêtre, where he is confined, on bread and water, in a dungeon ten feet underground.'[72] Latude had used a shirt and a pair of silk stockings to bribe a man to deliver a message from his prison to Versailles[73], and it had ended up discarded in a gutter. For once, however, fate was on his side. The woman who opened it, Madame Legros, was so moved by Latude's plight, that she would become a tireless campaigner for his freedom. For over two years she fought for his release, circulating copies of his letter around the city, securing interest in the case from lawyers of the Paris court, reaching the salons of Madame Necker, wife of the Controller-General of Finance, and even the queen herself.[74] In March 1784, Latude finally became a free man again. More than that, he was an instant celebrity – one supported by a royal pension of four hundred livres a year.[75]

His story was taken up by many French writers and published in a series of journals: an inspirational tale of one man's struggle against a corrupt justice system. Latude received hundreds of visitors to his Paris apartment, eager to meet the man in person and to hear his story from his own lips. At first, Latude would not publish an account himself, as he still had an understandable dread that at any moment he would be rearrested. Yet this fear was misplaced. Latude, the one time hapless adventurer, was on his way to becoming a national hero.[76]

Linguet, the lawyer, had taken the idea of an equal and fair society, and used it to demolish the Bastille in argument. Latude was the second half of the equation[77]: despite his many years of incarceration, he was cast as the embodiment of action, the man who had escaped the Bastille – who, even when returned to its clutches, had kept his hope alive, endured, and survived. Thirty years of despotism had not broken him. If one man could defeat the terrible miseries of state-sponsored oppression, what could an entire people do?

The campaign for the demolition of the fortress began in earnest. In a leaflet circulated widely at the start of 1789, the Bastille and the prison of Vincennes are shown in conversation. 'It is I... who rule the centre of the most enormous city of the world and openly unfurl the horrible armament of my power,' says the Bastille. 'Within my walls I have locked up the most excellent heroes, famous authors and people of divine lineage... we can pride ourselves in having carried out deadly tortures that would be the envy even of cannibals.' The prison of Vincennes, however, can tell which way the wind is blowing, and warns his counterpart: 'You will soon be forced to bury your colossus's presumptuous conceit in the dust.'[78]

In June 1789, the death warrant for the mighty Bastille was already being signed in official correspondence. The Royal Academy of Architecture had produced a series of plans that would see the fortress demolished, to be replaced by a broad, open space of public gardens and promenades, spreading out from a central fountain with a column of bronze – taller than the towers of the old prison – topped by a statue of Louis XVI, made out of melted Bastille chains and padlocks.[79]

As a famous sculptor of the day wrote, 'The idea of raising a monument to liberty on this spot where bondage has reigned hitherto seems to me a noble thought and one calculated to inspire a man of genius'.[80] The establishment had at last realised the true power of the Bastille to incite public unrest. It was an architectural insult to the bourgeoisie, a constant reminder of the fear and suspicion between the ordinary man and the monarchy. It had to go before it caused a revolution.

By July 1789, Paris was a tinderbox, just waiting for any stray spark. Two months earlier, the Estates-General – a meeting of the king, the nobility, the clergy, and the common people – had been convened at Versailles for the first time in over one hundred and seventy years.[81] The purpose of this extraordinary gathering was to address the dire financial crisis afflicting France: a legacy of the profligate monarchy and the huge costs involved in fighting to support the newly-constituted thirteen colonies of the United States in the American War of Independence.

Yet for the 'Third Estate', the representatives of ninety-five per cent of the French population[82], finance was a side issue. Instead, they used the meeting as their opportunity to agree a radical reform of the political landscape, one that would finally enshrine the Enlightenment ideals of equality and democracy in a written constitution. The American victory, billed as a triumph for the Age of Reason, had galvanised both the intellectuals in their salons and the masses on the streets.[83] As negotiations descended into an impasse, on 17 June the Third Estate unilaterally declared themselves to be the 'National Assembly' – the true representatives of the people of France, and the new body that would govern the affairs of the nation.[84]

At first Louis XVI moved to resist, but as members of the clergy and the most liberal among the aristocracy began to join the Assembly, he appeared to concede his political authority.[85] Had the Third Estate achieved a bloodless coup? As June turned into July, this hope would fade. News reached the National Assembly and the people of Paris that troops from the provinces, made up of foreign regiments thought to be loyal to the Crown[86], were marching on the city. On 11 July, the king dismissed the popular finance minister Jacques Necker and replaced him with the hard-line Baron de Breteuil.[87]

Hysterical reports spread that the approaching army was 30,000 strong and under orders to sack Paris and massacre its rebellious citizens. Breteuil himself was reported to have said, 'If it should be necessary to burn Paris, it shall be burned, and the inhabitants decimated: desperate diseases require desperate remedies'.[88] Unsurprisingly, the Bastille was at the centre of many of the rumours. Its cannons were armed, people said, and ready to fire into the suburb of Saint-Antoine[89]; it was already holding in its cells representatives of the National Assembly[90]; it had just received a delivery of 31,000 pounds of gunpowder.[91]

On the morning of 14 July, over nine hundred Parisians had massed below the walls of the fortress. Cannon may have bristled from its towers and ramparts, but in fact the Bastille was manned only by eighty-two ageing, retired soldiers known as *invalides*, and a small complement of thirty-two Swiss guards. Moreover, the prison's food supplies wouldn't last much more than twenty-four hours, and there were no reserves of drinking water.[92]

Nevertheless, the reputedly impregnable Bastille had found itself the last outpost of royal authority in Paris. And its governor, Bernard-René de Launay, had become, by default, the figurehead of the *ancien regime* in the city. As he looked out onto the growing crowd, made up largely of artisans from the surrounding suburbs[93], de Launay was in a state of extreme agitation.[94] He could not dishonour his command by handing the Bastille and its stores of gunpowder over to the mob, at least not without direct orders from his superiors in Versailles. Yet if the gathering erupted into violence, he knew his position would be hopeless.

As the morning progressed, emissaries from the Hôtel de Ville, the headquarters of the committee in control of Paris, were admitted to the Bastille to talk with de Launay. To demonstrate his desire to cooperate, the governor took a delegate up to the prison ramparts to witness the standing-down of the high cannons.[95] From the Rue Saint-Antoine below, the people saw only movement around the guns, and grew even more suspicious. The negotiators returned to the Hôtel de Ville to report their progress and to receive further instructions. In their absence, the pent-up emotion and excitement of the crowd broke free. Calls of 'We want the Bastille!' and 'Down with the troops!' became louder, and a mass of people rushed forward to press against the gates of the prison.

Emboldened by this first unhindered advance, a group clambered on to the roofs of a perfumer's shop adjacent to the gates leading to the inner courtyard, and cut the drawbridge chains.[96] As the first great wooden door crashed down, the crowd surged forwards and the panicked garrison, faced with a charging mob, opened fire. Musket shots and the single, thunderous detonation of a cannon – the only one fired in the course of the siege – rang out over the rooftops of Paris.[97] In the gaping mouth of the Bastille, the Revolution had begun.

Ideas had brought France to the brink. Now violence tipped it over the edge. As the fighting intensified, the Bastille was proving worthy of its formidable reputation. By around four o'clock, eighty-three of the citizens' army were dead, and only one of the *invalides* inside the fortress had been recorded as a casualty.[98] Yet through the thick smoke from carts of burning straw pushed into the entrance passage, the defenders of the fortress could see that the stakes were being raised. Companies of defecting soldiers had bolstered the civilian crowd – and brought with them two cannons of their own.

De Launay decided this was a battle he could not win. Instead, he resolved to secure honourable surrender before more lives were lost. Just after five o'clock, a white handkerchief was waved from one of the towers, and the governor delivered his terms. He wanted safe passage for the garrison, or he would ignite the whole stash of gunpowder in the fortress, taking the Bastille, and a large chunk of the suburb of Saint-Antoine, along with him. The besiegers called his bluff, and prepared to fire their cannon on the final barrier. Before the fuses could be lit, the gate was opened from the inside, and the crowd flooded forward to seize their prize.[99] The Bastille had fallen.

De Launay was the son of a former governor of the Bastille, and had been born inside its walls.[100] He had followed in his father's footsteps to take charge of the prison, and had carried out his duties with stolid efficiency rather than zeal. Yet for the crowd caught up in the melodrama, he was the arch-villain. The leaders of the siege tried to take him to the Hôtel de Ville, but once again, the will of the people could not be contained. De Launay was beaten, stabbed and shot to death, before a cook by the name of Desnot severed the governor's head. It was then stuck on a pike, the better to display it to onlookers.[101] De Launay's was yet another life – and death – played out in its entirety in the dark theatre of the Bastille.

News of the successful siege spread first through Paris and then into the provinces. The storming of the fortress rapidly took on a quasi-religious significance for the citizens of the Revolution, and the bloody pageantry of the event and its aftermath would be re-enacted in processions and ceremonies across France. *Papier-mâché* miniatures of the fortress were created, then 'stormed'. Actors dressed as wizened, white-bearded old men were 'freed' from heavy chains and paraded among village crowds. At a grisly extreme, children marched in the streets with the heads of stray cats on spear tips as substitutes for the head of de Launay.[102] Among the sacred *vainqueurs* of the Bastille – the officially-certified nine hundred and fifty-four who had taken part in the siege[103] – one man recognised the emotional currency of the fortress better than any other. So much so, in fact, that he would turn its destruction into the greatest show in France.

Pierre-François Palloy came from a modest family of Parisian wine merchants. Sent to a school for the children of the liberal aristocracy, Palloy entered the royal army at fifteen, and five years later, at the end of his commission, took an apprenticeship as a mason. His master was blessed with both a flourishing building contracting business and a daughter. At twenty-one, Palloy married the latter and a few years later, took charge of the former. By 1789, at the age of thirty-four, he was head of one of the largest construction firms in Paris, owned seven houses and assorted prime property across the city, and had a personal fortune of half a million livres.[104] The *ancien regime* had done little to harm Palloy's progress. Yet he was at heart a liberal and an idealist, and in the early days of the Revolution, was quick to give himself his own soubriquet: 'Patriot Palloy.'[105]

On 14 July, Palloy and a group of his workmen, drawn by the sounds of the battle below the walls of the Bastille, had gathered their weapons and joined the uprising. In Palloy's own account, written two years later and no doubt a mixture of exaggeration and fiction, he tells of receiving a musket ball through his hat while fighting alongside one of the charismatic leaders of the siege, Lieutenant Elie, and of being one of the first to enter the inner courtyard when the prison fell.[106] 'As a good citizen,' wrote Palloy, 'I climbed onto the stage of the Revolution'.[107] Once on that stage, the 'Patriot' barely stepped off it again.

The day after the siege, on 15 July, the Comte de Mirabeau, a leading figure in the National Assembly and a former inmate of the Bastille, appeared on the towers of the prison before a large crowd. Handed a ceremonial pick, he swung out at the battlements and sent the first fragment of the Bastille's walls crashing to the ground.[108] Greeted by cheers, this piece of showmanship put the official seal on the plan to demolish the fortress – a plan devised by Palloy on the very same day the prison was stormed. At its peak, over one thousand men were engaged on site for the demolition. It was a time of high unemployment and even higher living costs, and Palloy's Bastille job provided a significant boost to the workers of Saint-Antoine, offering excellent wages and choice incentives. Yet while the walls of the fortress, quite literally, fell down around his ears, Palloy was doing everything he could to shore up the notorious reputation of the prison.[109]

'*Adieu Bastille*' – a peasant holding a chained lion plays the bagpipes while puppets of an aristocrat and clergyman dance to his tune. In the background the fortress is being demolished. (July 1789). Artist unkown.

When the cell doors of the Bastille had been thrown wide in the aftermath of the siege, only seven men had walked out to freedom. Four were forgers, two were lunatics, and one, the Comte de Solages, had been detained at his family's request, to protect both himself and others from his libertine urges.[110] It was hardly an outpouring of the oppressed and the innocent. The *vainqueurs* were undaunted, though, and as they rushed through the fortress on the evening of 14 July, they saw in every empty cell the shadows of comrades lost and forgotten.[111]

As the demolition work continued apace, Palloy and his workers began to offer paid tours of the prison's basement, dungeons and 'torture chambers', recounting the harrowing, gothic stories of the likes of Renneville, Latude, and the mysterious 'Man in the Iron Mask'. Visitors were shown old bones and the remains of skeletons. Pieces of metal – and in one instance, a fragment of a printing press – were held up as examples of 'death machines unknown to man'.[112] Latude himself returned to visit the scene of so many years of torment, and was amazed to be presented with the rope ladder he had used to make his escape thirty years before, and which had been carefully preserved in the prison archives.[113]

The revolutionary press mined the dark seam of the Bastille for every nugget of cruelty and despotism they could find, whether real or fabricated. Pamphlets and newspapers reported on inscriptions deciphered from faint carvings on the prison walls, including the conveniently 'discovered' one: 'I have been chained to this stone for forty years. They covered my face with an iron mask.'[114] The public lapped it up. With Palloy at the helm, the people of Paris and rich travellers from all over Europe paid their fees, passed through the turnstiles, and descended into the dungeons of a proto-theme park.[115]

By the end of July, the fortress had taken on the aspect of a ruin, its beams and superstructure exposed as it was pulled apart from the top down. By November 1789, almost nothing was upstanding, and all that remained were the subterranean warrens of the *cachots*[116], still much in demand for guided tours. Yet Palloy was far from finished with the Bastille. In July 1790, on the first anniversary of the siege, he held a lavish commemoration ball, with large tents pitched over the foundations of the prison. The area was decorated with trees, Chinese lanterns and tricolour garlands, featured a fireworks display and an orchestra, and was advertised at its entrance with giant placards bearing a simple slogan: *Ici l'on danse* – 'Here, we dance'.[117] Palloy recognised the importance of the site of the fortress as a place of revolutionary pilgrimage for the common man. Yet he was also aware that many fellow citizens throughout the provinces could never afford the journey to Paris. With this in mind, he took the Bastille on the road.[118]

France at that time comprised 83 districts, or *départements*, and Palloy's scheme involved creating for each one a travelling show made up of '*reliques patriotiques*' packaged into a kind of revolutionary sacrament.[119] He employed 'Apostles of Liberty' to transport the relics, held in three heavy chests loaded onto carts, and conduct dedication ceremonies in each individual *département* capital. The centrepiece of each show was an intricate scale model of the Bastille, carved from a single slab of stone taken from the walls of the prison. Alongside would be arranged a cannonball and breastplate from the siege, the official history of the storming of the fortress by the writer Jean Dusaulx, Latude's memoirs of his 30-year incarceration, portraits of revolutionary figures, and even an engraved portrait of the king.[120]

Scale model of the Bastille carved out of a stone slab taken from the prison's walls. © Pierre-Yves Beaudouin

The intention was for Latude to accompany these shows – with his rope ladder – to deliver in person the account of his unimaginable ordeals.[121] 'France is a new world,' wrote Palloy. 'And in order to hold on to this achievement, it is necessary to sow the rubble of our old servitude everywhere... These striking artefacts will remind posterity of the memorable times that led the French to liberty and equality after eighteen centuries of disgraceful slavery.'[122]

Palloy may come across as the archetypal entrepreneur – half pioneer in brand merchandising, half impresario – but his rhetoric appeared to be heartfelt. That he exhausted almost all of his fortune in the course of spreading the gospel of the Revolution was compelling evidence of his sincerity.[123] It did him little good. The brave new world of the people's uprising was losing its way in conspiracies and paranoia. On 21 January 1793, Louis XVI was executed by guillotine in the *Place de la Revolution*, after attempting to flee from France to Austria. His prosecutor, the implacable lawyer Robespierre, justified the violence as 'the despotism of liberty against tyranny'. The executions of the king and a great many of the French nobility marked the beginning of an ideological purge, a wave of mass beheadings carried out under the banner of 'Reason'.

Palloy himself was in danger of being swept up in the 'Terror', as it became known, and was imprisoned in March 1794 on charges of embezzlement.[124] Even as he faced death by guillotine, he could not let go of his obsession with the Bastille. His final request was to be buried with a piece of the fortress as his headstone, bearing the engraved epitaph: 'Here lies Palloy, who in his youth laid siege to the Bastille, destroyed it, and scattered the limbs of this infernal monster over the face of the earth.'[125] In the end he escaped the guillotine, and lived for another forty years. His youthful enthusiasm, however, curdled into desperation. Palloy campaigned for decades to receive a state pension in recognition of his role as a *vainqueur* of the Bastille, and eventually succeeded in 1832 – only to die three years later, in near poverty, at his home in Sceaux.[126]

As for the Bastille, the debate over what form *its* headstone should take had begun before the storming of the 14 July, and continued long after its demolition. For a time, all that remained where the fortress had once stood was the lone and level ground of a dusty, empty urban square, renamed the *Place de la Bastille.* On 17 July 1792, the French parliament authorised the laying of a foundation stone for a 'Freedom Column', a monument matching closely a design prepared by Palloy.[127] Yet no other stone would follow this first, as the attention and the finances of the government were distracted by war with Austria and Prussia. Instead, a year later, in July 1793, a plaster statue of the goddess Isis was erected, with breasts spouting water as a metaphor for the 'milk of liberty'.[128] Isis would last for eight years, before she crumbled to pieces and was swept away.[129]

The space would remain empty again until 1813, when one man commissioned the construction, not of a symbol of the struggle for equality and freedom, but of Empire. Napoleon Bonaparte, the son of a poor Corsican lawyer, was in many ways an embodiment of the revolutionary ideal. In the new meritocracy, he rose from humble beginnings through the ranks of the French military, led his armies to stunning victories in Italy and Austria, mounted a brutal campaign across the Mediterranean in Egypt and Syria, and, like a latter-day Caesar, exploited the political instability in the Parisian government to proclaim himself emperor.

Napoleon's vision for the Bastille was of a huge bronze elephant, cast from enemy Spanish cannon, that could be climbed by an internal staircase to a tower, and that would fountain water from its trunk. This bronze colossus, intended to overshadow the memory of the revolution with a gleaming icon of imperial French might and exotic conquests, would never be realised. Instead a giant plaster model was erected as understudy, a temporary structure to be replaced when more funds were available.[130] This facsimile monument would stand over the Bastille for thirty years. When it was finally pulled down in 1846, its passing was mourned only by the packs of rats nesting in its hollow legs. In his epic novel *Les Misérables*, Victor Hugo used Napoleon's elephant as the home of the street urchin Gavroche, and painted a picture of sublime decay:

> 'There it stood in its corner, melancholy, sick, crumbling, surrounded by a rotten palisade, soiled continually by drunken coachmen; cracks meandered athwart its belly, a lath projected from its tail, tall grass flourished between its legs... by that slow and continuous movement which insensibly elevates the soil of large towns, it stood in a hollow, and it looked as though the ground were giving way beneath it. It was unclean, despised, repulsive, and superb, ugly in the eyes of the bourgeois, melancholy in the eyes of the thinker.'[131]

Despised, repulsive, superb, ugly and melancholy: Hugo could have been describing the Bastille itself. In life, the fortress was an icon of tyranny and despotism. In death, it stood for – indeed, still stands for – freedom and democracy. On 24 March 1988, nearly two hundred years after its demolition, the French presidential candidate André Lajoinie marched to the Rue Saint-Antoine at the head of eighty thousand student supporters, all chanting, 'End the inequalities, the Bastilles must Fall'. In his speech, delivered on the spot where the prison had once stood, Lajoinie called on his supporters to, 'Fight a new French Revolution, found a new Republic, storm new Bastilles.'[132] On 11 January 2015, as many as 2 million people took to the streets of Paris to march in defiance of terror in the wake of the *Charlie Hebdo* murders. For a few days, people throughout the world joined in solidarity by expressing the sentiment '*Je suis Charlie*'. On the column which now stands at the centre of the Place de Bastille, a banner was draped bearing a slogan that echoed Descartes: '*Je pense, donc je suis Charlie*' – 'I think, therefore I am Charlie'.[133]

The fourteenth-century fortress is a symbol, not just of the Paris Revolution of 1789, but of all revolutions. The message: as long as there is inequality and social injustice in the world, more Bastilles will be stormed. In their complacency and arrogance, France's *ancien regime* had allowed the fortress to become the poster building of political emancipation. But it had to be destroyed and dismantled before it could be transformed from an icon of despotism into one of freedom.

By and large, today's Bastilles are no longer bricks and mortar. They are dictatorships, corruption and human rights violations; firewalls and super-injunctions; banks and bonuses and CCTV cameras. The crowds no longer gather beneath Gothic towers; they mass in cyber-space and on social media, share and coordinate their discontent in instant messages of less than 140 characters. Many have never heard of the Bastille, or Richelieu, or Latude, or Linguet, or de Launay, or Palloy or Robespierre. Yet as they strike out into the night, called on by the digital hum of the virtual mob, they are following the path trodden by the artisans of Saint-Antoine. The extraordinary political act of 1789 – glorious, ambiguous, subversive and violent – remains the template, the ultimate demonstration of the will of the people. From Tunis to Benghazi, Cairo to Damascus, Wall Street to St Paul's, it is really one fortress they all still seek to destroy. The Bastille.

Chapter Fourteen

Virtual City

Vilcabamba, Espiritu Pampa – Peru
(Born 1539 – Died 1572)

Sometimes, the fate of a civilisation can turn on the most banal event: for instance, an argument between a husband and his wife. In June 1572, on a riverside in the Amazonian rainforest, a young couple engaged in a lengthy squabble. The husband wanted his wife to climb into a canoe in order to speed up their journey into the jungle interior. The wife, who was heavily pregnant, refused.[1]

She had already left their home behind, watching her own people set it alight as they gathered up their most precious possessions and dispersed into the wilderness. After enduring a journey downriver of over a hundred kilometres, the wife was insistent that she would spend no more time in the canoe navigating vicious currents and fast-flowing rapids. It was too dangerous for her, and too dangerous for their unborn baby. The husband begged, but she would not relent.[2]

Instead, they carried on into the Amazon on foot. Another larger and safer river was nearby, and they set up camp for the night, just three hours walk from its banks.[3] At around nine o'clock that same evening, as the husband and wife crouched around a fire, the darkness of jungle surrounding them began to flicker with the tiny spots of distant, but fast approaching, torchlight. Then a party of barefoot soldiers emerged from the dense undergrowth.[4] The soldiers had been following the trail of the husband and wife for days after arriving at their city and finding it burnt out and deserted. Both the pursuers and their quarries were exhausted. There was no attempt to fight or flee. The husband's surrender was polite and amiable.[5] They all spent the night clustered around the same camp-fire, and in the morning began the long journey back to a city called Cuzco, set high in the shadow of the Andes Mountains.[6] The soldiers fixed a gold chain around the neck of the husband[7]: a gesture of respect to a prized prisoner. He was an emperor, after all.

In the summer of 1911, Hiram Bingham, Lecturer in South American history at Yale University, arrived in Cuzco to lead an expedition into the uncharted lands of south-eastern Peru.[8] At first Bingham's enterprise had only the vaguest of goals. He may not have liked to admit it, but it was a strike into the unknown. Unable to secure financial backing from any academic institution[9], Bingham had turned to his former classmates. In an after-dinner speech given at the Yale Club in New York in the winter of 1910, he described to his friends and colleagues 'an expedition now fairly launched in my mind's eye'.[10]

His proposed itinerary included mapping the terrain to the west of Cuzco, on the 73rd meridian – a task barely attempted before, let alone accomplished – and climbing Mount Coropuna, which he believed was the highest peak in South America. Bingham's charismatic and opportunistic pitch convinced his friends to fund the trip. In fact, a number were so enthused that they decided to join him. Whether qualified for the roles or not, erstwhile classmates filled the positions of 'collector-naturalist', 'surgeon', 'archaeological engineer' and 'topographer'. Bingham took to calling his party the 'Yale Peruvian Expedition of 1911'.[11]

The party's starting point, Cuzco, sits on a plateau set 11,000 feet above sea level on the fringes of the Andes. By the beginning of the twentieth century, it had been reduced to something of a frontier town: a gateway to a landscape where mountains collide with tropical jungle, where bleak tundra and high altitude glaciers loom thousands of feet above 'cloud' forests and precipitous river valleys. It was a gateway through which few modern western men had passed. The place held an irresistible appeal for Bingham. In a previous visit to Cuzco, travelling across Peru in February 1909 after attending an academic conference in Chile, he had been transfixed by the views of the Andes, and the possibilities of what they might conceal.

As he wrote in his memoirs in 1948, which drew together diary entries, field notes, photographs, and added a huge dash of artistic licence:

> 'These snow-capped peaks in an unknown and unexplored part of Peru fascinated me greatly. They tempted me to go and see what lay beyond. In the ever famous words of Rudyard Kipling there was "Something hidden! Go and find it! Go and look beyond the ranges – Something lost behind the ranges. Lost and waiting for you. Go!"'[12]

In Peru, Bingham's 'something hidden' was the remains of a civilisation that had flourished over five hundred years before. Cuzco had once been the capital of an empire that controlled territories stretching into large parts of Ecuador, Bolivia, Chile and Argentina. This society had, with no influence from the outside world, developed advanced skills in architecture, engineering, agriculture, metalwork and textile manufacturing. And in the fifteenth century, it had expanded aggressively under the leadership of a mountain tribe from the Cuzco valley. At its head was a king or emperor, known as the Inca. Today, this honorific is the word used to describe the entire race.[13]

'Few people realise how much they owe to the ancient Peruvians,' wrote Bingham. 'They gave us the white potato, many varieties of Indian corn, and such useful drugs as quinine and cocaine.'[14] Instead – apart, perhaps, from cocaine – the Incas were most famous for one thing: the dramatic fall of their empire.

This story, which in its most basic form has become a dark fairy tale of European exploration, remains one of the most fantastical in history. A party of Spanish *conquistadors,* made up of less than two hundred men, conquered native armies numbering in the hundreds of thousands, and claimed a South American landmass larger than all of continental Europe. Over four decades in the middle of the sixteenth century, the Incas of the New World were wiped out by a handful of adventurers from the Old.

During his stay in Cuzco in 1909, Bingham had been approached by J. J. Nunez, Prefect of the province of Apurimac, and persuaded to embark on a trip to explore the ruins of a place said to be 'the home of the last of the Incas'. Known as Choqquequirau, which translates as 'Cradle of Gold', it had been visited just three times over the previous hundred years – including one trip by Nunez himself.[15] Each time, the travellers had returned with tales of enormous hardships endured en route. But then travellers always do. Far more intriguing were their stories of palaces and temples 'all covered by dense jungles and luxuriant tropical vegetation'. Although Bingham was, in his own words, 'not on the lookout for new Inca ruins and had never heard of Choqquequirau'[16], he was intrigued enough to agree to the journey.

'We had entered a new world,' Bingham later wrote of the moment his party left the Cuzco valley.[17] Over the following days, he experienced a landscape of stark contrasts and incredible beauty. There were 'great green mountains piling upon one another, their precipitous sides streaked with many lovely waterfalls'; 'green parrots overhead and yellow iris underfoot'; and 'a maze of hills, valleys, tropical jungles and snow peaks'.[18] What he did not find at the end of his first Peruvian expedition, however, was a lost city.

Choqquequirau had, however, clearly been the site of an Inca fortress.[19] Set on a rocky saddle between an isolated hilltop and a mountain range, and roughly constructed as if in a hurry, it commanded panoramic views, both of the mountain approach on one side and a 5,000-foot drop down into the jungle valley of the Apurimac River on the other.[20] In one of the ruined buildings, Bingham discovered, written on a slab of slate, the name of a previous visitor, someone calling themselves the 'Comte de Sartiges', who had noted the date of their arrival at Choqquequirau as 1834.[21]

Back at Cuzco, Nunez was downcast to learn that the expedition had failed to locate any buried treasure in the so-called 'Cradle of Gold'. Bingham was less concerned. He may not have found gold, but he had uncovered an intriguing thread of inquiry.[22] Taking advantage of his role as curator of the 'South American Collections' of the Harvard and Yale libraries – collections that had not existed before Bingham began assembling them – he tracked down in a June 1850 edition of the French cultural magazine *Revue de Deux Mondes* an account of an excursion in Peru. The Comte de Sartiges, writing under the pseudonym 'E. de Lavandais', was the author of the article.[23] Sartiges was a young French diplomat based in South America, and he appeared to be the source of the theory that Choqquequirau had been the Incas' final refuge.[24]

Bingham's own interest in the subject coincided with the discoveries of several chronicles dating from the time of the *conquistadors*. The Peruvian historian, Carlos Romero had studied these contemporary accounts in depth, and in correspondence with Bingham concluded that the 'tradition, so generally accepted' of the central role of Choqquequirau was 'totally without foundation'.[25] Instead, it appeared this mountain fortress was merely an outpost and a lookout built by the Incas as they retreated from the Spanish threat into the remote hinterlands to the north-west of Cuzco, where the Andes drop down into the Amazon basin. The last city of the Incas was still out there, maintained Romero, waiting to be found.

In July 1537, the Inca Emperor Manco was forced to concede that his rebellion against the Spanish had failed. The siege of Cuzco had been repelled, although for a time the battle had been in the balance, as tens of thousands of native troops threatened to overwhelm a city garrison numbering just one hundred and ninety men.[26] In the end, however, the remarkable fortitude of the defenders had demoralized the Inca forces. On top of that, the rainy season was about to begin, and news had reached Manco that another Spanish army was marching on his position from Lima. He retreated to a place called Ollantaytambo, to confer with his advisors.[27]

The choice of Ollantaytambo was not accidental. To the south-east is Cuzco, and the traditional Inca domain of grassy highland plateaus, bare, rocky mountains, and valleys where corn and potatoes grow on terraces cut into the hillsides. Immediately to the west, however, the landscape changes completely. The Yucay River cuts a gorge through a sheer granite rock face, dropping below Ollantaytambo into the Amazon basin, and transforming into the fast-flowing Urubamba.[28] Here the great grey Peruvian peaks become green foothills, the climate switches almost instantly to tropical humidity, and the land falls away to dense misty forests, eventually merging with Amazonian jungle to continue, almost uninterrupted, to the Atlantic coast.[29] From the west, another river, the Vilcabamba, joins up with the Urubamba, and this large tributary carries on to meet the Amazon. These two rivers mark the northern boundary of a territory known itself as the Vilcabamba: a wild, largely uninhabited borderland. Manco was faced with a difficult choice. He could regroup his forces and strike out against the advancing Spanish army. Or he could retreat to where he was sure that the *conquistadors* could not follow, into a territory the Incas themselves could navigate only with the help of the jungle tribes.

Manco decided that his duty was to preserve the Inca Empire, even if it meant subsisting in exile, away from their true highland home. The departure from Ollantaytambo was marked by a lavish and mournful ceremony, as prayers and sacrifices were offered to the gods. Precious religious ornaments were packed up in readiness for the journey, including the most sacred Inca idol – the great disc of Punchao, god of the sunrise. The size of a man, and cast entirely in gold, this disc was surrounded by golden medallions and had a chalice at its centre, containing the mummified hearts of dead emperors.[30] As Manco set off into the Vilcabamba, the people signalled his departure with shouts and lamentations that, as his son Tuti Cusi later recalled, 'seemed as if they would sink the hills'.[31]

Less than five years had passed since the first meeting between the Incas and the *conquistadors*. The narrative of the Spanish conquest is often presented as a collision between naïve natives and a rational if rapacious modernity. It is a common myth that the Incas saw the tall, bearded Europeans, clad in shining armour and mounted on beasts far larger than any llama, as gods. This was never really the case.[32]

The Peruvian *conquistadors*, 180 men led by a soldier from Extremedura called Francisco Pizarro[33], possessed one quality required by all the greatest explorers: luck. When the Spanish landed on the Pacific coast in 1532 and began to advance inland, they found a landscape scarred by the ruins of conflict. The Inca Empire was just emerging from a civil war – a not uncommon occurrence, as rival tribal leaders vied for overall supremacy. More debilitating, however, was a recent epidemic of smallpox. Even before the *conquistadors* and the Incas had met face to face, this Old World disease had spread overland across South America from the Spanish colonies around Panama. The native population had no natural immunity, and the impact had been devastating.[34]

Even so, when these two alien worlds first collided, at the town of Cajamarca in northern Peru, the Incas were in a position of overwhelming strength. When Pizarro and his men saw the scale of the forces set against them, they were thrown into blind panic. Having arranged a meeting with the Inca Emperor Atahualpa, they decided in desperation that their only chance of survival was to mount a surprise attack and to take the native king hostage.[35]

This gambit had worked before. It had been employed by the father of all *conquistadors*, Hernán Cortés, when he seized the Aztec ruler Moctezuma in Mexico in 1520.[36] The Inca Atahualpa, for his part, was also intending to take the Spaniards prisoner: some he would sacrifice to the sun god; others would be castrated to serve as eunuchs for the ladies of his royal household.[37] First, though, he wanted to indulge his curiosity: a mistake that would prove fatal. Pizarro's ambush worked. Atahualpa had been carried to the meeting on a throne of gold and silver, lined with multi-coloured parrot feathers. At the signal of a volley from the Spaniards' arquebuses – forerunners of the musket – the emperor's honour guard was sent into disarray. The *conquistadors* rode into the mêlée on horseback, hacked down any natives in their way, and snatched Atahualpa.[38]

By taking the Inca ruler captive, Pizarro had in one stroke attained effective control over the whole empire. At first he used Atahualpa to acquire the thing prized by *conquistadors* above all others: gold. The emperor offered a ransom to secure his release, promising to fill an entire room in Cajamarca, measured by Pizarro's secretary at 3,000 cubic feet, with precious metals.[39] As this great haul accumulated, with objects seemingly arriving from all corners of Peru, the *conquistadors* began to suspect Atahualpa was also sending out messages to his armies to mobilise for an attack.

Urged on by a representative from the Spanish royal court, who maintained that the Inca emperor was too dangerous to keep alive, Pizarro ordered Atahualpa's execution.[40] In the words of the sixteenth-century historian Pedro de Cieza de Leon, they 'put him to death with great cruelty and little justice'.[41] The emperor's murder created a new power vacuum. Different Inca factions again began to vie for control, and many tribes saw collaboration with the Spanish incomers as the best way of achieving supremacy.[42] The *conquistadors* used this to their advantage, marching 750 miles down the spine of the Andes to seize the capital, Cuzco. There they installed Manco as the new Inca emperor: a seventeen-year-old prince from the family that had recently lost the civil war to Atahualpa.[43]

For three years Manco acted as a puppet king, helping to quell native uprisings, and giving the seal of legitimacy to the *conquistadors'* presence in Peru. It soon became clear to him, however, that the Spanish had no intention of leaving. On 18 April 1536, at the end of the rainy season, Manco left Cuzco, on the pretext that he was required to perform ceremonial duties at a religious event in a nearby province. Instead he joined a vast army of native warriors which had been assembling for months in the hills surrounding the capital. It was the beginning of the first Inca rebellion.[44]

Within a year, Manco's uprising had collapsed. As he fled from Ollantaytambo in the summer of 1537, his conviction that the

Spaniards would not follow him into the jungle proved wrong. The young *conquistador*, Rodrigo Orgonez hounded the rebels through the valleys and mountains with three hundred cavalry and foot-soldiers.[45] When the Incas destroyed the bridge of Chuquichaca, the main route over the river Urubamba into western Vilcabamba, Orgonez simply had his men rebuild it in a day, and the hunt resumed.

Manco had no intention of turning to fight. He moved further and further into the wilderness, leaving spoil-heaps of precious royal gold behind in an attempt to distract his pursuers.[46] At last, the Spanish were forced to turn back. Manco, however, was deeply disturbed by how far the *conquistadors* had been prepared to advance into this unforgiving terrain. This was at the forefront of his mind when he began, at the beginning of 1539[47], to build a new capital in exile. The site he chose was beyond the borders of the Inca Empire – a *terra incognita* in the western fringes of the Amazonian forest. He called the new city Vilcabamba.

Hiram Bingham and the Yale Peruvian Expedition of 1911 arrived at Ollantaytambo, along with their substantial mule caravan, in mid-July. Like the *conquistadors* nearly four centuries before, their timing was fortuitous. Almost every previous explorer had entered the Vilcabamba region by the Pass of Panticalla, a high mountain road winding over the towering granite peaks that define the territory's eastern border.[48]

The Urubamba River cuts directly through this rocky perimeter to drop into the tropical valley immediately below, but this natural gateway, with its sheer cliffs and impassable rapids[49], had always been considered too dangerous to navigate. When Bingham and his party arrived, however, a boom in the Amazonian rubber trade had seen a new route blasted through the mountains. This road followed the course of the Urubamba in order to allow trees to be transported more quickly back from the jungle floor. According to Bingham's account, there was more than a hint of Arthur Conan Doyle's *The Lost*

World about this intrusion into nature by modern man.[50] The 'wilderness' on the other side of the mountains 'was practically unknown and had been inaccessible for almost four centuries,' he wrote.[51]

It was an exaggeration to suggest this area had been cut off from the rest of the world, but it was certainly a remote and overlooked stretch of terrain. The mountain route into Vilcabamba rejoined the Urubamba many miles further down the valley, so most travellers simply pressed onwards rather than doubling back to investigate the land that lay immediately beyond the gorge.[52] On the evening of 23 July, Bingham's party stopped to make camp at a place called Mandor Pampa, a small, floodplain of flat, open ground between the road and the river. They were approached by a local farmer, Melchor Artega, who was curious to know what the foreign strangers were doing in the valley. When the purpose of the expedition was explained to Artega, he told them about some Inca ruins that could be found just across the river, on a nearby hillside.[53]

It was a common occurrence in the life of an explorer to be presented with vague rumours and tenuous gossip. There was always 'something in the next valley' or 'just over this mountain pass'. The tendency of travellers to pay locals to help them find ruins and, as Bingham himself put it, offer 'cash prizes for good ones'[54], meant that they were rarely short of advice. The trick, of course, was to filter out the dead-ends and follow the genuine leads.

The next morning, Bingham set off with Artega. He was on his own, the rest of the party being less inclined than their colleague to embark on a substantial hike with no guarantee of finding anything. As the day progressed, Bingham himself became more and more sceptical. Exhausted by the heat and humidity, he arrived with Artega at a grass-covered hut some 2,000 feet above the river, where they were greeted by two farmers. After enjoying a brief meal and several 'gourds of cool, delicious water', Bingham was tempted simply to rest, take in the view, and then return to camp. When he asked how far there was to go, he was told that the ruins were 'a little further along'.[55]

Despite his doubts – '"He may have been lying" is a good footnote to affix to all hearsay evidence,'[56] he wrote later in his memoir – Bingham did continue. And shortly after leaving the hut, he rounded a promontory to be greeted by his first glimpse of ruins: hundreds of stone terraces climbing up the hillside for a further 1,000 feet. They led to a summit wreathed in thick green jungle. Scrambling to the top, Bingham was astonished to find among the dense undergrowth and bamboo thickets a series of massive stone buildings, showing the distinctive and exquisite craftsmanship of the Incas.[57] The setting was unquestionably dramatic. Clouds hung low over the steep Urubamba river valley below, and overlooking the site, linked to it by a narrow spur, was a second, even higher sugar-loaf peak. The mountain Bingham could see beyond was Huayana Picchu. The one on which he stood was Machu Picchu.

Bingham spent a few hours making notes and sketches, then made his way back down to his party. It was an auspicious start to the expedition, but he saw nothing particularly momentous in this discovery. The site was surely too close to Cuzco and Ollantaytambo to have been the Incas' last retreat. They had barely entered the Vilcabamba region, and all the evidence had suggested that their true goal lay much deeper into the landscape. Bingham left some of his companions behind to map the ruins at Machu Picchu, and pressed on.[58]

Soon afterwards they made the crossing at Chuquichaca, the bridge destroyed by Manco during his flight into the wilds. They were about to enter the most treacherous terrain, but here there were signs of modern progress. The crossing was constructed out of steel and iron rather than cables of vegetable fibre and vines.[59] As their journey progressed, they continued to uncover more remarkable Inca ruins: the sites the chroniclers had described in Vilcabamba. There was Vitcos, the great fortress of the region, where the natives had mounted increasingly desperate defences against the incursions of the *conquistadors.* And nearby, at the head of a natural spring, was the gigantic carved boulder Chuquipalta, the White Rock, a sacred site for sacrifices and religious ceremonies.[60] Yet Manco's capital, Vilcabamba itself, continued to elude them.

By this point, Bingham's party – excepting guides, porters and mules – was down to just two: Bingham himself, and his Yale colleague, Professor Harry Foote. The others had returned to less remote territory, but this pair had already ventured so far that they felt compelled to carry on. They travelled first to the only place whose name seemed to reference the lost city – San Francisco de la Vitoria de Vilcabamba. But there was nothing Inca about this settlement. It was a Spanish mining town, built at the end of the sixteenth century in an attempt to exploit the silver said to be in the surrounding hills. Aside from the odd farmer's hut, it had been abandoned centuries ago.[61]

Yet rumours persisted of a great Inca ruin in the jungles to the north-west, beyond the Pampaconas valley – an area blank on every map. And with good reason, it seemed. Bingham was told that the region was 'terrible to reach', and was 'inhabited by savage Indians who would not let strangers enter their villages'.[62] Aside from the Indians, only one man was known to live there: Saavedra, owner of a sugar cane plantation, who was said to be extremely hostile to outsiders, and to employ the jungle tribesmen and their poisoned arrows as security. Bingham was warned that 'no one had been there recently and returned alive'.[63]

First the party had to cross the Pampaconas watershed, a route that opened up to 'a long chain of snow-capped mountains towering above and behind the town of Vilcabamba'. As Bingham wrote, 'we searched in vain for [the mountains] on our maps... we were on top of a lofty mountain pass surrounded by high peaks and glaciers... Our surveys opened an unexplored region, 1,500 square miles in extent, whose very existence had not been guessed before 1911. It proved to be one of the largest undescribed glaciated areas in South America.'[64]

As they rested at the village of Pampaconas, set some 10,000 feet up the mountainside, they met the first native claiming to have visited Vilcabamba. He told Bingham of a series of ruins at a place called '*Espiritu Pampa*' – the *plain of the ghosts* – a site far below them on the western fringes of the Amazon jungle. For several days, the two men descended further and further, dropping below the cloud level and into a tropical valley. After sheltering for a night on a tiny ledge set

1,000 feet above a river, they moved on into dense woodland 'until presently we saw sunlight ahead, and, to our intense astonishment, the bright green of waving sugar cane'.[65] They had arrived at Saavedra's plantation. Contrary to the rumours, the owner was delighted to meet the Americans, and confirmed that there were indeed Inca ruins close by, in the very next valley. For two days, Saavedra had his son and his workers clear a path to *Espiritu Pampa*, and then, at last, Bingham and Foote made their way to the site.

'Would the ruins turn out to be ghosts?' Bingham asked himself. 'Would they vanish on the arrival of white men with cameras and measuring tapes?'[66] It was a playful remark, but one that would soon have an answer: yes. Or rather, they had already vanished. Led on by Campa Indian tribesmen, they spotted, just beyond a clearing, their first signs of Inca buildings: a series of artificial terraces and the denuded foundations, stones about a foot high, of a near 200-foot-long rectangular structure.[67] The faintest traces of more buildings began to emerge, but everywhere the jungle dominated, with visibility often reduced to just a few feet in any direction.

The jungle reclaiming the ruins of Vilcabamba at *Espiritu Pampa* - the 'Plain of the Ghosts'. © Despedes

They camped for the night, and in the morning their guides attempted to clear away the thick undergrowth. They discovered the walls of two substantial houses set on a small terrace, which, apart from one or two slabs of bare masonry, had otherwise been consumed completely by vines and creepers. 'Nothing gives a better idea of the density of the jungle than the fact that the savages themselves had often been within five feet of these fine walls without being aware of their existence,' remarked Bingham.[68] These were undoubtedly Inca ruins, but as Bingham and his party continued their search, the only other remains they could find were the stones of a well-built bridge: 'Saavedra's son questioned the savages carefully. They said they knew of no other ruins.' The expedition's supplies were running low, and the guides were growing increasingly nervous of lingering too long in the jungle. It was time to turn back, and leave the 'plain of the ghosts' behind.[69]

Bingham was both excited and confused by what he had found. Could these isolated jungle remains really be Vilcabamba? The chroniclers described it as the 'largest city' in the province.[70] Yet the ruins they had uncovered seemed evidence of a modest settlement, nothing more. Even so, all the other clues seemed to fit: accounts of the Spanish incursions into this landscape provided a trail that led beyond the Pampaconas to the basin of the Amazon jungle. Bingham puzzled over this as he made his return journey, but was soon distracted by another task. It had been one of the stated aims of the Yale expedition to climb Mount Coropuna, which lay several hundred miles south of Cuzco, on the fringes of the dry desert region of Peru leading to the Pacific coast. Bingham made the ascent, but was disappointed to record the altitude at the summit as a mere 21,703 feet.[71] He had scaled the nineteenth highest peak in South America.[72]

On 24 June 1572, a Spanish army, led by the veteran *conquistador* Martin Hurtado de Arbieto, made a final advance on the Incas' remote jungle capital. 'They marched off, taking the artillery,' wrote Arbieto in his own account of the campaign, 'and at 10 o'clock they marched into the city of Vilcabamba, all on foot, for it is the most wild and rugged country, in no way suitable for horses'. What they discovered was a city built for 'about a thousand fighting Indians, besides many other women, children and old people', filled with 'four hundred houses'.[73] It was also, however, completely deserted. The Incas had retreated into the jungle, setting fire to their houses and food stores before they left. As another chronicler put it: 'the entire town was found to be sacked, so effectively that if the Spaniards had done it, it could not have been worse... When the expedition arrived it was still smoking.'[74]

This was not the first time the *conquistadors* had succeeded in penetrating as far as Vilcabamba. In 1539, the same year that the city was first established, Gonzalo Pizarro – the half-brother of Francisco – had led three hundred men on a mission to extinguish the continuing threat of the rebel Emperor Manco.[75] They had been confronted with the exact same scene as Arbieto when they reached the city: a mass of ruins and deliberately spoiled supplies. Manco had escaped by swimming across the Urubamba River, and concealed himself in the jungle on the far side. As the Spanish struggled to find a place to cross, Manco was said to have shouted to his pursuers that 'he intended to kill them all and regain possession of the land that had belonged to his forefathers'.[76] Pizarro's men occupied Vilcabamba while they searched for the emperor, but, with their resources dwindling, they were forced to give up the city and return to Cuzco.

For the next thirty years, the Incas survived in this remote kingdom, although they remained embroiled in a continuing diplomatic stand-off with the *conquistadors*. Successive emperors teased the Spanish with suggestions that they were considering conversion to Christianity, and even allowed missionary priests in to preach. This was just a ploy, however – a trick to make the Europeans believe they could conquer the Inca state by a means other than force.

When Emperor Tuti Cusi, the son of Manco, died of illness in 1571, he was replaced on the throne by his brother, Tupac Amaru. This new leader of the Incas had been brought up in the priesthood, and was something of a religious hard-liner.[77] While Tuti Cusi had amused himself in conversations with two Spanish missionaries, Marcos Garcia and Diego Ortiz, even dictating an account of the life story of his father to be written down and translated by Garcia[78], Tupac Amaru and his advisors had little tolerance for the Christians. Ortiz was blamed for the death of Tuti Cusi, and in particular for not being able to bring him back to life after saying a mass over his body. In retribution, the priest was tortured for three days, and then murdered. Spanish emissaries who ventured into Vilcabamba with messages from Cuzco were similarly despatched by the natives.[79]

This increased aggression played into the hands of the recently appointed viceroy of Peru, Francisco de Toledo. He had explicit instructions from the king of Spain to resolve the problem of the rebel Incas, by any means necessary. When it was confirmed that a Spanish messenger carrying letters to Vilcabamba from the viceroy, the king and the pope had also been murdered, it was held up as the baldest act of provocation. On 14 April 1572 – Palm Sunday – Toledo resolved 'to be rid of that robbers' den and scarecrow bogey, and to launch total war on the Inca as an apostate, prevaricator, homicide, rebel and tyrant'.[80]

'Total war', however, continued to elude the viceroy's army as it made its way into Vilcabamba. The Incas repeated the tactics that had served them for decades. They staged a series of skirmishes at fortified outposts, all the while retreating deeper into jungle, moving the Spaniards further away from their own supply lines. Even when the army reached the capital city itself, the very heart of the empire, there was no climatic battle. The Incas had disappeared into the jungle like a fine mist, leaving their homes behind and the *conquistadors* chasing ghosts – *Espiritu Pampa* indeed.

The Spaniards faced an embarrassing return to Cuzco, and the disheartening prospect of a never-ending guerrilla war. Search parties scoured the surrounding jungle, but while they captured some natives, Tupac Amaru remained elusive. The suspicion was that the emperor had escaped down the Masahuay River with the help of a tribe of Chuncho Indians.[81] Martin Garcia de Loyola, a young, ambitious captain, volunteered to lead a contingent deeper than ever before into the Amazonian jungle.

Taking forty men, Garcia journeyed 140 miles downriver to a mangrove swamp, where his party captured a group of the Chuncho tribesmen. The natives told Garcia that the emperor was hiding another 170 miles further along the course of the Masahuay, at a place called Momori. Travelling on five crudely built rafts, the *conquistadors* continued their pursuit. At Momori, they learned that they were five days behind Tupac Amaru. The Inca was burrowing deep into the rainforest, but his pace was being slowed by his heavily pregnant wife. The Spaniards marched for another 50 miles into the jungle, throughout the day and into the night, without food or provisions, having lost them somewhere in the river. At last they spotted a campfire in the darkness. There they found Tupac Amaru and his wife.[82] Garcia had his prize – the last emperor of the Incas.

The journey back to Cuzco took almost two months, the war party arriving in the capital at the end of September 1752.[83] Tupac Amaru was tried and sentenced to death. On the day of his execution, a vast crowd gathered, so dense that 'since there was no more room on the ground, the Indians climbed the walls and the roofs of the houses... even the many large hills that are visible from the city'.[84] Another chronicler described streets so crowded that 'if an orange had been thrown down it could not have reached the ground.'[85] It was almost exactly forty years since Atahualpa had been killed by Pizarro at Cajamarca. When the executioner brandished his knife, 'the whole crowd of natives raised such a cry of grief that it seemed as if the day of judgement had come'.[86] Tupac Amaru was beheaded, and the last vestiges of Inca resistance died with him. The Spanish conquest of Peru was complete.

Once he had returned to Yale University, Bingham began to collate the various findings and records from his 1911 expedition. The sheer volume of discoveries suggested that the trip had been a success, yet he was still struggling to piece together what they all meant.[87] In particular, his thoughts kept straying back to the magnificent ruins above the Urubamba River, on the hilltop of Machu Picchu.

In his memoirs written forty years later, Bingham claimed he had known nothing of this site before the farmer, Melchor Artega, had tipped him off.[88] This was disingenuous. His journal entries of the time mention an encounter with a drunk official in Cuzco, who told him of Inca remains on the Urubamba by 'Huainapichu'.[89] The nineteenth-century French explorer, Charles Weiner, had mentioned ruins at 'Huana Picchu and Matcho Picchu' in a book published in 1875[90], a reference very unlikely to have escaped Bingham's notice. Furthermore, during his first exploration of the site, he had spotted the name 'Augustin Lizarraga' scratched on a wall in charcoal, alongside the date '1902'.[91] Bingham must have realised that he was not the first modern visitor to Machu Picchu, yet no one in the academic community or in the wider world seemed to know anything about it. Here was a wonderfully preserved archaeological site of remarkable size in a location of sublime beauty, which, thanks to new roads, could be reached easily from Cuzco. Set against this spectacular site, and in stark contrast to it, were the strange, mysterious fragments of a settlement he had found deep in the undergrowth of the Amazon jungle at *Espiritu Pampa*.

Bingham returned to Peru the following season to carry out further explorations and excavations. A year later, in 1913, he was ready to go public. He had approached the National Geographic Society, and pitched to them a discovery that he believed was so momentous it should fill an entire issue of their magazine. The Society awarded Bingham a grant of $10,000 – with Yale contributing the same – to continue his work in Peru, and offered up the April 1913 edition of *National Geographic* to showcase the results. The magazine was titled 'In the Wonderland of Peru', and its editor, Gilbert H. Grosvenor promised a thrilling account of the Inca's 'wonderful city of refuge', illustrated by '250 marvellous pictures'.[92] Bingham had made his choice: the *National Geographic* included a large fold-out poster with the issue. On the poster was a photograph of Machu Picchu.

Over the next few years, Bingham worked with his own excavation results and the accounts left behind by the *conquistador* chroniclers to advance the theory that Machu Picchu was in fact Vilcabamba, lost city of the Incas.[93] Though he often ignored the most basic issues of geography – by most accounts Machu Picchu was simply in the wrong place – Bingham's argument rapidly gained credence. The contemporary sources left enough room for interpretation for Bingham to get away with asserting what he saw as the true significance of Machu Picchu. He proposed that the last Inca city had been under the noses of the Spanish all the time, but hidden behind the 'sheer granite precipice' of the Urubamba gorge, which 'defied all efforts to pass it'.[94]

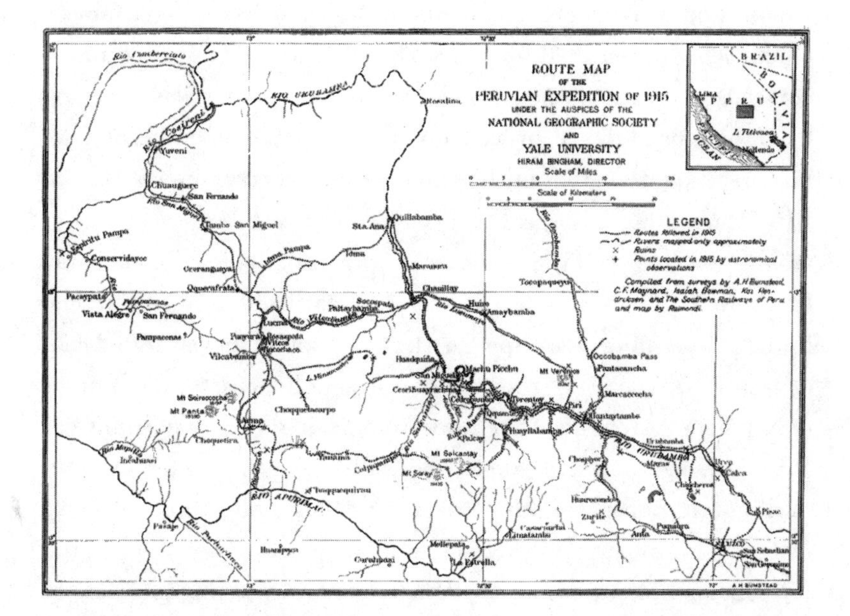

A map of the area explored on the joint Yale University / N.G.S. expedition of 1915, led by Hiram Bingham. Machu Picchu is near the centre, while *Espiritu Pampa*, and the real Vilcabamba, are at the far left. Courtesy the private collection of Roy Winkelman.

It was only the new road, blasted through the mountain at the very end of the nineteenth century, that had had made its discovery possible. Rather than a jungle sanctuary, Bingham recast the Incas' city-in-exile as a 'sacred shrine hidden on top of great precipices in a stupendous canyon where the secret of its existence was safely buried under the shadow of Machu Picchu mountain. Its ruins have taken the name of the mountain because when we found them no one knew what else to call them'.[95] For Bingham, one of the most compelling pieces of evidence was the sheer size of the site. The chronicler Antonio de Calancha had been quite specific in his description of Vilcabamba as the 'largest city' in the province.[96] Over the course of several expeditions, Bingham had travelled perhaps more than any other explorer throughout the wilds of Peru, and he had still found nothing comparable in scale or grandeur to the monolithic ruins of Machu Picchu.

During the first half of the twentieth century, the identification of Machu Picchu as Vilcabamba became widely accepted as fact. This did not stop new explorers, however, from being drawn to the jungles around *Espiritu Pampa*. Rumours persisted of Inca ruins as yet undiscovered. At the same time, new documentary evidence was emerging from the time of the Spanish conquest. Perhaps most significant of all was an account written in the late sixteenth century by the Basque friar, Martin du Murua, entitled *Historia General de Peru*.

The provenance of this manuscript was a story in itself. Filed away for centuries, first in the possession of a Castilian statesman and then in the private library of King Charles IV, it found its way into a haul of archival and artistic treasures that Joseph Bonaparte, the brother of Napoleon, attempted to remove from Spain during the Peninsular War. Pursued by British forces under the command of the Duke of Wellington, Bonaparte was forced to ditch his spoil in order to make his escape.[97] Murua's work came into the possession of Wellington himself, and he sent it on to Walter Scott. Scott was too busy to undertake the translation, though, and returned it without having read the contents. It remained in Apsley House, the ancestral home of the Wellingtons, for another century, until, in 1945, it was 'rediscovered' by a descendant of the First Duke.[98]

Murua's history was drawn from eyewitness accounts of the Spanish soldiers who had taken part in the final assault on Vilcabamba. As such, it contained the most comprehensive description yet found of the lost city and its location.[99] The friar had listed the sites and landmarks passed by the Spanish army as they advanced through Vilcabamba; the route taken bore a striking similarity to Bingham and Foote's journey during their 1911 expedition: over the Chuquicha Bridge, through the fortress of Vitcos, over the mountains at Pampaconas, and then down into a tropical valley.[100]

Murua's text repeated continually that Vilcabamba was located in 'hot country', and he provided detailed information of the plants, trees, birds, insects and animals that could be found there. He summarised the setting of the city as being in a wide valley with pastures for cattle, around four miles long and two miles wide. As for the city itself, he described houses and sheds 'covered in good thatch' and a palace set 'on different levels', with 'doors of fragrant cedar', and 'covered in roof tiles' and a 'great variety of paintings'.[101] There was very little in Murua's history that pointed to Machu Picchu rather than *Espiritu Pampa* as the lost city of Vilcabamba.

In July 1964, another American explorer, Gene Savoy, led an expedition to *Espiritu Pampa*. Savoy made his way to the same clearing that the Yale party had entered fifty years before[102], and set his team to work among the undergrowth. Very quickly, it became clear that Bingham had been on the cusp of a major discovery, before the seductive allure of Machu Picchu pulled him away. The buildings he had examined in the dense undergrowth had not been the isolated dwellings of a remote settlement. Instead, they marked the fringes of an extensive Inca city.

Savoy and his party hacked at the jungle for weeks on end. Little by little, they uncovered the ruins of fifty major buildings and almost three hundred houses. There were streets, temples, canals, bridges, squares and public fountains.[103] The remains of some buildings were over three hundred feet long, while others seemed to have been built on platforms, perhaps as protection against flooding. Fragments of Spanish-influenced roofing tiles were dug out of the thick rainforest vegetation, just as Murua had described on the houses – and just as Bingham himself had discovered, and discounted.[104] Everywhere, the stonework displayed distinctive scorch-marks[105], the result, almost certainly, of the fire the Incas had set in their own city, before they fled into the jungle for the last time.

There is a telling line in Bingham's memoirs when he comes to describe Machu Picchu: 'Surely this remarkable lost city which has made such a strong appeal to us on account of its striking beauty and the indescribable grandeur of its surroundings appears to have had a most interesting history.'[106] The 'surely' speaks volumes: it was inconceivable to Bingham that a site of such size and magnificence might not hold a special place in the story of the Incas. Perhaps more than anything else, it was this that led him to conclude that Machu Picchu was Vilcabamba.

It does not, however, always follow that a civilisation's most spectacular ruins were once its most important buildings. Survival alone does not equate with significance. Indeed, sometimes it is a site's very obscurity that explains its preservation. What Bingham had actually found at Machu Picchu was not the capital of a kingdom, but a country retreat – the pleasure palace of a former emperor, abandoned, it turned out, before the Spanish had even arrived in Peru.[107]

Nevertheless, Bingham's work transformed the fortunes of Machu Picchu: 'This marvellous Inca sanctuary, which was lost for three hundred years, has at last become a veritable Mecca for ambitious tourists,' he wrote in 1948.

> 'Everyone who goes to South America wants to see it. It used to be two or three days' hard journey from Cuzco, on mule-back and on foot, but now it can be reached by train and car in one day... Cuzco, which used to be a week away from Lima, can now be reached by aeroplane in a few hours! Pilgrims come from Buenos Aires and Santiago as well as from New York and Washington.'[108]

Sometimes the face just fits. The fact is that Machu Picchu is exactly what we want our mysterious lost cities to look like. It is a bedtime story for all would-be explorers – the acme of the sublime ruin. As Ernesto Che Guevara put it: 'Machu Picchu was to Hiram Bingham the crowning of all his purest dreams as an adult child.'[109] It remains the popular face of the Inca civilisation, and one of the most recognisable ancient sites on earth.

It obscures, however, a darker story: of a people who retreated until they could retreat no more. Ruins are almost always melancholy places. That is an essential part of their appeal. Sometimes, however, the sense of loss can be almost too acute. The few people who have visited Vilcabamba report a powerful atmosphere of unease among the remains.[110] The locals go even further, and talk of dread and curses.[111] This lost city has become a metaphor for the fall of the Inca.

When Martin du Murua described Vilcabamba in the sixteenth century, he was already composing a lament. 'The climate is such that bees make honeycombs like those of Spain in the boards of the houses, and the maize is harvested three times a year,' he wrote. 'In it are raised parrots, hens, ducks, local rabbits, turkeys, pheasants, curassows, macaws and a thousand other species of birds of different vivid colours... The Indians savoured scarcely less of the luxuries of greatness and splendour of Cuzco in that distant, exiled land. And they enjoyed life there.'[112]

Vilcabamba today is unlikely to become a great attraction. It is inaccessible, set in harsh and dangerous terrain, and its ruins are fragmentary and underwhelming. It exists in permanent gloom, as the jungle canopy cuts out the light from above. And always the undergrowth is creeping to reclaim it, to pull it down, beneath vines and moss and lichen – so deep that it will never be found. The hidden city still seeks to hide itself, as if in fear that some new *conquistadors* may arrive at any moment.

Part Four

You Say Utopia, I Say Dystopia – Let's Call the Whole Thing Off

Since the creation of the very first structure, a tension has existed in architecture – between utility and ornament, beauty and function. Are buildings extensions of us – of our power, piety, wealth, taste and refinement? Or are we extensions of them – mere products of environments designed to control how we feel, think and behave? It is the nature-versus-nurture debate in stone, steel, glass and concrete.

Modern architecture, particularly in the early twentieth century, came to be dominated by the idea that better designs could make better people. Great buildings were devised to turn criminals into honest citizens, or the poor into the rich. Walls rose to protect not against the threat of physical assault, but subversive political ideas. And the two tallest buildings the world had ever known were erected with a purpose as laudable as it was ludicrous – to bring about world peace.

Yet history has always been tough on utopias (and tough on the causes of utopias). The modern world has left behind its fair share of ruins, albeit ones paved, clad, glazed, burnished, and pre-cast with good intentions. Instead, it has often been in the cracks and wildernesses of society that genuinely new communities have flourished. By stepping outside design and regulation, organic structures have sometimes succeeded where architecture has failed. And now, among the infinite realities of the web, there is the potential to create – and destroy – on a scale never seen before.

Chapter Fifteen

Little Brother's Big Brother House

The St Petersburg Panopticon – Okhta, Russia
(Born 1806 – Died 1818)

Imagine a circular building with many rooms. The rooms are filled with people – perhaps one to each room, perhaps more – and they are positioned on the circumference of the circle, which rises several storeys high. Every room has two windows. One takes in light from outside the building, while the other faces inward, towards a central, cylindrical tower. Inside this tower is just one person. He can see into every single room. The people in the rooms, though, cannot see into the tower: their view is obscured by a series of blinds, or curtains, or opaque, one-way mirrors. They could be being watched at any time.

This uncertainty leads them to believe that they are, in fact, being watched at *all* times. Very quickly, their behaviour changes. With the eyes of the person in the tower felt as 'omnipresent', there is no opportunity for private indulgence. For instance, if the people in the rooms are working on manufacturing, then they do not take more breaks than they are allowed, because they think their foreman will see. If they are students tasked with reading, or sitting exams, then they do not neglect their work or cheat, because they are convinced their teacher will spot them. If they are prisoners, then they do not misbehave, for fear that they will receive further punishments.

The applications for this 'simple idea in architecture'[1] go on and on. And, if you believe those responsible for its design, the potential benefits are remarkable: 'morals reformed – health preserved – industry invigorated – instruction diffused – public burthens lightened – economy seated, as it were, on a rock'.[2] Others are not so sure. They see it as a 'diabolical piece of machinery' for social control[3], a 'cruel, ingenious cage'[4], and a 'haunting symbol' of totalitarianism.[5] Its creation represents a singular event in 'the history of the human mind'.[6] From now on, the state will not seek merely to control bodies; it will look to exert its power over the *soul*.

This building takes its name from the Greek for 'all-seeing'. It is called the Panopticon.

At one end of the South Cloisters of University College, London, there is a wooden cabinet containing a figure of a seated man dressed in smart clothes and sporting a straw hat. The body is an actual preserved skeleton – it reputedly still attends meetings of the College Council, and is marked in the minutes as 'present but not voting'[7] – but the head is a wax replica. The original was damaged during the preservation process, and so the replica was preferred – although for a time the original sat on the cabinet floor between the seated man's legs.

The mummified head did not remain in place for long, however: its travails included being stolen and ransomed by students of the rival King's College; being deposited in a luggage locker in Aberdeen railway station; even being used for football practice in the college quadrangle. It is a bizarre fate for the head of one of the greatest and most prolific thinkers in English history – Jeremy Bentham. Yet perhaps it was how Bentham would have wanted it. He had, after all, requested in his will that his body be dissected as part of a public anatomy lecture, and that his skeleton and mummified head be preserved in the wooden cabinet, which he called an 'auto-icon'.[8]

Born in Spitalfields, London on 15 February 1748, Bentham was quick to display the hallmarks of a child prodigy. As a toddler he was discovered at his father's desk reading a multi-volume history of England; by five he was studying Latin and was known by family and friends as the 'Philosopher'; and at twelve he was enrolled in Queen's College, Oxford as the youngest person ever to be admitted.[9] His father Jeremiah, a prosperous attorney, was adamant that his son would follow him into the law, and would one day become Lord Chancellor.

The free-thinking Bentham rebelled: instead of going into practice, he became an arch-critic of the legal system, devoting his life to its philosophical dissection, and proposing endless theories for its improvement. Although far from a man of action in the physical world, in the intellectual sphere he existed in perpetual motion. He spent his days at his desk in Westminster, producing page after page of letters and manuscripts. Today he is most famous for the doctrine of 'utilitarianism', summed up by the principle of seeking 'the greatest happiness for the greatest number'. With this as an objective standard, Bentham tested the utility of existing institutions, practices and beliefs; proposed radical reforms in every domain from poor relief to animal welfare[10]; and well before his time argued for universal suffrage and the decriminalisation of homosexuality.[11] It should come as no surprise that he was an eldest child.

Five of Jeremy's younger siblings died in infancy before one managed to survive to adulthood – Samuel.[12] Born in 1757, Samuel shared his brother's fierce curiosity, yet his talents were more practical in nature. From an early age, he showed an aptitude for mechanics and engineering and became a prolific inventor. At thirteen, he was apprenticed to a master shipwright in Woolwich, and for the next decade he devoted himself to shipbuilding and the administrative organisation of naval dockyards.[13]

While Jeremy was perhaps happiest in the comfort of his home and study, Samuel nursed a passionate desire to travel. In particular he was fascinated by Russia. In July 1762, the Prussian princess, Sophie Frederike Anhalt-Zerbst, was crowned Catherine II, Empress of Russia. Better known today as 'Catherine the Great', she inherited a vast but primitive state, separated from central and western Europe both geographically and intellectually. Her goal was to bring Enlightenment principles to bear on the Russian Empire: to turn a cultural backwater into a paragon of rational, modern civilisation.[14]

Catherine recruited thinkers and innovators from across Europe to her court. Russia became a land of opportunity for intellectual fortune-seekers: 'I need not recall to you the feasts we have so often heated our imaginations with, when we have been contemplating the progress of improvement in that rising country,' Samuel wrote to Jeremy in May 1779. Any opportunity to lend a helping hand to such a grand project, he continued, interested him greatly.[15] Two months later, in August 1779, he sailed by boat from London to Holland, and began the long journey overland to St Petersburg.[16]

Along with eighty-one letters of introduction to notable figures in Holland, Germany, Sweden and Russia, Samuel carried with him a message from Jeremy to the Empress Catherine. The elder Bentham saw this newly progressive Russia, under the reign of its 'Enlightened Autocrat' Tsarina, as the perfect testing ground for the new rational code of law he had drawn up. Once Samuel had established his status in the royal court, he was to present the proposal – Jeremy even gave instructions on how the document should be bound – to Catherine and her ministers.[17] The Bentham brothers could never be accused of lacking confidence.

It was this combination of intellectual restlessness and precocious self-worth that prevented Samuel from taking up any permanent employment on his arrival in Russia. He refused the position of 'Director-General of all the Shipbuilding and Mechanical Works Relating to the Marine' because he felt the salary was too low.[18] Instead, he set off to discover more about the country, travelling south to the Black Sea coast and then on to a nobleman's estate in Chernobyl, before, in the summer of 1781, embarking on an expedition into the remote hinterlands of Siberia. He did not make it back to St Petersburg until October 1782.[19] By this point, he had been in Russia for three years. Still without employment, and with his finances close to exhaustion, he began to contemplate a return to England. That he remained in Russia was due largely to the abundant distractions and intrigues – particularly those of a romantic nature – to be found in the royal court.

For a time, Samuel's courtship of Countess Sophia Matushkina, niece and ward of Field-Marshal Prince Alexander Golitsyn, was the talk of St Petersburg. It was even observed with amusement, much to Golitsyn's dismay, by the Empress Catherine. Eventually, the Tsarina did intercede to end the affair, dashing Samuel's hopes of marriage. Nevertheless, he had succeeded in attracting attention at the highest echelons of Russian society. On 11 December 1783, he was invited to the St Petersburg residence of Prince Grigory Alexandrovich Potemkin, a prosperous industrialist, high-ranking statesman – and a lover of the Empress.[20]

Potemkin wanted Samuel to run his large estate at Krichev in White Russia, on land newly annexed from Poland. The task was to take a diffuse collection of cottage industries – Krichev contained a distillery, a malt-house and a brewery; glass, rope and sailcloth factories; a pottery, tannery, textile mill and copper-works; and large tracks of farmland – and turn them into a model production estate along Enlightenment principles.[21] Once up and running, it would act as a centre of excellence, a hub from which specialist skills and technical expertise would be disseminated to the surrounding regions. Samuel was also to oversee a major new development at Krichev – the construction of a large-scale inland shipyard.[22] The estate sat on the Dnieper River, a long, navigable stretch of water running south to the Black Sea. The shipyard was key to Potemkin's grand military plan to fortify Russia's southern coast and develop a substantial fleet. At Krichev, Samuel would help the prince build and supply a navy large enough and strong enough to challenge the Ottoman Empire.[23]

This intellectual ambition of this project so piqued Jeremy's interest that, for about the only time in his life, he was inspired to leave his London study and set out into the wider world to visit his younger brother. He left for Russia in August 1785, travelling via Paris, Lyons, Nice, Genoa, Smyrna and Constantinople. The journey took over six months, and he did not arrive at Krichev until February 1786.[24] Once there, however, he reverted to type. For the next two years, he devoted himself to a number of legal treatises. He had, it seemed, merely swapped one writing desk for another, several thousand miles distant. Although he picked up some knowledge of the Russian language, it was only, he later said, as much as he knew 'of the language of cats – I could speak their language and obtain an answer, but the answer I never understood'.[25]

Samuel was busier than ever. Potemkin was in the process of organising a 6,000-mile tour of his southern provinces for the Empress Catherine – a tour intended to showcase the region as an 'Enlightenment garden' in a 'Russian Eden'.[26] Samuel had already designed a new type of vessel to carry the royal party: a flexible, 250-foot-long barge made up of a series of joints and hinges which allowed it to navigate the tightest of river bends. Its rather wonderful name was the 'vermicular'.[27] The estate at Krichev was intended as one of the key stopping points, demonstrating to Catherine how manufacturing, science and agriculture could be combined in one ideal community. And at its centre, there would be an entirely new kind of structure, the first of its kind to be built anywhere in the world – the Panopticon.

As Jeremy wrote to his friend Charles Brown in December 1786: 'My brother has hit upon a very singular new and I think important, though simple, idea in Architecture.'[28] To tackle the problems of teaching an entirely unskilled peasant workforce – at the same time as managing a knowledgeable but disobedient contingent of specialists imported from Britain – Samuel had devised 'the plan of what we call an Inspection-house... a circular building so contrived that any number of persons may therein be kept in such a situation as either to be, or – what comes nearly to the same thing – to seem to themselves to be, constantly under the eye of a person or persons occupying a station in the centre which we call the Inspector's Lodge'.[29]

The peasants were to be watched by their trainers, but the trainers, in turn, were to be watched by the highest authority in the system, that is, Samuel himself. Potemkin was a keen supporter of the idea,[30] and saw it as a potent architectural metaphor for the Russian state: the population developing new skills under the guidance of an enlightened nobility, beneath the unwavering, all-seeing gaze of a benevolent Empress.[31] It fitted perfectly with his vision for the royal tour. At the very moment of its construction, however, the Krichev

Panopticon became a victim of circumstance. At the end of 1787, war broke out between Russia and Turkey. Samuel was appointed a commander in Potemkin's navy and sent into battle in the Black Sea. The plans for the building were shelved, and Potemkin later sold the Krichev estate to a Polish industrialist.[32]

Jeremy left Russia for England in November 1787, but he could not forget his brother's revolutionary idea. In a series of letters written in Krichev and sent home to his father, he turned the concept of the Panopticon inside and out, exploring 'the efficacy which this simple and seemingly obvious contrivance promises to the business of schools, manufactories, prisons and even hospitals'. Here, he continued, was a 'new mode of obtaining power of mind over mind, in a quantity hitherto without example... such is the engine: such the work that may be done with it'.[33]

On 31 May 1793, Sir Charles Bunbury, Member of Parliament for the county of Suffolk, delivered an impassioned speech to the House of Commons, advocating a radical reform of the British prison system. He damned the policy of 'transportation', which sentenced convicts to be sent to Australia, yet often left them languishing for years in squalid ships moored in the Thames. Bunbury recommended instead a new and ingenious plan, the adoption of which, he claimed, would lead to 'well-regulated prisons calculated to reform offenders, and to convert the dissolute and idle into good and industrious subjects'. Crucially, it could also be put into effect at a much 'cheaper rate than vessels in the Thames'.[34] The author of this plan was Jeremy Bentham.

For five years, Jeremy had been revising and developing the idea of the Panopticon, and in particular, he had adapted it to the area where he felt it was most pressingly needed: prisons. He published his Krichev letters on the subject, and supplemented them with two extended postscripts, containing 'further particulars and alterations relative to the plan of construction originally proposed; principally adapted to the purpose of a Panopticon Penitentiary-House'.[35] This document was both an ideological prospectus and an architectural blueprint for a new national prison based on the Panopticon principle. Jeremy sent it to influential figures throughout the political establishment in an attempt to win support. In August 1790, Sir John Parnell, Chancellor of the Irish Exchequer, remarked that he had 'never read a more ingenious essay' and that he was 'so convinced of the utility of the plan' that he would advocate its adoption in Ireland.[36] Although this came to nothing, Jeremy was sufficiently encouraged to write directly to the Prime Minister William Pitt in January 1791, enclosing a short summary of his proposal.[37] Pitt did not reply.

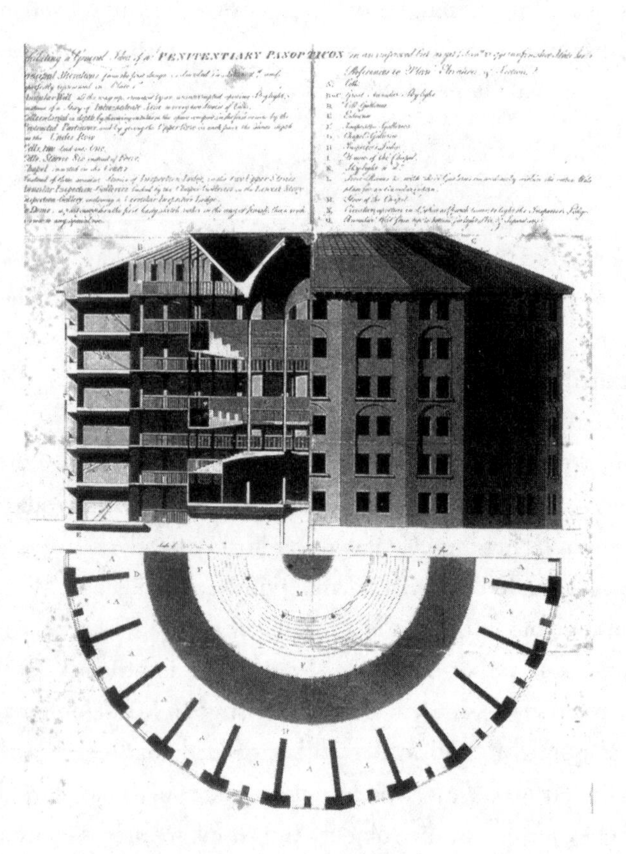

Elevation, section and plan of Jeremy Bentham's Panopticon Prison, as envisioned by Willey Reveley in 1791.

Jeremy's enthusiasm was undimmed. He explored the potential of building Panopticon prisons in both Edinburgh and Paris, and in December followed up his first letter to Pitt with a second, informing the Prime Minister that he was 'now ready to execute the plan stated in that proposal', taking on 'all expense of building, and without any advance to be made by government for that purpose'.[38] He also mentioned Bunbury's 'most zealous wishes' for the adoption of the Panopticon prison. This endorsement was not insignificant. Bunbury was a veteran of penal reform, and had been appointed to a three-man government committee on prison construction and administration established by the 1779 Penitentiary Act.[39]

By this time, Samuel Bentham had returned from Russia, and was working diligently alongside Jeremy to promote the Panopticon project. The two brothers set up a display in Jeremy's house at Queen's Square Place, consisting of a scale model of the prison and a machine for wood and stone-working, invented by Samuel to be powered by prisoners' physical exertions. Politicians and backers were invited to demonstrations, and in September 1792, the Benthams succeeded in attracting the Home Secretary Henry Dundas. Almost a year later, in July 1793, Dundas returned to Queen's Square Place with William Pitt.[40] Stung into action by Bunbury's speech in the House of Commons two months before, the Prime Minister agreed that the scheme for the construction of the prison should go ahead on a site already marked out in Battersea. 'The "Panopticon" plan,' wrote a triumphant Jeremy, 'is approved by everybody.'[41]

The design had developed considerably from the workers' inspection house first devised by Samuel in Russia. Jeremy had endeavoured to turn a general concept into a structural reality, commissioning the architect Willey Reveley to draw up a series of detailed schematics.[42] Special adaptations had to be made so that the Panopticon could operate effectively as a prison, and Jeremy devoted a huge amount of time to working out the practical implications of the original idea. What had not changed, however, was the basic shape. The prison remained circular, with the cells around the circumference, and separated by empty space from a central inspection area. From this lodge or tower, the inspectors could watch the prisoners, while remaining invisible themselves.

However, the surveillance did not stop there. As the Panopticon concept evolved in Jeremy's mind, it took on a structure akin to that of the *matryoshka* – the Russian doll. The prisoners could inform on each other. The inspectors who watched the prisoners were watched by a governor. The governor was watched by the government. And the government was watched by the press and the public: 'the great *open committee* of the tribunal of the world'.[43] The concentric circles of the Panopticon expanded ever outwards, acting as a model not only for a prison, but for a whole society.

The Panopticon was becoming the architectural extension of Jeremy's philosophy. He saw it as an essentially humane construction, far removed from the cruelties of the prevailing penal system. The inspection principle, he argued, removed the need for chains and irons. Inmates were to be safe from violence or torture, but were never to forget that they were being punished. The ultimate goal was the reformation of character and morality. 'They suffer neither hunger, thirst nor cold; true,' he wrote, 'but not a moment of their time is at their own disposal... They are not worn down by excessive labour: true: but except what is absolutely necessary for meals and sleep there is not a moment of their time during which they are not either at work or under discipline. They work and what they do is more for others than for themselves'.[44]

Jeremy saw incarceration as analogous to a religious experience. On arrival, prisoners would be washed in a warm bath, inspected by a surgeon, and supplied with completely new, clean clothing – all to the accompaniment of hymnal organ music. 'Ablution – regeneration – solemnity – ceremony – form of prayer – the occasion would be impressive,'[45] wrote Jeremy. He had even tinkered with the architecture to allow a chaplain to preach to the whole prison every Sunday, from a pulpit made temporarily visible inside the central inspection tower.

A strict physical regime would be integral to the running of the prison. Inmates' heads would be shaved, and they would be forced to maintain cleanliness, with handkerchiefs and spit boxes supplied. They would wear wooden shoes, and their coats would have one sleeve shortened at the elbow, to allow their bare arms to be tattooed with a prisoner number. For exercise they would walk alone for an hour each day on a giant tread-wheel that powered a device for working stone and wood – an enlarged version of the prototype created by Samuel – or pump the water for an internal heating system. 'Certainty, promptitude, and uniformity,' wrote Jeremy, 'are qualities that may here be displayed in the extreme.'[46]

He had also devised a system of communication tubes running from the inspection tower to every cell, allowing the disembodied voice of the warder or governor to instruct the prisoners at any time. So taken was Jeremy with this device that he had it installed in his own home.[47] As a final, rather gothic measure, he decided that inmates should wear masks whenever they came into contact with the public, with expressions painted on the masks reflecting the severity of the crime committed. Jeremy intended the Panopticon to be open to visitors, and so he saw the mask system as essential in preserving a prisoner's privacy and dignity.[48]

For five months, from October 1793 to February 1794, Jeremy was engaged in drafting a new Penitentiary Bill to lay before Parliament, the basis for what was intended to become the 'Panopticon Act'. His tendency to verbosity did not serve him well. The Bill was of an exceptional and unnecessary size: 15 sections and 257 clauses that added up to 50,000 words.[49] It was packed with arguments and justifications rather than concise statements, and its unwieldy form and style was anathema to parliamentary approval. From this point on, what had seemed so certain unravelled at remarkable speed.

Political support for the project began to wane while considerable and influential opposition grew, often coming from wealthy Lords horrified at the prospect of a giant Panopticon prison being built on or near their land. For the next decade-and-a-half, Jeremy's hopes that the project would receive official government and legal sanction were raised again and again, only to be dashed summarily. One bureaucratic obstacle followed another. Between 1796 and 1798, four separate sites were identified for the Panopticon. In each instance, fierce objections forced the project to move elsewhere.[50]

Jeremy compared himself to Homer's Odysseus: 'Four Ithacas each in its turn within a rope's length of my weather beaten back had already each in its turn vanished from my pursuit, after four such voyages little appetite was left to me for a fifth.'[51] Jeremy's fifth Ithaca was Millbank: a foul, frequently flooded swamp that overlooked the Thames. These were not the salubrious surroundings he had at first sought for his prison, but he pressed on once again, and bought the land himself in November 1799. Yet by August 1800 the Home Office and Treasury Board had started to voice their concerns, suggesting that the project should either be abandoned altogether, or built on a small, experimental scale, involving just 500 prisoners.[52]

This uncertainty dragged on for over another decade. In 1812, a government penal reform committee resurrected the Panopticon, only to dismiss it as a well-intentioned but misguided anachronism. Giving evidence to the committee, the Reverend John Thomas Becher, a magistrate from Nottingham and a prison administrator, delivered a savage indictment of Jeremy's design:

> 'To convey an adequate representation of a Panopticon Penitentiary, we may suppose a watch tower encircled by an external gallery, and surrounded at a small distance with six rows of cages, nearly similar to those used for the restraining of wild beasts. Let the whole be connected under the same roof, with a sky-light over the area, and we shall have a Panopticon. Occupy these cages with 1,000 convicts, and the whole will exhibit an assemblage of human beings with the same ferocious dispositions, the same offensive exhalations, and the same degrading propensities, that characterize this brute creation.'[53]

Jeremy's project had passed from one political generation to another.

The era of the privately run prison was over, to be replaced by the state-run penitentiary.

With Becher as advisor, Millbank became the site of a brand new state prison. Constructed at enormous cost, there was nothing of Bentham's design in this building. It was a vast, impenetrable labyrinth: warders ended up marking the walls with chalk to avoid getting lost in their own institution.[54] Conditions were so poor that, on one occasion in 1823, every inmate had to be transferred back to the prison boats in the Thames due to an epidemic of fever. The marshy ground had clearly been no place to erect a structure of such size. By the 1840s, it ceased to be a penitentiary, and was used as a clearing-house for convicts awaiting transportation to Australia; and in 1892 the building was demolished and replaced with the National Galley of British Art, known today, of course, as Tate Britain.[55]

Jeremy never got over the failure of his revolutionary scheme. Just months before his death in 1832, he chanced upon his collection of materials relating to the prison. 'I cannot look among the Panopticon papers,' he remarked. 'It is like opening a drawer where devils are locked up – it is breaking into a haunted house.'[56]

In the Russian State Naval Archives is a single-sheet architectural drawing of a remarkable building. A plan, an elevation and two sections present a simple yet vivid picture of the structure. The centre of the building is a twelve-sided drum. Twelve segments radiate out from this drum, with five alternate segments extending out like the spokes of a wheel to meet a large circular perimeter wall. Where the sixth spoke should be, there is instead an entrance portico aligned with a main gate in the exterior wall. The spokes are all three storeys high, and form long, open-plan hallways. The segments on the outer part of the drum are four storeys high, while the centre rises to six storeys. The sketch also reveals a rather strange interior: the floors at the centre are circular platforms with no walls, and there is an empty, circular space between them and the floors of the drum exterior.

Also, the inner floors do not line up with the outer floors – rather they are a little above one floor, a little below the other, meaning that a view of two floors is possible from the central platforms.

At the very centre of the building, there is one more circle. Just a metre in diameter, this is a cylinder running through every storey, from the basement to the roof. The elevation shows that the entire exterior of the building is studded with large, regularly spaced lines of windows – a strikingly modernist style that calls to mind the 'classical socialist' architecture of the Soviet era. A brief inscription on the bottom right of the drawing reveals, however, that this design was produced almost a century-and-a-half earlier. It is the 'Plan, façade and profile of the Panoptical Institution on the Great Okhta'[57], and it is dated 1810.

The history of the Panopticon is often presented as the story of a building never built, and perhaps un-buildable. Jeremy Bentham portrayed his travails with the British government as a tale of petty bureaucracy and elitist self-interest thwarting grand innovation. Yet the suspicion remained that the real reason for the Panopticon's failure had been its sheer impracticality. Jeremy's endless revisions of the style and structure of his building did not help his cause: he called it variously an 'iron cage glazed', a 'glass bee-hive', and a 'glass lantern', and at times imagined it taking the elegant form of Bath's Royal Circus.[58] Some found this delicate, fragile-looking structure laughable as a prison. On seeing the plans, Lord Westmorland, the Lord Lieutenant of Ireland, made the perfunctory remark: 'They will all get out'.[59]

Yet at the start of the nineteenth century, something happened to make Jeremy even more certain, if that were possible, of the feasibility of his building. In 1806, he received word from Russia of a plan to construct a 'Panopticon Institute' at the mouth of the River Okhta in St Petersburg. Its aim was to house children and young adults between the ages of seven and twenty-two, and to train them in 'the acquisition of practical knowledge in various arts and professions.'[60]

Six years later, in a letter written on 24 January 1812 to George Holford, chairman of the government committee that would finally scrap the Panopticon prison, Jeremy was able to cite the success in

Russia of 'an Establishment on the Panopticon principle for educating and employing boys in a variety of trades subservient to the business of the Naval Department'. It had, he said, not only been finished and 'employed with success', but also 'copied in several other private as well as Government establishments in that Empire.'[61] There was a reason Jeremy knew so much about this 'St Petersburg Panopticon'. It had been designed and built by his brother, Samuel.[62]

In May 1791, after eleven years in Russia, Samuel returned to England. Still a colonel in Catherine's navy, his intention had been merely to visit for three months, before journeying back east. The three months passed, and then turned to years. Samuel had been drawn into supporting his brother's scheme for the Panopticon prison, and he obtained an extended leave of absence from the Russian navy. In March 1796, however, he accepted an offer from the British Admiralty to take up the role of Inspector General of Naval Works.[63]

It was during this time that Samuel returned to the original idea behind the Panopticon – the Krichev workers' factory. He began collaborating with an Admiralty architect called Samuel Bunce on a school for 'gentlemen cadets' at Woolwich. The building they devised was semi-circular, divided into four 'pie' segments: three set up as lecture rooms, one left open for 'fencing and dancing'.[64] At the point where the wedges of the segments met, they planned an elevated glass room with views over the entire school, to be occupied by the governor.

In 1797, Samuel and Bunce took this concept further, extending it into a design for a paupers' workhouse, which they called a 'House of Industry'.[65] The aim was to construct 200 of these throughout Britain, each providing capacity for 2,000 people. To meet this purpose, the semi-circle of the Woolwich cadets' school evolved into a five-storey, twelve-sided drum, made almost entirely out of glass set in a steel frame. Published drawings showed a central viewing platform with floors positioned to look across an empty space into the twelve exterior segments – almost exactly the same as the later design for the drum in St Petersburg.[66] However, neither the cadets' school nor the 'House of Industry' was ever built. Like his brother,

Samuel failed to convince the British establishment to support his radical ideas.

In 1805, the Admiralty posted Samuel back to Russia. His task was to build warships to aid in the wars against Napoleon, but he could not resist taking his revised Panopticon plans with him. Not long after arriving in St Petersburg, he convinced Admiral Chichagov, the head of the Russian Navy, and Tsar Alexander I, grandson of the Empress Catherine, to allow him to build what he called a 'School of Arts' on the Okhta River on the outskirts of the city. Employing the same principles first conceived in Krichev, workers were to be trained in the manufacture of materials and equipment for the Russian Navy, from wooden parts and navigational instruments, to clothing and sailcloth.[67]

This time there were to be no obstacles. Construction began in 1806. Samuel's wife, Mary Sophia, gave an account of the interior of the building as it was nearing completion: 'From the central chamber, a perfect view was obtained of all that passed within the walls on each of the two floors, the rays inclusively'.[68] These 'rays' were Samuel's newest addition to his original design: the three-storey hallways that extended out beyond the circumference of the central drum. Mary Sophia also described the misaligned floors, commenting that surveillance of workers was 'effected by a very nice adjustment of the relative height of floors – one of the two principal floors being below, the other above, the floor of the inspection room.'[69]

Finally, she explained the purpose of the mysterious cylindrical tube at the centre of the building. It was to be used by the chief inspector of the school, and contained a chair 'suspended by a counterpoise, regulated in its movements up and down by a simple and safe apparatus, and easily managed by the inspector himself'.[70] Concealed within this tube, the inspector could move quickly, unseen, between floors, appearing at will to monitor both staff and students. This quite bizarre adaptation was the Panopticon principle in action: scrutiny could descend at any time, and therefore must be assumed to be there at all times.

In a report passed from Admiral Chichagov to Tsar Alexander in

1806, Samuel reported that 'all the supervisors, together with those participating in the membership of the institution, by being turned to the continuous gaze of the main authority, or even the Supreme Power Himself, will be forced to the highest possible perfection regarding its activity'.[71] The building was completed in 1808, and so effective was its regime – claimed Mary Sophia – that, almost from the very beginning, it was producing model workers who were exported to other businesses and factories 'fifty at a time'.[72] Samuel had succeeded in building the world's first – and perhaps its only – Panopticon. He did not, however, ever get to see his School of Arts completed. War broke out between Britain and Russia in September 1807, and he was forced to return to England.[73]

Samuel continued to campaign for reform in the structure of the Naval Dockyards, and pushed tirelessly for the adoption of the Panopticon principle. 'Of the great advantage resulting from this arrangement,' he wrote, 'experience has already been obtained in the instance of a building constructed under my direction in a foreign country'.[74] But the Admiralty remained unmoved by this account of his Russian experiment.

On one aspect of the design for the St Petersburg School of Arts, Samuel had not got his way. Rather than being constructed out of iron, the structural columns were made of wood.[75] In 1818, a stray spark, probably from machinery housed in the basement of the central drum, caught hold. After barely a decade, the first and last Panopticon was destroyed completely.

An idea, however, is harder to demolish than a building. Towards the end of the twentieth century, the French philosopher Michel Foucault identified the invention of the Panopticon as a watershed moment in social history: 'The fact that it should have given rise, even in our own time, to so many variations, projected or realised, is evidence of the imaginary intensity that it has possessed for almost two hundred years.'[76] Writing in 1975 in his landmark book *Discipline and Punish*,

Foucault stressed that the Panopticon should not be seen as a 'dream building', but as 'a mechanism of power reduced to its ideal form... a figure of political technology that may and must be detached from any specific use'.[77]

Foucault believed that the Bentham brothers had hit on a device for social control that was both ingenious and deeply insidious. They had, inadvertently or otherwise, opened the Pandora's Box that housed totalitarianism and the surveillance society. Here, for instance, could be found the origin point of George Orwell's *1984* and the ever-watchful 'Big Brother'. Here was the picture of the future summed up by 'a boot stamping on a human face... forever'.[78] According to Foucault, once discovered, 'Panopticism' gathered a stealthy, unstoppable momentum: the idea was 'destined to spread throughout the social body'.[79]

The Benthams believed they had failed: one prison never built, one 'School of Arts' destroyed by fire. Yet perhaps they succeeded to a greater degree they can possibly have imagined. For Foucault, the 'inspection principle' gave the state a way of accessing people's minds as never before, a mechanism for transforming individuals into obedient subjects. It was the simplicity of Panopticism that was its strength: the more closely someone is watched, the more certain they are that they are being watched, the more likely that they will behave according to the expectations of the watcher. Over time, conscious action becomes unconscious. Behaviour is transformed.

In 1836, some twenty years after the British government's final rejection of Jeremy's prison, the 'Eastern Penitentiary' was built in Philadelphia. Its architect was an English émigré called John Haviland, and its design borrowed a number of the key features of Panopticism. At its centre was a small, octagonal building. Seven long corridors led off to the seven 'spokes' of the prison: lines of cells on one or two stories, with each cell designed to be occupied by a single prisoner. The eighth side of the central chamber was the main entrance. The intention was for prisoners never to meet, speak or interact. This principle of 'solitary confinement', first proposed and then rejected by Jeremy in his writings – except as a special punishment – became known as the 'Pennsylvania System', an extension of the ideals of the reformist Quaker religion which dominated the state administration.[80]

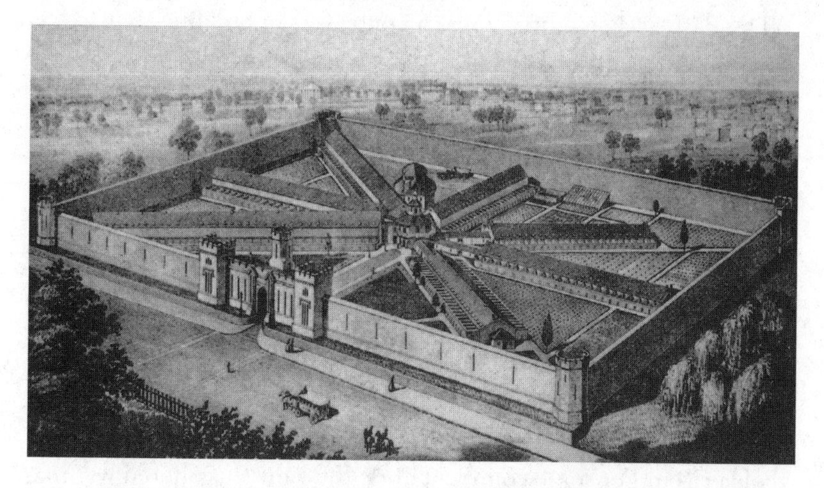

John Haviland's 'Eastern Penitentiary' in Philadelphia. Lithograph by P. S. Duval & Co., 1855

The roof of each cell contained a single skylight, a symbol of the all-seeing eye of God. On admission to the prison, inmates had their clothing and belongings removed; they were given baths and had their hair cut short; they were issued with woollen trousers, a jacket, a shirt, two handkerchiefs, two pairs of socks and two pairs of shoes. As they were taken to their cells, a hood was placed on their heads to prevent them from seeing other prisoners or gaining any knowledge of the layout of the prison. Guards walked the corridors to oversee the prisoners, visiting every prisoner every day, and from the central octagon, the chief warder watched the guards.[81]

On 8 March 1842, Charles Dickens visited the Penitentiary. The writer was appalled by what he saw there. 'The system here, is rigid, strict, and hopeless,' he wrote. 'I believe it, in its effects, to be cruel and wrong.' As he continued, he seemed to anticipate Foucault by over a century: 'I am persuaded that those who devised this system of Prison Discipline, and those benevolent gentlemen who carry it into execution, do not know what it is that they are doing... I hold this slow and daily tampering with the mysteries of the brain, to be immeasurably worse than any torture of the body.' It was, he concluded, 'a secret punishment which slumbering humanity is not roused up to stay.'[82]

The Eastern Penitentiary was a controversial building, but it was also a sensation. Its unique design was copied throughout the world. Over three hundred 'radial prisons', as they were called, were built all over the world: from France, Italy and Germany to Argentina, Peru, China and Japan.[83] The English version was Pentonville in London. Completed in 1842 to a design produced by Haviland himself, it was the first of thirty radial prisons to be built across Britain.[84] It tinkered with the original form established in Philadelphia, using just four 'spokes', but with three floors of cells – later extended to four – rising above each corridor. Where the corridors met, there was a raised structure, surrounded by glazing, which offered a view of the whole prison. For some commentators, the view this offered was like 'a bunch of Burlington Arcades, that had been fitted up in the style of the opera box lobbies with an infinity of little doors'.[85] This was perhaps unsurprising, given that, along with radial prisons, Haviland also built some of America's first shopping malls.[86] Just as Foucault wrote, Panopticism could get everywhere.

Did the Benthams' idea influence Haviland? Although there is no explicit evidence, it seems likely. Haviland began his apprenticeship as an architect with James Elmes, who built a number of prisons in the late nineteenth century, and in 1817, had published a pamphlet called *Hints for the Improvement of Prisons*, which suggested the adoption of a radial principle.[87] It is inconceivable that the two men were not aware of Bentham's protracted political campaign to build the Panopticon prison. Perhaps most telling of all is the fact that Haviland travelled to St Petersburg in 1815 to visit his aunt, who had married a Russian count.[88] While there, he would surely have visited Samuel Bentham's School of Arts. Certainly, the similarities between the plan of the St Petersburg building and the Eastern Penitentiary are striking.

At the beginning of the twentieth century, some prison architecture moved away from the radial design, and back towards Jeremy Bentham's own 'purist' plan. Between 1916 and 1924, five 'rotundas' were built at Stateville Penitentiary near Joliet in Illinois. Beneath a ceiling of glass panels and wrought iron, a central glazed lookout post was surrounded by four levels of sixty-four cells each. This was the closest the world had ever come to the design produced by Jeremy and his architect collaborator Willey Reveley.

A guard tower sits at the centre of the 'roundhouse' of the Stateville Penitentiary, Illinois. From the postcard collection of Alex Wellerstein.

It was also inherently flawed. The renowned American prison architect Alfred Hopkins called Stateville 'the most awful receptacle of gloom ever devised'.[89] A former inmate was more specific: 'They figured they were smart building them that way. They figured they could watch every inmate in the house with only one screw in the tower. What they didn't figure is that the cons know all the time where the screw is.'[90] Stateville botched the central principle of the inspection house: that the watching only went one way. Nevertheless, its design was copied by the Presidio Modelo, a prison built on the Isle of the Pines in Cuba in 1931. Modelo once counted Fidel Castro as an inmate, before Castro in turn used it to hold political dissidents and counter-revolutionaries attempting to undermine his own regime. It was finally closed in the 1960s, yet remains today as a national monument and tourist attraction. Its five rotundas, each with five floors of cells surrounding a central inspection tower, are well-maintained ruins, though the glass has now gone from the many cell windows. Only the shells of the prison blocks remain.

One wonders what Jeremy Bentham would have made of Closed Circuit Television. The Panopticon of his day foundered because architecture and technology could not match the ambition of the concept. Yet, at the end of the twentieth century and the beginning of the twenty-first, the rapid spread of CCTV throughout towns and cities appears, for the first time, to allow a near perfect realisation of the inspection idea. Britain is at the forefront of this surveillance culture, boasting twenty per cent of the world's CCTV cameras. The average British citizen can expect to be captured on film some three hundred times a day.[91] Some cameras now even deploy loudspeakers, which use a child's voice to reprimand anyone spotted committing an offence.[92] Here is the Panopticon without walls, a society governed by constant observance. Except it doesn't work.

Statistics suggest that only one crime is solved for every one thousand CCTV cameras in use.[93] While footage has often proved crucial *after* an event for tracking down potential suspects, the system seems to have little impact on the actual commission of crime. Surveillance is not curtailing bad behaviour, merely documenting it. It is less Panopticism, more voyeurism.

The inefficacy of modern CCTV cameras may have its roots in its failure to adhere to one of the key aspects of Bentham's prison scheme – the involvement of private enterprise. Bentham intended the prison governor to work to commercial incentives, with a financial reward attendant on the smooth running of the institution and the reform of prisoners. A state-operated surveillance programme, even one as far-reaching as today's CCTV network, is passive and reactionary by comparison. Modern technology's first engagement with Panopticism has been a failure. But it is learning – and fast.

The solution – whether it is perfect or nightmarish depends on one's stance on civil liberties – rests in your pocket: inside your smart-phone, to be exact. In this gadget, owned now, at least in First World societies, by almost everyone apart from the very old and the very young, there exists a sophisticated means of documenting the world around you, and at the same time of tracking your own exact location. Cameras and recording devices are everywhere, or to borrow Jeremy Bentham's phrase, they are 'a kind of omnipresence'.

Increasingly, footage shot by ordinary bystanders and passers-by dominates our news broadcasts. Almost without thinking, people pull out their phones to capture anything unusual or out of the ordinary. Within an instant the result can be uploaded to blogs or websites like YouTube, and shared with global communities via Twitter and Facebook.[94] In July 2005 in South Korea, a young woman was captured on camera after her dog defecated on the subway, and she did not clean up the mess. Fellow passengers, angry at her behaviour, posted the pictures on social media with the caption *gae-ttong-nyue – dog shit girl.* Within hours, the images had gone viral. Within days, the story had made the national news. Details of the girl's identity – and of her family – spread across the internet. She began to be recognised in the street and subjected to abuse. Eventually she dropped out of her university course.[95]

In the above example, it was righteous indignation rather than financial reward that sparked a digital witch-hunt. But imagine a system where governments paid ordinary citizens to provide evidence of anti-social behaviour or criminal activity. Rewards could be credited anonymously to accounts linked to the phones that supplied the photographs or videos.[96] Anyone and everyone around you could be an informer – and with all-encompassing surveillance, your behaviour would change. At first it would take an effort to stop yourself from doing the wrong thing: dropping litter, talking on your phone while driving, smoking in a public place. But soon it is second nature. You are reprogrammed. And all this from a 'simple idea in architecture'.

Chapter Sixteen

No-Man's City

Kowloon Walled City – Kowloon, Hong Kong
(Born 1843 – Died 1994)

The most densely populated city on earth had only one postman. His round was confined to an area barely a hundredth of a square mile in size. Yet within that space was a staggering number of addresses: 350 buildings, almost all between ten and fourteen storeys high, occupied by 8,500 premises, 10,700 households and over 33,000 residents.[1]

The city's many tall, narrow tower-blocks were packed tight against each other – so tight as to make the whole place seem like one massive structure: part architecture, part organism. There was little uniformity of shape, height or building material. Cast-iron balconies lurched against brick annexes and concrete walls. Wiring and cables covered every surface: running vertically from ground level up to forests of rooftop television aerials, or stretching horizontally like innumerable rolls of dark twine that seemed almost to bind the buildings together. Entering the city meant leaving daylight behind. There were hundreds of alleyways, most just a few feet wide. Some routes cut below buildings, while other tunnels were formed by the accumulation of refuse tossed out of windows and onto wire netting strung between tower-blocks. Thousands of metal and plastic water pipes ran along walls and ceilings, most of them leaking and corroded. As protection against the relentless drips that fell in the alleyways, a hat was standard issue for the city's postman. Many residents chose to use umbrellas.[2]

There were only two lifts in the entire city. At the foot of some of the high-rises, communal and individual post boxes were nailed to the walls.[3] But often the only option for the postman was to climb. Even several storeys up, the maze of pathways continued: knotted arteries that burrowed into the heart of the city along interconnecting bridges and stairwells.

Sometimes the postman would reach a top floor and climb out onto the roof. Gangways and rusting metal ladders let him move quickly from building to building, before he dropped back down into the darkness. While some alleys were empty and quiet, others overflowed with life. Hundreds of factories produced everything from fish balls to golf balls. Entire corridors were coated with the fine flour-dust used for making noodles. Acrid, chemical smells filled the streets that lay alongside metal and plastic manufacturers. Unlicensed doctors and dentists clustered together, electric signs hanging over their premises to advertise their services. Many patients came from outside the city, happy to pay bargain fees in return for asking no questions. Shops and food stalls were strung along 'Big Well' Street, 'Bright' Street and 'Dragon City' Road. For the adventurous, dog and snake meat were specialities of the city.[4]

Moving deeper, long corridors offered glimpses into smoke-filled rooms. The incessant click of *mahjong* tiles echoed along the walls. Gambling parlours lined up alongside strip clubs and pornographic cinemas. Prostitutes – including children – solicited in the darkness, leading clients away to backroom brothels. And everywhere there were bodies lying in the gloom. At Kwong Ming Street – known as 'Electric Station' – wooden stalls sold cheap drugs. Addicts crouched down to inhale heroin smoke through tubes held over heated tinfoil.[5] Bare rooms, enticingly referred to as 'divans', were filled with prone men and women, all sunk in opium stupors. Many of the city's rats were addicts too, and could be seen writhing in torment in dark corners, desperate for a hit.[6]

There was no law to speak of. This was an anarchist society, self-regulating and self-determining. It was a colony within a colony, a city within a city, a tiny block of territory at once contested and neglected. It was known as Kowloon Walled City. But locals called it something else. *Hak Nam* – the City of Darkness.[7]

In April 1810, a commoner by the name of Yang was caught bringing six boxes of opium into Peking's Forbidden City.[8] This was a serious crime: opium had been made illegal by imperial decree eighty years before, and its discovery behind the walls of the governmental palace came as an enormous shock.

The Jiaqing emperor of the Qing dynasty issued an immediate order, to be sent from his grand secretariat to all provinces, reiterating in the strongest possible terms the prohibition on the purchase, sale and use of the substance. 'Opium has a very violent effect,' he began. 'When an addict smokes it, it rapidly makes him extremely excited and capable of doing anything he pleases. But before long, it kills him. Opium is a poison, undermining our good customs and morality.'[9] Yang's crime was bad enough, but the emperor recognised that it was no isolated occurrence, rather a sign of the rapid increase in the illicit use of opium throughout Chinese society. 'Recently the purchases and eaters of opium have become numerous,' he lamented. 'Deceitful merchants buy and sell it to gain profit.'[10]

The extent of the problem was greater than the Jiaqing emperor realised. In the first decade of the nineteenth century, Jiaqing's son Minning wrote in his journal of a spring day when he found himself wearying of his studies and eager to seek some distraction. 'A new morning has begun with much free time,' he began. Bored and tired, Minning asked his servant to bring him his pipe. 'Each time, my mind suddenly becomes clear, my eyes and ears refreshed... When you desire happiness, it gives you happiness. And it is not vulgar like some of the popular customs today.'[11] As he smoked his *yan* – tobacco soaked in opium – the young prince began to scribble down a poem to capture the sensations he was experiencing: 'Watch the cloud ascend from nostril; Inhale and exhale, fragrance rises; Ambience deepens and thickens'. And then, in almost no time, 'Mountains and clouds emerge in distant sea'.[12]

Opium comes from the pods of immature poppy seeds. When cut or lanced, these pods exude a sticky gum, which is then dried and pressed into cakes.[13] A major natural ingredient of this gum is morphine, which, whether eaten, drunk, smoked or injected, takes rapid effect on the nerve receptors, dulling or removing feelings of pain. At the same time, it stimulates a massive surge in the production of dopamine, the chemical which feeds positive 'reward' signals back to the brain after pleasurable experiences.[14] Just as the emperor's son had written, it gave happiness whenever happiness was desired.[15] Such a substance was, of course, highly addictive.

Dependency makes opium the centre of a user's life, to the exclusion of all other things. The Chinese government described the unsavoury consequences when they first imposed a ban in 1729. If users 'cease to drink it only for a day, the skin on their faces will suddenly shrink and their lips and teeth loosen and drop off. So exhausted are they that they seem to be dying. Only after they resume drinking it can they temporarily recover.'[16] For the habitual addict, opium consumption can lead to a gradual shutting down of the body's systems – in particular the lungs and respiratory functions – and, ultimately, to death.[17]

The imperial authorities were acutely aware of the deleterious effects of the drug on society. Yet just as distressing to them was how opium was reaching the people: 'on the ships of foreign barbarians who smuggle it in, after which it spreads throughout the country'.[18] At the vanguard of these 'barbarians' – the term employed by the imperial Chinese to describe all incomers[19] – were the British, in the guise of the East India Company. For decades, Britain had been racking up a substantial trade deficit with China. There was huge domestic demand for silks, porcelain, and especially tea, and the East India Company operated a massive import business. Yet all the Chinese wanted for themselves was silver, and trade was becoming increasingly costly. That was, however, until the British came into possession of the vast poppy fields of Bengal.[20]

The East India Company managed the processing and packaging of opium gum, transported it to Calcutta, and from there sold it on to private merchants. What the merchants did with it after that was their business.[21] The East India Company knew very well, however, that it would make its way to the Chinese coast, to the wholesalers and smugglers based around the only port permitted to conduct international trade: Canton, in the southernmost province of the Chinese Empire.[22] In the early years of the nineteenth century, the opium trade, despite the imperial ban, experienced a massive boom, and very quickly began to offset the British deficit. In 1816, just over 3,000 chests of opium were trafficked into China. By 1836, this figure had risen to over 27,000.[23] Dealing in the drug was so lucrative that both the importing agents, and the many customs officials and Chinese buyers – the 'Hong' merchants who regulated foreign trade on behalf of the imperial government – ignored the emperor's increasingly irate decrees.[24]

In 1820, Jiaqing was succeeded by his son. The new emperor's official title was Daoguang, but his original name had been Minning – he was the same young student prince who had once dabbled so pleasurably in the delights of opium.[25] The pressures of power were a far cry, however, from lazy days reading history books and smoking *yan*. By 1829, Chinese imports were exceeding exports for the first time. To cover the deficit, silver had to be exported – a direct reversal of the favourable economic situation enjoyed by the empire in the eighteenth and early nineteenth centuries.[26] Daoguang was confronted with a hard truth: opium was draining his country's wealth. On top of that, there was the dire impact on public health. By 1835, it was estimated that two million of the Chinese population were addicts.[27]

For years, the emperor and his government vacillated over the best course of action, even at one point coming close to legalising opium.[28] Finally, however, they settled on a policy of zero tolerance, and on the very last day of 1838, Daoguang appointed an Imperial Commissioner, Lin Zexu, to wipe out the illegal traffic.[29] Zexu had a reputation for incorruptibility, and he set about his task with uncompromising zeal. The success of the opium trade had relied on a largely non-interventionist imperial policy, as well as the collusion of the Canton merchants, who benefited from the enormous profits.

Suddenly, the climate changed completely. Zexu hunted down and imprisoned Chinese dealers and users, and in March 1839 he ordered British merchants to turn over their stocks of opium. When they refused, he held them captive in their factories and warehouses in Canton.[30]

After six weeks, Captain Charles Elliot, the British Superintendent of Trade, stepped in. He negotiated to hand over 20,000 chests of opium, and at the same time promised the merchants that the British government would underwrite the value of their loss, which amounted to the considerable sum of £2 million.[31] A delighted Zexu took the consignments, mixed the drug with salt and lime, and flushed it all out to sea. He followed up this victory by proposing that foreign traders sign a bond renouncing trafficking the drug, 'on pain of death'.[32]

Zexu believed that he was making good progress with his appointed task, but Elliot's involvement – and the governmental guarantee he had offered to protect British commercial interests – had escalated a trading quarrel into something bigger. 'This is the first time in our intercourse with this empire that its government has taken unprovoked initiative in aggressive measures against British life, liberty and property, and against the dignity of the British Crown,' wrote Elliot to the Foreign Secretary Lord Palmerston on 2 April 1839.[33] The seizure by Zexu had become a prelude to war. To British hawks, the Chinese were the enemies of the free market, an outmoded, supercilious empire ignoring the economic realities of the modern world, and, indeed, the wishes of their own people. This conveniently ignored the origins of the dispute: the importation of an illegal, harmful narcotic. If China were not prepared to engage with the international community, then, the British Empire resolved, they should be forced to see sense.

The 'Opium War' of 1839 to 1842 was actually a series of skirmishes, interposed with fractious negotiations. Agreements were settled, only to break down again almost instantly. The Chinese were both surprised and irritated by this British belligerence in a remote province of their empire – indeed, for some time they saw it as more of a border dispute than a war.[34] Either way, they had no hope of winning a military encounter. The conflict was finally settled in August 1842 with the Treaty of Nanking, the first treaty the Chinese had ever signed with a foreign nation. It was also the first of what modern Chinese historians describe as the 'unequal treaties', because the terms saw China ceding various rights while gaining nothing in return, and the beginning of the 'century of humiliation': a hundred-year struggle ending with the 'rebirth' of the nation in the communist People's Revolution of 1949.[35]

For the British, Nanking had several important outcomes. They were compensated handsomely for the chests of opium destroyed by Zexu. Better still, they succeeded in instituting free trade throughout China, removing the restrictive system that had forced all goods to pass through Canton. Furthermore, and although it was never mentioned specifically in the treaty terms, they assumed a legal right to import opium.[36] Most significantly of all, Britain gained a colonial foothold in China: a near-deserted, mountainous island with a sheltered, deep-water harbour at the entrance to the Canton River, opposite the Kowloon Peninsula. This was Hong Kong.

A year later, in 1843, the Chinese began to build a fort at the very tip of the Kowloon Peninsula[37] – a fort that looked out directly across the bay towards Britain's newest colony. A high-ranking assistant magistrate was transferred to the site, along with the region's chief military officer and a garrison of 150 soldiers.[38] The viceroy of Canton oversaw the construction, and in 1846, he contacted the imperial court in Peking to propose a number of improvements. Along with introducing offices, barracks and a training ground, his chief recommendation was for the construction of a substantial wall, mounted with cannons. The wall was built of ashlar granite, thirteen feet high, fifteen feet wide, and studded with six watchtowers, forming a rough parallelogram around the fort, 700 feet long by 400 feet wide.[39] For the viceroy, this wall would have a 'constraining' influence on 'barbarian' activity in the area, and act as a highly visible symbol of the continuing authority of imperial China.[40]

To emphasise that this was as much about moral as military fortitude, a school was founded on the site: an ideological bulwark against western decadence.[41] A face-saving recasting of the Treaty of Nanking presented its terms as a series of generous gifts granted by a benign emperor. Foreigners should be in no doubt as to who still ruled the region. By 1847, the fort was complete. Kowloon Walled City trained its imperial eyes on Hong Kong.[42]

In 1860, continuing disputes over trade sparked a second 'Opium War'. This time, British and French forces devastated Chinese resistance, and marched to the very walls of the Forbidden City, burning down the architectural wonder of the imperial Summer Palace en route in retaliation for the torturing of a diplomatic delegation. Robert Swinhoe, a naturalist who took part in the campaign, recalled walking through the charred remnants of the palace and its once wondrous gardens: 'it betokened to our minds a sad portent of this antiquated empire.'[43]

For all the Chinese posturing, the armies of the west had once again demonstrated their overwhelming superiority. This second conflict ended with the signing of the Convention of Peking, which both reaffirmed and extended the major clauses of the 1842 Treaty, including freedom of trade and travel, and the full legalisation of opium, and added the right of foreign nations to establish embassies in Peking. It also ceded the Kowloon Peninsula 'to have and hold as a dependency of Her Britannic Majesty's Colony of Hong Kong'.[44]

The Walled City remained, however, a Chinese administrative outpost within the region. Suburbs grew up around the city to service the flow of trade between Hong Kong and the mainland. The site became the major market centre for the surrounding villages, and a large number of shops and factories sprang up in a strip along the coastline.[45]

What Kowloon also acquired, rather quickly, was a louche reputation. Along with British trading ships, the waters of the Hong Kong and Kowloon bays were filled with Chinese junks, many of which belonged to smugglers. The legalisation of opium had allowed the imperial government to impose taxes on the trade, but many of the traders who had once colluded with the British in sneaking contraband imports past customs proved reluctant to take a hit to their profits.[46] There were the first signs of civil insurrection and organised crime in the region. Secret societies supporting republicanism and the overthrow of imperial rule – gangs known as Triads – were rumoured to be operating in Kowloon.[47] Gambling dens became a key attraction on the peninsula. Special steamer ships operated through the night, ferrying passengers between Hong Kong and the gaming tables. As an extra incentive, the trip was free, as were the cigars and coffee handed out on the journey.[48] To cope with the increased traffic, the 700-foot-long Lung Chun pier was built out into the bay.[49]

It was the free market in action: the very principle that the British had waged war to uphold. That did not mean, however, that they were happy with the situation in Kowloon. 'It is not too much to say that this place, with its encouragements to vice and dishonesty, adds enormously to the task of preserving order and good government among the large Chinese population of the Colony,' was the verdict of the Hong Kong General Chamber of Commerce. 'The inclusion of this small city within British boundaries would greatly assist in the detection and repression of crime.'[50]

Not the detection of all crime, however. One of the main reasons for the continued presence of Chinese officials right next to Hong Kong was to police the smuggling trade. Writing in private correspondence in 1875, the Governor of Hong Kong, Sir Arthur Kennedy, admitted the danger that imperial customs officers presented to the prosperity of the port:

> 'It is beyond doubt that a not inconsiderable number of Chinese junk owners are in the habit of consulting their individual interests by violating Chinese customs laws, and making the Colony the basis of smuggling operations, for which its geographical location affords every facility... The Chinese Customs Officers and Revenue

> Collectors, with a knowledge of these facts, lose no opportunity seizing and confiscating every Chinese junk for which they can find a pretext.'[51]

The result was that 'honest and innocent traders are often grievously harassed and plundered'.[52] Too much Chinese government intervention in Hong Kong's merchant traffic, and trade might move south, to the Portuguese port of Macau.

Another pressing consideration for the administrators and businessmen of Hong Kong was the long-term security of the colony. 'Without some such arrangement and readjustment of boundaries, the position of this Colony in the event of any war must I think be very insecure from a defensive point of view,' wrote Sir William Robinson, Governor from 1891, in a despatch to the Colonial Office.[53] His missive included supporting memoranda from the commanding officer of the British troops in Hong Kong, and from the prominent merchant, Catchik Paul Chater. As he considered the prospect of a resurgent Chinese nation in the future, Chater asked: 'If then the boundaries of Hong Kong are no more extensive than they are now, where will we be with a Chinese fleet in Kowloon Bay, and hills and islands close around, in Chinese possession?' His answer was clear: 'At their mercy at any moment.'[54]

In March 1898, Sir Claude MacDonald, the British Minister in Peking, began negotiations with the *Tsungli Yamen,* the Chinese Foreign Office, to lease additional territory on the mainland opposite Hong Kong. The imperial government was open to discussion – and in fact had just embarked on similar negotiations with other nations, including France, Russia and Germany – but on one issue they remained resolute. The Walled City had to remain under Chinese jurisdiction. 'Is it a question of dignity or of money?' Lord Arthur Balfour, head of the British Foreign Office, asked in a telegraph to MacDonald. 'If money compensation is required, we could offer reasonable terms, or some arrangements might be made leaving Chinese officials in the town undisturbed but subjecting them to paramount British authority.'[55] MacDonald replied that it was pride at stake, and that money would be of little use: 'doubtless they are afraid of being denounced for selling their country.'[56]

In a detailed message to the Prime Minister Lord Salisbury, MacDonald reiterated that the status of Kowloon City was the sticking point. His recommendation was to concede. Once the Chinese had saved face, he reasoned, the British would quickly assume *de facto* control of the fort. 'It is not to be supposed that the city of Kowloon will long remain outside British jurisdiction with the surrounding district subject to it,' he wrote, 'but I think that no harm can result from allowing it to do so for a few years longer, and that little inconvenience will be caused by it, especially as the authority of the Chinese officials will be subject to the stipulation that it does not interfere with military requirements.'[57]

The agreement was drafted by MacDonald himself, a military man with no legal background. The result was a very short – and very ambiguous – contract, which left much room for interpretation. It granted over 350 square miles of the Canton province to Britain, with the specific exception of the six-and-a-half acre plot of land at the tip of the Kowloon Peninsula occupied by the Walled City.[58] But on the actual details of the transfer, it was remarkably vague. The first clause, which admitted that 'the exact boundaries shall be hereafter fixed when proper surveys have been made,' was typical of the rushed nature of the agreement. It was the second and third clauses, however, which would prove most problematic: 'It is at the same time agreed that within the city of Kowloon the Chinese officials now stationed there shall continue to exercise jurisdiction except so far as may be inconsistent with the military requirements for the defence of Hong Kong... It is further agreed that the existing landing place near Kowloon City shall be reserved for the convenience of Chinese men-of-war, merchant and passenger vessels, which may come and go and lie there at their pleasure; and for the convenience of movement of the officials and people within the city.'[59]

MacDonald believed that the 'New Territories', as the lands were called, were in effect being absorbed into the British Empire. A rather arbitrary 99-year term was apportioned to the lease, presumably on the basis that, by the time it expired, Hong Kong and its mainland holdings would be recognised as indisputably British. The 'Convention Respecting an Extension of the Hong Kong Territory' was signed in Peking on 9 June 1898. Its end date, after which Britain was required, in theory, to hand the territory back, was 30 June 1997.[60] No one believed this would ever happen.

At 3pm on 16 May 1899, two hundred Welsh Fusiliers and one hundred Hong Kong Volunteers marched through the dirty, dilapidated suburbs of Kowloon to the south gate of the Walled City.[61] Two days earlier, the Secretary of State for the Colonies, Joseph Chamberlain, had received authorisation from the Foreign Office to order the occupation of the city. The operation had been planned in strictest secrecy. This did not, it seemed, prevent a large crowd of Chinese locals from gathering on the beach to watch the arrival of the British troops. Landing at Lung Chun Pier, the party unloaded their Maxim machine guns and their seven-pounders, and began hauling them through the mud of Kowloon's main street.[62]

According to their intelligence reports, 300 imperial soldiers, under the command of the viceroy of Canton, were waiting behind the walls of the city. No one knew what kind of reception they would face. One thing, however, was certain: if the Chinese troops did put up any resistance, there could be another war. As the British approached the fortress, they found the main gate wide open. Advancing inside the walls, they still saw no sign of Chinese soldiers. Apart from a few hundred residents, and the Kowloon Mandarin, who argued furiously with the British commanders, the city appeared to be deserted.[63]

Britain had not found the occupation of the 'New Territories' a smooth process. It was a full ten months after the hasty drafting and signature of the Peking Convention before planning began for a flag-raising ceremony to mark the official beginning of British jurisdiction in the region. In part this delay was caused by the need to agree the precise extent of the territory being leased. While the necessary boundary survey was in progress, diplomatic wrangles continued over the exact meaning of the terms of the agreement MacDonald had drafted.

On one side, the viceroy of Canton announced that he would only agree to the lease subject to a list of his own 'regulations'. On the other, the British continued to look for a way to circumvent the Walled City clause.[64] More seriously, the drawn-out nature of the transfer was giving disaffected local clan-leaders time to organise support for a rebellion against their new masters. As the day of the flag-raising ceremony approached – 17 April 1899 – officials scoping out locations for the event were attacked, and the temporary structures they had erected were burnt down. British troops moved into the region, and at the same time a request was made to the viceroy of Canton to send Chinese forces to help preserve order: 300 of the viceroy's men were to advance to Kowloon City, while 300 more were to occupy another fort at the border town of Sum Chun.[65]

A site was eventually chosen for the ceremony near the village of Tai Po, and named Flagstaff Hill. As the British continued with their preparations, they came under attack again – and this time, alarmingly, they spotted uniformed Chinese soldiers among the rebels. The commander of the British army in China and Hong Kong, Major-General William Gascoigne, arrived at Tai Po on 16 April at the head of a large contingent of troops. Accompanied by James Stewart Lockhart, the Colonial Secretary, Gascoigne ordered the raising of the Union Flag, a day earlier than planned.[66]

The wisdom of this decision soon became clear. The local Hong Kong press had written of looking forward to 'a pleasant little outing and an opportunity for indulging in an outburst of patriotic fervour'.[67] In fact, the ceremony at Tai Po was interrupted almost immediately by another attack from thousands of Chinese. While the British soon routed the rebels, a pitched battle was hardly an auspicious start to British jurisdiction. Suspicions grew over the role of the viceroy in the disturbances. The Colonial Office and the Foreign Office made representations to Peking, and on 20 April the order was transmitted from the imperial government for all Chinese troops to leave the

New Territories.[68] Weeks passed, however, and reports continued to confirm that 300 of the viceroy's soldiers remained within the Walled City.[69] The Foreign Office decided the only option was force.

When the British entered Kowloon on 16 May 1899, the Chinese troops *had* gone. But their commanders were still there. The following day, on 17 May, the civilian population of the Walled City was loaded onto a junk on Lung Chun Pier and taken away. The military personnel, however, refused to leave their posts without orders from the viceroy. Once again, telegraphs rattled back and forth between Hong Kong, London and Peking. The Yamen in particular expressed astonishment at the British occupation of Kowloon: 'In connection with this affair China has shown the most accommodating spirit, and the conduct of England in sending soldiers to Kowloon City and expelling the Chinese officials and troops... and hoisting the British flag, is indeed an unexpected return.'[70]

Lord Salisbury was categorical in his response: 'It is impossible for Her Majesty's Government to allow the resumption of Chinese authority within the walls of that City.'[71] The viceroy's actions had provided the perfect opportunity for the British to draw further concessions from the imperial government, and in particular to resolve the vexed issue of the Walled City clause. Peking continued to protest, but the British would not budge. Here, they insisted, was a clear violation of the terms of the 1898 Convention.

On 27 December 1899, Queen Victoria signed an Order in Council at Windsor Palace which stated that the continued presence of Chinese officials in Kowloon had been 'found to be inconsistent with the military requirements for the defence of Hong Kong'. As a consequence, the Walled City was to become 'part and parcel of Her Majesty's Colony of Hong Kong, in like manner and for all intents and purposes as if it had originally formed part of the said Colony'.[72] As far as the British were concerned, the Chinese had lost all rights to Kowloon.

Five years later, in May 1904, an article in the *Hong Kong Weekly Press* described 'nothing but desolation' inside the Walled City.[73] The British may have succeeded in removing the Chinese officials, but they had done little to claim Kowloon as their own. On the other hand, the Yamen had not returned to the issue of the city's occupation, or made any attempt to reinstate a Chinese imperial presence in the city. For both sides, it seemed, Kowloon had become a diplomatic embarrassment.

In time the Hong Kong government began to grant short-term land leases in the city, but only for 'public purpose'. Missionaries of the Protestant and Anglican churches moved in, occupying the old administrative buildings and turning them into schools, hospitals, a home for the elderly, and an alms house. The city's Chinese temple was converted into a chapel, which held sermons every Wednesday and Sunday evenings.[74] Pig farmers from the surrounding hills began to migrate down to the peninsula; some took over empty plots within the walls of Kowloon.[75] There remained a total absence of development or administrative control within the city.

By the mid-1920s the former office of the Mandarin, a once-grand official building, was in ruins, and the main south wall had started to crumble away.[76] At the same time, land reclamation at the tip of the peninsula had extended Kowloon's suburbs into the bay area, and had removed the city from the waterfront. Set back behind modern factories, shops and tenement housing, it had become 'a little bit of China in the Heart of Hong Kong' as the governor, Sir William Peel, disapprovingly described it to the Secretary of State for the Colonies, Sir Philip Cunliffe-Lister, in 1934.[77]

All land leases were set to expire in December 1934, and Peel informed the city's residents – with the exception of the Church Missionary Society and a free school – that their grants of ownership would not be renewed. They were offered compensation, either in the form of money or land, for relocation. At this time there were some 400 people living in the Walled City, in 64 houses – many of them little more than squatters' hovels.[78] The Hong Kong government proposed the demolition of all insanitary dwellings, and the redevelopment of Kowloon into 'a place of popular resort and antiquarian interest'.[79]

A number of the residents objected, appealing to the provincial government of Canton, who passed their complaints on to the *Wai Chiao Pu*, the Ministry of Foreign Affairs in the new Republic of China. For the first time in three decades, the issue of jurisdiction in the Walled City was raised. Citing the terms of original 1898 Convention, and ignoring the Order in Council of the following year, the *Wai Chiao Pu* questioned the legality of the British attempt to evict the residents, and backed the right of the people to remain in what they maintained was still Chinese territory.[80]

Eager to avoid a diplomatic incident, the Hong Kong government proceeded cautiously with the scheme, relocating a number of willing families while continuing negotiations with those who remained recalcitrant. Throughout the process the Chinese authorities appeared to be actively encouraging residents to protest. By 1940, however, all the city's buildings, apart from the Mandarin's house, the former Lung Chun School and one private dwelling, had been demolished.[81] With the onset of the Second World War, there was no opportunity to complete the development of Kowloon as a historic garden and 'popular resort'. It lay neglected and empty. And things would get even worse.

In late December 1941, Japanese forces occupied the New Territories. Hong Kong had long been a key strategic naval base in the Pacific, but the Japanese army also began to extend the nearby Kai Tak Airport, a landing strip first established on the peninsula in the late 1920s. The granite walls of Kowloon made perfect building material. The Japanese ordered them to be torn down[82], and set POWs to work carrying the rubble to Kai Tak to add into a new runway. The Walled City was gone.

In the aftermath of the Second World War, refugees flooded south to the Kowloon Peninsula. The only trace of the old city was the derelict shell of the Mandarin's house. Yet people gravitated almost instinctively to this rough rectangle of ground. Perhaps it was the *feng shui.* The Walled City had originally been laid out according to the ancient principles of Chinese philosophy: facing south and overlooking water, with hills and mountains to the north.[83] This ideal alignment, it was said, brought harmony to all citizens. In their desperate plight some refugees may have believed that Kowloon would be a much-needed source of luck and prosperity. Others, however, recalled that this had once been a Chinese exclave in British colonial territory. The stone walls of the 'Walled City' had gone, but the refugees were convinced the diplomatic ones remained.

By 1947 there were over 2,000 squatters camped in Kowloon[84], their ramshackle huts arranged in almost the exact footprint of the original city. No one wanted to find themselves outside the borders – those on the wrong side of the line risked losing the protection of the Chinese government. The people kept coming, and the camp grew ever more squalid and overcrowded.

Appalled by the conditions, the Hong Kong authorities made plans to clear the refugees. On 5 January 1948, the Public Works Department, supported by a large police presence, removed the squatters and demolished all the slum housing. Within a week, however, the occupiers had returned to rebuild their shacks. When the police attempted to intervene, a riot broke out. News of the disturbances spread across China, and the plight of the 'residents' of Kowloon became a *cause célèbre.* The British consulate in Canton was set on fire, and a group of students in Shanghai staged a protest strike. Officials from the Chinese government travelled to the Walled City – and officially encouraged the refugees to continue the struggle against their British oppressors.

The provincial Canton government sent a delegation on a 'comfort mission' to the region, supplementing the distribution of food and medical aid with messages advocating militant action. The Chinese Foreign Ministry continued to argue that they retained jurisdiction over the city and its people. Amid mounting tension, the Hong Kong government relented. The eviction programme was halted, and the police withdrew.[85] From a temporary refugee camp, Kowloon now began to evolve into something more permanent. A new city was being founded on the ruins of the old.

What kind of city? Naturally, the judgement of Sir Alexander Grantham, Governor of Hong Kong from 1947 to 1957, was damning. Kowloon, he wrote, had become 'a cesspool of iniquity, with heroin divans, brothels and everything unsavoury'.[86] The Chinese claims to sovereignty over Kowloon did not extend to any day-to-day administration; they merely used its uncertain status as a convenient tool for political point-scoring. After the disturbances in 1948, the Hong Kong government had settled on a similar policy of non-intervention. The result was a city outside the law: there was no tax; no regulation of businesses; no health or planning systems; no police presence. People could come to Kowloon, and, in official terms, disappear. It was little surprise that criminal activity flourished. Five Triad gangs: the King Yee, Sun Yee On, 14K, Wo Shing Wo and Tai Ho Choi, took up residence.[87] Kowloon's extra-legal status made it the perfect place for the manufacture, sale and use of drugs like opium and heroin. The city that had been founded to police the traffic of opium became the epicentre of Hong Kong's narcotics trade.

Organised crime may have dominated much of Kowloon, but it did not define the city. Entrepreneurs, attracted by low rents offered by private landlords, saw a unique opportunity. Hundreds of factories were established, with entire families manning the production lines. Conditions were often appalling, yet productivity – and profit – remarkable. Goods made in Kowloon were exported throughout Hong Kong, China, and even, in some cases, the world. Plastics and textile manufacturing were a speciality, as was food production. To the blissful ignorance of Hong Kong's well-heeled residents, the dumplings and fish balls served in their restaurants were frequently sourced from Kowloon.[88]

The citizens of the Walled City demonstrated an extraordinary capacity for change and adaptation. The boundaries of their world were tightly constrained, yet, as more people continued to enter the city, their architecture met the demand. As modern high-rises grew up in Hong Kong, the builders of Kowloon copied what they saw, erecting tower-blocks of their own. Thin columns, established on foundations often consisting of thin layers of concrete poured into shallow trenches[89], started to extend skywards. With no requirement for planning permission, structures were thrown up with amazing speed. Subsidence and settlement were common. Because the high-rises would often lean against each other, residents called them 'lovers' buildings'.[90]

As the blocks began to merge together, the city became less a collection of buildings, and more a single structure, a solid block filled with thousands of individual units designed to meet every requirement of a city: living, working, learning, production, commerce, trade, and leisure. Increasingly, residents were physically sealed-off from the outside world. Light did not penetrate down to the narrow lanes leading between the high-rises. It was the beginning of the 'City of Darkness'.

A system of self-government gradually emerged. In 1963, for the first time in over a decade, the Hong Kong authorities attempted to intervene in Kowloon, issuing a demolition order for one corner of the city, and proposing to relocate the displaced residents to a new estate development nearby. When the plans were made public, the community instantly formed a 'Kowloon City anti-demolition committee'.[91]

They sought support from Peking, and once again the Chinese government – now in the form of Chairman Mao's Communist People's Republic – raised their objections at the highest diplomatic level. 'The City of Kowloon is China's territory, and within China's jurisdiction and... this has all along been so in history,' was the message conveyed to the British Foreign Office.[92] When the Hong Kong government went ahead with publishing a schedule and dates for demolition, the Chinese accused Britain of a 'gross violation of China's sovereignty'.[93] Once again, broader diplomatic issues – namely the future of Hong Kong and the New Territories as a whole – forced the British authorities to relent.

Emboldened by their success, the 'Kowloon City anti-demolition committee' became a permanent association, with the aim of representing all the needs of their residents. Known as the *Kai Fong*, they set up their office in the old Mandarin's house, and handled everything from hygiene and fire-prevention to providing administrative support for property transactions – notarising bills of sale and deeds of ownership on strips of rice paper.[94] From 1968 to 1979, until the Hong Kong government introduced compulsory free education, they even ran a school in the city.

One of their chief tasks, however, was to lobby the authorities for a permanent water supply. The government had always refused to connect Kowloon to the mains – not least to avoid encouraging further population growth – and for decades residents had taken matters into their own hands. Some paid the Triads for supplies tapped illegally from the mains system. Others sunk wells beneath the city, and used electric generators to pump water to tanks built on the rooftops of the tower-blocks. From there, a network of makeshift pipes spread out across the city, supplying water to any resident paying a subscription.[95]

Over time the wells were drilled deeper, until some reached up to 100 metres below ground.[96] Under pressure from the *Kai Fong*, the Hong Kong government eventually agreed to install standpipes, but only one was actually placed inside the city. The others were pointedly positioned just outside the perimeter of Kowloon. In the 1970s, mains sewage was provided; prior to that, human and industrial waste had merely run out of the city in open drains. As it filtered down below the city foundations, this sewage must have contaminated many of the water sources from which the wells drew.[97]

For all the ingenuity of the residents and the *Kai Fong*, there was no denying the unsavoury conditions within Kowloon. The city was dank, fetid and filthy, home to an accumulation of dirt and smells that amounted to an assault on the senses of obscene proportions. As time passed, the contrast grew even more acute between the respectable face of the city, represented by the *Kai Fong*, and its popular reputation as a warren of criminal activity.

While police had begun to conduct irregular raids of Kowloon in the 1960s[98], making hundreds of arrests, many felt these incursions were barely scratching the surface. 'The Walled City remains the vice centre of Hong Kong,' wrote the *Hong Kong Standard* in June 1968, 'with an estimated 5,000 drug addicts.'[99] When another concerted police campaign was undertaken in the mid-1970s, 500 pounds of heroin and nearly 4,000 pounds of opium were seized.[100] At the same time, the city became a magnet for evangelical Christian missionaries, who set up Salvation Army outposts and drug rehabilitation centres in the heart of Kowloon, often leasing properties and arranging protection from the same Triad gangs who were feeding the addicts' habits.[101] So many souls to save – and in such a small space – was clearly too much to resist.

'Inside the Walled City', 1998
© Patrick Zachmann / Magnum Photos

For decades the city had stolen electricity from the mains supply, yet in the late 1970s and early 1980s, the Hong Kong authorities approved official installation, probably as a safeguard against the extreme fire-risk posed by the makeshift wiring which riddled Kowloon's infrastructure. Employees of 'China Light and Power' led cables into the city 'inch by inch': sometimes attaching them to alleyway ceilings; at other times being forced to dig below the pavements. 'The city was just a maze of pipes and wires all over the place,' explained one engineer. 'We had to invent many new ways of installing cables'.[102] Even then, often the technicians could only lead the mains cables to the lower floors of the tower-blocks, leaving it to the residents to connect the supply higher up the buildings. All the same, it was symptomatic of changing official attitudes towards Kowloon. Light was shining into the deepest corners of the City of Darkness.

At 9.20am on 14 January 1987, thirty trucks pulled up around the perimeter of Kowloon Walled City. Within the trucks were over 400 officials from the Hong Kong Housing Department. They were organised into 60 teams, each containing a police officer, and they immediately began to erect cordons around the 83 streets and alleys leading into and out of the city. At 10am, they entered Kowloon, on a mission to contact and survey every single resident.[103]

At 9am, the Hong Kong government had announced that Kowloon was to be cleared and redeveloped as a public park, and that all residents would be re-housed and compensated for any costs incurred. Of course, the city had been in this position before. The difference this time, however, was that an agreement was already in place with the Chinese government.[104] Just minutes after the first notice, the Foreign Ministry in Beijing released a supporting statement. They backed the move as being essential 'for fundamentally improving the living environment of the inhabitants of Kowloon Walled City', and continued that they wished 'to express our full understanding of the decision made by the British Hong Kong government to take appropriate measures to clear the Kowloon Walled City and build it into a park'.[105]

The city's fate had been sealed just over two years before. On 19 December 1984, the governments of China and Great Britain signed a joint declaration, affirming that the transfer of sovereignty over Hong Kong would take place on 1 July 1997.[106] The Chinese Foreign Ministry had always used Kowloon as a political pawn to remind the

British and the world of their claim of ownership over the New Territories. With a diplomatic solution in place, the Walled City lost its special status. Almost instantly, this protected exclave, once praised by a high-ranking communist party official for 'doing a good job in self-administration'[107], was reclassified as an unhealthy slum. In the 1960s, the leader of the *Kai Fong* had explained that, 'as long as the Communist flag is flying here, Peking knows it's their duty to protect us... This is part of China. The Walled City will never become part of Hong Kong. One day Hong Kong will become part of us.'[108] And so it would, in a sense. Except that no Walled City would be there to see it happen.

The plans for clearance and demolition were kept secret. Compensation was a key element of the eviction process, so there was the permanent danger of a sudden influx of people keen to grab a slice of government money. For six months at the beginning of 1986, Housing Department officials kept Kowloon under surveillance, working to produce an estimate of population numbers, and a record of the exact physical dimensions of the city. Once this initial report was complete, planning began for the door-to-door survey. The purpose of the operation remained under wraps until the last minute. It was only on the morning of 14 January, as the Housing Department inspectors arrived for work, that they were informed of their task.[109]

The joint statement from Britain and China had stunned the residents of the Walled City, leaving many simply resigned to their fate. The *Kai Fong* had always presented itself as the champion of the rights of Kowloon citizens. Now it found it hard to argue against a government-sanctioned, comprehensive resettlement package that placed residents' welfare at its heart. Although a resistance movement did develop after the survey, its main outlet was a series of anonymous posters stating that Kowloon had been built with 'blood and sweat', and demanding appropriate compensation.[110] The demolition, it seemed, was inevitable.

The compensation package for residents and business owners totalled $2.76 billion.[111] On average, resident owners received

$380,000 for their individual flats – the equivalent to around £430,000 today. Negotiations progressed over the course of several years, and by November 1991, only 457 households were still to agree terms.[112] By this time, a large proportion of the 33,000 residents had already moved out. Some, however – described as 'difficult clearances' – clung on till the end. Section by section, the Walled City was closed down and condemned. Demolition teams began to move through the emptied units, stripping buildings of hazardous materials – in particular, of huge amounts of asbestos sheeting – and removing all inflammable or chemical substances. Once the sweep of a block was complete, it was sealed with mesh windows and padlocked gates, to prevent residents or squatters from returning.

During every phase of the clearance, police were required to break into flats to evict small numbers of residents. At the same time, pest control teams moved through the deserted alleyways, in an attempt to destroy Kowloon's massive rat population before it decamped to other housing estates nearby.[113] Finally, on 2 July 1992, riot police with shields and clubs forced out the last remaining residents. Already evicted from their homes, a group of twenty or so had set up a protest camp in a small Buddhist temple on the city's kerbside.[114] A tall wire fence was erected to encircle the whole site, following almost exactly the line once marked out by the old granite wall. Kowloon was closed and sealed up for good.

On 23 March 1993, a wrecker's ball smashed into the side of an eight-storey tower-block on the edge of the Walled City. This was a solitary, ceremonial swing. The real work of demolishing Kowloon, piece-by-piece, would begin several weeks later. The moment was applauded by a crowd of invited guests and dignitaries. It was also greeted with shouts of anger from former residents who had gathered for one last, futile protest.[115] It took almost exactly a year to reduce the rest of the city to dust and rubble.[116]

Remarkably, from within the modern wreckage, fragments of the original city emerged. There were two granite plaques, each marked with Chinese characters: one read 'South Gate', and the other 'Kowloon Walled City'. Once the ruins of the tower-blocks had been cleared away, developers uncovered segments of the foundations of the original wall, along with three of the iron cannons that had once bristled from the city's ramparts.[117] A solitary building still stood at the centre of Kowloon, the one structure to have survived throughout its whole turbulent history – the office of the Mandarin. Over the course of the next year, the ruins began their rapid conversion into a landscaped park, modelled on the famous seventeenth-century Jiangnan gardens built by the Qing dynasty.

The paths running through these new gardens were named after the streets and buildings of the demolished slum. The Kowloon Walled City Park was officially opened on 22 December 1995 by the British Governor of Hong Kong, Chris Patten.[118] It had taken some six decades, but at last Kowloon was transformed into the 'place of popular resort' envisaged by Sir William Peel, the Governor of Hong Kong in 1934: six-and-a half acres of ornate bamboo pavilions, pretty water-features and vibrant greenery.

This is the story of the rise and fall of a slum. It was born out of a quirk of history; it exploited its unsavoury reputation; and, as is the fate of all slums, it became an embarrassment before being levelled by the authorities. Is there any greater significance to its story than that? Many would argue not. But while locals and tourists now enjoy the park, some still crave the claustrophobic darkness. Theorists from the wilder shores of architecture keep returning to the idea of Kowloon. On this tiny rectangle of ground, a single community created something that had only existed before in the *avant garde* imagination: the 'organic megastructure'.[119]

The concept of the megastructure emerged in the late 1960s, as a radical departure from the conventional idea of the city. Instead of buildings being arranged around public spaces, streets and squares, the megastructuralists envisioned one continuous city binding citizens together in a set of modular units, capable of unlimited expansion. It was a city designed to live, evolve and adapt, fulfilling all the needs of its people, and with the capacity to endlessly 'plug in' more units to meet changing desires.[120]

Architects pushed this idea to extremes, most sensationally in the work of Alan Boutwell and Michael Mitchell, who in 1969 proposed a 'continuous city for 1,000,000 human beings'.[121] They envisaged a single, linear city, sitting on 100-metre-high pillars, running in a straight line between the Atlantic and Pacific coasts of North America.[122] Kowloon, in effect, was proof of concept. Within its anarchist society, argued the megastructuralists, was the kernel of an architectural utopia.

Others, however, saw Kowloon not as a Petri dish for urban theory, but a model or diorama for a new kind of construction – one that did not exist in the ordinary physical plane, yet was as real as anything that could be seen or touched. The renowned American science fiction writer, William Gibson, described Kowloon, not long before its demolition, as a 'hive of dream'.[123] What Gibson saw in the unregulated, organic chaos of the City of Darkness was an embodiment of his famous concept of 'cyberspace' – or, as we would call it today, the internet.

In its formative years, the internet provided the perfect environment for the establishment of multiple, self-regulating communities. Just like the Walled City, it operated outside of law or external oversight. It was post-design and post-government.[124] Thousands, even millions of Kowloons could spring up at will in cyberspace: digital enclaves thriving on creative and political freedom, possessing an autonomous, dynamic structure that allowed them to grow at a frightening, near-exponential rate. It was also, just like the Walled City, living on borrowed time. 'I'd always maintained that much of the anarchy and craziness of the early internet had a lot to do with the fact that governments just hadn't realised it was there,' commented Gibson. 'It was like this territory came into being, and there were no railroads, there were no lawmen, and people were doing whatever they wanted, but I always took it for granted that the railroads would come and there would be law west of Dodge.'[125]

Yet to Gibson's mind, the people of Kowloon – and the

megastructuralists – were groping towards the next stage in human evolution. He saw the Walled City, that accident of urban birth, as a crude, subconscious schematic of the future, a blueprint for coders and hackers, the architects of the web, to follow. In his 1996 novel *Idoru*, Gibson imagined a virtual Kowloon, a Walled City 2.0 recreated as an ultra-libertarian web sanctuary: 'These people, the ones they say made a hole in the net, they found the data, the history of it. Maps, pictures... They built it again.'[126]

So the wrecking ball may not only have been destroying a notorious slum. Perhaps Kowloon was also the first, true, physical monument to the internet. The city offered a glimpse into the infinite horizons, the structural possibilities – and the inherent amorality – of the digital realm. And as a result, it may also serve as an origin point for an ever-growing, secret structure that lives between the strands of the web. When Gibson's 'They' rebuilt Kowloon digitally, did they create an internet bogeyman? Has the City of Darkness evolved into the 'Dark Net'?

Chapter Seventeen

The Day the Architecture Died

Pruitt-Igoe – St Louis, Missouri
(Born 1951 – Died 1976)

On 4 October 1982, 5,000 people crowded into the Radio City Music Hall in New York[1] to watch the world première of an 87-minute-long feature film with no actors, plot, story or dialogue. The film was the work of a first-time director called Godfrey Reggio, and it had a wilfully obscure and wonderfully unpronounceable title: *Koyaanisqatsi*. While Reggio was an unknown – he had once been an ascetic monk in a Roman Catholic teaching order called the Christian Brothers[2] – his collaborators were not. The *avant-garde* composer, Philip Glass wrote the soundtrack; the renowned experimental cinematographer Ron Fricke shot much of the footage; and Francis Ford Coppola, Oscar-winning director of *The Godfather* and *Apocalypse Now,* was the film's patron.[3]

Koyaanisqatsi opens with a lingering shot of an ancient cave painting in Horseshoe Canyon, Utah. This shifts to a slow-motion explosion, set to repeated chanting of the film's title in a deep bass – revealing that it sounds just like it reads: 'Koy-an-is-kat-si'. What follows is a long, lyrical sequence of sweeping views of the natural environment. The score by Glass is at once seductive and melodic, discordant and oppressive, shifting from repetitive synthesizer lulls to full-blown operatic bombast: 'a sonic weather that surrounds, twists, turns, develops', in the words of one commentator.[4]

Aerial shots drift over the sandstone peaks of Colorado's Monument Valley, the landscape immortalised by the director John Ford as the backdrop to the American West. The camera then moves down to weave through valleys, caves and rock formations. Stop-motion footage – a technique now familiar beyond the point of cliché, but pioneering in 1982 – allows clouds and shadows to race across mountains and deserts. Just under twenty minutes in, humans arrive for the first time. A huge truck fills the screen, spewing out and then disappearing into a cloud of its own black engine smoke. Pipelines cut through the earth, massed ranks of giant electricity pylons march across the plains. A woman and her son are shown lying on a beach. When the camera pans out, however, it reveals that their sunbathing spot is overlooked by the giant concrete spheres of a nuclear power plant. A mushroom cloud from an atomic bomb-test rises up from a desert floor.

At around the half-hour mark, the music pauses, and the camera tracks across the New York skyline – a shot in direct echo of the earlier footage of Monument Valley. Just as before, the viewer is taken down into the landscape, only instead of rock there are gridiron canyons of glass, chrome and steel. Soon, however, the gleaming optimism of these Manhattan skyscrapers gives way to a stark scene of ruin. A tall, stocky, concrete tower-block stands empty and abandoned. Every window appears to be smashed, street-light casings hang limp and loose, and walls are covered in graffiti. The open spaces that surround the block are overgrown and scattered with rubbish and debris.

At this point, Glass's score explodes into propulsive life. A helicopter view shows us that there is not just one tower, but many, lined up in ordered rows, and all in the same state of extreme disrepair. The camera sweeps low over the rooftops, and tracks alongside the broken façades. One shot closes in on a single, shattered window. The darkness beyond it – inside the building – is absolute. As the music reaches a crescendo, we see a tower-block blown up, or rather blown down, in extreme slow-motion. First, great plumes of white dust shoot out from its base; the building remains still for an instant; and then it goes slack, sags, and seems almost to melt into the ground, lost in clouds of rubble.

It is a visceral moment. And, when *Koyaanisqatsi* premiered at the beginning of the 1980s, it was also still a profoundly shocking one. Ruins were supposed to belong to the Old World, yet here they were in the New. Something had gone badly wrong. The building Reggio captured crashing to the ground was already infamous. Its downfall had been picked over in lurid detail by the mass media, in everything from live CBS broadcasts to features in *Time* magazine and the work of the celebrated author Tom Wolfe. It was said to encapsulate a wrong turn in the national dream – and a warning. Set on a 57-acre site to the north of downtown St Louis in the State of Missouri, it was called Pruitt-Igoe. The first great American ruin.

On 16 March 1972, the demolition of Pruitt-Igoe began.[5] According to the influential critic Charles Jencks, this was the moment modern architecture died.[6] 'Boom, boom, boom,' the dynamite blew, and Pruitt-Igoe, 'vandalised, mutilated and defaced', was put out of its misery. Jencks did not want anything built in its place. 'Without doubt, the ruins should be kept,' he wrote.

> 'The remains should have a preservation order slapped on them, so that we keep a live memory of this failure in planning and architecture... As Oscar Wilde said, 'experience is the name we give to our mistakes', and there is a certain health in leaving them judiciously scattered around the landscape as continual lessons.'[7]

The death of Pruitt-Igoe would have huge repercussions for the future of American politics. It came to represent the failure of the vision and ideals of a whole generation. From a shining symbol of postwar optimism, it deteriorated, in a handful of years, into the supreme icon of modernist architectural hubris.

A promotional photograph for Pruitt-Igoe, taken in the mid-1950s, shows a young black family, four children and a mother and father, standing in a glazed internal gallery near the top floor of one of the tower-blocks. These galleries were referred to as 'streets in the air'[8], along which residents would walk to enter their apartments. The family are dressed in their Sunday Best: suits for the father and his three sons, a skirt-suit for the mother, and a plaid skirt, plain shirt and bobby-socks for the daughter.

Promotional shot of a family 'dressed in their Sunday Best' at Pruitt-Igoe, mid-1950s.

They stand backlit by the sun flooding through the gallery window, looking out through the glass, their faint reflections just visible. Much of the view is taken up by another tall tower-block, its flat front sporting similar long lines of windows. The white tiles leading up to the windowsill, and the bare concrete floor, are gleaming in the light. It is an image of remarkable power – its framing profoundly aspirational and unmistakeably American. The fact that the family are wearing their 'church clothes' is no coincidence. It suggests a spiritual reverence for their new home, as well as the none-too-subtle idea of 'salvation'. The implication is that modernist architecture promotes moral values and upward mobility. This photograph captures the attitude recalled many years later by a former resident of Pruitt-Igoe: 'the day I moved in was one of the most exciting of my life'. Or, as another put it, the family had left the slums to live in 'all this newness... the poor man's penthouse'.[9]

Image-making is at the heart of the Pruitt-Igoe story. It was one of the flagship developments to emerge from the 1949 United States Housing Act. For the first time, this Act made large-scale government funding available to city officials for slum clearance, urban redevelopment, and the construction of public housing.[10] Between 1930 and 1940, St Louis was one of only four cities in the whole of the United States to experience a population decline[11] – and this at a time when increased mechanisation in farming was driving agricultural labourers away from the countryside, towards the cities. In part, the decline was a symptom of the growth of the suburb: the bright, new and spacious living areas that were appearing on city fringes, attracting both businesses and the affluent middle class. As the wealth left downtown, it was replaced by chaotic and insanitary slums, filled with poor, unskilled workers: a 'hollow city', where growth flourished on the periphery, and stagnated at the centre.[12]

In 1949, Joseph M. Darst was elected Mayor of St Louis on a ticket of reviving and rebuilding the inner-city. In his campaign, he had made 'the great need of rental housing for the lower income groups' his first priority. He reiterated this vision in his inaugural address: 'If we can clear away the slums and blighted areas of this city, and replace them with the modern, cheerful living accommodations, people will stop moving out of the city... and many will start moving back'.[13] Darst looked to New York as his model. After being given a tour of Manhattan by the city's Mayor William O'Dwyer, he saw St Louis as the perfect place to replicate the thrusting confidence of high-rise living.[14] Pruitt-Igoe was the centrepiece of this ambitious plan.

Between 1951 and 1956, thirty-three identical, eleven-storey, concrete-slab blocks rose up from a vast rectangle of cleared ground that had once housed the DeSoto-Carr ghetto – said to be the worst neighbourhood in the city.[15] The contrast between the dense, organic masses of the surrounding slums, and the tall, pristine and aloof tower-blocks, lined up in rows as if in marching formation, was stark. There can be few better illustrations of the 'shock of the new'.

Darst had taken a leading role in appointing the architectural practice that would build this public housing project. The original firm, which presented rather modest designs for low-rise, terraced row-houses, was replaced swiftly by Leinweber, Yamasaki & Hellmuth. The practice's founder, George Hellmuth, had worked alongside Darst in the 1930s, as architect for the St Louis Division of Bridges and Buildings while Darst was Director of Public Welfare. He brought with him a young and ambitious partner called Minoru Yamasaki. A Japanese-American from Seattle, Yamasaki had previously worked for the New York architectural practices that had been responsible for the Empire State Building and the Rockefeller Centre.[16]

Yamasaki adhered to the purist principles of architectural modernism: a movement characterised by belief in the decadence of all previous architectural forms, subscribing instead to ideals of rationalism and utility, and to the mantra 'form follows function'. Modernist structures were built not to celebrate the greatness of sovereigns or the ruling elite, but wholly to serve the needs of those who lived, worked and played within them. As the godfather of the movement, the Swiss-French architect Le Corbusier, so famously put it, modernists built 'machines for living'. It was just such machines that Darst wanted to fix inner-city St Louis.

Yamasaki's design for the Pruitt-Igoe tower-blocks showcased two – until that point largely theoretical – modernist ideas: skip-stop elevators and glazed internal galleries.[17] By stopping only at the fourth, seventh and tenth floors, the elevators aimed to create mini-community spaces, as residents would be obliged to walk up and down stairwells, and along what Yamasaki called the 'vertical neighbourhoods'[18] of the windowed galleries, to reach their apartments.

The galleries were eleven feet deep and eighty-five feet long, and were intended to be light, open spaces where children could play high up in the sky, still under the watchful eye of their parents. 'Mother can be doing laundry within sight and hearing of child playing in the sun,' explained an article in the *Architectural Forum*, 'not too far away from what may be cooking on the stove'.[19] And, at least to begin with, this architectural vision appeared to become a vivid reality. One former resident recalled the 'smells of pies, cookies and cakes' wafting out of apartments to fill his nostrils as he ran 'up and down these little breezeways' in the midst of groups of excited children. Another recalled her first Christmas in Pruitt-Igoe, when, after receiving a second-hand record player as a present, she put on *Martha Reeves and the Vandellas* 'Dancing in the Streets', threw open her apartment door, and sparked an impromptu party all along the windowed gallery.[20]

Vestibules next to the elevator stops opened out to laundry and storage rooms – further shared spaces intended to promote community living. At the base of the towers were wide expanses of trees and grass: what Yamasaki described as a 'river' of green.[21] Concluding that the high-rise environment was the only solution to the problem of replacing the old slums, the *Architectural Record* commented in 1956 that Yamasaki had managed to design buildings which still allowed 'communities with individual scale and character' to flourish whilst retaining 'all that is possible of the small neighbourhood'.[22]

On completion, Pruitt-Igoe comprised 2,870 housing 'units'[23] with space for over 15,000 tenants[24]: an even higher population density than the slums it replaced. That this public good could be achieved through a design that embraced Le Corbusier's 'three essential joys of urbanism' – 'sun, space and greenery'[25] – seemed a remarkable achievement. The project was also planned as a racially mixed community. The name Pruitt-Igoe came from Wendell O. Pruitt, a black fighter pilot who had won the Distinguished Flying Cross in the Second World War, and William Igoe Homes, a white congressman who had represented the state of Missouri in the 1920s. With 1,736 units, Pruitt was intended for black residents; and with 1,134 units, Igoe was allocated to whites. In 1954, the Supreme Court ruled that this segregation was unconstitutional. As it turned out, the project failed from the outset to attract any white tenants, and Pruitt-Igoe became an entirely black residential area.[26]

The pristine new tower blocks of Pruitt Igoe surrounded by the old downtown slums. 'There can be few better illustrations of the "shock of the new".' © Arthur Whitman, 1954

Darst was delighted with the scheme, and, as early as 1950, before construction of the first blocks had even begun, he was praising the design of Pruitt-Igoe in a speech given at a conference of US city mayors in New York. Indeed, the new development was just the beginning of his plans for the transformation of St Louis. In 1951, he commissioned Leinweber, Yamasaki & Hellmuth to envision an even larger high-rise housing development, aimed at bringing affluent white-collar workers back to the inner-city. The resulting designs proposed three, gigantic, thirty-storey concrete slabs, each of which would contain 1,200 apartments – more than the whole of Igoe.[27] Darst died in June 1953 and saw neither Pruitt-Igoe completed, nor his colossal new modernist scheme advance beyond the drawing board.

In December 1965, James Bailey, a writer for the *Architectural Forum*, took a tour through the galleries and hallways of Pruitt-Igoe. 'The undersized elevators are brutally battered,' he wrote:

> '...and they reek of urine from children who misjudged the time it takes to reach their apartments. By stopping only on every third floor, the elevators offer convenient settings for crime... The galleries are anything but cheerful social enclaves. The tenants call them "gauntlets" through which they must pass to reach their doors... Heavy metal grilles now shield the windows... The steam pipes remain exposed both in the galleries and the apartments, frequently inflicting severe burns... The storage rooms are also locked, and empty. They have been robbed of their contents so often that tenants refuse to use them'.[28]

The title of Bailey's piece was 'The Case History of a Failure'.

Two years later, the journal *Social Work* published the article 'Survival in a Concrete Ghetto'. This brought together the results of a floor-to-floor survey of the residents of Pruitt-Igoe – originally compiled in 1966 in a document called 'A Dream Deferred' – and a statement given to the United States Senate by Dr Lee Rainwater of Washington University, St Louis, who had just completed a three-year sociological study of the housing project.[29] The *Social Work* article painted a horribly bleak picture of decline: 'A visitor driving or walking into Pruitt-Igoe is confronted with what looks like a disaster area.' Broken windows were noted in every building, along with street lights which did not work, and debris – glass, rubble, tin cans – scattered everywhere across the muddy sidewalks. Parking lots were full of abandoned cars and piles of tyres. 'As the visitor nears a building entrance, the filth and debris intensify.'[30]

Rooms at the base of the blocks, originally intended for communal storage, had had their light bulbs removed and their locks broken. They had become dumping grounds for waste, and a haven for mice, rats and cockroaches: 'It takes little imagination to conceive of the dangers that lurk in these dark and filthy rooms,' continued the *Social Work* article. Even after this initial greeting, the lifts came as a shock to the writer: their paint peeling, their walls covered in unidentifiable stains. With no ventilation, the stink of urine inside them was overpowering.[31]

Moving on, the windowed galleries brought to mind 'caricatures of nineteenth-century insane asylums... institutional grey walls line one side of the institutional grey concrete floors. On the other side, rusty screens cover windows whose glass panes have long since disappeared'.[32] The garbage chutes leading down to the incinerators were stuffed and overflowing, and refuse littered the corridors in thick piles. Everywhere, the smell of rot and decay was inescapable. Lights had been smashed from the stairwells connecting lift stops. Once intended as settings for neighbourly chats, these were now places of darkness and fear.[33] As Rainwater summarised adeptly in his testimony to the Senate: 'What started as a precedent-breaking project to improve the lives of the poor in St Louis... has become an embarrassment to all concerned... The words Pruitt-Igoe have become a household term for the worst in ghetto living'.[34]

The occupancy rate of Pruitt-Igoe reached 91 per cent in 1957. It would never go any higher.[35] From that moment on, just a year after the last tower-blocks were completed, it entered a steady, rapid decline. As the numbers of residents dropped, so did the living standards. Petty vandalism and delinquency evolved into serious crime. The fabric of the buildings, from doors and windows to elevators and incinerators, began to degrade.[36] One winter, the pipes burst in several blocks, leaving residents without heating. The cascades of water froze to icicles in the stairwells.[37] Repairs were slow, if they even happened at all. Gangs began to roam the galleries, made up of opportunists who did not even live in the project, and of the children who had once joyfully raced up and down their 'streets in the air'.

One resident recalled how, as a nine-year-old, he had rushed with his mother into a corridor to see his older brother collapsed from a close-range shotgun wound. He described how all his brother's 'innards were out'; and as his mother vainly tried to push them back into his body, he died. 'It took me eight years to stop dreaming about it every night,' he recalled, 'and all I could think about as a kid was how to murder somebody.'[38] By the late 1960s, more of Pruitt-Igoe was empty than was occupied – vacancies had increased to around 70 per cent.[39] Squatters and criminals moved into the vacant apartments, and the cycle of decline and violence intensified.

In 1958, barely two years after Pruitt-Igoe was completed, the St Louis Housing Authority approached the federal government for funds to renovate the tower-blocks. It would be several years before their pleas were answered. In 1965, millions of dollars *were* sunk into Pruitt-Igoe, but by then the hole was too deep.[40] In one year, tenant rents were increased three times, as the city authorities desperately tried to supplement the funds for the renovations.[41] In 1969, Pruitt-Igoe's residents organised a nine-month rent strike in protest.[42] The project was doomed. Even before the strike, the Housing Authority had started to look for a way out. In 1967, they asked the federal government to take over administrative control of Pruitt-Igoe, or let them demolish it.[43] Five years later, in 1972, the government sanctioned the demolition.

Pruitt-Igoe's remaining residents were moved into eleven of the project's thirty-three tower-blocks. On 16 March 1972, a trial demolition of one building was attempted. Only half was destroyed in the detonation, and the event was covered only by the local press, poor weather having kept the television crews away.[44] A month later, however, on 21 April, one of Pruitt-Igoe's largest slab blocks, 92 metres long, was scheduled for a second trial demolition. The building was just 18 years old. CBS news cameras and Associated Press photographers took their positions high up in an adjacent tower.[45] Their vantage point gave them a view – far in the distance and just peeking above the roofs of the doomed blocks – of St Louis' most iconic architectural feature: the great curve of the 'Gateway Arch'.

Watched by the implacable façades of the surrounding slab towers, the block imploded from its base in a burst of white dust. This time, the images of the destruction were circulated across the nation, and around the world. At first the St Louis Housing Authority did not intend to level all of Pruitt-Igoe; its aim was to reduce it to a more manageable size.[46] It had not counted on the demolition images becoming symbols of the general failure of public housing.[47] The first modernist dominoes had fallen, and amid the media clamour and public outcry, the rest would have to go with them. As is often the case, however, once the cameras had been switched off, the show did not remain quite so spectacular. Over the next five years, Pruitt-Igoe endured a slow and methodical death. Wrecking ball crews worked their way systematically over the vast site.[48] The flattened rubble of the towers was left behind, just where it lay.

The second, widely televised demolition, in April 1972.

So what went wrong? In the aftermath of the demolitions, critics did not have to look far for a culprit. The blame was placed squarely at the – functionalist, utilitarian and most likely concrete – door of modern architecture. There was something, it was claimed, inherently flawed in the design, an inbuilt propensity for failure. As Charles Jencks argued in his own barbed verdict on Pruitt-Igoe, the project was a slavish devotee of the ideals of modernism, and as such was 'heir' to its 'congenital naiveties'. Chief among these naiveties was the belief that 'good form was to lead to good content, or at least good conduct; the intelligent planning of abstract space was to promote healthy behaviour'. The 'purity of design' principle running throughout the architectural DNA of Pruitt-Igoe was 'meant to instil, by good example, corresponding virtues in the inhabitants'.[49] Modernism had placed its faith in the power of design to act as a social corrective. The disintegration and demolition of the project seemed to toll the death knell of the movement.

In 1972, just as the first demolitions of Pruitt-Igoe were taking place, the architectural theorist Oscar Newman published a hugely influential work called *Defensible Space*. Exploring the connection between physical environments and human behaviour, it grew directly out of Newman's own experiences – he was a teacher at Washington University in St Louis – of watching Pruitt-Igoe fall apart. Pruitt-Igoe, wrote Newman, 'was designed by one of the country's most eminent architects and was hailed as the new Enlightenment'.[50] It was dominated by communal spaces: walkways, stairwells, laundry and garbage rooms, and Yamasaki's 'river of trees'. These were meant to belong to everyone, but, for Newman, they belonged ultimately to no one. They were 'indefensible spaces'.

> 'Because all grounds were common and disassociated from the units, residents could not identify with them. The areas proved unsafe. The river of trees soon became a sewer of glass and garbage... Such anonymous

> public spaces made it impossible for even neighbouring residents to develop an accord about acceptable behaviour in these areas. It was impossible to feel or exert proprietary feelings, impossible to tell resident from intruder'.[51]

Directly across the street from Pruitt-Igoe was Carr Square Village, one of the older downtown slums. Throughout the decline of the modernist housing project, Carr Square had remained fully occupied and relatively untroubled by deprivation, crime or violence. Newman could only conclude that the difference in behaviour in these two, near-identical, side-by-side populations was environment.[52] Ironically, the project designed specifically to promote community and harmony had succeeded in destroying them.

This narrative of Pruitt-Igoe as a failure of design acquired widespread currency. Standard textbooks such as Mark la Gory and John Pipkin's *Urban Social Space* used the project as a template for what not to do. 'Pruitt-Igoe,' they wrote, 'has proved an instructive, albeit costly, error'.[53] Like Newman, they made unfavourable comparisons between modernism's austere purity and the vibrancy of the old slums.

> 'Lower-class slums may not normally be healthy environments, but they are vital and bursting with social activity. The dirty streets and littered back alleys provide space where informal social networks may flourish. Such semi-private spaces were not available in the high-rise, in which hallways were designed for access to the home only.'[54]

For La Gory and Pipkin, Yamasaki's design was more conducive to confrontation than community. In a rather cheap aside, they remarked that it was hardly surprising that the project's most famous resident had been the prize fighter, Leon Spinks. Pruitt-Igoe, they argued, was simply in the vanguard of a wider problem. 'Public housing has been a failure,' they wrote, as 'social structures have disintegrated in the desolate high-rise settings'. Modernism – and Pruitt-Igoe – had to be abandoned. 'When built it won an architectural prize, but it epitomized the ills of public housing.'[55]

This last sentence is revealing. In fact, Pruitt-Igoe never won any architectural prize. Yet this mistake recurs continually in accounts of the housing project.[56] Charles Jencks even names the prize and the date, claiming it won a design award from the American Institute of Architects in 1951.[57] Accolades and acclamation for Pruitt-Igoe have become a key part of the archetypal narrative of its failure – even though they are not true. Inevitably, this scholarly bout of Chinese whispers crossed into the popular domain, where it mutated even further. Author Tom Wolfe's journalistic polemic against the modern movement, *From Bauhaus to Our House*, first cited the fictitious award, before inventing a fantastical scene in which the demolition 'task force' convened a meeting with the residents of Pruitt-Igoe to ask them for their suggestions as to what to do with the project. 'The chant began immediately,' Wolfe wrote: '"Blow it... *up*! Blow it... *up*! Blow it... *up*!" The next day the task force thought it over. The poor buggers were right. It was the only solution.'[58]

Even Pruitt-Igoe's own architects bought into this story of inglorious failure. In a rather astonishing *mea culpa,* one of the project's associate designers, George Kassabaum, remarked that, 'You had middle class whites like myself designing for an entirely different group.'[59] Yamasaki, for his part, later insisted that he did not see high-rises as the *best* solution to the problem of public housing, but as the *most efficient* given the economic realities. 'If I had no economic or social limitations, I'd solve all my problems with one-storey buildings,' he said.[60] In his 1979 autobiography *A Life in Architecture*, he reflected that, 'no matter how good he may be, an architect is still to a great extent controlled by the attitudes and conceptions of the clients, people, and society that surround him.'[61] And when it came to Pruitt-Igoe, he lamented that, 'I never thought people were that destructive.'[62] At the same time as his first major work was being razed to the ground, Yamasaki was overseeing the design and construction of a great new

American monument: the Twin Towers of the World Trade Centre in New York City. He died of cancer in 1986. Fifteen years later, on 11 September 2001, people would prove more destructive than he could ever have imagined.

As the opponents of modernism grew, the movement and its ideals came under increasingly vociferous attack. Jencks, for instance, an adherent of that most elusive of concepts – post-modernism – was positively gleeful at the demise of Pruitt-Igoe. In his landmark 1977 treatise, *The Language of Post-modern Architecture,* he used the St Louis project as the launch-point for a scathing assault:

> 'Let us then romp through the desolation of modern architecture, and the destruction of our cities, like some Martian tourist out on an earthbound excursion, visiting the archaeological sites with a superior disinterest, bemused by the sad but instructive mistakes of a former architectural civilisation. After all, since it was fairly dead, we might as well enjoying picking over the corpse.'[63]

Jencks did not dispute the power of design. Indeed, in his criticism of Pruitt-Igoe he fingered it as the sole cause of the project's failure. Decades earlier, the father of modern American architecture, Frank Lloyd Wright, had written that he 'saw the architect as the saviour of the culture of modern American society... saviour now as for all civilisations heretofore'.[64] Of course, it suited the profession to assert its central importance to culture and society. 'Good' buildings could transform people for the better. 'Bad' buildings – among which Jencks included such woefully misguided modernist structures as Pruitt-Igoe – could trigger rapid breakdown. Architects, by implication, wielded enormous powers of salvation or destruction. The Italian theorist Giancarlo de Carlo wrote in 1972 of the 'broad and ambiguous meanings... of the architect', who, 'depending on reigning forces... has always been more of a chief bricklayer, or more of a god.'[65] Jencks and his twentieth-century contemporaries leaned decisively towards the role of 'god'. They disagreed only over what type of 'god' they should be.

In an article published in the *Journal of Architectural Education* in 1991, the academic Katherine G. Bristol took aim at this lofty conceit. She called the belief in the primacy of architecture '*The Pruitt-Igoe Myth*'. Elevating the demolition of one housing project to a watershed moment in architecture and a symbol of ideological failure was, Bristol argued, at best unhelpful, and at worst insidious. Instead, she returned to the historical context framing the modernist experiment in St Louis, and proposed an entirely different theory for Pruitt-Igoe's downfall.[66]

The scheme, she recalled, had been pushed through by a bullish mayor looking to reinvigorate a city in crisis: old industries failing, population declining, wealth deserting. Pruitt-Igoe had been intended to be revolutionary and transformative – the saviour of St Louis.[67] When the project was conceived, there was huge demand for new, affordable public housing. Pruitt-Igoe was built on the basis that this demand would continue rising: after all, if the city was going to embark on such a major government-funded construction project, then it needed to ensure that the finished product offered room for growth. Pruitt-Igoe wasn't built to house an existing population, but an anticipated one.[68]

As early as 1954, however, when the first tower-blocks opened, there were signs that this population influx would not materialise. The ongoing movement of the wealthy to the suburbs freed up housing in the inner-city, and many families chose these newly vacated private dwellings over the public housing of Pruitt-Igoe. The knock-on effect on the project was significant, and financially disastrous. The 1949 Housing Act had provided the seed money to build, but the local housing authorities were expected to fund the ongoing operation and the maintenance of projects through tenant rents. Housing schemes had to become self-sufficient.[69]

Moreover, it was clear even from the outset that the massive scale of Pruitt-Igoe was problematic. Yamasaki and his colleagues had neither design *carte blanche* nor an unlimited budget. They had to meet targets for population density, and were restricted by the dimensions and locations of the site. Their original proposal had mixed high-rise, mid-rise and low-rise structures. This was accepted in principle by the St Louis Housing Authority, but resulted in a cost-per-unit that exceeded federal government stipulations. The final layout of the thirty-three, eleven-storey slab blocks was a compromise imposed by budget.[70] The cost-cutting did not stop there. Plans drawn up to surround the towers with children's playgrounds, landscaping and ground-floor public toilets ended up being scrapped.[71] The materials used in the construction were often chosen on the grounds of cost rather than because they were the most suitable for the job[72]: 'The quality of the hardware was so poor that doorknobs and locks were broken on initial use,' wrote the political scientist Eugene Meehan in a 1979 study of the development. 'Windowpanes were blown from inadequate frames by wind pressure. In the kitchen, cabinets were made of the thinnest plywood possible.'[73] If Yamasaki was a god, the resources he commanded were curiously limited.

The original intention was for Pruitt-Igoe to house working families: that bright vision encapsulated in the promotional images that accompanied the project's opening. The housing authority's need to find tenants, however, saw a substantial shift towards those on welfare. By the late 1960s, adult males accounted for only 10 per cent of the project's entire population. Broken families became the norm in Pruitt-Igoe. This was exacerbated by a bizarre policy that forbade any able-bodied man from sharing an apartment with any woman receiving financial aid for dependent children.[74] Even fathers were not allowed to live with their families. Some stayed, hiding in cupboards when the authority inspectors made their visits[75], but many others felt they had no option but to leave.

The lack of rental income from the growing numbers of apartment vacancies caused a massive drop in the level of maintenance. Broken fittings, fixtures and windows were not repaired. A single janitor, expected to sweep the corridors, galleries and laundry rooms, mop the elevator and stairwells daily, and replace missing or burned-out bulbs, could be responsible for several buildings at once.[76] Ever poorer-quality materials were supplied for repairs, and the housing authority began to charge for replacing broken items. Everything from windows and door locks, to fuses and bath plugs, carried a price tag.[77]

Bristol dubbed Pruitt-Igoe a 'programmed failure'[78], arguing that it could never have worked. From the moment public housing projects began to appear, they were viewed as decidedly un-American. They carried with them the whiff of socialism, even of communism. It was one thing to build them – that provided work for private enterprise during the construction phase. It was quite another to keep them in good order once they were complete. Pruitt-Igoe could not be separated from the heated politics of welfare – and of race. Some blamed the black population. The *Washington Post* suggested that there was an 'incompatibility between the high-rise structure and the large poor families who came to inhabit it, only a generation removed from the farm.'[79] This attitude was symptomatic of the casual prejudice and social indifference with which America's inner-city poverty was regarded.

In Bristol's view, the city and the government steadily turned their backs on Pruitt-Igoe – and public housing policy in general – ultimately forcing it to fail. Architecture was just a sideshow. Yet the popular, media-friendly fable of modernism's fall continued to dominate, helping to obscure the deeper problems in American society. According to this story, it was not class, the poverty gap, race, or government policy that needed solving. It was merely the shape, size and design of a building.

Charles Jencks got his wish for Pruitt-Igoe – the ruins were kept. While there was no 'preservation order' or memorial plaque, the site has remained almost completely undeveloped up to the present day. It still sits just to the north of downtown St Louis, bounded by

Cass, Carr and Jefferson Avenues, and North Twentieth Street. It is surrounded by a chain-link fence and concertina wire. Inside, it has filled up with trees and vegetation, forming a dense urban wilderness. Myths and scare-stories continue to attach themselves to the site: venture into the interior, some say, and you will be hunted down and attacked by packs of feral stray dogs.[80]

Pruitt-Igoe's main function over the past four decades has been as official and unofficial city dumping ground. In 1993, the state authority unloaded hundreds of tonnes of rubble created by the demolition and reconstruction of large areas of central St Louis. While plans have emerged intermittently for the redevelopment of the Pruitt-Igoe site – as industrial park, golf course, retail centre, hotel complex, even a residential project called Gateway Village – none has taken hold.[81] Instead, it has become a graveyard for the castaways of the changing city. New deposits of broken concrete slabs, iron street-car rails and smashed bricks lie on top of the fragmentary remains of the tower-blocks. The original road networks still lead through the trees, providing convenient access for the city dump trucks. Here and there, sections of the old kerb-sides peek from the accumulated debris. One of Yamasaki's electricity substations remains completely intact, as does a solitary street-light. In places, piles of obsolete technology rise up: old phones and fax machines among layers of office furniture.[82] If Jencks' 'Martian archaeologists' ever excavate Pruitt-Igoe, one wonders what conclusions they will reach about twentieth-century humanity.

In 2011, an international design competition invited new proposals for the site's future, which the organisers explained 'had already been, in turn, both utopian and dystopian'.[83] Architects, planners, designers, writers and artists were asked the open-ended question: 'What is Pruitt-Igoe Now?' The symbolic deadline for entries was 16 March 2012, exactly forty years after the first trial demolitions. The competition received over 348 submissions from around the world.[84]

In the finalists' proposals, the fatalistic history of Pruitt-Igoe was addressed directly, and then turned on its head. The result was a series of visions for new 'urban utopias' driven not by architecture, but by systems. 'Carr Square Brick Yard' subverted the site's current role as a dump for building materials, by imagining it as a community-run *source* of them. From the ruins of Pruitt-Igoe there would emerge a storage site for salvaged bricks, along with a newly-built brick-works manufacturing more to meet demand.[85]

Another entry, 'Recipe Landscape', proposed an inner-city farm to feed the people. Pruitt-Igoe would become home to cattle and beehives, literally turning into 'the land of milk and honey'. A dairy and creamery would be built, and all ingredients for the production of ice-cream would be grown in or derived from the site, so that as its designers put it, 'a landscape of loss is transformed into one of production, growth and sustenance'. The ice cream – 'the 31 flavours of Pruitt-Igoe' – would be distributed to stores across St Louis.[86]

'Pruitt-Igoe National Park', meanwhile, advocated giving the site over to the National Park Service, to be managed as a protected wilderness, with paths and interpretive signs, picnic stops and public toilets. Apart from these visitor-friendly interventions, Pruitt-Igoe would remain untouched, its trees and vegetation growing unhindered.[87] Some of the other ideas were more literal. 'The Museum of Attempted Utopias' envisaged a giant 'burial mound for modern architecture' containing a series of underground exhibition spaces.[88] Others were positively surreal: 'Double Moon', for example, proposed a massive artificial moon above the site, its light ensuring that it would never become socially 'invisible' again.[89]

The winner of the competition was the 'St Louis Ecological Assembly Line: Pruitt-Igoe as a Productive Landscape'. In this proposal, the current wilderness of urban forest would be managed as a tree and plant nursery, supplying the 13,000 acres of parks throughout St Louis. At the same time, 'aquaculture' basins would be developed on-site to raise native fish and mussels, which would be used to replenish stocks in the Mississippi River, which have become endangered by industrial pollution. Rather than producing material goods, this 'assembly line' would be a source of ecological and biological diversity – a 'green corridor' whose values could radiate throughout all of St Louis.[90]

As the organisers concluded: 'Just as the paper utopias of the 1920s were realised, formally, in the 1954 Pruitt-Igoe towers, the utopian proposals advanced in this competition, too, have the potential to be built – *sparked? started? planted?* – in another twenty years, perhaps less.' At the same time, they pointed out that these new 'systems utopias raise as many questions as they answer.'[91] Who would manage them? How would workers be paid – if they were paid at all? What economies would sustain them, and who were they ultimately intended to benefit?

Pruitt-Igoe was always about utopia. In its first incarnation, it became utopia's graveyard. Could it one day – this unlikely rectangle of ground in a mid-western American city – become its birthplace?

Chapter Eighteen

The Mirrorwall

The Berlin Wall – Berlin, East and West Germany
(Born 1961 – Died 1989)

Berlin, in the latter half of the twentieth century, was a city of opposites, and because it was a city of opposites, it had to be divided in two. Running right through the middle of the city, for some 40 kilometres, there was a wall. The wall cut across streets; it passed between buildings; it extended over roads, railway tracks and even lakes[1]. Sometimes, it dropped down below the ground to block tunnels. When people on either side came to look at the wall, they saw themselves looking right back. Every day, the wall told them 'who was the fairest one of all'.[2]

On the eastern side, people were told the wall was built to keep other people out. On the western side, they were told it was built to keep other people in. On the east, people wanted to cross the wall, but they were forbidden from doing so. On the west, they were allowed to cross the wall, but they did not want to. For twenty-eight years, the wall split Berlin. On the west they stopped noticing it – or when they did notice it, they painted it with bright and colourful pictures, and wrote messages and slogans all over it. On the east it remained untouched, apart from a framing of barbed wire, reflecting everything back in an unwavering monochrome.

Then, one November evening, just like that, the news spread that the wall was gone. Everyone rushed to see, and on the site of the wall they shook hands and kissed and danced through the night. In that moment, the people of Berlin realised that they weren't opposites after all. And, as they watched the people of Berlin realising this, other people all over the world realised the same thing too. Deep down, everyone was the same. Everyone wanted peace and happiness and to get along. Everyone wanted an end to the violence that could be caused by opposites. The fall of the Berlin wall was not just the end of a story – it was also the end of *history.*[3]

Not everyone believes in fairy tales. It is nice to believe that a barrier that kept Berliners apart for nearly three decades could just disappear, as if by magic. But is anything ever really that simple? A physical wall can be demolished very quickly. What about the wall, though, that remains in people's heads?[4]

The Berlin Wall was born at 1am on 13 August 1961: a Saturday night, already turned into a Sunday morning, at the height of summer. Some 10,000 men – a mix of soldiers, police, government officials and co-opted factory workers – were the midwives.[5] Streetlights were extinguished across a swathe of the city, and organized units set to work in the darkness, unloading and erecting some 300 tons of barbed wire barricades; if they had been laid out straight, they would have stretched for over 3,000 kilometers.[6] Every one of the 193 streets leading between the west and east sides of Berlin was closed. S-Bahn and U-Bahn lines were blocked off. The *Volkspolizei*, the 'People's Police' of East Germany, even descended into the sewer systems to keep watch over the tunnels and shafts that united the two subterranean halves of the city. Beneath the neoclassical columns of the Brandenburg Gate, soldiers with pneumatic drills tore apart the road surface and broke up the pavements.[7]

All over the city, in places like the large central square of Potsdamer Platz, concrete posts were thrown up to act as pylons for the strings of barbed wire. By 6am, before the vast majority of Berliners on either side had even contemplated rising from their beds, the work was complete.[8] The city had been cut in half by a physical line of iron, steel, mesh and concrete.

Division was nothing new to Berlin. In the aftermath of the Second World War, the city had been carved up between the victorious Allies: four ways, into British, America, French, and Soviet quarters. It was soon obvious, however, that four really meant two. The city was becoming the postwar world in microcosm. By 1949, defeated Germany had re-emerged as two separate republics: one Federal, one, in name at least, Democratic. The former was capitalist, backed by the Western Allies; the latter communist, receiving the patronage of the Soviet Union. Two diametrically opposed ideologies met in the heart of a city devastated by global conflict. Berlin was bombed-out and bullet-scarred. It was a city of ruins and empty spaces, a city facing a stark choice: rebuild or die. The split in the city created a unique testing ground for two competing economic systems. Which of the two new Berlins would come out on top? The city of the free market, or the city of the worker's paradise?

A further complication was Berlin's location. The west side of the city, affiliated to the Federal Republic, was surrounded by territory belonging to the Democratic Republic. West Berlin was an island of capitalism in a communist sea. And that sea was frequently rough. The Soviet Premier, Nikita Khrushchev, hit on a characteristically indelicate metaphor: for him, the city was 'the testicles of the West.' He explained: 'When I want the West to scream, I squeeze on Berlin.'[9]

The Soviets had already made their intentions clear in June 1948, when they blockaded the city as a first step towards annexing it completely. The blockade lasted for nearly a year, but was foiled by a concerted campaign of Allied air-drops, with 1,500 cargo flights a day landing at Tempelhof airport.[10] The crisis ushered in new era in world politics – the 'Cold War'. This was a war characterized by entrenchment and stalemate, punctuated by incidents of almost unbearable tension. The nuclear age gave a terrifying new dimension to global conflict – the prospect of mutually assured destruction. Any flashpoint had the potential to trigger a worldwide holocaust and the end of the human race. And all this pressure, fear, suspicion, mistrust and dread began to centre on Berlin. On world maps, the city might as well have been represented by a big red button.

Throughout the 1950s, it appeared that capitalism was winning. West Berlin became known as the *Schaufenster* – the 'show window'. It offered a glittering demonstration of the consumer society and all that the communist East was missing out on. In just over a decade, nearly three million political refugees crossed from East to West Germany.[11] By July 1961, people were leaving at the rate of 30,000 a month. On 1 August, the East German leader Walter Ulbricht petitioned Khrushchev for approval to seal the border. The Soviets were very concerned about the repercussions of such a provocative act. The logistics also seemed torturous. What, Khrushchev asked Ulbricht, about the many places where the border crossed streets, or ran through houses?

'We have a specific plan,' replied the East German leader. 'In the houses with exits into West Berlin, they will be walled up. In other places, barbed wire will be erected. The barbed wire has already been delivered. It can all happen very quickly.'[12] Reluctantly, the Soviets agreed: one way or another, the exodus had to be stopped. Khrushchev's subsequent message to the West German ambassador in Moscow was almost apologetic. 'I know that the Wall is an ugly thing,' he wrote. 'It will also disappear. However, only when the reasons for its construction have gone.'[13] This was the final tug of the ropes that drew shut the 'Iron Curtain'. Thousands of kilometres of fencing already lined the border between the Eastern Bloc and Western Europe, but there was still relative freedom of movement between the two halves of Berlin. On 13 August, that last chink of light disappeared.

So quietly and efficiently did the wall go up that the city was taken wholly by surprise. The western intelligence services, for instance, had no inkling of what was about to happen. Ordinary people on both sides were too shocked to do anything. 'East Berlin was dead,' recalled one resident. 'It was as if a bell-jar had been placed over it and all the air sucked out.'[14] For some, however, particularly the younger generation, the mood changed quickly. In West Berlin, shock became anger; in East Berlin, it turned to panic.

Escape from Bernauer Strasse, 1961

Bernauer Strasse was one of the places Khrushchev had picked out as problematic. While front doors led out into the East, back windows looked over the West. Residents – and, as word spread, many others – began jumping or climbing from one half of Berlin to the other. A crowd gathered on the western side to help, including a group of eager firemen, holding out tarpaulins to catch people.[15] At the same time, the communist *Volkspolizei* were trying frantically to clear the buildings. In a highly symbolic moment, one man attempting to flee found himself half-out of a window, held by his arms by the East German police from above, and pulled by his ankles by West German citizens from below. After a brief struggle – it must have seemed interminable to the man himself – he tumbled down into the street. The windows of Bernauer Strasse were bricked up. Some still tried to escape over its rooftops, and a number died falling into the West.

Both sides had their iconic moments. On 15 August, on the corner of Bernauer Strasse and Ruppiner Strasse, a nineteen-year-old East German soldier, Corporal Conrad Schumann, deserted his post to hurdle the barbed wire barrier strung across the border he was supposed to be guarding. Remarkably, a photographer standing on the western side captured him mid-jump. In full uniform and helmet, with his rifle still slung over his shoulder, he is pictured hanging in the air, staring anxiously down at the thick rolls of wire directly below him. In this moment, he is neither in the East nor the West. He is a man in no-man's land.

On the same day, on Zimmerstrasse, at the border post known famously as 'Checkpoint Charlie', the twenty-one-year-old Hagen Koch, a private in East Germany's National People's Army with a background in cartography, was part of a unit tasked with surveying and mapping the new fortifications. Zimmerstrasse was near the centre of the city and had drawn a large and vocal crowd of demonstrators from the western side. One of Koch's jobs was to mark the exact line of the border between East and West. In places, this required actually drawing the line in white paint.[16]

'It was an ordinary summer day,' recalled Koch. 'I had my left leg in the East, my right leg in the West, and I drew my white line across the street.' The western crowd focused their abuse on Koch. 'I concentrated on the line and not what was happening around me,' he continued. 'I thought to myself that those in the West were enemies, looters and profiteers.'[17]

Koch's white line was presented as the product of the honest toil of the eastern worker in the face of aggressive western provocation. Its purpose was more than just metaphorical, though. Up to this point, the Berlin Wall was not strictly speaking a wall at all, but a stretch of barbed wire and fencing. On 18 August, however, that began to change. It started at prominent locations like Potsdamer Platz and the Brandenburg Gate, where there were large stretches of open ground. On top of Koch's white line, bulky square blocks of concrete were laid, each 1.2 metres high and 0.3m thick.[18] Originally prepared for use in prefabricated housing, they had now been requisitioned for the Wall. No foundations were dug, and the blocks were assembled at high speed. On top of these lowest slabs, layers of smaller blocks were added and mortared together. Finally, Y-shaped metal uprights were fixed at regular intervals for the stringing of barbed wire.[19]

It may have been structurally flimsy, but this wall was symbolically potent. Within days, similar stretches had sprung up throughout the centre of the city. The original, tangled lines of barbed wire may, in fact, have been more effective as practical barriers. But they lacked a certain psychological impact desired by the East German authorities. The monolithic grey blocks represented permanence.

Erecting the Wall was a supremely reductive act. It removed all political subtlety, and simplified the world to a series of competing dualities: East versus West; Capitalist versus Communist; Us versus Them; friend versus enemy. At stake was the ultimate judgment: who was good and who was evil? It was this that made the Wall not just a wall, but also a mirror. For those on either side, to look at it was not to see through it or over it, but to see their own reflections.

On 1 September 1961, two young, talented East German film-makers working for the state-run film studio – the director Frank Vogel and the scriptwriter Paul Wiens – began shooting a new feature called '*...und deine Liebe auch*' – '...and also your love'. Its subject, and its central dramatic device, was the Wall.[20]

The entire film crew consisted of Vogel and Wiens, two cameramen, and three professional actors. In the first few days after the Wall appeared, a 10-page 'memorandum' was produced, outlining a structure for the film, along with a series of artistic doctrines to underpin its production.[21] Although a fictional story, it was to be shot like a documentary. Almost two-thirds of the film was to be set in exterior, public locations. Make-up and costumes were not to be used; the use of artificial lighting was also excluded, even when shooting indoors. The crew had a van with an opening roof, 50,000 metres of film, an American Bell & Howell camera, and a French Cameflex camera.[22] This style of working – and, in the case of the Cameflex, the camera itself – were in homage to avant-garde French 'New Wave' film-making. Just over a year before, in March 1960, the director Jean-Luc Godard had released his seminal feature '*À Bout de*

Souffle' – 'Breathless' – to a rapturous critical reception. Starring the French actor Jean-Paul Belmondo and the American actress Jean Seaberg, it had been shot over just twenty-three days in Paris in August and September 1959.

Vogel and Wiens were eager to bring Godard's ground-breaking approach – his refined editing techniques combined with gritty visual authenticity – to bear on their story of the Wall. And, as in the work of another New Wave director – Alain Resnais' film '*Hiroshima mon Amour*' – they would use as their narrative vehicle 'a minor, personal story of three young people... meshed with the major history of our times'.[23]

In '*...und deine Liebe auch*', Berlin becomes the setting for a love-triangle between two half-brothers, Ulli and Klaus, and the object of their desire, Eva. The film begins on 12 August 1961, the anniversary of the death of the brothers' mother, and, of course, the day before the erection of the Wall. Ulli is a party official and administrator at an electrics factory, and Klaus is a taxi-driver working both sides of Berlin. Whereas Ulli's job contributes to the common good of the East German nation, his younger brother's is solitary and selfish. Klaus is, as outlined in the script notes, 'energetic, confident, eloquent and cheery'[24], yet he is also apolitical and thus, by implication, amoral. The two brothers go with Eva to the 'Budapest' dance club to celebrate their mother's memory. There, in a wonderful piece of socialist product-placement, they drink Russian champagne.[25] Ulli, however, has to leave early. He has important party work to do.

The next day, 13 August, Klaus and Eva come across Ulli standing guard on a bridge as the borders between the two halves of Berlin are sealed with barbed wire. Later on, Ulli meets a Cuban friend Alfredo, and as the two comrades stand by the bridge, they sing 'We are Socialists' together in Spanish. Ulli happens to have a guitar to hand, while Alfredo uses a Kalshnikov magazine for percussion.[26] As the film develops, Eva's turmoil grows over the competing affections of the two brothers. She is attracted to Ulli's principles and upright character, but ultimately succumbs to the charms of passionate, impulsive Klaus, and becomes pregnant with his child. One scene uses a real stand-off between American and Soviet armoured vehicles at Checkpoint Charlie in October 1961 to make an important political point.[27] Eva, the expectant East German mother, is frightened as she witnesses an open display of western belligerence. And she is thankful that the Wall is there to protect her and her unborn child.

Ultimately, Klaus decides to desert both Eva and his nation. In the climactic scene of the film he attempts to escape over the Wall to the West, via the graveyard alongside the infamous Bernauer Strasse. The scene is all the more dramatic because the cemetery is also where the two brothers' mother is buried. Ulli has followed Klaus, and they come to blows in the darkness. The commotion brings border guards from both East and West. As Klaus attempts to scale the Wall, Ulli is shot by a West Berlin police officer. The two brothers collapse to the ground on the eastern side. One is taken to hospital, while the other is arrested.

After visiting Ulli, who is recovering from his wound, Eva goes to see Klaus in a labour camp. She tells him that, with the birth of their child, she wants them to start 'a new life' together.[28] Wiens emphasised in his script that Klaus was not to be seen as a criminal. Instead he was 'our class-brother on whom we must use all measures possible to bring back to us and to educate... He is one of us but does not know it yet.'[29] His failed escape is his salvation. His reconciliation with Eva is a symbol of hope for East Germany. The erection of the Wall marks an optimistic new chapter in the history of the Democratic Republic. It marks the rebirth of the nation.[30]

'...*und deine Liebe auch*' was just one component of the Democratic Republic's concerted public relations and propaganda campaign. While some messages were cynical in the best (or worst) traditions of political spin, others demonstrated the strength of feeling and ideological pride behind the East's utopian socialist project. Wiens, for instance, admitted that his film had almost been titled '*German Democratic Republic – My Love*'.[31] Both he and Vogels believed they were making good art for a good cause. Often, there was a quasi-religious message: that only the selfless and the righteous could build the worker's paradise. As Hagen Koch, the painter of the white line of the Wall, said of defectors: 'These people were shirking the hard work that had to be done here in order to build a better future for themselves – they wanted to enjoy their lives right here, right now... they allowed themselves to be seduced by the lure of the West.'[32]

On the one hand, the East German government tried to play down the significance of the Wall. They were merely instituting, as *Neues Deutschland,* the official newspaper of the ruling Socialist Unity Party, explained, something found 'on the borders of every foreign state' – a 'method for the control and supervision'[33] of the movement of people between different nations. As the characters Ulli and Eva repeat matter-of-factly several times during '*...und deine Liebe auch*': 'You have to put a border somewhere.'[34]

At the same time, the authorities defined the Wall as a particular solution to a particular problem. They had given a name to the movement of citizens from East to West. It was not 'escape', but '*Menschenhandel*' – 'human trafficking'.[35] 'Spy headquarters' in West Germany and West Berlin, claimed *Neues Deutschland,* were responsible for the 'systematic recruitment' of citizens of the Democratic Republic.[36] It was, they said, a calculated policy of corruption – and, in some cases, even kidnapping.

In a state television interview broadcast five days after the Wall was erected, the East German leader Walter Ulbricht declared that the West was attempting to destabilize their nation to 'create the conditions in which... it would have been possible to launch an open attack'.[37] The Federal Republic was, he claimed, aggressive and imperialist – a new incarnation of the Third Reich. And so the Wall was built for defence. It was an essential measure to strengthen the position of the 'peaceful state' of the Democratic Republic and to secure 'the self-confidence of its citizens'.[38] The East German government never referred to the Wall simply as 'the Wall'. Instead it was always the '*Antifaschistischer Schutzwall*' – the '*Anti-fascist Protection Rampart*'.

The West certainly saw a Wall. Indeed, they saw a *'Schandmauer'* – a '*Wall of Shame*'. The Mayor of West Berlin, using his own Nazi analogy in return, labelled East Berlin – and by extension East Germany – 'the biggest concentration camp of all time'.[39] Others regarded this sealing of the border as a last, desperate act. What legitimacy could the Democratic Republic claim if the only way of stopping its citizens from leaving was to erect 'a dividing line of barbed wire, concrete walls and bayonets'?[40] On his visit to Berlin in 1963, John F. Kennedy called the Wall 'the most repulsive and strongest demonstration of the failure of the Communist system'.[41]

On 17 August 1962, just over a year after the Wall was erected, two East German teenagers, Peter Fechter and Helmut Kulbeik, attempted to make it across the city border. They hid in a carpenter's workshop in Zimmerstrasse, near Checkpoint Charlie, and watched the guards going through their daily routine. Finally, they broke cover, jumping out of the workshop window and sprinting to the base of the Wall. Kulbeik made it over, but Fechter did not. He was shot in the pelvis by East German soldiers, and collapsed screaming at the base of the Wall. Mutual distrust and fear prevented soldiers and civilians on either side from attempting to give medical help. Peter Fechter lay in the shadow of the wall for over an hour before he bled to death. Press photographs of the dying young man, taken from the western side through the barbed wire fixed to the top of the Wall, circulated around the world.[42] It was a shocking and visceral image – a terrible sequel to the photograph of Corporal Schumann vaulting the border. Schumann was merely frozen for an instant between sides. Fechter was caught there forever, his blood a permanent addition to the Wall's foundations.

The East Germans dismissed Fechter as a 'provocateur caught in the act'.[43] Look instead, they said, at twenty-one-year-old Peter Göring, the first border guard of the Democratic Republic to die at the Wall. Göring was shot and killed by a West German police officer on 23 May 1962, as he tried to stop a fourteen-year-old boy from swimming to the west across a canal. The East German press claimed Göring was the victim of an assassination plot, elevating him to the status of martyr. Obituaries depicted a perfect, humble socialist hero, who made the ultimate sacrifice for the 'great, just cause'.[44]

Göring's story was part of the training narrative for new recruits to the East German army, and a public monument was erected in his memory. This in turn became the model for a general 'Monument for Murdered Border Guards', which was used as the centrepiece of an annual military parade through East Berlin to mark each anniversary of the Wall. Streets in the city were named after Göring and other guards who had been killed carrying out their duties. As *Neues Deutschland* proclaimed, the sacrifices of these young men reminded the people why the Wall had to exist. In the face of Western aggression, it stood 'for the protection and consolidation of the power of the workers and peasants in our socialist Fatherland'.[45]

Spies and refugees. Traitors and heroes. Murderers and martyrs. Life went on in the city of opposites.

For some time, only a very small part of the Wall was actually *wall*. Just twenty per cent of the border was fitted with the concrete-block barriers; the rest remained a mixture of barbed wire and fencing.[46] Yet throughout the world – and even in Berlin itself – people believed from the start that the Wall was one unbroken structure that cut the city in two. In some ways, then, the Wall was an illusion. To understand its true, fragmentary nature would have meant following its course to see the reality with one's own eyes, but few outside of official circles would think of doing such a thing. The Wall's psychological power derived from its image as a single structure. That was how people saw it, even if no such structure existed – at least to start with.

After a few years, the East German government began to plan a substantial upgrade. The original fortifications had been thrown up at such speed that they had already begun to degrade. The concrete blocks showed a tendency to collapse, and guard towers and accommodation had been made out of wood. In 1964, a prototype 'border security strip' was tested by East German soldiers at a training facility in

Streganz to the south-west of Berlin.[47] It was made up of a series of obstacles: a fence, an anti-vehicle trench, a patrol road, a strip of gravel, and a concrete sentry tower with a panoramic view. In the West, this became known as the 'death strip'. On top of the wall, instead of barbed wire, there was single stretch of smooth, overhanging pipe, an ingenious addition that made it much harder to climb.[48]

In January 1965, this new border was demonstrated to the East German Defence Minister Heinrich Hoffman. While he observed that some elements still needed refinement – recommending the use of even more prefabricated concrete – Hoffman judged the fencing and updated Wall as *kulturvoll*: 'of high cultural standard'.[49] In the language of the Democratic Republic, this was high praise. There was no comprehensive programme of redevelopment, but over the next few years more and more stretches of the border began to take on this new *kulturvoll* appearance. The first phase of the Wall was over. Before, it had possessed a certain quality of improvisation, its structure determined largely by expediency and the re-purposing of existing materials. Now it had become a piece of carefully calculated and comprehensively tested design.

In 1976 work began to rebuild the entire Wall according to an ideal standard. The 1964 design was modified further, with a particular focus on large prefabricated concrete pieces that could slot together to form a new wall. Once again, the structure was tested on the training grounds, where it was subjected to attacks by hammers and chisels, attempts 'by athletic persons' to climb it, and even efforts to ram it with vehicles and blow it up. Some forty designs were tested. The most effective was found to be 'UL 12.41', an L-shaped pre-cast of steel-reinforced concrete.[50] The 'leg' of the L rested on the ground, while the 'body' rose to a height of 3.6 metres, and was topped once again by the large pipe. Each section weighed almost three tons, and slotted together with other pieces via lateral grooves. Factories began mass-producing UL 12.41.[51] Nearly a decade-and-a-half into its life, the long-imagined Berlin Wall was at last built for real: a single, seamless strip of industrially-designed concrete running through an entire city.

The irony was that, as the East Germans obsessively bolstered and refined their Wall, the citizens of West Berlin stopped even noticing it. This bizarre, 'shameful' structure had become a mere fact of everyday life. Yes, it was there. Yes, for those wanting to visit friends or relatives in the East, it was an inconvenience. But it was merely part of the fabric of the city – nothing special. Perhaps it was the tourists' fault. The Wall become a major attraction. And as such, it elicited the inevitable, stock response given by natives of every city when asked by visitors what it was like: 'Don't know. Never been.'

West Berliners were too sophisticated to gawp at a slab of concrete. This attitude is captured by the West German author Peter Schneider in his 1983 novel, *The Wall Jumper*. Whenever the narrator, who has lived in Berlin for twenty years, is asked how it feels to be 'surrounded by concrete and barbed wire', he replies: 'living here is no different from living in any other city. I really don't see the Wall anymore, even if it is the only structure on earth, apart from the Great Wall of China, that can be seen from the moon with the naked eye.'[52] This is not sarcasm, but a wry acknowledgement that, over time, even the strangest environments become normal.

For many, this strangeness was a large part of the city's appeal. West Berlin exerted a considerable attraction on a certain kind of person. Unlike in the rest of the Federal Republic, there was no compulsory military service for Germans living there. This policy was designed to boost the population of the western half of the city – to entice people to make their homes in this tiny exclave at once behind the Iron Curtain and on the front line of the Cold War. In his introduction to the 2005 translation of *The Wall Jumper*, the novelist Ian McEwan recalls how 'artists, perpetual students, ageing hippies and diverse lost souls' migrated to West Berlin 'to live and resurrect, albeit less daringly, the bohemian freedoms of the 1920s.'[53]

The western city was the original 'hipster' neighbourhood: faded, depressed, down-at-heel, yet, thanks to the patronage of a self-consciously cool counter-culture, on the inevitable road towards gentrification. 'In the Berlin quarter of Kreuzberg they found cheap, shabby, once grand apartments,' continues McEwan. 'Those high ceilings echoed to the sound of radical political talk and avant-garde jazz sweetened by the reek of cannabis. It was the presence of the Wall... that made West Berlin both edgier and yet intellectually more vital than other cities in the west.'[54] Or, as the narrator of *The Wall Jumper* puts it: 'after only a short stay in Berlin, all the cities in West Germany struck me as artificial.'[55] For those seeking truth and authenticity, it seemed, this was the place to be.

Once in Berlin, however, people appeared reluctant to talk about the Wall directly. The third incarnation of the border, the smooth, white-washed concrete barrier erected in the late 1970s[56], became on its western side, thanks to innumerable graffiti artists, the world's largest open-air gallery. This vibrant, defiant strip of colour defined the Wall in the western consciousness: here was art reclaiming a symbol of repression. But the awkward truth was that the art only covered one side – in the East, the Wall remained as drab and featureless as ever. Was the graffiti on the West side really just an act of meaningless self-congratulation?

McEwan suggests that the literary reticence over the Wall was perhaps 'because writers, whose politics were generally well to the left of centre, found the Wall an embarrassment as a subject, an intractable problem posed by socialism.'[57] For many of the more radical residents of West Berlin, the Wall was the gravestone of a cherished political dream. 'Merely to describe the Wall was to attack it,' continued McEwan, 'and thus to appear to be a stooge of the CIA.'[58]

Peter Schneider was an exception. Like '*...und deine Liebe auch*' – although from a very different perspective – *The Wall Jumper* is an attempt to understand, through a dramatic storyline set against a divided Berlin, what it means to be free. The novel is full of melancholy characters on both sides of the divide. The narrator, who feels compelled to keep travelling back and forth between West and East, seeks stories of other 'Wall Jumpers', literal and metaphorical. He is charmed by the tale of three East German teenagers, who, every Friday night, cross the Wall to a West Berlin cinema to watch Hollywood westerns, before crossing back once the film is over. Then there are the Westerners who visit the East to tell their friends how bad everything is in the

West, and that the only difference is 'freedom of movement', which is overrated anyway. Another story follows the escapades of an East German, Walter Bolle, who, after many attempts, finally makes it over the Wall. He later makes the journey the other way, and hands himself into the border guards: he wants to come home, he tells them, because 'there was nothing happening in the West.'[59] Finally, there is the narrator's own girlfriend, Lena, a defector from the East who maintains an attitude of constant intellectual and moral superiority. At least in the East, she tells the narrator, the state is open about its efforts to control the people. The West's citizens, on the other hand, have no idea how much they are being secretly manipulated under the guise of freedom. Schneider concludes that the Wall is merely a symptom of an unbreachable ideological divide, rather than its cause. Differences in belief and understanding existed before the Wall was put up, and will be there long after it has come down. 'Those walls,' says the narrator, 'will still be standing when no one is left to move beyond them.'[60]

At 6pm on 9 November 1989, the East German government spokesman Gunter Schabowski addressed the world's media. It was a standard, scheduled briefing, with a number of items on the agenda. At 6.53pm, Schabowski began his final announcement. It came from a document handed to him just before the press conference by the East German leader, Egon Krenz, and it concerned temporary new foreign travel arrangements for Democratic Republic citizens.[61] Schabowski read it out verbatim, and once he had finished, prepared to leave the briefing. The international media were, however, confused by what they had just heard. Many questions were asked in an attempt to clarify the exact meaning of this government statement. It appeared to signal a change to the Democratic Republic's border regulations, allowing both private travel and permanent exit, subject to an application procedure. Schabowski was asked when the new rules would come into effect. He scanned the document, spotted one phrase, and answered that the regulations applied '*Absofort*' – 'immediately'.[62]

Just after 7pm, Reuters reported that citizens of the Democratic Republic were to be permitted to travel out of the country at appropriate border points. While a significant development, the implication was that this was a temporary measure and that there remained a number of bureaucratic hurdles. The Associated Press took a bolder line. At 7.05pm they released a headline over the wires: 'The German Democratic Republic is opening its borders'. Soon, every other press agency had followed their lead.[63]

By the late 1980s, the idea that a wall could act as a serious barrier between people had become an almost comical anachronism. Technology defeated it over and over again. Even at the time when the Wall was first built, it could be crossed by radio waves. Now that televisions had become commonplace in every home, East Germans, in particular East Berliners, could turn their antennae westwards to pick up programmes from the Federal Republic.

For a time these 'ideological border-crossers'[64] were targeted by party zealots: their ox-horn-shaped aerials pointed across the Wall and gave them away. The houses of offenders were graffitied, and sometimes cardboard donkey ears, symbols of the foolish desire to listen out for western frequencies, were pinned to their doors. Soon, however, this policy was abandoned.[65] By 1989, East Berliners had been watching West German television stations for decades. At 8pm on the evening of 9 November, the bulletin of the Federal Republic's ARD network – the equivalent of the BBC – used the very same line as the Associated Press: 'The German Democratic Republic is opening its borders'.[66]

Within minutes, border officials telephoned government headquarters to report some eighty East Berliners at the Bornholmer Strasse, Heinrich-Heine-Strasse and Invalidenstrasse checkpoints, seeking to cross to the West.[67] The guards were told to ask the people to return the following day. By 10pm, however, the numbers had swelled to over a thousand. Half an hour later, the East German state television news reiterated that border crossings were still subject to an application process. Hardly anyone in East Berlin was watching, though. Those not swarming towards the Wall were all tuned into West Germany's late-night TV discussion programme, *Tagesthemen*.

This show began its broadcast by proclaiming: 'the ninth of November is a historic day: the German Democratic Republic has announced that its borders are open to everyone, with immediate effect, and the gates of the Wall stand wide open.'[68] It was too late for the East German government to hold back the tide.

Over the next two hours, the Berlin Wall fell. It had appeared over the course of one night, and, almost three decades on, it disappeared over the course of another. The next morning, the West German newspaper *Volksblatt* carried the headline, 'The Wall has fallen'. Yet a second leader on the same front page called 'for the demolition of the Wall'.[69] Once again, it seemed, the Wall was simultaneously there and not there. As the American historian Robert Darnton, an eye-witness working in East Germany at the time, put it: 'On ninth November it still cut the heart of Berlin, a jagged wound in the centre of a great city, the great division of the Cold War. But on the tenth it was a dance floor, a picture gallery, a black-board, a cinema screen, a video cassette, a museum and, as the cleaning lady in my office said, "just a pile of stones"'.[70]

Perhaps not *just* a pile of stones.

It is too easy, in hindsight, to suggest that the fall of the Wall was inevitable. At the beginning of 1989, the soon-to-be-deposed East German leader, Erich Honecker, predicted that the Wall would still be standing in a hundred years, continuing to protect the Democratic Republic 'from robbers'.[71] Plans were well advanced for another revamp of the border: the so-called 'Wall 2000', which, somewhat bizarrely, proposed a combination of cutting-edge security technology and landscape gardening. Along with infra-red sensors and laser tripwires, large sections of the Wall were to be recast as a 'green border', incorporating hedges, plants, flowers, and other wildlife.[72]

This willingness to spend money beautifying the Wall underlined its permanence in the minds of the East German government. It was also an attempt to cover up the structure's fundamental, unavoidable flaw: it was the wrong way round. As a former border-guard-turned-defector told the West German newspaper *Der Spiegel* in 1981: 'They always said – anti-fascist protection rampart. But the whole thing was built back to front... Everybody saw this. It was built so that no one from our side could go over.'[73]

In the end the Wall had no defence against the advance of history or the weight of circumstance. After coming to power in 1985, the Soviet leader Mikhail Gorbachev pursued progressive policies of *glasnost* and *perestroika* – 'openness' and 'restructuring' – which included relaxing controls over the Communist nations of the Eastern Bloc. The Hungarian and Czechoslovakian governments reacted by allowing East German citizens to cross their borders and go on into the West. The government of the Democratic Republic was then forced hurriedly to draft its own, unintentionally historic, statement on border regulations. In the words of one diplomat, the events of the night of 9 November 1989 were a 'mistake... one of the most colossal administrative errors in history'.[74]

Many in the West were eager to take credit. The American President Ronald Reagan, for instance, recalled his Berlin visit of 1987, when he had delivered the famous line: 'Mr Gorbachev, tear down this wall!'[75] Reagan's speech had gone through seven drafts. Each time, State Department and National Security Council advisors had removed that line. And every time, Reagan had put it back in.[76]

Even more influential, some say, was the intervention of another American – Bruce Springsteen. On 19 July 1988, he performed a concert behind the Iron Curtain in East Germany. It had been approved by the Democratic Republic's government as a measure to placate the nation's restive youth. Just a year before, policemen at the Wall had used truncheons and stun guns to hold back East Berliners trying to get as close to the border as possible in order to hear David Bowie and Michael Jackson giving concerts in the West. Secret police files described Springsteen as the 'undisputed pinnacle of contemporary rock music'[77], yet also emphasised his working-class roots and the 'hard and unadorned songs' he wrote about economic depression in America. During his performance, Springsteen told the crowd of

300,000: 'I'm not here for any government. I've come to play rock and roll for you in the hope that one day all the barriers will be torn down'. He followed his speech by singing Bob Dylan's *Chimes of Freedom*.[78]

Yet to seek out individuals is to miss the point. The most famous images from 9 November 1989 show ordinary Berliners, from both sides of the divide, climbing, sitting, standing and dancing on top of the Wall. Soon people were hacking away at the concrete, grabbing little pieces of the Wall for themselves, permanent mementoes of the night they personally played a part in changing the course of world history. The Wall had lost its original power – to stop people crossing from one nation to another – but had gained in its place a talismanic quality. What had been functional and brutal was suddenly imbued with immense significance.

For many, the initial urge to destroy may have been cathartic: a chance to hack away with joyous abandon at a structure that had once signified repression. But people also understood instinctively that the Wall was a relic – and an instant relic at that. The concrete chippings that fell to the floor in those first moments rapidly took on value. The Wall – the definitive dividing line between capitalism and communism – was being commodified.

Within days 'fragments of freedom' were on sale in the markets of both East and West Berlin. Foreigners descending on the city could hire hammers and chisels – 5 Deutschmarks for 20 minutes – to smash off pieces for themselves.[79] There are not many holidays where you can claim to have played your part in ending the Cold War, and return with the evidence to prove it. These vandalism tourists became known as *Mauerspechte* – 'wallpeckers' – and they set about their task with considerable gusto. Indeed, the chunks were so popular that demand quickly began to outpace supply.

Local entrepreneurs attacked the Wall with pneumatic drills, stockpiling fragments for sale. Six months after the fall, some sellers were complaining that the 'wall-peckers' had already chipped away the whole face of the West side.[80] Pieces from the East side were much less desirable, because they were not marked with graffiti.

In fact, without any splashes of colour, people did not believe that they were even real. As a consequence, market traders took to spray-painting genuine but unadorned Wall chippings to make them seem 'more authentic'.[81]

The East German government, showing a keen instinct for the free market, soon realised they were in possession of a unique asset. In January 1990 they placed a value on the whole Wall – 800 million Deutschmarks, around £3.7 million – and began selling pieces of it around the world.[82] The global appetite was astonishing. Slabs ended up in the garden of Vatican City, outside the European Court of Human Rights in Strasbourg, and in front of the CIA Headquarters in Washington DC.[83] One giant block taken from near the Brandenburg Gate was erected by the main entrance to the Imperial War Museum in London. Sporting an image by the graffiti artist 'Indiano', it shows a wide-open mouth filled with the slogan 'Change Your Life'. A 20-foot-long section was installed on the street at 520 Madison Avenue in New York City, near the Museum of Modern Art – to be passed unnoticed every day by hurrying office workers. The Main Street Station Casino and Hotel in Las Vegas bought several concrete slabs and used them to mount three men's urinals.[84]

The popularity of these fragments in North America is telling. The Wall was not just a symbol of freedom; it was also, to some, 'the trophy reserved for the winners of the Cold War'.[85] Rainer Hildebrandt, director of the newly-formed Checkpoint Charlie Museum, exploited this in December 1993 in his sales pitch for an original two-storey border tower. Here, Hildebrand said, was the opportunity to buy a unique 'trophy', a physical structure representing 'the victory of a political idea'.[86]

You can still buy pieces of the Wall today. Whether they are real or not is another question. Large segments continue to change hands between private collectors and major companies or institutions, often for hundreds of thousands or even millions of pounds. On 8 November 2013, the day before the twenty-fourth anniversary of the fall of the Wall, the photographer Markus Schreiber shot the site of a storage location for large, unsold fragments of the Wall at the town of Teltow, just outside Berlin. In Schreiber's image, the tall, L-shaped concrete slabs stand apart and irregularly spaced, and are reflected in a large puddle of water in what appears to be a tree-lined stretch of otherwise empty waste ground.

As the writer Geoff Dyer observes, seen together these slabs bear a striking resemblance to 'Stonehenge or the Standing Stones of Callanish', yet at the same time they are 'both ancient and post-apocalyptic – in a word, timeless – as if whatever they commemorate occurred in the future'.[87] It is an astute comment. The physical Wall was rapidly destroyed and scattered. But what it meant, what it still means, remains unclear. Schreiber's photograph captures a monument that is yet to be reconciled with the people who built it up and knocked it down.

Today, less than two of the forty-four kilometres of the Berlin Wall are still standing.[88] It is a surprise that anything remains at all. Just a day after the fall of the Wall, the West Berlin Mayor Willy Brandt suggested that 'a piece of this horrible edifice' should be preserved as a lasting reminder of 'a historical monstrosity'.[89] Very few agreed with him. Instead the mantra, chanted over the discordant percussion of the wall-peckers, was '*Die Mauer muss weg*!' – 'the Wall must go!'[90] Another city official, Dieter Havichek, proclaimed, 'There is no space for Walls in Berlin any more. The legacy of the Wall's victims demands that divisions be irrevocably removed.'[91]

While the lasting image of the 'destruction' of the Wall is of concrete slabs collapsing on a November night, the bulk of the work was done in the months after. Tourists chipped away merrily, but they were literally just scratching the surface. The Wall proved remarkably strong and durable. Breaking down steel-reinforced concrete needed more than a hammer, a chisel and some righteous zeal. Instead, it was East and West German soldiers who worked together to carry out the demolition, using bulldozers and wrecking balls.[92]

Soon enough, the Wall was gone. Despite the initial clamour for it to be wiped from the face of the city, its sudden absence came as a shock. 'It is typical for us Germans that at the end of an historical era we want to rip everything down and forget it ever happened,' said Berlin's chief archaeologist, Dr Alfred Kerndl. 'It occurred with the Nazi sites, now it's happening with the Berlin Wall'.[93] The cry 'Save the Wall!' began to be heard more and more. In October 1990, an opinion poll posed to Berliners the question, 'Do you want the Wall back?' One in three West Berliners and one in four East Berliners said they did. Of those in the West under the age of thirty, almost forty per cent confessed that they 'had shed a tear for the passing of the Wall'.[94]

The speed with which perspectives changed was dizzying. Western companies and workers spread out across the newly unified city. Many East Berliners lost their jobs in the process. For some, the fall of the Wall had not joined together two equal halves: it had allowed the West to 'colonise' the East, just as the communist party leaders had always warned. It became common to hear the muttered remark that 'not everything was so bad'[95] behind the barbed wire. You could knock the Wall down, but it didn't go away.

In the 1960s, East German psychologists had begun to see patients suffering from what became known as *Mauerkrankheit* – 'Wall Disorder'. Symptoms ranged from psychosis and schizophrenia, to alcoholism, depression, anger and dejection. Suicide rates for East Berliners – in particular those living closest to the Wall, saw a rapid increase.[96] The Wall, it seemed, was imprinting itself on the psyche of significant numbers of the population. Just as the concrete barrier prevented freedom of movement, so the psychological barrier restricted emotional freedom. For twenty-eight years, East Germans experienced a 'walled-in' existence. Many grew up knowing nothing of life without a Wall.

After the euphoria of 9 November 1989 had evaporated, '*Die Mauer in den Köpfen*' – 'the Wall in the Head' – reasserted itself, and came to dominate relations between Easterners and Westerners. It was a barrier, seen by some as insurmountable, to integration, and reflected a growing social and economic divide. A 'character wall'[97] was emerging. In the media, this has increasingly been used over the past three decades as a shorthand explanation of the cultural, linguistic, economic and political gap between East and West. It is the reason why one side still smokes different cigarettes, wears different clothes, shops at different stores, reads different newspapers and lives in different neighbourhoods from the other. It is the reason why Easterners are paid less than Westerners, or are more likely to be unemployed. It is the reason why people from one side even *walk* differently from people from the other.[98]

On 18 April 2013, the Canadian astronaut Chris Hadfield posted on Twitter a photograph of Berlin at night, taken through a window of the International Space Station as it orbited the planet. In the image, the city is clearly divided into two halves, in a way that seems almost to track the path of the vanished Wall.[99] The West shines out a bright white, while the East glows a softer, dimmer yellow. This could be for mundane, practical reasons – the Berlin authorities are in the process of replacing the city's old gas powered-lamps with modern electric street-lights. Or it could be hard evidence of the continuing economic imbalance between the two sides. Perhaps it is the perfect schematic – a brain scan, if you like – of the 'Wall in the head': the two hemispheres of Berlin lit by different, competing synaptic pulses. What, you want to ask, is this city *thinking*?

Even a quarter of a century after its downfall, the Berlin Wall can be seen from space.

Chapter Nineteen

No Day Shall Erase You From the Memory of Time

The Twin Towers of the World Trade Centre – New York City (Born 1973 – Died 2001)

There are many stories to be told about the rise and fall of New York's World Trade Centre. As many as there were floors in each building (110); as many as there were people who worked there (50,000), or visitors who came to see it every day (100,000); as many, even, as there were tons of collapsed steel and concrete left behind after it was destroyed (1.2 million).[1] There are many stories to be told. This is just one of them. It is about two towers, and two architects.

On 1 December 1912, an architect was born in Seattle, in Washington State. The architect's parents had emigrated from Japan to the Pacific Northwest of America in 1908; the father worked in a shoe factory and the mother was a pianist. This made the architect a *Nisei*, meaning literally 'second generation': he was Japanese, but a citizen of the United States. His name was Minoru Yamasaki.[2]

As he grew up, Yamasaki increasingly felt like an outsider. He looked different from his classmates, and was subjected to racist taunts from an early age. His cause was not helped by his mother, who insisted that her son always wear bright bow ties to school. Inspired by his maternal uncle, an architecture graduate from the University of California at Berkeley, Yamasaki enrolled at the age of sixteen as a student in the architectural programme of the University of Washington. It was the beginning of the Great Depression, and to pay for his education he spent five summers working 100-hour weeks in a fish cannery in Alaska, for $50 a month.[3] His father was a domineering presence throughout his early life, and even demanded that Yamasaki end his relationship with his first girlfriend so that nothing would distract him from his studies.[4]

In 1934, as soon as he had graduated, Minoru looked to escape for good the 'uncompromising and personally degrading circumstances'[5] of the life he had known in Seattle. With no job and just $40 to his name, he moved to New York City. Once there, he spent his days wrapping dishes for an import company, while completing his master's degree at night school.[6] Over the next decade, he found work as a draughtsman and engineer with a number of Manhattan's most prestigious architectural practices – most notably Shreve, Lamb and Harmon, creators of the iconic Empire State Building; and Harrison, Fouilhoux and Abramovitz, who were behind the recently completed art deco skyscraper known as the Rockefeller Centre.

The Second World War, and in particular the attack on Pearl Harbour, brought back the toxic racism that had tainted Yamasaki's childhood. This time however, the discrimination and paranoia were coordinated by the state. He was investigated by the FBI, and reported repeatedly to the authorities as a suspected spy, purely on the basis of his appearance. Unlike many Japanese-Americans, however, he escaped the government 'interment camps', as did his parents, whom he moved away from Seattle and installed in the one-bedroom Manhattan apartment he already shared with his wife and brother.[7]

In 1945, despite the anti-Japanese sentiment still pervading American society, Yamasaki secured the position of Head Designer at a large architectural firm in Detroit. Six years later he set up his own practice, and then, in 1956, won the American Institute of Architects' First Honour Award for his design for a new air terminal in St Louis.[8]

In the same year and in the same city, he completed one of America's first and largest state-funded public housing schemes. This was Pruitt-Igoe, whose thirty-three modernist concrete tower-blocks were intended to offer a new start to working-class families from the downtown slums.

Yamasaki had overcome hardships and prejudice to become an establishment architect. Then, in 1962, he received the commission of a lifetime. The Port Authority of New York and New Jersey selected his firm from a short-list of forty to design a major new complex at the southern tip of Manhattan Island. On receiving the brief for the project, Yamasaki called a staff meeting and held up the Port Authority letter as an example of the dangers of careless writing. The budget was set at $280 million. Someone, he said, had clearly been remiss in counting their zeroes, and had added one too many.[9] It was Yamasaki, however, who was wrong. The Port Authority wanted to construct what they called 'the first buildings of the twenty-first century', a 'vertical port'[10] that would stand as the greatest monument ever built in the name of commerce – the World Trade Centre. Money was no object. Or rather, money was the whole object.

Yamasaki's first thought was that he should avoid an 'over-all form which melts into the multi-towered landscape of Lower Manhattan'.[11] That would not achieve the symbolic effect his employers were looking for: 'It should be unique, have excitement of its own,' he said.[12] At the same time, he would 'scale it to the human being so that, rather than be an overpowering group of buildings, it will be inviting, friendly and humane'.[13] In 1963, as media excitement mounted over the sheer immensity of the project, Yamasaki joined the select list of architects who had made it onto the cover of *Time* magazine. In an interview, he expanded on his design concepts: 'A building should not awe but embrace man... Instead of overwhelming grandeur in architecture, we should have gentility. And we should have the wish mentally and physically to touch our buildings.'[14]

A decade later, in 1973, the World Trade Centre opened. It was defined by two colossal towers, at that time the largest and tallest built in the history of the world.[15] At the inauguration ceremony, Yamasaki explained that 'world trade means world peace'. What he had created, he said, was 'a representation of man's belief in humanity, his need for individual dignity, his beliefs in the cooperation of men, and through cooperation, his ability to find greatness'.[16]

When the towers were complete, Yamasaki had made his way onto the roof with two of his colleagues – his partner in the practice, Henry Guthard, and a designer, Modris Pudists – and they had opened a bottle of champagne to celebrate. The view from the summit was startling. At that moment, as they stood gazing out over the city, they saw beneath them the aircraft landing and taking off from Newark airport. 'Looking down on the planes,' said Pudists, 'was an extraordinary feeling'.[17]

On 1 September 1968, an architect was born in Kafr el-Sheikh, in Egypt's Nile Delta. He was the youngest of three siblings, but the first son – a privileged position in a Middle Eastern family. His father was a lawyer, while his mother was the home-keeper. When he was ten years old, they moved to Cairo, to live in the middle-class suburb of Giza. The city was growing very fast: in the three decades between 1950 and 1980, the number of people in Cairo quadrupled, from 2 million to 8 million. It had become one of the most densely populated places on earth. When the Egyptian leader, Anwar al-Sadat, came to power in 1970, he opened the country to western capitalist influences and private investment.[18] Cairo became a vast building site. The architect lived with his family in one of the products of all this construction: a modernist-style apartment block, surrounded by row after row of other modernist-style apartment blocks.[19] His name was Mohammad Atta.

As he grew up, Atta felt like an outsider. His father was ambitious and authoritarian. Giza was just a stopping point for the family on the way to greater things, he said. They did not mix with the neighbours, they kept their doors closed.[20] Atta's elder sisters excelled at school: one became a zoologist, the other a medical doctor. Both earned their PhDs. Atta himself was shy, sometimes withdrawn. His father called him *Bolbol* – the Arabic slang for a little singing bird, and told him continually that he needed to 'toughen up'.[21] He was small and skinny – as an adult he was just 5 foot 7 inches – and preferred chess to physical, outdoor games.[22]

In 1985, Atta enrolled to study architecture at the University of Cairo. He had never shown any interest in politics – his father had drummed into him that 'politics equals hypocrisy'[23] – yet it was difficult to avoid it on campus. Four years earlier, President Anwar al-Sadat had been murdered by Islamic fundamentalists posing as soldiers. Sadat's successor, Hosni Mubarak, had instituted a zero-tolerance policy towards religious militancy – and he had no qualms about using mass imprisonment and torture. Student bodies became highly politicised. Atta's engineering faculty was effectively controlled by the Muslim Brotherhood, a religious and political group promoting hard-line Islamic values, and railing against the corrupting, 'colonising' influence of the west. Mubarak's government regarded the Brotherhood as a hotbed of revolutionaries and organised terrorism.[24] Atta's generation was confronted with a barren economic landscape and a society dominated by harsh military rule, cronyism and corruption. Graffiti and posters all over Egypt told the country's youth there was only one way to channel their anger and frustration: Islam.[25]

Meanwhile, Atta's father continued to try to control his son's life. The only way to improve his career prospects at home, he told his son, was by securing an advanced degree abroad. For several years Atta had been taking lessons in English and German, paid for by his father, and in October 1992 he secured a scholarship to study for a Masters in town-planning at Hamburg Technical University. He was reluctant to leave Egypt and his family behind, but his father kept up the pressure. He said that he 'needed to hear the word "doctor"'[26] in front of his son's name.

Atta lived in student accommodation in the Harburg district of Hamburg, just minutes away from the university. Whilst working on his degree, he found a part-time job with an architectural and planning firm called Plankontor. His new colleagues were impressed with the skill and elegance of his draughtsmanship. Atta was a quiet and conscientious worker: the only thing that stood out about him was his tendency, at midday every day, to stop whatever he was doing, kneel down beside his drawing board, and pray.[27] It was a habit he had acquired in his early teens, around the time of President Sadat's assassination.

In 1994, Atta began to look for a subject for his doctoral thesis. In December of that year, he travelled to the Syrian city of Aleppo with a German friend and fellow student – Volker Hauth – with a view to co-writing a study of the conflict between traditional Arab structures and modern western buildings in Middle Eastern cities.[28] Hauth listened with interest to Atta as he described the social injustices of Egyptian society. Atta would joke about Arab dictators, but would also talk earnestly and passionately of his distaste for President Mubarak and his coterie of 'fat cats', a cabal that persisted unchallenged due to the lack of democracy in the country.[29]

In Aleppo, Hauth watched Atta flirt with a young Palestinian woman, also an architectural student, who teased him that 'All Egyptians are Pharaohs'. Atta admired the girl, but concluded with regret that there could be no future between the two of them because she was 'emancipated' and 'challenging'.[30] In 1995, he won a prestigious scholarship from a German research institute to spend three months back in Cairo, writing about Egyptian public policy and, as he put it in his application, 'how this so-called first world sees us and how it treats our third world'.[31] While he was there, he investigated a 'renovation' project in a poor quarter around the old city gates. As he told his fellow students when he returned to Hamburg, this redevelopment was merely an excuse to knock down a traditional neighbourhood and improve views for tourists. The authorities, he said, were attempting to 'make a Disneyworld' out of the city.[32]

Atta completed his thesis in August 1999. That it took five years was not unusual in a German university, where students face less strict deadlines for the submission of research work.[33] During that time he had often left Hamburg to travel abroad. One several-month-long trip in 1995 was accounted for as a pilgrimage to Mecca; another – this time lasting over a year between 1997 and 1998 – was explained to his tutor as being 'for family reasons'.[34] Although the plan to co-author his thesis with Hauth had been abandoned, the original concept remained in place: a discourse on eastern tradition versus western modernism, using part of one Syrian city as a case study. The paper stretched to 162 pages[35], and centred on a detailed critique of the old quarter of Aleppo, the oldest continually inhabited city in the world.

Atta saw a community and a way of life being eroded steadily by unsympathetic contemporary architecture. Building styles alien to Aleppo were being transplanted, without thought, from an entirely different culture. The fabric of the city was being changed irrevocably. For instance, careless urban planning was destroying the souks and leaving shopkeepers with no natural environment in which to carry out their business. Atta's deepest anger, though, was reserved for the high-rises that had sprung up all over the old quarter to loom over the courtyards of older houses, denying ordinary families their private spaces.

Worst of all was the skyscraper, a structure inherently western, yet emerging all over the Middle East as identikit hotels and offices were constructed throughout the region.[36] These tall buildings were, Atta implied, nothing less than the architectural tools with which the west was colonising the east. In his conclusion, he proposed an entirely low-rise scheme for the redevelopment of Aleppo, a master-plan eschewing western modernism and flowing from Arabic cultural values. This included notes on how to keep women inside their homes, in accordance with strict religious practice. The title page of his thesis, a last-minute addition, used a verse from the Koran: 'My prayer and my sacrifice and my life and my death are for Allah, the Lord of the worlds'.[37]

Atta's thesis was awarded a 1.0 – the best grade possible.[38] His tutor, Professor Dittmar Machule, was extremely impressed with the work. Here was a model student for a multicultural world, someone who would perhaps 'one day go back to his country as a sort of ambassador between the secular west and the religious east... to explain our cultural differences'.[39] Atta, however, had resolved to go not east, but further west. He arrived in America for the first time in the spring of 2000. After travelling briefly back to Europe, he returned, flying from Prague into Newark on a six-month tourist visa. In July, he and a friend from the United Arab Emirates began taking flying lessons at a training school in Venice, Florida.

Fourteen months later, on 10 September 2001, Atta spent the night at the Comfort Inn motel in Portland, Maine.[40] The next morning, he followed the simple routine that he had set down for himself on paper. He showered, shaved, evacuated his bowels and splashed on some cologne. He had prayed through the night, and now told himself, over and over, to be happy, optimistic and calm, because he was about to perform a good deed. He dressed carefully, and laced his shoes tightly over his socks. He double-checked that he had his passport, ID and papers. His notes reminded him to smile.[41] Perhaps he even practised in the bathroom mirror.

At 5.30am, Atta checked out of his motel, and drove with his friend Abdulaziz Al-Omari in a rental car to Portland airport. From there, he caught a commuter flight to Boston's Logan airport. When he boarded his connection – the 7.45am American Airlines flight 11 to Los Angeles – he put to the back of his mind his fear of flying[42], and recalled instead his instructions to take his seat and offer up a prayer to God.

At 8.46am, Mohammad Atta sat at the controls of the flight 11 Boeing 767. Ahead of him, growing larger in the cockpit window with every passing second, was the steel and glass façade of the north tower of the World Trade Centre.

Atta had arrived at his last instruction from his checklist for the day. 'Either end your life while praying, seconds before the target,' he had written. 'Or make your last words: "There is no God but God, Muhammad is His messenger"'.[43]

There are many stories to be told about the rise and fall of New York's World Trade Centre. As many as there were terrorists on board the four hijacked aircraft (19); as many as there were minutes between the moment Mohammad Atta's plane hit the north tower and its final collapse (102); as many as there were victims who died in the carnage

(2,792); as many, even, as there were people around the world witnessing the events unfold live on television, radio and the internet (2 billion).[44] Many stories, but they all end in the same place: Ground Zero.

It was, perhaps, a curious term to apply to the disaster site, having been coined in the 1940s to describe the epicentre of a nuclear blast – the origin point of the atomic chain-reaction that surges unstoppably outwards. In truth, the World Trade Centre's ground zero was more about implosion than explosion. It was a black hole that sucked everything inwards.

Unconnected stories, like the lives of a Japanese-American architect and a disaffected Egyptian architect born a generation apart, were suddenly pulled together. As viewers across the world tuned in to their televisions to watch reports of what seemed a terrible aviation accident, their own individual stories were drawn within the dense gravitational field of this new ground zero. Then came the second plane, 'sharking in low over the Statue of Liberty', as Martin Amis put it. 'That was the defining moment,' he added.[45] In the instant that the second Boeing struck the south tower, it became clear that this was no accident. It was an assault. The pull of the black hole became exponentially stronger. This was 'terror doubled, or squared'.[46] Story after story – thousands, millions, billions – flowed into Lower Manhattan. The world was a witness, and all our stories met in one place, in one day, joined in disbelief.

Nearly a century earlier, the famous American architect Frank Lloyd Wright had volunteered a morbid prediction about the fate and future of the skyscraper: 'Millions of tons of brick and stone go high up into thin air by way of rivets driven into thin webs of perishable steel. Therefore millions of tons of stone and brick will have to come down again. Come down when? – Come down how?'[47] September 11 provided an answer that few could have imagined, let alone anticipated. The terrorists' impossible aim was for the towers to collapse. And somehow, they succeeded. 'No visionary cinematic genius,' wrote Amis, 'could hope to recreate the majestic abjection of that double surrender, with the scale of the buildings conferring its own slow motion. It was well understood that an edifice so comprised of concrete and steel would also become an unforgettable metaphor.'[48] In those minutes, the greatest story of all – history itself – was consumed by the black hole, by Ground Zero.

In September 2005, the Museum of the City of New York held an exhibition of a series of sixty-seven photographs titled *The Destruction of Lower Manhattan.* All in black and white, these images captured sombre scenes of desolation and ruin in the heart of the city: exposed ironwork, shattered walls and an overall sense of emptiness. Perhaps the most remarkable thing about the photographs, however, was when they were taken – in 1966 and 1967. The World Trade Centre site, which had been reduced to ruins by a terrorist atrocity, had itself been built on top of ruins. Some three decades before 9/11, 'a neighbourhood fell, and barely made a sound'.[49]

The Destruction of Lower Manhattan was the work of the photographer Danny Lyon. After spending two years in the mid-1960s riding and living with a Chicago motorcycle gang – an experience he documented in a book called *The Bikeriders* – Lyon, a Brooklyn native, returned to New York City. He found a loft apartment on the corner of Beekman and Williams Streets. This was one of the oldest surviving parts of the city, full of mercantile structures built in the nineteenth century, including one of the first multi-storey cast-iron buildings in the world, dating from 1848. It was also an area living on borrowed time. Lyon had moved into a neighbourhood, comprising some sixty acres of lower Manhattan, which was scheduled for demolition. It was the essential levelling of the ground, before construction of the World Trade Centre could begin.

Lyon was both disturbed and captivated by the eerie atmosphere of the downtown city. He secured a commission from the prestigious Magnum photo agency, and began documenting the buildings' last days. In many of the images, people remain firmly in the background. The occasional lone figure is pictured from a distance, crossing a deserted street and casting a long shadow, like a painting by Giorgio de Chirico.

As a result, the structures themselves take on characters and personalities. The delicate compositions of Lyon's photographs give the doomed buildings – their stout arches and frames, surrounded by emptiness and divested of their people and purposes – an aura of noble grace. As the *New York Times* puts it, they are 'like hulking creatures prepared for sacrifice', standing with 'proud dignity and unsettling quietude'.[50]

80 and 82 Beekman Street from 'The Destruction of Lower Manhattan' 1967 © Danny Lyon / Magnum

Lyon made his way up exposed fire escapes to take shots from rooftops, climbed through empty window frames to explore derelict warehouses and apartment blocks. He worked on the project for almost a year, keeping diary entries as he went, which would later serve as extended captions for his photographs. 'I came to see the buildings as fossils of a time past,' he wrote.

> 'These buildings were used during the Civil War. The men were all dead, but the buildings were still here, left behind as the city grew around them. Skyscrapers emerged from the rock of Manhattan like mountains growing out from the earth. And here and there near their base, caught between them on their old narrow streets, were the houses of the dead... In their last days and months, they were kept company by bums and pigeons.'[51]

As time moved on, Lyon's focus shifted a little away from the buildings and more towards the men tearing them down. As early as 18 June 1966, he wrote in his diary that the wrecking work was proceeding at such a pace that buildings were disappearing overnight. Yet the erasure of the historical fabric of the city remained a 'non-event'. No one in New York cared, said Lyon. During the six months it took to tear all the buildings down, he did not see another photographer.[52] The task of recording what was lost appeared to be his alone. 'As I see it now I might weave a kind of song of destruction,' he wrote. 'There will be portraits of housewreckers and anyone left in the neighbourhood. In a way the whole project is sad; except for the demolition men and their work.'[53] He saw the same nobility in these men – many of them first or second-generation immigrants – as he saw in the doomed buildings. They were, Lyon wrote, all 'American workers of 1967 drinking pop-top soda on their beams at lunch time, risking their lives for $5.50 an hour, pulling apart, brick by brick and beam by beam, the work of other American workers who once stood on the same walls and held the same bricks, then new, so long ago.'[54]

In July 2010, the remains of an eighteenth-century wooden merchant ship emerged from the earth and mud near the foundations of the former World Trade Centre. As bulldozers worked to excavate the site to build a new underground car park, workmen spotted curved timbers, which led down to a thirty-two-foot-long hull. An anchor weighing forty-five kilograms was also discovered, just a few yards away.[55] Years had been spent clearing millions of tons of concrete and twisted steel from the site: the accumulated debris left behind as two 1,360-foot-high buildings collapsed into 65 feet of rubble in a mere 10 seconds.[56]

When the World Trade Centre was built forty years earlier, the construction crews had worked down far below the water table to build an ingenious impermeable concrete base – nicknamed 'the Bathtub' – in order to house the foundations of the two towers.[57] In the clear-up operation they had to excavate deep into the earth once again, through the Bathtub to the original bedrock of Manhattan. It was, as one workman commented, rock that was never supposed to have seen the light of day again.[58]

It was also rock that had, over millennia, felt the footsteps of Lenape Indians; rock that had met the boots of the first Dutchman to step from his boat onto Manhattan Island at the beginning of the seventeenth century.[59] It was rock that, in 1625, was transformed into a fur-trading post by the Dutch West India Company, and that began sprouting long piers, built first out of wood but soon out of stone, that stretched into the water beyond the tip of the island: fingertips beckoning merchants to the port of New Amsterdam. And it was rock that, in 1664, was seized by the English, and was renamed New York.

Throughout the eighteenth and nineteenth centuries, Manhattan Island expanded both to the east and west, encroaching on the rivers in large tracts of reclaimed land, which quickly grew more piers, harbours and warehouses. The wooden ship that rose out of the ground alongside the World Trade Centre in 2010 was just one fragment of the accumulated mass of debris that had been used to create these dock-sides two hundred years earlier.

By the nineteenth century, New York was one of the world's largest and busiest ports, a city shaped by the tides of foreign trade. It was built on money and ruled by the market, its fortunes joined to the worldwide economy. A boom-and-bust culture created boom-and-bust architecture. And New York proved itself adept at renewal and reinvention. Fires in 1776 and 1835 consumed a third and a quarter of the city respectively. The march of progress barely skipped a beat. Just one day after the last flames of the 1835 fire were doused, architects set about designing replacements for the seven hundred buildings that had been lost.[60]

By the end of the nineteenth century, New York developers were pioneering a solution to the problems of building on an island. There was a limit to how much land could be reclaimed from the river, and so instead, architects looked upwards. The sky was prime real estate, and with advances in structural engineering, in particular in the use of iron and steel, it was there to be claimed. Writing in the 1890s, the architecture critic Montgomery Schuyler was the first to use the term 'skyline' to evoke the silhouette of Manhattan and its 'chain of peaks rising above the horizon... struggling or shooting towards the sky.'[61]

Schuyler was dubious about the architectural merits of these tall, blocky towers, but saw clearly what they represented: business. The novelist Henry James agreed. When he visited New York in 1905, he looked with awe on these raw expressions of power, but could muster little affection for them. Skyscrapers, he said, had unmoored themselves from history to float on the treacherous sea of the economy. They were 'consecrated by no uses save the commercial at any cost... monsters of the mere market'.[62]

On 16 September 1920, a first attempt was made on the life of these 'monsters'. Just a few blocks south-east of the site of the future World Trade Centre, where Wall and Broad Streets meet, there was a plaza surrounded by gleaming, high-rise buildings. This was the very centre of American finance. At almost exactly noon, as workers left their offices for lunch breaks, they walked past an uncoupled, horse-drawn cart parked directly outside the Morgan Bank. Seconds later, the cart exploded. Forty people died in what the *New York Herald* described as an 'unprecedented horror'.[63] Until 11 September 2001, this was the worst terrorist attack in New York's history.

The crime remains unsolved to this day: no one claimed responsibility and no one was caught. The target, however, seems clear enough: capitalism. Not just capitalism as an intangible political ideology, but capitalism in its physical form – represented most purely in the architecture of downtown Manhattan. The city's response was instant. By the morning of 17 September, the carnage caused by the explosion had been almost completely erased. Crews had worked through the night to clear the bomb-site of rubble and bloodstains. Everything continued as normal, and everyone – except, of course, for the dead and injured – returned to work, including the staff of the Morgan Bank.[64] When the stock exchange opened, the market went up. It was not boom and bust, but boom and boom.

It seemed that nothing could halt the rise of the skyscraper. It was, in a sense, architecture reduced to its simplest, most infantile form. First build high, then build even higher: this was something that a child piling up wooden blocks could understand. The 1920s and 30s witnessed the golden age of the New York skyscraper. And, as this race to 'verticality' intensified, midtown Manhattan left downtown behind. The Empire State, Chrysler and Rockefeller buildings were giant, stylish and unambiguous statements of power and prestige. They were the kings of Schuyler's skyline, unmatched by anything at the tip of the island. The World Trade Centre, conceived in the late 1950s, was an attempt to redress the balance, to shift the scales back towards downtown.

By the mid-twentieth century, Lower Manhattan contained what was left of the historic core of the city. In the words of a 1939 city guidebook, it was 'grimy with age': full of narrow, cobbled streets and buildings that revealed their 'pre-Civil War glory in carved lintels, arched doorways and ornate cornices.'[65] This was the part of town where people still *made things*. Before the Second World War, New York was one of the largest manufacturing centres in all of America, providing employment for two-fifths of the city's entire workforce.[66] By the end of the 1950s, however, the manufacturing industries were confined to an island within Manhattan Island, an enclave at the very tip of downtown. Small businesses selling everything from shoes, jewellery, textiles and electronic goods, to sporting equipment, garden seeds, pets and fireworks[67], operated out of predominantly low-rent, low-rise, mixed-use buildings, and the area played host to a remarkably diverse ethnic mix. This was the traditional fabric of the seaport city. On the east side, covering some six city blocks, there was Fulton Fish market – 'the largest on the Atlantic coast' – which from '2 to 9 am' (the 1939 guide tells us) was 'bedlam, as rubber-booted men in the street and in the narrow stalls' cleaned, boned, iced, unpacked and repacked 'approximately one hundred varieties of fish'.[68]

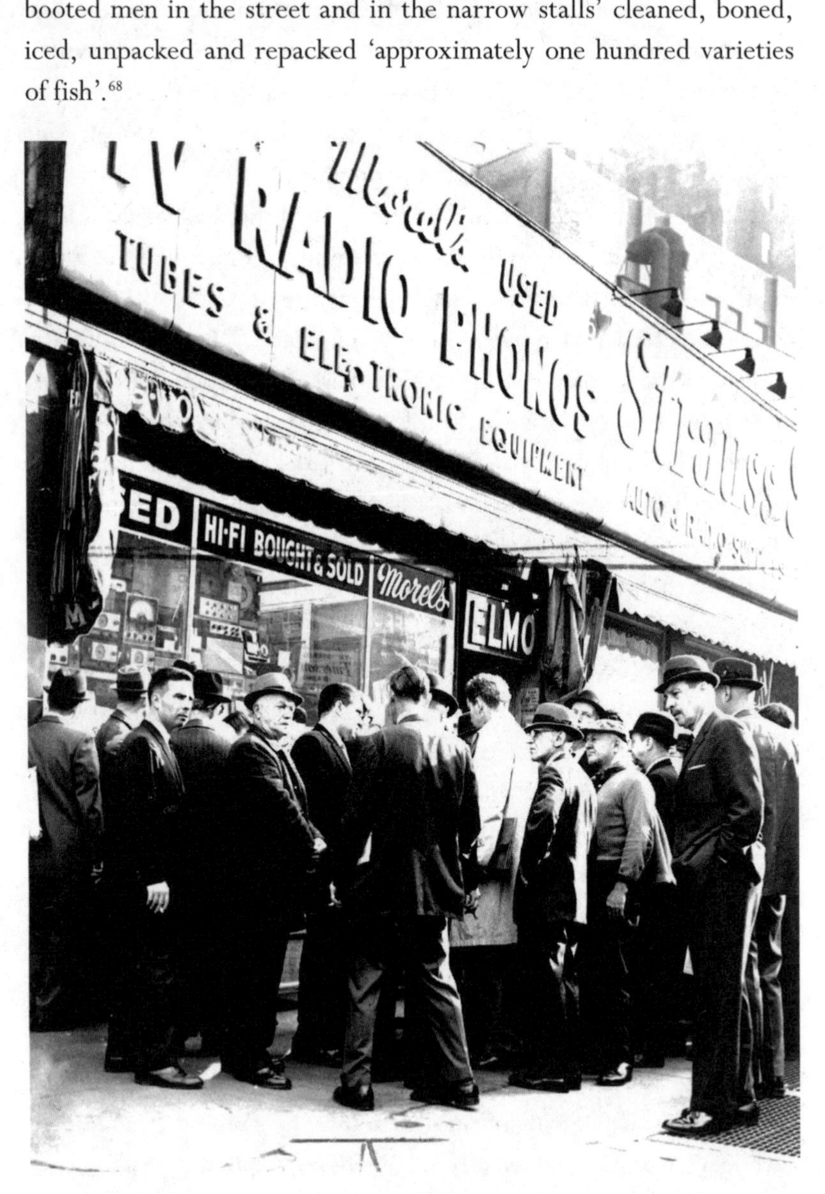

A crowd gathers on Lower Manhattan's Radio Row to listen to news of President Kennedy's death © Orlando Fernandez

On the west side was the great Washington Market. First established in 1812, it was said to handle and process one-eighth of all the food produce entering and leaving America. Its stalls offered a glimpse of the whole world: 'caviar from Siberia, Gorgonzola cheese from Italy, hams from Flanders, sardines from Norway, English partridge, native quail, squabs, wild ducks and pheasants; also fresh swordfish, frogs' legs, brook trout, pompanos, red snappers, codfish tongues and cheeks, bluefish cheeks and venison and bear steaks'.[69] Just two blocks east and south of Washington Market was Cortlandt Street, nicknamed 'Radio Row'. Filled with shops selling consumer electronics, it was the street, famously, that you heard long before you saw. According to the *New York Times,* it blasted out into the streets 'a confusion of sounds which only an army of loudspeakers could produce'.[70] Radio Row stood on the exact spot that would be marked out for the World Trade Centre.

In 1958, David and Nelson Rockefeller – the two brothers at the head of the enormously wealthy American family – announced a $1 billion public urban renewal plan for Lower Manhattan. As their family money gravitated away from oil and towards banking, the Rockefellers looked to transform the city's downtown financial district by creating a massive modern complex of trading and banking offices, hotels, exhibition centres and customs services. Or, to put it another way, a World Trade Centre.

This would be, in the words of David Rockefeller's faithful aide and confidant Warren Lindquist, 'the heart pump of the capital blood that sustains the free world'[71], a new home for all companies and agencies in the city, public and private, engaged in international commerce. A *New York Times* editorial gave front-page approval for the scheme, noting that 'some of the poorest people live in conveniently-located slums on high price land', just 'a stone's throw from the stock exchange'. Such a situation, continued the editorial, 'outrages one's sense of order', and the Rockefellers' plan would 're-arrange the hodge-podge and put things where they belong'.[72]

It would also remove the last vestiges of 'blue-collar' infrastructure from Manhattan. This new district of corporate capitalism would be built on the ruins of those traditional manufacturing industries that had allowed it to come into being in the first place. But progress has little time for sentimentality: 'We realise that all changes bring some hardship,' David Rockefeller told the downtown property owners, businessmen and residents. 'We want to work with you in minimizing any hardship.'[73]

From the very start, the World Trade Centre was deeply political, both in the domestic and the international realm. It emerged within the context of the Cold War and its intense atmosphere of East-West competition, from the arms race to the space race. A new construction project on such a colossal scale in one of the world's richest and most dynamic cities could not avoid acquiring a symbolic significance. Many in the west believed that economics rather than military might would win the battle against communism. The World Trade Centre was intended as an icon of the free market, the collective property of everyone prepared to come to the table to do business.[74] Perhaps, it suggested, money really could buy everything – even global peace.

New Yorkers about to lose a large portion of their history and heritage had to be persuaded that the project represented the natural evolution of the city. The new structure had to take all that was being lost – the historic buildings, the small businesses, the manufacturing industries, the merchant spirit of the port city – and memorialise them in its architecture. It was on account of this civic sensitivity that the Port Authority of New York and New Jersey – the large, part public, part private agency responsible for the flow of goods, people and vehicles through the city's seaports, airports, bridges and tunnels – assumed control of the project in 1961.[75]

The involvement of the Port Authority was intended to shore up the claim that the development was for the public good, rather than merely a vehicle for private enterprise. It was at this juncture that the term 'vertical port' first emerged.[76] The Port Authority Director, Austin Tobin, diagnosed a need to change the popular understanding of what a port could be. Physical ports might be characterised by harbours, docks and warehouses tasked with processing and handling goods, but there were other ways that valuable products could make their way to and from markets across the world. What would the port of the future look like – the port that handled the flow of services, money and information? New York's new World Trade Centre was the answer.

As Lower Manhattan was cleared to make way for the redevelopment, the debris of the demolished buildings was used to extend the tip of the island even further into the Hudson River. The foundations of the World Trade Centre cleared away the landfill of the previous centuries – itself composed of the fragments of outmoded merchant ships – and used it to bury a host of piers still operating on the south-western tip of the city. The port of the future was literally being built on the port of the past.

Minoru Yamasaki was afraid of heights. It is a curious fact about a man who once built the tallest buildings in the world. This private phobia even became part of the architecture of the World Trade Centre towers. The walls were made up entirely of glass dressed by 18-inch-wide, aluminium-clad steel columns, regularly spaced so that all the windows in the building were just 22 inches wide. For Yamasaki, this 'humanised' the windows and the view. He had, he believed, designed a defence against vertigo.[77] All the same, when the proposal drawings were first made public in 1964, they left out almost all the views looking downwards.[78]

Perhaps it is wrong, however, to start at the top. The Port Authority did not, and nor did Yamasaki. The World Trade Centre began as a large open plaza, of similar dimensions to the Piazza San Marco in Venice, and 'like that lovely plaza... surrounded by a great square of... buildings, beautifully designed'.[79] History's most famous merchant republic was an obvious starting point for a development that aspired to become the modern acme of international trade.

The illustrator working alongside Yamasaki, a Brazilian-American named Carlos Diniz, had undergone his military service in Venice, and retained an enduring affection for its romantic, Renaissance cityscape. His drawings imagined a plaza, just like San Marco, always filled with people and activity, a setting for ceremonies and celebrations, a vibrant public space.[80] At ground level, the World Trade Centre buildings employed a variety of architectural styles in a curious blend of global cultures. Yamasaki described the plaza as a 'Mecca'[81], and referred to Arab mosques, the Taj Mahal, and Gothic cloisters. At the bases of the two towers, the parallel steel columns on the faces of the buildings curved together in groups of three to meet the plaza floor, creating a series of archways – a modernist take on a Venetian palace. 'What really matters in Manhattan is the scale near the ground,' said Yamasaki. 'It doesn't matter... how high you go. So I concentrated on providing human scale – a broad plaza, arcades, restaurants and fountains'.[82]

Except how high you go does matter a great deal. The development promised a vast 10-million-square-feet of office space. The Campanile of this modernist San Marco was not one tower, but two – and they kept going up and up into the sky above the plaza. The Port Authority was delighted. 'When Yamasaki began to design the wide plazas,' said Austin Tobin, 'and then, to meet our space requirements, to throw his towers towards the sky, we knew that our objective of a beautiful as well as functional complex of Trade Centre buildings was going to be accomplished.'[83]

One of the towers' greatest innovations related directly to this need for maximising the usable floor area. Despite, or perhaps because of their size, Yamasaki settled on a remarkably simple plan. The towers were exact squares, 208 feet by 208 feet, and at their centre was an internal core 87 feet by 135 feet. This core housed all the service functions – elevators, stairways, bathrooms and utility shafts – and was surrounded by huge steel columns running from bedrock to the summit of the towers.[84] The steel columns rising up the exterior of the buildings also acted as load-bearing structural supports. This meant floors and ceilings could be suspended between the outer walls and the inner core with no other form of support. Each office area was an 8-foot 7-inch-high-segment of entirely empty space: 'open plan' in its purest form.[85]

To cope with the mass movement of people through an unprecedented 110 storeys, Yamasaki designed what he called 'sky lobbies'. The 44th and 78th floors became elevator interchanges. Workers would take an express elevator to a sky lobby, then ascend to their specific floor via one of a number of 'local' elevators. In the design for the exterior of the buildings, there was a subtle acknowledgement of this break in the traditional, regimented office-upon-office structure. For three floors, including the sky-lobbies themselves and the floors immediately above and below them, the steel columns on the façades widened and protruded outwards from the towers by just a few inches. This tiny alteration was only perceptible from a distance, creating a series of bands that broke up the otherwise uniform appearance of the towers' identical faces, giving them a continually shifting texture depending on the time of day or the quality of light.[86]

Some of the first critical responses to the plans for the towers bordered on the rapturous. Ada Louise Huxtable, the architectural critic for the *New York Times,* saw them as a 'breakthrough' in skyscraper design, heralding 'a second great period of the skyscraper because the two factors that have limited the height of the tall building until now – construction cost and elevator space – have been solved'.[87]

For the *Houston Chronicle*, it was a 'stunning creation' whose 'soaring metallic structures will be clean but not sterile'.[88] Within a decade, however, the mood changed significantly. The costs had risen as rapidly and relentlessly as the towers themselves. $280 million became $400 million – and the Trade Centre complex was still not complete. Furthermore, Yamasaki's reputation had taken a considerable knock from the very public demolition in 1972 of his Pruitt-Igoe public housing project in St Louis, described with some relish by the architecture critic Charles Jencks as the moment modern architecture died.[89]

Against the backdrop of the Vietnam War and an impending oil crisis, the vaulting optimism of the World Trade Centre towers appeared shockingly naïve. They were called dinosaurs, 'towers of Mammon', 'monuments to boredom', and the 'Colossus that nobody seems to love'.[90] On 5 April, the day after the opening, Huxtable reversed her original opinion. Her *New York Times* review was titled 'Big But Not So Bold', and she wrote that 'the towers are pure technology, the lobbies are pure *schmaltz* and the impact on New York is... pure speculation'.[91] She was horrified that the 'grill-like metal façade' on the interior of the building – part of the technical innovation she had earlier praised for allowing the towers to grow so high – had 'destroyed' one of the 'miraculous benefits of the tall building, the panoramic view out'. She concluded that 'these are big buildings but they are not great architecture'.[92]

Yamasaki had always emphasised his desire to provide human scale and depth in the World Trade Centre. Yet now most reactions seemed to dwell on the 'inhumanity' of the towers. They had no front, back or sides. They were like two giant, anonymous, corporate filing cabinets standing side-by-side, more suggestive of places to store information and data than of environments in which human beings should work. The *Architectural Review* saw them as a 'dire warning' of the 'latest and most terrifying stage in that relentless process which in American cities seems to know no bounds, of putting more and more accommodation on less and less land'.[93]

Charles Jencks popped up again to attack the towers as examples of 'late Capitalist extreme repetition' that equated to 'mental torture'.[94] The French theorist Jean Baudrillard followed Jencks by suggesting that, in their capacity for repetition, the towers threatened the historic and symbolic fabric of all cities. 'The twin towers are clones of each other,' he wrote. 'It's the end of the city.'[95] The pair of identical towers seemed to threaten to multiply – to produce clones of themselves everywhere. In his compelling 1999 'biography' of the World Trade Centre, *Divided We Stand*, the American author Eric Darton argued provocatively that Yamasaki's architecture was a form of terrorism.[96] Mohammad Atta, the architect-turned-terrorist who destroyed the North Tower, might well have concurred, albeit for his own, different reasons.

Outside architectural circles, however, the public reaction was more benign. While the neutral, unadorned style of the buildings undoubtedly left many cold, their scale and their audacity exerted awe and fascination. As the years passed, millions from across the globe rode the fastest elevators in America to the breathtaking open terrace of the World Trade Centre roof. More postcards of the towers were sent each year than of any other building in the world.[97] The power of this 'vertical port' was unmistakable, anchoring every New Yorker to their place in the city. No other buildings were so visible. The towers oriented people and guided them home. They were mostly glimpsed from a distance, their tops appearing above the foreground skyline, or at the end of long canyons of blocks and avenues. Gradually, their unchanging, identical faces became reassuring and familiar – exerting an aura of permanence amid the uncertainties of daily life. When Yamasaki was interviewed by *Time* magazine in 1963, he talked of how 'the element of surprise' offered by architecture was 'little explored'. One of his greatest joys, he said, was 'the experience of moving from a barren street through a narrow opening in a high wall to find a quiet court with a lovely garden and still water; or to tiptoe through the mystery and dimness of a Buddhist temple and come upon a court of raked white gravel dazzling in the sunlight; or to walk a narrow street in Rome and suddenly face an open square with graceful splashing fountains'.[98]

Some saw the towers as the ultimate backdrop, great sculptures in the landscape. As the dean of the architecture school of Yale University, Robert A. M. Stern, put it, they were 'powerful symbols of American and modern life' and, as symbols, 'as successful as the pyramids'.[99] Constantly shifting in and out of view, they could lend a sense of mystery, even magic, to the everyday urban experience.

Today, there are two black holes at the heart of Ground Zero: two cuboid black granite basins, matching exactly in size and position the footprints of the twin towers. Water cascades thirty feet from each side down to the basin floor, into another, smaller, empty square at the centre. This second square is stark in its blackness and blankness. It is the 'void' – meant to symbolise the void left in the lives of so many people after the September 11 attack. Around the rim of the basins, the names of the victims have been perforated into an otherwise seamless strip of bronze. Perforated, rather than carved, to emphasise absence. Four hundred oak trees, all the same height, surround the fountains. And surrounding this memorial, there is a new World Trade Centre. Its most prominent feature is its *single* dominant tower, which now rises, with the help of a large crowning spire, 1,776 feet into the New York sky. The height is a reference to the date of the signing of the Declaration of Independence. Once known as the 'Freedom Tower', this building is now called simply 'One World Trade Centre'.[100]

Set between the two basins is a wedge of glass, containing an atrium clad in blond wood.[101] Inside are two of the original steel columns that once rooted the exterior framework of the north tower to the ground. With no building to attach to anymore, they stand as battered and rusted tridents. This is the entrance to the September 11 Memorial Museum. Some 110,000 square feet have been excavated below ground level, dropping 70 feet – seven storeys – to the original granite schist bedrock of Manhattan Island.[102] From the entrance atrium, a long ramp, based on the road used by the clear-up trucks to remove the rubble from Ground Zero, leads visitors downwards. Its walls are lined with projections of the thousands of 'Missing Person' posters that covered the public spaces of New York in the weeks and months after the attack. Part of the way along the ramp is a balcony overlooking a massive chamber. The far side of this chamber is made up of the monolithic slurry wall, the last line of defence that stopped the Hudson River pouring into Lower Manhattan as the towers fell.[103]

Standing spotlit in front of the slurry wall is the 'Last Column', the final piece of debris removed from Ground Zero. Over the years, this long, slim 36-foot-high slice of steel had been covered in personal memorials. There is bright, spray-painted graffiti detailing the casualties suffered among the various emergency services, along with taped-up photographs, pictures and prayer cards. It is presented as a sacred object – a totem pole and shrine to the towers and to the victims. Touch-screens allow visitors to navigate the Column, to investigate the individual stories behind each image or message.[104]

Other objects are similarly preserved. There is a fire truck with a smashed cabin, an ambulance, a fragment of battered aeroplane fuselage, and a section of a staircase used by workers to escape the towers before they fell, christened the 'Survivors' Stair'. Over 10,000 artefacts have been gathered from the debris to form the museum's 'collection': on display are everything from wallets, handbags and lipsticks, to a fireman's helmet, a Bible and transcripts of victims' final phonecalls.[105] These prosaic items are transformed into poignant relics.

At the lowest level is the most sombre – and the most controversial – part of the museum. A concrete wall is marked, using original steel taken from Ground Zero, with a phrase from Virgil's *Aeneid*: 'No day shall erase you from the memory of time.'[106] Behind the wall are the unidentified bodily remains of people who died in the attack – almost 8,000 individual pieces belonging to the 1,115 victims still officially unaccounted for.[107]

At 7am on 10 May 2014, these remains were transferred to the museum from the repository of the city medical examiner. Three coffin-sized, metal military cases, draped in American flags, were carried by uniformed bearers through the memorial plaza, past watching family members, and down into the museum. Some relatives were there, however, as protesters, wearing black gags over their mouths, symbolising the lack of consultation over the treatment of the remains.[108] It does not sit easy with them that what may be the last resting place of their loved ones has become a tourist attraction charging $24 dollars for entry, and selling fridge-magnets and souvenir T-shirts.[109] The official line is that the remains are still in the custody of the medical examiner, and, as DNA technology advances, so the identification process will continue.[110]

In the wake of September 11, Ground Zero was given 'landmark' status and made subject to federal preservation law. This brought with it a legal requirement to make the artefacts that were salvaged there accessible to the public. It was the unique nature of what was left – in particular huge fragments like the surviving slurry wall – that led to the decision to build a museum on the exact spot where the attacks and the devastation occurred. As the museum's director, Alice Greenwald, puts it: 'where most museums are buildings that house artefacts, this museum has been built within an artefact'.[111]

When it opened on 14 May 2014, the *New York Times* called it 'as powerful as a punch to the gut', but acknowledged the museum's somewhat uncomfortable role as both memorial and attraction, asking: 'How many theme parks bring you, repeatedly, to tears?'[112] The *Washington Post*, on the other hand, condemned the museum as 'an oversized pit of self-pity, patriotic self-glorification and voyeurism' that turned 'grief on a loop' into a bizarre ritual.[113]

Are the twisted metal fragments that fill the museum, the giant steel beams bent and broken by unimaginable pressures, worthy of preservation as artefacts from one of the most significant days in modern history? Or, mounted on plinths and bathed in atmospheric light, have they become art installations, curiously, queasily beautiful? Perhaps most uncomfortable of all is the quote from Virgil on the wall that contains the remains of the fallen. In the original epic poem, this line refers to two male warriors, and lovers: Nisus and Euryalus. They have just slaughtered countless enemy soldiers, and once captured, are executed together. It is a fate they embrace gladly, an act of self-sacrifice for a greater political cause. It is a sentiment that seems to fit more closely the hijackers of September 11 than their victims.[114]

Such discord was perhaps inevitable. The billions of threads of story knotted together at Ground Zero could not remain as one for very long. History has passed through the black hole, and on the other side narratives are unravelling again, splitting off, diverging, multiplying, and racing away. It is easy to forget – or deny – that there was a moment when the world stopped still in a shared paralysis of fear, amazement and shame. The further it recedes from memory, the more people question the significance of what happened on that September morning. Two buildings fell down, they say, and then we picked up again just where we left off.

When they were first completed, Yamasaki's towers were widely pilloried as blank, modern obelisks, out of place in a nuanced, post-modern world. But if the towers were anachronisms from the very beginning, then what did that make the attack on them, a full thirty years later? What does it actually mean to destroy a building in the modern, digital world, where data – and power – resides not in any one place, but in all places, and all at once? The majority of businesses based in the Trade Centre continued to operate seamlessly, despite the catastrophe. If capitalism was the target, then it barely noticed. Perhaps the attack itself, despite its implausible scale and terrifying spectacle, was itself a relic: unoriginal and derivative, the product of too many Hollywood movies. Perhaps the hijackers hit the towers, but missed the point. Perhaps.

There are many stories to be told on the other side of Ground Zero. This is just one of them.

Chapter Twenty

The Deleted City

GeoCities – The World Wide Web
(Born 1994 – Died 2009)

It was a perfectly normal day in the city. The sun rose over the streets and neighbourhoods. At the same time, it also set. Somewhere in the city it was always mid-morning, just as it was always late evening somewhere else: the city was so big that it crossed every time zone. It truly was a city that never slept. Or rather, it was a city that was always awake. As this particular day unfolded, the people of the city continued to gather together in their favourite places.

Some went to Athens to talk about ancient history and philosophy. Across town, Bourbon Street was busy with hipsters discussing jazz music and Cajun food. Round the corner at Colosseum, the topic of conversation was the previous day's sports results; while across the road at Capitol Hill, it was politics. On Left Bank and SoHo, writers and artists shared ideas and opinions. On Wall Street they shared business advice. In Napa Valley, there were fierce arguments over wines and grapes. In Area 51, groups gathered close together, communicating in low whispers about UFOs and government secrets. In Petsburgh, they let their favourite animals roam free.

Yet, despite the appearance of 'business as usual', things had not been normal in the city for some time. All of the city's neighbourhoods – which had once overflowed with so many people that they had grown their own suburbs – had suffered a steady fall in population. For years, residents had been leaving. Their homes remained just where they had built them, but they no longer answered when their neighbours came round to call. It was the same story everywhere across the city. Some streets were completely empty. All the lights were on, flickering and flashing in garish repetitions, but no one was home. Some worried that they were living in a ghost city. Others persisted. Many of the original residents stayed on. They did not feel the need to move away, or to find anywhere new. They had met many friends in the city – friends who shared the same passions and interests. And they had built so much. They had created the city from scratch. This meant something. It was important. The city had been home to 38 million people.[1] It was the biggest collective cultural endeavour in history. It was a city for the ages.

The end came in an instant. One moment, every single neighbourhood, suburb and individual home was still there. The next, they were gone. There had been no storm clouds on the horizon, no rumbles deep within the earth, no shadowy armies gathering in the distance.

On 27 October 2009, at 12.30pm Pacific Standard Time[2], the city simply ceased to exist.

Fifteen years previously, in November 1994, a pair of young entrepreneurs named David Bohnett and John Rezner had set up a company called Beverley Hills Internet. Bohnett was a business graduate from Chicago with a passion for computers, while Rezner was a systems engineer for the aerospace firm McDonnell Douglas.[3] They based their company in Los Angeles, and joined the vanguard of the early prospectors of the World Wide Web. It was a time when so much seemed worth doing, if only because it had never been done before. Bohnett and Rezner saw the digital realm as a place for experimentation, as a place to be explored – and, once explored, *colonised*. What this all meant in business terms, however, nobody really knew.

In May 1995, the company came to the attention of the media for broadcasting, live on their website, the feeds from two video cameras left running around the clock in separate locations in Beverly Hills.

The first camera was fixed on the corner of Hollywood and Vine. The second filmed the bus stop outside their office.[4] For Bohnett and Rezner, this was no idle gimmick. Their idea was to bring 'a sense of place to the sometimes confusing world of cyberspace'. According to their company philosophy, 'the Internet becomes easier to understand and relate to when it is rich with content and closely identified with an actual idea or location'.[5] The webcams were a bridge between the physical and the digital world. For months, Beverly Hills Internet had been creating virtual online communities based on real places in Los Angeles. 'Rodeo Drive' was dedicated to shopping; 'Hollywood' was all about movies and actors; 'Sunset Strip' focused on rock music; and West Hollywood catered for Gay, Lesbian, Bisexual and Transgender issues – 'just like their real life namesakes!' as the company press release said.[6]

By July, they had installed webcams on the Champs-Élysées in Paris, and in the Ginza shopping precinct of Tokyo, and extended the number of their digital communities to ten.[7] For the first time, locations were featured outside the city of Los Angeles: there was Silicon Valley (for computers and programming), Wall Street (for business and finance), Capitol Hill (for politics), Colosseum (for sports), Paris (for romance and poetry), and Tokyo (for everything to do with the Far East). 'The problem with the Internet and the Web,' said Bohnett, 'is that it can be a confusing place. If we created communities based on a theme, it would give people a sense of familiarity, of comfort.'[8] The communities were also given a collective name: *GeoCities*.

It was one thing to attract people to a website, but it was quite another to get them to stay. Bohnett and Rezner had, however, hit on a revolutionary idea. They offered anyone with internet access the space and the tools to build, for free, their own web-pages within the GeoCity of their choice. For the first time, ordinary people were able to 'homestead' cyberspace, to create and develop residences that were uniquely personal. 'This is the next wave of the net,' said Bohnett. 'Not just information, but *habitation*.'[9]

Every 'homesteader' – or 'netizen'[10] – was given a unique address on the web, and even a GeoCity street number. Bohnett encouraged users to 'put down roots in a GeoCity they feel comfortable and familiar with to call home, where they can express themselves, create their own content, build their own neighbourhoods.'[11] This was both a staging post they could use to explore the rest of web, and a permanent base, a constant and reassuring point of return within the vastness of cyberspace. 'You may surf the net via access utilities or online services, but you'll live in GeoCities,' continued Bohnett. 'There, on the street or in the city of your choice, you'll dwell in a home that reflects the context of your life, become part of the fabric of the community and establish your own net culture.'[12] What they were offering was 'land' within the digital frontier. Anyone who filled out their personal details on a form was entitled to two megabytes – which would later grow to fifteen – of free space to create their home.[13] Crucially, the users did not own the land. Bohnett and Rezner did. Every resident of GeoCities was a tenant.

What did it actually mean to 'live' in the internet? Primarily, it was about 'uploading' your personality into the digital world. The 'homes' in GeoCities were web-pages. Once they were allocated their plot of land, users were given a basic tool-kit that allowed them, with little or no programming knowledge, to create simple web structures. They could then populate these structures with their own content, and decorate them to their personal tastes, with such items as looping music files (known as MIDI – for Musical Instrument Digital Interface) and animations (GIFs – for Graphics Interchange Format).[14]

The results were often garish in the extreme. For professional graphic artists and web developers, exploring the 'streets' of a GeoCity was like entering the seventh circle of design hell. Bright, clashing primary colours, outlandish fonts – including an obsession with the *comic sans* typeface that seemingly crossed all national boundaries – a determination to fill all available space with *something*, were common themes. This chaotic development was, however, quite understandable. It was GeoCities that first introduced the concept of the personal webpage.[15] The users who filled their 'homes' with family photographs, crude digital artwork, rambling text and, most common of all, manically flickering GIFs, were pioneers, groping blindly towards some standard of web culture. GeoCities offered, on a scale never seen before, a forum for free art and unfettered expression.[16]

Bohnett and Rezner wanted their site to 'make the world smaller'.[17] The simple idea at the very heart of this was that users were free to choose where they lived based on their interests. Once their homes were built, they could walk out of their virtual front doors into a neighbourhood of like-minded residents. Anyone, from anywhere in the world, could bond in a GeoCity over anything from blue whales to Baked Alaska, from Mozart to muscle cars.

'Everything we do is based on shared interests,' explained Bohnett. 'We give people an opportunity to share their thoughts on their favourite subject. It's about one-to-one communication.'[18] Once people had found their feet (their web feet?), they were encouraged to play a part in the 'management, stewardship and growth'[19] of their neighbourhoods. GeoCity administrators would identify enthusiastic and active homesteaders, and appoint them as community leaders, with a responsibility to welcome and assist new residents, and give the community itself a sense of drive and direction. At all times, the familiar structural model of the city remained in place: streets, blocks, neighbourhoods, downtown, suburbs.

The concept proved popular with early users of the web. In December 1995, when Beverley Hills Internet changed its name to GeoCities, visitor numbers to their website had surged to over 6 million per month. Over 20,000 people had taken a plot of land in a GeoCity, and had created over 25,000 webpages.[20] The number of residents continued to increase at an incredible rate. On 14 May 1996, GeoCities welcomed its 50,000th homesteader. Just three months later, on 7 August, it had reached 100,000 citizens. By 9 October 1997, the population of GeoCities had increased tenfold to over a million.[21] 'I knew right from the beginning this was going to be big,' said Bohnett. 'I got an email every time someone would register. There were ten a second at one point.'[22] From zero to one million people in two years. This was the fastest growing city in history.

In June 1999, protesters crowded the streets of GeoCities in a virtual demonstration that threatened to turn into a virtual riot. Many left the city, never to return. What had caused such an impassioned outcry? It was all to do with the management of their digital home. The millions of tenants of GeoCities had a new landlord – the internet giant Yahoo. And they were not happy about the changes being made to their city.

A year earlier, on 11 August 1998, GeoCities had launched on the stock market. The Initial Public Offering valued the shares at $17. Over the course of the trading day, they shot up in value, settling at $34.[23] By the time the market closed, GeoCities was a billion dollar public company.[24] Just two days later, on 13 August, it also became the first-ever internet company to be charged with violating the privacy of its users. It signed a decree with the Federal Trade Commission, admitting no wrongdoing, but agreeing to adjust the terms for sign-up to its services.[25] GeoCities had been sharing residents' personal registration information with advertisers. As more and more people had moved into the streets of the digital city, more and more virtual advertising hoardings had followed them.

A change of virtual landlord: Yahoo takes over GeoCities.

It was no coincidence, for instance, that a resident of MotorCity would see promotions for cars, or that a homesteader in Yosemite would find their web-page surrounded by inducements to buy hiking and camping gear. Some residents had willingly agreed to this; others believed they had not. There were isolated pockets of vociferous discontent, but most GeoCities residents were willing to accept that there had been a misunderstanding – a symptom of the original vague terms of service.[26] It was a sign, however, of a changing landscape. GeoCities was no longer the frontier city of the web, an enclave of blissful freedom. The mainstream and the establishment were catching up. Lawyers, regulators and big businessmen were following the original netizens across the virtual border, into the digital world.[27]

On 29 January 1999, Yahoo paid a remarkable $4.58 billion in stock to buy GeoCities. The sale made the front page of the *Wall Street Journal*.[28] By this time, it was the third most visited website on the internet – the original 'social network'. 'GeoCities has built the web's most popular and widely used community,' said Yahoo Chairman Tim Koogle, as he announced the deal. 'Through this acquisition, we are accelerating our global leadership position by combining two of the web's strongest brands and most heavily used services into one powerful offering.'[29] The GeoCities Chief Executive Officer, Tom Evans explained that 'Yahoo has a proven capability of monetizing their user base.' Working with them, he said, 'gives us the ability to put GeoCities on steroids.'[30]

Bohnett, whose three million shares were worth $367 million at Yahoo's closing price, claimed not to see the buy-out as a 'financial event'; he had not, he said, started the company 'with money in mind'.[31] GeoCities was still about 'giving people a chance to speak up', and its goal was to 'stake out a broader territory and create a community of interests, just as Yahoo was helping people find their way around the web.'[32] All the same, it was a business. At some point, Bohnett acknowledged, they were going to have to find a way 'to monetize that base of users'. When Yahoo bought GeoCities, the company was yet to turn a profit.[33]

Many, however, were not happy being 'monetized'. The colonisers of the web, the digital frontiersmen who had made their way to GeoCities, had believed that things were going to be different this time. For them, the internet represented a free society: free of regulation, ownership, censorship, free of rules, barriers, government and the grey, business-suited authority of *The Man.* Yet again, though, it seemed that the fate of the many was being decided by the few, in some distant, real-world, corporate boardroom. Six months after the stock purchase, Yahoo took the step that sent the GeoCities community into uproar. One morning, as residents made their way from their physical to their digital homes, they found that Yahoo had, effectively, changed all the locks.

In order to interact with their web-pages – or enter their homes – residents were asked to re-register, and agree to new terms of service.[34] GeoCities had always owned the 'land' on which residents' home-pages were built. Now Yahoo wanted to own the content as well; in effect, anything created in GeoCities would become their property. In response, homesteaders took to the streets of their digital city, bombarding Yahoo with protest emails. The dispute soon made its way into the mainstream media. 'Yahoo Angers GeoCities Members with Copyright Rules,' reported the *New York Times* on 30 June 1999.[35] Many residents were so incensed that they simply uprooted their homes and rebuilt them in the internet wilderness, lone outposts far beyond the GeoCities walls.

Protest websites encouraged users to migrate away from their old neighbourhoods to new digital land elsewhere. After just a few days, with the online protests growing, and media scrutiny intensifying, Yahoo amended its terms of service, adding the line: 'Yahoo does not own content you submit, unless we specifically tell you otherwise before you submit it.'[36]

Yahoo said they had never intended to seize intellectual property: rather, they needed users to sign up to the terms to allow them to migrate members' homes to the Yahoo servers, which would allow everything in GeoCities to become much quicker and more reliable.[37] At this point, most residents signed up, but a significant number did not. In every neighbourhood, homes were left empty and abandoned. It was a troubled start for the new owners of GeoCities. And it was also the warning sign that the first city of the internet might have reached its peak. While the population as a whole continued to grow, thanks to the inevitable surge from Yahoo users, parts of GeoCities were in decay. Little by little, the digital city was beginning to fall.

In July 2009, Yahoo sent a 'service announcement' email to every resident of GeoCities. 'Dear Yahoo GeoCities customer,' it began, 'we're writing to let you know that Yahoo GeoCities, our free web site building service and community, is closing on October 26, 2009. On October 26, 2009, your GeoCities site will no longer appear on the web, and you will no longer be able to access your GeoCities account and files... Please be aware that after October 26, your GeoCities files will be deleted from our servers, and *will not be recoverable*'.[38]

It was confirmation of the rumours that had been circulating for months. In April, Yahoo had announced that it was about to make five per cent of its staff redundant.[39] Just days later, it had provided a list of unprofitable sites to be closed down or, as the web terminology puts it, 'shuttered'. GeoCities had been on the list. The July email merely gave the exact date. An entire city was condemned. The 'service announcement' was its demolition notice.

For a time, life in the Yahoo-owned GeoCities had been as good, if not better, than before. After the initial clashes with residents, Yahoo settled down as a seemingly ideal administrator and governor of the digital city. More people than ever before filled the neighbourhoods. Services and amenities improved, residents were able to get around their great, growing city much faster than in the past. The sense of global community was stronger than ever, as a flood of new users immigrated. And yet, as history has demonstrated many times, the peak is often reached after the decline has already begun.

In the early years of the twenty-first century, competitors began to emerge. In the streets of GeoCities, residents began to talk openly about places called MySpace and Facebook, and later something called Twitter. They began to question exactly why they were living in a 'city' online. Why were they slavishly copying the conventions of the real world, when really they should be enjoying the unstructured freedoms of the digital?

As their disquiet over city-living grew, they also noticed that the city itself was changing. Yahoo had helped to improve the basic 'urban' infrastructure, but it wanted something in return: money.

As the city grew, and more land was needed, Yahoo had to find some way to fund the expansion. Advertising became more prevalent than ever before. Yahoo offered a premium, paid-for, ad-free service.[40]

For $158 a year, residents could buy themselves a much larger plot in 'gated' communities, where advertising was not permitted.[41] But this imposed hierarchies on the city where none had existed before: virtual walls began to divide neighbourhoods. Despite these measures, the high costs of simply maintaining GeoCities left little scope for investment and civic redevelopment on Yahoo's part.

Compared to other sites on the web, the city was starting to look and feel *old*. Services began to break down, and the community fabric became frayed and tired. In October 2006, there were some 18.9 million visitors to GeoCities. By March 2008, this had dropped to 15.1 million. Another year on, in March 2009, this figure was down to 11.5 million.[42] It was still one of the most visited sites on the web, but it was clearly in a steady and sustained decline. It was a virtual exodus. Yahoo decided they could not justify the upkeep. The only option, they said, was to level the whole city, leaving no trace.

Many simply left GeoCities behind and did not look back. It was seen increasingly as something of an embarrassment, a ramshackle internet shanty-town, full of crude structures belonging to a different age. In April 2009, the computer magazine *PC World* ran a joke obituary for the site. Titled 'So Long GeoCities: We Forgot You Still Existed', it began by announcing that 'GeoCities, a free web hosting service that achieved fame in the mid-90s, died Thursday at the Yahoo headquarters in Silicon Valley. GeoCities was 15 years old.'[43] A cause of death, it said, had still to be determined, but it noted that the site had been growing weaker by the month: 'The proliferation of low-cost housing options, combined with the increasing popularity of social network-style services in place of personal home-pages, only contributed to its demise.' The obituary concluded that 'the GeoCities site is expected to remain functional through midyear as a tribute to its life. Funeral arrangements are now pending.'[44]

For others, there was dismay at the very principle of mass-deletion, and what it meant for the future of everything created within the digital world. 'While the natural urge by some would be to let GeoCities sink into obscurity and death, leaving nothing its wake,' said the Archive Team, a group dedicated to preserving the 'digital heritage' of the internet, 'the fact remains that GeoCities was for millions of people the first experience of dealing with the low-cost, full-colour world-accessible website and all the possibilities this contained.' Its destruction, they said, 'would be a loss of the very history of the web.'[45]

When Yahoo announced in April 2009 that GeoCities was to be closed, Jason Scott, a former systems administrator from New York and one of the leaders of the Archive Team, put together a group of thirty volunteers from around the world, and began trying to download as much as he could of GeoCities before it was destroyed.[46]

When it comes to the preservation and 'archaeology' of the internet, speed is very much of the essence. Scott and his team were engaged in a race against time. At first, they feared that GeoCities would be razed at any moment and without warning. Then, in July, Yahoo pinned the zero hour to a specific day – 26 October.

For six months, the Archive Team set almost 100 computers running non-stop, sending 'crawling' programmes known as Wgets (a name derived from World Wide Web and 'get') into the Yahoo servers to copy every available public file they could find.[47] Because of the size of GeoCities, the amount of data being harvested was vast: copied pages were filling terabyte after terabyte of hard drive space. Scott put out a call for more hard drives to cope with the relentless stream of files.[48] The programmes kept running, copies of the city's millions of homes flooding cyberspace right up until the last day in the life of GeoCities. 26 October came and went, and still the work continued. Then finally, at around 12.30pm Pacific Standard Time, the following day, the Wget crawlers ground to a halt.[49]

On the screen of every computer still attempting to archive the GeoCities pages, and the screen of every city resident still attempting to access their internet 'home', there appeared a message from Yahoo: 'Sorry, GeoCities has closed.' There was little further explanation, merely the line, 'The GeoCities service is no longer available, but there's a lot more to explore on Yahoo!'[50] Just like that, the largest city in history was dead.

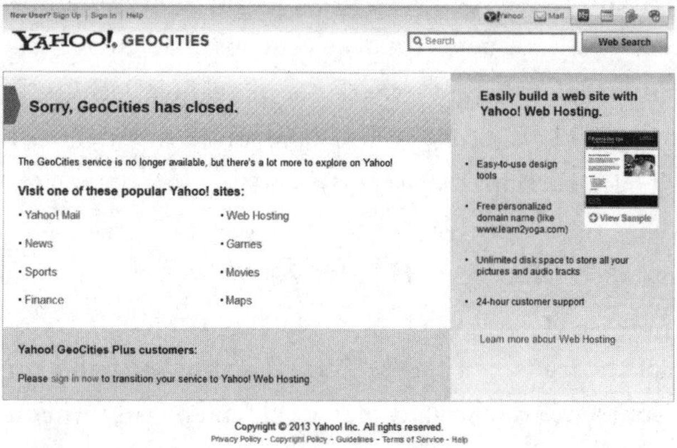

'Sorry, GeoCities has closed.'

With the virtual city razed, Scott and his team turned to the task of working methodically through the data files, compiling the copies held on all the various different servers and hard drives across the globe, to work out how much they had managed to save.[51] On 9 November 2009, just a few weeks after the fall of GeoCities, Scott was interviewed by *Time* magazine. In an article with the provocative title, 'Internet Atrocity! GeoCities' Demise Erases Web History'[52], Scott and other internet preservationists compared what Yahoo had done to the environmental depredations of rapacious nineteenth-century industrialists, even to the Taliban's destruction in 2001 of the ancient Buddha statutes of Bamiyan in Afghanistan. 'GeoCities was the largest self-created folk-art collection in the history of the world,' claimed Scott. And Yahoo, he said, had 'found the way to destroy the most massive amount of history in the shortest amount of time with absolutely no recourse.'[53]

In September 2011, a Dutch designer and artist called Richard Vijgen – head of the Studio for Object Oriented Information Design and Research – went public with an 'interactive visualisation' he had created, called 'The Deleted City'.[54] The installation has now toured galleries from Los Angeles and Denver to Amsterdam and London, and takes the form of a touch-screen containing a top-down digital map. The map is drawn with green lines against a black background, 'reminiscent of old phosphorescent computer screens'[55], and it begins with a view of a great many clusters of green squares: the brighter the green, the denser the accumulation of squares in any particular area. By pinching and dragging the screen, you can zoom further and further into the map to explore it in more and more detail.

Many of the larger squares reveal names: 'Heartland', 'SunsetBeach', 'EnchantedForest', 'FashionAvenue'. Zooming takes you into a kaleidoscope of more and more squares, which appear to expand almost exponentially outwards. Finally, you arrive at the base level. There, the squares reveal themselves as web-pages, their contents defined by the context of the larger squares in which they are found. The squares in 'Heartland' are all about families; in 'FashionAvenue' they are full of countless images of shoes and dresses. At the highest zoom, animated GIFs flicker across the touch-screen, and as you drift over certain areas, MIDI files play tinny snatches of music. Vijgen's installation is made up of everything that remains of GeoCities.[56]

Scott and his Archive Team spent a full year sifting through the data they had gathered from the doomed GeoCities. Once they had pieced together all the salvaged pages, they released a copy of the site through one, massive 'BitTorrent': a data-transfer system which coordinates the downloading of often very large files from multiple locations holding all or part of the original file.[57] In effect, the remnants of GeoCities are now 'seeded' throughout the web. Partly a necessity due to the sheer amount of data archived, this is also a means of ensuring that there is no single copy that can be destroyed: replication and 'backups' are fundamentals of the internet preservation process.

It took Vijgen several months to download the whole of GeoCities from the Archive Team torrent. The extraction of the compressed files then took days, producing a database of over 36 million files.[58]

Vijgen's next step was to produce an algorithm sorting the data into a two-dimensional grid. The sizes of the individual neighbourhoods on the grid were determined by the number of home-pages they had housed in the original GeoCities structure.[59] Smaller neighbourhoods slotted into the gaps between the larger ones, 'mimicking a city that tries to use the land efficiently'.[60] This interactive map transforms GeoCities into one vast, sprawling archaeological site: as Vijgen memorably puts it, a 'digital Pompeii'. His analogy is a good one. The Archive Team managed to save a significant proportion of the site before it was destroyed – exactly how much will never be known – but what they preserved is still merely a snapshot, not a living environment: a 'virtual city frozen in time'.[61]

'The Deleted City' © Richard Vijgen

Like Pompeii, the nature of GeoCities' death has allowed it to be seen just as it was at the moment of its destruction, in all its everyday banality. As Scott explains: 'a lot of people see GeoCities as this sea of amateurish, poorly written websites. I understand that thinking: I certainly don't want people to think that I'm saying GeoCities is an example of the best the web could be, but I do think it is an example of what the web was.'[62]

The ruins of GeoCities are a place to browse, explore and commune with the early history of the internet, to see the beginnings of a technology that is continually and rapidly superseding itself. Buried within its virtual streets are artefacts bearing witness to the very origins of the web. And it may be years before there is any broad appreciation of the significance of what has been preserved. Most will see it as worthless detritus: the formative, multi-coloured vomitus of an infant internet; one vast and useless rubbish dump. Yet one of the most basic rules of archaeology is that much can be learnt from what has been thrown away. Who knows? Perhaps those facile GeoCities web-pages, to which we today ascribe negligible cultural value, will in the distant future be treated as 'no less important than the cave paintings of Lascaux'.[63]

GeoCities was the very first internet city. It will also likely be the last. Basing web structures on real-world counterparts is already outmoded. The city has been replaced by the cloud. Instead of digital earth, we have digital heaven, an omnipotent repository of data that is nowhere and everywhere all at once. We are no longer citizens of the net, but consumers. We do not have to live in the web anymore, because the web lives with us, carried in our pockets or even broadcast onto the lenses of our glasses.

In any case, the 'land' once occupied by GeoCities has been built on by massive corporations. They watch, monitor and analyse our every digital move. 'The sense that you were given some space on the internet, and allowed to do anything you wanted to in this space, it's completely gone from these new social sites,' said Scott. 'Like prisoners, or livestock, or anybody locked in an institution, I am sure the residents of these new places don't even notice the walls anymore.'[64]

In June 2014, Facebook announced that it had been conducting a secret experiment on 600,000 of its users, to see if manipulating the content of their 'news feeds' could affect their emotions. 'The results show emotional contagion,' concluded the Facebook researchers. 'When positive expressions were reduced, people produced fewer positive posts and more negative posts; when negative expressions were reduced, the opposite pattern occurred.' The company claimed users had opted in to this secret psychological testing by ticking a box agreeing to assist in 'internal operation, including troubleshooting, data analysis, testing, research and service improvement.'[65]

There can be no ruins in the cloud, no tangible traces, no relics, no artefacts. The cloud represents the end of ruins. Or does it? After all, the cloud still has an engine: the cloud-making machines that keep it floating above us all. This engine is found in 'server farms': what the internet pioneer and historian of information technology James Gleick describes as so many 'unmarked brick buildings and steel complexes, with smoked windows or no windows, miles of hollow floors, diesel generators, cooling towers, seven-foot intake fans, and aluminium chimney stacks.'[66] We have not yet transcended the physical, despite what the metaphorical 'cloud' might like you to think.

GeoCities represents the ruins of web 1.0. How long before we find ourselves picking through the debris of the second generation? The empires of the internet believe they will last forever, but history shows that this cannot be. It is inevitable that Google, Facebook and all the other giants of our current digital age will succumb to the eternal cycle of rise, decline and fall.

Chapter 21

Let the Past Meet the Future

Palmyra – Tadmor, Syria (Born 41 BC – Died 2015)

In mid-July 2015, an 82-year-old retired archaeologist called Khaled al-Assad was seized at his home in the Syrian city of Tadmor by the militant fundamentalist group Islamic State. He was held for twenty-seven days.[1] On Tuesday 18 August, he was led into a square in front of the city museum. There, a crowd watched as al-Assad was beheaded. His corpse was strung up with twine, and his head was left resting on the ground beneath his feet. A sign was hung from his waist listing his crimes: he had visited Iran; he had represented Syria abroad at 'infidel conferences', he was 'apostate'; and, as a former head of Tadmor's museum, he was a 'director of idolatry'.[2]

Tadmor is a city of some 70,000 people[3] set in the middle of the Syrian Desert, halfway between the Mediterranean coast and the river valley of the Euphrates. Its name derives from the Arabic word for dates, *tamar*[4], of which it boasts more than twenty different varieties.[5] It is a city that has grown out of the remains – and the memory – of another, much older city, a city that is known across the world by its Latin name. *Palmyra.* The 'place of palm trees'. Today's settlement is a scruffy town which has grown up to service Syria's phosphate mining, natural gas and oil industries. Its nondescript urban sprawl lives in the shadow of one of the world's most spectacular ruins – the near 2,000-year-old remains of a trader oasis-enclave shaped uniquely by ancient Roman, Greek and Eastern influences. Or rather it *lived* in the shadow. Because the grotesque murder of al-Assad came in the midst of one of the most shocking acts of iconoclasm in the modern era. With crude symbolism, al-Assad's body was suspended from one of Palmyra's thousand or so ancient columns.[6] Now there are significantly fewer remains standing from which to hang anything. The name Palmyra has become universal shorthand for deliberate cultural annihilation.

The battle for these two desert cities – ancient and modern, celebrated and obscure – was short and brutal. On Wednesday 13 May 2015, Islamic State surged westwards in a rapid offensive from their bases in Iraq and the Euphrates Valley. They swiftly overran the town of al-Amiriya, around 2km to the north of Tadmor, and the site of a number of weapons and fuel depots. At the same time, they attacked Palmyra's military airport, subjecting it to heavy shelling.[7] On Saturday 16 May they infiltrated the northern districts of the city, engaging the Syrian government forces in fierce fighting in the streets. The following day the tide appeared to have turned. Isis were pushed out by a counter-offensive, and the city borders seemed once again secure – although the army continued to sweep the streets for bombs and explosive devices left behind during the retreat. After just four days of fighting, some 300 were dead, including over 50 civilians.[8]

By Monday 18 May, the government forces – spearheaded by a heavily-armoured tank battalion – had recaptured al-Amiriya.[9] Yet what they discovered stashed within the Isis forward positions was ominous: sophisticated combat armour; stacks of suicide vests; thermal missiles; Muslim prayer books printed in Russian, indicating the involvement in the offensive of battle-hardened Chechen rebels; vast quantities of small-arms ammunition, enough for each Isis fighter to carry 10,000 rounds; and a huge hoard of Snickers chocolate bars.[10] Two days later, the Syrian army was in full retreat, fleeing westwards and – depending on which news reports were to be believed – either evacuating Tadmor's civilian population as they went, or leaving them to their fate.[11]

On the evening of 20 May, two very different messages rang out. A government soldier radioed Syrian army headquarters with the abrupt, anguished cry of 'We're finished'[12], while an Isis fighter announced over the internet that 'Praise God, Palmyra has been liberated'.[13] An injection of some 800 Isis reinforcements, including veteran soldiers from Afghanistan and Chechnya, had smashed the resistance of the government troops.[14]

As the battle raged, Mamoun Abdulkarim, Syria's Director General for Antiquities and Museums, tried to arrange the transfer of as many ancient artefacts as possible from Palmyra's museum. Staff had barricaded themselves in the building, and were engaged round the clock in wrapping everything from statues and stone fragments to jewellery, coins and mosaics, and packing them in crates. Abdulkarim's original plan was to use military planes to fly the antiquities to safety, but the airport was one of the first sites to fall into Islamic State hands.[15] His only option was to move them by road – packing two trucks with a collection that was at once 'priceless' and, in real market terms, worth millions. The museum staff worked up to the last second. Early in the morning of 21 May, with the city fallen and militants advancing on the last pockets of resistance, the trucks were still being loaded. As the final crates were being stowed, armed insurgents moved towards the museum through the ruins of Palmyra's colonnaded boulevard and opened fire, wounding three staff members.[16] The casualties were pulled bleeding into the trucks, which drove away under a heavy barrage, escaping to the desert highway that runs west all the way to the Syrian capital, Damascus.

Abdulkarim's questionable assessment was that 95 percent of the museum's artefacts had been rescued.[17] Several objects, however, had been too heavy to carry. For instance the 2,000-year-old, three-metre-tall, 15-tonne limestone sculpture known as the 'Lion of Al-lat' was left behind, sealed up with foam padding and large sheets of metal plating. Then there was the ancient city of Palmyra itself. There was nowhere for it to go, nowhere for it to hide. By the middle of June, reports were filtering out that its columns, buildings and tombs had been rigged with mines. At first it wasn't clear whether the explosives were there for strategic or ideological purposes. It was standard practice for Isis to booby-trap newly seized frontline sites to make them harder to recapture. At the same time, they had demonstrated that they viewed all remnants from the pre-Islamic world as heretical. In February 2015, after capturing the Iraqi city of Mosul, they had ransacked its museum, destroying a host of ancient artefacts. The whole episode was captured on video, showing militants overturning millennia-old Assyrian and Akkadian statues, and smashing them with sledgehammers and pneumatic drills. Addressing the camera, one man used Mohammed's destruction of idols at Mecca as a reference point, explaining that God had ordered the 'removal' of these works, because they had been created by 'devil worshippers'.[18] The anguished reaction of the western media to these acts of cultural violence was, of course, exactly what Islamic State wanted.

In seizing Palmyra Islamic State had captured a site of world-wide renown – one that, before the onset of the Syrian civil war, had attracted some 150,000 tourists a year. They were well aware of its symbolic potency. The re-purposing of the historic city began almost instantly. On 27 May, soldiers herded 25 captives onto the stage of the ruined Roman amphitheatre, lined them up, and ordered 25 teenage recruits to shoot them in the backs of their heads.[19] A few weeks later this atrocity was circulated on the internet as a 10-minute-long propaganda video. At the start of July, they unwrapped the Lion of Al-lat, and promptly blew it up.[20] In an interview on Alwan FM, an anti-government Syrian radio station, the Isis military commander in Tadmor explained that, while the destruction of the lion was demanded by their strict beliefs, Palmyra itself would be safe. 'Concerning the historic city,' he said, 'we will preserve it and it will not be harmed, God willing. What we will do is break the idols that the infidels used to worship. The historic buildings will not be touched and we will not bring bulldozers to destroy them like some people think'.[21]

This pledge did not last long. Towards the end of July, Isis detonated a large quantity of explosives placed inside the temple of Baal

Shamin.[22] This huge building, which dates back to AD 23[23], was instantly shattered, reduced to fragments and rubble. It took until late August for its fate to become known to the world. A week later, the Temple of Bel, Palmyra's most significant ruin, was also confirmed as destroyed. Its demise was revealed in satellite imagery captured by the United Nations Institute for Training and Research. Pictures showed an expanse of flat, rubble-strewn desert where, perhaps just days before, great walls and columns had risen high above the sands.[24] More ancient buildings and tombs followed, including the majestic 'Arch of Triumph'. At the end of October, three captives were tied to three columns, and executed by high explosives, taking the columns with them.[25] Satellites continued to monitor the site, and as the weeks passed they built up a systematic picture of erasure.[26] Palmyra was being wiped from the face of the earth.

Two years earlier, at 5pm on Wednesday 15 May 2013, armed Lebanese security forces broke into a shop in a flea market in a suburb of southern Beirut.[27] The shop was full to bursting with artefacts: trinkets, jewellery, bowls, vases, vessels, statues and sculptures. The goods on offer were a typical mix of the faked, the forged and the genuine. The Lebanese Directorate General of Antiquities had received a tip-off from Interpol and UNESCO's Cultural Heritage Protection division – aided by a sting operation carried out by an undercover reporter from *The Sunday Times* – that a small group of dealers were attempting to sell into the hands of private collectors a haul of 2,000-year-old statues worth up to £1.4 million.[28]

The dealers told the reporter, posing as the agent of a wealthy collector, that the statues, all sculpted busts, had been smuggled into Beirut from Syria via the Abboudieh-Dabbousieh border crossing, hidden in crates of fruit and vegetables.[29] They originated, it was claimed, from 'Tadmor'. The dirt-encrusted busts were displayed leaning against sandbags and propped up by wooden planks. The dealers offered the reporter a brush to clean the earth and dust from the surfaces[30], and even allowed photographs of the busts to be taken and sent on to the 'buyer' for verification before any sale could take place. In fact the images were forwarded to five independent experts, including the Keeper of Middle East Collections at the British Museum and a senior antiquities consultant at the fine art auctioneers Bonhams. Their verdict was that the statues were real – and they were indeed from Palmyra.[31]

During the raid, the Lebanese security forces were accompanied by an archaeological expert from the Directorate General of Antiquities. It soon became clear that the statues had been moved to a second site: a sculpture workshop where objects were cleaned and restored prior to sale. Nevertheless, the expert identified a host of suspect artefacts in the flea market. He grabbed a piece of charcoal and rapidly marked each one with an X, before setting off in pursuit of the statues with a detachment of police and security forces.[32]

Fourteen Palmyrene stone busts, dating from the second century AD, were seized at the workshop, out of a total of 83 items identified as Syrian in origin, from the Roman, Byzantine, early Islamic and early Ottoman periods. The next day three Lebanese men were arrested and charged with the attempted sale of illicit artefacts. They confessed to being part of an antiquities smuggling ring receiving stolen goods from Syria to sell into the international art market.[33]

There is more to the story of Palmyra than mere destruction. In some reports, it was suggested that al-Assad, the archaeologist and former site director of Palmyra, was murdered by Isis because he refused to give up information about the location of ancient relics that had been stashed away by museum staff before they fled.[34] Their propaganda machine may churn out images of demolition by detonator and sledgehammer, but it seems that religious principles are quickly set aside where there is money to be made.[35] There is evidence that Isis are granting permits to looters to access ancient sites, then taking a hefty cut from the proceeds of illegal sales[36] – anywhere from 20 to 50 percent.[37] When images circulated in July 2015 of militants whipping an antiquities smuggler in the street, it was speculated that this was punishment not for dealing in heretical works, but rather for tax avoidance.[38]

Yet Isis did not create this black market. They are just the latest in a long line of people and groups to exploit it. Syrian artefacts have been exiting the country at an alarming rate since the outbreak of the civil war in March 2011.[39] The fourteen Roman busts found in Beirut left Palmyra at least two years before its seizure by militant forces. Other evidence has surfaced online, including, from August 2012, a video of artefacts piled up in the flatbed of an open-top truck, along with photographs of two Syrian loyalist soldiers posing with the heads of Palmyrene statues. In June 2015, weeks before Islamic State destroyed the Temple of Baal Shamin, a limestone Palmyrene funerary statue of a seated female figure was put up for at auction by Christie's New York. In a macabre detail, it was missing its head. The only mention of its provenance was a reference to a private collection in Santa Barbara, with no indication of how – or when – it made its way from Syria to California. The statue was listed at $25,000. It sold for $45,000, almost double the asking price.[40] But then, of course, fame and the prospect of scarcity will do that to market value...

The longer a structure lasts – and Palmyra has lasted for some two thousand years – the greater the likelihood that it will fall victim to history's unique capacity for irony. Once upon a time, all goods travelling from east to west, west to east, had to pass through this desert city. Two millennia on and the process has reversed. The very fabric of ancient Palmyra – stones, statues and artefacts – is travelling outwards to the four corners of the globe and changing hands for large sums of money.[41] The wheel has turned. The ultimate trader city now finds *itself* being traded.

Occupying an entire wall of room 91 of the State Hermitage Museum in St Petersburg's Winter Palace are four massive, fractured slabs of inscribed stone. Together they are five-and-a-half metres long and just under a metre and three-quarters tall, although in their original state they would have been double that height.[42] The slabs were discovered among the ruins of Palmyra in 1882 by the Russian prince Semyon

Abamelek-Lazarev. At that time, they were still fused together as one complete stone with just the top poking out above a mound of accumulated earth and sand. Abamelek-Lazarev had his workmen dig down, revealing that the slab was covered entirely with inscriptions.

He took rubbings of the text and commissioned a Beirut photographer to come and capture the remains in situ; these images appeared in a summary of the expedition written up by the prince for the Imperial St Petersburg University in 1884.[43]

The city of Palmyra as photographed by Abamelek-Lazarev's expedition of 1882.

Almost twenty years later, the Russian Academy of Sciences entered into negotiations with the Ottoman Sultan Abdel Hamid to remove it from Palmyra and deliver it as a gift to Tsar Nicholas II. In the summer of 1901, an expedition set out from the Russian Consulate in Jerusalem to collect the stone. Owing to its great size and weight, they could shift it only by sawing it vertically into four pieces, with each piece following a column of the dense inscription text.[44] The slabs were taken across the desert from Palmyra to Damascus, transported by railway from Damascus to Beirut, carried by boat from Beirut to Odessa, and finally moved overland through Russia to St Petersburg.[45]

The acquisition was a major coup for the Russian Archaeological Institute, not least because the Sultan's gifting of the slabs contravened an 1884 Ottoman law prohibiting the transfer of antiquities abroad. Then as now, when the circumstances, price or diplomatic incentives are right, the art market turns a blind eye to attempts at regulation.

The inscription – written in both Greek and Palmyrene, an Aramaic dialect unique to Palmyra – set out the tax law and regulations for goods transferred through the ancient city, along with the costs of various services. Dated AD 137, the text was comprehensive, even exhaustive. It was a revision of an earlier law and associated tariffs, and this older version was included as part of the inscription, to make clear where changes had been made and to avert any disputes between tax collectors, merchants and tradesmen.[46]

As though to emphasise the central role of import and export duties to the life of the city, the inscription formed the entire wall of one side of the street facing Palmyra's a*gora,* its central square and gathering place.[47] It was visible at all times for public consultation. Ignorance of the law could clearly be no excuse when the law was right there, opposite the very spot where deals were made, carved in stone in two languages. The inscription set out the tax rates for a host of potential transactions: one denarius was levied per camel-load of wheat and wine; three denarii per camel-load of dry goods; eight denarii per fleece of dyed purple wool; ten denarii per load of salt fish imported by camel; 13 denarii per donkey-load of ointment in alabaster vessels (of the kind described in the New Testament being used by the prostitutes to anoint the head and feet of Jesus Christ[48]); 13 denarii per load of olive oil imported by camel in four goatskins. The list went on and on. Slaves were taxed at different rates depending whether or not they were bought and sold within the city (12 denarii), or imported from other regions (22 denarii). Prostitutes paid a monthly tax on their earnings equivalent to their rates for a single act.[49] Everything was recorded in stone: 'the publican will collect from prostitutes, from the one who charges 1 denarius he will collect 1 denarius, from the one who charges 8 assarii he will collect 8 assarii, and from the one who charges 6 assarii, 6 assarii, and so on'.[50] The bronze statues imported by rich Palmyrenes to adorn their homes were taxed at half their value, calculated by weight. Salt was taxed too and was to be sold only in the main square to ensure its careful control and regulation.[51] Perhaps most significant of all, though, was Clause 88: 'for the use of the two water sources which are in the city, each year: 800 denarii'.[52]

By the second century AD, a huge amount of investment had gone into water management, from the creation of a network of underground cisterns and wells, to reservoirs and aqueducts that captured and transported the region's infrequent but sometimes heavy rainfall from the surrounding hills and mountains to the civic centre.[53] There were public baths and private gardens and fountains, an advanced sewage system and a growing population, estimated at anything from 40,000 to 200,000 people.[54] Demand for water was constantly on the increase. In the heart of the desert, there was no commodity more precious.

Palmyra itself was born out of water: a sulphurous spring called Efqa, which bubbled up through a limestone cave to irrigate the surrounding land via a series of natural canals. Hunter-gatherers and Neolithic peoples came to this site; the faint traces of their presence are preserved in fragments of discarded flints and arrowheads. Pottery shards suggest that the first settlement was over 4,000 years ago. An ancient text dating from around 1100 BC boasts of the conquests of the 'courageous hero' Tiglath-Pileser, 'King of the World, King of Assyria, King of all the four rims of the earth', who sacked 'Tadmor' and took its 'possessions as spoils'.[55] In the first millennium BC, communities of Arab nomads came down from the surrounding mountains and out of the deserts to put down roots in the oasis. But for centuries life remained simple, pastoral, with a small population managing the water and the surrounding resources to support a humble community living in basic, mud-brick houses.[56]

The Palmyra we know today was born out of something else, a trend we associate more closely with our own time: globalisation. In the fourth century BC, it became part of the vast empire of Alexander the Great. When Alexander died, much of the Middle East was carved up between the two generals Ptolemy and Seleucus. Palmyra found itself in the no-man's land between two territorial blocks: Ptolemaic Egypt to the south and west and Seleucid Babylonia to the east. As relations between the former compatriots and their descendants worsened, the harsh Syrian desert, with Palmyra at its heart, emerged as a natural bulwark. The oasis remained in a state of relative peace – and relative obscurity.

Soon, however, new powers began to emerge and disrupt the status quo. The Roman Republic embarked on its inexorable journey towards Empire. By 64 BC the legionnaires had overrun the last Seleucid territories in northern Syria. Further east, the Seleucids had already been forced out of Babylon and the Euphrates valley by civil war with the Parthians, who had risen in the region of modern day Iran to conquer their Hellenic masters. Palmyra was once again caught between the tectonic plates of two vast imperial powers.[57]

The armies of Rome and Parthia ventured back and forth across the divide, but neither side was able to make lasting territorial gains. From time to time the oasis caught the eye of the advancing and retreating generals. The Roman historian Appian recounted how, in 41 BC, Mark Antony 'sent his cavalry to plunder the city of Palmyra', but that the people were forewarned, and 'moved their essentials to the other side of the river and stood on the bank armed with bows, a weapon with which they are extraordinarily expert . . . The cavalry found the city abandoned and sacked it without any fighting and without obtaining any booty'.[58] It is telling that the Palmyrenes withdrew to the Euphrates' eastern bank.. Despite the Greek and Roman elements that came to dominate the aesthetic of their city, they retained their deep-rooted eastern Arabic culture.[59]

Over time, war settled into détente. Little by little, trade began to flow between Rome and Parthia. When it did, it flowed by the path of least resistance, through the Syrian mountain passes and across the desert – through Palmyra.[60] The city was both island and crossroads, and evolved a unique character. It was neutral and independent, yet reliant on the bureaucratic infrastructure of Rome and the trade that flowed to and from Parthia.[61] It was isolated but also richly cosmopolitan. This was not just a case of east meeting west, but also north, south and every point in between. A spider web of routes led out of Palmyra into the wilderness, the most important of which was the road to the cities of Dura, Ana and Hit on the Euphrates. From there connections led further downriver to Babylon, and, at the mouth of the Persian Gulf, Charax. This was the landing point for goods arriving by sea from as far afield as the Saka Kingdoms of northwest India.[62] These kingdoms in turn were trading with the rest of the subcontinent and with China. Almost all the goods that fed the Roman love of luxury and exoticism passed through Palmyra, from Chinese silk and jade, to Indian spices, muslin, ivory, pearls, gemstones and perfumes.[63] The Palmyrenes, former nomads who had made the oasis their home, proved accomplished businessmen, spreading out along this nexus of trade routes to become bankers, merchants and middlemen, all maintaining the flow of commerce through their desert home. Through a combination of their own trading and the duties they levied on others, they became quite stupendously rich.

Increasingly they saw themselves not just as a city-state, but a discrete territory. Stone boundary columns were erected at points 60km to the southwest and 75km to the northwest of the oasis. Another inscription, some 200km due south, was dedicated to the 'reapers' who had been working 'here at the boundaries', evidence of a networked economy based not only on foreign trade, but also agriculture.[64] Although the stones were erected under the aegis of Rome, they signalled the persistent spirit of Palmyrene pride and independence.

For a time the city itself must have resembled one vast building site. The great Temple of Bel alone was under construction for over a century. Its huge porticos were first raised around AD 19, but work was ongoing in AD 175.[65] The greatest single piece of monumental architecture in the city, it was a physical metaphor for Palmyrene identity. From the outside it seemed a clear product of the Greco-Roman style: a huge 205m by 210m courtyard, formed by a double row of massive Corinthian columns, surrounded a central temple. But the temple within was plated in silver and gold and must have dazzled in the relentless desert sun. In this the building seemed to owe more to another tradition and a another construction: King Herod's vast temple in Jerusalem.

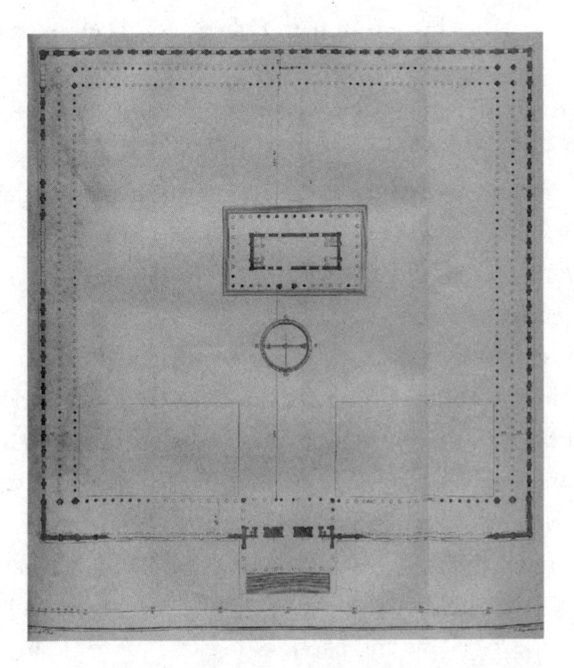

Plan of the Temple of Bel from *The Ruins of Palmyra*, by Woods and Dawkins

The gods the Palmyrenes worshipped are lost to us now: Bel, Herta, Nanai, Reshef, Yarhibol, Belhammon, Manawat, Bolastor and Baaltak. This structure, however, along with others in the city, honoured men as well as the gods: it was a community-funded project, a display of civic munificence. The merchants of Palmyra used their new-found wealth to transform their urban environment, and in the process they inscribed into the very fabric of the city the stories of the people that had helped make them wealthy men. Dedications in Bel's exterior courtyard honoured the Palmyrene caravan leaders who had chaperoned and guarded goods from one far-flung location or another as they passed through the desert. Statues were erected to the greatest of these men, like 'Soados, son of Boliades, son of Soados', who, it was said, 'saved the recently arrived caravan from Vologesias from the great danger that surrounded it'.[66] No fewer than four statues of Soados stood over the city's agora, and still more could be found in the eastern cities with which Palmyra traded.[67] Soados was even honoured in dispatches by two Roman Emperors – Hadrian and Antoninus Pius.[68]

The streets of Palmyra grew dense with self-reference. Statues abounded among the colonnades. Walls and buildings were covered with inscriptions, friezes and relief carvings. Most often the subjects of these artworks were not gods or legendary historical figures, but rather the Palmyrenes themselves, either those who were still living or the recently deceased.

Indeed, sculptured portraits were commissioned at such a rate that it is possible to trace the growth of the city's trade networks through the changing jewellery worn by its marble-hewn women.[69] In the first half of the second century, the fashion was Greek in style: simple tiaras and modest earrings and finger rings, with the most prominent adornment being the small but intricate 'fibula' that fastened the cloak to the left shoulder. After AD 150 necklaces and bracelets began to appear. Tiaras and earrings became more flashy, with the addition of large, conspicuously placed jewels. By the third century, the fashion was to wear several necklaces at once: whole sets that were carefully spaced apart as they moved from the throat down to the chest. Heavy, bejewelled amulets and brooches also became commonplace. The clothing was heavier and more luxurious, featuring embroidery and tassels. Tiaras and headdresses positively exploded in size and ostentation, and were festooned with gemstones. Bracelets were joined by armlets and anklets. The women of Palmyra wore their wealth on their sleeves – and by this time, just about everywhere else as well. The style was increasingly eastern and oriental, with the fashions of India particularly in vogue.[70] Yet, precisely because it mashed together widely varying influences and trends, the Palmyrene look remained distinctive. Nowhere else was so exposed to the traffic of world goods and culture, or so eager to adapt what it could see, touch and buy to shape its own identity.

Palmyra was in danger of buckling under the weight of its own spectacular wealth. Or rather *ambition*. It had risen so far and so fast, and had acquired such broad horizons through its trade, that it began to look out from the oasis and beyond the desert. Perhaps it was inevitable that a city built on money and the market would be unable to check its forward momentum. For a time the Palmyrenes believed that there was nothing that they could not do – including becoming an Empire.

In the summer of AD 272, a young woman slipped away from Palmyra, riding eastwards on the back of a she-dromedary.[71] This was said to be the fastest way of crossing the desert: the females were quicker than their male counterparts, and beat camels and even horses for speed.[72] Sixty miles away, on the banks of the Euphrates, a boat waited to take her over the river, to safety. Her appearance was striking. She rode bare-armed but wore a jewelled helmet embellished with purple trim. She was dark-skinned, with black hair and black eyes, which were described by those who saw them as 'powerful beyond the usual wont'. Her teeth were pearl-white and her beauty was held to be 'incredible'.[73] In pursuit was a detachment of light cavalry commanded by the Roman Emperor Aurelian, himself a onetime cavalry officer.[74]

At last the woman reached the Euphrates and her waiting ship, but she was too late. The thunder of Roman hooves was close behind. Before she could unmoor her vessel to escape across the river, she was seized and taken back the way she had come, to where Aurelian waited in camp outside the walls of Palmyra.[75] The woman was Zenobia, leader of the Palmyrene Empire, 'Queen of the East', and the mother of Vaballathus, whom she had proclaimed 'Augustus', the rightful ruler of all Rome.[76]

For a brief instant, it had seemed that a remote desert city could conquer the world. The Palmyrenes had embarked a power struggle with their protectors, administrators and long-term allies in commerce, and they had been on the cusp of victory. But it was not to be. As the enlightenment historian Edward Gibbon put it, 'the competition was fatal, and ages of prosperity were sacrificed to a moment of glory'.[77] Palmyra had taken all of its great wealth and placed it on one grand, heroic gamble – not on red or black, but on the imperial purple. And they had lost.

Perhaps, however, the city had been left with no choice. As the third century progressed, the two great tectonic plates of power in the east – Roman and Parthian – began to shift again. Where once they had knit together at the very site of the oasis city, now they were grinding against each other, threatening seismic and – for Palmyra – even catastrophic change. In AD 224, the Persian king Ardashir won a climactic battle against Artabanus V, the last ruler of the Parthians. Ardashir now controlled the lands to the east of Palmyra, and he wanted more. His empire, known as the Sassanian Empire, harked back almost a millennium to the reigns of Darius and his son, Xerxes. Ardashire aimed to remake Persia in the image of its former greatness.[78] This meant sweeping westwards, through Mesopotamia and Syria to the Mediterranean and Africa. It meant going to war with the Romans. The timing was favourable. The death of Emperor Severus Alexander in AD 235 had thrown Rome into one of its periodic bouts of internal strife and chaos.[79] The imperial grip on territories at the extremities loosened.

Ardashir was succeeded by his son Shapur, who shared his father's expansionist vision. For a decade he tormented the Romans on their eastern frontier, before, around AD 252, he made a major breakthrough. Advancing through the Fertile Crescent to the north of Palmyra, Shapur reached the port city of Antioch and sacked it.[80] Now the Sassanians, like the legendary Persians of old, could once again gaze out over the Mediterranean Sea – and look for more worlds to conquer.

The Palmyrenes watched these events with mounting concern. War was not good for business. Fewer and fewer caravans were travelling to or from the east. Even before the rise of the Sassanians, relations between Rome and Parthia had started to break down.[81] Bandit raids and seizures were on the rise, and some merchants never returned from their expeditions.[82] The Palmyrene army, established over a century before to protect business interests and police the desert territory, had grown in size and strength. But it could do little to stop distant trading networks closing down and the flow of goods from drying up. The city's economic lifeblood was spilling into the sands. It had to act.

At the mid-point of the third century, Palmyra's leader and un-crowned king, Septimius Odenathus – the husband of Zenobia – made contact with the Sassanian Emperor.[83] He sent camel-loads of luxury gifts from Palmyra to Shapur, and letters explaining that he had no quarrel with Persia. On the contrary, he suggested that his city could be the conduit through which goods from all over the world could be supplied to the Sassanians. This diplomatic entreaty was rather less than successful: Shapur ordered his slaves to throw the gifts in the river and tear the letters to pieces. 'Who is he and how has he dared to write letters to his master?' he fulminated. 'If then he wants to obtain a lighter punishment, let him know that I shall destroy him and his people and his land.'[84]

Far from being perturbed, Odenathus's next move demonstrated the extent of Palmyrene self-belief. The fall of Antioch had finally prompted Rome to mount a campaign, with the Emperor himself at the helm, to reclaim its lost provinces in the east. Unfortunately, that Emperor, Valerian, was neither an accomplished general nor tactician, preferring, as some historians put it, an 'effeminate, loose way of life'.[85] Depending which account is to be believed, when he came up against the Persians at the city of Edessa in modern day Turkey in AD 260, he was either surrounded and taken in battle; seized after obtaining audience with Shapur to negotiate a truce; or surrendered out of fear that he would be murdered by his own men.

This was an ignominious defeat for Rome, and with its leader taken by its great enemy, the entire eastern empire stood on the brink. Its saviour was Odeanthus. Having bolstered his own Palmyrene army with Syrian peasants and whatever Roman troops he could find, he began to strike back. Victory followed victory, and by AD 262, he had succeeded in taking almost all of Mesopotamia. It was, of course, no coincidence that this opened up the Euphrates trade routes for Palmyrene caravans. Five years later Odenathus advanced once again, pushing the Persians all the way back to their capital Ctesiphon on the banks of the Tigris. There, as the historian Zosimus put it, 'he shut the Persians up in their fortifications, and rendered them content to save their wives, their children and themselves, while he restored order as best he could to the pillaged territory'.[86]

Odenathus wore many faces. He was Arabic by birth, but had grown to prominence in the wealthy, cosmopolitan, Greco-Roman culture of his desert city, with its sophisticated salons frequented by the era's greatest philosophers, rhetoricians and sophists, including the famous Athenian thinker Cassius Longinus. He was at once a senator of Rome, and a semi-independent prince, the leader of his people. After defeating the Persians, he was accorded by Valerian's successor Gallienus the title of *Restitutor totius Orientis* – 'Restorer of all the East'. Only Roman emperors had ever previously received this honour. Yet he also claimed for himself the Persian title used by Shapur, of 'King of Kings'.[87]

Odenathus and Zenobia must have made an impressive couple. The two would hunt together, pursuing 'with ardour the wild beasts of the desert, lions, panthers and bears'.[88] She preferred to ride a horse rather than travel in comfort by carriage, and would drink with her husband and their generals, commanding authority with her clear, masculine voice.[89] When Odenathus was killed in AD 267 – victim of a petulant assassination by a nephew, Maeonius, whom he had chastised for bad behaviour during a hunt[90] – Zenobia was more than capable of taking the reigns of power. She was 'inured to hardship and held by many to be even braver than her husband . . . the noblest of all the women of the East, and ... the most beautiful'.[91]

Following their victory against the Persians, Zenobia and the Palmyrenes commanded the loyalty of many of the provinces – and armies – of the Eastern Roman Empire. Paradoxically, though, their new-found power, wealth and success made them insecure. They had become a target. To truly protect their people, and their *commercial* empire, they believed that they had to expand.

In AD 269 they pushed south into Arabia, capturing the capital Bostra, then advanced west and north to take all of Roman Syria. That same year, they invaded Egypt with an army of 70,000 men.[92] By AD 270, Egypt had fallen and Zenobia was sweeping northwards past the port city of Antioch, reaching as far as Ankara. Now Palmyra controlled almost all of Asia Minor, and was within striking distance of Constantinople and the Black Sea. No single force had ever challenged the might and authority of Rome in quite this way. They erected milestones along the Roman roads as they went, with proclamations claiming the territories in the names of Zenobia and her son Vaballathus. It was telling that these inscriptions were in Latin, and that the titles they bestowed on mother and son were conventional Roman ones. Zenobia was playing a political game, attempting to project, like Odenathus before her, an image that was all things to all people. She was both an Arabic queen and a Roman Augusta; both a defender of the empire and an ethnic freedom fighter. She was a mirage.

Yet behind all this posturing was economic pragmatism. Money remained the real driving force of Palmyrene expansion. Egypt, thanks to its abundantly fertile Nile valley, was the key supplier of food to the Roman Empire.[93] To the north lay the Black Sea and the overland route to the east via the famous Silk Road. Here was an opportunity to replicate on a vast scale the model that had served their desert city so well. Zenobia and the Palmyrenes did not so much want to overthrow Rome as take control of its bureaucratic economic networks in a bid to dominate world trade. It was a plan of breath-taking confidence and ambition.

In AD 271, coins were struck at Antioch proclaiming Vaballathus as 'Augustus'. This was an explicit claim of supremacy over Rome[94], and the new emperor Aurelian's response was instant and devastating. Aurelian was cut from very different cloth from Valerian: a career solder, he took personal charge of the campaign in Asia Minor, leading his armies against the Palmyrenes, pushing them back from Ankara and then retaking the city of Antioch. Zenobia's finest general Zabdas retreated to the city of Emesa, modern day Homs. This was the site of the decisive battle. Wary of the skilled Palmyrene horseman, Aurelian ordered his own cavalry to pretend to flee from the field to tire the enemy out in the chase and bring them within range of his infantry. The deception was a success and, as the historian Zosimus put it, 'a confused slaughter ensued, some falling by the sword and others ... by their own horses'.[95]

Zenobia and what was left of her army were forced to retreat across the desert to Palmyra itself. Aurelian pursued relentlessly. In the spring of AD 272, with the Roman army in siege camp outside the walls of the oasis city, the emperor dispatched a message offering terms. 'You should have done of your own free will what I now command in my letter. For I bid you surrender, promising that your lives shall be spared, and with the condition that you, Zenobia, together with your children, shall dwell wherever I, acting in accordance with the wish of the most noble senate, shall appoint a place. Your jewels, your gold, your silver, your silks, your horses, your camels, you shall all hand over to the Roman treasury. As for the people of Palmyra, their rights shall be preserved'.[96]

Zenobia's response was full of pride and indignation. 'Whatever must be accomplished in matters of war must be done by valour alone,' she admonished Aurelian. 'You demand my surrender as though you were not aware that Cleopatra preferred to die a Queen rather than remain alive, however high her rank.' Zenobia was relying on hunger, the extremes of the desert, and Syrian and Persian reinforcements to come to her aid. Nothing could subdue Aurelian. In a last, desperate act, she made her dash for the Euphrates, hoping to persuade the Sassanians, whom her own husband had defeated just a decade earlier, to join her in the fight against Rome. She never made the crossing, and was brought back before Aurelian.

What happened next is a matter of dispute. Some writers attest to Zenobia's execution, either outside Palmyra or on the route back westwards, at Antioch.[97] Others describe in great detail how Aurelian brought her all the way to Rome and made her the star attraction of a triumphal procession.[98] These accounts depict the emperor leading the way on a Goth chariot drawn by four stags – which he sacrificed once he arrived at the Capitol. Behind him were elephants, tigers, giraffes and elks, eight hundred gladiators, and a great many captives from the lands he had subdued. Zenobia herself was led through the crowds on foot, barely able to walk under the weight of gold and jewels covering her body. After subjecting the queen to this crudely symbolic humiliation, the story goes, Aurelian remained true to his word, granting Zenobia a pension and a villa in Tivoli, where she lived out the rest of her life in peace and obscurity.[99]

Palmyra made a brief – and disastrous – show of defiance. In AD 273, the city rose up and slaughtered the garrison Aurelian had stationed there. The Romans promptly returned and smashed the city, killing, looting and burning as they went. It is difficult to know how much was destroyed. What is certain, though, is that Palmyra's golden age was over. In their hubristic bid for power, the Palmyrenes had given up their role as middlemen. The city no longer held favour with the Romans in the west or the Persians in the east.[100] New trade routes had opened up, offering alternatives to the desert crossing. Palmyra had defaulted on its neutrality and the consequences were clear. The *money* was gone, and it would never return. The city shrank back in on itself, leaving behind the skeleton of one of the classical era's most extraordinary economic powerhouses. By the fourth century, the Temples of Bel and Baal Shamin had been converted into churches. By the eighth century, they were mosques.[101] History occasionally passed through Palmyra, but now largely passed it by. The columns and colonnades whitened and crumbled in the desert sun, and the monumental architecture became a site for the tents and hovels of semi-nomadic squatters.

On 12 March 1751 two Englishmen – Robert Wood and James Dawkins – made camp in the heart of the Syrian Desert. They had begun their journey in Rome in the autumn of 1749, travelling first to Naples, and then sailing across the Aegean to the Anatolian coast. After exploring the ancient ruins of Smyrna, Sardis and Pergamon, they carried on to Constantinople, before spending the best part of a year exploring the Turkish interior. By December 1750, they had reached the port of Alexandria in Egypt, and by February 1751, they had arrived in Damascus. On 6 March, they set out eastwards, into the desert.[102]

'The tiresome sameness of our road and manner of travelling,' they wrote, 'was now and then relieved a little by our Arab horsemen, who engaged in mock fights with each other for our entertainment . . . When the business of our day was over, coffee and a pipe of tobacco made their highest luxury, and while they indulged in this, sitting in a circle, one of the company entertained the rest with a song or story, the subject love, or war'. On 14 March, they reached the end of the flat plain they had been crossing, where two hills met. There, they found the broken remains of an aqueduct, and as they continued onwards, they observed a series of square towers. 'We had scarce passed these venerable monuments, when the hills opening discovered to us, all at once, the greatest quantity of ruins we had ever seen, all of white marble, and beyond them towards the Euphrates a flat waste, as far as the eye could reach, without any object which showed either life or motion.'[103] They had arrived at Palmyra.

Wood and Dawkins were not the first modern travellers to rediscover the city. Indeed, they were not even the first Englishmen. In 1678, a group of merchants based in Aleppo had ventured into the desert, enticed by rumours of fabulous ruins. They were within sight of Palmyra when a group of Bedouins descended on them and stripped them of all their belongings – including their clothes. Thirteen years later they made another attempt, this time heavily armed and, as one of their party, a Dr Halifax, explained, 'having obtained a promise of security' from the local Arab 'king'.[104] This time there was no bandit attack to halt their progress. They ascended a hillside topped by an Ottoman castle built in the sixteenth century, and looked out over the remains of Palmyra. 'The city itself appears to have been of a large extent,' wrote Halifax, 'by the ruins that lie scattered here and there at a good distance from one another, but there are no footsteps of any walls discernible, nor is it possible to judge the ancient figure of the place'. He went on to describe the present inhabitants: thirty or forty families of 'poor miserable dirty people' living in 'little huts made of dirt within the walls of a spacious court which enclosed a most magnificent heathen temple.' Halifax was stunned by the contrast of 'remains of the greatest state and magnificence together with the extremes of filth and poverty'.[105] Over the course of a millennium-and-a-half Palmyra had shrunk to a muddy village, its boundary walls marked by the ancient colonnades of the courtyard of the Temple of Bel. Halifax's lengthy if rather prosaic account of the site proved remarkably alluring to other adventurers. Precisely because he had been unable to evoke the appearance of the ruins with any vividness, others wished to experience them for themselves.[106]

Wood and Dawkins were accompanied by an Italian architect by the name of Giovanni Battista Borra, whom they had recruited in Rome at the outset of the journey. Borra was the expedition draughtsman and it was he, perhaps more than anyone else, who was responsible for the resurrection of Palmyra in the modern consciousness. 'The drawings he made,' wrote Wood, 'have convinced all those who have seen them that we could not have employed anybody more fit for purpose.'[107]

The travellers stayed in Palmyra for almost two weeks, with the Englishmen engaged in measured survey while the Italian sketched tirelessly. The results were published by Wood two years later as *The Ruins of Palmyra*. This volume aimed to 'rescue from oblivion the magnificence of Palmyra'[108]; it featured a short history, an even shorter travelogue, and fifty-seven plates showcasing Borra's exquisitely detailed drawings. Readers could relive the experience of a visit to the desert city, moving from sweeping vistas to intricate renderings of specific architectural details.

Plate XXXV of Giovanni Battista Bora's etchings of the ruins of Palmyra, showing one side of the city's great colonnaded avenue.

The book was a tremendous success. The library of almost every country house in Britain was soon in possession of a copy.[109] Edward Gibbon himself commended 'the magnificent descriptions and drawings of Wood and Dawkins' who had 'transported into England the ruins of Palmyra.'[110] An edition was brought out in Paris, and found an avid reader in the Russian Empress Catherine the Great. A forgotten city had suddenly become the height of fashion. The leading architects of the day were quick to react. *The Ruins of Palmyra* became the pre-eminent 'mood book' for purveyors of the neo-classical. In 1753, the year of publication, the Scottish stuccoist Thomas Clayton invoiced the owners of Blair Castle in Perthshire for creating a 'Palmyra ceiling' and a 'Palmyra cornice'.[111] A year later, again in Scotland, the prolific and influential architect Robert Adam began work alongside his two brothers John and James on Dumfries House in Ayrshire. For the ceiling of the building's main drawing room, Adam created a pattern of repeating octagons surrounding a central, circular floral motif set inside a square. This design drew direct inspiration from Plate XIX of Wood and Dawkins' book – Borra's drawing of the ceiling of the Temple of Bel.

The ceiling design of the Temple of Bel, captured in Plate XIX of *The Ruins of Palmyra*

Adam created further variations on his 'Palmyra ceiling' throughout his career, including at Croome Court in Worcestershire and, most strikingly, at Osterley Park House in Middlesex. Many others followed suit, such as George Pitt with his dining room ceiling at

Stratfield Saye House in Berkshire, and master plasterer Joseph Rose in his library ceiling at Milton Abbas in Dorset.

Artists and poets were also drawn to the romance of this exotic and mysterious oasis city. In 1758, the neo-classical Scottish artist Gavin Hamilton produced *The Discovery of Palmyra by Wood and Dawkins*, a baroque, Ruben-esque oil painting. In Hamilton's picture, the two Englishmen are depicted wearing togas, surrounded by turbaned Arab horsemen. They gaze out from a darkened foreground, past a palm tree, towards the distant, almost supernatural brightness of a row of colonnades and a striking classical arch – the ghostly glow of the ancient city.

John Hall's etching of Gavin Hamilton's painting of the discovery of Palmyra by Woods and Dawkins

A teenage Percy Shelley was similarly affected, seeing in Palmyra's blend of grandeur and obscurity a metaphor for man's never-ending yet futile attempts to seek immortality through architecture. In one of his first extended works, the 1813 poem *Queen Mab* – forerunner of the more famous *Ozymandias* – he chose Palmyra as his symbol of fallen glory:

> 'Behold the Fairy cried,
> Palmyra's ruined palaces! –
> Behold! Where grandeur frowned;
> Behold! Where pleasure smiled;
> What now remains? – the memory
> Of senselessness and shame –
> What is immortal there?
> Nothing – it stands to tell
> A melancholy tale, to give
> An awful warning: soon
> Oblivion will steal silently
> The remnant of its fame'[112]

More and more travellers were inspired to make the long and arduous journey into the Syrian Desert. In the same year that Shelley published *Queen Mab*, the eccentric English socialite Lady Hester Stanhope, daughter of the Earl of Stanhope and niece of the British Prime Minister William Pitt, made a flamboyantly bizarre entry into the ruins of Palmyra. 'Seldom was witnessed a caravan of a few individuals on a more magnificent scale,' wrote the narrator of Lady Stanhope's memoirs, her personal physician Charles Meryon. 'Twenty-two camels were to bear the tents, luggage, firewood, rice, flour, tobacco, coffee, sugar, soap, saucepans, spare horseshoes, and other provisions; eight carried water, and nine corn for the horses. We were to be escorted by a tribe of Bedouins, headed by a prince's son; and our own cavalcade amounted to twenty-five horsemen.'[113] As they advanced along Palmyra's great colonnaded boulevard, they spotted with astonishment that, on the broken summits of a number of columns and pedestals, beautiful Arab girls had been positioned 'in the most graceful postures, and with garlands in their hands; their elegant shapes being but slightly concealed by a single loose robe.' These 'living statues' remained motionless until Lady Hester passed, at which point they jumped down and danced alongside, placing a wreath of flowers over her head, and leading her on to the gates of the Temple of Bel. 'Without joke,' she wrote in a letter to her friend Henry Williams Wynn, 'I have been crowned Queen of the Desert under the triumphal arch at Palmyra.'[114]

By the end of the nineteenth century the ruined city had become an established tourist fixture, albeit one that was accessible only to the more determined traveller. 'During ten years, I had seen many tourists arrive at Damascus, eager as devotees to gaze on this queen of ruins,' commented the English adventurer Dr William Wright in an 1895 memoir, before observing that 'owing to the expense, danger, and general hardships of the journey, few of the multitude had been permitted to look upon her beauty.'[115] Wright himself, of course, was speaking as one of the 'few'. His own account of visiting Palmyra in the summer of 1874 has more than a whiff of traveller one-upmanship about it:

> 'After the bare monotonous desert, we come gradually on a scene of enchantment. And though we have come expressly to see the scene, it breaks upon us as a surprise; not all at once, but increasing at every step. Castle and tower and temple, and serried lines of Corinthian capitals, seen in part, and in such a way as to suggest more, lead up with the most dramatic effect to the most splendid denouement. The thrill of expectancy and delight is a rich reward for all our fatigue.'

Wright described how his party 'hastened over prostrate columns, and along silent streets, till we reached the beautiful little temple . . . we pitched our camp beside it, and my bed was spread within its once sacred fane'. There, he had 'ample leisure by starlight and sunlight' to read, relax, and commune with the faded grandeur of antiquity.

Wood and Dawkins had set something in motion when they published *The Ruins of Palmyra*. They had given the breath of life to a dead city. Something stirred anew among the colonnades. For the first time in over a thousand years, Palmyra was being talked about again, and all over the world. The great network of trade routes that had once spread out from the oasis began to flicker, like electrical synapses. Palmyra had become a fashion and a style. The design of its great pagan temple now graced the ceilings of many of Britain's grandest aristocratic houses. Travellers like Lady Hester and Dr Wright were prepared to fork out vast sums to see the city. Palmyra meant something again. Or rather it was *worth* something again. Fragments of the ancient city – its statues, its stonework, its artefacts – had acquired a value. Ancient culture was being commodified as something to experience – and something to own. At long last, the money had returned

Today the most visited single building on earth – welcoming over 80 million visitors each year – is not ancient, cultural, beautiful or sacred. Instead, it is a vast, shed-like structure set in the middle of a barren landscape: the Dubai Mall. Yet goods and people from all over the globe flow ceaselessly through its doors. In a single day its turnover can be more than £10 million, and it takes in over £3 billion annually.[116] It is tempting to suggest that Dubai is the natural descendant of Palmyra. A desert city built on, living on – living *for* – money. A city where all points of the compass meet. A twenty-first century caravan city.

On 19 April 2016 Palmyra's monumental Arch of Triumph was raised up out of the dust and rubble to stand once again – not in Syria, but in London, right in the middle of Trafalgar Square, overlooked by Nelson's Column and the National Gallery. How was this possible, less than a year after the arch had been blown up by Isis? In the summer of 2015, with fears mounting over the safety of the site, local volunteers had started to smuggle pieces of the archaeology of Palmyra out of the city, out of the country, and halfway across the world. These pieces were not physical, however. They were digital. The Oxford and Massachusetts-based Institute for Digital Archaeology (IDA) had launched a technological offensive against the iconoclasm of Isis. Thousands of lightweight but robust 3D cameras, designed by IDA, were distributed throughout the region. Brave Syrians were prepared to risk their lives to capture images of ancient sites and upload them to the cloud. At the same time, an open call was put out to anyone who had ever visited Palmyra to supply copies of their tourist photographs to a central repository to help build the most accurate picture possible.[117] As Roger Michel, the Executive Director of IDA explained: 'by placing the record of our past in the digital realm, it will lie forever beyond the reach of vandals and terrorists'.[118]

The Arch of Triumph, from *The Ruins of Palmyra* by Woods and Dawkins

The technology involved is (at times quite literally) cutting edge. The data was used to build a full digital 3D model of the original Arch of Triumph. After the 'copy' came the 'paste'. First, raw matter – cement and what is known, rather enigmatically, as 'geocomposite' material, a predominantly synthetic aggregate – was used to approximate the density of the original. The exterior of the arch, however, is Egyptian marble carved, with 'sub-millimetre'[119] precision, by robot stonemasons working to the schematic offered by the digital model. The robots carried out their work in the symbolic setting of Tuscany's Carrara marble quarry (used, famously, by Augustus to rebuild the republican city of Rome as an imperial capital). At this point, the arch was still in pieces: it was only when it arrived on site between the fountains of Trafalgar Square, that the jigsaw was fitted together, relying on steel rebar to keep it all in place. Curiously, it is not a one-to-one scale reproduction: whether due to cost or logistical problems, it is two-thirds of the size of the original.

The Arch of Triumph *in situ* in Trafalgar Square © James Crawford

After London, the arch went on tour – first to New York's Times Square (the *second* most visited place on earth); then (no irony intended) on to Dubai. Its final destination, though, is home: Tadmor. Palmyra. The intention is to erect it close to, but not within, the ancient city, in honour of the now demolished arch, and of Khaled al-Assad, the archaeologist who lost his life attempting to protect his country's cultural heritage. On the other side of the proposed setting for the new arch is Tadmor, the modern oasis settlement – bombed-out, broken, and deserted; a warren of rubble and corpses.

In some respects it seems rather antiquated to move this reconstructed arch from place to place. Surely the very point of its digital existence is that it can be recreated anywhere, at any time – and as many times as we might like. Palmyra replicas could be seeded throughout the museums of the world, either *in toto* or piecemeal, a colonnade here and an architrave there. When the Syrian government recaptured Tadmor and Palmyra from Isis in March 2016, IDA announced their desire to use their ground-breaking technology to rebuild everything that Isis had destroyed. 'This is the moment we have been waiting for', said Michel: 'if they knock it down, we will rebuild it. If they knock it down again, we will rebuild it again'.[120]

Yet the question arises: why be bound by such limited horizons? Why not also plant Palmyra in the Nevada desert, or stick it on an empty stretch of Greenland tundra? Why not rebuild it wholesale in Central Park or Hyde Park – another attraction for the millions of tourists passing each year through New York and London? Why not think cosmically, and put it on the moon, or in outer space?* In an interview with the *Washington Post*, IDA director of technology Alexy Karenowska expressed the desire to make their antiquities database 'open access', at which point, she explained, 'it will indeed be possible for people to print their own 3D models of a range of structures and artefacts'.[121] We could replicate Palmyra everywhere and anywhere, for any conceivable purpose: Palmyra key-rings, doorstops or garden ornaments. We could transform the Arch of Triumph into a marketable trademark, like the Nike swoosh (a classical Greek goddess turned sportswear retailer). One suspects that the savvy ancient Palmyrenes would have approved. Resurrection can take many forms, and mass-produced reincarnation would perhaps come closest to the entrepreneurial spirit of the people who built the city in the first place.

So maybe Shelley was wrong. 'Oblivion' has not stolen 'the remnant' of Palmyra's fame. Speaking to a world summit on cultural heritage at Yale University in April 2016, United Nations Secretary General Ban Ki-moon expressed his hope that 'one day, Palmyra, Aleppo, Nineveh and the other devastated cities of Syria and Iraq will again serve as symbols of unity and diversity.'[122] It is a measure of Palmyra's fortitude in the face of destruction, and its newfound global celebrity, that you could argue that it already does.

---

* In 2015 the International Astronomical Union agreed to rename the planet Errai in the Cephus constellation as Tadmor, at the request of the Syrian Astronomical Association.

Endnotes

CHAPTER 1

1 Genesis 11: 1-5, *The Holy Bible,* Oxford University Press, 1984
2 www.globalsecurity.org/military/world/iraq/tallil
3 www.globalsecurity.org/military/world/iraq/tallil, ibid
4 Michael Taylor, 'Letter from Iraq: The Ziggurat Endures, An American Soldier reflects on his experiences at the ancient city of Ur', *Archaeology,* Vol 64, No.2, March/April 2011
5 Gwendolyn Leick, *Mesopotamia: The Invention of the City,* Penguin, 2002
6 Donny George and McGuire Gibson, 'The Looting of the Iraq Museum Complex' in *Catastophe! The Looting and Destruction of Iraq's Past*, George Emberling and Katharyn Hanson editors, The Oriental Institute of the Museum of the University of Chicago, 2008
7 Tim Judah, 'Death in Baghdad', *The New York Review,* 1 May 2003
8 Matthew Bogdanos, 'The Casualties of War: The Truth About the Iraq Museum', American Journal of Archaeology, Vol 109, No 2, July 2005
9 Matthew Bogdanos, ibid
10 McGuire Gibson, 'The Looting of the Iraq Museum in Context', in *Catastophe! The Looting and Destruction of Iraq's Past,* ibid
11 Donny George and McGuire Gibson, ibid
12 Matthew Bogdanos, ibid
13 Donny George and McGuire Gibson, ibid
14 Matthew Bogdanos, ibid
15 Matthew Bogdanos, ibid
16 Donny George and McGuire Gibson, ibid
17 'Museum Treasures Now War Booty', *Associated Press,* 12 April 2003
18 'Plunder of past in new Iraq', *Reuters,* 12 April 2003
19 'Iraqi art "stolen to order"', *BBC News*, 29 April 2003
20 'Pillagers Strip Iraq Museum of Its Treasure', *New York Times,* 13 April 2003
21 'US blamed for failure to stop sacking of museum', *Independent,* 14 April 2003
22 '"Experts" Pleas to Pentagon Didn't Save Museum', *New York Times*, 16 April 2003
23 Eleanor Robson, quoted in *Independent*, ibid
24 Piotr Michalowski, quoted by David Aaronovitch, 'Lost from the Baghdad museum: truth', *The Guardian,* 10 June 2003
25 US Secretary of Defense Donald Rumsfeld, Department of Defense News Briefing, 11 April 2003, www.defense.gov/transcripts/transcript.aspx?transcriptid=2367
26 Quoted by Alexandra Zavis in 'Ancient civilization ... broken to pieces', *LA Times,* 22 January 2008
27 McGuire Gibson, ibid
28 Elizabeth Stone, 'Archaeological Site Looting: The Destruction of Cultural Heritage in Southern Iraq', in *Catastophe! The Looting and Destruction of Iraq's Past*, ibid
29 Joanne Farchakh Bajjaly and Peter G. Stone, *The Destruction of Cultural Heritage in Iraq*, Boydell & Brewer Ltd, 2008
30 Joanne Farchakh Bajjaly, 'History lost in dust of war-torn Iraq', *BBC News,* 25 April 2005
31 'Lion sculpture gets record price', *BBC News,* 6 December 2007
32 Christopher Witmore and Omur Harmansah, 'The endangered future of the past', *The New York Times,* 21 December 2007
33 McGuire Gibson, ibid

34 'Really old money', *Fortune*, 23 October 2008

35 Martin Chulov, 'A sledgehammer to civilisation: Islamic State's war on culture', *The Guardian,* 7 April 2015

36 Mark V Vlasic, 'Islamic State sells 'blood antiquities' from Iraq and Syria to raise money', *The Washington Post,* 14 September 2014

37 Gwendolyn Leick, ibid

38 John Gloag, *The Architectural Interpretation of History,* A & C Black, 1975

39 Herodotus, *The Histories,* translated by Tom Holland, Penguin 2013

40 Herodotus, ibid

41 Paul Kriwaczek, *Babylon: Mesopotamia and the Birth of Civilization,* Atlantic Books, 2010

42 Diodorus Siculus, *Bibliotecha Historica,* translated by C. H. Oldfather, William Heinemann, 1933-1967

43 Herodotus, ibid

44 A. R. George, 'The Tower of Babel: archaeology, history and cuneiform texts', *Archiv f□r Orient-forschung,* Vol 51, 1 January 2005

45 N. K. Sandars, introduction to *The Epic of Gilgamesh,* Penguin, 1972

46 *The Epic of Gilgamesh,* translated by N K Sandars, ibid

47 Gwendolyn Leick, ibid; and A. R. George, ibid

48 Translated by A. R. George, in 'The Tower of Babel: archaeology, history and cuneiform texts', ibid

49 A. R. George, The Tower of Babel: archaeology, history and cuneiform texts', ibid

50 Daniel 5: 6-28,*The Holy Bible,* ibid

51 Strabo, *The Geography of Strabo VII*, translated by Horace Leonard Jones, William Heinemann, 1932

52 Gwendolyn Leick, ibid

53 Joanne Morra, 'Utopia Lost: Allegory, Ruins and Pieter Bruegel's Towers of Babel', *Art History,* Vol 30, Issue 2, April 2007

54 Stephanie Porras, 'Rural Memory, Pagan Idolatry, Pieter Bruegel's Peasant Shrines', *Association of Art Historians,* 2011

55 S. A. Mansbach, 'Pieter Bruegel's Towers of Babel', *Zeitschrfit fur Kunstgeschichte,* Vol 45. Issue 1, 1982

56 *The Itinerary of Rabbi Benjamin of Tudela,* translated by A. Asher, A. Asher & Co., 1840

57 Giovanni Villani, *Corniche Fiorentine of Giovanni Villani,* translated by Rose E. Selfe, Archibald Constable & Co, 1906

58 *The Travels of Sir John Mandeville,* Macmillan and Co., Limited, 1900

59 Leonhart Rauwolf, *A Collection of Curious Travels and Voyages,* edited by John Ray for S. Smith and B. Walford, London 1693

60 Claudius James Rich, 'Extracts from a Memoir on the Ruins of Babylon', published in *The North-American Review and Miscellaneous Journal,* Vol. 2, No. 5, January 1816

61 Claudius James Rich, ibid

62 Gwendolyn Leick, ibid

63 Gwendolyn Leick, ibid

64 Gwendolyn Leick, ibid

65 Gwendolyn Leick, ibid; and Paul Kriwaczek, ibid

66 Gwendolyn Leick, ibid

67 Quoted in Paul Kriwaczek, ibid

68 A. R. George, 'The Tower of Babel: archaeology, history and cuneiform texts', ibid

69 A. R. George, 'A Stele of Nebuchadnezzar II', in *Cuneiform Royal Inscription and Related Texts in the Schoyen Collection,* Cornell University Studies in Assyriology Sumerology, CDI Press, 2011

70 A. R. George, 'A Stele of Nebuchadnezzar II', ibid

71 Gwendolyn Leick, ibid

72 Fuad Matar, *Saddam Hussein: A Biographical and Ideological Account of His Leadership Style and Crisis Management*, Highlight Publications, 1990, quoted, by David Lamb, 'Saddam Hussein Held Hostage by His Obsession with the Arab Myth', *Los Angeles Times*, 12 October 1990

73 Eric H. Cline, *Jerusalem Beseiged, From Ancient Canaan to Modern Israel,* University of Michigan Press, 2000

74 Paul Kriwaczek, ibid

75 Neil MacFarquhar, 'Saddam Hussein had Oppressed Iraq for More than 30 Years', *New York Times,* 29 December 2006
76 Colin Freeman, 'Saddam Hussein's Palaces', *The Telegraph,* 16 July 2009
77 Dan Crucikshank, 'Letter from Baghdad', *The Architectural Review,* March 2003, Vol 213, Issue 1273
78 A. R. George, 'The Tower of Babel: archaeology, history and cuneiform texts', ibid
79 Dr John E. Curtis, *Report on Meeting at Babylon 11-13 December 2004*, British Museum
80 Dr John E. Curtis,, ibid
81 A. R. George, 'A Stele of Nebuchadnezzar II', ibid
82 A. R. George, 'A Stele of Nebuchadnezzar II', ibid
83 A. R. George, 'A Stele of Nebuchadnezzar II', ibid
84 Christopher de Hamel, *The Book: A History of the Bible,* Phaidon, 2001
85 N. K. Sandars, *The Epic of Gilgamesh*, ibid
86 N. K. Sandars, introduction to *The Epic of Gilgamesh*, ibid
87 Dale S. DeWitt, 'The Historical Background of Genesis 11:1-9: Babel or Ur?', *Journal of the Evangelical Theological Society,* 22, No 1, 1979
88 Gwendolyn Leick, ibid
89 Gwendolyn Leick, ibid
90 Gwendolyn Leick, ibid
91 Leonard Woolley, *Ur excavations: publications of the joint expedition of the British Museum and of the Museum of the University of Pennsylania to Mesopotamia,* Oxford University Press, 1935
92 *Lamentation over the Destruction of Sumer and Ur,* translated by Piotr Michalowski, Winona Lake, Eisenbrauns, 1989
93 Gwendolyn Leick, ibid
94 Genesis 11-12, *The Holy Bible,* Oxford University Press, 1984
95 Gwendolyn Leick, ibid
96 Mohammed Fuad Safar and Seton Lloyd, *Eridu,* Ministry of Culture and Information, State Organization of Antiquities and Heritage, Baghdad, 1981
97 Thorkild Jacobsen, 'The Eridu Genesis', *Journal of Biblical Literature,* Vol 100, No 4, 1981
98 Alexander Heidel, *The Babylonian Genesis: The Story of Creation,* University of Chicago Press, 1963
99 Gwendolyn Leick, ibid
100 Mohammed Fuad Safar and Seton Lloyd, ibid
101 Paul Kriwaczek, ibid
102 Gwendolyn Leick, ibid

CHAPTER 2

1 Leonard Cottrell, *The Bull of Minos,* I B Tauris, 1953
2 Arthur Evans, *Cretan Pictographs and Prae-Phoenician Script,* Bernard Quaritch, 1895
3 Arthur Evans, *Cretan Pictographs and Prae-Phoenician Script,* ibid
4 Joan Evans, *Time and Chance,* Longmans, Green and co, 1943
5 Leonard Cottrell, ibid
6 J. Alexander McGillivray, *Minotaur: Sir Arthur Evans and the Archaeology of the Minoan Myth,* Pimlico, 2001
7 J. Alexander McGillivray, ibid; and Leonard Cottrell, ibid
8 Leonard Cottrell, ibid
9 J. Alexander McGillivray, ibid
10 J. Alexander McGillivray, ibid
11 J. Alexander McGillivray, ibid
12 Homer, *The Odyssey,* translated by Robert Fagles, Penguin, 1997
13 Thucydides, *The Peloponneisan War,* translated by Martin Hammond, Penguin, 2009
14 Homer, *The Iliad*, translated by Robert Fagles, Penguin, 1990
15 Jenny March, *The Penguin Book of Classical Myths,* Penguin, 2008
16 J. Alexander McGillivray, ibid
17 Robert Pashley, *Travels in Crete,* John Murray, 1837
18 Claude-Etienne Savary, *Letters on Greece,* Dublin, 1788
19 Claude-Etienne Savary, ibid
20 Rodney Castleden, *The Knossos Labyrinth: A New View of the 'Palace of Minos' at Knossos,* Routledge, 1990

21 Robert Pashley, ibid
22 Cathy Gere, *Knossos and the Prophets of Modernism,* University of Chicago Press, 2009
23 J. Alexander McGillivray, ibid
24 Michael Wood, *In Search of the Trojan War,* BBC Books, 1989
25 W. J. Stillman, 'Extracts of Letters from W. J. Stillman, respecting ancient sites in Crete', *Archaeological Institute of America*, 1881, quoted by J. Alexander McGillivray, ibid
26 Dilys Powell, *The Villa Ariadne,* Hodder & Stoughton, 1973
27 *Athenaeum, Nov 6 1886,* quoted by J. Alexander McGillivray, ibid
28 J. Alexander McGillivray, ibid
29 Joan Evans, ibid
30 Arthur Evans, *Cretan Pictographs and Prae-Phoenician Script,* ibid
31 Michael Wood, *In Search of the Trojan War*, BBC Books, 1985
32 Arthur Evans, *The Times,* 29 August 1894
33 Arthur Evans, *The Times,* 29 August, ibid
34 Arthur Evans, 'A Mycenaean System of Writing in Crete and the Peloponnese', *Athenaeum*, 23 June 1894
35 Arthur Evans, 'A Mycenaean System of Writing in Crete and the Peloponnese', ibid
36 Arthur Evans, 'Explorations in Eastern Crete. II. A 'Town of Castles'', *Academy,* 1259, 20 June 1896
37 Arthur Evans, 'Archaeological News. Krete. A Mycenaean Military Road', *American Journal of Archaeology,* 10, 1895
38 Arthur Evans, *The Times,* 29 August, ibid
39 Arthur Evans, 'Archaeological News. Krete. A Mycenaean Military Road', ibid
40 Joan Evans, ibid
41 Joan Evans, ibid
42 Joan Evans, ibid
43 Leonard Cottrell, ibid
44 Leonard Cottrell, ibid
45 Arthur Evans, *Through Bosnia and the Herzegovina on Foot During the Insurrection, August and September 1875,* Longmans, Green and Co, 1876
46 Arthur Evans, *Through Bosnia and the Herzegovina on Foot During the Insurrection,* ibid
47 Leonard Cottrell, ibid
48 Joan Evans, ibid
49 Leonard Cottrell, ibid
50 Leonard Cottrell, ibid
51 J. Alexander McGillivray, ibid
52 Joan Evans, ibid
53 Sir John Myres, quoted in Leonard Cottrell, ibid
54 Joan Evans, ibid
55 Dilys Powell, ibid
56 Dilys Powell, ibid
57 Dilys Powell, ibid
58 Arthur Evans, *Letters from Crete,* reprinted from the Manchester Guardian, 1898, quoted in Cathy Gere, ibid
59 Arthur Evans, 'Summary Report of the Excavations in 1900: I. The Palace', *The Annual of the British School at Athens,* Vol. 6, 1899/1900
60 Arthur Evans, 'Summary Report of the Excavations in 1900: I. The Palace', ibid
61 As recorded by Harriet Boyd and quoted by M. Allesbrook, *Born to Rebel: The Life of Harriet Boyd Hawes,* Oxbow 1992, from J. Alexander McGillivray, ibid
62 Quoted by Leonard Cottrell, ibid
63 Quoted by Leonard Cottrell, ibid
64 Arthur Evans, *The Palace of Minos,* Vol 1, Macmillan, 1921
65 Arthur Evans, *The Palace of Minos,* Vol 1, ibid
66 From the diaries of Arthur Evans, quoted in J. Alexander McGillivray, ibid
67 Joan Evans, ibid
68 Arthur Evans, 'Summary Report of the Excavations in 1900: I. The Palace', ibid
69 Quoted by Leonard Cottrell, ibid
70 Arthur Evans, 'Exploration in Crete', *The Times,* 31 October 1900

71 Dilys Powell, ibid
72 John Pendlebury, Letter of 12 February 1928, Pendlebury Archive, JP/L/292, quoted in J Alexander McGillivray, ibid
73 Cathy Gere, ibid
74 Arthur Evans, 'Summary Report of the Excavations in 1900: I. The Palace', ibid
75 Arthur Evans, *The Palace of Minos,* Vol 1, ibid
76 Cathy Gere, ibid
77 Arthur Evans, 'Work of Reconstitution in the Palace of Knossos', *The Antiquaries Journal,* The Society of Antiquaries of London, Vol 7, Issue 3, July 1927
78 J. Alexander McGillivray, ibid
79 R. G. Collingwood, quoted in Sinclair Hood, 'Collingwood on the Minoan Civilisation of Crete', in *Collingwood Studies*, R. G. Collingwood Society, 1995, quoted by Cathy Gere, *Knossos and the Prophets of Modernism,* ibid
80 Evelyn Waugh, *Labels: a Mediterranean Journal,* Duckworth, 1930
81 Arthur Evans, *The Palace of Minos,* Vol 4, Macmillan, 1935
82 Mary Beard, 'Knossos: Fakes, Facts and Mystery', *New York Review of Books,* 13 August 2009
83 Mary Beard, 'Knossos: Fakes, Facts and Mystery', ibid
84 Evelyn Waugh, ibid
85 Mary Beard, 'Knossos: Fakes, Facts and Mystery' ibid; and Cathy Gere, ibid
86 Cathy Gere, ibid
87 Arthur Evans, 'Work of Reconstitution in the Palace of Knossos', *Antiquities Journal* 7, Mo 3, 1927; and quoted in Leonard Cottrell, ibid; and Cathy Gere, ibid
88 Dilys Powell, ibid
89 Arthur Evans, *The Palace of Minos,* Vol 1, ibid
90 Cathy Gere, ibid
91 Homer, *The Iliad,* translated by Robert Fagles, ibid
92 Arthur Evans, 'The Palace of Knossos', *Annual of the British School at Athens* 7, 1901
93 Cathy Gere, ibid
94 Arthur Evans, 'The Palace of Knossos', *Annual of the British School at Athens* 9, 1903
95 Cathy Gere, ibid
96 Cathy Gere, ibid
97 Cathy Gere, ibid
98 Joseph Conrad, *Heart of Darkness and Other Tales,* Oxford University Press, 1990
99 www.art.tfl.gov.uk/labyrinth/about/
100 Mark Wallinger, www.art.tfl.gov.uk/labyrinth/about/
101 Mark Wallinger, ibid
102 Cathy Gere, ibid; and Mary Beard, 'Knossos: Fakes, Facts and Mystery' ibid
103 Cathy Gere, ibid
104 Cathy Gere, ibid
105 Henry Miller, *The Colossus of Maroussi,* New Directions Publishing, 1958
106 Cathy Gere, ibid
107 Quoted by Leonard Cottrell, ibid
108 Norman Davies, *Europe: A History,* Pimlico, 1997
109 John Pendlebury, *The Archaeology of Crete: an introduction,* Methuen, 1939
110 John Pendlebury, *The Archaeology of Crete,* ibid
111 Dilys Powell, ibid
112 Quoted by Dilys Powell, ibid
113 Dilys Powell, ibid
114 Dilys Powell, ibid
115 Norman Davies, ibid
116 Peter Warren, 'Knossos: New Excavations and Discoveries', *Archaeology*, Vol 37, No. 4, July/August 1984

CHAPTER 3

1 Hesiod, *Works and Days*, edited by T. A. Sinclair, Macmillan, 1932
2 Homer, *The Iliad,* translated by Robert Fagles, Penguin, 1990

3 Leonard Cottrell, *The Bull of Minos,* I. B. Tauris, 1953
4 Homer, *The Iliad,* translated by Robert Fagles, ibid
5 Alan B. Wace, W. A. Heurtley, Winifred Lamb, Leicester B. Holland, C. A. Boethius, 'The Report of the School Excavations at Mycenae, 1920-1923', *The Annual of the British School at Athens,* Vol 25, 1921/1922 – 1922.1923,
6 Aeschylus, *The Oresteia (Agamemnon, The Libation Bearers, The Eumindes),* translated by Robert Fagles, Penguin, 1979
7 Aeschylus, translated by Robert Fagles, ibid
8 Cathy Gere, *The Tomb of Agamemnon*, Profile, 2006
9 Aeschylus, translated by Robert Fagles, ibid
10 Cathy Gere, ibid
11 Cathy Gere, ibid
12 Cathy Gere, ibid
13 Chrestos Tsountas, *The Mycenaean Age,* Macmillan, 1897
14 Alan B. Wace, 'Mycenae', *Antiquity,* Vol 10, No 40, 1936
15 George E. Mylonas, *Mycenae Rich in Gold,* Ekdotike Athenon, 1983
16 Helen Wace, *Mycenae: Guide*, 1962
17 Nicholas G. Blackwell, 'Making the Lion Gate Relief at Mycenae: Tool Marks and Foreign Influences', *American Journal of Archaeology,* Vol 118, No 3, July 2014
18 Chrestos Tsountas, ibid
19 George E. Mylonas, ibid
20 Flemming Kaul, 'The Nordic razor and the Mycenaean lifestyle', *Antiquity,* Vol 87, No 336, 2013
21 Bettany Hughes, *Helen of Troy: Goddess, Princess, Whore,* Pimlico, 2006
22 Alan B. Wace, 'Mycenae', *Antiquity*, ibid
23 Cathy Gere, ibid
24 Thucydides, *History of the Peloponnesian War,* translated by Rex Warner, Penguin, 1972
25 Cathy Gere, ibid
26 Heinrich Schliemann, 'The Tomb of Agamemnon', *The Times,* 22 December 1876
27 Heinrich Schliemann, telegram published in *Ephemeris,* 21 November – 3 December 1876, from *Myth, Scandal and History: The Heinrich Schliemann Controversy And A First Edition of the Mycenaean Diary,* edited by William Calder and David Traill, Wayne State University Press, 1986
28 Cathy Gere, ibid
29 Heinrich Schliemann, *Ilios: The City and Country of the Trojans*, John Murray, 1880
30 Heinrich Schliemann, *Ilios: The City and Country of the Trojans*, ibid
31 Heinrich Schliemann, *Ilios: The City and Country of the Trojans*, ibid
32 Heinrich Schliemann, *Ilios: The City and Country of the Trojans*, ibid
33 Leonard Cottrell, ibid
34 Susan Heuck Allen, '"Finding the Walls of Troy": Frank Calvert, Excavator', *American Journal of Archaeology*, Vol 99, No 3, July 1995
35 Frank Calvert, quoted by Heinrich Schliemann, *Ithaque, le Peloponnese et Troie,* quoted in Mark Lehrer and David Turner, 'The Making of an Homeric Archaeologist: Schliemann's Diary of 1868', *The Annual of the British School at Athens,* Vol 84, 1989
36 Mark Lehrer and David Turner, ibid
37 Heinrich Schliemann, *Ithaque, le Peloponnese et Troie*, quoted in Leo Deuel, *Memoirs of Heinrich Schliemann: A Documentary Portrait Drawn from His Autobiographical Writings, Letters and Excavation Reports,* Hutchinson, 1978
38 Heinrich Schliemann, *Ithaque, le Peloponnese et Troie,* in Leo Deuel, ibid
39 Heinrich Schliemann, *Ilios: The City and Country of the Trojans*, ibid
40 Leo Deuel, ibid
41 Heinrich Schliemann, *Troy And Its Remains,* John Murray, 1875
42 Heinrich Schliemann, *Troy And Its Remains,* ibid
43 David Traill, *Schliemann of Troy: Treasure and Deceit*, St Martin's Press, 1995
44 David Traill, *Schliemann of Troy*, ibid
45 Pausanias, *Pausanias's Description of Greece,* translated by J. G. Frazer, Macmillan and Co, 1898
46 Heinrich Schliemann, *Mycenae: A Narrative of Researches and Discoveries at Mycenae and Tiryns,* John Murray, 1878
47 Heinrich Schliemann, *Mycenae,* ibid

48 Heinrich Schliemann, *Mycenae,* ibid
49 Heinrich Schliemann, *Mycenae,* ibid
50 Heinrich Schliemann, *Mycenae,* ibid
51 Heinrich Schliemann, *Mycenae,* ibid
52 Heinrich Schliemann, *Mycenae,* ibid
53 David Traill, *Schliemann of Troy*, ibid; and Cathy Gere, ibid
54 Cathy Gere, ibid
55 Heinrich Schliemann, *Mycenae,* ibid
56 Heinrich Schliemann, *Mycenae,* ibid
57 *The Times,* 18 December 1876
58 William Gladstone, 'Preface', in Heinrich Schliemann, *Mycenae,* ibid
59 *The Times,* 18 December 1876, ibid; and quoted in Cathy Gere, ibid
60 Cathy Gere, ibid
61 *The Times,* 18 December 1876, ibid; and quoted in Cathy Gere, ibid
62 Rupert Brooke in a letter to Jacques Raverat, March 1915, *The Letters of Rupert Brooke,* edited by Geoffrey Keynes, Faber and Faber, 1968
63 Rupert Brooke in a letter to Violet Asquith, February 1915, *The Letters of Rupert Brooke,* ibid
64 Rupert Brooke, *The Collected Poems of Rupert Brooke: With a Memoir,* Sidgwick & Jackson, 1918
65 Patrick Shaw Stewart, 'I saw a man this morning', quoted by Elizabeth Vandiver, 'Homer in British World War One Poetry', in *A Companion to Classical Receptions,* edited by Lorna Hardwick and Chrsitopher Stray, Blackwell, 2008
66 Maurice Baring, 'In Memoriam AH', in *Poems: 1914-1919,* Martin Secker, 1920
67 Siegfried Sassoon, 'On Passing the New Menin Gate', *The War Poems,* Faber, 1983
68 Cathy Gere, ibid
69 Friedrich Nietzsche, *On the Genealogy of Morality,* quoted in Cathy Gere, ibid
70 Cathy Gere, ibid
71 Oswald Spengler, *The Decline of the West: Perspectives of World-History,* translated by Charles Francis Atkinson, George Allen & Unwin, 1928
72 Oswald Spengler, ibid
73 Oswald Spengler, ibid
74 Oswald Spengler, ibid
75 Oswald Spengler, ibid
76 Malcolm Quinn, *The Swastika: Constructing the Symbol,* Routledge, 1994
77 Malcolm Quinn, ibid
78 Malcolm Quinn, ibid; and Cathy Gere, ibid
79 Heinrich Schliemann, *Troy And Its Remains,* ibid
80 A. H. Sayce, 'Preface' to Henirich Schliemann, *Troja: Results of the Latest Researches and Discoveries on the Site of Homer's Troy*, John Murray, 1884
81 Karl Blind, quoted by Malcolm Quinn, ibid
82 Heinrich Schliemann, *Mycenae,* ibid
83 Emile Burnouf, quoted in Cathy Gere, ibid
84 Otto Grabowski, *Das Geheimnis der Hakenkreuzes und die Wiege des Indogermanentums (The Secret of the Swastikas and the Cradle of the Indo-Germanic Race),* quoted in Malcolm Quinn, ibid; and Cathy Gere, ibid
85 Adolf Hitler, *Mein Kampf,* translated by Ralph Manheim, Hutchinson, 1969
86 George Seferis, *Collected Poems, 1924-1955, Princeton University Press, 2014;* Cathy Gere, ibid
87 Alan B. Wace, W. A. Heurtley, Winifred Lamb, Leicester B. Holland, C. A. Boethius, 'The Report of the School Excavations at Mycenae, 1920-1923', ibid
88 Cathy Gere, ibid
89 Cathy Gere, ibid
90 Cathy Gere, ibid
91 Charlotte Higgins, 'The Iliad and what it can still tell us about war', *The Guardian,* 30 January 2010
92 Henry Miller, *The Colossus of Maroussi,* New Directions, 1958
93 Henry Miller, ibid
94 Henry Miller, ibid

CHAPTER 4

1 Cyril Aldred, *Akhenaten: King of Egypt,* Thames & Hudson, 1988
2 Barry Kemp, *The City of Akhenaten and Nefertiti: Amarna and its People,* Thames & Hudson, 2012
3 Cyril Aldred, ibid
4 Cyril Aldred, ibid
5 Cyril Aldred, ibid
6 Barry Kemp, *The City of Akhenaten and Nefertiti*, ibid
7 Frances J. Weatherhead, *Armana Palace Paintings,* Egypt Exploration Society, 2007
8 Barry Kemp, *The City of Akhenaten and Nefertiti*, ibid
9 Barry Kemp, *The City of Akhenaten and Nefertiti*, ibid
10 Barry Kemp, *The City of Akhenaten and Nefertiti*, ibid
11 William J. Murnane, *Texts from the Amarna Period in Egypt,* Scholars Press, 1995
12 Norman de Garis Davies, *The Rock Tombs of El Amarna,* Egypt Exploration Fund, 1903-1908
13 Norman de Garis Davies, *The Rock Tombs of El Amarna,* ibid
14 Anne Godlewska, 'Map, Text and Image. The Mentality of Enlightened Conquerors: A New Look at the Description de l'Egypte', *Transactions of the Institute of British Geographers, New Series*, Vol 20, No 1, 1995
15 *Description de l'Egypte,* Chez Louis Genneau et Jacques Rollin, 1809-1822
16 Cyril Aldred, ibid
17 Cyril Aldred, ibid
18 Cyril Aldred, ibid
19 H. R. Hall, 'Egypt and the External World in the Time of Akhenaten', *The Journal of Egyptian Archaeology,* Vol 7, No 1/2, April 1921
20 John Ray, 'Akhenaten: ancient Egypt's prodigal son?' *History Today,* Vol 40, January 1990
21 Cyril Aldred, ibid
22 Norman de Garis Davies, *The Rock Tombs of El Amarna,* ibid
23 William J. Murnane, ibid
24 Cyril Aldred, ibid
25 Norman de Garis Davies, *The Rock Tombs of El Amarna,* ibid
26 Barry Kemp, *The City of Akhenaten and Nefertiti*, ibid
27 Stanley Casson, *Progress and Catastrophe: An Anatomy of Human Adventure,* Hamish Hamilton, 1937
28 James Henry Breasted, *A History of the Ancient Egyptians,* John Murray, 1924
29 Quoted in Barry Kemp, *The City of Akhenaten and Nefertiti*, ibid
30 James Henry Breasted, *A History of the Ancient Egyptians*, 1909
31 William Matthew Flinders Petrie, *Tell El-Amarna,* Methuen, 1894
32 Sigmund Freud, *Moses and Monotheism,* translated by Katherine Jones, Hogarth Press, 1939
33 John Ray, ibid
34 Donald B. Redford, *Akhenaten: The Heretic King, Princeton University Press, 1984*
35 Arthur E. P. Weigall, *The Life and Times of Akhnaton, Pharaoh of Egypt,* Thornton Butterworth, 1922
36 Irwin M. Braveman, Donald B. Redford, Philip A. Mackowiak, 'Akhenaten and the Strange Physiques of Egypt's 18th Dynasty', *Annals of Internal Medicine*, Vol 150, Issue 8, 21 April 2009
37 Cyril Aldred, ibid
38 Dominic Montserrat, *Akhenaten: History, Fantasy and Ancient Egypt,* Routledge, 2000
39 Barry Kemp, *The City of Akhenaten and Nefertiti*, ibid
40 Barry Kemp, *The City of Akhenaten and Nefertiti*, ibid
41 Barry Kemp, *The City of Akhenaten and Nefertiti*, ibid
42 William Matthew Flinders Petrie, ibid
43 Norman de Garis Davies, *The Rock Tombs of El Amarna,* ibid
44 Norman de Garis Davies, *The Rock Tombs of El Amarna,* ibid
45 Cyril Aldred; and Barry Kemp, *The City of Akhenaten and Nefertiti*, ibid
46 Barry Kemp, *The City of Akhenaten and Nefertiti*, ibid
47 Barry Kemp, *The City of Akhenaten and Nefertiti*, ibid
48 Barry Kemp, *The City of Akhenaten and Nefertiti*, ibid
49 Barry Kemp, *The City of Akhenaten and Nefertiti*, ibid
50 Cyril Aldred, ibid
51 Ludwig Borchardt, *Porträts der Konigin Nofret-ete,* Liepzig, 1923, quoted by Joyce Tyldesley in

Nefertiti: Unlocking the Mystery Surrounding Egypt's Most Famous and Beautiful Queen, Penguin, 1999

52 Camille Paglia, *Sexual Personae: Art and Decadence from Nefertiti to Emily Dickinson,* Yale University Press, 1990, quoted by Joyce Tyldesley, ibid

53 Barry Kemp, Anna Stevens, Gretchen R. Dabbs, Melissa Zabecki, Jerome C. Rose, 'Life, death and beyond in Akhenaten's Egypt: excavating the south tombs cemetery at Amarna', *Antiquity,* Vol 87, Issue 335, March 2013,

54 Barry Kemp, *The City of Akhenaten and Nefertiti*, ibid

55 Heather Pringle, 'Beyond the Palace Walls', *Archaeology,* May/June 2014

56 *BBC News*, 'Grim secrets of Pharaoh's city', 25 January 2008

57 John Ray, ibid

58 Cyril Aldred, ibid

59 Cyril Aldred, ibid

60 Cyril Aldred, ibid

61 William J. Murnane, ibid

62 Cyril Aldred, ibid

63 Rick Gore, 'Pharaohs of the Sun', *National Geographic,* 199, Part 4, 2001

64 Rick Gore, ibid

65 William J. Murnane, ibid

66 Barry Kemp, *The City of Akhenaten and Nefertiti*, ibid

67 Rick Gore, ibid

68 Rolf Krauss, quoted by Rick Gore, ibid

69 Barry Kemp, *The City of Akhenaten and Nefertiti*, ibid

CHAPTER 5

1 Genesis 22: 1-19, *The New Oxford Annotated Bible*, edited by Bruce Metzger and Roland Murphy, Oxford University Press, 1991

2 John Gray, *A History of Jerusalem,* Robert Hale, 1969

3 Motta Gur, quoted in *Six Days of War: June 1967 and the Making of the Modern Middle East,* Michael B. Oren, Penguin, 2003

4 Michael B. Oren, ibid

5 www.isracast.com, recording and transcript of 'Liberation of the Temple Mount and Western Wall', 7 June 1967

6 Simon Goldhill, *The Temple of Jerusalem,* Harvard University Press, 2004

7 Michael B. Oren, ibid

8 Gershom Gorenberg, *The End of Days: Fundamentalism and the Struggle for the Temple Mount,* Free Press, 2000

9 Amos Oz, 'Alien City' in *Under This Blazing Light,* Cambridge University Press, 1995

10 2 Samuel 5: 6-8

11 Eric H. Cline, *Jerusalem Besieged,* University of Michigan Press, 2004

12 1 Samuel 16: 12-18

13 Kathleen M. Kenyon, *Jerusalem: Excavating 3000 Years of History,* Thames and Hudson, 1967; Eric H. Cline, ibid, John Gray, ibid

14 F. E. Peters, *Jerusalem: The Holy City in the Eyes of Chroniclers, Visitors, Pilgrims, and Prophets from the Days of Abraham to the Beginnings of Modern Times,* Princeton University Press, 1985

15 John Gray, ibid

16 Exodus 25: 10-22

17 Alan Balfour, *Solomon's Temple: Myth, Conflict and Faith,* Wiley-Blackwell, 2012

18 2 Samuel 6: 12-16

19 Alan Balfour, ibid

20 Josephus, *Antiquities, Vol 3,* translated by H. Thackery and Ralph Marcus, William Heinemann, 1926

21 2 Samuel 7: 2-3

22 2 Samuel 24: 18-24

23 Josephus, *Antiquities, Vol 7,*

24 1 Chronicles 28: 2-20

25 1 Kings 2: 19-46

26 1 Kings 6: 1-37
27 Josephus, *Antiquities, Vol 8*, ibid
28 Simon Goldhill, ibid
29 Josephus, *Antiquities, Vol 8*, ibid
30 Josephus, *Antiquities, Vol 8*, ibid
31 1 Kings 8: 13
32 1 Kings 9: 1-5
33 Exodus 20: 4-6
34 Simon Goldhill, ibid; and Alan Balfour, ibid
35 Simon Goldhill, ibid
36 Simon Sebag Montefiore, *Jerusalem: The Biography,* Weidenfeld and Nicholson, 2011
37 Acts 2: 5
38 Josephus, *The Jewish War, Book 6,* translated by H. Thackery, William Heinemann, 1926
39 Mark 13: 1
40 Luke 19: 41-44
41 Jeremiah 52: 2
42 1 Kings 16: 31-33, and 2 Kings 9: 22
43 Alan Balfour, ibid
44 Isaiah 1: 7
45 Isaiah 2: 2-4
46 Simon Goldhill, ibid; and Alan Balfour, ibid
47 Eric H. Cline, ibid
48 Lamentations 4: 10
49 Cahill, Jane M., Karl Reinhard, David Tarler, and Peter Warnock, 'It Had to Happen: Scientists Examine Remains of Ancient Bathroom', *Biblical Archaeology Review*, 17, No 3, 1991, in Eric H. Cline, ibid
50 Eric H. Cline, ibid
51 Josephus, *Antiquities, Book 10*, ibid
52 Psalm 137
53 Simon Goldhill, ibid
54 Isaiah 52: 1
55 Matthew 21: 1-11
56 Luke 19: 38
57 Luke 19: 39-40
58 Alan Balfour, ibid
59 Josephus, *The Jewish War, Book 5,* ibid
60 Josephus, *The Jewish War, Book 5,* ibid
61 Josephus, *The Jewish War, Book 5,* ibid
62 Alan Balfour, ibid
63 Simon Sebag Montefiore, ibid
64 Pliny the Elder, *Natural History,* translated by H. Rackham, William Heinemann, 1938
65 Ezra 6: 6-15
66 Ezra 3: 11-13
67 Haggai 2: 3
68 Josephus, *Antiquities, Book 15*, ibid
69 Josephus, *Antiquities, Book 15*, ibid
70 Simon Goldhill, ibid
71 Josephus, *Antiquities, Book 15*, ibid
72 Alan Balfour, ibid
73 Josephus, *Antiquities, Book 15*, ibid
74 Simon Goldhill, ibid
75 Mark 11: 17
76 Mark 13: 1-2
77 Matthew 24: 7
78 Mark 14: 43-50
79 Mark 14: 53-65
80 Matthew 27: 27-50

81 Theophanes, *Chronographia,* quoted in Guy Le Strange, *Palestine Under the Moslems: A Description of Syria and the Holy Land from AD 650 to 1500,* Houghton, Mifflin and Company, 1890
82 Guy Le Strange, ibid
83 Guy Le Strange, ibid
84 Josephus, *The Jewish War, Book 2,* ibid
85 Josephus, *The Jewish War, Book 5,* ibid
86 Eric H. Cline, ibid
87 Tacitus, *The History of Tacitus, Book 5,* translated by Alfred John Church and William Jackson Brodribb, Macmillan and Co, 1894
88 Josephus, *The Jewish War, Book 5,* ibid
89 Josephus, *The Jewish War, Book 5,* ibid
90 Simon Goldhill, ibid
91 Josephus, *The Jewish War, Book 6,* ibid
92 Josephus, *The Jewish War, Book 6,* ibid
93 Josephus, *The Jewish War, Book 6,* ibid
94 Josephus, *The Jewish War, Book 6,* ibid
95 Alan Balfour, ibid
96 Josephus, *The Jewish War, Book 7,* ibid
97 Dio Cassius, *Dio's Roman History, Book LXIX,* translated by Earnest Cary, William Heinemann, 1914-1927
98 Dio Cassius, ibid
99 Eric H. Cline, ibid
100 Washington Irving, *Life of Mahomet,* Henry G. Bohn, 1850
101 Guy Le Strange, ibid
102 Simon Goldhill, ibid
103 Simon Sebag Montefiore, ibid
104 Guy Le Strange, ibid
105 Arculf, *Pilgrimage of Arculfus in the Holy Land,* quoted in F. E. Peters, ibid
106 F. E. Peters, ibid
107 Al-Muqaddasi, quoted in F. E. Peters, ibid
108 Al-Muqaddasi, quoted in Guy Le Strange, ibid
109 Alan Balfour, ibid
110 Alan Balfour, ibid
111 Nasir-i-Khusrau, quoted in Guy Le Strange, ibid
112 Muthir al Ghiram, quoted in Guy Le Strange, ibid
113 Edmund H. H. Allenby, *A Brief Record of the Advance of the Egyptian Expeditionary Force under the Command of General Sir Edmund H H Allenby,* Her Majesty's Stationery Office, 1919
114 Amos Elon, *Jerusalem: City of Mirrors*, quoted by Simon Sebag Montefiore in *Jerusalem: The Biography,* Weidenfeld & Nicolson, 2011
115 Edmund H. H. Allenby, ibid
116 Edmund H. H. Allenby, ibid
117 T. E. Lawrence, *Seven Pillars of Wisdom,* Jonathan Cape, 1926
118 David Lloyd George, quoted in John Grigg, *Lloyd George: War Leader, 1916-1918,* Faber and Faber, 2011
119 David Lloyd George, quoted in John Grigg, ibid
120 Quoted in Eric H. Cline, ibid
121 Quoted in Jeremy Wilson, *Lawrence of Arabia: The authorised biography of T. E. Lawrence,* William Heinemann, 1988
122 Quoted in John Grigg, ibid
123 Alan Balfour, ibid
124 Hazem Nusseibeh, quoted in Simon Sebag Montefiore, ibid
125 Eric H. Cline, ibid
126 Pope Urban II, quoted in August C. Krey, *The First Crusade: The Accounts of Eye-Witnesses and Participants,* Princeton University Press, 1921
127 D. C. Monro, 'The Speech of Pope Urban II At Clermont, 1095, *The American Historical Review,* Vol 11, No 2, Jan 1906
128 August C. Krey, ibid

129 Quoted in August C. Krey, ibid

130 Quoted in August C. Krey, ibid

131 Fulcher of Chartres, quoted in Eric H. Cline, ibid

132 Eric H. Cline, ibid

133 Edward Robinson, *Biblical Researches in Palestine, Mount Sinai and Arabia Petraea: A Journal of Travels in the Year 1838, Vol 1,* John Murray, 1841

134 Michael Dumper, 'Israeli Settlement in the Old City of Jerusalem', *Journal of Palestine Studies,* Vol 21, No 4, Summer 1992

135 Alan Balfour, ibid

136 Alan Balfour, ibid

137 Ariel Sharon, quoted by Ross Dunn, 'Muslims shot in clash at Jerusalem site', *The Times,* 30 September 2000

138 Suzanne Goldenberg, 'Rioting as Sharon visits Islam holy site', *The Guardian,* 29 September 2000

139 Yair Bar-El, Rimona Durst, Gregory Katz, Josef Zislin, Ziva Strauss and Haim Y. Knobler, 'Jerusalem Syndrome', *British Journal of Psychiatry*, 176, 2000

140 Moshe Brilliant, '"God's will' statement at mosque fire trial', *The Times,* 7 October 1969

141 Christopher Walker, 'Gunman shatters Jerusalem calm', *The Times,* 12 April 1982

142 Quoted in Simon Goldhill, ibid

143 Dennis Ross, *The Missing Peace: The Inside Story of the Fight for Middle East Peace,* Farrar, Straus and Giroux, 2005

144 Susan M. Akram, Michael Dumper, Michael Lynk, Iain Scobie, *International law and Israeli-Palestinian Conflict: A Rights-Based Approach to Middle East Peace,* Routledge, 2010

CHAPTER 6

1 Edward Gibbon, *The History of the Decline and Fall of the Roman Empire, Vol III, Chapter LXXI,* edited by David Womersley, Penguin, 1994

2 Samuel Ball Platner, *A Topographical Dictionary of Ancient Rome,* Oxford University Press, 1929

3 Samuel Ball Platner, ibid

4 Poggio Bracciolini, *De Varitae Fortunae,* quoted by Edward Gibbon, ibid

5 L. Richardson, *A New Topographical Dictionary of Ancient Rome,* John Hopkins University Press, 1992; David Watkin, *The Roman Forum,* Profile Books, 2009

6 Poggio Bracciolini, *De Varitae Fortunae,* quoted by Edward Gibbon, ibid

7 Poggio Bracciolini, *De Varitae Fortunae,* quoted by Edward Gibbon, ibid

8 Poggio Bracciolini, *De Varitae Fortunae,* quoted by Edward Gibbon, ibid; Revd William Shepherd, *The Life of Poggio Bracciolini,* Cadell and Davies, 1802

9 Stephen Greenblatt, *The Swerve: How the Renaissance Began,* Bodley Head, 2011

10 Stephen Greenblatt, 'The Answer Man', *The New Yorker,* 8 August 2011

11 Poggio Bracciolini in *Two Renaissance Book Hunters: The Letters of Poggius Bracciolini to Nicolaus de Niccolis,* translated by Phyllis Walter Goodhart Gordon, Columbia University Press, 1974

12 Helmut Illbruck, *Nostalgia: Origins and Ends of an Unenlightened Disease,* Northwestern University Press, 2012

13 Adrian Goldsworthy, *Caesar,* Weidenfeld & Nicholson, 2006

14 Appian, *The Civil Wars, Book II,* translated by John Carter, 1996

15 Plutarch, *Fall of the Roman Republic: Six Lives by Plutarch,* translated by Rex Warner, Penguin, 1958

16 Appian, ibid

17 Appian, ibid

18 Plutarch, ibid

19 Samuel Ball Platner, ibid

20 David Watkin, ibid

21 Appian, ibid; and Plutarch, , ibid

22 Appian, ibid

23 Adrian Goldsworthy, ibid; and Robin Lane Fox, *The Classical World: An Epic History of Greece and Rome*, Penguin, 2005

24 Appian, ibid

25 Appian, ibid, and Suetonius, *Lives of the Caesars,* translated by Catherine Edwards, Oxford University Press, 2000

26 Plutarch, ibid
27 Appian, ibid
28 Plutarch, ibid
29 Plutarch, ibid
30 Plutarch, ibid
31 Plutarch, ibid
32 Robin Lane Fox, ibid
33 Robin Lane Fox, ibid
34 Tom Holland, *Rubicon: The Triumph and Tragedy of the Roman Republic*, Little Brown, 2003
35 Samuel Ball Platner, ibid
36 Augustus, quoted by Pliny, *Natural History,* translated by H. Rackham, William Heinemann, 1938
37 David Watkin, ibid
38 Suetonius, *Lives of the Caesars,* ibid
39 R. M. Ogilvie, introduction to Livy, *The Early History of Rome,* translated by Aubrey de Selincourt, Penguin, 2002
40 Livy, *The Early History of Rome*, ibid
41 Livy, *The Early History of Rome*, ibid
42 Virgil, *The Aeneid,* translated by Robert Fagles, Penguin, 2006
43 Livy, *The Early History of Rome*, ibid
44 Livy, *The Early History of Rome*, ibid
45 Livy, *The Early History of Rome*, ibid
46 Livy, *The Early History of Rome*, ibid
47 Norman Davies, *Europe: A History,* Pimlico, 1997
48 Livy, *The Early History of Rome*, ibid
49 Samuel Ball Platner, ibid
50 Samuel Ball Platner, ibid
51 Samuel Ball Platner, ibid
52 Livy, *The Early History of Rome*, ibid
53 Livy, *The Early History of Rome*, ibid
54 R. M. Ogilvie, introduction to Livy, *The Early History of Rome,* ibid
55 R. M. Ogilvie, introduction to Livy, *The Early History of Rome,* ibid
56 David Watkin, ibid
57 Suetonius, *Lives of the Caesars,* ibid
58 Suetonius, *Lives of the Caesars,* ibid
59 Rodolfo Lanciani, *The Destruction of Ancient Rome,* Macmillan, 1899
60 John Gloag, *The Architectural Interpretation of History,* A & C Black, London, 1975; and David Watkin, ibid
61 Samuel Ball Platner, ibid
62 Samuel Ball Platner, ibid
63 L. Richardson, ibid
64 L. Richardson, ibid; and David Watkin, ibid
65 David Watkin, ibid
66 David Watkin, ibid
67 David Womersley, introduction to Edward Gibbon, *The History of the Decline and Fall of the Roman Empire, Vol I,* ibid
68 Edward Gibbon, *The Autobiographies of Edward Gibbon,* John Murray, 1896, quoted by David Womersley, ibid
69 Edward Gibbon, *The Autobiographies of Edward Gibbon,* quoted by David Womersley, ibid
70 Edward Gibbon, Preface to *The History of the Decline and Fall of the Roman Empire, Vol I,* ibid
71 Edward Gibbon, *The History of the Decline and Fall of the Roman Empire, Vol II, Chapter XXXI,* ibid
72 Edward Gibbon, *The History of the Decline and Fall of the Roman Empire, Vol II, Chapter XXXI,* ibid
73 Orosius, quoted by Edward Gibbon, *The History of the Decline and Fall of the Roman Empire, Vol II, Chapter XXXI,* ibid
74 Livy, *The Early History of Rome*, ibid
75 Edward Gibbon, *The History of the Decline and Fall of the Roman Empire, Vol III, Chap LXXI,* ibid
76 Saint Jerome, quoted by Christopher Woodward in *In Ruins,* Chatto & Windus, 2001
77 Jonathan Scott, *Piranesi,* Academy Editions, 1975; and David Watkin, ibid

78 Giovanni Battista Piranesi, quoted by Arthur Samuel, *Piranesi,* Batsford, 1910

79 Jonathan Scott, ibid

80 John A. Pinto, *Speaking Ruins: Piranesi, Architects and Antiquity in Eighteenth-Century Rome,* University of Michigan Press, 2012

81 *Piranesi,* Taschen, 2011

82 Edward Gibbon, *The History of the Decline and Fall of the Roman Empire, Vol III, Chap LXXI,* ibid

83 Rodolfo Lanciani, ibid

84 Rodolfo Lanciani, ibid

85 Samuel Ball Platner, ibid

86 Ferdinand Gregovorious, *History of the City of Rome in the Middle Ages,* Cambridge University Press, 2000

87 Ferdinand Gregovorious, ibid

88 David Watkin, ibid

89 Rodolfo Lanciani, ibid

90 David Watkin, ibid

91 Edward Gibbon, *The History of the Decline and Fall of the Roman Empire, Vol III, Chap LXXI,* ibid

92 J. W. Goethe, *Italian Journey, 1786-1788,* translated by W. H. Auden and Elizabeth Mayer, Collins, 1962; David Watkin, ibid

93 Patricia Mainardi, 'Assuring the Empire of the Future: The 1798 Fête de la Liberté', *Art Journal,* Vol 48, Issue 2, 1989

94 Dorothy Mackay Quynn, 'The Art Confiscations of the Napoleonic Wars', *The American Historical Review,* Vol 50, No 3, Oxford University Press, April 1945

95 Patricia Mainardi, ibid

96 Patricia Mainardi, ibid

97 Dorothy Mackay Quynn

98 Patricia Mainardi, ibid

99 Dorothy Mackay Quynn, ibid; Patricia Mainardi, ibid; and David Gilks, 'Attitudes to the Displacement of Cultural Property in the Wars of the French Revolution and Napoleon', *The Historical Journal*, Vol 56, Issue 1, March 203

100 Patricia Mainardi, ibid

101 Dorothy Mackay Quynn, ibid

102 David Watkin, ibid

103 Quoted in David Watkin, ibid

104 David Watkin, ibid

105 David Watkin, ibid

106 David Watkin, ibid

107 R. J. B. Bosworth, *Mussolini,* Arnold, 2002

108 R. J. B. Bosworth,, ibid

109 Borden W. Painter, *Mussolini's Rome: Rebuilding the Eternal City,* Macmillan, 2005

110 Benito Mussolini, *Opera Omnia,* quoted in Borden W. Painter, ibid

111 Benito Mussolini, *Opera Omnia,* quoted in Borden W. Painter, ibid

112 Borden W. Painter, ibid

113 David Watkin, ibid

114 Martin Clark, *Mussolini,* Pearson, 2005; and Borden W. Painter, ibid

115 Paul Baxa, 'Capturing the Fascist Moment: Hitler's Visit to Italy in 1938 and the Radicalization of Fascist Italy', *Journal of Contemporary History,* Vol 42 (2), SAGE Publications, 2007

116 David Watkin, ibid

117 Leo Longranesi, *In piedi e seduti, 1919-1943,* quoted by Paul Baxa, ibid

118 Albert Speer, *Inside the Third Reich,* translated by Richard and Clara Winston, Phoenix, 1995

119 Albert Speer, *Inside the Third Reich,* translated by Richard and Clara Winston, Phoenix, 1995

120 Albert Speer, *Inside the Third Reich,* translated by Richard and Clara Winston, Phoenix, 1995

121 David Watkin, ibid

122 Emile Zola, *The Three Cities Trilogy, Complete Rome, Lourdes and Paris,* translated by Ernest A. Vizetelly, 1896, Project Gutenberg 2005

123 David Watkin, ibid

CHAPTER 7

1 Lawrence Durrell, quoted by Jan Morris in the 2012 introduction to *The Alexandria Quartet: Justine, Balthazar, Mountolive, Clea*, Faber and Faber, 1962
2 Jan Morris, ibid
3 Lawrence Durrell, *The Alexandria Quartet,* ibid
4 Lawrence Durrell, *The Alexandria Quartet,* ibid
5 Lawrence Durrell, quoted by Helena Smith, 'Capital of Memory', *New Statesman,* 3 September 2001
6 Plutarch, *The Age of Alexander: Nine Greek Lives by Plutarch*, translated by Ian Scott-Kilvert, Penguin, 1973
7 Homer, *The Odyssey,* translated by Robert Fagles, Penguin, 1997
8 Strabo, *The Geography of Strabo,* translated by Horace Leonard Jones, William Heinemann, 1917; and Plutarch, ibid
9 Dr Henri Riad, Youssef Hanna Shehala and Youssef El-Gheriani, *Alexandria: An Archaeological Guide to the City and the Graeco-Roman Museum,* Balagh Press, 1960
10 Strabo, ibid
11 Plutarch, *The Age of Alexander,* ibid
12 Angela M. H. Schuster, 'Mapping Alexandria's Royal Quarters', *Archaeology,* Vol 52, No 2, March/April 1999
13 Andrew Lawler, 'Raising Alexandria', *Smithsonian,* April 2007
14 Lawrence Durrell, *The Alexandria Quartet,* ibid
15 Athenaeus, quoted by Posidonius, *Posidonius: Volume 3, The Translation of the Fragments,* edited by L. Edelstein and I. G. Kidd, Cambridge University Press, 2004
16 Iota Sykka, 'Aristotle's Lyceum to Open this Summer', www.ekathimerini.com, 25 February 2013
17 Michael Rowan Robinson, 'Was Aristotle the First Physicist', *The Guardian,* 15 January 2002
18 R. G. Tanner, 'Aristotle's Works: The Possible Origins of the Alexandrian Collection', in *The Library of Alexandria: Centre of Learning in the Ancient World,* edited by Roy Macleod, I. B. Tauris, 2010
19 Eleni Banou, quoted by Iota Sykka, 'Aristotle's Lyceum to Open this Summer', ibid
20 Plutarch, *The Age of Alexander* ibid
21 Peter Green, *Alexander of Macedon, 356-323* BC*: A Historical Biography,* University of California Press, 1970
22 Peter Green, ibid
23 Plutarch, *The Age of Alexander,* ibid
24 Plutarch, *The Age of Alexander,* ibid
25 Daniel Heller-Roazen, 'Tradition's Destruction: On the Library of Alexandria', *October,* Vol 100, Obsolescence, Spring 2002
26 *Demetrius of Phalerum: Text, Translation and Discussion,* edited by William W. Fortenbaugh and Eckart Schutrumpf, Transaction Publishers, 2000; and Roy Macleod, 'Alexandria in History and Myth', in *The Library of Alexandria, ibid*
27 *Demetrius of Phalerum:* William W. Fortenbaugh and Eckart Schutrumpf, ibid
28 Aristeas, *Aristeas to Philocrates,* edited and translated by Moses Hadas, Harper & Brothers, 1951
29 Aristeas, *Aristeas to Philocrates,* ibid
30 *Demetrius of Phalerum:* William W. Fortenbaugh and Eckart Schutrumpf, ibid
31 Strabo, ibid
32 Roy Macleod, 'Alexandria in History and Myth', in *The Library of Alexandria, ibid*
33 Galen, *Commentary in Hippocratis Epidemias III,* quoted in Roy Macleod and Daniel Heller-Roazen, ibid; and Andrew Erskine, 'Culture and Power in Ptolemaic Egypt: The Museum and Library of Alexandria', *Greece and Rome*, Second Series, Vol 42, No 1, April 1995, Cambridge University Press
34 From *Hippocratis librum de natura hominis,* quoted in Daniel Heller-Roazen, ibid
35 Roy Macleod, 'Alexandria in History and Myth', in *The Library of Alexandria,* ibid
36 Roy Macleod, 'Alexandria in History and Myth', in *The Library of Alexandria,* ibid
37 Pliny, *Natural History, Voume XIII,* translated by H. Rackham, William Heinemann, 1945
38 Andrew Erskine, ibid

39 Andrew Erskine, ibid
40 Athenaeus, quoted in Daniel Heller-Roazen, ibid
41 Vitruvius, *De Architectura,* quoted in Daniel Heller-Roazen, ibid
42 Robert Barnes, 'Cloistered Bookworms in the Chicken-Coop of the Muses: The Ancient Library of Alexandria', in *The Library of Alexandria,* ibid; Daniel Heller-Roazen, ibid; and Andrew Erskine, ibid
43 Roy Macleod, 'Alexandria in History and Myth', in *The Library of Alexandria,* ibid
44 Celus, *De Medicina,* quoted by John Vallance, 'Doctors in the Library: The Strange Tale of Apollonius the Bookworm and Other Stories', in *The Library of Alexandria,* ibid
45 John Vallance, in *The Library of Alexandria,* ibid
46 T. L. Heath, introduction to *The Thirteen Books of Euclid: translated from the text of Heiberg,* Cambridge University Press, 1908
47 Roy Macleod, 'Alexandria in History and Myth', in *The Library of Alexandria,* ibid
48 Hero, *The Pneumatics of Hero of Alexandria,* translated and edited by Bennet Woodcroft, Taylor Walton and Maberly, 1851 (reprinted Macondald, 1971)
49 Hero, ibid
50 Hero, ibid
51 Noel Sharkey, 'A programmable robot from AD 60', *New Scientist,* 4 July 2007
52 Hero, ibid
53 Hero, ibid
54 Plutarch, *Fall of the Roman Republic*, translated by Rex Warner, Penguin, 1958
55 Julius Caesar, *Caesar's Commentaries on the Gallic and Civil Wars,* translated by W. A. McDevitte and W. S. Bohn, Bell & Daldy, 1857
56 Julius Caesar, *Caesar's Commentaries on the Gallic and Civil Wars,* ibid
57 Plutarch, *Fall of the Roman Republic,* ibid
58 Julius Caesar, *Caesar's Commentaries on the Gallic and Civil Wars,* ibid
59 Lucan, *Civil War,* translated by Susan H. Braund, Oxford University Press, 1992
60 Luciano Canfora and Antonia Coleman, 'The Vanished Library', *Index on Censorship,* 28: 46, 1999
61 Seneca, *De Animi tranquilitate, Book IX,* quoted in Daniel Heller-Roazen, ibid
62 Daniel Heller-Roazen, ibid; and James Raven, editor, 'The Resonances of Loss', in *Lost Libraries: The Destruction of Great Book Collections Since Antiquity,* Palgrave Macmillan, 2004
63 Plutarch, *Fall of the Roman Republic,* ibid
64 Aulus Gellius, *The Attic Nights of Aulus Gellius, Book VII,* translated by John C. Rolfe, Willia Heinemann, 1948
65 Edward Gibbon, *The History of the Decline and Fall of the Roman Empire, Vol II, Chapter XLVII,* edited by David Womersley, Penguin, 1995
66 Socrates Scolasticus, *The Ecclesiastical History of Socrates: Comprising a History of the Church in Seven Books, from the Accession of Constantine AD 305 to the 38th Year of Theodosius II,* Henry G. Bohn, 1853
67 Edward Gibbon, *Decline and Fall of the Roman Empire, Vol II, Chapter XLVII*, ibid
68 Bishop John of Nikiu, *The Chronicle of John, Coptic Bishop of Nikiu: Being a History of Egypt Before and During the Arab Conquest,* translated by Robert Henry Charles, APA – Philo Press, 1981
69 Edward Gibbon, *Decline and Fall of the Roman Empire, Vol II, Chapter XLVII*, ibid
70 Socrates Scolasticus; and Bishop John of Nikiu, ibid
71 Bishop John of Nikiu, ibid
72 Socrates Scolasticus, ibid
73 Michael A. B. Deakin, 'Hypatia and Her Mathematics', *The American Mathematical Monthly,* Vol 101, No 3, March 1994
74 Edward Gibbon, *Decline and Fall of the Roman Empire, Vol II, Chapter XXVIII*, ibid
75 Tom Holland, *In the Shadow of the Sword: The Battle for Global Empire and the End of the Ancient World*, Abacus, 2012
76 James Raven, ibid
77 Edward Gibbon, *Decline and Fall of the Roman Empire, Vol II, Chapter XXVIII*, ibid
78 Edward Gibbon, *Decline and Fall of the Roman Empire, Vol II, Chapter XXVIII*, ibid
79 Edward Gibbon, *Decline and Fall of the Roman Empire, Vol III, Chapter LI*, ibid
80 Alfred J. Butler, *The Arab Conquest of Egypt: And the Last Thirty Years of the Roman Dominion,* Clarendon Press, 1978
81 James Raven, ibid

82 Ibn Al-Qifti, *History of Wise Men, quoted in* James Raven, ibid
83 Edward Gibbon, *Decline and Fall of the Roman Empire, Vol III, Chapter LI*, ibid
84 Edward Gibbon, *Decline and Fall of the Roman Empire, Vol III, Chapter LI*, ibid
85 James Raven; Daniel Heller-Roazen; and Luciano Canfora and Antonia Coleman, ibid; Robert Barnes, 'Cloistered Bookworms in the Chicken-Coop of the Muses: The Ancient Library of Alexandria' in *The Library of Alexandria,* ibid
86 Dio Cassius, quoted Daniel Heller-Roazen; James Raven; and Luciano Canfora and Antonia Coleman, ibid
87 Jon Thiem, 'The Great Library of Alexandria Burnt: Towards the History of a Symbol', *Journal of the History of Ideas,* Vol 40, No 4, University of Pennsylvania Press, October – December 1979
88 Mostafa El-Abbadi, *The Life and Fate of the Ancient Library of Alexandria, quoted in* James Raven, ibid
89 Christoph Kapeller, 'The architecture of the new Library of Alexandria', *The Massachusetts Review,* Vol 42, Issue 4, Winter 2001
90 The Aswan Declaration, UNESCO, 12 February 1990, www.unesco.org/new/en/communication-and-information/access-to-knowledge/libraries/bibliotheca-alexandrina/the-aswan-declaration/
91 Christoph Kapeller, ibid
92 Helena Smith, 'Capital of Memory', *New Statesman,* 3 September 2001
93 Bibliotheca Alexandrina, www.bibalex.org/aboutus/overview_en.aspx
94 Moshen Zahran, quoted by Bruce Watson, 'Rising Sun', *Smithsonian,* April 2002
95 Bibliotheca Alexandrina, www.bibalex.org/InternetArchive/IA_en.aspx
96 Brewster Kahle, quoted by Jack Schofield, 'The Time Machine', *The Guardian,* 19 November 2007
97 Rick Pellinger, quoted by Rory Carroll, 'Brewster's Trillions: Internet Archive strives to keep web history alive', *The Guardian,* 26 April 2013
98 As of 1 January 2015, archive.org/web/
99 Rory Carroll, ibid
100 Alexis Rossi, quoted by Rory Carroll, ibid
101 Jorge Luis Borges, 'The Library of Babel', in *Labyrinths: Selected Stories and Other Writings,* Penguin, 2000; and James Gleick, *The Information: A History, A Theory, A Flood,* Fourth Estate, 2012
102 James Gleick, ibid
103 Jorge Luis Borges, ibid
104 Rory Carroll, ibid
105 Jorge Luis Borges, ibid
106 Noam Cohen, 'Wikipedia goes to Alexandria, home of other great reference works', *International New York Times,* 17 July 2008
107 James Gleick, ibid
108 As of 1 January 2015, meta.wikimedia.org/wiki/List_of_Wikipedias#Grand_Total
109 As of 1 Jaunary 2015, tools.wmflabs.org/wmcounter/
110 en.wikipedia.org/wiki/Wikipedia:There_is_a_deadline
111 wikipedia.org/wiki/User:Emijrp/All_human_knowledge
112 Jon Thiem, ibid
113 Seneca, *De Tranquillitate Animi,* quoted by Jon Thiem, bid
114 Louis LeRoy, *Of the Interchangeable Course, or Variety of Things in the Whole World,* translated by R. Ashley, 1594, quoted by Jon Thiem, ibid
115 Edward Gibbon, *Decline and Fall of the Roman Empire, Vol III, Chapter LI*, ibid
116 George Bernard Shaw, 'Caesar and Cleopatra: A History', *Collected Plays with their Prefaces, Vol II,* edited by D. H. Laurence, 1971, quoted in Jon Thiem, ibid
117 Rory Carroll, ibid
118 Stewart Brand, quoted in archive.org/about/
119 Danny Hills, quoted in archive.org/about/
120 Jorge Luis Borges, ibid

CHAPTER 8

1 Procopius, *The Secret History,* translated by G. A. Williamson and Peter Sarris, Penguin, 2007
2 Procopius, *The Secret History,* ibid

3 Procopius, *The Secret History,* ibid
4 Anthony Burgess, *A Clockwork Orange,* William Heinemann, 1962
5 Cassius Dio, *Dio's Roman History, Book LXXV,* translated by Earnest Cary, on the basis of the version of Herbert Baldwin Foster, William Heinemann, 1914-1927
6 Edward Gibbon, *The History of the Decline and Fall of the Roman Empire, Vol I, Chapter XVII,* edited by David Womersley, Penguin, 2005
7 Cassius Dio, *Dio's Roman History, Book LXXV,* ibid
8 Cassius Dio, *Dio's Roman History, Book LXXV,* ibid
9 Cassius Dio, *Dio's Roman History, Book LXXV,* ibid
10 Cassius Dio, *Dio's Roman History, Book LXXV,* ibid
11 Juvenal, *Thirteen Satires of Juvenal,* with commentary by John E B Mayor, Macmillan, 1889
12 Sotiris G. Giatsis, 'The organization of chariot-racing in the great Hippodrome of Byzantine Constantinople', *The International Journal of the History of Sport,* 17:1, Routledge, 2000; and Alan Cameron, *Circus Factions: Blues and Greens at Rome and Byzantium*, Clarendon Press, 1976;
13 Rodolphe Guilland, 'The Hippodrome at Byzantium', *Speculum,* Vol 23, No 4, Medieval Academy of American, October 1948
14 *Accounts of Medieval Constantinople: The Patria*, translated by Albrecht Berger, Harvard University Press, 2013
15 Edward Gibbon, *Decline and Fall of the Roman Empire, Vol I, Chapter XVII*, ibid
16 *Accounts of Medieval Constantinople: The Patria*, ibid;
17 Edward Gibbon, *Decline and Fall of the Roman Empire, Vol I, Chapter XIII*, ibid
18 Edward Gibbon, *Decline and Fall of the Roman Empire, Vol I, Chapter XIII*, and XIV, ibid
19 Edward Gibbon, *Decline and Fall of the Roman Empire, Vol I,* XIV, ibid
20 Eusebius, quoted in Timothy Barnes, *Constantine,* Wiley-Blackwell, 2014
21 Edward Gibbon, *Decline and Fall of the Roman Empire, Vol I,* XX, ibid
22 Edward Gibbon, *Decline and Fall of the Roman Empire, Vol I,* XIV, ibid
23 Edward Gibbon, *Decline and Fall of the Roman Empire, Vol I,* XVII, ibid
24 Edward Gibbon, *Decline and Fall of the Roman Empire, Vol I,* XVII, ibid
25 Philostorgius, *History of the Church by Sozomen and Philostorgius,* translated by Edward Walford, Henry G. Bohn, 1855
26 Edward Gibbon, *Decline and Fall of the Roman Empire, Vol I,* XVII, ibid
27 Michael Maclagan, *The City of Constantine,* Thames and Hudson, 1968; John Julius Norwich, *A Short History of Byzantium,* Penguin, 1998
28 John Julius Norwich, ibid
29 *Accounts of Medieval Constantinople: The Patria*, ibid; Edward Gibbon, *Decline and Fall of the Roman Empire, Vol I,* XVII, ibid
30 *Accounts of Medieval Constantinople: The Patria*, ibid
31 *Accounts of Medieval Constantinople: The Patria*, ibid
32 Livy, *The Early History of Rome,* translated by Aubrey de Selincourt, Penguin, 1971
33 Livy, ibid
34 Livy, ibid
35 Edward Gibbon, *Decline and Fall of the Roman Empire, Vol II, Chapter XL;* and Sotiris G. Giatsis, ibid; and Alan Cameron, ibid
36 Cassiodorus, *Variae Epistolae Of Magnus Aurelius Cassiodorus Senator,* quoted in Edward Gibbon, *Decline and Fall of the Roman Empire, Vol II, Chapter XL*, ibid*;* and Alan Cameron, ibid
37 Pliny the Younger, *The Letters of the Younger Pliny,* translated with an introduction by Betty Radice, Penguin, 1969, quoted by Alan Cameron, ibid
38 Galen, *Methedo Medendi*, quoted in Alan Cameron, ibid
39 Alan Cameron, ibid
40 Pliny, *Natural History, Book XXXIII,* translated by H. Rackham, William Heinemann, 1938-1963; Alan Cameron, ibid
41 Alan Cameron, ibid
42 Alan Cameron, ibid
43 Alan Cameron, ibid
44 Josephus, *Jewish Antiquities, Book XIX,* translated by L. H. Feldman, William Heinemann, 1965
45 Josephus, *Jewish Antiquities, Book XIX,* ibid
46 Cassius Dio, *Dio's Roman History, Book LIX,* ibid

47 Josephus, *Jewish Antiquities, Book XIX*, ibid; Alan Cameron, ibid
48 Pliny, *Natural History, Book XXXIV*, ibid, from Alan Cameron, ibid
49 Tacitus, *Tacitus' Annals, Book II and XIII*, from Alan Cameron, ibid
50 Pliny the Younger, *Panegyric,* quoted in Alan Cameron, ibid
51 Stanley Casson, *Preliminary Report Upon the Excavations carried out in the Hippodrome of Constantinople in 1927*, Oxford University Press, 1928
52 Stanley Casson, ibid
53 Rodolphe Guilland, ibid
54 Niketas Choniates, *O City of Byzantium: Annals of Niketas Choniates*, translated by Harry J. Magoulias, Wayne State Universtiy Press, 1984; Sotiris G Giatsis, ibid
55 Sarah Guberti Bassett, 'The Antiquities in the Hippodrome of Constantinople', *Dumbarton Oaks Papers,* Vol 45, 1991
56 Sarah Guberti Bassett, ibid; Anthony Cutler, 'The Designis of Nicetas Choniates: A Reappraisal', *American Journal of Archaeology*, Vol 72, No 2, April 1968; Niketas Choniates, *O City of Byzantium*, ibid
57 R. M. Dawkins 'Ancient Statues in Medieval Constantinople', *Folklore,* Vol 35, No 3, 30 September 1924, Taylor and Francis; Sarah Guberti Bassett, ibid; Anthony Cutler, ibid; Niketas Choniates, *O City of Byzantium*, ibid; and Edward Gibbon, *Decline and Fall of the Roman Empire, Vol III, Chapter LX*, ibid
58 Sarah Guberti Bassett, ibid;
59 Sarah Guberti Bassett, ibid; and Sotiris G. Giatsis, ibid
60 Sotiris G. Giatsis, ibid
61 Sotiris G. Giatsis, ibid; and Alan Cameron, ibid
62 Eusebius, *Life of the Blessed Emperor Constantine,* Samuel Bagster and Sons, 1845
63 R. M. Dawkins, ibid
64 Niketas Choniates, *O City of Byzantium*, ibid; and R. M. Dawkins, ibid
65 Sotiris G. Giatsis, ibid; Alan Cameron, ibid; and Rodolphe Guilland, ibid
66 Sotiris G. Giatsis, ibid; Alan Cameron, ibid; and Rodolphe Guilland, ibid
67 Procopius, *The Secret History,* ibid; and Edward Gibbon, *Decline and Fall of the Roman Empire, Vol II, Chapter XL*, ibid
68 Peter Sarris, introduction to Procopius, *The Secret History,* ibid
69 Procopius, *The Secret History,* ibid
70 Procopius, *The Secret History,* ibid
71 Procopius, *The Secret History,* ibid
72 Procopius, *The Secret History,* ibid
73 Procopius, *The Secret History,* ibid; and Edward Gibbon, *Decline and Fall of the Roman Empire, Vol II, Chapter XL*, ibid
74 Procopius, *The Secret History,* ibid
75 Procopius, *The Secret History,* ibid
76 Chronicle of John Malalas, quoted in J. B. Bury, 'The Nika Riot', *The Journal of Hellenic Studies*, Vol 17, 1897
77 Alan Cameron, ibid
78 Theophanes, quoted in Edward Gibbon, *Decline and Fall of the Roman Empire, Vol II, Chapter XL*, ibid
79 Theophanes, quoted in Edward Gibbon, *Decline and Fall of the Roman Empire, Vol II, Chapter XL*, ibid; and Alan Cameron, 'A Circus Dialogue' Appendix to *Circus Factions*, ibid
80 Edward Gibbon, *Decline and Fall of the Roman Empire, Vol II, Chapter XL*, ibid; Alan Cameron, ibid; and J. B. Bury, ibid; and Geoffrey Greatrex, 'The Nika Riot: A Reappraisal', *The Journal of Hellenic Studies,* Vol 117, 1997
81 J. B. Bury, ibid; and Geoffrey Greatrex, ibid
82 John Malalas, *The Chronicle of John Malalas*, translated by Elizabeth Jeffreys, Michael Jeffreys and Roger Scott, University of Sydney, 1986; and Edward Gibbon, *Decline and Fall of the Roman Empire, Vol II, Chapter XL*, ibid
83 Geoffrey Greatrex, ibid
84 Geoffrey Greatrex, ibid
85 Geoffrey Greatrex, ibid; J. B. Bury, ibid; Alan Cameron, ibid; and Edward Gibbon, *Decline and Fall of the Roman Empire, Vol II, Chapter XL*, ibid
86 Procopius, *History of the Wars, Book I, Chapter XXIV,* translated by H. B. Dewing, William Heine-

mann, 1914; and J. B. Bury, ibid; Alan Cameron, ibid; and Edward Gibbon, *Decline and Fall of the Roman Empire, Vol II, Chapter XL*, ibid

87 Geoffrey Greatrex, ibid; Alan Cameron, ibid; and J. B. Bury, ibid

88 J. B. Bury, ibid; Alan Cameron, ibid; and Edward Gibbon, *Decline and Fall of the Roman Empire, Vol II, Chapter XL*, ibid

89 Procopius, *History of the Wars, Book I, Chapter XXIV,* ibid

90 Geoffrey Greatrex, ibid; and Edward Gibbon, *Decline and Fall of the Roman Empire, Vol II, Chapter XL*, ibid

91 Procopius, *History of the Wars, Book I, Chapter XXIV,* ibid; and Edward Gibbon, *Decline and Fall of the Roman Empire, Vol II, Chapter XL*, ibid

92 Procopius, *History of the Wars, Book I, Chapter XXIV,* ibid

93 Procopius, *History of the Wars, Book I, Chapter XXIV,* ibid

94 Procopius, *History of the Wars, Book I, Chapter XXIV,* ibid

95 Edward Gibbon, *Decline and Fall of the Roman Empire, Vol II, Chapter XL*, ibid

96 Edward Gibbon, *Decline and Fall of the Roman Empire, Vol II, Chapter XL*, ibid

97 Geoffrey Greatrex, ibid;

98 Procopius, *History of the Wars, Book I, Chapter XXIV,* ibid; and Edward Gibbon, *Decline and Fall of the Roman Empire, Vol II, Chapter XL*, ibid; J. B. Bury, ibid;

99 Geoffrey Greatrex, ibid;

100 Procopius, *History of the Wars, Book I, Chapter XXIV,* ibid; and Edward Gibbon, *Decline and Fall of the Roman Empire, Vol II, Chapter XL*, ibid; and John Julius Norwich, ibid

101 Rodolphe Guilland, ibid

102 Robert de Clari, *The History of Them That Took Constantinople: Being an Account of the Fourth Crusade, which Robert of Clari in Amienois, Knight, caused to be written down in the Picard Tongue about 1216*, translated by Edward Noble Stone, The University of Washington, 1939

103 Edward Gibbon, *Decline and Fall of the Roman Empire, Vol III, Chapter LX*, ibid; John Julius Norwich, ibid; and Michael Angold, *The Fourth Crusade,* Pearson, 2003

104 John Julius Norwich, ibid

105 Edward Gibbon, *Decline and Fall of the Roman Empire, Vol III, Chapter LX*, ibid

106 Geoffrey de Villehardouin, quoted by John Julius Norwich, ibid

107 John Julius Norwich, ibid; and Michael Angold, ibid

108 John Julius Norwich, ibid; and Michael Angold, ibid

109 Niketas Choniates, *O City of Byzantium,* ibid

110 Niketas Choniates, *O City of Byzantium,* ibid

111 Niketas Choniates, *O City of Byzantium,* ibid; Edward Gibbon, *Decline and Fall of the Roman Empire, Vol III, Chapter LX*, ibid

112 John Julius Norwich, ibid

113 Michael Jacoff, *The Horses of San Marco and the Quadriga of the Lord,* Princeton University Press, 1993

114 Michael Jacoff, ibid

115 Michael Jacoff, ibid

116 Charles Freeman, 'St Mark's Square: an imperial hippodrome?', *History Today,* Vol 54, Issue 4, April 2004

117 Edward Gibbon, *Decline and Fall of the Roman Empire, Vol III, Chapter LXVIII*, ibid

118 Edward Gibbon, *Decline and Fall of the Roman Empire, Vol III, Chapter LXVIII*, ibid; and John Julius Norwich, ibid

119 Edward Gibbon, *Decline and Fall of the Roman Empire, Vol III, Chapter LXVIII*, ibid

120 *The Oxford Dictionary of Byzantium*, edited by Alexander P. Kazhdan, Oxford University Press, 1991

121 Jonathan Harris, *Byzantium and the Crusades,* Bloomsbury Publishing, 2014

122 Saadi, quoted in John Julius Norwich, ibid; and Edward Gibbon, *Decline and Fall of the Roman Empire, Vol III, Chapter LXVIII*, ibid

123 Edward Gibbon, *Decline and Fall of the Roman Empire, Vol I, Chapter XVII*, ibid

124 R. M. Dawkins, ibid; and Edward Gibbon, *Decline and Fall of the Roman Empire, Vol III, Chapter LXVIII*, ibid

125 Edward Gibbon, *Decline and Fall of the Roman Empire, Vol I, Chapter XVII*, ibid

126 Zeynip Çelik, 'Bouvard's Boulevards: Beaux-Arts Planning in Istanbul', *Journal of the Society of Architectural Historians,* Vol 43, No 4, December 1984

CHAPTER 9

1 Ann Christys, 'Picnic at Madinat Al-Zahra', in *Cross, Crescent and Conversion: Studies on Medieval Spain and Christendom*, edited by Simon Barton and Peter Linehan, Brill, 2008

2 Ibn Khaqan, quoted by Ann Christys, ibid; and D. Fairchild Ruggles, 'Arabic Poetry and Architectural Memory in al-Andalus', *Ars Orientalis,* Vol 23, Pre-Modern Islamic Palaces, University of Michigan, 1993

3 Ann Christys, ibid; D. Fairchild Ruggles, 'Arabic Poetry and Architectural Memory in al-Andalus', ibid; and D. Fairchild Ruggles, *Gardens, Landscape and Vision in the Palaces of Islamic Spain*, University of Pennsylvania Press, 2000

4 Ibn al-Arabi, quoted in D. Fairchild Ruggles, 'Arabic Poetry and Architectural Memory in al-Andalus', ibid; and D. Fairchild Ruggles, *Gardens, Landscape and Vision in the Palaces of Islamic Spain*, ibid

5 Ibn Hayyan, quoted in Ann Christys, ibid

6 Antonio Vallejo Triano, 'Madinat Al-Zahra: Historical Reality and Present-Day Heritage', *Reflections on Qurtuba in the 21st Century,* Casa Arabe, 2013

7 Abdulwahid Dhanun Taha, *The Muslim Conquest and Settlement of North Africa and Spain,* Routledge, 1989; and Joseph F. O'Callaghan, *A History of Medieval Spain,* Cornell University Press, 1983

8 Abdulwahid Dhanun Taha, ibid; and Joseph F. O'Callaghan, ibid

9 Joseph F. O'Callaghan, ibid

10 D. Fairchild Ruggles, *Gardens, Landscape and Vision in the Palaces of Islamic Spain*, ibid

11 Joseph F. O'Callaghan, ibid

12 Maribel Fierro, *Abd al-Rahman III: The First Cordoban Caliph*, Oneworld, 2005; Abdulwahid Dhanun Taha, ibid; and Joseph F. O'Callaghan, ibid

13 Maribel Fierro, ibid; Abdulwahid Dhanun Taha, ibid; and Joseph F. O'Callaghan, ibid

14 Joseph F. O'Callaghan, ibid

15 John Gill, *Andalucia: A Cultural History,* Oxford University Press, 2008; and Henry George Farmer, *A History of Arabian Music,* Luzac & Co, 1929

16 Renata Holod, 'Luxury Arts of the Caliphal Period', in *Al Andalus: The Art of Islamic Spain,* The Metroploitan Museum of Art, 1992; John Gill, ibid; Maribel Fierro, ibid

17 Joseph F. O'Callaghan, ibid

18 Maribel Fierro, ibid

19 Henry George Farmer, ibid and John Gill, ibid

20 Henry George Farmer, ibid

21 John Gill, ibid

22 Renata Holod, ibid; and John Gill, ibid

23 D. Fairchild Ruggles, *Gardens, Landscape and Vision in the Palaces of Islamic Spain*, ibid

24 Maribel Fierro, ibid

25 Maribel Fierro, ibid; and Joseph F. O'Callaghan, ibid

26 Maribel Fierro, ibid; and Joseph F. O'Callaghan, ibid

27 Joseph F. O'Callaghan, ibid

28 Ibn Abd Rabbihi, quoted in Maribel Fierro, ibid

29 Maribel Fierro, ibid; and Joseph F. O'Callaghan, ibid

30 Abd al-Rahman III, quoted in Joseph F. O'Callaghan, ibid

31 Abd al-Rahman III, quoted in Joseph F. O'Callaghan, ibid

32 D. Fairchild Ruggles, *Gardens, Landscape and Vision in the Palaces of Islamic Spain*, ibid; and Antonio Vallejo Triano, 'Madinat al-Zahra: The Triumph of the Islamic State', in *Al Andalus: The Art of Islamic Spain*, ibid; and Joseph F. O'Callaghan, ibid

33 D. Fairchild Ruggles, *Islamic Gardens and Landscapes,* University of Pennsylvania Press, 2008

34 *The Arabian Nights: Tales of 1001 Nights,* translated by Malcolm C. Lyons, introduction by Robert Irwin, Penguin 2008

35 D. Fairchild Ruggles, *Islamic Gardens and Landscapes,* ibid; and Ann Christys, ibid

36 *The Arabian Nights: Tales of 1001 Nights,* Vol 1, Night 278 ibid

37 *The Arabian Nights: Tales of 1001 Nights,* Vol 1, Night 278 ibid

38 *The Arabian Nights: Tales of 1001 Nights,* Vol 1, Night 278 ibid

39 *The Arabian Nights: Tales of 1001 Nights,* ibid; and D. Fairchild Ruggles, *Islamic Gardens and Landscapes,* ibid

40 D. Fairchild Ruggles, *Islamic Gardens and Landscapes,* ibid

41 *The Arabian Nights: Tales of 1001 Nights,* Vol 2, Night 574, ibid
42 *The Arabian Nights: Tales of 1001 Nights,* Vol 2, Night 574, ibid
43 *The Arabian Nights: Tales of 1001 Nights,* Vol 2, Night 576, ibid
44 D. Fairchild Ruggles, *Islamic Gardens and Landscapes,* ibid
45 K. A. C. Creswell, *Early Muslim Architecture,* Clarendon Press, 1969; John D. Hoag, *Islamic Architecture,* Harry N. Abrams, 1977; Martino Tattara, 'The Multiplicity of Al-Mansur's Baghdad', *ARQ,* No 80, Santiago, April 2012; and D. Fairchild Ruggles, 'The Mirador in Hispano-Umayyad Garden Typology', *Muqarnas,* Vol 7, BRILL, 1990
46 D. Fairchild Ruggles, *Gardens, Landscape and Vision in the Palaces of Islamic Spain*, ibid
47 D. Fairchild Ruggles, *Islamic Gardens and Landscapes,* ibid; and D. Fairchild Ruggles, *Gardens, Landscape and Vision in the Palaces of Islamic Spain*, ibid
48 Al-Mutawakkil, quoted in D. Fairchild Ruggles, *Gardens, Landscape and Vision in the Palaces of Islamic Spain*, ibid; and John D. Hoag, ibid
49 Maribel Fierro, ibid; John Gill, ibid; D. Fairchild Ruggles, 'Arabic Poetry and Architectural Memory in al-Andalus', ibid; D. Fairchild Ruggles, *Gardens, Landscape and Vision in the Palaces of Islamic Spain*, ibid; and R. A. Jairazbhoy, *An Outline of Islamic Architecture*, Asia Publishing House, 1972
50 D. Fairchild Ruggles, *Gardens, Landscape and Vision in the Palaces of Islamic Spain*, ibid
51 Al-Maqqari in D. Fairchild Ruggles, *Gardens, Landscape and Vision in the Palaces of Islamic Spain*, ibid
52 Ibn Hayyan in D. Fairchild Ruggles, *Gardens, Landscape and Vision in the Palaces of Islamic Spain*, ibid
53 Antonio Vallejo Triano, 'Madinat Al-Zahra: Historical Reality and Present-Day Heritage', ibid
54 Antonio Vallejo Triano, 'Madinat Al-Zahra: Historical Reality and Present-Day Heritage', ibid; Antonio Vallejo Triano, 'Madinat al-Zahra: The Triumph of the Islamic State', ibid; D. Fairchild Ruggles, 'The Mirador in Hispano-Umayyad Garden Typology', ibid
55 Al-Himyari, quoted in D. Fairchild Ruggles, *Gardens, Landscape and Vision in the Palaces of Islamic Spain*, ibid
56 Antonio Vallejo Triano, 'Madinat Al-Zahra: Historical Reality and Present-Day Heritage', ibid
57 Antonio Vallejo Triano, 'Madinat Al-Zahra: Historical Reality and Present-Day Heritage', ibid; and D. Fairchild Ruggles, *Gardens, Landscape and Vision in the Palaces of Islamic Spain*, ibid; and Antonio Vallejo Triano, 'Madinat al-Zahra: The Triumph of the Islamic State', ibid; and Maribel Fierro, ibid
58 D. Fairchild Ruggles, *Gardens, Landscape and Vision in the Palaces of Islamic Spain*, ibid; D. Fairchild Ruggles, 'The Mirador in Hispano-Umayyad Garden Typology', ibid; and Antonio Vallejo Triano, 'Madinat al-Zahra: The Triumph of the Islamic State', ibid
59 Ibn Idhari, quoted in Ann Christys, ibid
60 Al-Maqqari, quoted in D. Fairchild Ruggles, *Gardens, Landscape and Vision in the Palaces of Islamic Spain*, ibid
61 D. Fairchild Ruggles, 'The Mirador in Hispano-Umayyad Garden Typology', ibid
62 Antonio Vallejo Triano, 'Madinat al-Zahra: The Triumph of the Islamic State', ibid
63 Renata Holod, 'Luxury Arts of the Caliphal Period', ibid
64 Al-Maqqari in Renata Holod, 'Luxury Arts of the Caliphal Period', ibid; D. Fairchild Ruggles, *Gardens, Landscape and Vision in the Palaces of Islamic Spain*, ibid; Maribel Fierro, ibid; and A. Jairazbhoy, ibid
65 Ibn Hayyan, in Robert Hillenbrand, *Studies in Medieval Islamic Architecture,* The Pindar Press, 2001, and Renata Holod, 'Luxury Arts of the Caliphal Period', ibid
66 Al-Maqqari, quoted in Antonio Vallejo Triano, 'Madinat Al-Zahra: Historical Reality and Present-Day Heritage', ibid
67 Al-Maqqari, quoted in D. Fairchild Ruggles, *Gardens, Landscape and Vision in the Palaces of Islamic Spain*, ibid
68 Maribel Fierro, ibid; and D. Fairchild Ruggles, 'The Mirador in Hispano-Umayyad Garden Typology', ibid
69 Joseph F. O'Callaghan, ibid; and D. Fairchild Ruggles, *Gardens, Landscape and Vision in the Palaces of Islamic Spain*, ibid
70 Maribel Fierro, ibid
71 Joseph F. O'Callaghan, ibid
72 D. Fairchild Ruggles, *Gardens, Landscape and Vision in the Palaces of Islamic Spain*, ibid
73 D. Fairchild Ruggles, *Gardens, Landscape and Vision in the Palaces of Islamic Spain*, ibid; and Joseph F.

O'Callaghan, ibid

74 Joseph F. O'Callaghan, ibid

75 Joseph F. O'Callaghan, ibid

76 Joseph F. O'Callaghan, ibid; and D. Fairchild Ruggles, *Gardens, Landscape and Vision in the Palaces of Islamic Spain*, ibid

77 D. Fairchild Ruggles, *Gardens, Landscape and Vision in the Palaces of Islamic Spain*, ibid

78 Al-Himyari, quoted in D. Fairchild Ruggles, *Gardens, Landscape and Vision in the Palaces of Islamic Spain*, ibid

79 Al-Maqqari, in D. Fairchild Ruggles, *Islamic Gardens and Landscapes,* ibid; and D. Fairchild Ruggles, *Gardens, Landscape and Vision in the Palaces of Islamic Spain*, ibid

80 Al-Himyari, quoted in D. Fairchild Ruggles, *Gardens, Landscape and Vision in the Palaces of Islamic Spain*, ibid; and Joseph F. O'Callaghan, ibid

81 Joseph F. O'Callaghan, ibid

82 Joseph F. O'Callaghan, ibid; and D. Fairchild Ruggles, *Gardens, Landscape and Vision in the Palaces of Islamic Spain*, ibid

83 Joseph F. O'Callaghan, ibid

84 D. Fairchild Ruggles, *Gardens, Landscape and Vision in the Palaces of Islamic Spain*, ibid; and Ann Christys, ibid

85 Ann Christys, ibid; D. Fairchild Ruggles, 'Arabic Poetry and Architectural Memory in al-Andalus', ibid; and D. Fairchild Ruggles, *Gardens, Landscape and Vision in the Palaces of Islamic Spain*, ibid

86 Ibn Hazm, quoted in D. Fairchild Ruggles, 'Arabic Poetry and Architectural Memory in al-Andalus', ibid; and D. Fairchild Ruggles, *Gardens, Landscape and Vision in the Palaces of Islamic Spain*, ibid; and Ann Christys, ibid

87 Ibn Shuhayd, quoted in D. Fairchild Ruggles, 'Arabic Poetry and Architectural Memory in al-Andalus', ibid; and D. Fairchild Ruggles, *Gardens, Landscape and Vision in the Palaces of Islamic Spain*, ibid

88 Al-Maqqari, quoted in D. Fairchild Ruggles, *Gardens, Landscape and Vision in the Palaces of Islamic Spain*, ibid

89 Al-Sumaysir, quoted in D. Fairchild Ruggles, 'Arabic Poetry and Architectural Memory in al-Andalus', ibid; and D. Fairchild Ruggles, *Gardens, Landscape and Vision in the Palaces of Islamic Spain*, ibid

90 Ann Christys, ibid; D. Fairchild Ruggles, 'Arabic Poetry and Architectural Memory in al-Andalus', ibid; and D. Fairchild Ruggles, *Gardens, Landscape and Vision in the Palaces of Islamic Spain*, ibid

91 D. Fairchild Ruggles, 'Arabic Poetry and Architectural Memory in al-Andalus', ibid; and D. Fairchild Ruggles, *Gardens, Landscape and Vision in the Palaces of Islamic Spain*, ibid

92 Joseph F. O'Callaghan, ibid; and Robert Hillenbrand, ibid

93 Joseph F. O'Callaghan, ibid; and D. Fairchild Ruggles, *Gardens, Landscape and Vision in the Palaces of Islamic Spain*, ibid

94 Joseph F. O'Callaghan, ibid

95 Antonio Vallejo Triano, 'Madinat Al-Zahra: Historical Reality and Present-Day Heritage', ibid; John Gill, ibid; and Antonio Almagro, 'Preserving the Architectural Heritage of al-Andalus. From Restoration to Virtual Reconstruction', *Al-Masaq,* Vol 19, No 2, Routledege, September 2007

96 Joseph F. O'Callaghan, ibid

97 Ann Christys, ibid; and D. Fairchild Ruggles, *Gardens, Landscape and Vision in the Palaces of Islamic Spain*, ibid

CHAPTER 10

1 John Orrell, 'A New Hollar Panorama of London', *The Burlington Magazine,* Vol 124, No 953, August 1982; Gillian Tindall, *The Man Who Drew London: Wenceslaus Hollar in Reality and Imagination,* Chatto & Windus, 2002; Peter Ackroyd, *London: The Biography,* Vintage, 2001; and John Bold, 'Bird's-Eye Views: From Hollar to the London Eye', *The London Journal,* Vol 35, No 3, November 2010

2 Gillian Tindall, ibid

3 Gillian Tindall, ibid

4 Leo Hollis, *The Phoenix: St Paul's Cathedral and the Men Who Made Modern London,* Weidenfeld & Nicolson, 2008

5 Gillian Tindall, ibid; and Leo Hollis, ibid

6 Thomas Howard, quoted by Marion Roberts, *Dugdale and Hollar, History Illustrated,* University of Delaware Press, 2002
7 Gillian Tindall, ibid
8 Gillian Tindall, ibid
9 Gillian Tindall, ibid
10 William Dugdale, *The History of St Pauls Cathedral in London,* Tho Warren, 1658
11 William Dugdale, ibid; and William Longman, *A History of the three Cathedrals dedicated to St Paul in London*, Longman's Green and Co, 1873
12 John Schofield and Derek Keene, 'Before St Paul's', *St Paul's – The Cathedral Church of London 604 – 2004,* edited by Derek Keene, Arthur Burns and Andrew Saint, Yale Univeristy Press, 2004; and William Benham, *Old St Paul's Cahtedral,* Seeley and Co Ltd, 1902
13 Peter Ackroyd, ibid
14 John Schofield and Derek Keene, 'Before St Paul's' in Derek Keene, Arthur Burns and Andrew Saint, ibid
15 William Dugdale, ibid; and John Schofield and Derek Keene, 'Before St Paul's', in Derek Keene, Arthur Burns and Andrew Saint, ibid
16 John Schofield and Derek Keene, 'Before St Paul's', in Derek Keene, Arthur Burns and Andrew Saint, ibid
17 Peter Ackroyd, ibid
18 William Dugdale, ibid; Pamela Taylor, 'Foundation and Endowment: St Paul's and the English Kingdoms, 604-1087', in Derek Keene, Arthur Burns and Andrew Saint, ibid; William Benham, ibid; and Sir Israel Gollancz, *Select Early English Poems,* Oxford University Press, 1922
19 Pamela Taylor, 'Foundation and Endowment: St Paul's and the English Kingdoms, 604-1087', in Derek Keene, Arthur Burns and Andrew Saint, ibid
20 William Benham, ibid
21 Sir Israel Gollancz, ibid; and Cynthia Turner Camp, *Spatial Memory, Historiographic Fantasy, and the Touch of the Past in St Erkenwald, New Literary History, Volume 44, Number 3,* John Hopkins University Press, 2013
22 Sir Israel Gollancz, ibid
23 *St Erkenwald,* translation by Cynthia Turner Camp, ibid
24 Sir Israel Gollancz, ibid; and Cynthia Turner Camp, ibid
25 Cynthia Turner Camp. ibid
26 Cynthia Turner Camp, ibid
27 Quoted in Peter Ackroyd, ibid
28 *St Erkenwald,* translation by Sir Israel Gollancz, *Select Early English Poems,* ibid
29 Sir Israel Gollancz, ibid
30 Sir Israel Gollancz, ibid
31 Cynthia Turner Camp, ibid
32 Alan Thacker, 'The Cult of Saints and the Liturgy', in Derek Keene, Arthur Burns and Andrew Saint, ibid
33 William Dugdale, ibid;
34 Pamela Taylor, 'Foundation and Endowment: St Paul's and the English Kingdoms, 604-1087', in Derek Keene, Arthur Burns and Andrew Saint, ibid; and Derek Keene, 'From Conquest to Capital: St Paul's c1100-1300', in Derek Keene, Arthur Burns and Andrew Saint, ibid
35 Alan Thacker, 'The Cult of Saints and the Liturgy', in Derek Keene, Arthur Burns and Andrew Saint, ibid
36 Cynthia Turner Camp, ibid
37 William Dugdale, ibid
38 William Dugdale, ibid; and William Longman, ibid
39 William Benham, ibid
40 Derek Keene, 'From Conquest to Capital: St Paul's c1100-1300', in Derek Keene, Arthur Burns and Andrew Saint, ibid
41 William Dugdale, ibid
42 Sir Israel Gollancz, ibid; and Cynthia Turner Camp, ibid
43 William Dugdale, ibid
44 William Dugdale, ibid
45 Caroline M. Barron and Marie-Helene Rousseau, 'Cathedral, City and State', in Derek Keene,

Arthur Burns and Andrew Saint, ibid

46 William Benham, ibid; and William Longman, ibid

47 Caroline M. Barron and Marie-Helene Rousseau, 'Cathedral, City and State', ibid

48 Caroline M. Barron and Marie-Helene Rousseau, 'Cathedral, City and State', ibid

49 Caroline M. Barron and Marie-Helene Rousseau, 'Cathedral, City and State', ibid

50 Edward Hall, *Hall's chronicle: containing the history of England, during the reign of Henry the Fourth, and the succeeding monarchs to the end of the reign of Henry the Eighth, in which are particularly described the manners and customs of those periods,* 1547, printed for J. Johnson, 1809

51 Edward Hall, ibid

52 Edward Hall, ibid

53 Edward Hall, ibid

54 Edward Hall, ibid

55 Leviticus, xviii, 16; xx, 21

56 David J. Crankshaw, 'Community, City and Nation: 1540-1714', in Derek Keene, Arthur Burns and Andrew Saint, ibid; and William Benham, ibid

57 Quoted in William Benham, ibid

58 David J. Crankshaw, 'Community, City and Nation: 1540-1714', ibid

59 William Longman, ibid; and David J. Crankshaw, 'Community, City and Nation: 1540-1714', ibid

60 Quoted in *A History of the three Cathedrals dedicated to St Paul in London*, William Longman, Longman's Green and Co, 1873

61 William Longman, ibid

62 David J. Crankshaw, 'Community, City and Nation: 1540-1714', ibid

63 David J. Crankshaw, 'Community, City and Nation: 1540-1714', ibid

64 Francis Osborne, *Works,* quoted in *The Retrospective Review, Vol VII,* Charles Baldwyn, 1823

65 John Earle, *Microcosmography: or, a piece of the world discover'd. In essays and characters,* London, 1628, reprinted E. Say, 1732.

66 William Haughton, quoted by Helen Ostovich in the introduction to Ben Jonson, *Every Man Out of His Humour,* Manchester University Press, 2001

67 Ben Jonson, ibid

68 James Shapiro, *1599, A Year in the Life of William Shakespeare,* Faber, 2005

69 James Shapiro, ibid

70 John Stockwood, quoted in James Shapiro, ibid

71 David J. Crankshaw, 'Community, City and Nation: 1540-1714', ibid

72 John Timbs, *Curiosities of London,* J S Virtue, 1885

73 John Evelyn, *The Diary of John Evelyn,* edited by E. S. de Beer, Clarendon Press, 1955

74 John Evelyn, ibid

75 William Longman, ibid

76 Christopher Wren, Wren Society, Volumes 1-20, quoted in William Longman, ibid

77 Christopher Wren, Wren Society, quoted in William Longman, ibid

78 Christopher Wren, Wren Society, quoted in William Longman, ibid

79 Leo Hollis, ibid

80 Leo Hollis, ibid; and William Longman, ibid

81 Dean Milman, quoted in William Longman, ibid

82 Dean Milman, quoted in William Longman, ibid

83 Dean Milman, quoted in William Longman, ibid; and David J. Crankshaw, 'Community, City and Nation: 1540-1714', ibid; Leo Hollis, ibid; William Benham, ibid;

84 Leo Hollis, ibid

85 David J. Crankshaw, 'Community, City and Nation: 1540-1714', ibid; William Benham, ibid;

86 David J. Crankshaw, 'Community, City and Nation: 1540-1714', ibid

87 David J. Crankshaw, 'Community, City and Nation: 1540-1714', ibid

88 William Longman, ibid

89 Thomas Fuller, *The Church History of Britain: from the birth of Jesus Christ, until the year M DC XLVIII,* 1655

90 Marion Roberts, ibid

91 Marion Roberts, ibid

92 Gillian Tindall, ibid

93 Christopher Wren, Wren Society, ibid, quoted in William Longman, ibid
94 Kerry Downes, 'Wren and the New Cathedral', in Derek Keene, Arthur Burns and Andrew Saint, ibid;
95 John Evelyn, ibid
96 John Evelyn, ibid
97 John Evelyn, ibid
98 John Evelyn, ibid
99 Samuel Pepys, *The Diary of Samuel Pepys*, edited by Robert Latham and William Matthews, G. Bell & Sons Ltd, 1970
100 Samuel Pepys, *The Diary of Samuel Pepys*, edited by Robert Latham and William Matthews, G. Bell & Sons Ltd, 1970
101 Thomas Vincent, *God's Terrible Voice in the City,* Bridgeport, 1811
102 John Evelyn, ibid
103 Samuel Pepys, ibid
104 John Evelyn, ibid
105 Samuel Pepys, ibid
106 Samuel Pepys, ibid
107 John Evelyn, ibid
108 John Evelyn, ibid
109 John Evelyn, ibid
110 Leo Hollis, ibid
111 Christopher Wren, *Parentalia: or Memoirs of the family of the Wrens,* T. Osborn, 1750
112 Christopher Wren, *Parentalia,* ibid
113 Samuel Pepys, ibid
114 Samuel Pepys, ibid
115 James W. P. Campbell and Robert Bowles, 'The Construction of the New Cathedral', in Derek Keene, Arthur Burns and Andrew Saint, ibid;
116 Christopher Wren, *Parentalia,* ibid
117 Winston Churchill, quoted by W. R. Matthews in *St Paul's Cathedral in Wartime 1939-1945,* Hutchinson, 1946
118 Ernie Pyle, *Ernie's War: The Best of Ernie Pyle's World War II Dispatches*, Random House, 1986

CHAPTER 11

1 Ala al-din Ata-Malik Juvaini, *Genghis Khan: The History of the World Conqueror,* translated from the text of Mirza Muhammad Qazvini by J A Boyle, Manchester University Press, 1997
2 Ata-Malik Juvaini, ibid
3 Ata-Malik Juvaini, ibid
4 J. J. Saunders, *The History of the Mongol Conquests,* Routledge, 1971
5 Ata-Malik Juvaini, ibid
6 Ata-Malik Juvaini, ibid
7 Ata-Malik Juvaini, ibid
8 Ata-Malik Juvaini, ibid
9 Noriyuki Shiraishi, 'Seasonal Migrations of the Mongol Emperors and the Peri-Urban Area of Kharakhorum', *International Journal of Asian Studies,* 1, 1, Cambridge University Press, 2004; and J. Daniel Rogers, Erdenebat Ulambayar and Matthew Gallon, 'Urban centres and the emergence of empires in Eastern Inner Asia', *Antiquity,* 79, 2005
10 Leo de Hartog, *Genghis Khan: Conqueror of the World*, I. B. Tauris, 1999
11 Ata-Malik Juvaini, ibid
12 Ata-Malik Juvaini, ibid
13 David Morgan, *The Mongols,* Basil Blackwell, 1986
14 Leo de Hartog, ibid
15 Jack Weatherford, *Genghis Khan and the Making of the Modern World',* Broadway Books, 2004
16 Ata-Malik Juvaini, ibid
17 David Morgan, *The Mongols,* ibid
18 Francis Woodman Cleaves, *The Secret History of the Mongols,* Harvard University Press, 1982; and Igor de Rachewiltz, *The Secret History of the Mongols: A Mongolian Epic Chronicle of the Thirteenth*

Century, Brill, 2004

19 Igor de Rachewiltz, ibid; David Morgan, ibid; Leo de Hartog, ibid; Francis Woodman Cleaves, *The Secret History of the Mongols,* ibid; Francis Woodman Cleaves, 'The Sino-Mongolian Inscription of 1346', *Harvard Journal of Asiatic Studies,* Vol 15, No 1/2, 1952; and William Hung, 'The Transmission of the Book Known as the Secret History of the Mongols', *Harvard Journal of Asiatic Studies,* Vol 14, No. 3/4, Dec 1951

20 Igor de Rachewiltz, ibid; and David Morgan, *The Mongols,* ibid

21 Igor de Rachewiltz, ibid; and David Morgan *The Mongols*, ibid; and Urgunge Onon, *The History and Life of Chinggis Khan,* Brill, 1990

22 Igor de Rachewiltz, ibid

23 David Morgan, *The Mongols,* ibid

24 David Morgan, *The Mongols,* ibid

25 *The Secret History of the Mongols,* translated by Igor de Rachewiltz, ibid

26 *The Secret History of the Mongols,* translated by Igor de Rachewiltz, ibid

27 *The Secret History of the Mongols,* translated by Igor de Rachewiltz, ibid

28 *The Secret History of the Mongols,* translated by Igor de Rachewiltz, ibid

29 *The Secret History of the Mongols,* translated by Igor de Rachewiltz, ibid

30 David Morgan, *The Mongols,* ibid

31 *The Secret History of the Mongols,* translated by Igor de Rachewiltz, ibid

32 *The Secret History of the Mongols,* translated by Igor de Rachewiltz, ibid; David Morgan, *The Mongols,* ibid; and Leo de Hartog, ibid

33 David Morgan, *The Mongols*, ibid; and Leo de Hartog, ibid

34 J. J. Saunders, ibid; and Jack Weatherford, ibid

35 David Morgan, *The Mongols,* ibid; and Leo de Hartog, ibid; and J J Saunders, ibid

36 David Morgan, *The Mongols,* ibid

37 Matthew Paris, *Chronica Majora,* in *Matthew Paris's English History: From 1235 to 1273*, translated by J. A. Giles, Henry G. Bohn, 1852

38 Matthew Paris, translated by J. A. Giles, ibid

39 Matthew Paris, translated by J. A. Giles, ibid

40 Matthew Paris, translated by J. A. Giles, ibid

41 David Morgan, *The Mongols,* ibid

42 David Morgan, *The Mongols*, ibid; and J J Saunders, ibid

43 Jack Weatherford, ibid; and Timothy May, *The Mongol Conquests in World History,* Reaktion Books, 2012

44 David Morgan, *The Mongols,* ibid

45 P. Pelliot, *Notes on Marco Polo, quoted in* J. J. Saunders, ibid; and David Morgan, *The Mongols*, ibid

46 J. Daniel Rogers, Erdenebat Ulambayar and Matthew Gallon, ibid

47 Leo de Hartog, ibid

48 Rashid al-Din, *The Successors of Genghis Khan,* translated by J. A. Boyle, Columbia University Press, 1971

49 Rashid al-Din, ibid

50 Rashid al-Din, ibid

51 Noriyuki Shiraishi, ibid

52 Ministry of Education Science and Culture, Republic of Mongolia, *The Ancient City of Kharakhorum,* UNESCO, 1997

53 Ata-Malik Juvaini, ibid; Rashid al-Din, ibid; Noriyuki Shiraishi, ibid; and J. Daniel Rogers, Erdenebat Ulambayar and Matthew Gallon, ibid

54 J. Daniel Rogers, Erdenebat Ulambayar and Matthew Gallon, ibid

55 Timothy May, ibid

56 J. A.Boyle, introduction to Rashid al-Din, *The Successors of Genghis Khan*, ibid; and David Morgan, *The Mongols,* ibid

57 Rashid al-Din, ibid

58 Rashid al-Din, ibid

59 Rashid al-Din, ibid

60 Rashid al-Din, ibid

61 Ata-Malik Juvaini, ibid; and Jack Weatherford, ibid

62 J. J. Saunders, ibid

63 J. J. Saunders, ibid; Leo de Hartog, ibid; Timothy May, ibid; and Jack Weatherford, ibid

64 Peter Jackson, 'The Crusade Against the Mongols', *Journal of Ecclesiastical History,* Vol 42, No 1, January 1991

65 Leo de Hartog, ibid

66 Rashid al-Din, ibid

67 Jack Weatherford, ibid

68 J. J. Saunders, ibid

69 Jack Weatherford, ibid

70 David Morgan, *The Mongols,* ibid

71 Peter Jackson, introduction to Friar William of Rubruck, *The Mission of Friar William of Rubruck: His journey to the court of the Great Khan Mongke, 1253-1255,* translated by Peter Jackson, Hackett, 2009

72 Peter Jackson, introduction to *The Mission of Friar William of Rubruck,* ibid

73 Peter Jackson, introduction to *The Mission of Friar William of Rubruck,* ibid; and A. J. Watson, 'Mongol inhospitality, or how to do more with less? Gift giving in William of Rubruck's Itinerarium', *Journal of Medieval History*, 37, 2011

74 Friar William of Rubruck, *The Mission of Friar William of Rubruck,* Chapter I, ibid

75 Friar William of Rubruck, *The Mission of Friar William of Rubruck,* Chapter I, ibid

76 Friar William of Rubruck, Chapter IX, ibid

77 Friar William of Rubruck, Chapter XIII, ibid

78 Friar William of Rubruck Chapter XVI, ibid; and A. J. Watson, ibid

79 Friar William of Rubruck, Chapter XIX ibid

80 Friar William of Rubruck, Chapter XIX, ibid

81 Friar William of Rubruck, Chapter XIX, ibid

82 A. J. Watson, ibid

83 Friar William of Rubruck, Chapter XX, ibid

84 Friar William of Rubruck, Chapter XXII ibid; and A. J. Watson, ibid

85 Friar William of Rubruck, Chapter XXVII, ibid

86 Friar William of Rubruck, Chapter XXVII, ibid

87 Peter Jackson, introduction to *The Mission of Friar William of Rubruck,* ibid; and Friar William of Rubruck, ibid

88 Friar William of Rubruck, Chapter XXVIII, ibid

89 Friar William of Rubruck, Chapter XXX, ibid

90 Friar William of Rubruck, Chapter XXX, ibid

91 Friar William of Rubruck, Chapter XXIX, ibid

92 Friar William of Rubruck, Chapter XXXII, ibid

93 Peter Jackson, introduction to *The Mission of Friar William of Rubruck,* ibid

94 Friar William of Rubruck, Chapter XXXIII, ibid

95 Friar William of Rubruck, Chapter XXXIII, ibid

96 Friar William of Rubruck, Chapter XXXVI, ibid

97 Friar William of Rubruck, Chapter XXXVI, ibid

98 Ronald Latham, introduction to *The Travels of Marco Polo*, translated by Ronald Latham, Penguin, 1958

99 Marco Polo, *The Travels of Marco Polo*, ibid

100 Marco Polo, *The Travels of Marco Polo*, ibid

101 Timothy May, ibid

102 David Morgan, *The Mongols,* ibid; Timothy May, ibid; J. J. Saunders, ibid; Jack Weatherford, ibid; and David Morgan, 'The Decline and Fall of the Mongol Empire', *Journal of the Royal Asiatic Society,* Vol 19, Issue 4, January 2009

103 David Morgan, *The Mongols,* ibid; and Jack Weatherford, ibid

104 J. J. Saunders, ibid; and Morris Rossabi, *Khubilai Khan: His Life and Times,* University of California Press, 1988

105 Manfred Rosch, Elske Fischer and Tanja Markle, 'Human diet and land use in the time of the Khans – Archaeobotanical research in the capital of the Mongolian Empire, Qara Qorum, Mongolia', *Vegetation History and Archaeobotany,* Vol 14, Issue 4, 2005

106 Jack Weatherford, ibid

107 Timothy May, ibid

108 Samuel Taylor Coleridge, *The Complete Poetical Works of Samuel Taylor Coleridge,* edited by Earnest Hartley Coleridge, Clarendon Press, 1912
109 Marco Polo, *The Travels of Marco Polo*, ibid
110 Morris Rossabi, ibid
111 Jack Weatherford, ibid
112 Marco Polo, *The Travels of Marco Polo*, ibid; J. J. Saunders, ibid
113 Marco Polo, *The Travels of Marco Polo*, ibid
114 Marco Polo, *The Travels of Marco Polo*, ibid
115 Jack Weatherford, ibid
116 Jack Weatherford, ibid; and Marco Polo, *The Travels of Marco Polo*, ibid
117 Timothy May, ibid
118 Timothy May, ibid; J. J. Saunders, ibid
119 David Morgan, 'The Decline and Fall of the Mongol Empire', ibid; and Jack Weatherford, ibid; and Timothy Brook, *The Troubled Empire: China in the Yuan and Ming Dynasties,* Harvard University Press, 2010
120 Michael Pradwin, *The Mongol Empire: Its Rise and Legacy,* Allen and Unwin, 1940
121 Timothy Brook, ibid
122 Jack Weatherford, ibid
123 Michael Pradwin, ibid
124 Peter Young, *Tortoise*, Reaktion Books, 2003
125 Jehangir S. Pocha, 'Mongolia sees Genghis Khan's good side', *New York Times,* 10 May 2005
126 Jehangir S. Pocha, ibid; and Jack Weatherford, ibid
127 Jehangir S. Pocha, ibid
128 Dan Levin, 'Genghis Khan Rules Mongolia Again, in a PR Campaign', *International New York Times,* 2 August 2009
129 'Reviving the Ancient Capital of Karakorum', *Foreign Affairs,* Vol 84, Issue 3, May/June 2005

CHAPTER 12

1 John Keats, *The Complete Works of John Keats*, edited by H Buxton Forman, T Y Cromwell & Co, 1817
2 *Maasir-i-Alamgiri, A History of the Emperor Aurangzib-'Alamgir (reign 1658-1707 AD)*, Jadunath Sarkar translator, The Asiatic Society, Calcutta, 1990
3 Jadunath Sarkar, *History of Aurangzib, Volume IV,* M. C. Sarkar and Sons, Calcutta, 1924; and Rocco Sha, *A Guide to Golconda Fort and Tombs,* Government Central Press, Hyderabad, 1929
4 Jean de Thévenot and Giovanni Francesco Gemelli Careri, *Indian Travels of Thévenot and Careri: Being the third part of the travels of M. De Thévenot into the Levant and the third part of a voyage round the world by D. John Francis Gemelli Careri*, National Archives of India, New Delhi, 1949
5 Rocco Sha, ibid
6 *Indian Travels of Thévenot and Careri,* ibid
7 Aurangzeb, quoted in Stanley Lane-Poole, *Rulers of India, Aurangzib*, Clarendon Press, Oxford, 1893
8 Quoted in H. G. Rawlinson, *India: A Short Cultural History*, The Cresset Press, 1937
9 Quoted in H. G. Rawlinson, ibid
10 *The Nature of Diamonds,* edited George E. Harlow, Cambridge University Press in association with the American Museum of Natural History, 1998
11 George E. Harlow, ibid; and George Frederick Kunz, *The Curious Lore of Precious Stones*, Halcyon House, 1938
12 George Frederick Kunz, ibid
13 George Frederick Kunz, ibid, citing Dr Julius Ruska, *Das Steinbuch aus der Kosmographie des al-Kazwini,* Heidelberg, 1894
14 George Frederick Kunz, ibid
15 George Frederick Kunz, ibid
16 *The Arabian Nights: Tales of 1,001 Nights, Volume 2,* translated Malcolm C. Lyons, Penguin, 2010; and George Frederick Kunz, ibid
17 *The Arabian Nights,* ibid
18 *The Arabian Nights,* ibid

19 Marco Polo, *The Travels of Marco Polo,* Marco Polo, translated Ronald Latham, Penguin, 1958
20 Marco Polo, ibid
21 Marco Polo, ibid
22 George Frederick Kunz, citing Dr Valentine Ball, ibid
23 Marco Polo, ibid
24 George E. Harlow, ibid
25 Marco Polo, ibid
26 *Indian Travels of Thévenot and Careri*, ibid
27 *Indian Travels of Thévenot and Careri,* ibid
28 *Indian Travels of Thévenot and Careri,* ibid
29 Marika Sardar, *Golconda through Time: A Mirror of the Evolving Deccan*, PhD dissertation, New York University, 2007
30 Marika Sardar, *The Early Foundations of Golconda and the Rise of Fortifications in the Fourteenth-Century Deccan,* Metropolitan Museum of Art, New York, 2011
31 From the *Tarikh-i Ferishta*, translated by John Briggs, in Marika Sardar, *The Early Foundations of Golconda and the Rise of Fortifications in the Fourteenth-Century*
32 Rocco Sha, ibid
33 Marika Sardar, *Golconda through Time: A Mirror of the Evolving Deccan,* ibid
34 Marika Sardar, *Golconda through Time: A Mirror of the Evolving Deccan,* ibid; and Rocco Sha, ibid
35 Laura Weinstein, *Variations on a Persian Theme: Adaptation and Innovation in Early Manuscripts from Golconda*, PhD dissertation, Columbia University, 2011; and Richard Maxwell Eaton, *A Social History f the Deccan, 1300-1761: Eight Indian Lives,* Cambridge University Press, 2005
36 Marika Sardar, *Golconda through Time: A Mirror of the Evolving Deccan,* ibid
37 Ferishta, *Ferishta's History of Dekkan from the First Mahummedan Conquests*, translated by Jonathan Scott, John Stockdale, London, 1794
38 Ferishta, *Ferishta's History of Dekkan from the First Mahummedan Conquests*, ibid
39 Rocco Sha, ibid; and Ferishta, *Ferishta's History of Dekkan from the First Mahummedan Conquests*, ibid; and Marika Sardar, *Golconda through Time: A Mirror of the Evolving Deccan,* ibid
40 Ferishta, *Ferishta's History of Dekkan from the First Mahummedan Conquests*, ibid
41 Marika Sardar, *Golconda through Time: A Mirror of the Evolving Deccan* ibid
42 Ferishta, *Ferishta's History of Dekkan from the First Mahummedan Conquests*, ibid
43 Ferishta, *Ferishta's History of Dekkan from the First Mahummedan Conquests*, ibid
44 Jean Baptiste Tavernier, *The Six Voyages of Jean-Baptiste Tavernier, Baron of Aubonne, through Turkey, into Persia and the East-Indies,* translated by V Ball, Munishram Manoharlal Publishers, 1995
45 Jean Baptiste Tavernier, ibid
46 Jean Baptiste Tavernier, ibid
47 Jean Baptiste Tavernier, ibid
48 Jean Baptiste Tavernier, ibid
49 Jean Baptiste Tavernier, ibid
50 Jean Baptiste Tavernier, ibid
51 Jean Baptiste Tavernier, ibid
52 Jean Baptiste Tavernier, ibid
53 Jean Baptiste Tavernier, ibid
54 Jean Baptiste Tavernier, ibid
55 Jean Baptiste Tavernier, ibid
56 Jean Baptiste Tavernier, ibid; and *Maasir-i-Alamgiri, A History of the Emperor Aurangzib-'Alamgir (reign 1658-1707 AD),* Jadunath Sarkar translator, ibid
57 Jean Baptiste Tavernier, ibid
58 Jean Baptiste Tavernier, ibid
59 Jean Baptiste Tavernier, ibid
60 Jean Baptiste Tavernier, ibid
61 *Indian Travels of Thévenot and Careri*, ibid
62 *Indian Travels of Thévenot and Careri*, ibid; and W W Hunter, *The Imperial Gazetteer of India, Vol XII*, 1908, Clarendon Press, Oxford
63 *Indian Travels of Thévenot and Careri*, ibid
64 *Indian Travels of Thévenot and Careri*, ibid
65 *Indian Travels of Thévenot and Careri*, ibid

66 *Indian Travels of Thévenot and Careri*, ibid
67 Stanley Lane-Poole, ibid
68 Sir George Dunbar, *A History of India, From the Earliest Times to the Present Day*, Nicholson and Watson, London, 1939
69 Stanley Lane-Poole, ibid
70 Stanley Lane-Poole, ibid
71 Sir George Dunbar, ibid; and Stanley Lane-Poole, ibid
72 Sir George Dunbar, ibid; and Stanley Lane-Poole, ibid
73 Stanley Lane-Poole, ibid
74 Stanley Lane-Poole, ibid
75 Stanley Lane-Poole, ibid
76 Stanley Lane-Poole, ibid
77 Stanley Lane-Poole, ibid
78 Sir George Dunbar, ibid; and Stanley Lane-Poole, ibid
79 Francois Bernier, quoted in Stanley Lane-Poole, ibid
80 Stanley Lane-Poole, ibid
81 Sir George Dunbar, ibid; and Stanley Lane-Poole, ibid
82 Sir George Dunbar, ibid
83 H. G. Rawlinson, ibid.
84 *Maasir-i-Alamgiri,* ibid
85 H. G. Rawlinson, ibid
86 Khafi Khan, quoted in H. G. Rawlinson, ibid.
87 Sir George Dunbar, ibid; and Stanley Lane-Poole, ibid
88 H. G. Rawlinson, ibid, Sir George Dunbar, ibid; and Stanley Lane-Poole, ibid
89 Quoted in Jadunath Sarkar, *History of Aurangzib, Mainly based on Persian sources, Volume I*, M. C. Sarkar and Sons, Calcutta, 1912
90 Jadunath Sarkar, *History of Aurangzib,Volumel I*, ibid
91 *Maasir-i-Alamgiri,* ibid
92 *Maasir-i-Alamgiri,* ibid
93 *Maasir-i-Alamgiri,* ibid
94 *Maasir-i-Alamgiri,* ibid
95 *Maasir-i-Alamgiri,* ibid
96 *Indian Travels of Thévenot and Careri,* ibid
97 Jadunath Sarkar, *History of Aurangzib, Volume IV,* ibid
98 Jadunath Sarkar, *History of Aurangzib, Volume IV,* ibid
99 *Maasir-i-Alamgiri,* ibid
100 Jadunath Sarkar, *History of Aurangzib, Volume IV,* ibid; Stanley Lane-Poole, ibid
101 Contemporary source quoted in Jadunath Sarkar, *History of Aurangzib, Volume IV,* ibid
102 Khafi Khan, quoted in Stanley Lane-Poole, ibid
103 Khafi Khan, quoted in Stanley Lane-Poole, ibid
104 Khafi Khan, quoted in Stanley Lane-Poole, ibid
105 Jadunath Sarkar, *History of Aurangzib, Volume IV,* ibid; Stanley Lane-Poole, ibid
106 *Maasir-i-Alamgiri,* ibid
107 Quoted in Jadunath Sarkar, *History of Aurangzib, Volume IV,* ibid
108 Quoted in Jadunath Sarkar, *History of Aurangzib, Volume IV,* ibid
109 *Maasir-i-Alamgiri,* ibid
110 *Maasir-i-Alamgiri,* ibid
111 Jadunath Sarkar, *History of Aurangzib, Volume IV,* ibid; Stanley Lane-Poole, ibid
112 Stanley Lane-Poole, ibid
113 Stanley Lane-Poole, ibid
114 Jadunath Sarkar, *History of Aurangzib, Volume IV,* ibid
115 *Maasir-i-Alamgiri,* ibid
116 Jean Baptiste Tavernier, ibid
117 Jean Baptiste Tavernier, ibid
118 Jean Baptiste Tavernier, ibid
119 Jean Baptiste Tavernier, ibid
120 Jean Baptiste Tavernier, ibid

121 Jean Baptiste Tavernier, ibid
122 William Crooke, Introduction to *The Six Voyages of Jean-Baptiste Tavernier,* ibid
123 George E. Harlow, ibid
124 William Crooke, Introduction to *The Six Voyages of Jean-Baptiste Tavernier,* ibid
125 William Crooke, Introduction to *The Six Voyages of Jean-Baptiste Tavernier,* ibid
126 William Crooke, Introduction to *The Six Voyages of Jean-Baptiste Tavernier,* ibid
127 Sir George Dunbar, ibid; and Stanley Lane-Poole, ibid; and H. G. Rawlinson, ibid
128 Khafi Khan, quoted in Stanley Lane-Poole, ibid
129 Khafi Khan, quoted in Stanley Lane-Poole, ibid
130 *Indian Travels of Thévenot and Careri*, ibid
131 Niccolao Manucci, quoted in H. G. Rawlinson, ibid
132 Quoted in Jadunath Sarkar, *History of Aurangzib, Volume V,*, in H. G. Rawlinson, ibid
133 Quoted in Stanley Lane-Poole, ibid
134 Stanley Lane-Poole, ibid; and H. G. Rawlinson, ibid
135 Quoted in H. G. Rawlinson, ibid
136 H. G. Rawlinson, ibid; and Sir George Dunbar, ibid
137 Sir George Dunbar, ibid
138 H. G. Rawlinson, ibid
139 W.W. Hunter, *The Imperial Gazetteer of India, Vol III*, Trubner and Co, London, 1881
140 W.W. Hunter, ibid
141 W.W. Hunter, ibid
142 Priya Ramachandran, 'Golconda Fort: Hyderabad's time machine', *The Times of India,* 9 January 2013
143 George E. Harlow, ibid
144 V. R. Ball, *Appendix I, The Six Voyages of Jean-Baptiste Tavernier,* ibid; and *Appendix II* to Francois Bernier's, *Travels in the Mogul Empire*, translated by Irving Brock and annotated by Archibald Constable, Munishram Manoharlal Publishers, 1992
145 V. R. Ball, ibid; and *Appendix II* , *Travels in the Mogul Empire,* ibid

CHAPTER 13

1 Henry Masers de Latude, *Memoirs of Henry Masers de Latude – who was confined during thirty-five years, in the different state prisons of France*, translated by John William Calcraft, W F Wakeman, 1834
2 Simon Schama, *Citizens: A Chronicle of the French Revolution,* Penguin, 1989
3 Henry Masers de Latude, *Memoirs,* translated by John William Calcraft, ibid
4 Henry Masers de Latude, *Memoirs,* translated by John William Calcraft, ibid
5 Masers de Latude, *Memoirs,* J. Johnson, 1787
6 Henry Masers de Latude, *Memoirs,* translated by John William Calcraft, ibid
7 Henry Masers de Latude, *Memoirs,* translated by John William Calcraft, ibid
8 Simon-Nicolas-Henri Linguet, *Memoirs of the Bastille: Containing a full exposition of the mysterious policy and despotic oppression of the French Government, in the Interior Administration of that State-Prison, interspersed with a Variety of Curious Anecdotes,* J A Husband, 1783
9 Frantz Funck-Brentano, *Legends of the Bastille,* Downey & Co, 1899
10 Hans-Jurgen Lusebrink and Rolf Reichardt, *The Bastille: A History of a Symbol of Despotism and Freedom,* Duke University Press, 1997
11 R. A. Davenport, *The History of the Bastille and of its Principal Captives,* Thomas Tegg and Son, 1838
12 R. A. Davenport, ibid
13 Brossais du Perray, *Historical Remarks on the Castle of the Bastille,* 1789; and R. A. Davenport, ibid
14 R. A. Davenport, ibid
15 R. A. Davenport, ibid
16 R. A. Davenport, ibid; and Frantz Funck-Brentano, ibid
17 Hans-Jurgen Lusebrink and Rolf Reichardt, ibid; and Frantz Funck-Brentano, ibid
18 William Robson, *The Life of Cardinal Richlieu,* Routledge, 1854; and Joseph Bergin, *Cardinal Richlieu: Power and the Pursuit of Wealth,* Yale University Press, 1985
19 Joseph Bergin, *The Rise of Richlieu,* Yale University Press, 1991
20 Jean Vincent Blanchard, *Eminence: Cardinal Richlieu and the Rise of France,* Walker & Company, 2011
21 Joseph Bergin, *Cardinal Richlieu: Power and the Pursuit of Wealth,* ibid; and William Robson, ibid

22 Joseph Bergin, *The Rise of Richlieu,* ibid
23 Simon Schama, ibid
24 Henry Kissinger, *Diplomacy,* Pocket Books, 2003, quoted in Jean Vincent Blanchard, ibid
25 Quoted in Jean Vincent Blanchard, ibid
26 Quoted in Jean Vincent Blanchard, ibid
27 Simon Schama, ibid; and R.A. Davenport, ibid
28 Simon Schama, ibid
29 David A Coles, *The French Revolution,* Friesen Press, 2014
30 R.A. Davenport, ibid
31 Claude le Petit, *Chronique scandaleuse, ou Paris ridicule,* quoted in Hans-Jurgen Lusebrink and Rolf Reichardt, ibid
32 Georgia Cowart, *The Triumph of Pleasure: Louis XIV and the Politics of Spectacle,* University of Chicago Press, 2008
33 Hans-Jurgen Lusebrink and Rolf Reichardt, ibid
34 Constantin de Renneville, *The French Inquisition: or, the History of the Bastille in Paris, the State Prison in France,* A. Bell, 1715
35 Constantin de Renneville, ibid
36 Hans-Jurgen Lusebrink and Rolf Reichardt, ibid
37 Andre Morellet, quoted in Simon Schama, ibid
38 Simon Schama, ibid; and Hans-Jurgen Lusebrink and Rolf Reichardt, ibid
39 Frantz Funck-Brentano, ibid; and Simon Schama, ibid
40 Hans-Jurgen Lusebrink and Rolf Reichardt, ibid
41 Simon Schama, ibid
42 The Marquis De Sade, quoted in *The Marquis de Sade: A Life,* Neil Schaeffer, Harvard University Press, 2000
43 Frantz Funck-Brentano, ibid
44 Neil Schaeffer, ibid
45 Neil Schaeffer, ibid
46 Frantz Funck-Brentano, ibid
47 Simon Schama, ibid
48 Bucquoy de Manican, *The Hell of the Living, or the Bastille in Paris, quoted* in Hans-Jurgen Lusebrink and Rolf Reichardt, ibid
49 Hans-Jurgen Lusebrink and Rolf Reichardt, ibid
50 Voltaire, *The Age of Louis XIV,* quoted in R.A. Davenport, ibid; Frantz Funck-Brentano, ibid; and Hans-Jurgen Lusebrink and Rolf Reichardt, ibid
51 Frantz Funck-Brentano, ibid; and Hans-Jurgen Lusebrink and Rolf Reichardt, ibid
52 Voltaire, *Age of Louis XIV,* quoted in R.A. Davenport, ibid
53 R.A. Davenport, ibid
54 Keith Reader, *The Place de la Bastille: The story of a quartier*, Liverpool University Press, 2011
55 From the *Declaration of the Rights of Man and Citizen, August 26, 1789,* in Georges Lefebvre, *The Coming of the French Revolution,* translated by R R Palmer, Princeton University Press, 1947
56 William Doyle, *The Oxford History of the French Revolution,* Oxford University Press, 1990; and Georges Lefebvre, ibid
57 Simon-Nicolas-Henri Linguet, ibid; R.A. Davenport, ibid; Simon Schama, ibid; Hans-Jurgen Lusebrink and Rolf Reichardt, ibid; and Frantz Funck-Brentano, ibid
58 Simon-Nicolas-Henri Linguet, ibid;
59 Simon-Nicolas-Henri Linguet, ibid; Simon Schama, ibid; and Hans-Jurgen Lusebrink and Rolf Reichardt, ibid
60 Simon-Nicolas-Henri Linguet, ibid
61 Simon-Nicolas-Henri Linguet, ibid
62 Fyodor Dostoevsky, *The House of the Dead,* 1862, translated by Constance Garnett, Heinemann, 1915
63 Simon-Nicolas-Henri Linguet, ibid
64 Frantz Funck-Brentano, ibid; R.A. Davenport, ibid; Hans-Jurgen Lusebrink and Rolf Reichardt, ibid; and Simon Schama, ibid
65 Frantz Funck-Brentano, ibid; R.A. Davenport, ibid;
66 R.A. Davenport, ibid; and Hans-Jurgen Lusebrink and Rolf Reichardt

67 Henry Masers de Latude, *Memoirs,* translated by John William Calcraft, ibid
68 Henry Masers de Latude, *Memoirs,* translated by John William Calcraft, ibid
69 R.A. Davenport, ibid
70 Henry Masers de Latude, *Memoirs,* translated by John William Calcraft, ibid
71 Frantz Funck-Brentano, ibid; Hans-Jurgen Lusebrink and Rolf Reichardt ibid; Simon Schama, ibid; and R.A. Davenport, ibid
72 Henry Masers de Latude, *Memoirs,* translated by John William Calcraft, ibid
73 Henry Masers de Latude, *Memoirs,* translated by John William Calcraft, ibid
74 Henry Masers de Latude, *Memoirs,* translated by John William Calcraft, ibid; Simon Schama, ibid; Hans-Jurgen Lusebrink and Rolf Reichardt, ibid; and R.A. Davenport, ibid
75 Frantz Funck-Brentano, ibid
76 Frantz Funck-Brentano, ibid; Hans-Jurgen Lusebrink and Rolf Reichardt ibid; Simon Schama, ibid; and R.A. Davenport, ibid
77 Simon Schama, ibid
78 *Dialogue entre le donjon de Vincennes et la Bastille,* 1787-88, quoted in Hans-Jurgen Lusebrink and Rolf Reichardt ibid
79 Jacques Godechot, *The Taking of the Bastille: July 14th 1789,* translated by Jean Stewart, Faber and Faber, 1970; Simon Schama, ibid; and Hans-Jurgen Lusebrink and Rolf Reichardt ibid
80 Houdon, quoted in Jacques Godechot, ibid
81 Jacques Godechot, ibid
82 Hans-Jurgen Lusebrink and Rolf Reichardt ibid
83 Jacques Godechot, ibid; Hans-Jurgen Lusebrink and Rolf Reichardt ibid; William Doyle, ibid
84 William Doyle, ibid
85 Jacques Godechot, ibid; Hans-Jurgen Lusebrink and Rolf Reichardt ibid; William Doyle, ibid
86 William Doyle, ibid; Jacques Godechot, ibid; and R.A. Davenport, ibid
87 Jacques Godechot, ibid
88 Quoted in R.A. Davenport, ibid
89 Jacques Godechot, ibid
90 Hans-Jurgen Lusebrink and Rolf Reichardt ibid;
91 Jacques Godechot, ibid; R.A. Davenport, ibid; and Simon Schama, ibid
92 Jacques Godechot, ibid; R.A. Davenport, ibid; and Simon Schama, ibid
93 Jacques Godechot, ibid
94 Jacques Godechot, ibid
95 Jacques Godechot, ibid; R.A. Davenport, ibid
96 Jacques Godechot, ibid; R.A. Davenport, ibid
97 Jacques Godechot, ibid; William Doyle, ibid; and Hans-Jurgen Lusebrink and Rolf Reichardt ibid
98 Jacques Godechot, ibid
99 Jacques Godechot, ibid; Nesta H Webster, *The French Revolution: A Study in Democracy,* Constable, 1926
100 Simon Schama, ibid
101 Jacques Godechot, ibid; Frantz Funck-Brentano, ibid; and Jules Michelet, ibid
102 Hans-Jurgen Lusebrink and Rolf Reichardt ibid; and Frantz Funck-Brentano, ibid
103 Jacques Godechot, ibid
104 Hans-Jurgen Lusebrink and Rolf Reichardt ibid; and Simon Schama, ibid
105 Jacques Godechot, ibid
106 Hans-Jurgen Lusebrink and Rolf Reichardt ibid; and Simon Schama, ibid
107 Pierre-Francois Palloy, *Adresse á la Convention nationale, le 26 Vendemiare, l'an II*, 1794, quoted in Hans-Jurgen Lusebrink and Rolf Reichardt ibid
108 Simon Schama, ibid
109 Jacques Godechot, ibid; Simon Schama, ibid; and Hans-Jurgen Lusebrink and Rolf Reichardt ibid
110 Jacques Godechot, ibid; and Jules Michelet, ibid
111 Jacques Godechot, ibid; Hans-Jurgen Lusebrink and Rolf Reichardt ibid; Simon Schama, ibid
112 Quoted from *Revolutions de Paris I,* 12-17 July 1789, in Hans-Jurgen Lusebrink and Rolf Reichardt ibid; see also Jacques Godechot, ibid; Simon Schama, ibid, and Rolf Reichardt, 'The Bastille as a Revolutionary Symbol', in *Revolution in Print: The Press in France 1775-1800,* edited by Robert Darnton and Daniel Roche, University of California Press, 1989
113 Henry Masers de Latude, *Memoirs,* translated by John William Calcraft, ibid

114 *Chronique de Paris*, 13 August 1793, quoted in Hans-Jurgen Lusebrink and Rolf Reichardt ibid
115 Hans-Jurgen Lusebrink and Rolf Reichardt ibid; Simon Schama, ibid
116 Simon Schama, ibid
117 From anonymous etching of Bastille for the 14 July 1790, from Bibliotheque Nationale, in Hans-Jurgen Lusebrink and Rolf Reichardt ibid
118 Jacques Godechot, ibid
119 Simon Schama, ibid; Jacques Godechot, ibid; and Hans-Jurgen Lusebrink and Rolf Reichardt ibid
120 Jacques Godechot, ibid; Hans-Jurgen Lusebrink and Rolf Reichardt ibid; Simon Schama, ibid
121 Simon Schama, ibid;
122 Pierre-Francois Palloy, *Eloge, Discours, Lettres et vers, addresses á la Section du Theatre-Francais*, 1793, quoted in Hans-Jurgen Lusebrink and Rolf Reichardt ibid
123 Simon Schama, ibid
124 Hans-Jurgen Lusebrink and Rolf Reichardt ibid
125 Pierre-Francois Palloy, *Adresse aux Représentants du Peuple, le 15 Messidor, l'an II*, 1794, quoted in Hans-Jurgen Lusebrink and Rolf Reichardt ibid
126 Hans-Jurgen Lusebrink and Rolf Reichardt ibid; and Jacques Godechot, ibid
127 Hans-Jurgen Lusebrink and Rolf Reichardt ibid; and Jacques Godechot, ibid
128 Hans-Jurgen Lusebrink and Rolf Reichardt ibid; Simon Schama, ibid
129 Simon Schama, ibid
130 Keith Reader, ibid; Hans-Jurgen Lusebrink and Rolf Reichardt ibid; and Simon Schama, ibid
131 Victor Hugo, *Les Misérables,* translated by Isabel F. Hapgood, Huntington Smith and Helen B. Dole, The Kelmscott Society, New York, 1887
132 Hans-Jurgen Lusebrink and Rolf Reichardt ibid
133 'Everyone is Charlie', *The Economist,* 11 January 2015

CHAPTER 14

1 Martin de Murua, *Historia general del Peru,* quoted in John Hemming, *The Conquest of the Incas*, Macmillan, 1993
2 Martin de Murua, *Historia general del Peru,* quoted in John Hemming, *The Conquest of the Incas*, ibid
3 John Hemming, *The Conquest of the Incas*, ibid
4 Martin Garcia de Loyola, quoted in John Hemming, *The Conquest of the Incas*, ibid
5 Martin de Murua, *Historia general del Peru,* quoted in John Hemming, *The Conquest of the Incas*, ibid
6 John Hemming, *The Conquest of the Incas*, ibid; Hiram Bingham, *Lost City of the Incas,* Phoenix, 1952; and Hugh Thomson, *The White Rock,* Weidenfeld & Nicolson, 2001
7 Antonia Bautista de Salazar, *Relacion sobre el periodo de gobierno de los Virreyes Don Francisco de Toledo y Don Garcia Hurtdao de Mendoza,* 1596, quoted in John Hemming, *The Conquest of the Incas*, ibid
8 Hiram Bingham, *Lost City of the Incas,* ibid
9 Hugh Thomson, introduction to Hiram Bingham, *Lost City of the Incas,* Weidenfeld & Nicolson, 2002
10 Hiram Bingham, *Lost City of the Incas,* ibid
11 Hiram Bingham, 'Preliminary Report of the Yale Peruvian Expedition', *Bulleting of the American Geographical Society,* Vol 44, No 1, 1912; and Hiram Bingham, *Lost City of the Incas,* ibid
12 Rudyard Kipling, quoted in Hiram Bingham, *Lost City of the Incas,* ibid
13 Hiram Bingham, *Lost City of the Incas,* ibid
14 Hiram Bingham, *Lost City of the Incas,* ibid
15 Hiram Bingham, 'The Ruins of Choqquequira', *American Anthropologist,* New Series, Vol 12, No 4, Oct-Dec 1910
16 Hiram Bingham, 'The Ruins of Choqquequira', ibid
17 Hiram Bingham, *Lost City of the Incas,* ibid
18 Hiram Bingham, *Lost City of the Incas,* ibid
19 Hiram Bingham, 'The Ruins of Choqquequira', ibid
20 Hiram Bingham, 'The Ruins of Choqquequira', ibid; and Hiram Bingham, *Lost City of the Incas,* ibid
21 Hiram Bingham, 'The Ruins of Choqquequira', ibid; and Hiram Bingham, *Lost City of the Incas,* ibid
22 Hiram Bingham, 'The Ruins of Choqquequira', ibid

23 Hiram Bingham, *Lost City of the Incas,* ibid
24 Hiram Bingham, 'The Ruins of Choqquequira', ibid; and John Hemming, *The Conquest of the Incas,* ibid
25 Carlos A. Romero, quoted in John Hemming, *The Conquest of the Incas*, ibid; and Hiram Bingham, *Lost City of the Incas,* ibid
26 John Hemming, *The Conquest of the Incas*, ibid
27 John Hemming, *The Conquest of the Incas*, ibid; and Hiram Bingham, *Lost City of the Incas,* ibid
28 John Hemming, *The Conquest of the Incas*, ibid
29 John Hemming, *The Conquest of the Incas*, ibid
30 Hugh Thomson, *The White Rock,* ibid; and John Hemming, *The Conquest of the Incas*, ibid
31 John Hemming, *The Conquest of the Incas*, ibid; and Hiram Bingham, *Lost City of the Incas,* ibid
32 John F. Guilmartin, 'The Cutting Edge: An Analysis of the Spanish Invasion and Overthrow of the Inca Empire, 1532-1539', in *Transatlantic Encounters: Europeans and Andeans in the Sixteenth Century*, edited by Kenneth J. Andrien and Rolena Adorno, University of California Press, 1991
33 Pedro Sarmiento de Gamboa, *History of the Incas*, translated by Clements Markham, Hakluyt Society, 1907
34 John F. Guilmartin, ibid; John Hemming, *The Conquest of the Incas*, ibid; and Craig Morris and Adriana Von Hagen, *The Incas,* Thames & Hudson, 2011
35 John Hemming, *The Conquest of the Incas*, ibid; and Craig Morris and Adriana Von Hagen, ibid
36 John Hemming, *The Conquest of the Incas*, ibid; and Thomas C. Patterson, *The Inca Empire: The Formation and Disintegration of a Pre-Capitalist State,* Berg, 1991
37 John Hemming, *The Conquest of the Incas*, ibid
38 Pedro de Cieza de Leon, *The Discovery and Conquest of Peru,* translated by Alexandra Cook and Noble Cook, Duke University Press, 1998; John Hemming, *The Conquest of the Incas*, ibid; Craig Morris and Adriana Von Hagen, ibid
39 Pedro de Cieza de Leon, ibid
40 John Hemming, *The Conquest of the Incas*, ibid; and Craig Morris and Adriana Von Hagen, ibid
41 Pedro de Cieza de Leon, ibid
42 Pedro de Cieza de Leon, ibid
43 John Hemming, *The Conquest of the Incas*, ibid
44 John Hemming, *The Conquest of the Incas*, ibid
45 John Hemming, *The Conquest of the Incas*, ibid
46 John Hemming, *The Conquest of the Incas*, ibid
47 John Hemming, *The Conquest of the Incas*, ibid
48 Hiram Bingham, *Lost City of the Incas,* ibid; and Craig Morris and Adriana Von Hagen, ibid
49 Hiram Bingham, *Lost City of the Incas,* ibid
50 Hugh Thomson, introduction to Hiram Bingham, *Lost City of the Incas,* ibid
51 Hiram Bingham, *Lost City of the Incas,* ibid; and Hugh Thomson, *The White Rock,* ibid
52 John Hemming, *The Conquest of the Incas*, ibid; and Craig Morris and Adriana Von Hagen, ibid
53 Hiram Bingham, *Lost City of the Incas,* ibid
54 Hiram Bingham, *Lost City of the Incas,* ibid
55 Hiram Bingham, *Lost City of the Incas,* ibid
56 Hiram Bingham, *Lost City of the Incas,* ibid
57 Hiram Bingham, *Lost City of the Incas,* ibid
58 John Hemming, *The Conquest of the Incas*, ibid; and Hugh Thomson, introduction to Hiram Bingham, *Lost City of the Incas*, ibid
59 Hiram Bingham, *Lost City of the Incas,* ibid
60 Hiram Bingham, *Lost City of the Incas,* ibid; and John Hemming, *The Conquest of the Incas*, ibid
61 Hiram Bingham, *Lost City of the Incas,* ibid; and John Hemming, *The Conquest of the Incas*, ibid
62 Hiram Bingham, *Lost City of the Incas,* ibid
63 Hiram Bingham, *Lost City of the Incas,* ibid
64 Hiram Bingham, *Lost City of the Incas,* ibid
65 Hiram Bingham, *Lost City of the Incas,* ibid
66 Hiram Bingham, *Lost City of the Incas,* ibid
67 Hiram Bingham, 'The Ruins of Espiritu Pampa, Peru', *American Anthropologist,* New Series, Vol 16, No 2, Apr-Jun 1914
68 Hiram Bingham, *Lost City of the Incas,* ibid
69 Hiram Bingham, *Lost City of the Incas,* ibid
70 Antonio de Calancha, quoted in Hiram Bingham, *Lost City of the Incas,* ibid

71 Hiram Bingham, 'Preliminary Report of the Yale Peruvian Expedition', ibid
72 James Wilson, *The Andes,* Oxford University Press, 2009
73 Martin Hurtado de Arbieto, quoted in John Hemming, *The Conquest of the Incas*, ibid
74 Martin de Murua, *Historia general del Peru,* quoted in John Hemming, *The Conquest of the Incas*, ibid
75 Pedro Pizarro, *Relation of the Discovery and Conquest of the Kingdom of Peru,* translated by Philip Ainsworth Means, Cortes Society, 1921; and quoted in John Hemming, *The Conquest of the Incas*, ibid
76 John Hemming, *The Conquest of the Incas*, ibid
77 John Hemming, *The Conquest of the Incas*, ibid
78 Hiram Bingham, *Lost City of the Incas,* ibid
79 John Hemming, *The Conquest of the Incas*, ibid
80 Antonio Bautista de Salazar, quoted in John Hemming, *The Conquest of the Incas*, ibid
81 Martin Garcia de Loyola, quoted in John Hemming, *The Conquest of the Incas*, ibid
82 Martin Garcia de Loyola, quoted in John Hemming, *The Conquest of the Incas*, ibid
83 John Hemming, *The Conquest of the Incas*, ibid
84 Vega Loaiza, quoted in John Hemming, *The Conquest of the Incas*, ibid
85 Captain Baltasar de Ocampo, *The Execution of the Inca Tupac Amaru,* translated by Clements Markham, Hakluyt Society, 1907
86 Captain Baltasar de Ocampo, ibid
87 Hiram Bingham, 'The Yale Peruvian Expedition: Preliminary Report', *The Geographical Journal*, Vol 39, No 3, March 1912
88 Hiram Bingham, *Lost City of the Incas,* ibid
89 Alfred Mitchell Bingham, *Portrait of an Explorer: Hiram Bingham, Discoverer of Machu Picchu,* Iowa State University Press, 1989
90 Hugh Thomson, introduction to Hiram Bingham, *Lost City of the Incas,* ibid; and Hugh Thomson, *The White Rock*, ibid
91 Amy Cox Hall, 'Collecting a "Lost City" for Science: Huaquero Vision and the Yale Peruvian Expeditions to Machu Picchu, 1911, 1912, and 1914-15', *Ethnohistory*, Vol 59, Issue 2, Spring 2012; and Hugh Thomson, introduction to Hiram Bingham, *Lost City of the Incas,* ibid
92 Gilbert H. Grosvenor, 'In the Wonderland of Peru', *National Geographic*, April 1913
93 Hiram Bingham, *Lost City of the Incas,* ibid; Hiram Bingham, 'The Ruins of Espiritu Pampa, Peru', ibid; Hiram Bingham, 'Preliminary Report of the Yale Peruvian Expedition', ibid; John Hemming, *The Conquest of the Incas*, ibid; Hugh Thomson, *The White Rock*, ibid;
94 Hiram Bingham, *Lost City of the Incas,* ibid
95 Hiram Bingham, *Lost City of the Incas,* ibid
96 John Hemming, *The Conquest of the Incas*, ibid
97 Hugh Thomson, *The White Rock*, ibid
98 John Hemming, *The Conquest of the Incas*, ibid
99 Hugh Thomson, *The White Rock*, ibid; and John Hemming, *The Conquest of the Incas*, ibid
100 Martin de Murua, *Historia general del Peru,* quoted in John Hemming, *The Conquest of the Incas*, ibid
101 Martin de Murua, *Historia general del Peru,* quoted in John Hemming, *The Conquest of the Incas*, ibid
102 Hiram Bingham, 'The Ruins of Espiritu Pampa, Peru', ibid
103 John Hemming, *The Conquest of the Incas*, ibid
104 Hiram Bingham, 'The Ruins of Espiritu Pampa, Peru', ibid
105 John Hemming, *The Conquest of the Incas*, ibid
106 Hiram Bingham, *Lost City of the Incas,* ibid
107 Craig Morris and Adriana Von Hagen, ibid
108 Hiram Bingham, *Lost City of the Incas,* ibid
109 Ernesto Che Guevara, 'Machu Picchu: Enigma de Piedra en America', quoted in Hiram Bingham, *Lost City of the Incas,* ibid
110 Hugh Thomson, *The White Rock*, ibid; Colin Thubron, *To The Last City,* Vintage, 2003
111 John Hemming, *The Conquest of the Incas*, ibid
112 Martin de Murua, *Historia general del Peru,* quoted in John Hemming, *The Conquest of the Incas*, ibid

CHAPTER 15

1 Jeremy Bentham, *The Collected Works of Jeremy Bentham Vol. 3,* Ian R. Christie editor, The Athlone Press, University of London, 1971

2 Jeremy Bentham, *The Panopticon Writings,* edited by Miran Bozovic, Verso, London, 2010
3 Michel Foucault, *Power/Knowledge, Selected Interviews and Other Writings, 1972-77,* edited Colin Gordon, Longman, 1980
4 Michel Foucault, *Discipline and Punish, The Birth of the Prison,* Penguin, 1975
5 Michael Ignatieff, *A Just Measure of Pain: the Penitentiary in the Industrial Revolution,* New York, 1978
6 Michel Foucault, *Discipline and Punish,* ibid
7 E. Smallman, '181-year-old corpse of Jeremy Bentham attends UCL board meeting', article in *The Metro*, 12 July 2013.
8 C.F.A. Marmoy, 'The "Auto-Icon" of Jeremy Bentham at University College London', *Medical History*, 2, 77-86, 1958; and Miran Bozovic, intorduction to *The Panopticon Writings,* ibid
9 Charles Milner Atkinson, *Jeremy Bentham: His Life and Work*, Methuen, 1905
10 Charles Milner Atkinson, ibid
11 Jeremy Bentham, 'Paederasty', in 'Jeremy Bentham's Essay on "Paederasty"', Louis Crompton, *Journal of Homosexuality,* Vol 3 (4), Summer 1978
12 Catherine Pease-Watkins, 'Jeremy and Samuel Bentham – the Private and the Public', Journal of Bentham Studies Vol 5, 2002
13 Matthew S. Anderson, 'Samuel Bentham in Russia 1779-1791', *American Slavic and East European Review,* Vol 15, No. 2, 1956
14 Matthew S. Anderson, ibid; and Simon Werret, *Potemkin and the Panopticon: Samuel Bentham and the Architecture of Absolutism in Eighteenth Century Russia*, Journal of Bentham Studies Vol 2, 1999
15 Samuel Bentham to Jeremy Bentham, May 5 1779, *British Museum Manuscripts*, quoted in Matthew S. Anderson, ibid
16 Matthew S. Anderson, ibid
17 Matthew S. Anderson, ibid
18 Matthew S. Anderson, ibid
19 Matthew S. Anderson, ibid; and Walther Kirchner, 'Samuel Bentham and Siberia', *The Slavonic and Easat European Review,* Vol 36, No 87, June 1958
20 Simon Sebag Montefiore, 'Prince Potemkin and the Benthams', *History Today*, August 2003; Matthew S. Anderson, ibid; and Walther Kirchner, ibid
21 Simon Sebag Montefiore, ibid; Matthew S. Anderson, ibid; Alessandro Stanziani, 'The Travelling Panopticon: Labour Institutions and Labour Practices in Russian and Britain in the Eighteenth and Nineteenth Centuries', *Comparative Studies in Society and History*, 51 (4), 2009; and Ian R. Christie, 'Samuel Bentham and the Western Colony at Krichev, 1784-1787', *The Slavonic and East European Review,* Vol 48, No. 111, 1970
22 Ian R. Christie, ibid
23 Ian R. Christie, ibid
24 Matthew S. Anderson, ibid
25 Charles Milner Atkinson, ibid
26 Simon Werret, ibid

27 Philip Steadman, *Samuel Bentham's Panopticon*, Bartlett School (Faculty of the Built Environment) University College London
28 Jeremy Bentham, *The Collected Works, Vol 3* Ian R. Christie editor, ibid
29 Jeremy Bentham, *The Collected Works, Vol. 3,* Ian R. Christie editor, ibid
30 Alessandro Stanziani, ibid
31 Simon Werret, ibid
32 Ian R.Christie, ibid; and Matthew S. Anderson, ibid
33 Jeremy Bentham, *The Panopticon Writings,* Miran Bozovic, ibid
34 *Parliamentary History*, 30, 31 May 1793, 953, quoted by Janet Semple, *Bentham's Prison: A Study of the Panopticon Penitentiary,* Oxford University Press, 1993
35 Jeremy Bentham, *The Panopticon Writings,* Miran Bozovic, ibid
36 Janet Semple, *Bentham's Prison: A Study of the Panopticon Penitentiary,* Oxford University Press, 1993
37 Jeremy Bentham, *The Collected Works, Vol. 3,* Ian R. Christie editor, ibid
38 Jeremy Bentham, *The Collected Works of Jeremy Bentham Vol. 4,* Ian R. Christie editor, The Athlone Press, University of London, 1971
39 Janet Semple, ibid
40 Janet Semple, ibid

41 Jeremy Bentham, quoted by Janet Semple, ibid

42 Janet Semple, ibid; and Simon Werret, ibid; and Philip Steadman, *Samuel Bentham's Panopticon*, ibid

43 Jeremy Bentham, *The Panopticon Writings,* edited by Miran Bozovic, ibid

44 Jeremy Bentham, quoted by Janet Semple, ibid

45 Jeremy Bentham, *The Panopticon Writings,* edited by Miran Bozovic, ibid

46 Jeremy Bentham, *The Panopticon Writings,* edited by Miran Bozovic, ibid

47 Janet Semple, ibid

48 Jeremy Bentham, *The Panopticon Writings,* edited by Miran Bozovic, ibid

49 Janet Semple, ibid

50 Janet Semple, ibid

51 Jeremy Bentham, quoted by Janet Semple, ibid

52 Janet Semple, ibid

53 John Thomas Becher, *First Report from the Committee on the Laws Relating to Penitentiary Houses. Ordered by the House of Commons to be printed, 31 May 1811* quoted by Janet Semple, ibid

54 A. Griffiths, *Memorials of Millbank and Chapters in Prison History* London, 1875, in Janet Semple, ibid

55 Janet Semple, ibid

56 Charles Milner Atkinson, ibid

57 Rossiiskii Gosudarstvennyi Arkhiv Voenno-Morskogo Flota, St Petersburg, fond 326, opis' 1, delo 10043.

58 Janet Semple, ibid

59 Lord Westmorland, quoted in Janet Semple, ibid

60 Jeremy Bentham, *The Correspondence of Jeremy Bentham*, Vol VII, edited by J. R. Dinwiddy, Oxford, 1988

61 Jeremy Bentham, *The Correspondence of Jeremy Bentham*, Vol VIII, ed. S. Conway, Oxford, 1988

62 Simon Werret, ibid

63 Catherine Pease-Watkins, ibid

64 Philip Steadman, *Samuel Bentham's Panopticon*, ibid

65 Jeremy Bentham, 'Outline of a Work Entitled Pauper Management Improved', Annals *of Agriculture,* 1797, cited in Philip Steadman, *Samuel Bentham's Panopticon*, ibid

66 Philip Steadman, *Samuel Bentham's Panopticon*, ibid

67 Philip Steadman, *Samuel Bentham's Panopticon*, ibid

68 Mary Sophia Bentham, 'Dockyards and Manufactories', quoted in Philip Steadman, ibid

69 Mary Sophia Bentham, 'Manufactories and Schools', quoted in Philip Steadman, ibid

70 Mary Sophia Bentham, quoted in Philip Steadman, ibid

71 Admiral Chichagov to Alexander I, June 15th 1806, British Library Add. MS. 33544, quoted in Simon Werret, ibid

72 Mary Sophia Bentham, 'Manufactories and Schools', quoted in Philip Steadman, *Samuel Bentham's Panopticon*, ibid

73 Catherine Pease-Watkin ibid; and Philip Steadman, *Samuel Bentham's Panopticon*, ibid

74 Samuel Bentham, *Desiderata in a Naval Arsenal,* quoted by Catherine Pease-Watkin ibid

75 Philip Steadman, *Samuel Bentham's Panopticon*, ibid

76 Michel Foucault, *Discipline and Punish,* ibid

77 Michel Foucault, *Discipline and Punish,* ibid

78 George Orwell, *1984,* Penguin, 1949

79 Michel Foucault, *Discipline and Punish,* ibid

80 Norman Johnston, *Eastern State Penitentiary: crucible of good intentions*, Philadelphia Museum of Art, 1994; and Philip Steadman, *Samuel Bentham's Panopticon*, ibid

81 Norman Johnston, ibid

82 Charles Dickens, quoted in Norman Johnstone, *Eastern State Penitentiary,* ibid

83 Norman Johnston, *Eastern State Penitentiary,* ibid

84 Philip Steadman, *The Contradictions of Jeremy Bentham's Panopticon Penitentiary,* Journal of Bentham Studies Vol 9, 2007

85 Quoted in Philip Steadman, *The Contradictions of Jeremy Bentham's Panopticon Penitentiary,* ibid

86 Philip Steadman, *The Contradictions of Jeremy Bentham's Panopticon Penitentiary,* ibid

87 Philip Steadman, *The Contradictions of Jeremy Bentham's Panopticon Penitentiary,* ibid

88 Norman Johnston, ibid

89 Quoted in Philip Steadman, *Building Types and Built Forms*, Matador, 2014

90 Quoted in Philip Steadman, *Building Types and Built Forms*, ibid

91 Jan Kietzmann and Ian Angell, *Panopticon Revisited,* Communications of the Association for Computing Machinery, June 2010, Vol 53, Issue 6

92 Bentham, M., 'CCTV spy cameras will TALK in London', *London Lite,* 2007, cited in Jan Kietzmann and Ian Angell, ibid
93 BBC Online, '1,000 Cameras 'Solve One Crime', August 24, 2009, cited in Jan Kietzmann and Ian Angell, ibid
94 Jan Kietzmann and Ian Angell, ibid
95 Daniel J. Solove, *The Future of Reputation: Gossip, Rumour, and Privacy on the Internet,* Yale University Press, 2007
96 Jan Kietzmann and Ian Angell, ibid

CHAPTER 16

1 Greg Girard and Ian Lambot, *City of Darkness: Life in Kowloon Walled City*, Watermark, 1993; Charles Goddard, 'The Clearance', in Greg Girard and Ian Lambot, ibid; Peter Popham, introduction to Greg Girard and Ian Lambot, ibid; and Peter Wesley Smith, *Unequal Treaty, 1898-1997: China, Great Britain and Hong Kong's New Territories,* Oxford University Press, 1980
2 Greg Girard and Ian Lambot, ibid
3 Greg Girard and Ian Lambot, ibid
4 Greg Girard and Ian Lambot, ibid; and Peter Wesley Smith, ibid
5 Jackie Pullinger, *Chasing the Dragon,* Hodder, 2010
6 Peter Chan, interviewed in Greg Girard and Ian Lambot, ibid
7 Jackie Pullinger, *Chasing the Dragon,* ibid; and Greg Girard and Ian Lambot, ibid
8 *A documentary chronicle of Sino-Western relations, 1644-1820,* compiled, translated, and annotated by Lo-shu Fu, University of Arizona Press, 1966
9 Jiaqinq Emperor, 4 April 1810, in *A documentary chronicle of Sino-Western relations, 1644-1820,* ibid
10 Jiaqinq Emperor, 4 April 1810, in *A documentary chronicle of Sino-Western relations, 1644-1820,* ibid
11 Minning, quoted in Zeng Yangwen, *The Social Life of Opium,* Cambridge University Press, 2005
12 Minning, quoted in Zeng Yangwen, ibid
13 Julia Lovell, *The Opium War: Drugs, Dreams and the Making of China,* Picador, 2011
14 Vaughn Bell, 'The Unsexy Truth About Dopamine', *The Guardian,* 3 February 2013
15 Minning, quoted in Zeng Yangwen, ibid
16 *A documentary chronicle of Sino-Western relations, 1644-1820*, ibid
17 Julia Lovell, ibid
18 *A documentary chronicle of Sino-Western relations, 1644-1820*, ibid
19 P. C. Kuo, *A Critical Study of the First Anglo-Chinese War,* Hyperion Press, 1973
20 Jack Beeching, *The Chinese Opium Wars,* Hutchinson, 1975; Julia Lovell, ibid;
21 Jack Beeching, ibid; Julia Lovell, ibid;
22 Edgar Holt, *The Opium Wars in China*, Putnam, 1964
23 P. C. Kuo, ibid
24 P. C. Kuo, ibid
25 Zeng Yangwen, ibid; and Julia Lovell, ibid
26 P. C. Kuo, ibid
27 Jack Beeching, ibid
28 P. C. Kuo, ibid; and Julia Lovell, ibid
29 P. C. Kuo, ibid
30 P. C. Kuo, ibid
31 Julia Lovell, ibid
32 Julia Lovell, ibid; and P. C. Kuo, ibid
33 Charles Elliot to Lord Palmerston, 2 April 1839, *Correspondence Relating to China,* quoted in Julia Lovell, ibid
34 Julia Lovell, ibid
35 Peter Wesley Smith, ibid
36 P. C. Kuo, ibid
37 Peter Wesley Smith, ibid
38 Elizabeth Sinn, 'Kowloon Walled City: Its Origin and Early History', *Journal of the Royal Asiatic Society Hong Kong Branch,* Vol 27, 1987
39 Elizabeth Sinn, ibid; and Peter Wesley Smith, ibid
40 Elizabeth Sinn, ibid
41 Elizabeth Sinn, ibid
42 Elizabeth Sinn, ibid
43 Robert Swinhoe, *Narrative of the North China Campaign of 1860,* quoted in Julia Lovell, ibid

44 *The Convention of Peking,* 24 October 1860, quoted in Steve Tsang, *Government and Politics,* Hong Kong University Press, 1995
45 Elizabeth Sinn, ibid
46 Peter Wesley Smith, ibid
47 Elizabeth Sinn, ibid
48 Peter Wesley Smith, ibid
49 Elizabeth Sinn, ibid
50 Quoted in Julia Wilkinson, 'A Chinese Magistrate's Fort', in Greg Girard and Ian Lambot, ibid
51 Sir Arthur Kennedy, quoted in Peter Wesley Smith, ibid
52 Sir Arthur Kennedy, quoted in Peter Wesley Smith, ibid
53 Sir William Robinson, 9 November 1894, quoted in Peter Wesley Smith, ibid
54 Catchik Paul Chater, 14 November 1894, quoted in Peter Wesley Smith, ibid
55 Lord Arthur Balfour to Sir Claude Macdonald, 26 April 1898, quoted in Peter Wesley Smith, ibid
56 Sir Claude Macdonald to Lord Salisbury, 28 April 1898, quoted in Peter Wesley Smith, ibid
57 Sir Claude Macdonald to Lord Salisbury, 27 May 1898, quoted in Peter Wesley Smith, ibid
58 Peter Wesley Smith, ibid
59 *The Convention of Peking*, 9 June 1898, in Peter Wesley Smith, ibid
60 Peter Wesley Smith, ibid
61 Elizabeth Sinn, ibid
62 Peter Wesley Smith, ibid; and Julia Wilkinson 'A Chinese Magistrate's Fort', in Greg Girard and Ian Lambot, ibid
63 Peter Wesley Smith, ibid; Elizabeth Sinn, ibid; and Julia Wilkinson, in Greg Girard and Ian Lambot, ibid
64 Peter Wesley Smith, ibid
65 Peter Wesley Smith, ibid; and Julia Wilkinson, in Greg Girard and Ian Lambot, ibid
66 Peter Wesley Smith, ibid;
67 *Hong Kong Weekly Press,* 22 April 1899, quoted in Peter Wesley Smith, ibid
68 Peter Wesley Smith, ibid;
69 Peter Wesley Smith, ibid; Elizabeth Sinn, ibid; and Julia Wilkinson, in Greg Girard and Ian Lambot, ibid
70 Tsungli Yamen to H. Bax-Ironside, 21 May 1899, quoted in Peter Wesley Smith, ibid;
71 Lord Salisbury, quoted in Julia Wilkinson, in Greg Girard and Ian Lambot, ibid
72 *The Walled City Order in Council,* 27 December 1899, quoted in Peter Wesley Smith, ibid
73 *Hong Kong Weekly Press,* 2 May 1904, quoted in Peter Wesley Smith, ibid
74 Elizabeth Sinn, ibid
75 Peter Wesley Smith, ibid
76 Elizabeth Sinn, ibid
77 Sir William Peel to Sir Philip Cunliffe-Lister, 9 January 1934, quoted in Elizabeth Sinn, ibid
78 Peter Wesley Smith, ibid
79 Sir William Peel to Sir Philip Cunliffe-Lister, 9 January 1934, quoted in Peter Wesley Smith, ibid
80 Peter Wesley Smith, ibid; and Elizabeth Sinn, ibid
81 Peter Wesley Smith, ibid; and Elizabeth Sinn, ibid
82 Peter Wesley Smith, ibid; and Elizabeth Sinn, ibid
83 Peter Popham and Chan Pui Yin, quoted in Greg Girard and Ian Lambot, ibid
84 Peter Wesley Smith, ibid; and Elizabeth Sinn, ibid
85 Peter Wesley Smith, ibid
86 Alexander Grantham, *Via Ports: From Honk Kong to Hong Kong*, Hong Kong University Press, 1965, quoted in Peter Wesley Smith, ibid
87 Peter Wesley Smith, ibid
88 Greg Girard and Ian Lambot, ibid
89 Greg Girard and Ian Lambot, ibid
90 Greg Girard and Ian Lambot, ibid
91 Peter Wesley Smith, ibid; and Greg Girard and Ian Lambot, ibid
92 Peter Wesley Smith, ibid
93 *Survey of China Mainland Press,* 22 January 1963, quoted in Peter Wesley Smith, ibid
94 Charles Goddard, in Greg Girard and Ian Lambot, ibid; and Peter Wesley Smith, ibid
95 Peter Popham, in Greg Girard and Ian Lambot, ibid
96 Greg Girard and Ian Lambot, ibid
97 Greg Girard and Ian Lambot, ibid
98 Peter Wesley Smith, ibid; and Julia Wilkinson, in Greg Girard and Ian Lambot, ibid

99 *Hong Kong Standard,* June 1968, quoted in Julia Wilkinson, in Greg Girard and Ian Lambot, ibid
100 Julia Wilkinson, in Greg Girard and Ian Lambot, ibid
101 Jackie Pullinger, *Chasing the Dragon,* ibid; and Jackie Pullinger, *Crack in the Wall,* Hodder, 1997
102 Mok Chung Yuk, interviewed in Greg Girard and Ian Lambot, ibid
103 Charles Goddard, in Greg Girard and Ian Lambot, ibid
104 Steve Tsang, ibid; and Charles Goddard, in Greg Girard and Ian Lambot, ibid
105 Quoted by Fionnuala McHugh, 'How Kowloon Walled City survived attempts to knock it down for almost a century', *South China Morning Post*, 31 August 2014
106 Steve Tsang, ibid
107 Quoted in Julia Wilkinson, in Greg Girard and Ian Lambot, ibid
108 Liu Kan, quoted by Julia Wilkinson, in Greg Girard and Ian Lambot, ibid
109 Charles Goddard, in Greg Girard and Ian Lambot, ibid
110 Charles Goddard, in Greg Girard and Ian Lambot, ibid
111 Charles Goddard, in Greg Girard and Ian Lambot, ibid
112 Charles Goddard, in Greg Girard and Ian Lambot, ibid
113 Charles Goddard, in Greg Girard and Ian Lambot, ibid
114 Jonathan Braude, 'Last squatters evicted in Kowloon', *The Times,* 3 July 1992
115 'Walled City's Last Days', *The Times,* 24 March 1993
116 John Carney, 'Living in the City of Darkness', *South China Morning Post,* 16 April 2013
117 'Kowloon Walled City Park' Leisure and Cultural Services Department, www.lcsd.gov.hk/en/parks/kwcp/index.html
118 'Kowloon Walled City Park' Leisure and Cultural Services Department, ibid
119 Peter Popham, in Greg Girard and Ian Lambot, ibid
120 Reyner Banham, *Megastructure: Urban Futures of the Recent Past*, Thames and Hudson, 1976
121 Alan Boutwell and Mike Mitchell, *Megastructure Reloaded,* Hatje Kanz, 2008
122 Alan Boutwell and Mike Mitchell, *Megastructure Reloaded,* ibid
123 William Gibson, 'Disneyland with the Death Penalty', *Wired,* Issue 1.04, Sep/Oct 1993
124 William Gibson, interviewed by Steven Poole, 'Tomorrow's Man', *The Guardian,* 3 May 2003
125 William Gibson, 'Tomorrow's Man', ibid
126 William Gibson, *Idoru,* Viking, 1996

CHAPTER 17

1 Vincent Canby, '"Koyaanisqatsi", Back to Psychedelia', *New York Times,* 4 October 1982
2 Michael Dempsey, *Qatsi Means Life: The Films of Godfrey Reggio, Film Quarterly, Vol 42, No.3,* University of California Press, 1989; and Carlo McCormick, 'Godfrey Reggio's fearful symmetry', *Aperture,* Issue 180, Fall 2005
3 Michael Dempsey, ibid; and Carlo McCormick, ibid
4 Tim Page, Quoted by Michael Dempsey, ibid
5 Michael R. Allen and Nora Wendl, 'After Pruitt-Igoe: An Urban Forest as an Evolving Temporal Landscape', *Studies in the History of Gardens & Designed Landscapes: An International Quarterly*, 34:1, 2014
6 Charles A. Jencks, *The language of post-modern architecture*, Academy Editions, London, 1977, updated 1984
7 Charles A. Jencks, *The language of post-modern architecture,* ibid
8 Quoted in Charles A. Jencks, *The language of post-modern architecture,* ibid
9 Sylvester Brown and Valerie Stills, interviewed in *The Pruitt-Igoe Myth,* Chad Friedrichs director, Unicorn Stencil Films, 2011
10 Alexander Von Hoffman, "Why They Built Pruitt-Igoe," in *From Tenements to the Taylor Homes: In Search of an Urban Housing Policy in Twentieth-Century America,* edited by John F. Bauman, Roger Biles, and Kristin M. Szylvian, University Park: Pennsylvania State University Press, 2000
11 Alexander Von Hoffman, ibid
12 Mary C. Comerio, *Pruitt-Igoe and Other Stories,* Journal of Architectural Education, Vol. 34, No. 4, Taylor & Francis, 1981; and Katherine G. Bristol, *The Pruitt-Igoe Myth,* Journal of Architectural Education, Vol. 44 No. 3, 1991
13 Alexander Von Hoffman, ibid
14 Alexander Von Hoffman, ibid
15 Alexander Von Hoffman, ibid
16 Alexander Von Hoffman, ibid
17 Alexander Von Hoffman, ibid; and Katherine G. Bristol, *The Pruitt-Igoe Myth,* ibid
18 Alexander Von Hoffman, ibid

19 'Slum Surgery in St Louis', *Architectural Forum* 94, April 1951

20 Sylvester Brown and Valerie Stills interviewed in *The Pruitt-Igoe Myth,* Chad Friedrichs, ibid

21 Quoted in Alexander Von Hoffman, ibid

22 'Four Vast Housing Projects for St Louis: Hellmuth, Obata and Kassabaum, Inc.', *Architectural Record* 120, August 1956

23 Alexander Von Hoffman, ibid

24 Katherine G. Bristol, *The Pruitt-Igoe Myth,* ibid

25 Charles A. Jencks, *The language of post-modern architecture,* ibid

26 Alexander Von Hoffman, ibid

27 Alexander Von Hoffman, ibid

28 James Bailey, 'The Case History of a Failure', *Architectural Forum* 123, December 1965; and quoted in Katherine G. Bristol, *The Pruitt-Igoe Myth,* ibid

29 Frances A. Koestler, Joan Miller, Eugene Porter and Lee Rainwater, 'Survival in a Concrete Ghetto', *Social Work,* October 1967, Vol. 12, Issue 4, Oxford University Press (US). Lee Rainwater's statement was titled 'Poverty and Deprivation in the Crisis of the American City'

30 Frances A. Koestler, Joan Miller, Eugene Porter and Lee Rainwater, ibid

31 Frances A. Koestler, Joan Miller, Eugene Porter and Lee Rainwater, ibid

32 Frances A. Koestler, Joan Miller, Eugene Porter and Lee Rainwater, ibid

33 Frances A. Koestler, Joan Miller, Eugene Porter and Lee Rainwater, ibid

34 Lee Rainwater, quoted in *Social Work,* ibid

35 Katherine G. Bristol, *The Pruitt-Igoe Myth,* ibid

36 Frances A. Koestler, Joan Miller, Eugene Porter and Lee Rainwater, ibid

37 *The Pruitt-Igoe Myth,* Chad Friedrichs, ibid

38 *The Pruitt-Igoe Myth,* Chad Friedrichs, ibid

39 Mary C. Comerio, ibid

40 Alexander Von Hoffman, ibid

41 Mary C. Comerio, ibid

42 Katherine G. Bristol, *The Pruitt-Igoe Myth,* ibid

43 Alexander Von Hoffman, ibid

44 Michael R. Allen and Nora Wendl, ibid

45 Michael R. Allen and Nora Wendl, ibid

46 Michael R. Allen and Nora Wendl, ibid

47 Michael R. Allen and Nora Wendl, ibid; and Katherine G. Bristol, *The Pruitt-Igoe Myth,* ibid

48 Michael R Allen and Nora Wendl, ibid

49 Charles A.. Jencks, *The language of post-modern architecture,* ibid

50 Oscar Newman, *Creating Defensible Space,* US Department of Housing and Urban Development Office of Policy Development and Research, 1996

51 Oscar Newman, ibid

52 Oscar Newman, ibid

53 Mark La Gory and John Pipkin *Urban Social Space*, Wadsworth Publishing Company, 1981

54 Mark La Gory and John Pipkin, ibid

55 Mark La Gory and John Pipkin, ibid

56 Katherine G. Bristol, *The Pruitt-Igoe Myth,* ibid

57 Charles A. Jencks, ibid

58 Tom Wolfe, *From Bauhaus to Our House,* Simon & Schuster, New York, 1981

59 'The Experiment that Failed', *Architecture Plus,* 1973, quoted in Katherine G. Bristol, *The Pruitt-Igoe Myth,* ibid

60 Minoru Yamasaki, 'High Buildings for Public Housing?' *Journal of Housing* 9, 1952, quoted in Katherine G. Bristol, *The Pruitt-Igoe Myth,* ibid

61 Minoru Yamasaki, *A Life in Architecture,* New York, Weatherill, 1979

62 *Architectural Review*, 1965, ibid

63 Charles A. Jencks, ibid

64 Frank Lloyd Wright, *A Testament,* Horizon Press, London, 1957

65 Giancarlo de Carlo, 'Legitimizing Architecture', *Forum,* 1972, quoted in Mary C Comerio, *Pruitt-Igoe and Other Stories,* ibid

66 Katherine G. Bristol, *The Pruitt-Igoe Myth,* ibid

67 Alexander Von Hoffman, ibid

68 Katherine G. Bristol, *The Pruitt-Igoe Myth,* ibid; and Alexander Von Hoffman, ibid; and Mary C. Comerio, ibid; and Joseph Heathcott, 'Pruitt-Igoe and the critique of pubic housing', *Journal of the American Planning Association,*

Vol 78, Issue 4, Autumn 2012

69 Katherine G. Bristol, *The Pruitt-Igoe Myth,* ibid; and Alexander Von Hoffman, ibid; and Mary C. Comerio, ibid

70 Katherine G. Bristol, *The Pruitt-Igoe Myth,* ibid; and Mary C. Comerio, ibid

71 Katherine G. Bristol, *The Pruitt-Igoe Myth,* ibid

72 Frances A. Koestler, Joan Miller, Eugene Porter and Lee Rainwater, ibid

73 Eugene Meehan, *The Quality of Federal Policymaking: Programme Failure in Public Housing,* Columbia, University of Missouri Press, 1979, quoted in Katherine G. Bristol, *The Pruitt-Igoe Myth,* ibid

74 Gideon Fink Shapiro, 'Review: The Pruitt-Igoe Myth', *Journal of the Society of Architectural Historians,* Vol 71, 2012

75 *The Pruitt-Igoe Myth,* Chad Friedrichs, ibid

76 Frances A. Koestler, Joan Miller, Eugene Porter and Lee Rainwater, ibid

77 Frances A. Koestler, Joan Miller, Eugene Porter and Lee Rainwater, ibid

78 Katherine G. Bristol, *The Pruitt-Igoe Myth,* ibid

79 Andrew B. Wilson, 'Demolition Marks Ultimate Failure of Pruitt-Igoe Project', *Washington Post*, 27 August 1973, quoted in Katherine G. Bristol, *The Pruitt-Igoe Myth,* ibid

80 Michael R. Allen and Nora Wendl, *After Pruitt-Igoe,* ibid

81 Michael R. Allen and Nora Wendl, ibid

82 Nora Wendl, 'Pruitt-Igoe, Now', *Journal of Architectural Education,* 67:1, 2013; and Michael R. Allen and Nora Wendl, ibid

83 Nora Wendl, 'Pruitt-Igoe, Now', ibid

84 Michael R. Allen and Nora Wendl, *After Pruitt-Igoe,* ibid

85 Sina Zekavat, 'Carr Square Brick Yard', in Michael R. Allen and Nora Wendl, *After Pruitt-Igoe,* ibid

86 Aroussiak Gabrielian and Alison Hirsch, 'Recipe Landscape', in Michael R. Allen and Nora Wendl, *After Pruitt-Igoe,* ibid

87 Jill Desinimi, 'Pruitt-Igoe National Park', in Michael R. Allen and Nora Wendl, *After Pruitt-Igoe,* ibid

88 Tyler Survant, 'The Museum of Attempted Utopias – A Burial Mount for Modern Architecture', in Nora Wendl, 'Pruitt-Igoe, Now', ibid

89 Clouds Architecture Office, 'Double Moon', in Michael R. Allen and Nora Wendl, *After Pruitt-Igoe,* ibid

90 Heather Dunbar and Xiaowei R. Wang, 'St Louis Ecological Assembly Line: Pruitt Igoe as a Productive Landscape', in Nora Wendl, 'Pruitt-Igoe, Now', ibid; and Michael R. Allen and Nora Wendl, *After Pruitt-Igoe,* ibid

91 Nora Wendl, 'Pruitt-Igoe, Now', ibid

CHAPTER 18

1 Frederick Baker, 'The Berlin Wall: production, preservation and consumption of a 20th-century monument', *Antiquity,* December 1993, Vol 67, Issue 257

2 Peter Schneider, *The Wall Jumper*, Penguin, 2005

3 Francis Fukuyama, *The End of History and the Last Man,* Penguin, 1992

4 Peter Schneider, ibid

5 Frederick Taylor, *The Berlin Wall: 13 August 1961 – 9 November 1989,* Bloomsbury, 2006

6 Leo Schmidt, The Architecture and Message of 'the Wall', 1961-1989, *German Politics and Society, Issue 99, Vol 29, No 2, Summer 2011*

7 Frederick Taylor, ibid

8 Frederick Taylor, ibid

9 Quoted by Ian McEwan in the introduction to the 2005 edition of *The Wall Jumper,* ibid

10 Roger Kimball, 'Tyranny Set in Stone', *New Criterion,* Foundation for Cultural Review, November 2009, Vol 28, Issue 3

11 Frederick Baker, ibid

12 From "Niederschift eines Gespraachs des Genossen N.S. Chruschtschow mit Genossen W. Ulbricht am 1. August 1961," *Die Welt On-Line,* 30 May 2009, quoted in Hope M. Harrison, 'The Berlin Wall After Fifty Years', *German Politics and Society, Issue 99, Vol 29, No 2, Summer 2011*

13 Quoted in Frederick Baker, ibid

14 Patrick Major, 'Walled In: Ordinary East Germans' Response to 13 August 1961', *German Politics and Society, Issue 99, Vol 29, No 2, Summer 2011*

15 Frederick Taylor, ibid

16 Frederick Taylor, ibid; and Anna Funder, *Stasiland: Stories from Behind the Berlin Wall,* Granta, 2003

17 Hagen Koch, interviewed by Anna Funder ibid

18 Leo Schmidt, ibid
19 Leo Schmidt, ibid
20 Cyril Buffet, 'Declaration of Love on Celluloid: The Depiction of the Berlin Wall in a GDR film, 1961-62', *Cold War History,* Vol 9, No 4, November 2009
21 Cyril Buffet, ibid
22 Cyril Buffet, ibid

23 Cyril Buffet, ibid
24 Wilkening an Rodenberg, 19 October 1961, Barch DR1/8917, quoted in Cyril Buffet, ibid
25 Cyril Buffet, ibid
26 Cyril Buffet, ibid
27 Cyril Buffet, ibid
28 Cyril Buffet, ibid
29 Cyril Buffet, ibid
30 Cyril Buffet, ibid
31 Cyril Buffet, ibid
32 Hagen Koch, interviewed by Anna Funder, ibid
33 'Klare Verhältnisse', *Neues Deutschland,* 14 August 1961, quoted in Pertti Ahonen, 'The Berlin Wall and the Battle for Legitimacy in Divided Germany', *German Politics and Society, Issue 99, Vol 29, No 2, Summer 2011*
34 Cyril Buffet, ibid
35 Pertti Ahonen, ibid
36 *Neues Deutschland,* 14 August 1961, in Pertti Ahonen, ibid
37 'Ansprache des Vorsitzenden des Staatsrates der Deutschen Demokratischen Republik, Walter Ulbricht,' *Neues Deutschland,* 19 August 1961, quoted in Pertti Ahonen, ibid
38 Pertti Ahonen, ibid
39 Willy Brandt's speech, 13 August 1961, 'Das grösste Konzentrationslager der Welt', *Die Rheinfpalz,* 16 June 1962, quoted in Pertti Ahonen, ibid
40 'Antwort auf den Gewaltakt von Berlin,' *Das Parlament,* 23 August 1961, quoted in Pertti Ahonen, ibid
41 Quoted in Frederick Baker, ibid
42 Pertti Ahonen, ibid
43 'Wir warnen Provokateure', *Neues Deutschland,* 19 August 1962, quoted in Pertti Ahonen, ibid
44 Lieutenant Tschitschke's radio address, *SBZ-Spiegel,* 26 May 1962, Generalstaatsanwaltschaft Berlin Archive, 27 2Js 102/91, Duplikatsakte 5, quoted in Pertti Ahonen, ibid
45 'Dank an alle, die unsere Grenze sicher schützen', *Neues Deutschland,* 13 August 1966, quoted in Pertti Ahonen, ibid
46 Leo Schmidt, ibid
47 Leo Schmidt, ibid
48 Leo Schmidt, ibid
49 Bundesarchiv Militararchiv (BA-MA) VA-07/9061, quoted in Leo Schmidt, ibid
50 Leo Schmidt, ibid
51 Leo Schmidt, ibid
52 Peter Schneider, ibid
53 Ian McEwan in the introduction to the 2005 edition of *The Wall Jumper,* ibid
54 Ian McEwan, ibid
55 Peter Schneider, ibid
56 Leo Schmidt, ibid
57 Ian McEwan, ibid
58 Ian McEwan, ibid
59 Peter Schneider, ibid
60 Peter Schneider, ibid
61 Frederick Taylor, ibid
62 Roger Kimball, ibid
63 Frederick Taylor, ibid
64 Patrick Major, ibid
65 Patrick Major, ibid
66 Frederick Taylor, ibid
67 Frederick Taylor, ibid
68 Frederick Taylor, ibid

69 Robert Darnton, *Berlin Journal: 1989-1990,* W W Norton & Company, 1982
70 Robert Darnton, ibid
71 *Berliner Zeitung,* 20 January 1989, quoted in Frederick Baker, ibid
72 Leo Schmidt, ibid
73 *Der Spiegel,* 10 August 1981, quoted in Leo Schmidt, ibid
74 Quoted by Victor Sebestyen in *Revolution 1989: The Fall of the Soviet Empire*, Pantheon, 2009, in Roger Kimball, ibid
75 Quoted in Roger Kimball, ibid
76 Roger Kimball, ibid
77 Quoted in Eric Kirschbaum, *Rocking the Wall: Bruce Springsteen, the Berlin Concert that Changed the World,* Berlinica, 2013
78 Eric Kirschbaum, ibid
79 Frederick Baker, ibid
80 Frederick Baker, ibid
81 Melanie van der Hoorn, 'Architectural Fragments as Intermediaries between History and Individual Experience, *Journal of Material Culture*, 2003, 8, 189, Sage
82 Frederick Baker, ibid
83 Melanie van der Hoorn, ibid
84 Melanie van der Hoorn, ibid
85 Lori Turner, 'The Berlin Wall: Fragment as Commodity', *Borderlines* 19, 1990, quoted by Yosefa Loshitzky, 'Constructing and Deconstructing the Wall', *CLIO*, 26, 3, 1997
86 'Berlin Journal: Wanted: A Home for 2 Watchtowers', *The New York Times,* 29 December 1993, quoted in Yosefa Loshitzky, ibid
87 Geoff Dyer, *New Republic,* Vol 244, Issue 20, 12 September 2013
88 Hope M. Harrison, 'The Berlin Wall and its Resurrection as a Site of Memory', *German Politics and Society, Issue 99, Vol 29, No 2, Summer 2011*
89 Quoted in Hope M. Harrison, 'The Berlin Wall and its Resurrection as a Site of Memory', ibid
90 Hope M. Harrison, 'The Berlin Wall and its Resurrection as a Site of Memory', ibid
91 Quoted in Frederick Baker, ibid
92 Tom Mueller, 'Berlin: Beyond the Wall: Nearly 17 years after the wall came down, Berliners are still trying to escape its shadow', *Smithsonian,* June 2006, Vol 37, Issue 3
93 Quoted in Frederick Baker, ibid
94 Frederick Baker, ibid
95 Quoted in Hope M. Harrison, 'The Berlin Wall and its Resurrection as a Site of Memory', ibid
96 Christine Leuenberger, 'The Berlin Wall: How Material Culture Is Used in Psychological Theory, *Social Problems,* Vol 53, No 1, February 2006
97 Christine Leuenberger, ibid
98 Tom Mueller, ibid
99 'Berlin satellite image reveals stark east-west division', *The Daily Telegraph,* 18 April 2013

CHAPTER 19

1 M. Christine Boyer, 'Meditations on a Wounded Skyline and Its Stratigraphies of Pain', *After the World Trade Center: Rethinking New York City,* Michael Sorkin and Sharon Zukin editors, Routledge, 2002
2 Minoru Yamasaki, *A Life in Architecture,* Weatherhill, New York, 1979
3 'Minoru Yamasaki, architect of World Trade Center, Dies', *New York Times,* 9 February, 1986

4 Eric Darton, *Divided We Stand: A Biography of the World Trade Center,* Perseus, 2011
5 Minoru Yamasaki, *A Life in Architecture,* ibid
6 *New York Times,* 'Minoru Yamasaki, Architect of World Trade Center, Dies', ibid

7 Rowan Moore, 'Minoru Yamasaki', *Prospect,* November 20, 2001
8 *New York Times,* 'Minoru Yamasaki, architect of World Trade Center, Dies', ibid
9 Danny Hakim, 'Watching a Creation from Infancy to Rubble', *New York Times,* 14 September 2001
10 Eric Darton, 'The Janus Face of Architectural Terrorism: Minoru Yamasaki, Mohammad Atta and Our World Trade Center', *After the World Trade Center: Rethinking New York City,* Michael Sorkin and Sharon Zukin editors, ibid
11 Eric Darton, 'The Janus Face of Architectural Terrorism: Minoru Yamasaki, Mohammad Atta and Our World

Trade Center', ibid

12 Minoru Yamasaki, quoted in M. Christine Boyer, 'Meditations on a Wounded Skyline and Its Stratigraphies of Pain', ibid
13 Minoru Yamasaki in a letter to Port Authority Director Austin Tobin, quoted in Eric Darton, *Divided We Stand*, ibid
14 Minoru Yamasaki, *Time*, quoted by Nicholas Olsberg, 'Memory In Ruins', *Architectural Review*, June 2014, Vol. 235 Issue 1408
15 Cathleen McGuigan, 'The Wolrd Trade Centre got a bad rap, but it became an indelible part of the Manhattan skyline', *Newsweek*, Vol 138, Issue 13, 24 September 2001
16 Quoted by Nicholas Olsberg, 'Memory In Ruins', ibid
17 Quoted by Danny Hakim, 'Watching a Creation from Infancy to Rubble', *New York Times,* ibid
18 Elena Lappin, 'Atta in Hamburg', *Prospect,* September 20, 2002
19 Brendan Threadgill, 'The Third Degree: Eyes Which Do Not See', *Art US,* 11, December 2005
20 Unni Wikan, 'My Son: A Terrorist? (He Was Such a Gentle Boy)', *Anthropological Quarterly*, Vol 75, No 1, Winter 2001
21 Unni Wikan, ibid
22 John Cloud, 'Atta's Odyssey: How a shy, well-educated young Egyptian became a suspected ringleader of the Sept. 11 attacks', *Time,* 8 October 2001, Vol 158, Issue 15
23 Unni Wikan, ibid
24 John Hooper, 'The shy, caring, deadly fanatic: Double life of suicide pilot', *The Observer,* 23 September 2001
25 Elena Lappin, ibid
26 Neil MacFarquhar, Jim Yardley and Paul Zielbauer, 'A portrait of the terrorist: From shy child to single-minded killer', *New York Times,* 10 October 2001
27 John Hooper, ibid
28 Elena Lappin, ibid
29 John Hooper, ibid
30 John Hooper, ibid
31 Elena Lappin, ibid
32 Neil MacFarquhar, Jim Yardley and Paul Zielbauer, ibid
33 Elena Lappin, ibid
34 John Hooper, ibid
35 Elena Lappin, ibid
36 John Cloud, ibid
37 John Hooper, ibid
38 John Hooper, ibid
39 Elena Lappin, ibid
40 Victoria Griffith, Peter Spiegel and Hugh Williamson, 'The hijackers' tale: How the men of September 11 went unnoticed', *Financial Times,* 30 November 2001
41 Translation of document released by the FBI, found in the baggage of Mohammad Atta, reported in 'Last words of a terrorist', *The Observer,* 30 September 2001
42 Unni Wikan, ibid
43 'Last words of a terrorist', *The Observer,* ibid
44 M. Christine Boyer, 'Meditations on a Wounded Skyline and Its Stratigraphies of Pain', ibid
45 Martin Amis, 'The Second Plane', *The Guardian,* 18 September 2001
46 Martin Amis, ibid
47 Frank Lloyd Wright, quoted by M. Christine Boyer, ibid
48 Martin Amis, ibid
49 Eric Banks, 'When a Neighbourhood Fell, and Barely Made a Sound', *New York Times,* 19 June 2005
50 Eric Banks, ibid
51 Danny Lyon, *The Destruction of Lower Manhattan,* Powerhouse, 2005, original edition Macmillan, 1969
52 Eric Banks, ibid
53 Danny Lyon, ibid
54 Danny Lyon, ibid
55 'Ground zero diggers uncover hull of 18th century ship', *The Guardian,* 15 July 2010
56 Mark Wigley, 'Insecurity by Design', *After the World Trade Center: Rethinking New York City,* Michael Sorkin and Sharon Zukin editors, ibid
57 George J. Tamaro, 'World Trade Center "Bathtub": From Genesis to Armageddon', *The Bridge,* Vol 32, No 1, Spring 2002

58 Quoted in the documentary *Rebuilding The World Trade Centre,* directed by Marcus Robinson, broadcast Channel 4, 2013, marcusrobinsonart.com/film-2/
59 George J. Tamaro, ibid
60 Mark Wigley, 'Insecurity by Design', *After the World Trade Center: Rethinking New York City,* Michael Sorkin and Sharon Zukin editors, ibid
61 M. Christine Boyer, 'Meditations on a Wounded Skyline and Its Stratigraphies of Pain', ibid
62 Henry James, quoted in M. Christine Boyer, ibid
63 Beverly Gage, 'The First Wall Street Bomb', *After the World Trade Center: Rethinking New York City,* Michael Sorkin and Sharon Zukin editors, ibid
64 Beverly Gage, ibid
65 *New York city guide: a comprehensive guide to the five boroughs of the metropolis: Manhattan, Brooklyn, the Bronx, Queens, and Richmond*, Random House, 1939
66 M. Christine Boyer, 'Meditations on a Wounded Skyline and Its Stratigraphies of Pain', ibid
67 *New York city guide,* ibid
68 *New York city guide,* ibid
69 *New York city guide,* ibid
70 'Bedlam on Radio Row', *New York Times,* 25 May 1930
71 Warren Linquist, quoted in Eric Darton, *Divided We Stand,* ibid
72 Quoted by John Kuo Wei Tchen, "Whose Downtown?!?', *After the World Trade Center: Rethinking New York City,* Michael Sorkin and Sharon Zukin editors, Routledge, 2002
73 David Rockefeller, quoted in Eric Darton, *Divided We Stand,* ibid
74 Nicholas Olsberg, ibid
75 Eric Darton, *Divided We Stand,* ibid
76 Eric Darton, *Divided We Stand,* ibid
77 Mark Wigley, 'Insecurity by Design', ibid
78 Nicholas Olsberg, ibid; and Cathleen McGuigan, ibid
79 Minoru Yamasaki, quoted in Eric Darton, *Divided We Stand,* ibid
80 Nicholas Olsberg, ibid
81 Rowan Moore, 'Minoru Yamasaki', *Prospect,* ibid
82 Minoru Yamasaki, quoted in Eric Darton, *Divided We Stand,* ibid
83 Austin Tobin, quoted in Eric Darton, *Divided We Stand,* ibid
84 Mark Wigley, 'Insecurity by Design', ibid
85 Mark Wigley, 'Insecurity by Design', ibid; and Cathleen McGuigan, ibid
86 Mark Wigley, 'Insecurity by Design', ibid
87 Ada Louise Huxtable, quoted in Eric Darton, *Divided We Stand,* ibid
88 Ann Holmes, quoted in Eric Darton, *Divided We Stand,* ibid
89 Charles A. Jencks, *The language of post-modern architecture*, Academy Editions, London, 1977, updated 1984
90 Quoted in Nicholas Olsberg, ibid
91 Ada Louise Huxtable, 'Big But Not So Bold', *New York Times,* 5 April 1973
92 Ada Louise Huxtable, 'Big But Not So Bold', ibid
93 Quoted in Eric Darton, *Divided We Stand,* ibid
94 Charles Jencks, quoted in Eric Darton, *Divided We Stand,* ibid
95 Jean Baudrillard, *The Singular Objects of Architecture,* quoted by Julian Reid in 'Architecture, Al-Qaeda, and the World Trade Centre', *Space and Culture*, Vol 7, No 4, 2004,
96 Eric Darton, *Divided We Stand,* ibid
97 Eric Darton, *Divided We Stand,* ibid
98 Minoru Yamasaki, *Time*, quoted in Nicholas Olsberg, ibid
99 Robert A. M. Stern, quoted by Danny Hakim, ibid
100 www.911memorial.org/museum
101 Holland Cotter, 'The 9/11 Story Told at Bedrock', *New York Times*, 14 May 2014
102 Holland Cotter, ibid
103 Holland Cotter, ibid; and Oliver Wainright, 'An emotional underworld beneath Ground Zero', *The Guardian*, 14 May 2014; and Robert Bevan, 'Memory In Ruins', *Architectural Review*, ibid
104 Holland Cotter ibid; Oliver Wainright ibid; and Robert Bevan, 'Memory In Ruins', *Architectural Review*, ibid
105 Holland Cotter, ibid; and Robert Bevan, 'Memory In Ruins', *Architectural Review*, ibid
106 Robert Bevan, 'Memory In Ruins', *Architectural Review*, ibid
107 Stephen Farrell, 'Ceremonial Transfer', *New York Times,* 11 May 2014
108 Stephen Farrell, ibid

109 Robert Bevan, 'Memory In Ruins', *Architectural Review*; and Stephen Farrell, ibid; and 'More than 300,000 people have visited 9/11 Memorial Museum', *The Guardian,* 25 June 2014
110 Stephen Farrell, ibid
111 Alice Greenwald, www.911memorial.org

112 Holland Cotter, ibid
113 Philip Kennicott, *Washington Post,* 7 June 2014
114 Philip Kennicott, ibid; and Robert Bevan, 'Memory In Ruins', *Architectural Review*, ibid

CHAPTER 20

1 Kate Lunau, 'Lessons from GeoCities' Death', *Maclean's*, 9 July 2009, Vol 122, Issue 34
2 *GeoCities, archiveteam.org/index.php?title=GeoCities#The_Closure*
3 Kara Swisher, 'Those Who Tied Fortune to GeoCities Yell Yahoo! All the Way to the Bank', *The Wall Street Journal*, 29 January 1999
4 'The Cutting Edge', *Los Angeles Times,* 31 May 1995
5 Mary Lou Roberts, 'GeoCities', *Journal of Interactive Marketing*, Vol 14, No 1, Winter 2000
6 Mary Lou Roberts, ibid
7 Mary Lou Roberts, ibid
8 David Bohnett, quoted by Gary Stern, 'GeoCities', *Link-Up,* Vol 14, Issue 4, 1997
9 David Bohnett, quoted in 'Beverley Hills Internet, builder of Interactive cyber cities, launches four more communities linked to real places', *Business Wire,* 5 July 1995
10 Mary Lou Roberts, ibid; and Gary Stern, ibid; and David Bohnett, quoted by *Business Wire,* ibid
11 David Bohnett, quoted by *Business Wire,* ibid
12 David Bohnett, quoted by *Business Wire,* ibid
13 Gary Stern, ibid
14 Joe Kloc, 'The Death and Life of Great Internet Cities', 25 November 2013, www.dailydot.com; and Angela Watercutter, 'Internet Archaeology: Behold the Most Hilarious Abandoned Websites', *Wired,* April 2013
15 Joe Kloc, ibid; and Phoebe Connelly, 'Neo Cities: How online communities are born and what happens when they die', *American Prospect,* 20, 7, September 2009
16 Joe Kloc, ibid
17 GeoCities user Linda Olmstead, quoted by Gary Stern, ibid
18 David Bohnett, quoted by Gary Stern, ibid
19 David Bohnett, quoted by Gary Stern, ibid
20 Mary Lou Roberts, ibid
21 GeoCities press releases, quoted by Mary Lou Roberts, ibid
22 Dennis Berman, 'For Facebook, GeoCities Offers a Cautionary Tale', *Wall Street Journal,* 25 September 2007
23 Mary Lou Roberts, ibid
24 Kate Lunau, ibid
25 Mary Lou Roberts, ibid
26 Mary Lou Roberts, ibid
27 Phoebe Connelly, ibid
28 Kara Swisher, 'Those Who Tied Fortune to GeoCities Yell Yahoo! All the Way to the Bank', *The Wall Street Journal*, 29 January 1999
29 'Yahoo! Moves in on GeoCities', *BBC News,* 29 January 1999
30 Kara Swisher and Don Clark, 'Yahoo Agrees to Buy GeoCities in $5 Billion Stock Transaction', *The Wall Street Journal*, 29 January 1999
31 David Bohnett, quoted by Kara Swisher, ibid
32 David Bohnett, quoted by Kara Swisher, ibid
33 Dennis Berman, ibid
34 Mary Lou Roberts, ibid
35 Lisa Napoli, 'Yahoo Angers GeoCities Members with Copyright Rules', *New York Times,* 30 June 1999
36 Lisa Napoli, ibid
37 Lisa Napoli, ibid
38 Yahoo GeoCities, 'Service Announcement', July 2009
39 Kate Lunau, ibid
40 Betsy Schiffman, 'A Community that Stays Together, Pays Together', *Forbes,* 28 August 2001
41 Betsy Schiffman, ibid

42 Leena Rao, quoting ComScore statistics in 'Yahoo Quietly Pulls the Plug on GeoCities', *Tech Crunch*, 23 April 2009

43 J.R. Raphael, 'So Long GeoCities: We Forgot You Still Existed', *PC World*, 23 April 2009

44 J.R. Raphael, ibid

45 The Archive Team, 'GeoCities', web.archive.org/web/20100722110205/http://www.archiveteam.org/index.php?title=GeoCities

46 Dan Fletcher, 'Internet Atrocity! GeoCities' Demise Erases Web History', *Time,* 9 November 2009; and Matt Schwartz, 'Fire in the Library', *MIT Technology Review,* 20 December 2011

47 Dan Fletcher, ibid

48 Matt Schwartz, ibid

49 *archiveteam.org/index.php?title=GeoCities#The_Closure*

50 *archiveteam.org/indexphp?title+File:Yahoo!_GeoCities_closed.png*

51 Matt Schwartz, ibid

52 Dan Fletcher, ibid

53 Jason Scott, quoted by Dan Fletcher, ibid

54 *deletedcity.net*

55 Richard Vijgen, 'The Deleted City: A Digital Archaeology', *Parsons Journal for Information Mapping,* Volume 5, Issue 2, Spring 2013

56 Richard Vijgen, ibid

57 Matt Schwartz, ibid; and Richard Vijgen, ibid

58 Richard Vijgen, ibid

59 Richard Vijgen, ibid

60 Richard Vijgen, ibid

61 Richard Vijgen, ibid

62 Jason Scott, quoted by Phoebe Connelly, 'Neo Cities', *The American Prospect*, September 2009

63 Internet Archaeology, 'Mission Statement', www.internetarchaeology.org/missionstatement.htm

64 Jason Scott, quoted by Joe Kloc, 'The death and life of great Internet cities', *The Daily Dot,* 25 November 2013

65 Quoted by Jennifer Faull, '600,000 Facebook users unknowingly take part in psychological experiment', *The Drum*, 29 June 2014

66 James Gleick, *The Information,* Fourth Estate, 2012

CHAPTER 21

1 Bel Trew, Tom Coghlan and Alice Richardson, 'Isis starts destruction of Palmyra after seizing city secrets', *The Times,* 25 August 2015

2 Ben Hubbard, 'Syrian Expert Who Shielded Palmyra Antiquities Meets a Grisly Death at ISIS' Hands', *New York Times,* 19 August 2015; 'Isis beheads leading Syrian relics scholar in Palmyra', *The Lebanon Daily Star,* 19 August 2015; Kareem Shaheen and Ian Black, 'Beheaded Syrian scholar refused to lead Isis to hidden Palmyra antiquities', *The Guardian,* 19 August 2015; Bel Trew, Tom Coghlan and Alice Richardson, ibid

3 'Syrian army pushes ISIS back from ancient Palmyra', *The Lebanon Daily Star,* 17 May 2015

4 Ian Browning, *Palmyra*, Chatto & Windus, 1979

5 Denys L Haynes, Preface to Iain Browning, *Palmyra,* Chatto & Windus, 1979

6 Ben Hubbard, ibid; 'Isis beheads leading Syrian relics scholar in Palmyra', *The Lebanon Daily Star,* ibid

7 'IS launches full-on assault of Palmyra', *Syria: direct,* 13 May 2015, syriadirect.org

8 'Syria army pushes ISIS back from ancient Palmyra', *The Lebanon Daily Star,* ibid; 'IS launches full-on assault of Palmyra', *Syria: direct,* ibid

9 Leith Fadel, 'ISIS Captures the Oil Fields Near Palmyra, While the Syrian Army Secures the Ancient City', Al Masdar News, 19 May 2015, www.almasdarnews.com

10 Robert Fisk, 'Syrian civil war: Can Assad's regime survive the onslaught from Isis and Jabat al-Nursa', *The Independent,* 12 June 2015

11 Annie Barnard and Hwaida Saad, 'ISIS Fighters seize control of Syrian City of Palmyra, and Ancient Ruins', *The New York Times,* 20 May 2015; Sylvia Westall and Tom Perry, 'Islamic State seizes ancient Palmyra city from Syrian forces', *Reuters,* 20 May 2015; 'IS seizes control of Syria's Palmyra', *The Lebanon Daily Star,* 25 May 2015; Kareem Shaheen, 'Palmyra: historic Syrian city falls under control of Isis', *The Guardian*, 21 May 2015

12 Annie Barnard and Hwaida Saad, 'Frantic Message as Palmyra, Syria, fell: 'We're Finished'' *The New York Times,* 21 May 2015

13 'IS seizes control of Syria's Palmyra', *The Lebanon Daily Star,* ibid

14 Tim McGirk, 'Syrians Race to Save Ancient City's Treasures from ISIS', *National Geographic,* July 2015

15 Tim McGirk, ibid

16 Tim McGirk, ibid; and Annie Barnard and Hwaida Saad, 'ISIS Fighters seize control of Syrian City of Palmyra, and Ancient Ruins', ibid

17 Tim McGirk, ibid

18 Kareem Shaheen, 'Isis fighters destroy ancient artefacts at Mosul Museum', *The Guardian,* 26 February 2015

19 'ISIS video shows mass execution in ruins of Syria's Palmyra', *The Lebanon Daily Star,* 4 July 2015; Kimberley Hutchinson, 'ISIS Video shows execution of 25 men in ruins of Syria amphitheatre', *CNN,* 5 July 2015

20 'Isis militants destroy 2,000-year-old statue of lion at Palmyra', *The Guardian,* 2 July 2015

21 Kareem Shaheen, 'Syria: Isis releases footage of Palmyra ruins intact and 'will not destroy them'', *The Guardian* 27 May 2015

22 'ISIS blows up temple in Palmyra: antiquities chief', *The Lebanon Daily Star,* 24 August 2015

23 I A Richmond 'Palmyra under the aegis of Rome', *The Journal of Roman Studies,* Vol 53, Parts 1 and 2, Cambridge University Press, 1963

24 'Images verify Palmyra's Temple of Bel destroyed', *The Lebanon Daily Star,* 2 September 2015

25 'ISIS blows up Palmyra columns to kill three', *The Lebanon Daily Star,* 27 October 2015

26 Dominic Bailey, 'Palmyra: Islamic State's demolition in the desert', *BBC News,* 5 October 2015

27 Assad Seif, 'Illicit Traffick in Cultural Property in Lebanon', *Countering Illicit Traffic in Cultural Goods: The Global Challenge of Protecting the World's Heritage,* Frances Desmaris,Frances Desmaris editor, ICOM, 2015

28 Assad Seif, ibid; 'Syrians Loot Roman Treasures to Buy Guns', Hala Jaber and George Arbuthnott, *The Sunday Times,* 5 May 2013; and 'Looted Roman treasures recovered in sting' Hala Jaber and George Arbuthnott, *The Sunday Times,* 26 May 2013

29 'Syrians Loot Roman Treasures to Buy Guns', Hala Jaber and George Arbuthnott, ibid

30 'Syrians Loot Roman Treasures to Buy Guns', Hala Jaber and George Arbuthnott, ibid

31 'Syrians Loot Roman Treasures to Buy Guns', Hala Jaber and George Arbuthnott, ibid

32 Assad Seif, ibid

33 'Three Lebanese arrested over attempted sale of rare artifacts', *The Lebanon Daily Star,* 17 May 2013

34 Kareem Shaheen and Ian Black, 'Beheaded Syrian scholar refused to lead Isis to hidden Palmyra antiquities', *The Guardian,* ibid

35 Brian I Daniels and Katharyn Hanson, 'Archaeological Site Looting in Syria and Iraq: A Review of the Evidence', *Countering Illicit Traffic in Cultural Goods: The Global Challenge of Protecting the World's Heritage,* Frances Desmaris editor, ICOM, 2015

36 Amr al-Azm, Salam Al-Kuntar and Brian I Daniels, 'ISIS's Antiquities Sideline', *The New York Times,* 2 September 2014

37 Amr al-Azm, Salam Al-Kuntar and Brian I Daniels, ibid

38 Tim McGirk, ibid; and Kareem Shaheen and Ian Black, 'Beheaded Syrian scholar refused to lead Isis to hidden Palmyra antiquities', *The Guardian,* ibid

39 Brian I Daniels and Katharyn Hanson, 'Archaeological Site Looting in Syria and Iraq: A Review of the Evidence', ibid

40 www.christies.com/lotfinder/ancient-art-antiquities/a-palmyrene-limestone-seated-female-figure-circa-5903819-details.aspx

41 www.christies.com/lotfinder/searchresults.aspx?searchtype=p&searchfrom=header&searchsubmit=-search&lid=1&sc_lan=en&entry=palmyrene&sid=4a434ab6-79b4-4a01-955d-538e6213cd0a&action=sort&sortby=dt

42 Michael Gawlikowski, 'Palmyra: reexcavating the site of the Tariff', *Polish Archaeology in the Meditteranean 23/1 (Research 2011),* University of Warsaw, 2014

43 Michael Gawlikowski, 'Palmyra: reexcavating the site of the Tariff' ibid; and Semyon Abamalek-Lazarev, 'Pal'mira. Archeologiceskoe izsledovanie', St. Petersburg, Tipografia Imperatorskoj Akademii, 1884

44 Michael Gawlikowski, 'Palmyra: reexcavating the site of the Tariff', ibid

45 Pinar Ure, *Byzantine Heritage, Archaeology, and Politics Between Russia and the Ottoman Empire,* London School of Economics Phd Dissertation, 2014

46 J F Matthews, 'The Tax Law of Palmyra: Evidence for Economic History In A City of the Roman East', *The Journal of Roman Studies,* Vol 74, 1984, Cambridge University Press; Iain Browning, *Palmyra,* ibid; and Andrew M Smith, *Roman Palmyra: Identity, Community and State Formation,* Oxford University Press, 2013

47 Michael Gawlikowski, 'Palmyra: reexcavating the site of the Tariff', ibid; J F Matthews, ibid
48 J F Matthews, ibid
49 J F Matthews, ibid; Iain Browning, ibid;
50 Translation in Iain Browning, ibid
51 J F Matthews, ibid
52 J F Matthews, ibid; Iain Browning, ibid
53 Andrew M Smith, ibid
54 Andrew M Smith, ibid
55 Iain Browning, ibid; Andrew M Smith, ibid
56 Iain Browning, ibid; Andrew M Smith, ibid
57 Michael Gawlikowski, 'Palmyra as a Trading Centre', *Iraq, Vol 56,* British Institute for the Study of Iraq, Cambridge University Press, 1994; J F Matthews, ibid; Iain Browning, ibid; Andrew M Smith, ibid; and I A Richmond, 'Palmyra under the Aegis of Rome', ibid
58 Appian, *The Civil Wars, Book V, 9*, translated by John Carver, Penguin, 1996
59 Iain Browning, ibid
60 Iain Browning, ibid; Andrew M Smith, ibid; I A Richmond 'Palmyra under the aegis of Rome', *The Journal of Roman Studies,* Vol 53, Parts 1 and 2, Cambridge University Press, 1963
61 I A Richmond 'Palmyra under the aegis of Rome', ibid
62 Michael Gawlikowski, 'Palmyra as a Trading Centre', ibid
63 Iain Browning, ibid; Michael Gawlikowski, 'Palmyra as a Trading Centre', ibid
64 J F Matthews, ibid
65 Andrew M Smith, ibid
66 J F Matthews, ibid; Andrew M Smith, ibid
67 J F Matthews, ibid; Andrew M Smith, ibid
68 Nathanael J Andrade, *Syrian Identity in the Greco-Roma World,* Cambridge University Press, 2013; G W Bowersock, *Roman Arabia,* Harvard University Press, 1983
69 D Mackay, 'The Jewellery of Palmyra and Its Significance', *Iraq*, Vol 11, No. 2 (Autumn 1949), British Institute for the Study of Iraq, Cambridge University Press, 1949
70 D Mackay, ibid
71 Zosimus, *Historia Nova, Book I,* translated by James T Buchanan, Trinity University Press, 1967; *The Scriptores Historiae Augustae, Book III,* translated by David Magie, Harvard University Press, 1932
72 Zosimus, ibid; Edward Gibbon, *The Decline and Fall of the Roman Empire, Vol 1, Chapter XI,* edited by David Womersley, Penguin, 1994
73 *The Scriptores Historiae Augustae*, ibid
74 Iain Browning, ibid; Edward Gibbon, ibid
75 Zosimus, ibid; Edward Gibbon, ibid; *The Scriptores Historiae Augustae*, ibid
76 Andrew M Smith, ibid; Iain Browning, ibid
77 Edward Gibbon, ibid
78 Andrew M Smith, ibid
79 Iain Browning, ibid; Edward Gibbon, ibid
80 Andrew M Smith, ibid
81 Iain Browning, ibid
82 Andrew M Smith, ibid
83 Andrew M Smith, ibid; Petrus Patricius, quoted in Michael Dodgeon and Sameul Lieu, *The Roman Eastern Frontier and the Persian Wars (AD 226-363): A documentary history,* Routledge, 1994
84 Petrus Patricius, ibid
85 Zosimus, ibid; Various, Michael Dodgeon and Sameul Lieu, ibid
86 Zosimus, ibid
87 Iain Browning, ibid
88 Edward Gibbon, ibid
89 *The Scriptores Historiae Augustae*, ibid; Edward Gibbon, ibid
90 *The Scriptores Historiae Augustae*, ibid; Edward Gibbon, ibid
91 *The Scriptores Historiae Augustae*, ibid
92 Michael Dodgeon and Sameul Lieu, ibid; Byron Nakamura, 'Palmyra and the Roman East', *Greek, Roman and Byzantine Studies*, Vol 34 (2), Summer 1993
93 Andrew M Smith, ibid; Byron Nakamura, ibid
94 Andrew M Smith, ibid; Byron Nakamura, ibid
95 Zosimus, ibid; Michael Dodgeon and Sameul Lieu, ibid;

96 *The Scriptores Historiae Augustae*,

97 Michael Dodgeon and Sameul Lieu, ibid; Zosimus, ibid;

98 Michael Dodgeon and Sameul Lieu, ibid; *The Scriptores Historiae Augustae*, ibid; Edward Gibbon, ibid

99 Michael Dodgeon and Sameul Lieu, ibid

100 Andrew M Smith, ibid

101 Iain Browning, ibid

102 C A Hutton, 'The Travels of 'Palmyra' Wood in 1750-51', *The Journal of Hellenic Studies*, Vol 47, Part 1, 1927

103 Robert Wood and James Dawkins, *The Ruins of Palmyra, otherwise Tedmor in the Desart,* Robert Wood, London, 1753

104 Dr William Halifax, *A Relation of A Voyage to Tadmor in 1691,* Trubner, 1890

105 Dr William Halifax, ibid

106 Robert Wood and James Dawkins, ibid

107 Robert Wood and James Dawkins, ibid

108 Robert Wood and James Dawkins, ibid

109 Iain Browning, ibid

110 Edward Gibbon, quoted in Iain Browning, ibid

111 Iain Browning, ibid; Geoffrey Beard, *Georgian Craftsmen and their Work,* A S Barnes, 1967

112 Percy Bysshe Shelley, *Queen Mab; A Philosophical Poem*, William Baldwin, New York, 1821

113 Charles Meryon and Lady Hestor Stanhope, *The Travels of Lady Hestor Stanhope, Forming the Completion of Her Memoirs, Narrated by Her Physician in Three Volumes, Volume II*, Henry Colburn, 1846

114 Lady Hester Stanhope, Letter to Henry Williams Wynn, 30 June 1813, excerpt in Frank Hamel, *Lady Hester Lucy Stanhope: A New Light on Her Life and Love Affairs,* Cassell and Company, 1921

115 Dr William Wright, *An Account of Palmyra and Zenobia with Travels and Adventures in Bashan and the Desert,* Thomas Nelson and Sons, 1895

116 John Arlidge, 'The Best Place in the World?', *The Sunday Times,* 22 June 2014

117 www.digitalarchaeology.org.uk

118 Ian Johnston, 'Modern Day Monuments Men take on Isis by 3D-mapping ancient sites militants are seeking to destroy', *The Independent,* 27 August 2015

119 Dr Alexy Karenowska, interview on *BBC Newsnight,* 30 March 2016

120 Roger Michel, quoted by Stephen Farrell, 'If All Else Fails, 3D Models and Robots Might Rebuild Palmyra', *New York Times,* 28 March 2016

121 Dominic Basulto, 'How 3D printers can help undo the destruction of Isis', *The Washington Post,* 7 January 2016

122 Ban Ki-moon, 12 April 2016, www.un.org/sg/statements/index.asp?nid=9605

Further Reading

Chapter 1 – Make a Name for Yourself!

For a forensically detailed and comprehensive – yet also wonderfully readable – account of the looting of the Baghdad Museum, there is no better place to start than 'Casualties of War: The Truth about the Iraq Museum', by Matthew Bogdanos in the *American Journal of Archaeology* (Vol 109, No. 3, July 2005). Bogdanos, an Assistant District Attorney in Manhattan, led the investigation into the antiquities thefts in 2003 while on duty as a Colonel in the United States Marine Corps Reserves. Equally compelling is *Catastrophe! The Looting and Destruction of Iraq's Past* (George Emberling and Kathryn Hanson editors, The Oriental Institute of the Museum of the University of Chicago, 2008), a series of essays looking at the impact of Second Gulf War on Iraq's cultural heritage; with particularly noteworthy contributions from Dr Donny George Youkhanna, the Baghdad Museum's former Director-General of Research. Both Gwendolyn Leick (*Mesopotamia: The Invention of the City*, Penguin, 2002) and Paul Kriwaczek (*Babylon: Mesopotamia and the Birth of Civilization*, Atlantic, 2010) provide excellent overviews of the history and importance of Mesopotamia as the cradle of civilisation. Leick is superb on the archaeology of the region, while Kriwaczek links skilfully the region's glorious past with its troubled present. To understand the connections between the Tower of Babel, the Temple of Entemenanki and ancient Babylon, two journal articles by A R George are essential reading: 'The Tower of Babel: archaeology, history and cuneiform texts' (*Archiv fur Orientforschung*, Vol 51, 1 January 2005) and 'A Stele of Nebuchadnezzar II' (*Cuneiform Royal Inscription and Related Texts in the Schoyen Collection*, Cornell University Studies in Assyriology Sumerology, CDI Press, 2011). The *Report on Meeting at Babylon 11-13 December 2004* by Dr John E Curtis of the British Museum (available on the British Museum website) also makes fascinating reading, illustrating in grim detail what happens when war and ancient monuments collide.

Chapter 2 - Modernism's Labyrinth

On the life of Arthur Evans, there are a number of places to look, but four books stand out for offering nicely competing perspectives. *Time and Chance,* written by Evans' half sister Joan (Longmans, Green and co, 1943), provides an excellent, if partial, biography, littered with wonderful details of family and personal interactions. J Alexander McGillivray's *Minotaur: Sir Arthur Evans and the Archaeology of the Minoan Myth* (Pimlico, 2001) is an impressive piece of scholarship, bringing a huge variety of sources to bear on the life of the man who excavated Knossos. After reading McGillivray's unvarnished account, it is clear that the author is not Evans' biggest fan. Leonard Cottrell's part-history, part-travelogue *The Bull of Minos: The Great Discoveries of Ancient Greece* (I B Tauris, 1953), draws heavily on Joan Evans in its affectionate account of Arthur and his work, but also provides a fantastically vivid and enticing account of exploring ancient ruins. Last, there is *The Villa Ariadne*, by Dilys Powell (Hodder, 1973), which includes beautifully-written accounts of the author's own personal experiences of Evans and Knossos during the 1920s and 30s. On Knossos itself, Evans' writings are prolific and compelling, from his multi-volume *The Palace of Minos* (I was using the original Macmillan editions from the 1920s and 30s) to his numerous journal articles and letters to *The Times*. Specifically on the strange symbols that led him to Crete, Evans' *Cretan Pictographs and Prae-Phoenician Script* (Bernard Quatrich, 1895) is a good place to start. On Knossos and its impact on art and culture at the beginning of the twentieth century, Cathy Gere's *Knossos and the Prophets of Modernism* (University of Chicago, 2009) is brilliant, witty and thought-provoking – and is augmented by a comment piece on the same subject by Mary Beard ('Knossos, Fakes, Facts and Mystery') in the *New York Review of Books* (13 August 2009). For a sober counterpoint to Evans, John Pendlebury's *The Archaeology of Crete* (Methuen, 1939) is superb.

Chapter 3 – The First War Memorial

You cannot read about Mycenae and Troy without reading Heinrich Schliemann. *Myceane: A Narrative of Researches and Discoveries at Mycenae and Tiryns* (John Murray, 1878), *Troy and its Remains* (John Murray, 1875), and *Ilios: The City and Country of the Trojans* (John Murray, 1880), are breathless accounts of momentous discoveries straight out of Homer. To understand the dark side of Schliemann, and in particular the accusations of forgery that followed his archaeological career almost from the outset, look at *Memoirs of Heinrich Schliemann: A Documentary Portrait Drawn from His Autobiographical Writings, Letters and Excavation Reports* (Leo Deuel, Hutchinson, 1978); *Myth, Scandal and History: The Heinrich Schliemann Controversy and a First Edition of the Mycenaean Diary* (William Calder and David Traill, editors, Wayne State University Press, 1986); 'The Making of an Homeric Archaeologist: Schliemann's Diary of 1868' (*The Annual of the British School at Athens*, Vol 84, 1989); and *Schliemann of Troy: Treasure and Deceit* (David Traill again, St Martin's Press, 1995). All four works take aim at Schliemann's lofty conceit of himself as the heroic archaeologist, and present fascinating arguments and evidence to the contrary. For more straightforward accounts of Mycenae and the Myceneans, there is *The Mycenean Age* by Christos Tsountas (Macmillan, 1897), and *Mycenae Rich in Gold,* by George E Mylonas (Ekdotike Athenon, 1983). Alan Wace's reports on the site are particularly rewarding, including 'Mycenae' in *Antiquity* (Vol 10, No 40, 1936) and, on the subject of the watchtower, 'The Report of the School of Excavations at Mycenae, 1920-23' (*The Annual of the British School at Athens*, Vol 25, 1921/22 - 1922/23). For an erudite and wonderfully accessible overview of the site, Cathy Gere's *The Tomb of Agamemnon: Mycenae and the Search for a Hero* (Profile, 2007) is a standout. Gere weaves together the history and mythology of Mycenae and is particularly good on the connections with Nietzsche, Hitler and the Nazis. For more information on the transformation of the Swastika from an archaeological curiosity to a symbol of hatred, see *The Swastika: Constructing the Symbol*, by Malcolm Quinn (Routledge, 1994). On the tragic fates of England's First World War poets, the boyishly optimistic letters of Rupert Brooke (*The Letters of Rupert Brooke*, edited by Geoffrey Keynes, Faber and Faber, 1968) make for particularly poignant reading. And if you haven't read Homer's *Iliad* or *Odyssey*, you must - I'd recommend the Robert Fagles verse translations (Penguin Classics, 1990 and 1996).

Chapter 4 – The Sun City Also Rises

Barry Kemp's *The City of Akhenaten and Nefertiti: Amarna and Its People* (Thames and Hudson, 2012) is a masterwork, the product of decades of excavation and research into the archaeological story behind this remarkable – and short-lived – city. Beyond Kemp, Cyril Aldred's *Akhenaten: King of Egypt* (Thames and Hudson, 1988) is a thrilling and engaging read, setting the city within the wider context of the life story of the rebel Pharaoh and the Amenhotep dynasty. For accounts of the remarkable carvings, paintings, inscriptions and letters found at Amarna, look at *The Rock Tombs of El Amarna* by Norman de Garis Davies (Egypt Exploration Fund, 1903-1908); *Amarna Palace Paintings* by Frances J Weatherhead (Egypt Exploration Society, 2007); and *Texts from the Amarna Period in Egypt* by William J Murnane (Scholars Press, 1995). On Akhenaten as history's first 'individual', read James Henry Breasted, *A History of the Ancient Egyptians* (John Murray, 1924); Flinders Petrie, *Tell El-Amarna* (Methuen, 1894); Donald B Redford, *Akhenaten: The Heretic King* (Princeton University Press, 1984); and Dominic Montserrat, *Akhenaten: History, Fantasy and Ancient Egypt* (Routledge, 2000). A fascinating account of Nefertiti's role in the Amarna story can be found in Joyce Tyldesley's *Nefertiti: Unlocking the Mystery Surrounding Egypt's Most Famous and Beautiful Queen* (Penguin, 1999). And, for a succinct overview of the confused circumstances that followed the death of Akhenaten, read 'Pharaohs of the Sun' by Rick Gore in *National Geographic,* (199, Part 4, 2001).

Chapter 5 – Jerusalem Syndrome

The two best books I have come across on the history of Jerusalem's Temple – in its Jewish, Islamic and Christian incarnations – are Alan Balfour's *Solomon's Temple: Myth, Conflict and Faith* (Wiley-Blackwell, 2012); and Simon Goldhill's *The Temple of Jerusalem* (Harvard University Press, 2004). Both are clever, witty and comprehensive, placing the story of the temple within its historical and modern cultural contexts. More generally on the history of Jerusalem, there is John Gray's *A History of Jerusalem (*Robert Hale, 1969); Kathleen M Kenyon's *Jerusalem: Excavating 3000 Years of History* (Thames and Hudson, 1967); F. E. Peters' *Jerusalem: The Holy City in the Eyes of Chroniclers, Visitors, Pilgrims and Prophets from the Days of Abraham to the Beginnings of Modern Times* (Princeton University Press, 1985); and Simon Seabag Montefiore's recent magnum opus, *Jerusalem: The Biography* (Weidenfeld and Nicholson, 2011). For a more unconventional history, Eric H Cline's *Jerusalem Beseiged* (University of Michigan Press, 2004) looks at the city through the prism of the many (many!) conflicts that have crashed up against, and through, its walls. The *Antiquities* and *The Jewish War* by Josephus (multiple volumes – I was using the William Heinemann editions) are invaluable sources of information on Jerusalem and the Temple during Roman times, and contain some fantastic and arresting descriptions of everything from architecture and Passover to famine and war. On the Islamic history of Jerusalem, Guy Le Strange's *Palestine under the Moslems: A Description of Syria and the Holy Land from AD 650 to 1500* (Hougton, Mifflin and Company, 1890) is a wonderful source of contemporary quotations and accounts. Similarly, when it comes to the Christian intervention in the city, August C Krey's *The First Crusade: The Accounts of Eye-Witnesses and Participants* (Princeton University Press, 1921) is invaluable. For information on the Six Day War, I found Michael B Oren's *Six Days of War: June 1967 and the Making of the Modern Middle East* particularly useful. And finally, of course, there is the Bible, which is filled with a great many references to the Temple, its destruction, its resurrection and its role in the life and death of Jesus Christ – I was using *The New Oxford Annotated Bible* (Oxford University Press, 1991).

Chapter 6 – The Rise, Decline and Fall of the Cow Pasture

I suspect it is unfashionable to admit these days, but I am huge fan of Edward Gibbon and *The History of the Decline and Fall of the Roman Empire* (Penguin, edited by David Womersley, Penguin Classics edition in three volumes, 2005 and 1995). Far from its popular reputation as a cure for insomnia, Gibbon to me is an enticing mix of detail and epic sweep, and is often deliciously gossipy and opinionated. For details of the sorry state of the Forum in the time of Poggio, look at *Vol III, Chapter LXXI.* For an invaluable overview of the remains of the Forum that survived to modern times, look at Samuel Ball Platner's *A Topographical Dictionary of Ancient Rome* (Oxford University Press, 1929), alongside Richardson's updated *A New Topographical Dictionary of Ancient Rome* (John Hopkins University Press, 1992). For a much more detailed consideration of the Forum and its changing uses and purpose throughout history, David Watkin's *The Roman Forum* (Profile, 2009) provides an excellent synthesis of a huge variety of source material, tracing the story of the site building by building – covering those that have gone alongside those that remain. Both Appian (*The Civil Wars, Book II*, translated by John Carter, Penguin, 1996) and Plutarch (*Fall of the Roman Republic,* translated by Rex Warner, Penguin, 1958) provide riveting accounts of the funeral of Caesar. On the early history of Rome, there is, unsurprisingly, no substitute for Livy's *The Early History of Rome* (translated by Aubrey de Selincourt, Penguin, 2002). For a wonderfully-written account of what happened to so much of the Roman Empire's architecture down the centuries, read Rodolfo Lanciani's *The Destruction of Ancient Rome* (Macmillan, 1899). *Piranesi* by Jonathan Scott (Academy Editions, 1975) and John A Pinto's *Speaking Ruins: Piranesi, Architects and Antiquity in Eighteenth-Century Rome (*University of Michigan Press, 2012*),* provide excellent summaries of the artist's life and influence. To look at Piranesi's work itself, Taschen's *Piranesi: The Complete Etchings* (Taschen, 2011) offers superb reproductions. On Napoleon and 'art theft', read Patricia Mainardi, 'Assuring the Empire of the Future: The 1798 Fete de la Liberté', (*Art Journal,* Vol 48, Issue 2, 1989) and Dorothy Mackay Quynn, 'The Art Confiscations of the Napoleonic Wars' (*The American Historical Review,* Vol 50, No 3, Oxford University Press, April 1945). On Mussolini's attempt to create a new Imperial Rome, Borden W Painter's *Mussolini's Rome: Rebuilding the Eternal City* (Macmillan, 2005) makes for fascinating reading. And for an excellent account of the circumstances and wider context of Hitler's visit to Rome, read Paul Baxa's 'Capturing the Fascist Moment: Hitler's Visit to Italy in 1938 and the Radicalization of Fascist Italy' (*Journal of Contemporary History*, Vol 42, 2007).

Chapter 7 – The Library of Babel

The Library of Alexandria: Centre of Learning in the Ancient World (Roy Macleod, editor, I B Tauris, 2010) is an ideal starting place – a series of essays by experts who have studied various different aspects of the library's convoluted history. Some of the best are R G Tanner's 'Aristotle's Works: The Possible Origins of the Alexandrian Collection'; Roy

Macleod's introduction 'Alexandria in History and Myth'; Robert Barnes' 'Cloistered Bookworms in the Chicken-Coop of the Muses'; and John Vallance's 'Doctors in the Library: The Strange Tale of Apollonius the Bookworm and Other Stories'. See also Andrew Erskine's excellent journal article 'Culture and Power in Ptolemaic Egypt: The Musuem and Library of Alexandria' (Cambridge University Press, *Greece and Rome*, Vol 42, No 1, April 1995). For some of the earliest written accounts of the library and its creation, look at *Demetrius of Phalerum: Text, Translation and Discussion* (Transaction Publishers, 2000) and *Aristeas to Philocrates* (Harper and Brothers, 1951). On the fantastic inventions that filled the streets of Alexandria, read *The Pneumatics of Hero* (with some excellent illustrations in the 1971 Macdonald edition I was using). On Caesar in Alexandria, the words of the great man himself can't be bettered: *Caesar's Commentaries on the Gallic and Civil Wars* (Bell and Daldy, 1857) is never less than enthralling. On the tragic fate of the library read Daniel Heller Roazen's, 'Tradition's Destruction: On the Library of Alexandria' (*October*, Vol 100, Obsolescence, Spring 2002); James Raven's 'The Resonance of Loss' in *Lost Libraries: The Destruction of Great Book Collections Since Antiquity* (James Raven, editor, Palgrave Macmillan, 2004); Jon Thiem's 'The Great Library of Alexandria Burnt: Towards the History of a Symbol' (*Journal of the History of Ideas,* Vol 40, No 4, University of Pennsylvania Press, 1979); and even Gibbon again, in *The Decline and Fall* (*Vol II, Chapter XXVIII*). On the modern incarnation of Alexandria as a repository of digital information – and its links to Borges and Wikipedia – see James Gleick's *The Information: A History, A Theory, A Flood* (Fourth Estate, 2012). For a live counter of Wikipedia edits, go to tools.wmflabs.org/wmcounter/. And on the Archive Team, there are two excellent *Guardian* articles: 'The Time Machine' by Jack Schofield (19 November 2007), and 'Brewster's Trillions', by Rory Carroll, (26 April 2013).

Chapter 8 – Anarchy's Theatre

On the history of the circus factions, there are a number of excellent sources: Procopius in *The Secret History* (translated by G A Williamson and Peter Sarris, Penguin, 2007), Livy in *The Early History of Rome (*translated by Aubrey de Selincourt, Penguin, 2002), Gibbon in *The Decline and Fall (Vol II, Chapter XL)* and Sotiris G Giastis in 'The organization of chariot racing in the great Hippodrome of Byzantine Constantinople' (*The International Journal of the History of Sport,* 17:1, Routledge, 2000). Best of all is Alan Cameron's wonderful *Circus Factions: Greens and Blues at Rome and Byzantium* (Clarendon Press, 1976), which provides a meticulously detailed analysis of the place of the sport of chariot racing - and its vociferous fan base - in the context of the Roman Empire. On the architecture of the Hippodrome, read Rodolphe Guilland, 'The Hippodrome at Byzantium' (*Speculum*, Vol 23, No 4, Medieval Academy of America, October 1948); Stanley Casson, *Preliminary Report Upon the Excavations carried out in the Hippodrome of Constantinople in 1927* (Oxford University Press, 1928); Sarah Guberti Bassett, 'The Antiquities in the Hippodrome of Constantinople' (*Dumbartion Oaks Papers,* Vol 45, 1991); and R M Dawkins, 'Anceint Statues in Medieval Constantinople' (*Folklore*, Vol 35, No 3, 30 September 1924). On the 'Nika' riot – after with Procopius (*History of the Wars,* William Heinemann, 1914) and Alan Cameron – J B Bury's 'The Nika Riot' *(The Journal of Hellenic Studies,* Vol 17, 1897) and Geoffrey Greatrex's 'The Nika Riot: A Reappraisal' *(The Journal of Hellenic Studies,* Vol 117, 1997) are essential reading. For fantastic contemporary detail of the Fourth Crusade, there is *The History of Them That Took Constantinople: Being an Account of the Fourth Crusade, which Robert of Clari in Amienois, Knight, caused to be written down in the Picard Tongue about 1216* (The University of Washington, 1939) and *O City of Byzantium: Annals of Niketas Choniates,* (Wayne State University Press, 1984). To put the overall history of Byzantium and Constantinople in context, read Cassius Dio *(Dio's Roman History,* multiple volumes, William Heinemann, 1914-1927), Gibbon, and John Julius Norwich's excellent and accessible *A Short History of Byzantium* (Penguin, 1998).

Chapter 9 – The Carpet of the World

The undoubted authority on the history of Islamic gardens – and their role in the culture of Al Andalus – is D Fairchild Ruggles. For a series of fascinating accounts and perspectives drawn from contemporary Arabic sources – and featuring the Madinat al Zahra – read *Gardens, Landscape and Vision in the Palaces of Islamic Spain* (University of Pennsylvania Press, 2000), *Islamic Gardens and Landscapes* (University of Pennsylvania Press, 2008), 'The Mirador in Hispano-Umayyad Garden Typology', (*Muqarnas,* Vol 7, Brill, 1990), and 'Arabic Poetry and Architectural Memory in al-Andalus', (*Ars Orientalis,* Vol 23, Pre-Modern Islamic Palaces, University of Michigan, 1993). For an excellent narrative of the construction and architecture of the palace city, see Antonio Vallejo Triano, 'Madinat Al-Zahra: Historical Reality and Present-Day Heritage', (*Reflections on Qurtuba in the 21st Century,* Casa Arabe, 2013) and 'Madinat al-Zahra: The Triumph of the Islamic State' in *Al Andalus: The Art of Islamic Spain* (The Metropolitan Museum of Art, 1992). Joseph F O'Callaghan's *A History of Medieval Spain* (Cornell University Press, 1983) and Adulwahid Dhanum Taha's *The Muslim Conquest and Settlement of North Africa and Spain* (Routledge, 1989) provide comprehensive overviews of the Islamic invasion, with the former particularly good on the rise and fall of Al Andalus. On the life of Abd al-Rahman III, Maribel Fierro's *Abd al-Rahman III: The First Cordoban Caliph* (Oneworld, 2005) is exceptionally useful. On the transformation of Madinat al Zahra into a site of romantic ruin and poetic lament, read – along with Fairchild Ruggles – Anna Christys' 'Picnic at Madinat Al Zahra', in *Cross, Crescent and Conversion: Studies on Medieval Spain and Christendom* (Simon Barton and Peter Linehan editors, Brill, 2008). And finally, if you haven't read the *Tales of 1,001 Nights* (translated by Malcolm C Lyons, Penguin complete edition in three volumes, 2008), please do.

Chapter 10 – 'London Was, But is No More'

On the life of Wenceslaus Hollar, Gillian Tindall's *The Man Who Drew London: Wenceslaus Hollar in Reality and Imagination* (Chatto & Windus, 2002) is excellent, exploring how London came to be his muse. Specifically on Old St Paul's, *Dugdale and Hollar: History Illustrated* (University of Delaware Press, 2002), details how Hollar worked with the historian William Dugdale in the late seventeenth century, recording the Cathedral in a series of beautiful engravings just before its destruction. Also of interest on Hollar, and more particularly the style he used to depict London, is John Bold's 'Bird's-Eye Views: From Hollar to the London Eye' (*The London Journal*, Vol 35, No 3, November 2010). The story of Old St Paul's is touched on in varied detail and quality by a huge number of sources – for me, the following are some of the best. *St Paul's – The Cathedral Church of London, 604 – 2004* (edited by Derek Keene, Arthur Burns and Andrew Saint, Yale University Press, 2004) is a spectacular volume, bringing together a series of essays – supported by superb illustrations – looking at every aspect of the building's history and architecture. William Dugdale's original history from 1658, *The History of St Paul's Cathedral in London* (Tho Warren), remains essential reading. Also very worthwhile are William Longman's *A History of the three Cathedrals dedicated to St Paul in London* (Longman's, Green and Co, 1873), William Benham's *Old St Paul's Cathedral* (Seeley and Co Ltd, 1902) and Leo Hollis's *The Phoenix: St Paul's Cathedral and the Men who Made Modern London* (Weidenfeld and Nicholson, 2008). On the fate of the Cathedral in the Great Fire, *The Diary of John Evelyn* (edited by E S de Beer, Clarendon Press, 1955) and *The Diary of Samuel Pepys* (edited by Robert Latham and William Mathews, G Bell & Sons Ltd, 1970) are utterly riveting.

Chapter 11 – The Tent at the Centre of the World

Four of the best sources of information on the inner workings of the Mongol Empire come from the pens of travellers who made the arduous journey east to Karakorum in the thirteenth century. Ala al-din Ata-Malik Juvaini's *Genghis Khan: The History of the World Conqueror* (translated by J A Boyle, Manchester University Press, 1997) provides wonderful detail on the seasonal palaces of the Great Khan (as do Noriyuki Shiraishi, 'Seasonal Migrations of the Mongol Emperors and the Peri-Urban Area of Kharakhorum', *International Journal of Asian Studies,* Cambridge University Press, 2004; and J. Daniel Rogers, Erdenebat Ulambayar and Matthew Gallon, 'Urban centres and the emergence of empires in Eastern Inner Asia', *Antiquity,* 79, 2005). Rashid al-Din's *The Successors of Genghis Khan* (J A Boyle, Columbia University Press, 1971) is particularly good on the life of Ogodei Khan, who established Karakorum as the urban capital of the nomadic steppes. Marco Polo's *The Travels of Marco Polo* (translated by Robert Latham, Penguin, 1958) is full of fantastical details of the later Mongolian Empire, and particularly the rule of Kubilai Khan. Best of all, is Friar William of Rubruck's *The Mission of Friar William of Rubruck: His journey to the court of the Great Khan Mongke, 1253-1255* (translated by Peter Jackson, Hackett, 2009). Rubruck plays the straight man, but his account of an accidental 7,000-mile round-trip to meet Mongke Khan in Karakorum is intimate, bizarre, and often hilarious. On the story of Genghis Khan's childhood, read Igor de Rachewitz's comprehensive *The Secret History of the Mongols: A Mongolian Epic Chronicle of the Thirteenth Century* (Brill, 2004); Leo de Hartog's *Genghis Khan:* Conqueror *of the World* (I B Tauris, 1999); Francis Woodman Cleaves' *The Secret History of the Mongols* (Harvard University Press, 1982); and Urgunge Onon's *The History and Life of Chinggis Khan* (Brill, 1990). More generally on Mongol history, see David Morgan's *The Mongols* (Basil Blackwell, 1986), and 'The Decline and Fall of the Mongol Empire' (*Journal of the Royal Asiatic Society,* Vol 19, issue 4, January 2009); Jack Weatherford's *Genghis Khan and the Making of the Modern World* (Broadway Books, 2004); J J Saunders' *The History of the Mongol Conquests* (Routledge, 1971); and Timothy May's *The Mongol Conquests in World History* (Reaktion Books, 2012). On the resurgence of Genghis Khan in modern day Mongolia, read 'Reviving the Ancient Capital of Karakorum' in *Foreign Affairs* (Vol 84, Issue 3, May/June 2005), and Jehangir S Pocha's 'Mongolia sees Genghis Khan's good side' in the *New York Times*, 10 May 2005.

Chapter 12 – The House of Diamonds

For a comprehensive overview of the history of diamonds – and in particular their discovery and exploitation by man – read *The Nature of Diamonds* (edited by George E Harlow, Cambridge University Press, 1998) and *The Curious Lore of Precious Stones* (George Frederick Kunz, Halcyon House, 1938). Both include details of India and Golconda as the earliest source of the world diamond trade. On the history of Golconda, both the region and the fortress, read Marika Sardar's *Golconda through Time: A Mirror of the Evolving Deccan* (New York University, 2007) and *The Early Foundations of Golconda and the Rise of Fortifications in the Fourteenth Century Deccan* (Metropolitan Museum of Art, 2011); *Ferishta's History of the Dekkan from the First Mahummedan Conquests* (translated by Jonathan Scott, John Stockdale, London, 1794); and Rocco Sha's *A Guide to Golconda Fort and Tombs* (Government Central Press, Hyderabad, 1929). Jean Baptiste Tavernier's travelogue is exceptional on the detail of seventeenth century Golconda (*The Six Voyages of Jean-Baptiste Tavernier, Baron of Aubonne, through Turkey, into Persia and the East-Indies,* translated by V Ball, Munishram Manoharlal Publishers, 1995); as is Jean de Thévenot and Giovanni Francesco Gemelli Careri's, *Indian Travels of Thévenot and Careri: Being the third part of the travels of M. De Thévenot into the Levant and the third part of a voyage round the world by D. John Francis Gemelli Careri,* (National Archives of India, New Delhi, 1949). On the life of Aurangzeb, and in particular the siege of Golconda, see the *Maasir-i-Alamgiri, A History of the Emperor Aurangzib-'Alamgir, reign 1658-1707 AD, (*Jadunath Sarkar translator, The Asiatic Society, Calcutta, 1990); *History of Aurangzib, Mainly based on Persian sources,* (M. C. Sarkar and Sons, Calcutta, multiple volumes: for the siege see *Volume IV*, 1924); and Stanley Lane Poole's *Rulers of India, Aurangzib* (Clarendon Press, Oxford, 1893).

Chapter 13 – Liberté for Sale

The writings of former prisoners of the Bastille provide some excellent and picaresque source material. Best of all are the *Memoirs of Henry Masers de Latude - who was confined during thirty-five years, in the different state prisons of France* (translated by John William Calcraft, W F Wakeman, 1834), and Simon-Nicolas-Henri Linguet's, *Memoirs of the Bastille: Containing a full exposition of the mysterious policy and despotic oppression of the French Government, in the Interior Administration of that State-Prison, interspersed with a Variety of Curious Anecdotes,* (J A Husband, 1783). Other notable examples are Constantin de Renneville's *The French Inquisition: or the History of the Bastille in Paris, the State Prison in France* (A Bell, 1715) and the experiences of the Marquis de Sade (for details of his living arrangements in the prison, see *The Marquis de Sade: A Life,* Neil Schaeffer, Harvard University Press, 2011). For a general history of the Bastille, there are several excellent places to look: R A Davenport's *The History of the Bastille and of its Principal Captives* (Thomas Tegg and Son, 1838); Frantz Funck-Bretano's *Legends of the Bastille* (Downey & Co, 1899); Keith Reader's *The Place de la Bastille: The story of a quartier* (Liverpool University Press, 2011); and Simon Schama's *Citizens: A Chronicle of the French Revolution* (Penguin, 1989). Perhaps best of all is Hans-Jurgen Lusebrink and Rolf Reichardt's, *The Bastille: A History of a Symbol of Despotism and Freedom* (Duke University Press, 1997), which is an exceptionally detailed and comprehensive study of the cultural impact of the prison before and after its destruction, drawing on an incredible range of sources. Specifically on the fall of the Bastille, read Jacques Godechot's *The Taking of the Bastille: July 14th 1789* (translated by Jean Sewart, Faber and Faber, 1970). On the eighteenth century media reaction to the prison, read Rolf Reichardt's 'The Bastille as a Revolutionary Symbol', in *Revolution in Print: The Press in France 1775-1800* (edited by Robert Darnton and Daniel Roche, University of California Press, 1989).

Chapter 14 – Virtual City

John Hemming's *The Conquest of the Incas* (Macmillan 1993) is a *tour de force* of narrative history, combining rigorous scholarship with an effortless ability to tell a great story. Hemming is particularly good at bringing together some of the key chroniclers of the *conquistadors*, including the writings of Martin de Murua (*Historia general de Peru* - which contains the best eye-witness account of Vilcabamba), and Martin Garcia de Loyola. Also excellent on the conquest is Pedro de Cieza de Leon's *The Discovery and Conquest of Peru* (translated by Alexandra Cook and Noble Cook, Duke University Press, 1998) and Pedro Sarmiento de Gamboa's *History of the Incas* (translated by Clements Markham, Hakluyt Society, 1907). Hiram Bingham has, of course, written a great deal about Peru and Vilcabamba. Key texts include his memoirs, *Lost City of the Incas* (Phoenix, 1959); the 'Preliminary Report of the Yale Peruvian Expedition' in the *Bulletin of the American Geographical Society* (Vol 44, No 1, 1912); 'The Yale Peruvian Expedition: Preliminary Report' in *The Geographical Journal,* (Vol 39, No 3, March 1912); 'The Ruins of Choqquequira' in *American Anthropologist* (New Series, Vol 12, No 4, Oct-Dec 1910); and 'The Ruins of Espiritu Pampa, Peru', also in *American Anthropologist,* (New Series, Vol 16, No 2, Apr-Jun 1914). For a perspective on the man behind the myth read *Portrait of an Explorer: Hiram Bingham, Discoverer of Mach Picchu* (Iowa Sate University Press, 1989), written by Bingham's son Alfred Mitchell Bingham. Hugh Thomson's *The White Rock* also offers an interesting take on Bingham's life, combining biography and history with an enthralling Peruvian travelogue which follows in the footsteps of the American explorer all the way to Vilcabamba. For the 'Lost City' announced to the world as Machu Picchu rather than Vilcabamba, see 'In the Wonderland of Peru' in the *National Geographic*, April 1913. On the same subject, read Amy Cox Hall's 'Collecting a "Lost City" for Science: Huaquero Vision and the Yale Peruvian Expeditions to Machu Picchu, 1911, 1912 and 1914-15' (*Ethnohistory*, Vol 59, Issue 2, Spring 2012).

Chapter 15 – Little Brother's Big Brother House

There is an enormous range of source material on the subject of the Panopticon – with a great deal produced by Jeremy Bentham himself. In general, see *The Collected Works of Jeremy Bentham* (Ian R Christie editor, Athlone Press, University of London, 1971), and to get straight to the heart of this 'simple idea in architecture', the Verso edition of *The Panopticon Writings* (edited by Miran Bozovic, 2010) is excellent. Charles Milner Atkinson's *Jeremy Bentham: His Life and Work* (Methuen, 1905) is a very useful biography of the elder Bentham. On little bother Samuel, read Catherine Pease-Watkins, 'Jeremy and Samuel Bentham - the Private and the Public', (*Journal of Bentham Studies,* Vol 5, 2002) Matthew

S. Anderson's, 'Samuel Bentham in Russia 1779-1791' (*American Slavic and East European Review*, Vol 15, No. 2, 1956); Simon Werret's, 'Potemkin and the Panopticon: Samuel Bentham and the Architecture of Absolutism in Eighteenth Century Russia' (*Journal of Bentham Studies,* Vol 2, 1999); and Ian R. Christie's, 'Samuel Bentham and the Western Colony at Krichev, 1784-1787' (*The Slavonic and East European Review,* Vol 48, No. 111, 1970). Specifically on the Russian Panopticon, read Philip Steadman's, *Samuel Bentham's Panopticon,* (Bartlett School, Faculty of the Built Environment, University College London). For a comprehensive history of the Panopticon idea, and in particular Jeremy's futile struggle to build it in Britain, read Janet Semple's excellent *Bentham's Prison: A Study of the Panopticon Penitentiary* (Oxford University Press, 1993). See also Philip Steadman's 'The Contradictions of Jeremy Bentham's Panopticon Penitentiary' (*Journal of Bentham Studies,* Vol 9, 2007). On the Panopticon as the model for a dystopian surveillance society, read Michael Foucault's seminal *Discipline and Punish: The Birth of the Prison* (Penguin, 1975). And for an account of mobile technology as an agent of Panopticism, read Jan Kietzmann and Ian Angell's 'Panopticon Revisted' (*Communications of the Association for Computing Machinery*, June 2010, Vol 53, Issue 6) and Daniel J Solove's *The Future of Reputation: Gossip, Rumour and Privacy on the Internet* (Yale University Press, 2007).

Chapter 16 – No-Man's City

For a visual record of the Walled City, Greg Girard and Ian Lambot's *City of Darkness: Life in Kowloon Walled City* (Watermark, 1993) is absolutely stunning. A great doorstep of a book, it is filled with remarkable photography – supplemented by interviews with the ordinary residents of an extraordinary place. On the history of opium as a recreational drug in China, see Zeng Yangwen's *The Social Life of Opium* (Cambridge University Press, 2005); and for a first hand account of its use and abuse within the Walled City, read Jackie Pullinger's *Chasing the Dragon* (Hodder, 2010). On Britain, China and the Opium Wars, there are a number of excellent sources, including, *A documentary chronicle of Sino-Western relations, 1644-1820,* (translated by Lo-shu Fu, University of Arizona Press, 1966); P. C. Kuo's *A Critical Study of the First Anglo-Chinese War,* (Hyperion Press, 1973); Jack Beeching's *The Chinese Opium Wars* (Hutchinson, 1975); and Julia Lovell's, *The Opium War: Drugs, Dreams and the Making of China,* (Picador, 2011). On the history of Kowloon Walled City as contested territory, Peter Wesley Smith's *Unequal Treaty, 1898-1997: China, Great Britain and Hong Kong's New Territories,* (Oxford University Press, 1980) is absolutely essential; as is Elizabeth Sinn's 'Kowloon Walled City: Its Origin and Early History' in the *Journal of the Royal Asiatic Society Hong Kong Branch* (Vol 27, 1987). On the last days of the Walled City, Charles Goddard's short essay 'The Clearance' in Girard and Lambot's *City of Darkness* is excellent. On the concept of the organic megastructure, read Reyner Banham, *Megastructure: Urban Futures of the Recent Past* (Thames and Hudson, 1976). And for William Gibson's take on Kowloon as a 'hive of dream' see 'Disneyland with the Death Penalty' in *Wired,* (Issue 1.04, Sep/Oct 1993); his interview with Steven Poole, 'Tomorrow's Man', in *The Guardian* (3 May 2003); and his novel *Idoru* (Viking, 2006).

Chapter 17 – The Day the Architecture Died

To learn more about the fascinating life of monk-turned-filmmaker Godfrey Reggio, read 'Qatsi Means Life: The Films of Godfrey Reggio' in *Film Quarterly* (Vol 42, No 3, University of California Press, 1989); and Carlo McCormick's 'Godfrey Reggio's fearful symmetry' in *Aperture*, (Issue 180, Fall 2005). *Koyaanisqatsi* has acquired cult following, and is well worth a watch – the scene involving the demolition of Pruitt-Igoe remains very powerful. Charles Jencks' gleeful commentary on the demise of Pruitt-Igoe comes at the beginning of *The language of post-modern architecture* (Academy Editions, 1977). On the origins of the housing project, Alexander Von Hoffman's 'Why They Built Pruitt-Igoe' in *From Tenements to the Taylor Homes: In Search of an Urban Housing Policy in Twentieth-Century America* (Pennsylvania State University Press, 2000) is excellent, and should be read alongside Mary C Comerio's 'Pruitt-Igoe and Other Stories' in the *Journal of Architectural Education* (Vol 34, No 4, Taylor & Francis, 1981). James Bailey's 'The Case History of a Failure' (*Architectural Forum* 123, December 1965) and Frances A. Koestler, Joan Miller, Eugene Porter and Lee Rainwater's 'Survival in a Concrete Ghetto' (*Social Work,* October 1967, Vol. 12, Issue 4, Oxford University Press US) provide vivid and shocking detail of the disintegration of conditions in Pruitt-Igoe. Further commentary comes from Oscar Newman in *Creating Defensible Space* (US Department of Housing and Urban Development, 1996) and Mark La Gory and John Pipkin in *Urban Social Space* (Wadsworth Publishing Company, 1981). For a brilliant analysis of the housing project as a 'programmed failure', read Katherine G Bristol's 'The Pruitt-Igoe Myth' in the *Journal of Architectural Education* (Vol 44, No 3, 1991). This was also the title of an excellent documentary film released in 2011 (Chad Friedrichs director, Unicorn Stencil Films). On the site of Pruitt-Igoe as inspiration for utopian development, read Nora Wendl's 'Pruitt-Igoe, Now' (*Journal of Architectural Education,* 67:1, 2013); and Michael R. Allen and Nora Wendl's, 'After Pruitt-Igoe: An Urban Forest as an Evolving Temporal Landscape' (*Studies in the History of Gardens & Designed Landscapes: An International Quarterly*, 34:1, 2014).

Chapter 18 – Mirrorwall

For a series of excellent and thought-provoking essays on the Wall, read *German Politics and Society, Special Issue: The Berlin Wall after Fifty Years, 1961-2011* (Issue 99, Vol 29, No 2, Summer 2011). In particular, look at Leo Schmidt's superb 'The Architecture and Message of 'the Wall', 1961-1989'; Hope M Harrison's title essay, 'The Berlin Wall After Fifty Years' and 'The Berlin Wall and its Resurrection as a Site of Memory'; Partick Major's 'Walled In: Ordinary East Germans' Response to 13 August 1961'; and Pertti Ahonen's 'The Berlin Wall and the Battle for Legitimacy in Divided Germany'. For a general, accessible history of the Wall from its creation to its collapse, read Frederick Taylor's *The Berlin Wall: 13 August 1961 - 9 November 1989* (Bloomsbury, 2006). On the Wall as inspiration for dramatic narrative, read Peter Schneider's wonderful *The Wall Jumper* (the Penguin 2005 edition, specifically for the introduction by Ian McEwan); and Cyril Buffet's utterly fascinating 'Declaration of Love on Celluloid: The Depiction of the Berlin Wall in a GDR film, 1961-62' (*Cold War History,* Vol 9, No 4, December 2009). The end of the Wall – and its cultural fallout – is explored in Melanie van der Hoorn's

'Architectural Fragments as Intermediaries between History and Individual Experience' (*Journal of Material Culture*, 8, 189, Sage, 2003); Roger Kimball's 'Tyranny set in Stone' (*New Criterion*, November 2009, Vol 28, Issue 3); Christine Leuenberger's 'The Berlin Wall: How Material Culture Is Used in Psychological Theory' (*Social Problems*, Vol 53, No 1, February 2006); Tom Mueller's 'Berlin: Beyond the Wall' (*Smithsonian*, June 2006, Vol 37, Issue 3); and Yosefa Loshitsky's 'Constructing and Deconstructing the Wall' (*CLIO*, 26, 3, 1997). And finally, for pivotal role played by 'The Boss' in the Wall coming down, see Eric Kirschbaum's *Rocking the Wall: Bruce Springsteen, the Berlin Concert that Changed the World* (Berlinica, 2011).

Chapter 19 – No One Day Shall Erase You From the Memory of Time

On the life of Minoru Yamasaki, unsurprisingly, the architect's own memoirs – *A Life in Architecture* (Weatherhill, 1979) – are an excellent place to start. See also Rowan Moore's 'Minoru Yamasaki' in *Prospect* (20 November 2011) and the *New York Times* obituary (9 February 1986). There are a number of key sources on the life of Mohammad Atta, and his transformation into a terrorist. Read Unni Wikan's 'My Son: A Terrorist? (He was Such a Gentle Boy)' (*Anthropological Quarterly*, Vol 75, No 1, Winter 2001); John Cloud's 'Atta's Odyssey' (*Time*, 8 October 2001, Vol 158, Issue 15); John Hooper's 'The shy, caring, deadly fanatic' (*The Observer*, 23 September 2001); Elena Lappin's 'Atta in Hamburg' (*Prospect*, 20 September 2002); and Neil MacFarquhar, Jim Yardley and Paul Zielbauer's 'A portrait of the terrorist: From shy child to single-minded killer' (*New York Times*, 10 October 2001). For an outstanding account of the story behind the construction of the Twin Towers, read Eric Darton's *Divided We Stand: A Biography of the World Trade Centre* (Perseus, 2011). On the aftermath of the attacks, look at the excellent *After the World Trade Centre: Rethinking New York City* (Michael Sorkin and Sharon Zukin, editors, Routledge, 2002). In a number of essays, it explores the past and the future of the site of the attack - in particular read M Christine Boyer's 'Meditations on a Wounded Skyline and Its Stratigraphies of Pain'; Eric Darton's 'The Janus Face of International Terrorism: Minoru Yamasaki, Mohammad Atta and Our World Trade Center'; Mark Wigley's 'Insecurity by Design'; and Beverly Gage's 'The First Wall Street Bomb'. On the 1960s clearance of downtown New York, Danny Lyon's photography in *The Destruction of Lower Manhattan* (Powerhouse, 2005) is haunting and beautiful. On Ground Zero recast as a museum and site of pilgrimage, see Nicholas Olberg and Robert Bevan's 'Memory in Ruins' in *Architectural Review* (Vol 235, Issue 1408, June 2014); Holland Cotter's 'The 9/11 Story Told at Bedrock' in the *New York Times* (14 May 2014); Philip Kennicott's 'The 9/11 Museum doesn't just display artifacts, it ritualizes grief on a loop', in the *Washington Post* (7 June 2014); and Oliver Wainwright's 'An emotional underworld beneath Ground Zero' in *The Guardian* (14 May 2014). See also the museum website www.911memorial.org.

Chapter 20 – The Deleted City

Mary Lou Roberts' 'GeoCities' in the *Journal of Interactive Marketing* (Vol 14, No 1, Winter 2000); and Gary Stern's 'GeoCities' in *Link Up* (Vol 14, Issue 4, 1997) provide fascinating overviews of the early history of the website. On the growth of the 'city' and its 'suburbs', see 'Beverley Hills Internet, builder of Interactive cyber cities, launches four more communities linked to real places' in *Business Wire* (5 July 1995). For details of the sale of GeoCities to Yahoo, read Kara Swisher's 'Those Who Tied Fortune to GeoCities Yell Yahoo! All the Way to the Bank' in *The Wall Street Journal* (29 January 1999). On the deletion of the city – and the frantic attempt to save it before the plug was pulled – read Dan Fletcher's 'Internet Atrocity! GeoCities Demise Erases Web History' (*Time*, 9 November 2009), Matt Schwartz's 'Fire in the Library' (*MIT Technology Review*); Phoebe Connelly's 'Neo Cities: How online communities are born and what happens when they die' (*The American Prospect,* September 2009); Joe Kloc's 'The Death and Life of Great Internet Cities' (www.dailydot.com, 25 November 2013); and the 'GeoCities' entry on the Archive Team website (www.archiveteam.org). On the creation of the art installation 'The Deleted City', read Richard Vijgen's 'The Deleted City: A Digital Archaeology' in *Parsons Journal for Information Mapping* (Vol 5, Issue 2, Spring 2013), and see www.deletedcity.net. For GeoCities as the first – but not the last – great internet ruin, read Dennis Berman's, 'For Facebook, GeoCities Offers a Cautionary Tale', (*Wall Street Journal,* 25 September 2007) and Kate Lunau's 'Lessons from GeoCities' Death' (*Maclean's,* 9 July 2009, Vol 122, Issue 3). On the seeming omnipotence of 'the Cloud', read James Gleick's excellent *The Information: A History, A Theory, A Flood* (Fourth Estate, 2012).

Chapter 21 – Let the Past Meet the Future

On the present-day battle for Palmyra and its subsequent capture, there are innumerable media sources. I found some of the most consistent, detailed and assiduous reporting in *The New York Times, The Guardian, Syria: direct* and *The Lebanon Daily Star.* For a specific focus on the fate of Palmyra's antiquities, Tim McGirk's July 2015 article in *National Geographic* makes for compelling reading. For a brilliant overview of the current state of global illicit trafficking in antiquities, read the series of essays in *Countering Illicit Traffic in Cultural Goods: The Global Challenge of Protecting the World's Heritage* (ICOM 2015), edited by Frances Desmaris, creator of the International Observatory on Illicit Traffic in Cultural Goods. On the history of Palmyra, two of the best books are Iain Browning's *Palmyra (*Chatto, 1979), and Andrew M Smith's *Roman Palmyra: Identity, Community and State Formation* (OUP, 2013). The latter in particular provides a fascinatingly detailed analysis of the social, political, economic and cultural life of the city and its people. Other important texts in this area include Michael Gawlikowski's 'Palmyra as a Trading Centre' (*Iraq, Vol 56,* CUP, 1994) and I A Richmond's 'Palmyra under the aegis of Rome' (*The Journal of Roman Studies*, CUP, 1963). Edward Gibbon's *Decline and Fall*... is, as ever, a useful reference. Primary sources – or as primary as you can get, as many were written some time after the events – include Appian's *Civil Wars* (Penguin 1996), the *Historia Nova* of Zosimus, and *The Scriptores Historiae Augustae.* See also Michael Dodgeon and Samuel Lieu's compilation of contemporary accounts in *The Roman Eastern Frontier and the Persian Wars (AD 226-363): A documentary history* (Routledge, 1994). Essential reading – and viewing – for anyone interested in Palmyra is, of course, the sumptuous *The Ruins of Palmyra* by Wood and Dawkins (Robert Wood, 1753).

ACKNOWLEDGEMENTS

Writing this book would not have been possible without a great deal of support. For the past few years, I have spent countless hours in the shelves and reading rooms of the National Library of Scotland and the Central Library of the University of Edinburgh (in the latter case, much more time than I ever did as an undergraduate…). I should like to thank the staff of both institutions for their patient and helpful assistance. The University Library – and its second floor in particular – became something of a home from home for me on long evenings, and over more weekends than I care to remember. Midnight oil was burnt like it was going out of fashion. Before I started writing *Fallen Glory*, I did not drink coffee. Now I have a two-a-day habit…

My publisher, Ben Yarde-Buller, has been calm, confident and quietly inspirational – exactly what a writer needs to keep him going. Thanks also to Matthew Baylis for his comprehensive copy-edit and commentary on the first draft, and to Toby Green, for his very useful input on an early treatment. Dr Jeff Sanders of the Society of Antiquaries of Scotland has been a consistently useful sounding board, and historian and Edinburgh University lecturer Dr Devon McHugh helped point me in the right direction in a number of key areas of my research. And I should also like to thank Fiona Brownlee, for her tireless work in getting the finished book out there into the world.

My agent, Maggie Hattersley, has been an absolute rock. Over the years, she has been a colleague, a mentor, an inspiration – and I am delighted to call her a friend. This book would not exist without her and her relentless dedication to the cause. She is, in the very best way, a force of nature. It is, and always has been, a privilege to work with her.

From as early as I can remember, I have been able to count on the unstinting support of my parents, James and Anne. Their enthusiasm and interest in my work means a great deal, and has always been a huge motivating factor.

Finally – and most importantly – I should like to thank to Hazel, Brodie and Nate. Their patience and good humour throughout has been bottomless. It has made all of this worthwhile. *Fallen Glory* is dedicated to them.